CW01083412

Charles Villier

Frontispiece   Charles Villiers Stanford by Sir William Orpen. By permission of the Masters and Fellows of Trinity College, Cambridge.

Charles Villiers Stanford

PAUL RODMELL

Routledge
Taylor & Francis Group

LONDON AND NEW YORK

First published 2002 by Ashgate Publishing

Published 2017 by Routledge
2 Park Square, Milton Park, Abingdon, Oxon OX14 4RN
711 Third Avenue, New York, NY 10017, USA

First issued in paperback 2017

*Routledge is an imprint of the Taylor & Francis Group,
an informa business*

British Library Cataloguing in Publication Data

Rodmell, Paul.
    Charles Villiers Stanford.
    (Music in Nineteenth-Century Britain)
    I. Stanford, Charles Villiers, 1852–1924. 2. Composers—
    Ireland—Biography.
    I. Title.
    780.9′2

Library of Congress Control Number: 2001098285

Typeset in Sabon by Q3 Bookwork

ISBN 13: 978-1-138-26903-3 (pbk)
ISBN 13: 978-1-85928-198-7 (hbk)

Contents

General Editor's Preface

The life and music of Charles Villiers Stanford represents a conspicuous absence for much of twentieth-century British musicology. Despite his central importance as a composer, teacher, conductor and writer, Stanford – like his times in general – was in part a casualty of the British self-uninterest engendered by the fallout from the 'land without music'. This malediction, which held sway for such a considerable time in the twentieth century, is only now beginning to be understood in its rich historiographical context, and it is because of this that its effects on the minds of musicologists and the listening public are beginning to be reconsidered. It is precisely because of works such as Rodmell's *Stanford* that our understanding of that period in time, and the musicians who lived in it, can achieve any level of clarity devoid of inherited prejudice. In Rodmell's book we have a 'land without "a land without music"'.

In addition to re-establishing Stanford as a musicological focal point, Rodmell also provides the first biography of Stanford since Henry Plunkett Greene's *Charles Villiers Stanford* (London, 1935). At the same time, he provides an extensive array of musical examples illustrative of his biographical considerations. These are informed by an equally extensive reading in issues of reception and the musical culture of Stanford's time. The combination of these affords the reader the first comprehensive investigation of its kind. For all this, however, Rodmell is not uncritical of Stanford's music, and neither does he indulge in analysis devoid of aesthetic judgement. Rather, he contextualizes his criticism in terms which relate to the continuum of Stanford's wide-ranging career, and through this there emerges a picture of the man and his music which is both humane yet discriminating. This is evident not only in the way individual compositions are treated, but also in the division of the book into two distinct parts, a life and works, and an appraisal and conclusion. Whilst the first part of the book explores the general inter-relationships between the man and his music, the second part underscores the significance of this in relation to Stanford's working environment as teacher, writer, and composer. This twofold methodology has obvious advantages in allowing the author to establish clear biographical information which can then be cast in increasingly specified ways. Rodmell's conclusion is framed in issues of national identity and multiple aspects of reception, and in this regard it affords as much a locus for critical overview as a vehicle for further debate. Taken as a whole, Rodmell's *Stanford* does this same thing on a wider basis, by providing scholars with an overview of one important figure, and also by situating him within a broader musicological debate about music and its cultural significance in late nineteenth- and early twentieth-century Britain.

Bennett Zon

University of Durham

List of Plates

List of Figures
and Tables

List of Music Examples

All music is by Stanford unless otherwise stated.

Acknowledgements

An item on a programme on BBC Radio 4 recently suggested that the purpose of acknowledgements in a book was to curry favour with the great and the good, and to ensure the support of all those whose help one might need in the future. I should not like to say to what extent that was true; the following acknowledgements recognise real support and encouragement over the five years that I have been writing this book and the nine years spent researching the life and works of Charles Villiers Stanford.

My first debt of gratitude is to the many libraries I have used and harried over the past few years; in no particular order, I should like to thank the following libraries and archives, and their staff: the British Library, old and new, especially in Rare Books and Music, Manuscripts, and the Newspaper Library at Colindale; Cambridge University Library, especially in Manuscripts; the Pendlebury Music Library at Cambridge; the Library of King's College, Cambridge, especially Margaret Cranmer; the Bodleian Library at Oxford; the National Library of Australia; the Pierpont Morgan Library in New York; the Beinecke Rare Books Library at Yale University; the Music Library at Yale University, especially Kendall Crilly for both help and hospitality; the West Yorkshire Archive Service at Leeds; the National Library of Scotland; the Berlin Staatsbibliothek, with sites in the old West (Tiergartenstraße) and the old East (Unter den Linden); Lincoln City Library; Birmingham Central Library; Leeds University Library; National Library of Ireland; the Library of Trinity College, Dublin; Kensington Library; and Worcester Records Office. In this area I owe especial debts to the libraries at Trinity College, Cambridge, with particular thanks to Jon Smith; the Royal College of Music and to Peter Horton; Robert Firth and Lesley Gordon at the Robinson Library, University of Newcastle; the University of Birmingham, Anna Greig and all her colleagues. Finally, to Laura Ponsonby and all her family at Shulbrede Priory for granting me access to the Parry archives there and for the warm hospitality (including croquet) given to me.

In formal terms I must particularly thank the Master and Fellows of Trinity College, Cambridge for permission to quote from various official college records and to reproduce the portrait of Stanford by Orpen as the frontispiece of this book; Laura Ponsonby for permission to quote extensively from Hubert Parry's diaries and correspondence; the Barber

Institute of Fine Arts at the University of Birmingham for allowing the reproduction of the drawings by Eric Kapp; West Yorkshire Archive Service for permission to quote from the Leeds Musical Festival Archives held by them; the Royal Academy of Music for allowing the reproduction of the portrait of Jennie Stanford by Hubert von Herkommer; and the Elgar Birthplace Trust for permitting the use of the photos of Stanford with Elgar at Bournemouth in 1910 and Gloucester in 1922.

Innumerable friends have given me support and/or floorspace or a bed over the past few years: for the latter grateful thanks to Anthony Geraghty, Fiona Donson, Paul Gardener and Bill Marlin, Duncan Campbell, Richard Hutt, and Michael Mehta. Other friends have been supportive and concerned ('how's the book?') and will I hope excuse me for giving them collective thanks rather than causing offence by trying to compile an accurate list of individuals. I also owe a debt to the late Geoffrey Bush, who was the external examiner for my doctoral thesis and who never ceased to take an interest in my work. Financial support has come from the British Academy, which funded the scholarship that allowed me to study for my doctorate; I should also mention here the various institutions which have kept me in gainful employment over the years, especially the University of Birmingham; without their money this book would not even be a twinkle in the eye.

My long-suffering editor, Rachel Lynch, supplied me with the contract for this book and has subsequently put up with lots of postponements, revisions and disorganisation: to her great thanks, although I suspect, as I write this, that the worst bit is yet to come. Thanks also to Bennett Zon for overseeing this project, to all the staff at Ashgate who will to bring this manuscript to a wider public, and especially to my copy-editor, Bonnie Blackburn, who spotted numerous slips and inconsistencies.

Closer to home there are several people to whom I owe substantial debts for help given over the years. First, to the late Frederick Hudson, whose unstinting work collecting information about Stanford made my life much easier (see the Preface). Secondly, to all my colleagues at the University of Birmingham, especially John Whenham for his support as my undergraduate tutor and Colin Timms for encouraging me to return to higher education. Thirdly to my parents, who have given me enduring encouragement and money(!) to keep going. Fourthly, back at Birmingham, to Jan Smaczny, who supervised the first year of my doctoral study and who suggested that Stanford's operas would be a subject worthy of investigation. Finally, and most importantly, to Stephen Banfield, who took over from Jan, and has provided almost limitless help over the years; he has read, criticised and refined my ideas; got me to the end of my thesis and done more than was called for to keep me in paid work – without which none of this would have been possible.

Preface

This is the first book to be devoted to the life and music of Charles Villiers Stanford since the biography written by his friend Harry Plunket Greene in 1935.[1] Since then Stanford's music has remained for a long time out of favour; it has only been in the last twenty years or so that the decline in interest in both the man and his music has been halted and reversed. This has been mainly attributable to the general growth in scholarly research on the 'English Musical Renaissance',[2] to a growing belief that Britain before 1914 was not 'das Land ohne Musik',[3] and to the rapid expansion of the recorded repertory which followed the success of the CD medium.

In the course of this wider resurgence Stanford has remained somewhat at the margin. Along with his contemporaries, Stanford has been examined in such general works as Nicholas Temperley's *Music in Britain: The Romantic Age* and Stephen Banfield's generic study *Sensibility and English Song*.[4] But while other 'renaissance' composers such as Vaughan Williams, Holst, Moeran, Parry, Stainer, Bax and Balfour Gardiner – to name just some – have been the subject of monographs or collections of articles,[5] Stanford has hitherto been substantially left

---

[1] Harry Plunket Greene, *Charles Villiers Stanford* (London, 1935).

[2] The term 'English [or British] Musical Renaissance' was coined by Morton Latham, who gave a lecture 'The Musical Renaissance in England' at Trinity College, Cambridge, in 1888; he later published a book, *The Renaissance of Music* (London, 1890). Latham focused on the sixteenth and seventeenth centuries in his work, but the term was soon taken up by musicians as a way to refer to the perceived growth in musical activity in Britain in the late nineteenth century and later became common currency. For further, provocative, discussion see Robert Stradling and Merion Hughes, *The British Musical Renaissance: Construction and Deconstruction* (London, 1995; 2nd rev. edn, Manchester, 2001); for a discussion of how perceptions of when the 'Renaissance' started have changed see Nicholas Temperley, 'Xenophilia in British Musical History', in Bennett Zon (ed.), *Nineteenth-Century British Music Studies*, 1 (Aldershot, 1999), 3–19.

[3] This term was first used by Oskar Schmitz late in 1914; see ch. 3 of Stradling and Hughes, *The British Musical Renaissance*.

[4] Nicholas Temperley (ed.), *Music in Britain: The Romantic Age 1800–1914* (London, 1981); Stephen Banfield, *Sensibility and English Song*, 2 vols (Cambridge, 1985).

[5] Respectively, Alain Frogley (ed.), *Vaughan Williams Studies* (Cambridge, 1996); Michael Short, *Gustav Holst: The Man and his Music* (Oxford, 1990); Geoffrey Self, *The Music of E. J. Moeran* (London, 1986); Peter Charlton, *John Stainer and the Musical Life of Victorian Britain* (Newton Abbot, 1984); Jeremy Dibble, *C. Hubert H. Parry: His Life and Music* (Oxford, 1992) and Bernard Benoliel, *Parry before Jerusalem: Studies of his*

alone. Since the mid-1960s, however, the late Frederick Hudson was tracing, collecting and cataloguing Stanford's music.[6] In attempting to produce a definitive list, Dr Hudson located nearly all of Stanford's manuscripts; it is regrettable that his death in 1994 prevented him from completing the catalogue to which he had devoted so much time. Stanford himself has also been the subject of scholarly and editorial interest, exemplified by the work of Geoffrey Bush, Heinrich van der Mescht, Jean Hoover, Michael Allis, Jeremy Dibble and myself.[7]

While finding and examining Stanford's music has proved to be relatively straightforward, I have been surprised at just how difficult it has been to piece together the story of the life of such a prominent pre-First World War musician. In addition to Greene's book, the most important sources of published information are Stanford's own autobiography,[8] his other published writings,[9] and a few other articles, such as those by Thomas Dunhill and Herbert Howells.[10] To a large extent, however, all of these works merely repeat each other, reiterate the same facts and figures, and concentrate, understandably, on Stanford's public life and work. Stanford himself was almost wholly reticent about his personal life after leaving Dublin in *Pages from an Unwritten Diary* (he does not, for example, mention his wife or marriage at all), while Greene, despite

---

Life and Music (Aldershot, 1997); Lewis Foreman, *Arnold Bax: A Composer and his Times* (Aldershot, 1983; 2nd edn, 1988); Stephen Lloyd, *H. Balfour Gardiner* (Cambridge, 1984).

[6] The ongoing results of this research were published in 'C. V. Stanford: Nova Bibliographica', *Musical Times*, 104 (1963), 728–31; 'C. V. Stanford: Nova Bibliographica II', *Musical Times*, 105 (1964), 734–8; 'C. V. Stanford: Nova Bibliographica III', *Musical Times*, 108 (1967), 326, and 'A Revised and Extended Catalogue of C. V. Stanford', *Music Review*, 37 (1976), 106–29.

[7] Respectively Geoffrey Bush's edition of Stanford's songs (*Musica Britannica*, 52); Jean Hoover and Heinrich van der Mescht both gave papers on Stanford at the Second Biennial Conference on Music in Nineteenth-Century Britain at Durham in 1999; Jeremy Dibble has played a crucial part in the issuing of several CDs of Stanford's music (see App. 2) and is also the author of 'Stanford's Service in B flat, op. 10, and the Choir of Trinity College, Cambridge', *Irish Musical Studies*, 2 (Dublin, 1993), 129–48; see also Michael Allis, 'Another "48": Stanford and "Historic Sensibility"', *Music Review*, 55 (1994), 119–37 and Paul Rodmell, 'A Tale of Two Operas: Stanford's *Savonarola* and *The Canterbury Pilgrims* from Gestation to Production', *Music & Letters*, 78 (1997), 77–91.

[8] Charles Stanford, *Pages from an Unwritten Diary* (London, 1914).

[9] From a biographical perspective the anthologies *Studies and Memories* (London, 1908) and *Interludes, Records and Recollections* (London, 1922) are the most useful. Other works, such as *Musical Composition* (London, 1911), are an exposition of Stanford's aesthetics rather than autobiographical comment.

[10] Thomas Dunhill, 'Charles Villiers Stanford: Some Aspects of his Work and Influence', *Proceedings of the Royal Musical Association*, 42 (1927), 41–65. Herbert Howells, 'Charles Villiers Stanford: An Address at his Centenary', *Proceedings of the Royal Musical Association*, 80 (1952–3), 19–31.

attempts to the contrary, was not only biased but often factually incorrect in his biography. Trying to go one step further, to build up a detailed picture of Stanford's day-to-day life and opinions, has proved to be a major stumbling block, for very few of Stanford's personal papers remain in existence. I have traced about 800 autograph letters in various locations, but this is only a small fraction of the conservative estimate of 28,000 letters which he probably wrote during his adult life.[11] Sources which might have proved particularly useful, for example his letters to such close friends as Greene, Fuller Maitland, Barclay Squire and George Grove, and to his own family, have proved impossible to trace and are presumed destroyed. Some rich sources of correspondence have survived, however, most notably Stanford's letters to Francis Jenkinson, Hans Richter and Joseph Joachim.[12] Research was further handicapped by the fact that hardly any letters written *to* Stanford survive;[13] it is not known when these letters were lost or destroyed but they have not found their way into any public depository; Stanford's own children, Guy and Geraldine, both died childless in the 1950s and there are, therefore, no direct living descendants. As Stanford himself was an only child, this leaves no close family to whom personal papers might have been left; in fact, the lack of any mention of such papers in the wills of either Guy or Geraldine Stanford suggests that they may already have been destroyed. To handicap research further, Stanford kept no diary.

The result is that Stanford remains, in many respects, a figure of mystery. Secondary sources have enabled a fairly thorough biography of his official tasks to be assembled; periodicals such as the *Musical Times*, *The Times* and the *Cambridge Review* have proved invaluable, as have the official records of the Royal College of Music, Cambridge University and Trinity College, Cambridge. Even here, however, it is very difficult to build a picture of Stanford's day-to-day schedule; while occasional flurries of activity enable one to trace brief periods in detail, there are frequently long periods where very little is known. In respect of Stanford's private life we still know next to nothing: his marriage,

---

[11] One can reasonably assume that Stanford wrote at least ten letters every week or 520 letters each year; taking his adult life only into consideration (from 1870 onwards), this amounts to a total of just over 28,000. Stanford probably produced far more than this, although many letters would have been brief notes and postcards; a more realistic estimate is at least twenty letters per week, or about 56,000 in total.

[12] These collections are to be found in Cambridge University Library, Royal College of Music Library and the Staatsbibliothek zu Berlin (Tiergartenstraße) respectively; specific references are given in the main body of the text.

[13] Most of these are to be found in Stanford's 'Autograph Book' (RCM, MS 4253), a collection of letters, postcards and autographs from significant people. There are only one or two items from each correspondent, however, so the value of the collection is sometimes limited.

his relationships with his children and with his parents, his view on most moral issues, and his opinion of most of his friends are all areas into which one gains only fleeting glimpses, mostly through his autobiography and Greene's book, both of which control the dissemination of facts carefully.

Those caveats aside, it is still the case that an immense amount of information on Stanford remains to be related. I have attempted in this book to convey much information on Stanford's activities, not least because it has never been assembled in one place until now. Inevitably, given his diverse workload and hectic life, there are many details that could not be included here. Rather I have aimed to give the reader an impression, backed by fact, of Stanford's life, taking time to deal with particular issues and incidents, public and private, which have struck me as being particularly significant. Hence there are discussions not only of Stanford's musical activities, such as conducting and teaching, but of other issues, most notably his attitude to Ireland. Generally speaking, I have dealt with these issues in Chapters 1 to 7 as they arise chronologically but, in some cases, where a subject was of central importance in Stanford's life, for example, his role as a teacher, I have dealt with it in Chapters 8 and 9 in order to avoid fragmentation.

I have taken a similar approach to Stanford's music in Chapter 9. He was renowned in his own lifetime for his rapid rate of production: he produced almost 200 works with opus numbers (the last known number is 194) and this total does not include many other works, most notably two symphonies, three operas and three concertos. Consequently I have examined in most detail the works which I consider to be the most interesting and important. I have used a number of criteria in this assessment, including contemporary popularity, stylistic innovation, formal innovation, and works which I consider to be of exceptional quality in his output. Inevitably this partially reflects my own research interests and the reader will no doubt find less or more on some works than s/he may expect. This may be particularly the case for the time devoted to Stanford's nine operas, but I make no apology for this; it is my contention, despite his general lack of popular success with this genre, that the composition of opera was one of his greatest loves and that he felt more passionately about converting Britain into a nation of opera-lovers than on almost any other musical issue.

My primary hope is that this book will prove to be a starting point for discussion and assessment of Stanford's life and of his contribution to musical life, as there is still much to be discovered, debated and assessed. He remains in many respects an enigma, a man of peculiar talents and frailties and, above all, a source of fascination.

P. R.
Birmingham, 2002

List of Abbreviations

Libraries and archives frequently referred to are denoted by the following abbreviations:

BCL	Birmingham Central Library
BerSt	Staatsbibliothek zu Berlin – Preußischer Kulturbesitz (sites at Unter den Linden and Tiergartenstraße)
BL	British Library, London
CUL	Cambridge University Library
FWC	Fitzwilliam Museum, Cambridge
KCC	King's College, Cambridge
LCL	Lincoln City Library (Tennyson Archive)
LUL	Leeds University Library
MA	Moldenhauer Archive, Northwestern University, Evanston, Ill.
NLI	National Library of Ireland, Dublin
NUL	Newcastle University Library
PML	Pierpont Morgan Library, New York
RAM	Royal Academy of Music, London
RCM	Royal College of Music, London
ShP	Shulbrede Priory, Lynchmere, West Sussex
TCC	Trinity College, Cambridge
WRO	Worcester Records Office
WYAS	West Yorkshire Archive Service, Leeds

Life and Work

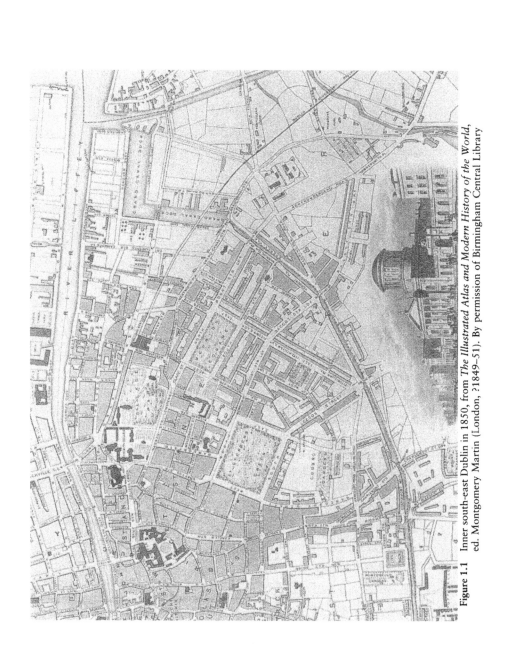

Figure 1.1 Inner south-east Dublin in 1850, from *The Illustrated Atlas and Modern History of the World*, ed. Montgomery Martin (London, ?1849–51). By permission of Birmingham Central Library

CHAPTER ONE

An Anglo-Irish Childhood

> A town mouse I was born and bred, and the town which sheltered
> me was one likely to leave its mark upon its youngest citizens, and
> to lay up for them vivid and stirring memories. Dublin, as I woke
> to it, was a city of glaring contrasts. Grandeur and squalor lived
> next door to each other, squalor sometimes under the roof of
> grandeur.[1]

One of the most striking architectural features of the Dublin in which
Stanford grew up was the network of residential streets (now mainly
converted into offices) which lay south of the Liffey and centred on St
Stephen's Green (see Fig. 1.1). Generally a product of eighteenth-century
prosperity, showing some elements of enlightened town-planning not
normally associated with Great Britain, the rows of Georgian terraces
and squares, with their deliberate symmetry and uniformity, are now
one of the most imposing remnants of the Anglo-Irish ruling class
which dominated Ireland from the eighteenth century to the formation
of the Irish Free State in 1922. Many street names reflect their Georgian
heyday, referring to famous politicians and other luminaries of the time
– Grattan, Fitzwilliam, Harcourt and Herbert – and it was here that
much of Ireland's political, social, cultural and bureaucratic elite made
its home, from the days of the area's first being built until the community's decline and virtual disappearance in the inter-war years.

The foundations of this ruling class are to be found in the sixteenth
and seventeenth centuries when successive monarchs, most notably
Elizabeth I and James I, and the republican Cromwell, encouraged
members of the English gentry and middle class to emigrate to Ireland
and to 'civilise' and subordinate the indigenous population. As in so
many aspects of British history, it was the outcome of Henry VIII's break
with Rome that led to this change in policy towards Ireland, which
had, by and large, been ignored by earlier monarchs except when insur-
rection was at its most blatant. The Catholic clergy of Ireland were
far more resistant to the Reformation than their English counterparts and Henry acted decisively against them and others. Land seized
from the monasteries was redistributed to a new wave of English immi-
grants and the Dublin parliament passed a law explicitly recognising

---

[1] Stanford, *Pages from an Unwritten Diary*, 1.

Henry's supremacy as monarch. The policy was sustained over decades; after monastic lands ran out property was seized from the indigenous population.

The policies of Henry, Elizabeth and James were relatively benign compared with what followed. Believing that Charles I had some pro-Catholic sympathies, much of Ireland supported the Royalist cause in the Civil War. After Cromwell's victory in 1649 the Irish were subjugated with little or no mercy. Land redistribution to English incomers took place on a vastly greater scale than hitherto and there was an attempt at 'ethnic cleansing' through a combination of slaughter of Catholics and the passing of a law (the Act of Settlement, 1652) which forced rebellious Catholic landowners to move west of the Shannon.[2] James was defeated in the Williamite Wars (1689–91), and the Protestant hegemony cemented.

The upshot of this last and most dangerous act of Catholic rebellion was the determination of successive English monarchs and governments to maintain Protestant supremacy. This was mostly achieved by a succession of Acts passed over the four decades from 1690 collectively known as the Penal Code (contemporaneously known as the 'Popery Laws'). This legislation forbade, amongst other things, the entry of any Catholic into the army or navy, the holding of posts in central or local government, entry into the legal profession, and the education of a child in the Catholic faith; it also removed the right of Catholics to vote. Catholic land could be passed from generation to generation but only on the old Merovingian principle of equal division of property between all sons – a simple method of ensuring that Catholic landholdings, already negligible as a part of the whole, became progressively more fragmented. The Penal Code cemented the Protestant domination of Ireland by emasculating the power of the remaining Catholic gentry.[3]

This social construction of Protestant, or rather more specifically Anglican, supremacy leads us directly to the physical construction of Dublin's Georgian terraces, a tangible manifestation of the domination and prosperity of the Anglo-Irish ruling class in the eighteenth century. Ireland was prosperous and Dublin was its thriving cultural, social and

---

[2] Displaced landowners received some property as compensation, but the amount was scaled according to the extent of their anti-Cromwellian actions. Some restoration of land was achieved under the Act of Settlement, 1662, but it far from cancelled out the resettlements of the 1650s.

[3] The provisions of the Penal Code, aimed principally at the professions and the laws of inheritance, had less direct effect on mercantile and lower classes than on the gentry. Legalised discrimination became, however, a rallying point for many, especially as the restrictions on the Catholic Church affected all classes; campaigns for relief started in the mid-eighteenth century. For further discussion see T. P. Power and Kevin Whelan (eds), *Endurance and Emergence: Catholics in Ireland in the Eighteenth Century* (Dublin, 1990).

commercial centre. Their position secured by prosperity combined with legalised discrimination, the Anglo-Irish easily became a ruling elite, confident and optimistic. Such was this degree of prosperity and self-sufficiency that during the course of the century the Anglo-Irish began to identify themselves less with England and more with Ireland. English rule seemed to them to comprise much taking but little giving. An economically strong but politically compliant Ireland was also in English interests and, in order to assuage the growing Anglo-Irish spirit of independence, the British government consented to the modification of the powers of the Irish Parliament in 1782. Its leader, Henry Grattan, supported the repeal of aspects of the Penal Code, but made little progress since many more of the Anglo-Irish were sceptical about the need for such action and there was little material change between pre- and post-1782 parliaments.[4] Grattan's lack of success was unfortunate, to say the least: growing frustration amongst Catholics and some Protestants, most notably Wolf Tone, allowed the success of the French Revolution to fire their imagination and culminated in the Irish Rebellion of 1798. This revolt was swiftly and brutally put down by the British Army but had so winded the Anglo-Irish that they voted their own Parliament out of existence and accepted the Act of Union – a concept to which most of them had previously been thoroughly hostile – with barely a murmur.

The Act of Union sounded the muted death knell of the Anglo-Irish. During the nineteenth century Dublin declined gradually as England became the overwhelmingly dominant partner in the relationship. The industrialisation of England was not matched in Ireland, not least because of its relative paucity of natural resources, and this dearth of heavy industry contributed greatly to the shift in England's favour. These unfavourable circumstances were amplified by poor agricultural conditions and unsympathetic rule from London, which preferred coercion to encouragement. Even the most tentative shoots of the welfare state which emerged in Great Britain in the nineteenth century were unknown in Ireland, while the circumstances in which the poor and needy lived were much worse than those on the mainland. Inhumane government was exacerbated by natural disasters, the worst of which was, of course, the potato famine of the late 1840s. Perhaps one million people died and the crisis triggered a wave of emigration, mainly to the United States, sustained for the rest of the century. The population declined rapidly and never recovered: in 2000 it was still barely two-thirds that of 150 years earlier.

---

[4] Limited emancipation was given in a succession of Catholic Relief Acts passed between 1775 and 1795.

In the midst of these crises the Anglo-Irish found themselves in an uncomfortable midway position, neither fully endorsing the actions of the British government nor supporting the demands of the Catholic majority. Had it not been for its own cohesiveness the community might well have disintegrated into two rival camps – one pro-Nationalist and one pro-Union – reflecting the potential schizophrenia inherent in its constitution and history. Of decreasing use to the British government, effectively undermined by Catholic Emancipation and other subsequent measures,[5] and regarded with increasing suspicion by the Catholic Irish, the Anglo-Irish found themselves steadily marginalised during the nineteenth century. They were, in effect, the forerunners of the last gasp of the British Raj of the twentieth century, upholding their social exclusivity, their dominance of the professions and civil service, and refuting their geographical isolation and declining status by a hectic social calendar of soirées, dances, concerts, nights at the theatre and days at the races.

The point from which the Anglo-Irish themselves perceived this decline is not clear. Joseph O'Brien asserts that

> Gradually the wealthiest segment of the population withdrew from Dublin, and the noble residences adorning the best streets and fashionable squares exchanged their occupants [the aristocracy] for the new pace-setters of society – the professional classes, especially the barristers and attorneys, who thrived on an admixture of law and politics in a city that retained in Dublin Castle a top-heavy bureaucracy.[6]

---

[5] Emancipation was passed for the whole of Great Britain and Ireland in 1828 (Grattan had introduced a bill to the Commons which failed by only two votes in 1819 and a bill introduced by William Conyngham Greene in 1821 passed in the Commons but failed in the Lords). Emancipation gave Catholics rights almost equal to those of Anglicans, including the right to vote, subject to the same property qualifications as Anglicans. University education remained one of the most contentious issues during the nineteenth century, not least because the possession of a degree was a prerequisite for entry into many professions. Technically, Catholics were allowed to attend Trinity College, Dublin, from 1793, but few did so because of its high-Church, high-Tory ethos, and religious 'tests' were not fully abolished until 1873. Various attempts during the nineteenth century to establish forms of higher education in Ireland widely acceptable to Catholics were unsuccessful and the situation was not resolved until the passing of the 1908 Irish Universities Act. It was not impossible for Catholics to enter either Oxford or Cambridge, but religious tests and requirements at both institutions made it extremely difficult; a succession of parliamentary Acts passed between 1854 and 1871 removed the tests gradually, enabling men to graduate without regard to religious affiliation and, eventually, to join the universities' staff. Practically speaking, in Ireland these various reforms together meant a gradual decline in the disproportionate dominance of various professions by Anglicans; for statistics see Mary E. Daly, *Dublin: The Deposed Capital* (Cork, 1984).

[6] Joseph V. O'Brien, *Dear Dirty Dublin: A City in Distress 1899–1916* (Berkeley, Calif., 1982), 5.

For those born in the centre of this professional, and especially legal, milieu, however, Dublin's status may well have grown during the nineteenth century: Harry Plunket Greene wrote that, 'Ireland in those days ... was a country of intensive brilliance, more of imagination even than culture.'[7] Certainly Georgian-style terraces were still being built in Dublin's exclusive Merrion Square area in the 1830s, suggesting that at this point, little or no decline was evident. Even at the beginning of the twentieth century, so close to the social upheavals leading to partition and independence, the city was still viewed by those looking back from the wholly different world of the inter-war years as a major social centre: 'Dublin at this time, about 1900, was amazingly gay and the season was a brilliant one. People used still to come up and take houses for the season, and wealthy and poor and good family mingled for a few weeks at dinners, dances, Court functions, and all sorts of miscellaneous sports and games.'[8] In truth, for the professions at least, post-Union Ireland was a rich and generally pleasant place with sour notes only creeping in towards the end of the century, when the number of people questioning their status and exclusivity exceeded the small group any elite can reasonably expect to have to deal with and to shrug off.

The nineteenth-century professional cadre comprised Dublin's most successful lawyers, merchants, clerics, doctors and civil servants. As in the eighteenth century their sense of cohesiveness was greatly reinforced by their being almost exclusively Anglican (this dominance declined steadily during the nineteenth century but Anglicans remained overrepresented in proportion to their population in most professions). The group was also content to stay in Ireland: summer was often spent on a rural estate or at a resort and the winter in Dublin. Visits to England were generally unnecessary, as well as being long and, especially in the earlier part of the century, sometimes dangerous (steamships commenced regular journeys across the Irish Sea shortly after the end of Napoleonic Wars, but the railway did not reach Holyhead until the late 1840s, meaning that any journey further than the British western coastal areas remained a gruelling expedition until well into the 1850s). Intermarriage reinforced insularity. As Harry Greene put it: 'The "home" spirit so pervaded the families that each fresh generation settled down comfortably to carry on the family tradition in the familiar sphere. With the exception of a few restless spirits its youth went into the Church or the Law or Medicine or took root in the land at home.'[9]

---

[7] Greene, *Stanford*, 19.
[8] Page L. Dickinson, *The Dublin of Yesterday* (London, 1929), 5.
[9] Greene, *Stanford*, 20.

As Joseph O'Brien has noted, it was the legal profession which led the Anglo-Irish elite. Law could lead to the very pinnacle of the social ladder and was a safe and eminently respectable occupation. This supremacy was recognised by all, as was the role the law played in Dublin social life:

> It is quite certain that the legal element dominates society in Dublin and is held in the highest respect. The leading members, i.e. the Chancellor and the Judges, do duty for the absentee nobility who have long since ceased to reside in the little capital, only putting in an appearance during the Castle season. Hence the lawyers and their wives do the 'representation', live in the finest houses, drive the finest carriages, and entertain the Lord Lieutenant.[10]

Even in this small group a noted pecking order was maintained: 'Judges entertained lavishly, or meanly (according to their personalities and the incomes of their wives). The Senior Bar did the same in a slightly modified way; and the Junior Bar dined out whenever and wherever it could, but more especially in the houses of solicitors with pretty daughters.'[11] If one takes 'law' as 'legal profession' then the perception of Anglo-Irish Dubliners was clearly that 'the law is the true embodiment of everything that is excellent'.[12] And it was into the geographical and social centre of this embodiment of excellence that Charles Villiers Stanford was born at 2 Herbert Street on 30 September 1852.

Stanford was indeed, both socially and geographically, the archetypal Anglo-Irishman. His birthplace lies towards the edge of the Anglo-Irish enclave (though the houses in and around Herbert Street were not built until about 1830, so their claim to be truly Georgian is marginal). His forebears, Stanfords on the one side, Henns on the other, comprised stalwart Anglo-Irish stock, able to trace their Irish lineage for almost two hundred years, following emigration from England in the seventeenth century. The men of both families played a significant role in Anglo-Irish society. Thus, in an atmosphere of comfort, some privilege and eminent respectability, the infant Charles started his life's journey.

Of the two sides of Charles's family, rather less is known of his paternal ancestry (see Fig. 1.2; letters refer to the notes in the figure). The earliest forebear resident in Ireland is Luke Stanford, a landowner and 'merchant of large dealing'[13] of Belturbet, Co. Cavan, who died in 1733. Quite how Luke Stanford acquired his land is unknown; nor is

---

[10] Frances A. Gerard, *Picturesque Dublin, Old and New* (London, 1898), 135.
[11] Dickinson, *Dublin of Yesterday*, 18.
[12] William Schwenk Gilbert, *Iolanthe* (opening line of the Lord Chancellor's Act I song).
[13] Quoted without source in Trinity College, Dublin, MS 5888.

it known from where in England he originated.[14] It seems likely, however, that he came to Ireland at some point during the reign of Charles
II since his son John was born in Killeshandra, Co. Cavan, in 1686. In
subsequent generations the men of the Stanford family, born and brought
up in Co. Cavan, were sent to Trinity College, Dublin for their university education,[15] and showed, in the eighteenth century, a disposition
towards careers in the army and navy (for example, Luke Stanford[b],
who was at one time Commander of HM Schooner 'Hope' and William
Luttrell Stanford[f], who was a Captain in the 56th Regiment). Several
Stanfords became High Sheriffs of Co. Cavan, an indication of the regard
in which the family was held (but all descended through Daniel, third
son of John Stanford[a] and grandson of the first Luke). Charles's
grandfather, William Stanford[g], returned to his great-grandfather's
profession and was described as a 'merchant', 'seller of woolen cloth'
and 'gentleman'.[16] He is known to have lived at 33 Lower Sackville
Street (now Lower O'Connell Street, at the heart of Dublin's northern
commercial district) and subsequently resided in the northern suburb of
Clontarf. In his wife, Sarah McCullan, daughter of James McCullan,
KC, Bencher of King's Inn, the Stanford family acquired one of its first
links to the legal profession.

   William fathered three sons and one daughter: William, Charles, John
and Mary. All three sons were educated at Trinity College; William and
Charles both entered the church and were rectors in Co. Cork and
Dublin respectively. William appears to have led a quiet life but Charles
had literary and quasi-political pretensions: he edited the *Dublin
University Magazine* and wrote several pamphlets attacking Catholicism,
the most successful of which was his *Handbook to the Romish
Controversy* in which he wrote, 'I believe it wholly impossible for any
one who accepts the doctrines of the Church of Rome as true, to know
anything of the Gospel of Christ, as being "the power of God unto salva-
tion to everyone that believeth"',[17] an ample demonstration of the
distance between Anglican and Catholic faiths at this time. Charles
Stuart Stanford was not only an author: he also composed. The 'Adelaide
Mazurka' (the sole piece held by the British Library) does not, however,
presage a great future for his nephew: it is an uninspiring piece

---

[14] Although the birth of a Luke Stanford in London in 1633 with siblings born in
Angmering in Sussex suggests, just possibly, that this was the origin of the family (assuming
that the two Lukes were father and son).

[15] See George Burtchaell and Thomas Sadler, *Alumni Dublinienses 1593–1846* (Dublin,
1924), 774.

[16] Ibid.

[17] Charles Stuart Stanford, *A Handbook to the Romish Controversy, being a Refutation
in Detail of the Creed of Pope Pius IV* (3rd edn, Dublin, 1870), p. i.

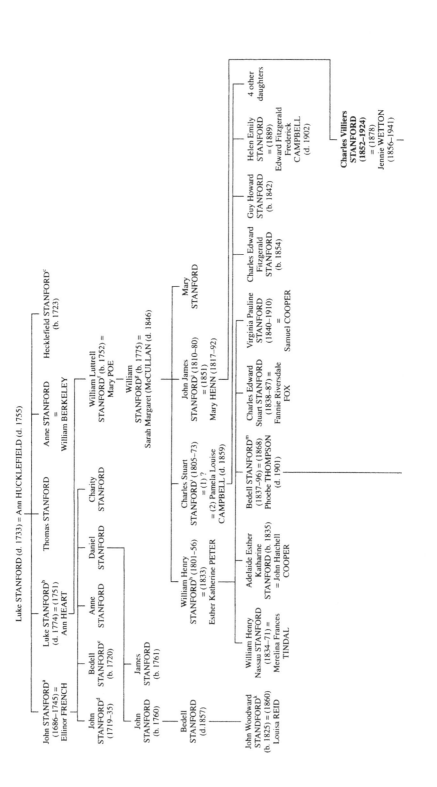

Luke STANFORD (d. 1733) = Ann HUCKLEFIELD (d. 1755)

John STANFORD[a]
(1686–1745) =
Ellinor FRENCH

Luke STANFORD[b]
(d. 1774) = (1751)
Ann HEART

Thomas STANFORD

Anne STANFORD
=
William BERKELEY

Hecklefield STANFORD[c]
(b. 1723)

John
STANFORD[c]
(1719–35)

Bedell
STANFORD[c]
(b. 1720)

Anne
STANFORD

Daniel
STANFORD

Charity
STANFORD

William Luttrell
STANFORD[f] (b. 1752) =
Mary POE

James
STANFORD
(b. 1761)

John
STANFORD
(b. 1760)

William
STANFORD[g] (b. 1775) =
Sarah Margaret (McCULLAN (d. 1846)

Bedell
STANFORD
(d.1857)

William Henry
STANFORD[h] (1801–56)
= (1833)
Esther Katherine PETER

Charles Stuart
STANFORD (1805–73)
= (1) ?
= (2) Pamela Louise
CAMPBELL (d. 1859)

John James
STANFORD (1810–80)
= (1851)
Mary HENN (1817–92)

Mary
STANFORD

John Woodward
STANFORD[k]
(b. 1825) = (1860)
Louisa REID

William Henry
Nassau STANFORD
(1834–71) =
Merelina Frances
TINDAL

Adelaide Esther
Katharine
STANFORD (b. 1835)
= John Hatchell
COOPER

Bedell STANFORD[m]
(1837–96) = (1868)
Phoebe THOMPSON
(d. 1901)

Charles Edward
Stuart STANFORD
(1838–87) =
Fannie Riversdale
FOX

Virginia Pauline
STANFORD
(1840–1910) =
Samuel COOPER

Charles Edward
Fitzgerald
STANFORD
(b. 1854)

Guy Howard
STANFORD
(b. 1842)

Helen Emily
STANFORD
= (1889)
Edward Fitzgerald
Frederick
CAMPBELL
(d. 1902)

4 other
daughters

**Charles Villiers
STANFORD
(1852–1924)**
= (1878)
Jennie WETTON
(1856–1941)

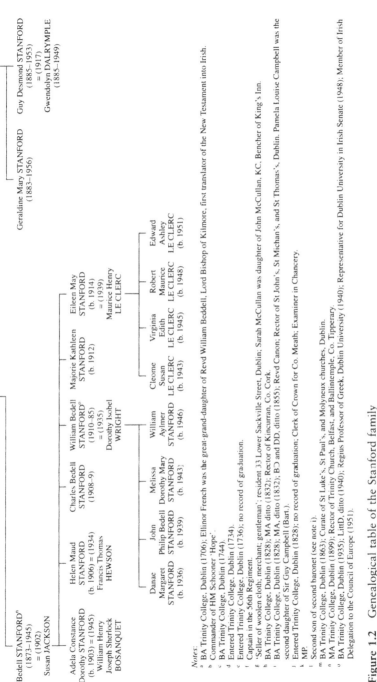

Notes:

a BA Trinity College, Dublin (1706); Ellinor French was the great-grand-daughter of Revd William Beddell, Lord Bishop of Kilmore, first translator of the New Testament into Irish.

b Commander of HM Schooner 'Hope'.

c BA Trinity College, Dublin (1744).

d Entered Trinity College, Dublin (1734).

e Entered Trinity College, Dublin (1736); no record of graduation.

f Captain in the 56th Regiment.

g 'Seller of woolen cloth; merchant; gentleman'; resident 33 Lower Sackville Street, Dublin; Sarah McCullan was daughter of John McCullan, KC, Bencher of King's Inn.

h BA Trinity College, Dublin (1828); MA ditto (1832); Rector of Kincurran, Co. Cork.

i BA Trinity College, Dublin (1828); MA, ditto (1832); BD and DD, ditto (1855); Revd Canon; Rector of St John's, St Michan's, and St Thomas's, Dublin. Pamela Louise Campbell was the second daughter of Sir Guy Campbell (Bart.).

j Entered Trinity College, Dublin (1828); no record of graduation; Clerk of Crown for Co. Meath; Examiner in Chancery.

k MP.

l Second son of second baronet (see note i).

m BA Trinity College, Dublin (1863); Curate of St Luke's, St Paul's, and Molyneux churches, Dublin.

n MA Trinity College, Dublin (1899); Rector of Trinity Church, Belfast, and Ballintemple, Co. Tipperary.

o BA Trinity College, Dublin (1935); LittD, ditto (1940); Regius Professor of Greek, Dublin University (1940); Representative for Dublin University in Irish Senate (1948); Member of Irish Delegation to the Council of Europe (1951).

Figure 1.2 Genealogical table of the Stanford family

Source: L. G. Pine (ed.), *Burke's Genealogical and Heraldic History of the Landed Gentry in Ireland*, London, 1958; George Burtchaell and Thomas Sadler, *Alumni Dublinienses*, Dublin, 1935.

comprising solely four-bar phrases and almost exclusively tonic and dominant chords in root position. Its existence, however, suggests that music had played a part in the Stanford family's life for many years.

While Charles Stuart Stanford exhibited some modest musical talents, his younger brother possessed far more ability, which manifested itself in his gift for singing. These talents, coupled with a strong degree of determination, caused his family much difficulty. The chronology is unclear but his son summed up the problem: 'As he was a born actor, with a great love for the stage, it was with the greatest difficulty that his very Low Church family prevented him from becoming an operatic singer, a scandal which in their opinion would have shaken their character and traditions to the core.'[18] In fact John Stanford matriculated at Trinity College, Dublin in 1828, aged 18, and entered King's Inn in 1831; he was evidently destined, so far as his family was concerned, for the legal profession. He is not noted as having graduated from Trinity and this may have been the reason that he became a legal administrator rather than a barrister. John held various posts in the Irish legal establishment, including Registrar to the Chief Justice of Common Pleas, Clerk of the Crown for Co. Meath, and Examiner in Chancery.[19] A flavour of his work can be given by citing some of the duties of the Clerks of the Crown:

> to receive and preserve all informations, examinations, and recognizances of magistrates and all depositions, inquests and recognizances of Coroners; to draw indictments in cases where they are not prepared by the Crown Solicitor; to swear the Grand Jury; to attend the Crown Court; to arraign the prisoners; to enter and record all pleas, orders and proceedings of the Court in the Crown book; swear and, if necessary, examine the several witnesses on the trials; prepare and keep all records of the Assizes, and prepare all warrants for the transmission of prisoners.[20]

Upon his death his obituarist tactfully referred to his legal career as 'a somewhat unobtrusive and uneventful one'.[21]

The Henns, Charles Stanford's maternal family, were of the cream of Dublin's legal elite (see Fig. 1.3). Like the Stanfords, they had come to Ireland during the reign of Charles II. Henry Henn[a] had been a Justice of the Court of Common Pleas for three years before being issued with

---

[18] Stanford, *Pages*, 28.

[19] According to A. E. M'Clintock and C. Brady, *The Law Directory for Ireland 1846* (Dublin, 1846) and his obituary notice (see n. 21) John Stanford held the first of these positions during the office of Lord Chief Justice Doherty; upon Doherty's death Stanford was recommended for the position of Clerk of the Crown by the Earl of Clarendon (the Viceroy), and held the post of Examiner in Chancery during the office of Master Fitzgibbon.

[20] M'Clintock and Brady, *Law Directory*, 78.

[21] *Dublin Daily Express*, 20 July 1880, p. 2.

his patent as Lord Chief Baron of the Court of Exchequer in Ireland in March 1679; another branch of the family had also at one time held a baronetcy[22] and claimed to be able to trace its ancestry as far as the Domesday Book. His career was not a smooth one: he was removed from office by James II in 1687, and replaced by Sir Stephen Rice (who was himself removed after the accession of William III and Mary); generations later the two families were linked when William Henn[f] (Charles's grandfather) married Mary Rice in 1809.

Henry's son Richard[b] was granted land at Paradise Hill, Co. Clare, by the Earl of Thomond in 1685 and from their settlement in Ireland the Henns were pillars of the Irish legal establishment. Following the obligatory degree invariably taken at Trinity, almost all the men became barristers and judges and thus were always at the centre of Irish professional society. Although they held land in Co. Clare, the Henns generally resided in Dublin's Georgian squares; the easy-going nature of the legal profession, however, no doubt allowed for extended visits to the family estate.

Charles's grandfather and great-grandfather rose highest and both became Masters in Chancery (William Henn[d] in 1793 and William Henn[f] in 1822). The post of Master in Chancery was that of a senior justice with the responsibility of 'executing the orders of the Court upon references made to them, and, by reports in writing to certify the result'.[23] This mundane description disguises the status of the Masters (of whom there were four in the 1840s) as only the Lord Chancellor had power to make rulings (a power often delegated to the Master of the Rolls) and the Masters were next in seniority to the Master of the Rolls. Furthermore, these powers were extensive as, being the highest judicial officer in Ireland, the Lord Chancellor appointed all Justices of the Peace, was Visitor of all hospitals and colleges of Royal Foundations, and was the 'guardian of all infants, idiots and lunatics'.[24] The small number of officers in the Court of Chancery led to long delays in the settlement of cases (the delays suffered in Chancery in England were, of course, witheringly portrayed in Dickens's *Bleak House* (1852–3)). In terms of social seniority the Masters appeared thirteenth in the table of precedence at Dublin Castle.[25]

---

[22] See John Burke, *A Genealogical and Heraldic History of the Extinct and Dormant Baronetcies of England* (2nd edn, London, 1844).

[23] M'Clintock and Brady, *Law Directory*, 8.

[24] Ibid.

[25] This disguises their importance since seven of the higher ranks were individuals (the Lord Chancellor, Lord Chief Justice, Master of the Rolls, Lord Chief Justice of Common Pleas, Lord Chief Baron, Attorney General and Solicitor General; the other five ranks were the Judges and Barons in the other courts: Queen's Bench, Common Pleas, Exchequer, Prerogative and Admiralty).

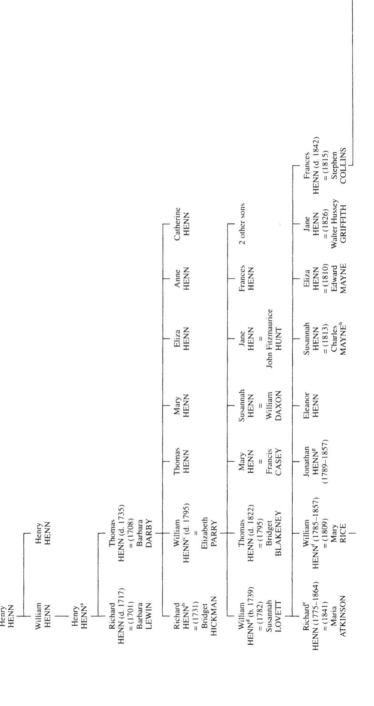

Henry
HENN

William
HENN

Henry
HENN[a]

Henry
HENN

Richard
HENN (d. 1717)
= (1701)
Barbara
LEWIN

Thomas
HENN (d. 1735)
= (1708)
Barbara
DARBY

Richard
HENN[b]
= (1731)
Bridget
HICKMAN

William
HENN[c] (d. 1795)
=
Elizabeth
PARRY

Thomas
HENN

Mary
HENN

Eliza
HENN

Anne
HENN

Catherine
HENN

William
HENN[d] (b. 1739)
= (1782)
Susannah
LOVETT

Thomas
HENN (d. 1822)
= (1795)
Bridget
BLAKENEY

Mary
HENN
=
Francis
CASEY

Susannah
HENN
=
William
DAXON

Jane
HENN
=
John Fitzmaurice
HUNT

Frances
HENN

2 other sons

Richard[e]
HENN (1775–1864)
= (1841)
Maria
ATKINSON

William
HENN[f] (1785–1857)
= (1809)
Mary
RICE

Jonathan
HENN[g]
(1789–1857)

Eleanor
HENN

Susannah
HENN
= (1813)
Charles
MAYNE[h]

Eliza
HENN
= (1810)
Edward
MAYNE

Jane
HENN
= (1826)
Walter Hussey
GRIFFITH

Frances
HENN (d. 1842)
= (1815)
Stephen
COLLINS

Genealogical table of the Henn family (rotated layout)

Generation (children, 1809 marriage of William Henn and Mary Rice):

- William HENN (1812–53)
- Thomas Rice HENN[i] (1814–1901) = (1845) Jane Isabella BLACKBURNE (d. 1902)
- Jonathar Lovett HENN (1818–88)
- George HENN (d. 1832)
- Richard HENN (d. 1836)
- Christiana HENN (1810–91)
- Jane HENN (d. 1905) = (1842) Robert HOLMES (d. 1870)
- Ellen HENN (d. 1913) = (1867) William LA TOUCHE (d. 1892)
- Mary HENN (1817–92) = (1851) John James STANFORD (d. 1880)
- Susanna HENN (d. 1891)

Next generation:

- William HENN (1847–94) = (1877) Susanna CUN'HAME-GRAHAM (d 1911)
- Francis Blackburne HENN (1848–1915) = (1880) Helen Letitia Elizabeth GORE (d. 1936)
- Thomas Rice HENN[h] (1849–80)
- Edward Lovett HENN (1852–1939) = (1878) Margaret HENRY (d. 1940)
- Adella Jane HENN (1853–93) = (1884) James Samuel GIBBONS (d. 1914)
- Richard HENN (1855–1929) = (1895) Elizabeth HEATON-ARMSTRONG (d. 1940)
- Mary Rice HENN (1857–83)
- Henry HENN (1858–1931) = (1905) Frances Helen COLLINS (d. 1938)
- **Charles Villiers Stanford** (1852–1924) = (1878) Jennie WETTON (1856–1941)
- Richard HENN-COLLINS[j] (1842–1911)

Next generation:

- Muriel Helen Isabella Rice HENN (1881–1966) = (1903) Frederick William O'HARA
- Maud Susan Beatrice HENN (1886–1967) = (1918) Philip BRACHI
- Lilian Adela Gore HENN (1883–1970) = (1919) Stanhope WILLIAMS
- William Francis HENN[m] (1892–1964) = (1915) Geraldine Frances Jane STACPOOLE-MAHON
- Thomas Rice HENN[n] (1901–74) = (1926) Mary Enid ROBERTS
- Eric HENN (1880–1915)

Notes:

[a] Lord Chief Baron of Ireland during reigns of Charles II and James II; removed by the latter in 1686 and replaced by Stephen Rice (whose descendant Mary Rice married William Henn in 1809).

[b] First member of the family to settle in Ireland, being granted land at Paradise Hill, Co. Clare, by the Earl of Thomond in 1685.

[c] BA at Trinity College, Dublin, (1739 or 1740); called to the Irish Bar (1744); Judge in the Court of King's Bench (1768).

[d] Entered Trinity College, Dublin (1755); called to the Irish Bar (1784); Master in Chancery (1793); Susannah Lovett was the fifth daughter of Sir Jonathan Lovett (Bart.) of Liscombe, Buckinghamshire.

[e] Commander in the Royal Navy.

[f] BA at Trinity College, Dublin (1805); called to the Irish Bar (1808); Master in Chancery (1822).

[g] BA at Trinity College, Dublin (1808); called to the Irish Bar (1811); Queen's Counsel; Chairman of Donegal Quarter Sessions.

[h] Eldest son of his Honour, Judge Mayne; ordained priest; his younger brother Edward married Susanna Henn's sister, Eliza.

[i] BA at Trinity College, Dublin (1837); called to the Irish Bar (1839); Queen's Counsel; Jane Blackburne was the second daughter of Hon. Francis Blackburne, Lord Chancellor of Ireland.

[j] Fellow of Downing College, Cambridge; King's Counsel; Master of the Rolls in England (1901–07).

[k] Killed at the Battle of Maiwand, Afghanistan.

[l] Ordained priest; Doctor of Divinity; Bishop of Blackburn; Frances Helen Collins was daughter of Rt. Hon. Lord Collins of Kensington and directly related to Stephen Collins, father of Richard Henn-Collins (note j above).

[m] Chief Constable of Gloucestershire; MVO; CBE.

[n] Fellow of St Catharine's College, Cambridge (1926); Chairman of Faculty Board of English. Cambridge University; FRSL; CBE; hon. Litt. D. and hon. LLD. Cambridge University; writer on Anglo-Irish literature, most notably on W. B. Yeats.

Figure 1.3 Genealogical table of the Henn family

Source: L. G. Pine (ed.), *Burke's Genealogical and Heraldic History of the Landed Gentry in Ireland*, London, 1958; George Burtchaell and Thomas Sadler, *Alumni Dublinienses*, Dublin, 1935; Thomas Rice Henn, *Five Arches: A Sketch for an Autobiography*, Gerrards Cross, 1980.

Charles's grandfather, William Henn[f], the younger of the two Masters, was remembered fondly by other members of the legal establishment: 'He discharged his very important duties with marked ability and unremitting attention. Always courteous in manner, patient and kind in conduct, he earned and retained to the last, the esteem of both branches of the profession and the confidence of the public.'[26] Inevitably, since he died when Charles was aged 4, the grandson's memories of his grandfather are second-hand, and it was Jonathan Henn[g], Charles's great-uncle, who made a far greater impact on the young boy. Indeed Jonathan Henn made an impression on almost everyone. He acquired a wide reputation as a brilliant yet modest barrister. Although many contemporaries were convinced that he could have risen to the top of his profession and/or entered parliament, Jonathan preferred to remain in practice on the Munster Circuit and maintain his free time:

> Mr Henn was in very independent circumstances and devoted to the sport of fishing. Having no domestic cares – he never married – chairman for the [Quarter Sessions of the] county of Donegal, with lucrative circuit practice and some private fortune, he preferred ease to labour, and the sport he loved to toil he disliked. Yet on circuit he flinched from no trouble in mastering his briefs. I never found him wanting either in reference to facts of law. His speeches were masterpieces of forensic oratory, unadorned it may be, yet perfectly suited to the occasion, and clear as a running stream.[27]

Only once did he rise to national prominence, when he was part of the team which defended the Irish nationalist Daniel O'Connell in 1843, securing his acquittal by the Law Lords after all lower courts had found against him.

This love of leisure was of great benefit to Charles. It is evident that it was from Jonathan Henn that Stanford gained his love of fishing, which became an ever greater leisure pursuit as he grew older; Harry Greene recalled that Charles would 'hold up a family dinner for a considerable time while he boned a herring in the way his granduncle had shown him when he was 6 years old'.[28] Charles himself writes fondly of him and devoted more space in his autobiography to Jonathan Henn than to any other relative except his father.[29] It was Jonathan who bought Charles his first grand piano (an early recognition of the boy's ability and an indication of the regard in which music was held in

---

[26] James R. O'Flanagan, *The Irish Bar* (London, 1879), 224.

[27] James R. O'Flanagan, *The Munster Circuit* (London, 1880), 357; for further writings on Jonathan Henn see Oliver J. Burke, *Anecdotes of the Connaught Circuit* (Dublin, 1885), 203, and Patrick Lynch, *Some Members of the Munster Circuit* (Cork, 1946), 50.

[28] Greene, *Stanford*, 15.

[29] See Stanford, *Pages*, 4–6.

the Henn family) and who taught him whist, which Stanford played all his life and which, like fishing, became more important to him as time went on.[30]

Before considering Charles's own childhood it is worthwhile pausing and looking at the Henns and Stanfords as they developed subsequently. Both families were of that type which somehow manages to produce a stream of talented men (and probably women, although in keeping with the social mores of the class and time the achievements of the female members of both families are much harder to trace). Coming from a class where such work was simply expected, their contribution to Irish and English society, principally in what might be defined as the 'broad public service', is notable. Charles's relatives in parallel and later generations have included, on the Henn side, Richard Henn-Collins[j] (b. 1842), Master of the Rolls in England, 1901–7; Rt Revd Henry Henn[l] (b. 1858), one time Bishop of Burnley; William Francis Henn CBE MVO[m] (b. 1892), a Chief Constable of Gloucestershire; and Thomas Rice Henn CBE FRSL[n] (b. 1901, the third of that name), Fellow of Downing College, Cambridge, scholar of Anglo-Irish literature (notably of W. B. Yeats); and numerous JPs. On the Stanford side there have been several more clergymen and, most notably, William Bedell Stanford[o] (b. 1910), Regius Professor of Greek in Dublin University, author of several scholarly texts, and a member of the Irish Senate and of the Irish Delegation to the Council of Europe in 1951. Curiously few of them seem to have had knowledge of their composing relative: *Burke's Landed Gentry in Ireland*, in its account of William Bedell Stanford's ancestry, mentions John Stanford, but refers only to him as having issue,[31] and Thomas Rice Henn, although educated at Cambridge within the time of Stanford's Professorship, makes no reference to him in his own autobiography.[32]

Returning to the years immediately prior to Charles's birth, both families are to be found in the Anglo-Irish enclave of Georgian squares. Several lived in close proximity to each other: John Stanford[j] at 14 Herbert Place, Jonathan Henn[g] at 16 Upper Merrion Street, Willam Henn[f] at 17 Merrion Square South, Thomas Rice Henn[i] at 48 Upper Mount Street and Richard Henn[e] (one time Commander in the Royal Navy, later Examiner in Chancery (like John Stanford) to his brother

---

[30] Stanford transferred his affections to bridge later in life when that game evolved from whist at the turn of the century.

[31] *Burke's Genealogical and Heraldic History of the Landed Gentry in Ireland*, ed. L. G. Pine (London, 1958), 648–9; see also pp. 364–5 for information on the Henns.

[32] Thomas Rice Henn, *Five Arches: Leaves from an Autobiography* (Gerrards Cross, 1980).

William Henn) at 17 Herbert Street (see Fig. 1.1).[33] Life was prosperous and enjoyable; the decline of the professional Anglo-Irish had yet to set in and even the consequences of the potato famine seemed far away.

John Stanford and Mary Henn married in 1851, taking up residence at 2 Herbert Street, the house in which they were both to live until John's death in 1880 (see Pl. 1). Neither Charles nor Harry Greene wrote much about the marriage, although the implication is that it was generally happy and stable. Although John's mercurial temper sometimes caused problems, Mary's acknowledged gentility complemented both the irritable and mischievous sides of her husband's personality. Having lived at a time when middle-class women were expected to be primarily concerned with domestic issues, it is inevitable that rather less is known about Mary Stanford than about her husband. She and her two sisters, Christiana and Susanna, were known as the 'hens of Paradise' (a pun on the surname and the family seat), which implies a degree of physical beauty. Charles noted that she appreciated her husband's wit and Harry Greene referred to her as being 'a woman of great charm and . . . gifted with all those Victorian gentle graces', but little flesh is put on these bare bones save for Greene's attributing to her Stanford's old-fashioned manners.[34] She remains, therefore, a shadowy figure in Charles's life, although there is certainly no implication that she was either inadequate or inept.

While the influence of his mother is generally unclear, it is much easier to see how John Stanford influenced his son. Both possessed short fuses and could explode with apparently little provocation and were sometimes remarkably obstinate over making amends. John Stanford's obituarist tactfully referred to his short temper as a 'somewhat nervous irritability (such as not seldom accompanies the finely organised mind)',[35] but its nature is more graphically illustrated by Alfred Graves,[36] who referred to John Stanford as 'An erratic person [whose] temper was not always to be relied upon. He fell out with my mother and was so rude to her on one occasion that a separation lasting several years took place between the two families, much to the distress of Mrs Stanford, a woman of the most peaceable disposition.'[37] On the other hand, John

---

[33] Information drawn from *Slater's Directory of Ireland*, 1846.

[34] Greene, *Stanford*, 29.

[35] *Dublin Daily Express*, 20 July 1880, p. 2.

[36] Alfred Graves (1846–1931), son of the Anglican Bishop of Limerick and father of the author Robert Graves, was a member of HM Inspectorate of Schools, but also published many volumes of Irish songs and ballads, mainly in collaboration with Stanford (see Ch. 8) and also wrote on Irish literature.

[37] Alfred Graves, *To Return to All That* (London, 1929), 24.

Stanford also had a lively sense of humour. Alfred Graves related another incident:

> John and his son Charlie Stanford once came on a visit to us at Limerick and on hearing that we were to have a charade party at the [Bishop's] Palace, John went out to Tait's big drapery shop and said 'I want a suit of clothes for a boy of three.' 'What size, Sir?' asked the shopman. 'My size!' answered Stanford seriously, as he stood six feet four. 'Measure me for it,' which the astonished tailor proceeded to do. In this strange garb Stanford quarrelled with our chief police magistrate's wife, Mrs Moore, who acted as a little girl, her long curls hanging down her back over her short frock and pinny.[38]

This mischievous nature was also evident in Charles, who showed a fondness for playing practical jokes and witty comments.[39]

Predictably, most of what is known of Charles's youth is derived from what he himself wrote in his autobiography and also from Greene's biography.[40] To the extent that both men were writing many years after the event, one should treat these reminiscences with some caution, but in general terms it seems reasonable to accept the essentials of what the two men have to say about Charles's life up to the age of 18, and it is from these two sources that all information about Charles's general education is to be drawn. Unusually for a boy of his class, Charles was not sent away to school but was educated locally by a martinet named Henry Tilney Bassett. Bassett seems to have run a small but exclusive school at the time of Charles's childhood which proved to be popular with many local Anglo-Irish professionals. Quite why Bassett's school should have been so successful is not clear, but Harry Greene, who was also taught by Bassett, indicated that many boys from the local area attended this small institution.[41] It is not evident when Stanford attended the school, but the implication is that he was a pupil for several years

---

[38] Ibid., 148.

[39] Greene gave several examples in his book, for example: '[Stanford] inherited this delight in bringing off a "sell", as on the occasion at the Royal College when he announced on the notice board that the first half of the afternoon's orchestral practice was to be devoted to the works of Strauss. Richard Strauss was at that time supposed to be the last word in modernism, and all the young bloods turned up to a man, and were entertained with the "Blue Danube" and other masterpieces of the immortal Johann' (Greene, *Stanford*, 28–9).

[40] Harry Plunket Greene (1865–1936) was Stanford's greatest personal friend from their first meeting in the 1870s. He was, from the late 1890s, one of the leading British baritone recitalists and also appeared at many provincial festivals; after the Great War he also produced several books. He married Hubert Parry's daughter Gwendolen in 1899 but they later separated.

[41] Greene, *Stanford*, 24–7.

prior to his admission to Cambridge; before this he was, presumably, educated at home by his mother and perhaps a governess (there are two references to there being a schoolroom at 2 Herbert Street which support this).[42] Greene acknowledged that, even by the standards of the 1930s, the school was basic and Bassett sometimes brutally so, so from the perspective of 2000, the regime would probably be found to be horrific. It appears that Bassett's school was somewhat backward, even in mid-Victorian terms, and the reforms seen at Winchester, Rugby and Uppingham had made no impression. The curriculum was heavily focused on Classics, with Maths seen as a very poor relation. The former was taught primarily by rote learning with only a secondary emphasis on understanding grammar, while Bassett was a disciplinarian for whom corporal punishment was a *sine qua non*. Yet both Stanford and Greene paid tribute to their schoolmaster, crediting him with an interest in his charges and a degree of inspiration as a teacher. And at a time when universities viewed accomplishment in Classics as the most important entrance requirement, Bassett's intensive, if regimented, drumming in of vocabulary, literature and grammar can be seen as having much to recommend it. Indeed, when it came to applying to university, Stanford's proficiency in Latin and Greek obviously stood him in good stead (see pp. 34–6).

As well as this general education, Stanford also gained considerable musical knowledge in Dublin, both through the offices of his parents and their families, but also through the wider cultural life of the Irish capital. Dublin's geographical isolation meant that front-rank musicians visited the city rarely and the Victorian attitude which required music to be a social accomplishment rather than a means of making one's living meant that there were very few resident professionals. Music may have been, therefore, an amateur sport, but it was still an essential part of life and evidence of good breeding. Even if some people had misgivings about music in church and a suspicion that the theatre was a place of loose morals, the Anglo-Irish community loved music in the home and in the concert hall, and entertained themselves with gusto:

> Music is a noted feature of afternoon parties. Passing through one of the fashionable squares during the season we note a block of carriages and cabs; and from the open windows come the strains of some popular duet or chorus. The Dublin amateur is somewhat ambitious and has a certain standpoint of excellence. The voices as a rule are tuneful and pleasing and show considerable cultivation. Tenors 'robust' and 'delicate' abound; and instrumentalists, although more rare, are of very fair quality.[43]

---

[42] Stanford, *Pages*, 64 and 74.
[43] Gerard, *Picturesque Dublin*, 407.

This love of music did not just manifest itself in these private parties but in many public concerts; Dublin possessed several choirs and concert societies in the mid-nineteenth century, all of which gave at least two or three concerts each season (roughly October to May), the most prestigious being the Society of Antient Concerts (*sic*), founded by John Stanford's friend Joseph Robinson in 1834.[44]

It seems certain that love of music was a prime factor in bringing John Stanford and Mary Henn together in marriage. The musical abilities of the Stanfords have already been alluded to; it is also known that Mary Henn was a gifted pianist and that her father was an adept flautist although, as usual, Mary's achievements seem almost exclusively to have taken place in private. By contrast, although John's family had succeeded in deflecting him away from a career as a musician, he was well known in Dublin musical circles and made regular professional appearances up until about 1851. He maintained his musical education over many years, taking lessons with Crivelli[45] and gaining some informal advice from Lablache.[46] The extensive holidays available to the legal profession at this time no doubt greatly facilitated his continuing education. Lablache was reportedly very impressed with him,[47] and although this may have caused John twinges of regret that he had not pursued the professional career after which he had hankered early in life, the status he acquired in Dublin in the 1840s may well have made up for this to a large extent.[48]

---

[44] Robinson was just 18 when he founded the Society of Antient Concerts and, according to Stanford, held the baton for twenty-nine years. Stanford went on to say 'He produced all the best of the old masters, and introduced into Dublin the works of Mendelssohn almost contemporaneously with their performances in this country [that is, England]. The chorus was small, but perfect in balance, and of beautiful quality. They sang well individually as well as collectively; for the conductor had the gift of training them not merely in the notes themselves, but in the manner of singing them' (Charles Stanford, 'Joseph Robinson', in *Studies and Memories*, 117–27). John Stanford took many solo parts with the 'Antients' (see below, n. 48), and Joseph was also conductor of the Dublin University Choral Society.

[45] Probably Domenico Crivelli (1793–1857), son of the tenor Gaetano Crivelli, who taught at the Real Collegio, Naples, and then relocated to London.

[46] Luigi Lablache (1794–1858) had an Irish mother, and was one of the most successful baritones of the early nineteenth century. He appeared in Paris and London regularly from 1830, and subsequently sang at many provincial festivals.

[47] See Stanford, *Pages*, 28–9.

[48] For example, two reviews from 1848 report that 'Mr Stanford, whose amateur performances are estimated for their intrinsic excellence, gave the animated air "Honour and Arms Score the Foe" boldly and with energy' (*Saunders's Newsletter*, 18 Feb. 1848, p. 2) and 'Mr Stanford, who had much devolved upon him during the evening, was never heard to greater advantage, and his distinct intonation, splendid organ and impressive manner constituted some of the material which contributed to his great success on this occasion' (*Saunders's Newsletter*, 18 Apr. 1848, p. 2), both referring to concerts given by the Society of Antient Concerts.

John Stanford became a member of 'a certain quartet of musicians who at one time were the pride and glory of Dublin society – Mrs Hercules MacDonnell, Mrs Edward Geale, Mr MacDonnell and Mr Stanford'.[49] The qualities of their voices were well remembered and Charles was evidently proud of the fact that his father sang in a trio with Mrs Geale and Jenny Lind in the presence of Queen Victoria at the Viceregal Lodge in August 1849.[50] Some greater objectivity might, perhaps, be expected from John Stanford's obituarist, but he, also, was unstinting in his praise:

> John Stanford ... was gifted with one of the noblest vocal organs we have ever heard – a bass voice of unusually extended compass: in the medium and upper part resembling the beautiful full quality of a well-played ophicleide, rather a baritone in timbre, while the lower register in power and depth and in resonance was a bass literally unequalled in excellence. But above all this great natural gift was chastened and guided by the purest, the most correct taste.[51]

His greatest achievement was to sing the part of Elijah in the first Dublin performance of Mendelssohn's oratorio, the première of which he and Joseph Robinson had attended in Birmingham in 1846. The two men determined to stage a performance in Dublin as soon as possible; this duly took place on 9 December 1847, with Robinson conducting, and Stanford acquitted himself so well that his performance was remembered for many years afterwards:

> The first concert of [the Society of Antient Concerts] for the season took place last evening and upon no previous occasion have we observed a more brilliant or crowded audience. The subject for

---

[49] Gerard, *Picturesque Dublin*, 407.

[50] Stanford wrote the following on this quartet of singers: 'Mrs Hercules MacDonnell, a dramatic soprano with a voice which would have rivaled even the greatest *prima donna* of her day, was in every sense an artist both technically and musically. So great a judge as [Sir Michael] Costa valued her powers at the highest estimate, and lamented that she was not enrolled in the ranks of the great public singers ... Mrs Geale (née Josephine Clarke), the cleverest and most gifted of them all, called by Prince Puckler Muskau "that pretty little devil, José", had by some extraordinary art manufactured for herself a tenor voice of rare Italian quality which she controlled with the best Italian skill ... When Queen Victoria came to Ireland during the Viceroyalty of Lord Clarendon, a musical evening was arranged at the Viceregal Lodge at which Jenny Lind was the star. A trio for soprano, tenor, and bass from an Italian opera was one of the items, the two other singers being Mrs Geale and my father. Madame Goldschmidt at the rehearsal wished to wait for the tenor, but to her amazement Mrs Geale said "I am she". When it was over, no one was more appreciative of her powers than that most critical of artists ... Of the men, the two most distinguished were Mr Hercules MacDonnell (a son of a former Provost of Trinity) who had a baritone voice of great power, and possessed a dramatic temperament which gave great incisiveness to his delivery; and my father, John Stanford, whose bass with a compass from high F to low C was one of the finest in quality and style that I have ever heard anywhere' (Stanford, *Pages*, 25–7).

[51] *Dublin Daily Express*, 20 July 1880, p. 2.

performance was well suited for the opening night and it speaks highly indeed for the musical resources of the 'Antients' that they should have been enabled to bring forward with such admirable effect the glorious oratorio of *Elijah*, the last and the greatest of the works of Mendelssohn ... Mr Stanford was the Staudigl of the evening [Joseph Staudigl (1807–61) had taken the solo bass part at the Birmingham première] and his fine voice and clear enunciation told admirably in the part of Elijah.[52]

Despite this glowing achievement there are few newspaper references to John Stanford after 1850, and it seems that he decided to give up appearing in public at this time. (Why? There are many possible reasons, such as his marriage, the birth of Charles, increased workload, but none have been traced. One public performance after Charles's birth has been traced – a Fund Raising Concert for the Royal Irish Academy of Music on 11 February 1861 at the Dublin Theatre Royal – but otherwise public performance appears to have been eschewed.) He did, however, remain active in private circles, for example, as a member of the Hibernian Catch Club. Founded in 1740 by the Vicars Choral of St Patrick's and Christ Church Cathedrals, the Catch Club was more significant from a social point of view than a musical one, and is another example of the nature of the Anglo-Irish enclave:

Its members consist of a limited number of professors of music, and amateurs, catch singers at sight, who are appointed by the committee, and such honorary members as may from time to time be elected. A catch singer at sight, professional or amateur ... [will have been] called on to take part in two or more glees or catches with which he is previously unacquainted, and if his capability be satisfactorily established, he is proposed and balloted for. The President is the Rt Hon Francis Blackburne, Lord Justice of Appeal in Ireland [later Lord Chancellor; his second daughter married Charles's uncle Thomas Rice Henn, QC; Charles's grandfather William Henn had been a past president] and the list of members contains the names of many of the nobility, gentry, members of the legal, medical, clerical and musical professions, and several of the leading mercantile gentlemen of Dublin ... The meetings take place on the second Tuesday in every month, and on the present occasion there was a numerous assemblage ... Amongst the talented amateurs, Mr John Stanford was present, whose glorious voice has so often been heard with delight by the members.[53]

As is the case for his school education, most of what is known of Stanford's early musical education derives from his own writings. The first instrument on which he received tuition was the piano, taught first

---

[52] *Saunders's Newsletter*, 10 Dec. 1847, p. 2.
[53] *Orchestra*, 12 Dec. 1863, p. 166. The four Robinson brothers (John, William, Francis and Joseph) were also prominent members of the club.

by his mother, then by his godmother Elizabeth Meeke, briefly by a
Miss Flynn, and then by Michael Quarry. If the chronology implied by
Stanford's account of his youth is correct then Elizabeth Meeke started
teaching him at about age 7, Miss Flynn at about age 10 and Michael
Quarry from about age 11. Additionally, in the summer of 1862,
Stanford had a few lessons with Ernst Pauer,[54] when the family visited
London. His three Dublin-based teachers had all been pupils of Ignaz
Moscheles.[55] Miss Flynn, perhaps due to the brevity of her tenure,
did not make much impact on him, but Stanford paid ample tribute
to Elizabeth Meeke and Michael Quarry – the former emphasised the
importance of touch and taught him to sightread; the latter introduced
him to both contemporary and early music, primarily Schumann,
Brahms, Bach and Handel.[56] These adventures with Michael Quarry
were made the more exciting by the companionship of Raoul de Versan,
with whom Stanford played many duets, and with whom he shared some
of his visits to Germany in the 1870s.[57]

Stanford had little systematic training in the theory of music but did
receive a few lessons from Francis Robinson (brother of Joseph, see
p. 21) and then Sir Robert Stewart.[58] Much of this time seems to have
been spent playing the organ, but through this Stanford surely greatly
extended his knowledge and understanding of harmony and counterpoint. Stewart is acknowledged to have had limited abilities as a
composer, so it is doubtful whether he was able to give Charles much
help other than that of a purely technical nature. He did, however, play
the organ with a great orchestral sense and almost certainly imbued in
the young Stanford a love and appreciation of the myriad colours obtain-
able by carefully planned registration. This love of colour was remarked
upon many times when Stanford occupied the organ lofts in Cambridge
(as was his ability to translate orchestral works to the organ, another

[54] Ernst Pauer (1826–1905) was an eminent pianist and teacher who settled in London
in 1851. He taught at the RAM and the National Training School for Music and examined at Cambridge in the 1870s, as well as publishing arrangements, editions and musical
primers.

[55] Ignaz Moscheles (1794–1870) was the foremost pianist between Hummel and Chopin
and was taught composition by Salieri. He first appeared in London in 1821 and settled
there in 1826, and was in constant demand as teacher and performer, and to a lesser
extent composer and conductor, for the next forty years.

[56] Stanford, *Pages*, 56–9 and 75–6.

[57] See Greene, *Stanford*, 31–5 and 54–61.

[58] Robert Prescott Stewart (1825–94) became organist of Trinity College, Dublin, in
1844, and conductor of the University Choral Society in 1846. He took both his B.Mus.
and D.Mus. at Trinity College in 1851 and was appointed Professor of Music there in
1861.

strength surely encouraged by Stewart, who could also manage this with ease) and probably contributed to the keen sense of orchestral colour manifest in Stanford's mature compositions.

Like most children of his generation Charles made only occasional trips out of Ireland before going up to Cambridge. His parents' interest in music and his father's numerous acquaintanceships, however, meant that he probably travelled more often to Great Britain than most of his contemporaries. It is known from his own writings that his first trip 'abroad' was to Anglesey in 1859 for a family holiday.[59] Whilst in Beaumaris Charles met J. S. Le Fanu, author of *Uncle Silas* and *Through a Glass Darkly*, who entertained him with ghost stories. This meeting was, in fact, something of a privilege since Le Fanu had been a virtual recluse since the death of his wife the previous year. It is significant that Charles recalled the return journey to Ireland as having been exceptionally rough:[60] it may have been this episode which led to his lifelong dislike of sea travel, a fear which sits somewhat paradoxically with his ability to evoke the sea musically, as exemplified in several of his finest works, for example, *The Revenge*, *Songs of the Sea* and *Songs of the Fleet*.

Of far greater significance, however, in Charles's childhood was his first visit to London, which took place in summer 1862. This trip marked the start of his wider cultural education. The 10-year-old was taken on a typical round of sightseeing but was also taken to the theatre, seeing Dion Boucicault in *The Colleen Bawn*, and on his first trip to the opera saw Adelina Patti in Flotow's *Marta* on 5 July at Covent Garden. In retrospect Charles described the opera as 'that old war horse',[61] but, despite this, the occasion made a lasting impression on the boy (see pp. 26–7). It is a little sad to record that on the same visit his parents neglected to take him to the first private hearing of Sullivan's incidental music to *The Tempest* or to see Lady Bancroft, as she later became, appearing in a burlesque at a theatre in the Strand. The Stanford family returned to London in the summers of 1864 and 1868 and Charles's cultural education continued. He particularly recalled meeting Frederic Clay, Sullivan and Grove, and attending many concerts at the Crystal Palace, hearing much music not generally available in Dublin and seeing many of the leading artists of the day.[62]

This is not to say that Charles gained no cultural experience in Dublin. The importance of small-scale music-making for social reasons has

---

[59] See Stanford, *Pages*, 53–4.
[60] Ibid., 54.
[61] Ibid., 62.
[62] See ibid., 70–73.

already been mentioned, but Dubliners, despite the lack of facilities, were enthusiastic concert- and opera-goers. Here too 1862 was a significant year: before going to London, Charles had been taken to his first public concert, at which he saw Joseph Joachim, whose programme included Beethoven's 'Kreutzer' Sonata, and, a few weeks later, he was also taken to see Henri Vieuxtemps.[63] From this point forward Charles seems to have been taken to concerts regularly by his parents and, later in his adolescence, allowed to go on his own. His appetite, especially for opera, appears to have been almost insatiable. The standard of performance was probably poor on average, but Charles still managed to acquaint himself with the popular end of the orchestral and operatic canon of the time, for example, Beethoven and Mendelssohn in the concert hall, and Meyerbeer, Verdi, Bellini, Donizetti and Gounod in the opera house.

In terms of his future development it is his knowledge of opera which is most significant. The Theatre Royal, Dublin, was usually visited by the company of Her Majesty's Theatre twice a year in the 1860s and the repertoire was dominated by French and Italian composers (see Table 1.1). By virtue of his friendship with Richard Levey, the leader of the orchestra (an alias – his real name was O'Shaughnessy),[64] Stanford gained admission to many rehearsals and spent his time at the top of the stage looking down on the cast below.

This insider's view of the theatre was coupled with a keen perception of the importance of the opera seasons in social terms. More than any other occasion in the year, the visits of the Opera Company of Her Majesty's Theatre were of primary social importance and attracted the cream of Dublin's Anglo-Irish elite. Although attendance was sometimes variable, in general the theatre was full and 'the Quality'[65] appeared in droves. It was not just the elite which appeared, however. Opera appealed to many Dubliners and the cheaper seats were filled by students, servants and less well-to-do tradesmen. In the galleries the audience behaved boisterously, making catcalls at the richer sections of the audience and lavishing both scorn and adulation on those on stage.

---

[63] See ibid., 61–2.

[64] Richard Michael O'Shaughnessy (1811–99) led the orchestra of the Theatre Royal from 1836 until it burnt down in 1880. Good friends with Balfe and Wallace, he claimed to have taught Stanford and Stewart, and also founded the Royal Irish Academy of Music (with John Stanford, Joseph Robinson and Sir Francis Brady) in 1850. He was also a prolific composer, producing substantial amounts of music for all manner of dramatic productions at the Theatre Royal, and also wrote operas and published two volumes of arrangements of Irish folksongs.

[65] The Irish term, according to Stanford, for those sitting in the best seats; see Stanford, *Pages*, 79.

Table 1.1   Selected operas performed by the company of Her
Majesty's Theatre, London, at the Theatre Royal, Dublin, 1862–70

Beethoven	*Fidelio*
Bellini	*I puritani, Norma, La sonnambula*
Donizetti	*Lucia di Lammermoor, Lucrezia Borgia*
Flotow	*Marta*
Gounod	*Faust, Mirella*
Meyerbeer	*Les Huguenots, Robert le Diable*
Mozart	*Don Giovanni, Le nozze di Figaro, Die Zauberflöte*
Rossini	*Il Barbiere di Siviglia, Semiramide*
Verdi	*Un ballo in maschera, Ernani, Rigoletto, La traviata, Il trovatore*
Weber	*Der Freischütz, Oberon*

Although many people criticised the extrovert behaviour of the audience, there is no doubt that it made a powerful impression on Stanford – for him this world of music, drama and extreme emotions, both on the stage and in the theatre, must have been the greatest source of excitement of his adolescent years. This experience is significant for two reasons. Firstly, it imbued in Stanford an abiding fascination with opera, a genre in which he always took the greatest interest and in which, more than any other, he longed to succeed. There is no doubt that he never forgot the heightened senses that characterised his early operatic experiences and that he longed to relive them. Secondly, the repertoire played in Dublin countered, to an extent, the heavily Germanic bias of music he heard and performed in every other context; although he never cared for Donizetti or Bellini, his grudging respect for Meyerbeer and his later love for Verdi were significant for his later development as a composer, evidenced particularly in his orchestration, his predisposition to the supremacy of the melodic line, and, of course, his periodic return to operatic composition throughout his life.

From the age of 11 or so a little more impartial information on Charles's musical progress, both as performer and composer, is to be found. Most of these references come in a burst in 1863–4, but it seems reasonable to assume that these were the start of Stanford's public career, rather than a brief spate of events. The earliest traced reference is to a song entitled 'Once more my love' which was performed by the baritone Richard Smith at a concert of the Dublin Philharmonic Society on 16 November 1863. Stanford was in exalted company since at the same concert Thalberg played the 'Emperor' Concerto. The music, unfortunately, does not survive, but the review in the *Orchestra* does give a hint of its nature:

> Mr Richard Smith ... also gave a new song 'Once more my love' from the pen of one who is but a child in years but who gives much promise of future musical excellence, Master C. V. Stanford, son of one of our well-known and most accomplished amateurs. The song betrays a depth of thought and feeling quite extraordinary for so young a writer; it is in three-eight time and in C Minor but leading at the end to the major with happy and telling effect. Mr Smith did every justice to the merits of the song which was received with well-deserved applause.[66]

The next performance is claimed by Stanford himself in a biographical article published in the *Musical Times* in 1898.[67] Here Stanford claims to have composed a march for inclusion in the annual Theatre Royal pantomime. The chronology is unclear: the typeset reproduction of the music in the article gives the date of composition as September 1860, but *Puss-in-Boots*, the pantomime to which Stanford refers in the article, was not played at the Theatre Royal until the winter of 1863–4. This piece is the earliest music by Stanford that appears to survive (see Ex. 1.1) but it does not (unsurprisingly, given the age of the composer) reveal a great deal about Stanford's style: the music is simple and straightforward and the elementary tonic and dominant harmonies and the characteristic rhythmic pattern of the accompaniment are derivative of marches found in many early to mid-nineteenth-century Italian and French operas. It has, unfortunately, not proved possible to trace any contemporary corroborative evidence for Stanford's claim of a theatrical performance.

In September 1864 another song was performed at a concert given by the Dublin Exhibition Choir:

> The other encores were 'When Green Leaves come Again', a charming song by the talented youth ... Master C. V. Stanford, who still continues to pursue his musical studies with a devotion which, with his precocious and wonderful capabilities both for performance and composition, must lead to fame. Miss Barry did full justice to the inspiration of the youthful but true artist.[68]

Again the music has not survived and the quoted review is the only tantalising evidence for the existence of this work. Nevertheless, the review strongly implies that Stanford's name was quite well known to music-loving Dubliners.

---

[66] *Orchestra*, 21 Nov. 1863, p. 118.
[67] 'Charles Villiers Stanford', *Musical Times*, 1 Dec. 1898, pp. 785–93.
[68] *Orchestra*, 17 Sept. 1864, p. 807.

Example 1.1 'Puss-in-Boots' March (?1864), bars 1–16

The longest account of Stanford's musical achievements at this time relates to a concert given at Herbert Street on 6 June 1864. Here Charles was given the opportunity, in a typical Anglo-Irish musical soirée, to show his skills both as a composer and performer:

A most interesting and delightful 'Pianoforte Recital' took place at the house of John Stanford, Esq., Herbert Street, on Tuesday last. Mr Stanford is well known as a most accomplished amateur in music both vocal and instrumental, a liberal patron of all that is good in art, and a kind and genial friend of artists. The pianist on this occasion was Master Charles V. Stanford, his son, a youth aged about 10 years, of rare talent, who is doubtless destined for a great position in the musical world should it be his choice to follow the 'divine art' as a profession. Here is the programme:-

PART I

Sonata in C Minor, op. 10	Beethoven
Trio	Heller
Song 'A Venetian Dirge'	C. V. Stanford
La Contemplazione	Hummel
Prelude and Fugue in C Minor	Bach

PART II

Sonata in C major	Dussek
La Gaiété	Weber
Song 'Serenade'	Gounod
Waltz in E flat minor	Heller
Trio in G Major, Pianoforte, Violin and Violoncello	Haydn

When it is considered that all the above pieces were performed by
Master Stanford from memory, it will be admitted as no mean proof
of talent and industry, but it must be recorded in addition that a
listener alone of whatever experience, not knowing of the youth, or
seeing the performer would suppose an artist at the instrument who
had passed through years of mature study, neatness and precision,
classic and elastic touch, expression and finish seem to have been
bestowed by nature in this case, for Master Stanford plays with his
head as well as with his hands. His performance of [the] Prelude
and Fugue was absolutely faultless, and Weber's *La Gaiété* quite
enraptured his audience. The premature 'applomb' and steadiness
displayed in the trio of Haydn were nothing short of wonderful,
and such as many of riper years might take example from. In addition to his talent *comme executant* Master Stanford already displays
a very high class feeling for composition, as evidenced in the song
'A Venetian Dirge' one of many of equal merit from his pen. It only
remains to wish him a great future and 'may we live to see it'.[69]

After allowing for the excessive gushing which often accompanies
reviews of adolescent performers, it is evident that Stanford was a
performer of no mean talent and that he must have had quite an accomplished technique, degree of stamina and well-developed sense of
musicianship to be able to execute a programme of this length, variety
and technical difficulty. What makes this concert review especially interesting, however, is the fact that the song 'A Venetian Dirge' was
published by Gunn & Sons of Grafton Street, Dublin; thus it is the
earliest of Stanford's works for which both music and a contemporary
review exist.[70]

The song is a simple strophic ballad, with each of the three stanzas
set identically (see Ex. 1.2) and is derivative of the Venetian gondola
songs in Mendelssohn's *Lieder ohne Worte* (see Op. 19 No. 6, Op. 30
No. 6, and Op. 62 No. 5). Although the melodic line and harmony are
simple, the music suggests that Stanford was already conversant with
the elementary aspects of good word-setting, strophic structure, a strong
melodic line and forward-moving harmonic progression. At the age of

---

[69] *Orchestra*, 11 June 1864, p. 590.

[70] Greene's claim that this song was written when Stanford was only 4 is surely incorrect (*Stanford*, 31) since the style shows more maturity than that of the 'Puss-in-Boots'
march.

Example 1.2 'A Venetian Dirge' (1864), bars 1–14 (text: Barry Cornwall)

12 one would hardly expect him to have developed a strong individual voice, but this song shows that he was at least well in control of the technical dimensions of his craft and that there was potential for development.

A later, isolated, reference to Stanford's development as a composer is another tantalising one in which the music referred to does not survive. Stanford himself supplied the following review to the *Musical Times* of a concert given by the Dublin Choral Society on 15 February 1867:

> The Kermesse chorus [from *Faust*] was followed by 'Heroes and Chieftains Brave', a song by Mr Kelly (and also with chorus)

composed by Master Charles Villiers Stanford, a little boy of tender
years, who continues to manifest not less remarkable talent as a
composer than as a pianist, but who is, we are credibly informed,
by no means to be ranked among 'enfants terribles', those impossible precocious children, those infant Mozarts, who are such a bore
to everybody. Master Stanford, with all his ability, is a lively, natural
and utterly unaffected boy. His song consists of an *Allegro maestoso*
in A Major, relieved by episodes in the relative minor keys, and
capped, as it were, by choral refrains of tenor and bass voices in
unison, breaking forth into bold harmony at the conclusion.[71]

With no music to examine little can be said about this song, although
the reference to 'episodes in the relative minor keys' suggests that
Stanford's sense of macro forms was developing gradually and that he
was able to manipulate dramatic tension in his music by pushing to a
climax at the end of the piece.

The story of Stanford's youth is bound to remain fragmentary and
occasionally incorrect: there is insufficient evidence to draw a complete
picture of his life in Dublin. Direct and a great deal more circumstan-
tial material, however, allows one to conclude that Stanford had, by the
standards of the day, a close and loving family, and a lifestyle typical
of that of the professional middle class. It is suggested that he was quite
shy (possibly a consequence of being very short-sighted), but it also seems
likely that he was far more extrovert around those he knew. Surviving
reviews give brief but sufficient confirmation of undoubted musical talent
which, importantly, both of his parents (plus other family members)
encouraged. His formal education was narrow but supplemented by a
much wider cultural education facilitated by the churches, concert halls,
theatres and well-to-do society of Dublin. It also seems likely that he
was aware of his own peculiar status as a member of a small privileged
minority. He certainly did not question this status, perhaps because, at
least in his memory, this divide was generally depersonalised:

> The division line between the two religions [Catholic and Protestant]
> was indelibly marked: great exceptions only accentuating the rule.
> But in spite of an antagonism which was only too naturally inten-
> sified by close contact, I was seldom if ever conscious of personal
> intolerance. It showed itself more in the markedly Low Church spirit
> of the Protestant inhabitants ... The feeling, as I afterwards came
> to know, was accentuated by the Oxford Movement, which in
> Ireland resulted in a twofold secession, the one in the direction of
> Rome, the other in that of Plymouth. It had split families, my own
> amongst them, and it took years for the bitterness to die down.[72]

---

[71] Quoted in 'Charles Villiers Stanford', *Musical Times*, 1 Dec. 1898, p. 788. The words
are reproduced on the preceding page.

[72] Stanford, *Pages*, 3.

This last sentence, however, indicates that personal breakdowns did occur and that Stanford was well aware of the negative implications of this religious intolerance. Consequently one can see in his later life various reflections of the strange nature of his upbringing. He was, for example, despite some rumours to the contrary, generally tolerant of other religions, especially Catholicism. He exhibited a strange mixture of formality and familiarity, reflecting on the one hand the heavily delineated class structure of Dublin society and the severe Victorian approach to manners, but on the other the small, enclosed nature of Anglo-Irish Dublin where many families were inter-related and those who were not generally knew each other. Predictably, above all, he was a child of his time: he was of the first generation of Anglo-Irish men and women for whom travel was a real possibility, following the construction of the railways in Great Britain and Europe and, like many of his contemporaries, he took full advantage of this freedom, so much more restricted for earlier generations, not only by travelling beyond Ireland, but by leaving his birthplace for good. Greene, his fellow Anglo-Irishman, looked on the matter sentimentally: 'He had left Dublin and was no longer in her ken, and her sun was setting. They closed their eyes, turned their faces to the wall and fell asleep.'[73] Yet stripped of sentiment, Greene is essentially right. Stanford strode forth to Cambridge, leaving Dublin behind. As is usually the case, his native city did not know what it was losing. By the time Stanford was of a status that he might have been able to return and succeed in his native city, Dublin itself had lost so much of its sparkle that such a decision was unthinkable.

---

[73] Greene, *Stanford*, 22.

CHAPTER TWO

Early Years at Cambridge

In spring 1870 Charles went with his father to Cambridge to try for a scholarship at Trinity Hall.[1] He did not win it but later obtained a scholarship to Queens' College, which he entered as a freshman on 1 October 1870. In choosing to study at Cambridge Stanford took the single most important decision in his life.

Traditionally both the Stanfords and the Henns had been educated at Trinity College, Dublin. Records of men in both families appear in the Trinity records from the early eighteenth century onwards and no Irish family members had attended any other university before 1870.[2] So, why did Charles go to Cambridge? Greene attributed the decision to a 'wanderlust' spirit prevalent in Dublin in the 1870s.[3] Although this no doubt arose primarily due to the growth in travel possibilities – it should be noted that attitudes to travel changed as much between 1810 and 1860 due to steam shipping and railways as they did between 1945 and 1995 due to mass air travel[4] – there was also a growing perception that the Anglo-Irish professional classes were being marginalised in British society by confining themselves to Ireland when their position there was gradually declining.[5] Gladstone's legislation disestablishing the Church of Ireland in 1868 was a particularly painful blow to the Anglo-Irish ego. The perception of decline led Anglo-Irish youth to broaden their horizons. Many other Irishmen, including members of both sides of Stanford's family, studied at Oxford and Cambridge in the late nineteenth century.[6] Specifically, Greene stated that the decision for Charles to study at Cambridge was taken by his father.[7] Stanford himself,

---

[1] Stanford, *Pages from an Unwritten Diary*, 105.

[2] See Burtchaell and Sadler, *Alumni Dublinienses 1593–1846* (London, 1924), 388 and 774, and above, pp. 9–17, for details of Stanfords and Henns educated at Trinity College, Dublin.

[3] Greene, *Stanford*, 20.

[4] The journey from Dublin to London took nineteen hours in 1850 (via steamer to Liverpool and then by train) but only eleven hours in 1863 (via Holyhead).

[5] See Ch. 1, n. 4.

[6] Stanford also noted that there were many other Irish students studying at Cambridge when he went up in 1870 (Stanford, *Pages*, 110).

[7] Greene, *Stanford*, 41.

however, gave credit for the original thought to his schoolmaster, the irascible Bassett, who argued for Cambridge because he believed that Stanford should enlarge his horizons by studying away from home.[8]

The decision was of vital importance. Had Stanford followed his forebears to Trinity College, Dublin, his career would surely have followed a very different path. It seems certain that he would not have left Ireland until much later in life, assuming that he would have left at all, and he would have been isolated in a city whose status was declining. From Ireland Stanford could never have had the same impact on British musical life as he did do when based in Cambridge and later in London. He would probably not have become Professor of Music at Cambridge – since he gained this post in part by being the internal candidate – and the lack of the status he had acquired at Cambridge in the 1870s would have greatly reduced the likelihood of his having been appointed to the staff of the Royal College of Music. And without Stanford teaching at either of those institutions, exercising his influence on the generation of composers which followed him, one can see that the course of British composition might well have been very different in the twentieth century. The significance of this change of environment was increased because both Oxford and Cambridge had been forced into change over the previous two decades, a process which was still under way when Stanford arrived. Religious tests had been abolished for undergraduates and the rule requiring the celibacy of fellows – who formed the majority of the teaching staff – was also soon to go. These changes, and others, were, steadily, to alter the character of Cambridge life and Stanford matriculated in the middle of this period of flux.

Stanford was drawn to Queens' College through Emily Pilkington, the Irish wife of the College President, George Phillips, and the latter was instrumental in securing Stanford his entrance scholarship.[9] Queens' was one of the smallest of the Cambridge colleges when Stanford matriculated, containing just thirteen new undergraduates.[10] Despite this,

---

[8] Bassett does not appear to have received a university education, but other related Bassetts appear in the Cambridge annals in the nineteenth century and this link is probably why Bassett argued for Cambridge rather than Oxford (see J. A. Venn, *Alumni Cantabrigienses, Part II: 1752–1900*, 6 vols (Cambridge, 1940), i, 140). Stanford set a trend within his family: the majority of those who were university-educated after him attended Cambridge.

[9] There is confusion as to which scholarship Stanford received as very few records of Queens' College survive before the 1880s; he asserted that it was an organ scholarship (see *Pages*, 106) but the *Cambridge Chronicle* stated that he was elected to a Choral Scholarship of £40 and made no mention of the Classical Scholarship to which Stanford also laid claim (see *Cambridge Chronicle*, 15 Oct. 1870, p. 5).

[10] It was in good company, however, with St Peter's, St Catherine's, Downing, King's, Pembroke, Christ's, Sidney Sussex and Magdalene, all of which admitted fewer than

Queens' was short of accommodation for undergraduates, and most lived in lodging houses kept by College servants.[11] The College had long had a reputation for evangelism but was strongly affected by the Oxford Movement and became more high-Church in the 1840s and 1850s; choral services had been reintroduced in 1854 after a long lapse and the Chapel was restored in neo-Gothic style in 1860. Stanford evidently felt at ease in his new surroundings since he composed a Magnificat and Nunc Dimittis in F for the College Choir in December 1872 (see pp. 70–72). Little information survives, however, about Stanford's academic career at Queens'. In the internal exams at the end of his first year he came sixth out of twelve in Maths and came first in Classics,[12] and it seems likely that this success led to Stanford's election to a foundation scholarship of £30 the following year.[13] In December 1871 he passed the Previous Examination 'with credit'[14] and also passed exams in December 1872.[15]

Stanford did not, of course, confine his activities to Queens'. His biggest contribution to Cambridge life was through the Cambridge University Musical Society (CUMS), which he joined on 25 October 1870. Although there were several talented musicians in Cambridge, there were not enough to organise large-scale concerts and the society was in a parlous state. It was not until the mid-1870s that Stanford really became the dynamo behind CUMS, but it is apparent that the young Irishman made an immediate impact on the society through his enthusiasm and talent.

Stanford's status in CUMS is evidenced by his appointment as Assistant Conductor to Dr John Hopkins on 5 June 1871. Stanford quickly realised that the refusal to admit women to the CUMS chorus curtailed the repertoire which it could perform – boys might supply all that was needed in the college chapels, but could never do justice to the works purposely written for mixed choruses. Later that year Stanford campaigned, with Ashton Dilke, for the admission of women to the chorus but was roundly defeated, demonstrating, on a small scale, the essential misogyny of the University. In response, Stanford – showing even now that if he did not get his way he would not be put off – decided

---

twenty-two undergraduates in 1870; of the remaining seven colleges, all took in fewer than fifty students except for St John's and Trinity, which admitted 125 and 152 respectively.

[11] There is no record, unfortunately, of where Stanford lived.

[12] *Cambridge Chronicle*, 10 June 1871, p. 4.

[13] *Cambridge Chronicle*, 14 Oct. 1871, p. 4. This could be the classical scholarship to which Stanford himself referred (see above, n. 9).

[14] *Cambridge Chronicle*, 26 Dec. 1871, p. 4.

[15] *Cambridge Chronicle*, 21 Dec. 1872, p. 4.

to show the advantage of a mixed chorus. He found an ally in a Mrs Dunn, with whom he founded the Amateur Vocal Guild. Their first concert appears to have been given on 22 February 1872 at the Cambridge Guildhall, the programme including Mendelssohn's setting of Psalm 95 ('O come, let us sing') and 'With a laugh as we go round' from Sterndale Bennett's *The May Queen*, as well as an unspecified piano solo performed by Stanford.[16] Another concert followed on 19 March, including Bach's Cantata No. 106 ('Actus Tragicus'), Mendelssohn's *Hear my Prayer*, and 'The Muleteer's Song' by Stanford himself.[17] On 19 November he organised a performance of Sir Robert Stewart's *The Eve of St John* conducted by Stewart himself. The *Cambridge Chronicle* declared that 'Mr C. V. Stanford of Queens' College ... deserves our thanks for affording us the opportunity of hearing from time to time such accurate rendering of such high-class music.'[18] The concert, held to raise money for the Town Hall organ, was, unfortunately, a financial disaster due to poor attendance and another concert was held two days later to reduce the losses – an early illustration, perhaps, of lack of interest in contemporary British music which Stanford bemoaned on many later occasions.

Faced with these examples of what could be done with a mixed chorus, the CUMS committee capitulated to Stanford's wish and voted to admit women to its choir on 27 November 1872. The Amateur Vocal Guild and another society, the Fitzwilliam, joined forces with CUMS. The first performance to be given by the new chorus was of Sterndale Bennett's *The May Queen*, acknowledging the work of Cambridge's Professor of Music and the fact that he had backed Stanford's move.[19] Bennett himself conducted, though Stanford could not persuade him to allow the orchestra to play in the solo numbers (having experienced the faltering of several earlier Cambridge ensembles) and Stanford had to accompany these numbers on the piano.

It was not just in CUMS that Stanford was active in musical life at Cambridge. The society's conductor, Dr John Hopkins, was also the organist of Trinity College. In 1872 he fell ill and his duties were taken over by Gerald Cobb, Junior Bursar of Trinity and close friend of Stanford. In spring 1873 it became evident that Hopkins needed a long

[16] Reviewed in *Cambridge Chronicle*, 24 Feb. 1872, p. 4. Mrs Dunn appears to have sung the tenor solos; the proceeds of the concert were donated to the new church of St Giles.

[17] See *Cambridge Chronicle*, 23 Mar. 1872, p. 4. 'The Muleteer's Song' was not published and the manuscript has not been traced.

[18] *Cambridge Chronicle*, 23 Nov. 1872, p. 4.

[19] See Stanford, *Pages*, 115.

period of convalescence and that Cobb could not keep up both jobs. Stanford was well placed for consideration as Hopkins's successor through his friendships with both Hopkins and Cobb; he had also given two recitals at Trinity in 1872. On 21 March 1873 the college's governing body, the Seniority, decided that 'in consequence of the continued illness of Dr Hopkins ... he should be relieved of his duties as organist for a year from Lady Day next and that Mr Stanford of Queens' College should be offered the post of Deputy Organist for that time; receiving £80, and also room and commons or a pecuniary equivalent for them'.[20] Stanford accepted the proposal within days.[21]

Stanford formally migrated from Queens' to Trinity on 19 April 1873 and took up residence in rooms previously occupied by Sir Isaac Newton. His friends included Gerald Cobb[22] and Francis Jenkinson[23] and several other contemporaries became, or were connected to, 'eminent Victorians', including A. W. Verrall (classicist), Edward Carpenter (philosopher and early campaigner for gay rights), Horace Darwin (youngest son of Charles) and Frank Balfour (brother of Arthur). Within days of Stanford's migration his position altered again, as Hopkins died unexpectedly on 25 April. Stanford was now organist in all but name and his enthusiasm manifested itself in the composition of a Magnificat and Nunc Dimittis in E flat, completed on 15 November. The Seniority was not to be hurried, however, and refrained from offering Stanford the post of Organist until the following February. He accepted, provided that the College allowed him to study in Leipzig for a substantial part of the two years after he had taken his degree. On 21 February 1874 the Seniority decided that

> Charles Villiers Stanford (undergraduate of the College) be appointed organist at a salary of £100 p.a. for the next two years, in addition to rooms and Commons when in residence. The organist to be allowed to be abroad during the two years mentioned for one term

---

[20] Seniority's Minutes 1872–4, pp. 77–8, TCC.

[21] Ibid., 88 (27 Mar. 1873), TCC.

[22] Gerard Cobb (1838–1904), educated at Marlborough and Trinity College, Cambridge, graduating BA Classics in 1861; he was elected a Fellow of Trinity in 1863 and then held several administrative and honorary posts, most notably Junior Bursar of Trinity (1869–94), President of CUMS (1874–83) and Chair of the Board of Musical Studies (1877–92). His principal leisure interest was music, and as well as being an organist he was also a prolific composer.

[23] Francis Jenkinson (1853–1923), educated at Marlborough and Trinity College, Cambridge, graduating BA Classics in 1876. Elected a Fellow of Trinity in 1878, he lectured in Classics (1878–89) until he was elected University Librarian, a post he held until his death. He acquired a substantial number of fifteenth-century books for the Library, and was also a noted collector of butterflies. He married Stanford's sister-in-law, Marian, in 1887.

and the vacations for the purpose of studying music in Germany, the college undertaking to find a substitute in his absence.[24]

Two days later Stanford's final exams started. In the newly introduced Classical Tripos, the degree result rested exclusively on the exams taken over a period of about six days in the Lent term four years after admission. Stanford had been taught at Trinity by Henry Jackson, R. C. Jebb, A. A. Vansittart, John Peile and C. A. M. Fennell, and sat papers involving translation into and etymology of Latin and Greek, Aristotle's *Rhetoric*, Plato's *Philebus*, *Gorgias* and *Phaedo* and Cicero's *Academica*. Results were published in order of merit and it is, perhaps, not surprising that, given the time he had devoted to his musical work, he came 65th out of sixty-five candidates and gained a third-class degree.

Distinguished in Classics he may not have been, but musically Stanford had everything for which he could wish. Having determined upon being a professional musician before he went up to Cambridge, he had achieved that ambition earlier than anyone could have expected. Not only had he gained the post of organist of Cambridge's most prestigious college, he also had an outlet for his talents as conductor, composer and pianist through his position in CUMS. And in persuading Trinity to allow him to study abroad, an unprecedented privilege granted by a body which did not take music seriously from an academic standpoint, Stanford ensured that he would gain the education needed to take him up through the ranks of his profession. His undergraduate days ended with appropriate celebrations. On 2 June he played in a concert of chamber music which included Schumann's Piano Quintet, Op. 44 and Raff's Grand Sonata for violin and piano in C minor, Op. 145. The *Cambridge Chronicle* recorded that 'this gentleman is so great a favourite as a pianist that his appearance was hailed with delight'.[25] On the following day he conducted CUMS in the first provincial performance of Schumann's *Paradise and the Peri*, a work which he himself had promoted, and the première of a Piano Concerto in B flat major of his own composition.[26]

This latter work was Stanford's first known attempt at such an extended form and, as such, is worthy of some consideration. The piano part is lyrical and grateful rather than virtuosic and showy, reflecting the more conservative aspects of the German aesthetic and repudiating showiness. As in other works of the period, one sees an elegant and lively mode of expression, and a mastery of the basics of form, which

---

[24] Conclusions Book 1811–1886, p. 407, TCC.

[25] *Cambridge Chronicle*, 6 June 1874, p. 8.

[26] This programme is preserved in the CUMS scrapbooks, Pendlebury Music Library, Cambridge University.

Example 2.1   Piano Concerto (1874), first movement: (*a*) first subject;
                        (*b*) second subject

give the concerto an engaging aspect. It is also clear, however, that
Stanford was still approaching composition very much from an
untrained perspective: the work is overly reliant on regular phrases,
which are not integrated into each other very well and, notably, a first
movement of just over 400 bars contains a development section of only
thirty-eight bars. This particular issue sums up the kernel of the compositional issue for Stanford at this point in his career: he was capable of
producing small blocks of music which were well wrought and crafted
(see Ex. 2.1 for the principal subject material of the first movement) but,
having got that far, was not really sure what to do next, especially over
extended periods – clearly he needed some professional training which
would enable him to consider structural issues, both harmonic and
formal, in a more open and flexible manner.

Few of Stanford's undergraduate compositions survive. The only ones
which can be dated with certainty are the two settings of the Magnificat
and Nunc Dimittis and Piano Concerto referred to above, plus a Rondo
for Cello and a Concert Overture (dating from August 1869 and July
1870 respectively, just before his migration to Cambridge) and five of
the Eight Songs from *The Spanish Gypsy*, Op. 1.[27] Some confusion arises
in the chronology of composition of these early works as, although
Stanford did almost always date his manuscripts, some are lost and he
did not start to assign opus numbers until the early 1880s.[28] It seems

---

[27] 'Spring comes hither' (no. 4), 'Came a pretty maid' (no. 5) and 'Bright, o bright
Fedalma' (no. 7) are referred to as complete in a letter from Stanford to George Eliot
dated 28 May 1873, reproduced in *The George Eliot Letters*, ed. G. Haight, 9 vols (London
and New Haven, 1954–78), vi, 96. All five songs published by Chappell had been acquired
by the British Library by May 1874.

[28] Stanford appears to have determined his opus numbers retrospectively in about 1881.
Quite why some compositions were disregarded is unknown. In some cases this was
doubtlessly because he decided that they were not worthy, but he also failed to assign
opus numbers to his first two symphonies and first three operas.

certain that he received no musical instruction when he was a student; had he done so he would almost certainly have referred to his teacher(s) in his autobiography, especially had he received tuition from Sterndale Bennett, for whom he had some admiration. Consequently these compositions were written with neither the restraining hand nor the guidance or encouragement of a teacher.

In light of these circumstances it is unsurprising that these early works generally show little individuality and that they have an air of the textbook exercise. In the orchestral works especially, Stanford handled harmony and form 'correctly', but in a thoroughly conservative and orthodox manner and there is no sign of a sense of adventure or of a mentor encouraging experimentation. In the Rondo for Cello in F, as in the Piano Concerto, Stanford's approach to harmony is based on a classical simplicity with modulations to the predictable keys of D minor and C major, and this lack of complication is emphasised by a strong preference for four- and eight-bar phrases, and clearly delineated closures. These two factors in particular imbue both works with a simplicity almost as if one could see the cogs turning in Stanford's mind, as he employed rules of form, phrasing and harmony which were learnt and generally understood but then applied without question.

In the *Spanish Gypsy* songs, perhaps aided by the fact of dealing with a miniature form, Stanford did much better. The songs aspire to be more sophisticated than the average British royalty ballad of the period, and indeed are far more ambitious in scale, complexity and execution. The influence of Schumann, both in terms of form and, especially, tonal language, is particularly strong. While the songs do not reach the standard of their German models, they are earnest in endeavour and Stanford brought a degree of harmonic and melodic finesse to them, which goes beyond the formulaic harmony and phrasing which characterises most other early works. In this sense 'The World is Great' (No. 6), with its dance-like rhythms and four-strophe structure, each of which begins with a fanfare signal in a different key (Ex. 2.2), and the tonal flexibility of 'Blue Wings' (No. 1) and 'Bright, o bright Fedalma' (No. 7) all show a desire to explore harmonic potential as well as to portray the meaning of the words. The final song, 'The Radiant Dark', stands somewhat apart from the others in that its chromaticism is clearly influenced, especially at the opening, by Wagner, while its main body betrays the influence of Liszt both in pianistic style and sense of grandeur. Further tonal ambiguity is demonstrated in the opening, focused on G, while the body of the song settles on G♭ (Ex. 2.3). Despite some weaknesses in these earliest songs, for example occasionally heavy piano writing and uncomfortable tonal wrenches, they are the best evidence, before 1878, of Stanford's ability and potential; the three published by

Example 2.2   'The world is great' (from Eight Songs from *The Spanish Gypsy*),
              Op. 1 No. 6, bars 1–6 (text: George Eliot)

Novello (nos 1–3) sold steadily, 'Sweet Isle' and 'Day is Dying' remaining in print until 1942, and 'Blue Wings' until 1956 (selling, together, 1,520 copies and earning £16.11.2 in royalties in Stanford's lifetime!).

Clearly Stanford felt that his own musical education was lacking or he would not have been so determined to study in Germany. Although he had taken part in a lot of music-making in Cambridge in his undergraduate years, Cambridge was, as has been seen, essentially backward as regards music in the early 1870s and Stanford found himself in the role of leader at a time when his own education was still incomplete. It seems highly unlikely that he made much progress in Cambridge or that he extended his own knowledge to any great extent; public music-making was more limited than in Dublin, so any new music with which he became acquainted would almost certainly have been chamber music or piano arrangements. It is probably for these reasons that Stanford's early compositions, even those which are undoubtedly successful, are so clearly indebted to stereotypical models and err on the side of caution: he needed to be in an environment where his own work would be scrutinised and questioned by other, more mature, musicians and where he would be exposed to music produced in more progressive surroundings. As it was, Stanford was left almost in a state of suspended animation in the early 1870s as he himself became the cutting edge of music in Cambridge, a position which brought him some notoriety in the town but did his development as a composer no good whatever. The conservative attitude to modern music of his friends such as Cobb and of his employers probably encouraged a degree of scepticism in Stanford

Example 2.3   'The Radiant Dark' (from Eight Songs from *The Spanish Gypsy*),
Op. 1 No. 8: (*a*) opening; (*b*) opening of main *Allegretto* (text:
George Eliot)

himself. Although Cambridge has a lot to answer for in this respect it
does not provide the complete explanation: he had become acquainted
in Dublin with music of a more radical nature (for example, Chopin
and Wagner's *Lohengrin*) but he seems to have shown little inclination
to explore the harmonic and formal avenues down which these two
composers travelled. In the case of Wagner this is perhaps understandable, since Stanford recalled that he found *Lohengrin* a disappointment,[29] but it is a mystery as to why Chopin's music did not spur him
on to greater experimentation. It is fortunate, therefore, that Stanford
was at least sufficiently self-aware to realise that he needed some intensive musical training away from England, for it was the time spent in
Germany which vitalised his music.

In the summer of 1874 Stanford went abroad for the first time, travelling with his friend Frank McClintock, going first to Bonn for the
Schumann Festival, and then to Heidelberg, Switzerland, and back to
England via Paris. In Bonn he met Joseph Joachim for the first time,
who was later to become one of his closest musical friends, and also
met Ferdinand Hiller, who introduced him to Brahms.[30] He continued
to compose, completing an eight-voice Latin setting of the Lord's Prayer
on 8 August, a setting for choir and orchestra of Klopstock's poem *The
Resurrection* (Op. 5), on 21 September, his Six Songs, Op. 4, to texts
by Heine, four days later, two Novelettes for piano on 30 October and

[29] See Stanford, *Pages*, 84–5.

[30] But not in such circumstances, it would seem, as to allow any sort of relationship to
develop: Stanford referred to him as 'silent and unapproachable'; ibid., 135.

4 November and a long anthem 'In memoria aeterna erit justus' (for the commemoration of Trinity benefactors) on 7 November.

His return to England was brief and he soon travelled to Leipzig to start studying with Carl Reinecke.[31] The reasons for Stanford's decision to go to Leipzig are given *in extenso* in his autobiography;[32] England, in his view, provided no facilities at all – Sterndale Bennett was 'wholly out of sympathy with any modern music',[33] and the Royal Academy was disregarded as a place at which to study composition. Anyone forced to look abroad turned to Germany, which was viewed in Britain as being the supreme musical nation, Italy and France being ignored by all except those who wanted to compose opera and who had no interest in any other genre. For Stanford, Germany meant Leipzig: Berlin had yet to attain a reputation for musical education and Weimar was dominated by Liszt, who was, in Stanford's opinion, only of real value for those dedicated to the piano.

In broad terms, Stanford's decision to go to Leipzig paid great dividends. Here he heard music never performed in England, first at concerts in the Gewandhaus, but especially at the opera. He became thoroughly acquainted with the works of Wagner, Marschner and Lortzing and broadened his knowledge of compositions by Verdi, Auber, Meyerbeer, Berlioz and Mozart. It is a sad reflection on the state of British theatre in this period that Stanford also saw more Shakespeare in Leipzig than he had in Britain, as well as seeing plays by Goethe and Schiller. In one sense, of course, Stanford was only broadening his knowledge to take in the canonic repertoire as it stood in the 1870s but, when compared with his previous experience, this wealth of music must have seemed both cosmopolitan and diverse. In this way Leipzig did him its greatest service: it broadened and extended his horizons.

Ironically, Stanford's experience with Reinecke was the least rewarding part of his time at Leipzig. Stanford described him as 'of all the dry musicians I have ever known he was the most dessicated'.[34] Reinecke was well known in Germany as a teacher and all-round musician and was also known to believe in upholding the German tradition represented by Bach, Haydn, Mozart and Beethoven. With these credentials it is not surprising that he gained Bennett's endorsement and it is

---

[31] Carl Reinecke (1824–1910) was initially trained as a violinst and then pianist, before being appointed, with Ferdinand Hiller's help, to the Professorships of Piano and Counterpoint at the Cologne Conservatoire in 1851; he became Professor of Composition at the Leipzig Conservatoire in 1860 and retired in 1902.

[32] Stanford, *Pages*, 138–9 and 142–3.

[33] Ibid., 138.

[34] Ibid., 156.

equally unsurprising that Stanford found Reinecke's approach restrictive, although in itself it may have been a good thing, as it may have encouraged Stanford to kick against the traces. Little is known about Stanford's work with Reinecke and he attributed any progress made at Leipzig to the interest shown in him by his piano teacher, one Papperitz. In retrospect, Stanford's judgement seems overly harsh; conservative Reinecke certainly was, but one can see in his music late classical clarity and concern for cleanliness that also became one of Stanford's hallmarks. Reinecke started to draw Stanford out of his harmonic shell too, and encouraged the young composer to experiment more in this aspect of his writing; while Reinecke was wedded to the styles of Mendelssohn, Schubert and Schumann, this was still more adventurous than much of Stanford's previous writing, and Reinecke should have been pleased with the Schumannesque milieu of Stanford's Heine settings in his Opp. 4 and 7. Almost certainly too, Reinecke reinforced Stanford's preference for melody-dominated writing and for a strict hierarchy of parts, for while Reinecke may have emphasised contrapuntal ability in his teaching, his music is much more strongly characterised by Schubertian lyricism, an attribute emulated by Stanford.

By March 1875 Stanford was back in Cambridge and had thrown himself into more music-making with CUMS as well as his regular duties as Trinity organist. He appeared in at least two concerts of chamber music, the one on 4 March including a Piano Trio in G of his own composition.[35] The most important concert of this Cambridge sojourn was the CUMS orchestral concert on 21 May, the programme of which comprised C. P. E. Bach's Symphony in D major, Beethoven's Piano Concerto in C minor with McClintock as soloist, the first performance of Stanford's orchestral anthem *The Resurrection*, Op. 5, and the British première of Part III of Schumann's *Faust*. It was this concert which brought Stanford to the attention of the musical fraternity outside Cambridge for the first time. His name had already been spreading through the musical grapevine – the first mention of Stanford in Hubert Parry's diary is in January 1875[36] – but to give the British première of a work by Schumann, a composer who, in English terms in the 1870s, was both modern yet respectable, was a great coup, showing both Stanford's capacity for innovation and organisation and, simultaneously,

---

[35] The manuscript of this work is lost.

[36] Parry wrote, '[Robin Benson] told me a great deal about rising men in the art whom I had not heard of, especially the new organist of Trinity College, Cambridge, called, I think Stanford, who according to him must be a tip-top man and is studying energetically in Germany with Reinecke' (Diary, 29 Jan. 1875, ShP).

illustrating the lack of vision displayed by most of England's professional musicians.[37]

Perhaps ironically for Stanford, the first performance of his own work attracted far less attention. *The Resurrection* sets an English translation of Klopstock's poem, although the work was subsequently published with both English and German words. As with the earlier works it is clear that Stanford had still to develop a distinctive style; the strongly reinforced tonic and dominant harmonies of the main triple-time sections, together with scalic crotchet movement in the common-time passages, show clear affinities with Beethoven in expansive mood, for example in the first movement of the Third and last movement of the Fifth Symphonies. In tonal terms in particular the work could hardly be said to be radical, but the final orchestral section is the first example of one of Stanford's many quiet conclusions (although in this case he did not manage to leave convention behind and the work ends with fortissimo chords). This preference for serenity at the end of a piece is an important trait in his work and reappeared on many subsequent occasions, for example, the Fifth Symphony and the *Stabat Mater*; it set him apart from his contemporaries and surely influenced Vaughan Williams

---

[37] Positive reception of Schumann's music in England was only gradual and characterised by pro and anti rivalries well into the 1870s. Sterndale Bennett had done some work to promote Schumann's music in Britain in the 1840s, and his symphonies and chamber music made the best progress (for example, the Philharmonic Society gave the British premières of the Overture, Scherzo and Finale in 1853, the 'Spring' Symphony in 1854, and *Paradise and the Peri* in 1856; August Manns gave the premières of the Fourth Symphony in 1856, the Overture 'Hermann and Dorothea' in 1869 and the Festival Overture for Chorus and Orchestra, Op. 123, in 1876). Schumann never came to Britain, and Clara came to London for the first time in 1856, shortly before Robert's death. Interest in his work increased rather in the 1860s, supported by John Ella and George Grove, but vehemently opposed by the critics James Davison and Henry Fothergill Chorley. These two critics not only disparaged Schumann's work but also attacked any British composer whose music, they believed, betrayed Schumann's influence. Despite this hostility, Clara Schumann was encouraged to come to England, particularly to promote Robert's music, in 1857, 1859, 1865, 1867, and then annually until 1877, with further visits, the last one taking place in 1888. Chorley's death in 1872 and Davison's retirement in 1879 reduced British press hostility to Schumann's work considerably, but by the 1870s the tide had already turned decisively in Schumann's favour, although many works, including his choral music, sole opera *Genoveva*, solo piano music and songs, still took some time to be appreciated and performed in Britain. For further discussion see Nicholas Temperley, 'Schumann and Sterndale Bennett', *Nineteenth Century Music*, 12 (1988–9), 207–20; Percy Young, *George Grove: A Biography* (London, 1980), 94; articles on Clara Schumann, Robert Schumann, Henry Fothergill Chorley, James Davison, and the Philharmonic Society in *Grove's Dictionary of Music and Musicians* ('Grove II'), ed. J. A. Fuller Maitland, 5 vols (London, 1904–10); Michael Musgrave, *The Musical Life of the Crystal Palace* (Cambridge, 1995); Myles Birket Foster, *History of the Philharmonic Society* (London, 1912).

and Holst, who also often used the same approach. Overall the work is technically proficient and coherently constructed, but hardly innovatory, although the generally simple writing may partly arise out of practicality, as Stanford was writing for mainly amateur performers.

In October 1875 Stanford returned to Leipzig for another six-month stint with Reinecke, although he also found time to travel to Vienna that autumn and to Paris in January 1876. He was continuing to compose and had set at least Part I of Longfellow's *The Golden Legend* before leaving England and had written a Violin Concerto. He had also started work on his incidental music for a production of Tennyson's play *Queen Mary* (Op. 6), completed on 31 January 1876 at Tours, and set Heine again in the Six Songs, Op. 7; the last of these, 'Schlummerlied', is the best of his songs before 'La Belle Dame sans Merci', being a lullaby over a sustained tonic pedal with careful and effective chromatic colouring above. He also made a choral and orchestral setting of Psalm 46 (*God is our hope and strength*, Op. 8), completed in Leipzig on 27 November 1875, and composed Six Waltzes for Solo Piano[38] and his First Symphony in B flat major. This last work was submitted for a competition organised by the Alexandra Palace for the best new symphony by a native composer; Stanford won the second prize of £5 but had to wait for three years for the first performance (Crystal Palace, 8 March 1879). Reviewers considered it to be technically proficient but lacking in inspiration and it was not well received; the work was compared unfavourably to another work which probably dates from 1876, the Festival Overture, which was premièred at the Gloucester Festival on 6 September 1877 and given at Crystal Palace on 17 November.[39] A fair review appeared in the *Pall Mall Gazette*,[40] which said the work was 'written throughout in masterly style', but the *Daily News* was more typical:

> After an attentive hearing of the symphony it is impossible to avoid the conclusion that it is throughout devoid of the interest and importance of the subject matter, the skill in treatment and development

---

[38] Completed on 27 February 1876 and initially allocated opus number 9 (whether by accident or design Stanford also used the number for his first Cello Sonata; this work was published and is the work to which Op. 9 has become linked). A version of the Six Waltzes for piano duet was completed on the following day but appears to have been refused for publication by Novello (see Stanford to Arthur(?) Littleton, undated, CUL, Add. MS 9370, item 71).

[39] See, for example, Ebenezer Prout in *The Academy* (15 Mar. 1879, pp. 249–50): 'As a whole we doubt whether the present work will rank as one of Mr Stanford's best compositions. The more recently written overture, played last season, appears to us decidedly superior to the Symphony'. See also *Monthly Musical Record*, 1 Apr. 1879, p. 63.

[40] Quoted in *Musical World*, 15 Mar. 1879, p. 163.

which are required in a work so ambitious in form . . . If Mr Stanford
again submits his symphony to a public hearing he will do well, in
the meantime, to recast and reduce it and revise some of its orchestral combinations.[41]

In fact, the Symphony has a sense of freshness and spontaneity which
is appealing, although it could hardly be called individual or innovatory
and, for many press reviewers, the first subject of the first movement
resembled 'The Campbells are Coming'. Curiously, the main *allegro*
of the first movement also shows a strong affinity to the equivalent
section of Dvořák's later Sixth Symphony (1880), but while both are
appealing in their *joie de vivre*, the comparison shows where Stanford
was still weak in his education, for he had yet to master successful development of material (in this work, themes are mainly only broken into
constituent elements and then reassembled) and to eliminate unsubtle
sectionalisation (too many blatant eight-bar phrases) and to acquire a
wider harmonic palette (little modulation and that which does take place
is too predictable; the harmony is generally regressive compared with
contemporaneous songs in Opp. 1, 4 and 7). The scherzo is laid out on
the same lines as that in Schumann's 'Spring' Symphony and includes a
'Ländler' section which points rather too firmly towards Teutonic lands,
while the 'hammer and tongs' subject of the final movement, while again
invigorating, is treated unsubtly, including a *fugato* section in the development wherein one almost sees a musical equivalent of the emissaries
of motor vehicles required under the 'Red Flag Act'.[42] As with his other
works, one should not be too hard on Stanford when considering the
First Symphony: at the age of 24 he was still learning his trade and this
work was probably viewed as an opportunity to try out the various techniques and disciplines which Reinecke had been teaching him in Leipzig;
one can see definite potential in the work, principally in the freshness
and vitality of the music; what is lacking at this point is the technical
mastery needed to bring about greater coherence and subtlety, and a
willingness to experiment more with tonal structuring.

Stanford was back in Cambridge again by late February 1876. Another
major triumph for CUMS took place on 23 May when he conducted
Brahms's *German Requiem* and Beethoven's Fifth Symphony. The
concert sold out weeks in advance; Gerald Cobb, Stanford's great friend
at Trinity and President of the CUMS, wrote to Joachim that 'compe-
tent critics pronounce [the rendition of the *Requiem*] to have been quite

---

[41] Ibid.
[42] The so-called 'Red Flag Act' was passed in 1865 and required, amongst other things,
any horseless road vehicle to travel at no more than four miles per hour and to be preceded
by an official waving a red warning flag. It was repealed in 1896.

the best performance of the work given in this country'.[43] In June Stanford asked the Seniority of Trinity for another period of leave, this time from the end of August until the beginning of the Lent term 1877, which was granted.[44] This final leave of absence was the most valuable of Stanford's visits to Germany. This time, having received a recommendation and introduction from Joachim, he had been accepted as a pupil of Friedrich Kiel in Berlin. And to cap this he started his sabbatical at Bayreuth, seeing the second performance of the complete *Ring* cycle, which took place between 20 and 23 August. His reaction to the 'Bayreuth experience' is very interesting. Stanford had acquired an immense admiration for *Die Meistersinger*, which he had seen at Leipzig,[45] but his opinion of *Der Ring* is altogether more circumspect. Although written many years later, with the benefit of hindsight, Stanford's words show a degree of detachment and illustrate the depth of his operatic knowledge acquired in Dublin and Leipzig:

> The stage effects were, with a few exceptions, in advance of most theatres. Steam was used, I believe, for the first time, for stage purposes; but the noise of its escape was so great that it often nearly drowned the music. The close of *Rheingold* and the Walkürenritt were, scenically speaking, failures, as was also the end of *Götterdämmerung*. The dragon ... was a gruesome beast, redolent of English pantomime. The best sets were the depths of the Rhine, the first two acts of *Die Walküre* and *Siegfried*. The outstanding moments in the music were then, as now, the first and last acts of *Die Walküre*, the second act of *Siegfried*, and the third act of *Götterdämmerung*. It seemed to me then, as it does now, far too long for the enjoyment of average human nature.[46]

Stanford also noted that he felt uncomfortable with the personality cult encouraged in Bayreuth, reflecting that his lack of wholehearted commitment to Wagner was not appreciated by some.

The reaction of Hubert Parry, who had seen the first performance of the cycle, forms an interesting contrast to that of Stanford: this was a man swept away by the experience, and a feeling that the sections which he found difficult reflected his own inadequacy, rather than weakness on Wagner's part:

> I never was so perfectly satisfied in my life. *Rheingold* was first of all perfect to my mind. *Die Walküre* came up to my anticipations which were of the very highest. *Siegfried* I found certainly hard to understand. I did not enjoy it so much as the others at the time –

[43] Cobb to Joachim, 24 May 1876, BerSt (Tiergarten), MS SM/12, item 1354.
[44] Seniority's Minutes 1876–78, p. 228 (9 June 1876), TCC.
[45] See Greene, *Stanford*, 59.
[46] Stanford, *Pages*, 169.

but upon looking back upon it I got to enjoy it more and the impression afterwards became very strong. As for *Götterdämmerung* it utterly surpassed my anticipation. I was in a whirl of excitement over it and quite drunk with delight. The last act satisfied me most with its great climaxes piled one on another like Andes or Himalayas.[47]

The difference between these two reactions illustrates well the difference between Parry and Stanford at this point in their respective careers. Stanford's reactions spring from a relatively cosmopolitan and varied background and he considered the weak parts of *Der Ring* as emanating from Wagner. Those of Parry demonstrate his more circumscribed education and naivety and a belief that it was his own lack of sophistication which caused him difficulties in appreciating what Wagner was trying to achieve.

From Bayreuth, Stanford went to Berlin to study with Friedrich Kiel.[48] Kiel may not have had the status of Reinecke, but he was a respected teacher who had been appointed by Joachim to the staff of the Berlin Hochschule für Musik in 1870. Stanford found him a far more sympathetic teacher than Reinecke and claimed to model his own teaching method on that of Kiel.[49] Little, unfortunately, is known of Stanford's lessons with Kiel and what little survives was written by Stanford himself. It is evident from the comments in his autobiography that Stanford appreciated, on the one hand, Kiel's ability in respect of 'traditional' skills, for example, counterpoint and fugue, and his veneration of Bach, but also, on the other, found his knowledge of and receptiveness to new music both encouraging and refreshing.[50] Certainly Kiel's writing was more chromatic than that of Reinecke and this must have encouraged Stanford further to broaden his harmonic palette and to experiment to a greater extent with chromatic inflection and modulation. Interestingly, however, Kiel's overtly contrapuntal approach to composition did not rub off on Stanford to such a great extent; while it is clear that Stanford did view composition as a 'horizontal' rather than 'vertical' process, Kiel's interest in Bachian counterpoint is only very occasionally reflected in Stanford's style and in this respect Stanford remained very much closer to Reinecke in his approach. Only one composition dates from Stanford's months with Kiel, a second setting of the commemoration text 'In memoria aeterna erit justus', completed on 25 November 1876.

---

[47] Parry's diary, [Aug.] 1876, condensed, ShP.

[48] Friedrich Kiel (1821–85) was trained as a violinist and pianist. He held various musical posts up until his appointment to the Berlin Hochschule and also became member of the Berlin Akademie der Kunst in 1869.

[49] Greene, *Stanford*, 53.

[50] Stanford, *Pages*, 164–5.

Example 2.4 *God is our hope and strength*, Op. 8, transition from No. 4 to No. 5 (text: Ps. 46)

Of the works which date from 1875 and 1876, *God is our hope and strength*, Op. 8, was the most successful in terms of performances and sales (remaining in print until 1930), and is one of the first works in which one sees Stanford's own voice emerging. The other works, especially the larger ones such as the First Symphony and the Violin Concerto (which Stanford appears to have suppressed after sending to Joachim for comments), suffer from a combination of undistinguished thematic

material and a conservative harmonic language; it was still to be some
time before he developed a more individual harmonic style, although
there are occasional instances of it in the works of the later 1870s (see
pp. 59–62 and 70–3). In *God is our hope* dynamic inspiration is lacking
and the long closing fugue suggests that the models prevalent at English
festivals were too close to Stanford's mind; the fugue is further handicapped by the fact that strict counterpoint was not a mode of expression
with which he felt comfortable and he generally avoided it except where
he felt the pressures of convention too strongly. At the earlier words 'Be
still then and know that I am God', however, the music becomes really
striking and individual: Stanford combined an eerie *pianissimo* with
some imaginative harmonic progressions (Ex. 2.4). The technique exemplified here, that is, the double use of a note as pedal and pivot, thus
allowing the juxtaposition of various chords, whether or not they are
diatonically related, is a quintessentially Stanfordian trait and one which
he used to great effect; it gave his music a harmonic interest and sophistication lacking in the work of many of his British contemporaries. Its
use also opens up a long list of modulations – whether real or implied
– not available to a composer devoted to the prevalent diatonic rules,
without the need to use Wagnerian chromaticism and sequences
which so many British composers regarded with distrust. The work was
first performed at a CUMS concert on 22 May 1877, in a programme
which also included the overture to *Die Meistersinger*, the British
première of Brahms's *Alto Rhapsody* and Schumann's Fourth Symphony,
and it is the first of Stanford's works which received significant coverage
in the national media. The performance was far from perfect, with
the orchestra breaking down completely at one point, and the critic of
Henry Labouchère's gossip-mongering newspaper *Truth* did not mince
his words:

> Mr Stanford's composition met with a very flattering reception,
> more flattering than it would have received anywhere out of
> Cambridge where he has done so much for music. This energetic
> young composer would do well to let his wings grow longer before
> he tries such high flights. The introduction and opening chorus have
> some good and skilful work, and the quartet is pretty and well
> harmonised; but the rest of this long psalm is pretentious and
> commonplace, and there is not an original idea from first to last. It
> would be better taste of Mr Stanford not to take up so much of
> these programmes with his own works.[51]

The critic of the *Musical Times* was more generous, declaring that
Stanford 'unless we be mistaken beyond common, has the right stuff in

---

[51] *Truth*, 31 May 1877, p. 684.

him',[52] and he gave the work a moderately favourable review, reflecting, accurately, the fact that, while the work was far from perfect, it was a cut above many contemporary efforts.

The work of greatest significance from 1875 and 1876 is the incidental music to Tennyson's *Queen Mary*, Op. 6, not so much because of the nature or quality of the music itself, but rather because it was *Queen Mary* which first brought Stanford and Tennyson together and which laid the foundations of a long and fruitful collaboration and friendship. Stanford subsequently set many texts by Tennyson and his poetry remained a source of inspiration long after the Laureate's death. Quite why Stanford's loyalty to Tennyson's poetry was so marked is unclear, but it was, in the mid-Victorian period, very popular, and no doubt Stanford entertained similar feelings of admiration as many others did. This was aided by his friendship, through Trinity, with Hallam and Lionel Tennyson, the poet's sons, and, later (from 1879), by his acquaintance with the man himself, whom Stanford found greatly impressive: 'There never was a more loyal friend. He was seventy when I first saw him on that stormy morning at Freshwater, but the mind was that of a man in his prime, and he had the rare faculty of adapting his age to his surroundings, a boy with boys and a man with men.'[53]

For *Queen Mary* it appears that Tennyson originally envisaged the adaptation of some music by Beethoven, and knowing of Stanford through his son Hallam, asked him to undertake the task.[54] Stanford persuaded the poet that this idea would bring down the wrath of many musicians and suggested new music, which Tennyson accepted. The play was to be produced at the Lyceum Theatre, then run by a Mrs Bateman, and Stanford soon came into conflict with her. The theatre conductor resented having not received the commission himself and encouraged Mrs Bateman to put gratuitous obstacles in the way.[55] In the end Stanford wrote to Tennyson:

> The writing of music to such an important play as *Queen Mary* naturally entailed much thought and work, but this was increased by the subsequent difficulty of adapting my music to a band of numerical proportion such as I never expected. Under all these circumstances I very much doubt the advisability of allowing the performance of the music of the songs and short incidental pieces, which [Mrs Bateman] offers still to perform [she having refused to

---

[52] *Musical Times*, 1 June 1877, p. 292.

[53] Stanford, *Pages*, 232.

[54] See Stanford to Hallam Tennyson, LCL items 4257 and 4258 (both undated, but probably Oct. 1875).

[55] Stanford, *Pages*, 229.

perform the overture and entr'actes], and which would lose much of their effect by the absence of the musical surroundings and unity.[56]

Tennyson subsequently offered to cover the losses which would result from the removal of two rows of stalls, needed to increase the size of the pit to accommodate the band required by the score. This offer was initially refused by Mrs Bateman, but when the play opened on 18 April 1876 the difficulties thrown up by the theatre management had, unexplained to Stanford, been solved, and the music was performed in its entirety. The play was not well received; Tennyson had adapted it from a much longer poem and his lack of comprehension of the stage was evident. *The Times* remarked that, 'in the poem we have leisure to admire the art of the poet, but on stage much of the art has necessarily been taken from us and its place has not been fulfilled by the art of the dramatist'.[57] Of the music the reviewer made no mention.

On his return to Cambridge from Berlin in early 1877, Stanford's period of formal education closed and he adapted to life as a full-time organist and conductor. At Trinity he became fully involved in the life of the chapel and the choir. The pattern of services was demanding: in a normal week there was choral evensong on Tuesdays, Thursdays and Saturdays, a communion service and evensong on Sundays plus occasional feasts and scarlet days.[58] A Seniority Minute from 1877 is, in effect, Stanford's job description:

> The duties of the College organist shall be:
> 1. to play the organ at all Chapel services which the Master and Seniors do now, or may hereafter require the organ to be used.
> 2. to prepare the choir, both men and boys, in the music to be sung at the Choral services [interpreted as comprising two rehearsals of 45 minutes each week during term and one rehearsal of at least 60 minutes each week during vacations].
> 3. to instruct the boys in reading music (so far as this is not provided for in their school course) and in the proper use of the voice, so that they may be duly qualified to take their part in the Chapel service [interpreted as comprising a minimum of 6 hours' instruction per week during term and a minimum of 4 hours' instruction per week during vacations, all in addition to the rehearsals set out in 2. above].
> 4. to see that the men singers are thoroughly conversant with the music to be sung and to give them where necessary individual instruction in the art of singing.

---

[56] Stanford to Alfred Tennyson, 14 Mar. 1876, LCL item 4260.

[57] *The Times*, 20 Apr. 1876, p. 8.

[58] A 'scarlet day' was an important day in the University calendar, so called as those who held doctorates were required to wear their formal scarlet gowns rather than day-to-day black.

5. in case of sickness or other necessary impediment, to provide a proper substitute to be approved of by the Choir Committee.

6. that on the days when anthems are performed in the Hall, he shall be present for the purpose of superintending the choir, and that on the commemoration day he do give his assistance in regulating the music.

7. that the tenure of his office be terminated by three months' written notice on either side.

8. that the precise interpretation of the above rules and conditions to be given by the Choir Committee for the time being, being subject to appeal to the Master and Seniors.[59]

Weekday services were low-key but at the weekend the music required was much more demanding. Trinity had a good and sizeable choir at its disposal, typically comprising about sixteen boys and eight men during Stanford's tenure.[60] Hopkins had succeeded in setting up an independent choir school shortly before he died and this made Stanford's task of training the boys much easier and allowed him to make the most of their potential. The service lists of Trinity College are preserved from Michaelmas 1876 onwards, so it is easy to map the repertory of the Choir during almost all of Stanford's time there. The musical tradition which Stanford inherited was ambitious but not auspicious and the lists are dominated by such composers as Spohr, Gounod, Mendelssohn, S. S. Wesley, Walmisley, Ouseley, Goss, Dykes, Barnby and Stainer, with a smattering of works by Classical and Baroque composers. While the great works of these composers represent the best of the Anglican tradition, most of the music performed indulged the Victorian predilection for vacuous sentimentality. Of the earlier Anglican tradition – the music of Byrd, Gibbons et al. – there was no sign apart from the occasional anthem by Tallis. Stanford endeavoured to overhaul the repertory and works of early composers steadily began to appear, while the worst excesses of the mid-Victorian period, about which Stanford had strongly held reservations, were weeded out. He also introduced the works of some contemporary composers, most notably movements of Parry's Service in D on 11 and 12 November 1876. He was rather reticent about his own music being performed in the Chapel: the Magnificat and Nunc Dimittis in F makes a solitary appearance on 5 May 1877; there is then none of his own music until the gradual introduction of the Service in B flat, Op. 10, in 1879. Indeed throughout his tenure at Trinity his music was heard much more frequently at the other two great Cambridge chapels, King's and St John's.

---

[59] Seniority's Minutes 1876–78, pp. 41–6 (21 Mar. 1877), TCC.

[60] For a longer discussion of the nature of the Trinity College Choir at this time see Dibble, 'Stanford's Service in B flat'.

Stanford's progress was not unimpeded. An intriguing note appears in the Seniority's Minutes as early as April 1875: 'Conversation on the character of the organ music in Chapel. The Junior Bursar will speak with the organist.'[61] This suggests that Stanford's catholic taste as an organist was not appreciated by all of the Fellows. Furthermore, the choice of choral music was not Stanford's responsibility: a minute from 1877 states that 'the Precentor shall be responsible for the selection of the music to be sung in Chapel and submit his selection to the Organist with reference to the Choir Committee if necessary'.[62] Stanford and the Precentor, Louis Borrisow, did usually agree on the choice of music, but there is evidence that the relationship became strained in later years (see pp. 111–14 and 164–6). It is clear, however, that Stanford was held in high regard by the college in the late 1870s and his salary, set at £100 per annum in 1874, was increased to £250 on 15 March 1877. A further £50 was added after his marriage in 1878 to compensate for his having moved out of college,[63] and the marriage was a sharp reminder to the Seniority that the rule requiring the celibacy of fellows had recently been abolished. Although not a fellow, Stanford's prominence as a member of Trinity was sufficient to highlight this change.

While Stanford worked steadily at Trinity, his career with CUMS was more trail-blazing. He often performed at chamber music concerts, appearing on at least eight occasions in 1877. The reticence which prevailed at Trinity did not recur in these concerts and one finds a performance of an Andante and Scherzo from a Serenade for piano duet on 7 March 1877,[64] the Violin Sonata, Op. 11 and 'Schlummerlied', Op. 7 No. 6 on 24 May, and 'La Belle Dame sans Merci' on 30 October. The programmes exemplify the predominance of nineteenth-century German music in British musical circles, with Schubert, Schumann, Beethoven, Mendelssohn and Brahms dominating, while composers of other nationalities and other periods are rarely represented. Thus in one more area Stanford's German-biased education was reinforced through the conservatism of the programme – but also was reflected, since there can be no doubt that he exercised considerable influence in the choice of music.

Stanford achieved most in the CUMS orchestral concerts. Performances of his own works and of music by Schumann and Brahms have been

---

[61] Seniority's Minutes 1874–76, p. 98 (30 Apr. 1875), TCC.

[62] Seniority's Minutes 1876–78, p. 46 (21 Mar. 1877), TCC.

[63] Ibid., p. 170 (16 May 1878), TCC.

[64] Could these be antecedents of two movements from the Serenade, Op. 18, written for the 1882 Birmingham Festival? This is possible: the Serenade does contain an Adagio and a Scherzo, although, in the final version, they appear the other way around. There is, unfortunately, no review of this 1877 concert so no firm conclusion is possible, and the piano work survives in neither published nor manuscript form.

referred to above, but the British première of Brahms's First Symphony on 8 March 1877 was a real coup. The seeds had been sown in 1874 when Joachim was invited to play in a fund-raising concert for the Bach Memorial at Eisenach. This event had been very successful and established a close relationship between Joachim and Cambridge which was to last for the rest of the century. Then, in 1876, there was a move, spearheaded by Cobb and Stanford, to secure honorary doctorates for Joachim and Brahms – triggered, perhaps, by the award of doctorates in March that year to Goss, Sullivan and Macfarren. The Council and Senate accepted the proposal and Cobb wrote to Joachim suggesting 1 March 1877 as a possible date for the congregation.[65] Joachim was delighted but the reaction of Brahms is less certain. It seems likely, however, that he was pleased – a later letter (see following quotation) suggests that he was willing to accept the doctorate and to allow CUMS the British première of his First Symphony. The acceptance came with a number of qualifications, however, and Cobb wrote to Joachim on 27 November 1876 setting out the position as it was understood in Cambridge:

> [Brahms] says there was a little misunderstanding about [the Symphony]: he is willing to send it to us for performance on March 8, but only *by your hands*, and with *your* kind promise to conduct it. I have written back to say that I fully understand this, and I feel sure that in his absence you will kindly undertake the matter for him.
>
> He writes that he definitely will *not* come; not that he dreads us and our ceremonies at Cambridge but because if he comes to England at all he feels bound to appear in London and it is *this* excitement and worry that he knows will be injurious to him.
>
> I am going to besiege our Vice-Chancellor and Council night and day to allow him to receive his degree *by proxy* but I am doubtful of success. The thing is not absolutely illegal, but it is altogether unprecedented.[66]

The authorities were immovable and Cobb wrote to Joachim again on 30 January 1877 asking if one more attempt could be made to induce Brahms to come to England. Many in Cambridge were frustrated that the prospect of having to appear in London had apparently put Brahms off but there was no solution to be found. No doubt Stanford was doubly disappointed since he must have desperately wanted to conduct Brahms's symphony himself.

The final schedule was settled soon afterwards and the personal arrangements for Joachim show a delightful mixture of convention and a desire to show a guest all that Cambridge had to offer. Cobb wrote:

[65] Cobb to Joachim, 24 May 1876, BerSt (Tiergarten), MS SM/12, item 1354.
[66] Cobb to Joachim, 27 Nov. 1876, BerSt (Tiergarten), MS SM/12 item 1356.

> Our present programme for you is as follows: you dine with me
> *after* the Senate House ceremony on Thursday and you sup with
> Stanford after the concert. On Friday morning he is expecting you
> to breakfast and I fancy Mrs Burn . . . will like to see you at lunch;
> then we take you down to see the Boat Races, and we dine in Hall
> at 7, and *adjourn* to the rooms of your *Tutor* (every member of the
> College has a Tutor) Mr Trotter for cigars etc. afterwards.[67]

Joachim received his Degree on 8 March. The ceremony was a raucous
affair as undergraduates viewed congregations as an opportunity to
make catcalls and, on this occasion, to throw coins at Sandys, the Public
Orator, whilst he was delivering his Latin eulogy of Joachim. The
evening concert was a triumph, and the concerns expressed a few weeks
previously that the tickets were too expensive[68] proved unfounded as
the Cambridge Guildhall was packed and the concert raised £40 for
Addenbrooke's Hospital. As well as Brahms's symphony the programme
included Beethoven's Violin Concerto and Joachim's Overture 'In
Memoriam Heinrich von Kleist', and Joachim received a tumultuous
reception.

In the view of the *cognoscenti*, many of whom were present, Stanford
had had a magnificent success. The day was the best evidence yet that
the Trinity organist was a force to be reckoned with and that he would
make a great contribution to British musical life in the future. From the
perspective of 2000 it seems remarkable that a University Music Society
should be allowed to stage such an important première, and it is evident
that without Stanford the event would not have happened. The inability
of anyone in London to show either the imagination to stage such an
event or the ability to organise it is all the more surprising, especially
as most members of the orchestra which played at Cambridge were
bought up from the capital for the occasion. It was, however, only the
cognoscenti who were aware of Stanford's contribution. The agenda of
the musical media was very different and demonstrates just how much
perceptions have changed. For both *The Times* and the *Musical Times*
it was the conferring of the honorary doctorate on Joachim that was
the main event, followed closely by his role in the evening concert as
composer, conductor and soloist. The première of what is now viewed
as one of the pillars of the symphonic canon attracted far less attention,
although the comments made were favourable. As for Stanford, his name
was mentioned only in passing and *The Times* could not even spell his
name correctly, he being referred to as 'Mr C. V. Stamford'.[69]

---

[67] Cobb to Joachim, 25 Feb. 1877, BerSt (Tiergarten), MS SM/12 item 1361. In order
to receive any degree a graduand had to be a member of a College, hence the references
to Joachim's tutor.

[68] See *Oxford and Cambridge Undergraduates' Journal*, 1 Mar. 1877, p. 266.

[69] *The Times*, 9 Mar. 1877, p. 10.

Example 2.5 Cello Sonata in A, Op. 9, first movement: (a) introduction, bars
1–2; (b) introduction, bars 12–17; (c) first subject, bars 21–5;
(d) second subject, bars 62–6; (e) exposition coda, bars 79–85;
(f) bars 228–35

From a purely musical point of view, the three most significant works
completed before Stanford's marriage are the Cello Sonata, Op. 9, the
Violin Sonata, Op. 11, and the song 'La Belle Dame sans Merci'. The
Cello Sonata was probably the first piece of Stanford's music to be
performed in Vienna, at a private concert organised by Ferdinand
Hiller on 2 October 1878 with Stanford himself playing the piano.[70]
The two sonatas are of interest because they show Stanford experimenting with various types of thematic manipulation. In the Cello Sonata
the first movement is laid out in the orthodox sonata manner, with slow

[70] Stanford to Bote & Bock, 13 Sept. 1878, BerSt (Unter den Linden), MS
Mus.ep.Stanford, item 3 (and see also items 1, 2 and 4–8).

introduction, but the themes of the movement are linked: the theme of the introduction (fig. *x*) becomes the second subject in the following *Allegro moderato* (Exs 2.5(*a*) and 2.5(*d*)), while the first subject (Ex. 2.5(*c*)) is also anticipated in the introduction (fig. *z*; Ex. 2.5(*b*)), and both figures *y* and *z* also recur in the exposition coda (Ex. 2.5(*e*)). Throughout the movement material is modified and developed with, for example, the recapitulation of the second subject appearing in the minor and moved from piano to cello (Ex. 2.5(*f*)). In the Violin Sonata, after a highly Beethovenian first movement (although the first subject is very close indeed to the opening of the final movement of Mozart's Piano Sonata in F, K.332), the influence of Liszt appears in the second movement, as Stanford experimented with thematic transformation, by the use of a descending four-note cell D–B–A–G. (It is probably coincidental that this cell is so similar to those of the first movement of the Cello Sonata and 'La Belle Dame sans Merci' (see below) but the resemblance of material between three works composed so closely together is striking.) The cell forms the theme of the opening major common time section, becomes a running semiquaver accompaniment figure in the succeeding minor key section, and is then used as the basis of the theme of the third section, which is a major-key quasi-minuet (Ex. 2.6). The movement is brought to a close by a coda based on the opening. The cell also appears at the beginning of the development of the finale and, at the beginning of the coda, the opening of the slow movement is quoted once more. Despite these formal adventures the sonata is lacking and the last two movements were described as 'scarcely [coming] up to the first' when it was first performed;[71] Stanford's experiments with motivic manipulation are of significance, however, since, while hardly revolutionary in themselves, they demonstrate a willingness to explore beyond the confines of standard classical forms and to achieve unity through other means.

While the Violin Sonata is only partially successful, 'La Belle Dame sans Merci' shows Stanford at his best and is the first example of his true ability as a song-writer. The developmental structure of the song betrays the influence of Schubert's 'Der Erlkönig' and again exploits the possibilities derived from manipulating a four-note cell. The song falls into four sections in varied strophic form, but Stanford also used the opening motif C–A♭–G–F (Ex 2.7(*a*)) as a means of binding the song together when the strophic form is abandoned. The opening section, in which the knight meets 'la belle dame', is tranquil and based on crotchet movement, and Stanford evoked the ride on horseback in the second section by transferring the opening motif into the piano in diminution

<hr>

[71] *Oxford and Cambridge Undergraduates' Journal*, 24 May 1877, p. 426.

Example 2.6 Violin Sonata in D, Op. 11, second movement: (a) bars 1–4; (b) bars 44–8; (c) bars 83–90

(Ex. 2.7(b)) as an accompanimental figure, while maintaining it as a melodic figure in the voice. These first two parts are tonally stable with Stanford sticking rigidly to the tonic of F minor and the related keys of A flat major and F major. In the third section, however, as the knight falls into a hallucinatory dream, the mood becomes much more agitated; the basic rhythmic unit diminishes again, this time to triplet quavers, the strophic structure is abandoned, with the music now driven forward by the insistent use of the opening motif, and the earlier tonal stability is discarded – Stanford avoided establishing keys, primarily by sequentially treated plagal progressions, so that there is no perceived overall tonic. In the final section, as the knight awakes alone, the artificiality of the stillness is emphasised by the constant repetition of the note C in the piano texture (Ex. 2.7(c)), a technique which Stanford surely borrowed from Schubert's use of F♯ in 'Der Doppelgänger' (Ex. 2.7(d)). Stanford's harmonic language also takes on a more individual character in this song and one can see some of the earliest instances of him

Example 2.7 *La Belle Dame sans Merci* (1877) (text: Keats): (*a*) opening theme, bars 1–5; (*b*) bars 57–62; (*c*) bars 131–4; (*d*) Schubert, 'Der Doppelgänger', bars 1–8; (*e*) (Stanford), bars 36–40

experimenting with modal inflections, principally by the use of flattened leading notes (Ex 2.7(*e*)). Although Stanford did not develop a full knowledge of the modes until he studied with W. S. Rockstro in 1890, he investigated this branch of harmony in an untutored fashion consistently from the late 1870s and these inflections helped to imbue his music with a degree of individualism. Stanford's imagination was evidently fired by Keats's poetry and his musical response shows a sensitivity to its drama which makes for a fine and taut song. The change in mood from one section to the next as the story unfolds is perfectly judged and he demonstrated an awareness of the importance of tonal (in)stability and rhythmic impetus as a means of illustrating the unfolding story.

Example 2.7 *(cont.)*

Although clearly indebted to Schubert, this song stands as easily the best work composed by Stanford before his marriage.

On 6 April 1878 Stanford married Jennie Wetton at St Margaret's Church, Ockley, Surrey. Little is known about Stanford's relationship with his wife apart from what Greene related, and this is another example of the general paucity of information relating to Stanford's home life.[72] Greene drew a rosy picture of the Stanfords' marriage but, as his book was written with the full cooperation of Jennie Stanford, this is hardly surprising. Conversely, however, there is no evidence to suggest that Greene's account is false. The Wettons were a Surrey family, but little is known of their antecedents. In the 1870s they were resident at Joldwynds, a large house near Holmbury St Mary, though it appears that the family did not stay there long and that some emigrated to Australia.[73] Greene related that Stanford first met Jennie in Leipzig,

---

[72] See Greene, *Stanford*, 62–8.

[73] The house was empty, apart from servants, at the time of the 1881 census. Champion Wetton, Jennie's father, appears to have died intestate and so there is little indication of the state of the family's finances at the time. There are several references to Australia in the diaries of Francis Jenkinson in the 1880s (CUL, Add. MSS 7407–12) and it is known that Jennie's mother went there at least twice, suggesting that several members of her family, perhaps even Champion Wetton himself, had emigrated.

where she was studying singing, suggesting a reasonable degree of family prosperity and liberal attitude to female education. Taken aback by her boldness at first, the relationship developed and the couple were soon engaged. John Stanford, however, did not approve of the match and forbade the pair from seeing each other for a year.[74] Edmund Holmes, one of Stanford's maternal cousins, acted as something of an intermediary in this period. The ties remained and the marriage took place with many friends from Cambridge and members of Jennie's large family present. Charles's family, however, stayed away because of his father's continuing disapproval, although the rapprochement came soon afterwards when the couple went to Dublin. According to Greene, John Stanford's reservations fell away when he first saw Jennie, and they got along famously.[75] It seems certain that Charles and Jennie enjoyed a successful marriage. The lively character attributed to Jennie was the perfect foil for Charles's mercurial temper and propensity to sulk and Jennie often acted as go-between, calming things down after Charles had vented his spleen; the most noted example of this is her role in heeling the rift with Parry in 1916 (see p. 308). Overall, little is known about day-to-day life in the Stanford household or of their domestic morals, although it is evident that Stanford was a lover of family life and had thoroughly Victorian views on the such subjects as the role of women; much later, Greene recalled:

> [Stanford] was devoted to Dilys Jones, both as a singer and as a woman – his intuitions were infallible. She told me that once, some time after she had left the [Royal] College, and was married, she suddenly met him in the street. He gave a great shout of joy, and said:
> 'Where have you been all this time, my girl?'
> 'Please, Sir Charles', she said, 'I've been having a son.'
> He took her by both arms, beaming all over, and said: 'And I *respect* ye, my dear!'
> He was first and last a family man, and he loved the woman who put motherhood before everything.[76]

Other documentation shows that Stanford also opposed the granting of degrees to women in most circumstances (see pp. 197–8) and women's suffrage (see pp. 262–4). In general, however, these are only fleeting and superficial glimpses into Charles's and Jennie's domestic life; Greene's memories of Jennie suggest that she was quite capable of holding her own sway; without evidence it is foolhardy to draw further conclusions.

---

[74] The relationship between father and son did not disintegrate completely, however: Charles still visited Dublin at Christmas 1877.

[75] Greene, *Stanford*, 67–8.

[76] Harry Greene, 'Stanford as I Knew Him', *RCM Magazine*, 20 (1923–4), 77–86.

By the time of his marriage Stanford's life had been transformed since his arrival in Cambridge in October 1870. In under eight years he had fulfilled his ambition of becoming a professional musician by taking one of the three most important organists' posts in Cambridge and had become a noted conductor through his work with CUMS. His skill as a performer was complemented by his enthusiasm and his innovative ideas, and it is these two latter qualities which distinguish him from many of his contemporaries and led to him being recognised outside Cambridge in the late 1870s. It is also true to say that Stanford was completely aware of his 'aims and objectives'. It is evident that, once he had his sights on a goal, he was not to be deflected easily from its pursuit or achievement. This assertion sits uncomfortably with the image promoted by Greene of a selfless Stanford, and that he did not make enemies at Cambridge in the 1870s is not because he lacked ambition or displayed false modesty, but because his ambitions were very focused and his natural ability meant that he was uncontestably the best man for the positions to which he aspired. Consequently he achieved his objectives without causing rancour. As a composer he was gradually finding his feet by refining and honing his technical knowledge. It could not be claimed by Stanford's most ardent admirer that the music which he produced before his marriage, with the certain exception of 'La Belle Dame', is of a standard comparable to his mature works, yet it is clear that these early compositions were a vital rite of passage and include several worthwhile pieces. He had gradually become more proficient at handling form, his harmonic language was beginning to show a greater degree of individualism and assurance, and he was already an accomplished orchestrator (the discipline in which he became most proficient most quickly). His time in Leipzig and Berlin had expanded his horizons and brought him, for the first time, into contact with rigorous and consistent appraisal; his studies with Kiel were especially fruitful. If one reflects on the small amount of tuition which Stanford received through these eight years, one realises that he was largely reliant on accomplished amateurs for criticism and on self-awareness as a means of discipline. It is surely these circumstances which allowed him to mature technically in the 1870s but prevented him from maturing emotionally at the same rate; no wonder he later discouraged the performance of many earlier works and cautioned his pupils from believing that they had done their best work in their youth.

CHAPTER THREE

From Proud Marriage
to Operatic Fall

An April marriage did not allow the newly-weds to go on honeymoon until the long vacation. Indeed, Jennie and Charles's time together started unsteadily as they were involved in a carriage accident in early May when Jennie was thrown clear of the vehicle. She had been due to sing at the CUMS chamber concert on 17 May and her absence was the cause of great disappointment. The concert went ahead with Charles taking as prominent a part as usual, and the programme included Parry's Grand Duo for Two Pianos in E minor, performed by Stanford and Fuller Maitland.[1] The circumstances of his appearance gave rise to another review:

> Mr Stanford deserved especial praise on this occasion. Though he had come off by no means unscathed in the accident which had befallen himself and Mrs Stanford, the closest observer could not have discovered the slightest lack of vigour either in his performances on the piano or in his general direction of the proceedings. Nothing was wanting but the presence of Mrs Stanford to make the concert of Friday last as perfect as any which have been given by the CUMS.[2]

Stanford was now working on his first opera, *The Veiled Prophet of Khorassan*, to a libretto by his friend William Barclay Squire.[3] The earliest traced reference to the work is in Parry's diary on 11 January 1878, when Stanford played some of it to him,[4] but, uncharacteristically for Stanford, work proceeded slowly, Act II being completed on 30 July

---

[1] John Alexander Fuller Maitland (1856–1936) was educated at Westminster School and Trinity College, Cambridge, gaining his MA in 1882. He subsequently studied the piano with Edward Dannreuther and then aspects of early music with W. S. Rockstro (see Ch. 4, n. 83). He worked as a music critic, most notably of the *Pall Mall Gazette* and *The Times,* and also edited the second edition of *Grove's Dictionary of Music and Musicians* (1904–10).

[2] *Oxford and Cambridge Undergraduates' Journal,* 23 May 1878, p. 414.

[3] William Barclay Squire (1855–1927) was educated privately before going to Pembroke College, Cambridge, graduating BA in 1879. He later worked at the British Museum, as well as being a music critic for several journals. Together with his brother-in-law John Fuller Maitland (see n. 1) he published the first modern edition of the *Fitzwilliam Virginal Book* between 1894 and 1899.

[4] Parry's Diary, 11 Jan. 1878, ShP.

1878 and Act III on 8 February 1879. Even before completion, however, Stanford was looking for a venue for its performance. Grand opera in Britain at this time was in a parlous state; since the collapse of the Pyne-Harrison Company in 1864 there had been no group specialising in the production of new British work. Neither Covent Garden nor Her Majesty's showed any willingness to move away from the Italian and French repertories favoured by their audiences, and Carl Rosa's Company, although it performed in English, had yet to embrace contemporary British work.

Stanford tried to interest Rosa in the work and almost gave him first refusal,[5] but Rosa was not willing to take a big financial risk on the first opera of an unknown composer: 'At present I am so very much engaged that it will be impossible for me to hear your work again. I strongly recommend you to have it first produced in Germany. Its success will (unfortunately) have much greater chances here if accepted abroad. Such is the feeling here ... If the work was of the *Pinafore* style it would be quite another matter.'[6] Stanford was not, however, inclined to give up. Even before Rosa's reply, he had written to Ernst Frank, Kapellmeister at the Frankfurt Stadttheater.[7] Frank had gained a reputation for innovation following his production of Goetz's *Der Widerspänstigen Zähmung* at Mannheim in 1874 and lived up to this by inviting Stanford to visit him.[8] Accordingly, Stanford went to Frankfurt during his honeymoon in September 1878. Unwilling to hedge his bets, he also tried the opera houses at Weimar, Berlin and Dresden but without success; he described the atmosphere at Berlin as being 'the most stiff and unsympathetic ... it was ever my misfortune to endure.'[9] At Frankfurt, however, Stanford received a friendly reception. Frank made many constructive suggestions and expressed great interest in producing the work, but, in early 1879, Frank resigned from Frankfurt and advised

---

[5] Stanford to Sir Robert Stewart, 2 Jan. 1881, Royal Irish Academy of Music, no MS number.

[6] Rosa to Stanford, 11 Feb. 1879, RCM, MS 4253, item 122.

[7] Stanford, *Pages from an Unwritten Diary*, 189.

[8] Ibid., 189. Ernst Frank (1847–89) was educated at Munich University and then held musical posts in Munich, Würzburg and Vienna before going to Mannheim in 1872. After Goetz's premature death Frank completed and produced his last opera, *Francesca*, at Mannheim in 1877 and also composed three operas himself; he moved to Frankfurt in 1878. His mental health later declined and he also suffered from tuberculosis. A valedictory article by Stanford was published in *Murray's Magazine* in 1890 and reproduced in Stanford, *Studies and Memories*, 99–106.

[9] See Stanford to Grove, undated, BL Add. MS 55239, fols. 3–4, for Dresden, and Stanford, *Pages*, 190–91, for Weimar and Berlin. In the former Stanford wrote that he was 'taking the opera to Dresden on Aug 26'; although the letter is undated it seems certain that it was written in 1878.

Stanford to try elsewhere.[10] As Stanford had almost finished the opera, this news was especially unwelcome.

Back in Cambridge, the Piano Trio in G was performed at the CUMS Chamber Concert on 8 November 1878, by Stanford and Frank and Percy Hudson. Ignored when first given in 1875, it now attracted a radiant review: 'Mr Stanford's Trio in G Major took us fairly by surprise. We could scarcely believe that a work of such originality, meaning, vigour, elaboration and melody was the production of any living composer and, further, that the composer was sitting before us.'[11] It seems likely, despite this glowing review and at least one more performance, that Stanford withdrew the work. The manuscript remains untraced and he assigned no opus number to it. On 5 February 1879 Jennie made her Cambridge debut, and gave the audience a preview of *The Veiled Prophet* by singing the song 'There's a bower of roses by Bendemeer's stream'. She was received enthusiastically, though the song, written strictly in the Phrygian mode (discussed below) caused some dismay in the audience: 'Mrs C V Stanford was the vocalist for the evening and her sweetly-toned voice was admirably adapted to reveal the beauty of Schubert's "Ganymed". The music of ['There's a bower of roses'] is very strange and tried the vocalist's powers a good deal.'[12]

More of Stanford's work was heard on 21 February when he and Fuller Maitland performed his *Fantasia Waltzes for Piano Duet*,[13] and on 26 March when the Cello Sonata, Op. 9, was performed by Stanford and Robert Hausmann. Another Cambridge première took place on 20 June when Stanford conducted Beethoven's Ninth Symphony. Stanford also to continued to compose: his Second Symphony (the 'Elegiac') was written during summer 1879, the second movement being completed on 18 July, the third seven days later and the finale on 7 August, though he had to wait almost three years for its first performance and revised it in the meantime (see below). A Cello Concerto dedicated to Hausmann followed this, but only the slow movement was performed and that not until five years later at a CUMS concert on 13 March 1884.

The Service in B flat, Op. 10, was introduced to the Trinity College Chapel at this time, the Te Deum and Jubilate appearing on 25 May, the Kyrie, Gloria and Credo on 10 August and the Benedictus, Magnificat and Nunc Dimittis on 24 August. The Service in B flat was the first piece of Stanford's liturgical music to be published and, due to its formal

---

[10] *Pages*, 190–91.

[11] *Oxford and Cambridge Undergraduates' Journal*, 21 Nov. 1878, p. 113.

[12] *Oxford and Cambridge Undergraduates' Journal*, 13 Feb. 1879, p. 212.

[13] Probably the duet version of the Six Waltzes for Piano composed in 1876.

innovations, it was his most significant contribution to the Anglican rite. The Service aspires to a cyclic unity previously unattempted, and achieved this by the application of instrumental forms. Earlier composers had been prevented from this – assuming they had entertained the idea – by the conservatism of the clergy and of congregations, who placed the communication of the words at the pinnacle of their aesthetic; the use of any cyclic form, and the setting of different texts to recapitulated music, had represented a desecration of this ideal. Stanford, it seems, shrugged his shoulders at this attitude and went straight ahead.

Cyclic unity is achieved by the reiteration of two sections of music: first, the doxology of the Te Deum, which is repeated in the Jubilate, Benedictus and Nunc Dimittis, and secondly, the 'Dresden Amen', which appears at the ends of the Jubilate, Benedictus, Credo, Sanctus, Magnificat and Nunc Dimittis. Although Stanford was not the first composer to adopt the wholesale repetition of sections of music, he was the first to do so so thoroughly and the first to modify the repeated music (in the case of the 'Dresden Amen') to fit into the context of the rest of the movement and to produce a unified musical experience spanning a whole day, from Matins to Evensong. Equally significant is the introduction of recapitulatory elements to the Te Deum, Benedictus, Kyrie, Gloria and Magnificat. S. S. Wesley had applied this formula long before (for example, in 'The Lord Hath Been Mindful of Us', the final part of *Ascribe unto the Lord*), but only where the words were also repeated; Stanford broke the taboo of setting different words to the same music – long since tackled by composers of Catholic liturgical music – without compunction. In the Te Deum a Gregorian intonation constitutes the main theme (Ex. 3.1(*a*)), which reappears at 'Day by day we magnify thee', the beginning of a highly condensed 'recapitulation'.[14] This is a procedure typical in instrumental forms but hitherto unheard of in the Anglican rite. The perception of recapitulation is greatly reinforced by the return to the tonic, which Stanford conspicuously avoided after the opening section, and its reappearance creates an impression of ternary form. The prominence of the intonation is emphasised by its occurrence in the organ pedals at 'Holy, Holy' (Ex. 3.1(*b*)). Ternary form is also used in the Magnificat where the principal theme (this time in the organ), home key and opening time signature reappear simultaneously at the doxology, there having been a conspicuous 'B' section before it.

---

[14] Stanford's published score contains the notes that 'The composer has . . . made use of Gregorian Intonations'; in the Gloria and Credo these are taken from the appropriate tones but in the Te Deum it would appear that he used the intonation of either the second or eighth tone of the Magnificat rather than the third-tone intonation of the Te Deum. I am grateful to Bonnie Blackburn for pointing out this peculiarity.

Example 3.1 Service in B flat, Op. 10, Te Deum: (*a*) bars 1–7; (*b*) bars 31–6

The prominent use of the organ is also notable. The puritan spirit of eighteenth-century clergy had frowned upon the soloistic use of the organ in choral music and composers used the organ merely as a support to the choir. This subservient role had been eroded by S. S. Wesley and Walmisley but Stanford took the organ one great step further forward in this Service – not only is the colour of the different stops vital to the interest of the music, but without the organ many of his unifying devices are redundant or greatly lose their impact. The Service in B flat is not, of course, all revolution. Stanford stuck to the expected homophonic vocal textures and concentrated on the communication of the words – both in terms of articulation and of meaning – to the congregation. But this finely judged use of convention and innovation helped propel the Service in B flat to such a prominent place in the life of the Anglican church, a position which it still occupies, along with its great freshness and confidence.

Perhaps the most encouraging feature of the work is that it shows how much progress Stanford had made over the previous few years; his time in Germany had been put to good use. This improvement is well

Example 3.2 Service in B flat, Op. 10, Magnificat, opening theme

Example 3.3 Service in B flat, Op. 10, Magnificat, bars 21–4 (organ doubles vocal lines)

Example 3.4 Service in B flat, Op. 10, Magnificat, bars 29–34

illustrated by comparing this Service to the Magnificat and Nunc Dimittis in F composed for Queens' College in 1872. First, Stanford had learnt the value of concision. In the earlier Magnificat the first section ('My soul doth magnify ... holy is His Name') occupies sixty-six bars; in 1879 this was reduced to thirty-three. Brevity may not be a virtue *per se*, but Stanford had clearly learnt that length had to be supported by strong thematic material and by its careful treatment; in Op. 10 he produced just the right amount of music from two short ideas (Ex. 3.2) and dispensed with the padding which is all too obvious in the earlier work. Furthermore, the earlier lack of long-term coherence, due to each short section being overly self-contained, had also been dealt with. Secondly, he was now much more adept in his manipulation of bass lines and chromaticism. Whereas in the earlier work the bass line is

Example 3.5   Service in B flat, Op. 10, Magnificat, bars 45–57

merely functional in a local sense, and chromatics are treated only as inflections, in the latter they are both used to drive the music forward and give a greater purpose (bass and alto lines in Ex. 3.3); similarly, Stanford applied the same directional principle to internal lines (scalic descent from G to C in the organ part in Ex. 3.4). A third important development was that of Stanford's ability to manipulate tonality.

In earlier works the key is always clearly established and there is a general reluctance to modulate to keys not closely related; by 1879 Stanford was able to deal quite easily with implied keys, lateral and pivot modulations, quick shifts of tonality, and even to hint at modulations which do not happen (all illustrated in Ex. 3.5); throughout this passage the implied key is C minor, but this is never established, the one resolution of the dominant pedal which appears at bar 53 being almost immediately discarded with a further descent back to the pedal; in bars 49–50 Stanford sets up the expected perfect cadence in C minor only to skew it by pivoting on G towards E minor, which is once again skewed back to C minor, retaining the pivot G and including an implied sequence on the way (bars 51–3). Clearly, therefore, he had needed his three years in Germany to secure his technical competence, which although good hitherto, had been partial and inhibiting. This extended vocabulary brought a far greater variety, and consequently interest, to his music. By the end of the 1870s he was beginning to put this new expertise to use and new realms of expression were opening to him, although to imply that this was a simple linear progression is erroneous: Stanford had shown some desire to experiment in his earlier works and later did not apply all the good practice he had learnt.

Charles and Jennie had now established a regular routine at Cambridge and the relatively uneventful Michaelmas term of 1879 exemplifies this. Charles's activities were still very much focused on the Trinity Chapel and CUMS, and his timetable was busy with the usual four choral services per week and at least six hours' rehearsal time for the chapel, plus weekly rehearsals for both CUMS orchestra and choir. On top of this would be added more rehearsals for the chamber concerts and his own practice at the organ and piano. Composition, it would seem, was squeezed into the remainder of the week, as was the couple's social life. The only activity which Charles eschewed at this time was teaching: Arthur Somervell, who studied with him between 1880 and 1883,[15] appears to have been the only pupil he accepted at Cambridge before his appointment to the Professorship in 1887, and he does not appear to have taken private organ or piano pupils. Jennie, meanwhile, seems to have fallen quite naturally into the newly created role of 'Cambridge wife' (still then something of an oddity since most fellows remained unmarried) and was occupied with running their domestic life at Chatham House, Chesterton Road, in circumstances

[15] And studied at the Berlin Hochschule für Musik from 1883 to 1885 (as Stanford had done some ten years earlier), presumably at Stanford's recommendation, and possibly studying with Kiel. Somervell does not, unfortunately, appear to have left any account of his lessons with Stanford.

which were comfortable but not luxurious. The end of term CUMS concert included works atypical of Victorian England which show a healthy interest in early music, such as Purcell's 'Yorkshire Feast Song', Bach's Violin Concerto in A minor, Leo's *Dixit Dominus* and Palestrina's *Hodie Christus natus est*. The critic of the newly founded *Cambridge Review* showed, however, that the audiences of 1879 were far from enthusiastic: 'Except for a motet by Brahms [*Es ist das Heil*], itself constructed on an antique model, the programme might have been drawn up 150 years ago [hardly!], instead of today. And, as a consequence, we have heard the programme described as uninteresting and dull.'[16]

During the Lent term 1880 Stanford continued to compose and perform. The Magnificat and Nunc Dimittis in A, Op. 12, written for the Festival of the Sons of the Clergy, was completed on 16 February and two days later his Three Intermezzi for Clarinet, Op. 13, were premièred at a CUMS chamber concert by Stanford and Frank Galpin, the dedicatee. Things were also moving on the opera front. In December 1879 Stanford had heard from Ernst Frank that he had been appointed Court Kapellmeister at Hannover and that he and his superior, Hans von Bronsart, were keen to produce *The Veiled Prophet*. On 30 March 1880 Stanford left for Hannover and came back with better news than he could have possibly expected: not only was his opera to be produced but Frank wanted another one from him. Stanford wrote to Hallam Tennyson:

> They have accepted my opera *The Veiled Prophet* and it is to be performed next January ... They want me to write a new one at once, and Arthur, you will be glad to hear, is out the question as a German has just written an opera on the subject. I at once thought of what you said about *Beckett* being a great subject for an opera. *But* I would not think of taking up that subject unless you and your father approved of my doing so ... The opera I may add could not be finished before the middle of next year, and it would be almost certainly produced in Germany, if it was not actually written to a German text.[17]

The reference to approval concerns Stanford's suggestion of adapting Alfred Tennyson's play *Beckett* (1876–9). The reaction of Tennyson *père* is not known but a negative one is likely as the subject does not reappear in the Stanford–Tennyson correspondence until early 1883 (see p. 91).

---

[16] *Cambridge Review*, 10 Dec. 1879, p. 138.
[17] Stanford to Tennyson, 18 Apr. 1880, LCL, item 4262. The Arthurian opera to which Stanford referred was probably Goldmark's *Merlin*, first performed at Vienna, 19 Nov. 1886.

The most important occasion in the first half of 1880 was the première of the Piano Quartet in F, Op. 15 on 26 May. The *Cambridge Review* declared that 'it seems to be the most masterful and most promising of Mr Stanford's writings', and, although this accolade should be taken with a pinch of salt as the notice was written by R. C. Rowe, one of Stanford's close friends, it is undoubtedly an individual work which only Stanford could have written.[18] Dedicated to Ernst Frank, the Piano Quartet is cast in four movements, with the middle movements reversed. In many respects the work is conventional but there are several manifestations of Irish folk music which raise it above the commonplace, and it is significant in that it was the first work in which Stanford consciously tried to exploit his knowledge of Irish music (apart from some brief inflections in the 'Gigue' from the Suite, Op. 2).

The first movement is in sonata form, but Stanford used his material carefully, taking the constituent elements of the first subject (Ex. 3.6(a)), for example, and juxtaposing them, and then presenting them in a different manner at the opening of the recapitulation (Ex. 3.6(b)). The second subject (Ex. 3.6(c)) has a distinctly Irish flavour with its two repeated figures y and z which, in the development, is reinforced by the accompanying circular harmonic movement (Ex. 3.6(d)). The themes of this movement are not Stanford's strongest, but he drew much from them, especially in the coda, which maintains the mood of tension, despite its length, by judicious postponement of the expected perfect cadence. The scherzo is also formally conventional, with a Beethovenian reference back to the trio just before the close; as in the first movement it is the repetitive figuration of the scherzo melody and the hop-jig compound triple rhythms (Ex. 3.6(e)) which emphasise the Irish characteristics of the movement together with the open-fifth drone of the trio. The slow movement is an unfortunately unsuccessful experiment in form: it is monothematic, with the melody used well and with some passion, but the music lacks direction and goes off at unjustified tangents, which include a modulation from the tonic of B flat to A, and references back to both the first and second movements which are gratuitous rather than purposeful. Irish melodic inflections come to the fore once more in the finale. The movement is too static harmonically since both subjects appear in the tonic in both exposition and recapitulation, and a reference back to the first subject of the first movement in the coda sits unhappily with the rest of the music; despite these drawbacks, however, the finale is, like the scherzo, a rapid and invigorating dash from beginning to end, and the momentum Stanford maintained more than compensates for the structural weaknesses.

---

[18] *Cambridge Review*, 26 May 1880, p. 121.

Example 3.6   Piano Quartet in F, Op. 15: (*a*) first movement, first subject; (*b*) first movement, recapitulation; (*c*) first movement, second subject; (*d*) first movement, development; (*e*) scherzo, first theme

Although the Piano Quartet was not an unqualified success, it was one of Stanford's strongest pieces to date. A mixture of formal convention and innovation, the work does not always hang together well but the vigour and commitment which spring from the music are appealing and cover up the other deficiencies. This is attributable to the use of Irish-influenced material, which induced Stanford to leave drawing-room manners behind and give way to the fire which evidently possessed him whilst writing this piece. The harmonic language may remain strongly redolent of Schumann and Brahms, but the use of rhythmic figures and melodic motifs derived from Irish folk music opened up to Stanford a whole new 'dialect' of writing. In time it was a dialect with which he became more comfortable, but he did not return so thoroughly to such a strong Irish aesthetic for another seven years, when he wrote the 'Irish' Symphony, with which this work has affinities (see Ch. 4).

On 17 July 1880 news came from Ireland that John Stanford had died suddenly and unexpectedly from laryngitis. Charles dashed to Dublin in time for the funeral and burial at Mount Jerome Cemetery three days later. It seems certain that he was greatly affected by his father's death. The rapprochement after his marriage to Jennie had been brief and although there is no possibility that Charles regretted his actions, he must have been deeply upset that he and his father had not had longer to rebuild their relationship, especially as a planned visit by his father to Cambridge in March 1880 had fallen through.[19] As Charles grew older there were undoubtedly periods of resentment between them as both men had the same determination and short fuse, and because Charles became his own man, ready to voice his feelings and opinions. But, despite this difficulty of communication, it is evident from his autobiography that Charles hero-worshipped his father and, according to his obituarist, John Stanford invested all his ambitions in his son: 'The chief object of Mr John Stanford's life may be said to have been the education and introduction to a public career of his gifted son Mr Charles Villiers Stanford in whom all his earthly hopes were centred, and it is gratifying to know that he was spared to see that son occupying the highest position of eminence.'[20] Jennie too was very upset by John Stanford's death, having formed a good if brief relationship with him; she remained in England, but the couple spent the latter part of August with Mary Stanford in north Wales.

In late December 1880 Charles and Jennie travelled to Hannover and were joined by several other friends in late January for the première of *The Veiled Prophet* on 6 February 1881. The optimistic mood was

---

[19] See Stanford to Joachim, 11 Aug. 1880, BerSt (Tiergarten), MS SM12/40, item 4599.
[20] *Dublin Daily Express*, 20 July 1880, p. 3.

further heightened when Charles received a commission to produce a
work for the 1882 Birmingham Festival, the product being the Serenade
in G, Op. 18.[21] The accounts given in the press of the opera's première
vary from the flattering to the highly sceptical. The positive account in
the *Musical Times* was written by Fuller Maitland and is best disregarded, but the account in the *Athenaeum* might be viewed as being
more impartial:

> The second performance of Mr Stanford's opera [on 11 February]
> ... was even more successful than the first. The composer was called
> before the curtain six times, a fact which proves that the warmth
> of its first reception was no mere compliment to it as a novelty. The
> *Neue Berliner Musikzeitung* ... says that Mr Stanford 'evinces the
> possession of a really extraordinary talent for dramatic composi-
> tion, such as seems destined to accomplish very great things in the
> domain of opera writing'.[22]

Due, according to Stanford, to local politics,[23] the Hannover press
reacted differently, the *Hannoverische Courier* commenting that 'Mr
Stanford appears not to have the least idea of how to write for the
stage'.[24] Back in Cambridge positive reports were received; on 10 March,
his first CUMS appearance after his return from Hannover, Stanford
was greeted with an ovation.[25] Such enthusiasm encouraged him once
more to try to secure a British performance. Carl Rosa showed some
interest but decided, after several months' deliberation, not to produce
the opera, much to Stanford's chagrin and to the dismay of many
friends.[26] Despite his hostility to the Italian Opera, Stanford also tried
Frederick Gye but without success.[27] An attempt to get Hans Richter to
produce the opera in Vienna also failed.[28]

That Stanford attached great importance to opera (expressed several
times in his published writing[29]) is shown by his willingness to compose

[21] See Stanford to Milward, 24 Jan. 1881, BCL, Lee Crowder MS 1171, item 105.

[22] *Athenaeum*, 19 Feb. 1881, p. 273.

[23] Stanford, *Pages*, 193.

[24] Quoted in *Allgemeine musikalische Zeitung*, 16 Feb. 1881, col. 110.

[25] *Cambridge Review*, 16 Mar. 1881, p. lix.

[26] See Cobb to Joachim, 22 Jan. 1882, BerSt (Tiergarten), MS SM 12/40, item 1368.

[27] See Stanford to Bote & Bock, 15 Jan. 1882, BerSt (Unter den Linden), MS
Mus.ep.Stanford, item 21.

[28] See Stanford to Richter, 3 Oct. 1881, RCM MS 4286, item 1.

[29] His most expansive article on this subject is 'The Case for National Opera' (*Studies
and Memories*, 3–23); in it he wrote: 'There was no question that the educational value
and civilising influence of such a great artistic plan [as the foundation and endowment of
a national opera house and company] was thoroughly realised even by men who had no
practical knowledge of or personal enthusiasm for music in itself [when a petition was
presented to the London County Council in 1898]. They were awake to the fact that every

a complete score – the lengthiest and most complex of any genre a composer might tackle – with no guarantee of performance or even that any producer would deign to look at it. He returned to opera on nine future occasions despite the effort required and, with the exception of *Shamus O'Brien*, with only fleeting success.

According to Greene, it was Raoul De Versan who suggested the subject matter of *The Veiled Prophet*,[30] probably whilst he and Stanford were in Leipzig in the mid-1870s, and he hit on a subject with definite (melo)dramatic potential. *The Veiled Prophet* is based on the first of the four poems in Thomas Moore's novel *Lalla Rookh* (1817). This was a phenomenally popular work across Europe, but especially in Ireland, and went through many reprints during the nineteenth century; it was just one element of Moore's enduring popularity with consumers of literature and music alike, providing inspiration for Félicien David (*Lalla Rookh*, opera, 1862), Anton Rubinstein (*Lalla Rookh*, later *Feramors*, opera, 1863), Schumann (*Paradise and the Peri*, cantata, 1843) and Sterndale Bennett (*Paradise and the Peri*, fantasy-overture, 1862).[31]

The Veiled Prophet, a story within the story of *Lalla Rookh*, is based on the life of Hakem Ben Haschem, a soldier who lost an eye in battle and who started wearing a veil to hide his deformity, but who pretended that he did so because his face was too magnificent to contemplate. Defeated by the Caliph Mahadi in 777, he committed suicide by throwing himself into a vat of acid after poisoning his followers.[32] Moore embellished this true story, adding many characters and the inevitable romantic element; Squire's libretto follows Moore's story almost exactly. Mokanna (the Veiled Prophet) rules despotically, aided by the mystique

---

other European country of importance possessed such institutions, and preserved them, and therefore that the collective wisdom of the Continent had gauged the value of it as a means of elevating and educating the masses of its people.' For further discussion of Stanford's petition to the LCC, see p. 200; for the impact of the publication of 'The Case for National Opera' see p. 257; for details of Stanford's proposed opera class at the Royal College of Music, see pp. 306–7.

[30] Greene, *Stanford*, 32.

[31] Other poetic works, particularly *The Loves of the Angels* (1823), were also very popular, but it was *Moore's Irish Melodies*, published in ten volumes between 1807 and 1834, which made him a rich man. Here Moore was able to exploit both his literary and musical gifts for, although the traditional Irish melodies which Moore used were given accompaniments mainly by Sir John Stevenson, it was Moore who chose the melodies, who adapted them (brazenly and with no scholarly concern for preservation of the form in which he found them), and who wrote the poems which went with them. This work formed the cornerstone of his reputation in Britain, such songs as 'The Minstrel Boy' and 'The Last Rose of Summer' (the latter incorporated into Flotow's opera *Martha*) being far better known than the originals, and acquiring authenticity as Irish art in their own right (see pp. 391–3).

[32] Moore found the story related in D'Herbelot's *Dictionnaire orientale* (1698).

of the veil. His city is under threat from the Caliph Mahadi's army and Mokanna puts Azim, a newcomer, in charge of its defence. Azim is the long-lost lover of Zelica, one of Mokanna's Priestesses, who happens to see him from a window; Zelica is overjoyed but Mokanna wants her for himself and insists that she remain true to her oath of loyalty to him. Mokanna removes his veil and Zelica realises that he is not a demi-god but a charlatan. Zelica next makes herself known to Azim and convinces him of the falsity of the Prophet; Azim urges her to desert with him, but Zelica is determined to remain true to her oath. Meanwhile, the Caliph's army has reached the city and the population is growing restless. Mokanna quells the crowd by appearing to make the moon rise on his command; the crowd is reassured and goes to celebrate, but Mokanna has poisoned the wine. He is about to commit suicide but Zelica appears and stops him, just as the Caliph's army arrives. Mokanna is detained but escapes and stabs himself; released from her oath, Zelica and Azim are reunited.

Stanford made an immediate break with the established traditions of British opera (practised, for example, by Balfe, Wallace and Macfarren) by eschewing spoken dialogue and writing continuous music, and in structural terms he followed the conventions of non-Wagnerian Continental opera: most of the music divides into self-contained separate numbers, with a superimposed system of reminiscence motifs representing characters and also the oath and the veil (Ex. 3.7). There are, however, sections which avoid set numbers, most notably the final scene of Act I, which comprises a mixture of short *arioso* passages, arias and duets, and which is given coherence by the use of the reminiscence motifs and a number of localised figures.

In light of Stanford's visit to Bayreuth in 1876, the most notable feature of the opera is the lack of the influence of Wagner. Stanford did

Example 3.7   *The Veiled Prophet* (1877), reminiscence motifs

not take on board Wagnerian chromaticism in *The Veiled Prophet* and, despite the use of reminiscence motifs and some *arioso*, he generally avoided the extensive and complex use of both these devices of the type found in *Der Ring*, preferring to stick to earlier conventions. In terms of structure, therefore, the opera is much closer to Meyerbeer and middle-period Verdi and its *mise-en-scène* owes most to French grand opera, especially in its use of the ballet in Act II. The harmonic and melodic language is firmly fixed in the mid-nineteenth-century pre-Wagnerian German tradition. An illusion of chromaticism is sometimes created, but this is due to the use of rapid modulations, harmonic pivots and occasional 'rogue' notes in otherwise conventional and expected chords; Stanford never attempted to emulate Wagner's pushing against the established tonal boundaries.

For a first attempt *The Veiled Prophet* is a remarkable achievement. The first version has faults, principally excessive length, and the autograph[33] shows the sections cut at Frank's suggestion, and the further cuts made for the opera's sole British performance at Covent Garden in 1893 (see Ch. 4). The autograph also contains an abandoned overture, a completed overture used at Hannover, and a Prelude for its later London presentation. The dramatic strength of Moore's story is of immense help and the opera contains a good balance of set pieces and dramatic incidents which are judiciously spread throughout the work. There is an ample supply of good music and Stanford showed particular strength in the choruses (mainly in terms of spectacle rather than drama), in the confrontation between Zelica and Mokanna at the end of Act I, and in the song 'There's a bower of roses' (the words being quoted directly from Moore). This song became the hit of the opera and, despite a passing resemblance to 'Denn alles Fleisch, es ist wie Gras' from Brahms's *German Requiem*, appeals because of the wistful and unsettled character created by the flattened second degree of the Phrygian mode in which the song is strictly written, both melodically and harmonically, and the simple strophic structure leading to (diatonic) catharsis. Perhaps more than any other section, this song emphasised the local colour and exoticism of the Middle Eastern setting, its modal writing, if not authentic, constantly reinforcing its presence through the most prominent characteristic of the Phrygian mode.

Equally, the opera has weak sections where Stanford should have exercised more rigorous self-criticism. While the structure of the work is usually coherent in a localised sense, taken globally the division between self-contained numbers in some scenes and the use of through-composed music with recurring motifs elsewhere is too sharp; Stanford had yet to

---

[33] RCM MS 4164.

work out how to integrate the two techniques and how to ameliorate the 'chop and change' effect. Inevitably, when compared with later operas, *The Veiled Prophet* looks staid, but Stanford's effort stands good comparison with its very few contemporaries, for example Mackenzie's *Colomba*, and his willingness to compose an opera at such an unpropitious time shows both his love of the genre and his desire to succeed; thus *The Veiled Prophet* cannot be dismissed merely as a reckless first attempt, but should be regarded as a great statement of faith and determination. From a modern standpoint, however, as in the case of *Queen Mary*, one can see that it was the opera's achievement in terms of the good it did Stanford's reputation rather than the actual music which was important: the performance in Germany of an opera which originated from a country well known for its insubstantial native tradition was a great coup, emphasising once more that the young Irishman was one to watch.

Stanford did not let the grass grow under his feet: he was already planning his next stage work.[34] It is not known when Stanford became acquainted with Gilbert A'Beckett,[35] the librettist of *Savonarola* and *The Canterbury Pilgrims*, but it seems likely that they became partners between April 1880 and May 1881. The reason for the choice of *Savonarola* for their first venture is unknown but, following the refusal of Tennyson to let Stanford set *Beckett*, *Savonarola* must have seemed an obvious alternative: there are clear parallels between the lives of Savonarola and Thomas Becket as both were charismatic clerics who fell out with the secular powers; Becket was murdered and Savonarola burnt as a heretic in order to destroy their authority. News of the new opera spread and the publisher John Boosey took the unprecedented step of offering Stanford £1,000 for its copyright, on condition that the opera was performed in London (or £500 if the opera was premièred on the Continent with a further £500 on the occasion of the first London performance). Stanford accepted Boosey's offer with enthusiasm. Boosey also offered A'Beckett £150 for the copyright of the libretto and commissioned another opera from Stanford to follow *Savonarola*. Boosey's actions – casting himself as the Richard D'Oyly Carte of British grand opera – show a degree of faith both in Stanford and in opera as a genre

---

[34] See also Rodmell, 'A Tale of Two Operas', *Music & Letters*, 78 (1997), 77–91.

[35] Gilbert Arthur A'Beckett (1837–91) was educated at Westminster School and Christ Church College, Oxford, taking his BA in 1860. He made his living from writing plays and satires, following his father, Gilbert Abbot A'Beckett. Together with his father and two brothers, he wrote for *Punch*, joining the staff in 1879. His most notable success was *The Happy Land* (1873), in which he collaborated with W. S. Gilbert. The family claimed to be descendants of the canonised Archbishop of Canterbury.

that was almost foolhardy. Certainly Stanford was perceived by many in the musical world as the coming man and showed, at this point, more potential to become an internationally recognised composer than any of his contemporaries (Parry, Sullivan, Mackenzie, Cowen and Goring Thomas), but Boosey's actions were still a great gamble, especially as there was no tradition of British grand opera and, consequently, no established market for the product.[36] To Stanford and A'Beckett, however, Boosey's business acumen was not then of consequence and the librettist set to work.

Back at Cambridge, Stanford's advocacy of Parry's *Prometheus Unbound*, performed by CUMS on 17 May 1881, caused some criticism in Cambridge musical circles, and a lively correspondence took place in the columns of the *Cambridge Review* on the subject. Evidently Parry's work, so often subsequently held up as the symbolic commencement of the 'British Musical Renaissance', provoked strong reactions, giving some legitimacy to the accolade. On the whole opinion went in Parry's favour, but not until some unflattering comments and proposals had passed; 'Battle of Prague' wrote: 'In consequence of the unpopularity of one of the works selected for performance by the chorus of the CUMS ... attention is likely to be drawn to the fact that the members have no power in the choice of the work which they will have to assist in performing.'[37] 'Battle' went on to propose that the members of the chorus should choose the works to be performed by ballot; this drew the following series of responses:

> The music chosen would be popular rather than good. New music would have no chance. The Society would probably give the same music over and over again at intervals of four or five years. [AJM]
>
> I am sure that very few members will be enrolled while the society rehearses such works as it is doing this term. Many members (ladies as well as undergraduates I have heard) object to one of the pieces; in fact two or three have gone so far as to denounce it as trash. It may contain good music but it does not suit the greater part of the society. [An Aggrieved Member]
>
> Might I suggest to ['Battle of Prague'] that he should attend the rehearsals ... [as] not only do I believe that he would find every

---

[36] Balfe, Wallace, Macfarren et al. had aimed at a more 'middle-brow' audience in their operas and did not compose works designed to compete with the Italian and French grand operas produced at Covent Garden and Her Majesty's Theatres. Since the collapse of the Pyne-Harrison Company in 1864 not even this type of opera had prospered and no premières of British works were given between 1864 and 1883, with the exception of Cowen's *Pauline* (1876) and the earliest of Sullivan's works; it was through the enthusiasm of Carl Rosa that British composers were given their first real opportunity to compose opera in the grand style and see it put on the stage in their native land and language.

[37] 'Battle of Prague' to the *Cambridge Review*, 9 Mar. 1881, pp. 213–14.

> one pleased with the choice [of *Prometheus*], but he would be
> obliged himself to change his opinions of it. Of course the work is
> hard, and it is not till after a closer acquaintance that the generality
> of persons will find out its beauties. [One of the Chorus][38]

Stanford had most of CUMS on his side, but the discussion is ample
demonstration of how a chorus (not unused to performing contemporary work) viewed Parry's music. To complicate matters, Parry had
reservations about Stanford's musical judgement; when Stanford had
first discussed *Prometheus* with him, Parry wrote, 'his criticisms were
confined to objections to passages which smelt too strong of Wagner
[*sic*], and on the whole not particularly useful or remarkably wise, and
whenever he played a bit to me it was cold and unmeaning to the touch,
but he read the notes wonderfully and is agreeable company'.[39] When
it came to the final rehearsals Parry still believed that Stanford had little
idea about what the piece meant: '[Stanford's] idea of the times were
[*sic*] often very wrong and I longed to have had the stick myself, as
things would have been much more intelligible.'[40] Although Parry had
reservations about Stanford's musicality – and these reservations were
expressed more frequently and trenchantly as years passed – it is clear
that in the late 1870s and early 1880s they had a good relationship and
were both generally happy to accept the differences in their temperaments and outlooks. Stanford, despite any private reservations he had
about Parry's music, still recognised that he was one of the most significant men in the new generation of British composers and promoted his
music enthusiastically. Indeed, after Stanford's own music, it was Parry
who most often represented contemporary British work in Cambridge
concert programmes at this time.

Despite Parry's doubts, the performance went well and was enthusiastically received. A long explanatory article in the *Cambridge Review*
had no doubt helped matters and suggests that the writer was aware of
the significance of the 'new' music facing him:

> It is difficult to assign Mr Parry's work to any particular school.
> Not that there are absent evident leanings towards the style of
> Wagner, more especially in the earlier portion of the work; but many
> strong characteristics of that composer are absent (notably the
> constant use of *Leit-motiv*), and in the last scene his influence may
> be said entirely to disappear. Let it therefore at once be said that
> Mr Parry need not be afraid to take his stand as a representative
> composer of the English school, influenced, as it is right he should

---

[38] *Cambridge Review*, 23 Mar. 1881, pp. 231–2.
[39] Parry's diary, 26 Nov. 1880, ShP.
[40] Parry's diary, 12 May 1881, ShP.

be, by the great men before him, but with his own remarks to make
and his own way of making them ... Mr Parry has done a good
work; he has stood out as a representative of the best school of
modern English music, and he has succeeded in adding to its perhaps
too scanty stores a work that is worthy of a musician of any nation.
For this alone he deserves the thanks of his country, and sooner or
later he will receive them, let us hope, in the shape of true appreciation of his great talent.[41]

At the concert Parry was cheered loudly and later wrote in his diary:

> The performance ... was for the most part superb ... Chorus fine
> though inclined to run away in the Furies' Chorus, and in the last
> King [bass] was perfectly magnificent ... Stanford all along was
> marvellously kind and genial. He has the Irishman's characteristic
> sweetness in companionship and is evidently worshipped almost
> universally at Cambridge.[42]

Well, perhaps not 'almost universally', but certainly substantially; and
here Stanford deserves a great deal of credit for pushing Parry's music
in the face of some opposition – the reactionary comments of some of
the *Cambridge Review*'s correspondents show that grudging reception
of contemporary music has a long been a feature of British musical life
and Stanford did well to overcome it. The musical success was not,
unfortunately, matched by the financial result and the concert lost
£159.10.11, the greatest of any CUMS concert, and this despite the
pairing of *Prometheus* with Schubert's 'Great' C Major Symphony.
Adventurous programming was not, however, the sole cause of the
problem: the performance of Beethoven's Ninth Symphony two years
earlier lost £150 and the chamber concerts had slipped from a profit of
£65 in Lent 1876 to a loss of £3 in Lent 1881. The *Cambridge Review*
carried Stanford's banner enthusiastically, but the rest of the population
was already inclined to forget how far music had come over the previous
ten years and appears to have been bloated by the lavish musical fare
on offer. It was an indifference about which Stanford was to feel increasingly annoyed.

A performance of *God is Our Hope* on 6 June at St James's Hall,
conducted by Hans Richter, and the completion of the Six Songs, Op.
14 brought a busy academic year to a close.[43] Charles and Jennie
must have looked forward to the onset of the long vacation; in September they travelled to the Continent, visiting, amongst other places,

[41] 'Mr Parry's *Prometheus*', *Cambridge Review*, 11 May 1881, pp. 307–9.

[42] Parry's diary, 17 May 1881, ShP.

[43] These had not been conceived as a set, are dedicated to different people, and are
settings of different languages, the earliest dating from 1873 ('Sweeter than the Violet'),
with 'Le Bien vient en dormant' the last one to be finished.

Switzerland, Vienna and Hanover, where they stayed with Ernst Frank, and Charles completed his commission for the 1882 Birmingham Festival, the Serenade in G, Op. 18. In the term after their return to Cambridge the *Cavalier Songs*, Op. 17 were premièred at the CUMS orchestral concert on 30 November and such was their success that they were encored on the night and performed again on 22 March 1882. Their straightforward, bucolic nature – all three songs are horseback gallops with easy yet brisk phrasing and melodic structure, supported by unpretentious but appropriate and vivid harmonies – was later applauded by George Bernard Shaw, who described them as 'fiery and original as they are vernacular from beginning to end'.[44] (See Ex. 3.8.) Stanford captured the spirit of Robert Browning's poetry excellently, his brisk, uncluttered settings displaying real vitality and go.

After revising the second, 'Elegiac', Symphony in January, the work was triumphantly premièred at the annual Joachim concert on 7 March 1882. The presence of Joachim added, as usual, an incentive to the audience and a sense of stature to the occasion. After a quiet few months, Stanford was back with a vengeance. The *Cambridge Review* was almost overcome with enthusiasm:

> We must really congratulate Mr Stanford on the great success of this concert and must still more congratulate the society of Mr Stanford's producing for its first performance what is in our opinion one of the finest pieces of modern music we have ever heard. An unusually demonstrative audience showed its appreciation of Mr Stanford's merits by calling for him no less than three times ... We need hardly add that Mr Stanford conducted the programme throughout with his usual facility and completed the success of the best concert, in the opinion of all, ever given here.[45]

The *Musical Times* also wrote positively about the new work.[46]

The work is prefaced by four stanzas from canto 70 of Tennyson's *In Memoriam*:

> I cannot see the features right,
> When on the gloom I strive to paint
> The face I know; the hues are faint
> And mix with hollow masks of night;
>
> Cloud-towers by ghostly masons wrought,
> A gulf that ever shuts and gapes,
> A hand that points, and pallid shapes
> In shadowy thoroughfares of thought;

[44] George Bernard Shaw, *Music in London 1890–94*, 3 vols (New York, 1973), ii, 327.
[45] *Cambridge Review*, 15 Mar. 1882, p. lxiv.
[46] See *Musical Times*, 1 Apr. 1882, p. 211.

Example 3.8   'Marching Along' (from *Cavalier Songs*), Op. 17 No. 1, bars 1–13
(text: Robert Browning)

And crowds that stream from yawning doors,
And shoals of pucker'd faces drive;
Dark bulks that tumble half alive,
And lazy lengths on boundless shores;

Till all at once beyond the will
I hear a wizard music roll,
And thro' a lattice on the soul
Looks thy fair face and makes it still.

It is not clear if Stanford intended to commemorate anyone in particular in the symphony; ironically, his father died between its composition and first performance. Although it is tempting, and possible, to match each stanza with a movement, it is not evident that this was what Stanford intended and this type of literal description is more evident in the Fourth and Fifth Symphonies (see pp. 143, 178–9 and 222–7). Musically, the work is vastly superior to its predecessor, even though only three years separate the two. Although the composers who influenced Stanford are still obvious (especially Beethoven and Brahms in the first movement, and Beethoven to an embarrassing extent in the Scherzo), there is an infinitely greater sense of assurance about the work and also of individuality; Stanford had now contained these influences to a greater extent than before, while retaining the spontaneity and *joie de vivre* which had characterised the First Symphony, along with a preference for melody-dominated texture and varied and illustrative orchestration. Again, Stanford's study in Germany had paid off; the symphony has a much better sense of proportion, propulsion and formal coherence, and Stanford showed that he had become more comfortable with rapidly moving tonality and lateral shifts of key, and could handle them confidently.

Whilst the Joachim concert was a success, the Cambridge audience remained fickle. On 17 May Stanford conducted a performance of Handel's *Hercules* at the Guildhall, with Jennie taking the role of Iole. Once again the *Cambridge Review* praised the concert, and particular attention was drawn to the new Guildhall organ. Stanford, however, was not happy and vented his frustration in a long and well-argued letter to the *Review*. He had, he wrote, been criticised in the past for spending too much time on contemporary work (*Prometheus?*) at the expense of older music, and especially the works of Handel, though the lack, until 1882, of an organ in the Guildhall had, in his view, prevented the effective performance of such works. He had also been castigated for bringing in orchestras from London. Each point was firmly rebutted:

> Cambridge ought to go with the age, and . . . we are in an exceptionally happy position for producing modern works and for aiding the development of contemporary genius (the proper object of a University) . . . [In recent years] an amateur orchestra, and a very fair one was collected; not, indeed, capable of playing the difficult modern orchestral works, but quite able to cope with the easier works of our older masters. An organ was also erected, and I thereupon suggested to the [CUMS] committee a performance of Handel's *Hercules* to be accompanied by our own orchestra; a performance, I may point out, exactly laid down upon the lines desired by [my] well-meaning amateur friends [that is, critics]. You will, of course, expect to hear that the concert room was crammed. Not at all! In spite of the very moderate prices of seats, the room was not half filled . . . and our well-meaning friends *were conspicuous by their absence*. What is the moral of this? There can be but one: firstly [*sic*], that the Cambridge public does not care to hear a local orchestra which is not equal to the best London orchestras; secondly, that the Cambridge public does not care to hear much about Handel,

and would prefer to go and hear the more modern compositions of the nineteenth century.

The half-empty room last Wednesday was a real disgrace to Cambridge. The performance was one of a most interesting and little-known work of Handel, interesting educationally as an illustration of ancient mythology treated dramatically, interesting musically as a specimen of what a Cambridge Musical Society orchestra could do unaided (save in the case of two solo singers and a double bass) by extraneous help . . . I only hope that my remarks may be partially the means, however feeble, of bringing the public to see that without their genuine support art cannot thrive, and that it is their duty to back up the efforts that are year by year made to advance it . . . and I can only trust that future performances will bring together an audience numbering more than 300 out of a population of nearly 40,000.[47]

It seems that with this devastating response, for once well-judged in its tone, Stanford silenced his critics for some considerable time (and several of his remarks still have astounding resonance today). He had given his critics a concert for which they had long argued and they and many others had stayed away. Stanford deliberately came to false conclusions: it is easy to see, of course, that what people really meant by Handel was the *Messiah* and, possibly, *Israel in Egypt*, and that they would have preferred either of *those* two works to many modern offerings, but in a university town it would hardly be acceptable to advocate openly a failure to explore the unknown and, by exploiting this taboo, Stanford won his argument decisively. But the poor showing of *Hercules* exemplified a recurrent problem in Cambridge music with which Stanford felt periodically annoyed: the town was not prepared to support the innovative programming he favoured and many of its musicians were happier performing a round of established standards. It was an attitude that led to a growing friction between Stanford and many other local people and which was a contributory factor to his decision in 1892 to leave for London.

Soon after the *Hercules* episode Stanford's attention was distracted by domestic matters, for it became apparent that Jennie was pregnant. Despite this he worked hard throughout the May term on *Savonarola* and by 5 May he had completed the Prologue and was well into Act I (finished 15 August). He wrote steadily throughout the autumn and the following spring, completing Act II on 26 December and Act III on 8 March 1883. 1882 also saw the publication of Stanford's first volume of arrangements of Irish folksongs (*Songs of Old Ireland*) and in late summer he gained much more public exposure through the première

---

[47] *Cambridge Review*, 24 May 1882, p. 339.

of his Serenade in G, Op. 18 (Birmingham Festival, 30 August) in a programme which also included the first performance of Alfred Gaul's highly successful *The Holy City*. Stanford conducted the work himself and it was well received both locally and nationally and was performed before the end of the year at Crystal Palace, St James's Hall, Manchester, and again at Birmingham. Though the form of the Serenade is evidently borrowed from Brahms's Op. 11, Stanford's composition is an altogether lighter affair and his intention was clearly to eschew the breadth and depth required of late romantic symphonies. This is especially true of the Intermezzo, with its *perpetuum mobile* filigree decoration, which approaches Saint-Saëns and Tchaikovsky in its playfulness (Ex. 3.9). Some of the music is derivative, especially the Beethovenian scherzo, but the best section is the Lullaby. This has the twin function of a separate movement and coda to the Finale and Stanford cocked one last effective snook at nineteenth-century symphonic bombast and obsession with 'argument', as the music proceeds over a tonic pedal sustained throughout (cf. 'Schlummerlied', Op. 7 No. 6), while placing a simple four-bar melody above it, which is merely repeated, with slight variations, through the whole forty-eight bars. This is the perfect foil to everything which has gone before, since four of the five preceding movements are lively and extroverted. The most important characteristic of the Serenade is its pretended lack of sophistication: Stanford retreated into a sort of child-like innocence in which all his high spirits were left to run wild before falling into a blameless sleep. The standard of technical workmanship is never compromised and the strength of the work is its sense of effortlessness; one can fully concur with Shaw's later criticism that Stanford too often felt that he was a 'professional man with a certain position to keep up',[48] for the Serenade shows that, when not standing on his dignity, Stanford could produce music with a splendid sense of spirit and fun.

Back in Cambridge the Michaelmas term saw the premières of two of the Six Songs, Op. 19 and *Awake My Heart*, Op. 16 at the CUMS orchestral concert on 2 December. Perhaps Jennie's pregnancy explains the relatively slow rate of progress Stanford made on *Savonarola* during the autumn and winter of 1882–3; in any case Jennie was safely delivered of a girl, subsequently christened Geraldine Mary, on 19 February 1883. It was probably this event, together with his appointment at the new Royal College of Music (see pp. 91–2), which led to the family moving to a large semi-detached house at 10 Harvey Road (conveniently close to the Cambridge station) in 1883, the house which they were to

[48] George Bernard Shaw, *London Music as Heard in 1888–89 by Corno di Bassetto* (New York, 1973), 395.

Example 3.9   Serenade in G, Op. 18, scherzo, bars 1–17

occupy until the relocation to London ten years later. Although there were no doubt considerable celebrations of Geraldine's birth and disruption caused by the move of house, the pace of work which Stanford maintained barely slackened. By early 1883 Tennyson's attitude to *Beckett* had altered and he gave permission for its adaptation. Plans for the production of *Savonarola* were also progressing well and Stanford wrote to Hallam Tennyson that Rosa was 'quite determined to do one of my two [*Savonarola* and *The Canterbury Pilgrims*] next season ('84).'[49] Stanford was confident this time that Rosa would not withdraw his offer, even though *Savonarola* was unfinished and *The Canterbury Pilgrims* not even begun. The première by Rosa of Mackenzie's *Colomba* (Drury Lane, 9 Apr. 1883), at which Stanford first made the Scotsman's acquaintance, probably spurred both Rosa and Stanford's enthusiasm.

Also in early 1883 Stanford was appointed Professor of Composition, Orchestration and Orchestral Conducting at the Royal College of Music. This was his first academic post and his appointment reflected his achievements at Cambridge, which were well known to the RCM Director, George Grove, who had followed his progress since meeting him as a boy in London, and who had encouraged his romance with

---

[49] See Stanford to Hallam Tennyson, 19 Jan. 1883, LCL, item 4265. The potential difficulty arising from setting two such similar stories – those of Thomas Becket and Savonarola – never seems to have occurred to Stanford.

Jennie. Parry, appointed Professor of Music History, was also expected to take on some composers and he and Stanford remained the principal teachers of composition at the RCM until Parry's death in 1918.[50] Stanford shared responsibility for the orchestra with Henry Holmes, but became its principal conductor in 1885 and remained so until his health began to decline in the early 1920s (the first public concert was given on 24 June 1885 and so Stanford monopolised the orchestra for thirty-five years). The appointment entitled him to a seat on the Board of Professors and he became a dominating figure in the College. His post at the RCM, although not attracting as much attention as that given to performances of his music, was the most tangible recognition Stanford had yet received of his standing as a composer. More importantly, he and Parry together were in the position of being able to influence cohorts of RCM students, including nearly all of the major British composers of the first half of the twentieth century. The list of Stanford's pupils, in particular, reads almost as a register of major composers of the next two generations, and it was through his work at the RCM that his aesthetic made itself most felt (see Ch. 8). The inception of the College took place on 7 May and was a gathering of both political and musical luminaries.[51] From this time Stanford's life was increasingly London-orientated; the College orchestra rehearsed on Tuesday and Friday afternoons so, for the next ten years, Stanford commuted up to London for at least two days each week during term, fitting in composition and orchestration classes before rehearsals.

It was probably at this time that Stanford and Parry were at their closest. Cambridge University had agreed to confer an honorary doctorate on Parry, which he received on 1 March 1883. He had also been asked by Stanford and Francis Jenkinson to compose the incidental music for the Greek Play Committee's production of Aristophanes's *The Birds*, a conspicuous honour as this was only the second in what became a long line of productions. Additionally Stanford had asked Parry to compose a symphony for CUMS, which Stanford conducted at the summer orchestral concert on 12 June 1883. The work, Parry's Second Symphony, thereafter nicknamed 'Cambridge', was well received and Parry himself was pleased with the performance.[52] Despite occasional chafing at this time, since the two men did not have complementary

---

[50] Parry reduced his teaching on his appointment as Director of the College in 1894; among the first six composition scholars admitted to the RCM were Hamish MacCunn, Charles Wood and Sydney Waddington.

[51] Term had actually started some three weeks earlier.

[52] Parry wrote: 'The Symphony got fair consideration, and in the afternoon went most admirably and sounded to me well. It was wonderfully received, and the friends I like to please seemed well delighted with it' (Parry's Diary, 12 June 1883, ShP).

temperaments, Stanford and Parry generally got on well and their relationship was mutually supportive.[53] Parry sometimes found Stanford's
manner overbearing and perhaps had felt a pang of regret that Stanford
had been appointed to the RCM Composition Professorship as, even at
this point, his view of Stanford's music was often ambivalent, but he
was quick to recognise Stanford's support and friendship. It is unclear,
due to lack of documentary evidence, precisely how Stanford viewed
Parry, but his advocacy of Parry's music suggests that he held him in
high regard and that he looked forward to the closer working relationship their twin appointments to the RCM created.

Two weeks after the opening of the RCM Stanford started composing
The Canterbury Pilgrims (22 May). He completed Act I on 19 July,
started Act II on 13 August, finishing it on 16 September, embarked on
Act III on 19 October and completed the opera on 2 December. Before
the opera was complete Rosa had settled on producing it in his 1884
season at Drury Lane.[54] Stanford had also secured performances of
Savonarola at the Hamburg Stadttheater, and at Covent Garden as part
of a German Opera season(!) conducted by Hans Richter. A highly
pleasurable piece of public recognition came at this time from Oxford
University, which conferred an honorary doctorate on Stanford on 14
June 1883; a more practical one had come four days previously when
he was approached by Robert Milward, representing the Birmingham
Triennial Festival Committee, who asked to compose another work for
them, this time a secular cantata for the 1885 Festival. Stanford accepted
immediately, and was equally happy when, a few days later, Milward
asked him if, instead, he would undertake to compose an oratorio.[55] In
terms of contemporary cultural values this commission, more than any
other, indicates how highly Stanford was then regarded. The patronage
of the three major musical Festivals (Birmingham, Leeds and the Three
Choirs) was the most highly valued in the country and the request for
an oratorio, the pinnacle of the British musical aesthetic at this time,
indicated that Stanford was recognised as a first-rank composer.

On 4 February 1884, Stanford's only piano sonata (in D flat major,
Op. 20) was premièred at St James's Hall by Agnes Zimmermann. The
work was well received and repeated five days later. It was reported that

---

[53] For example, Parry wrote '[We] talked much about the Irish situation, upon which
we of course differ, but we differed amicably and discussed long. [Stanford] played me
some of the new comic opera which seems excellent. He writes at an astounding pace. It
seems only necessary for him to take up his pen for the ideas to come as fast as he likes'
(Parry's Diary, 6 June 1883, ShP).

[54] Stanford to the Philharmonic Society, 2 Nov. 1883, BL MS Loan 48/13/32, fol. 212.

[55] See Stanford to Milward, 10 June 1883 and 22 June 1883, BCL, Lee Crowder MS
1171, items 108 and 109.

the work 'will certainly add to his reputation',[56] although when it was
performed in Cambridge a year later, the reaction was lukewarm and
the sonata was referred to as not possessing 'enough continuity, repose
or distinctive style'.[57] The sonata was not published and the manuscript
is lost. Meanwhile, the CUMS orchestra reached a crisis through lack
of size and proficiency. The problems had started in the previous year,
many blaming the growth of college music societies. But there was also
a feeling that Stanford was too ambitious and exceeded the capabilities
and enthusiasm of the orchestra on occasion. The *Cambridge Review*
reported that F. O. Carr would take over the rehearsals during the Lent
Term and that they would be 'of a more elementary character than
before'.[58] Possibly Stanford's heavy workload and intensive commuting
to London intensified the problem, but inevitably in a university the size
of 1880s Cambridge the orchestra would vary in standard, and the
implied source of the problem – Stanford's overambition for the
ensemble – was a further illustration of how Cambridge could easily
become too small for him; Stanford himself probably viewed dimly the
implied attack on his management.

In late February A'Beckett completed the libretto to *Beckett* and
read it to Rosa and Stanford. Stanford wrote to Hallam Tennyson
optimistically, convinced that Rosa would promise to produce the
opera and give him the go-ahead to start composing.[59] Lack of surviving
documentation necessitates supposition, but instead of giving approval
Rosa seems to have recommended alterations. In June 1884 Stanford
wrote that A'Beckett had amended the libretto and offered it to
Tennyson for his consideration,[60] but there are no further records of the
project.[61]

As the Hamburg première of *Savonarola* approached Stanford was in
high spirits. Parry wrote to Francis Jenkinson: 'I saw C.V.S. today. He
appears radiant, as well he may be.'[62] Charles crossed over to Hamburg
shortly before the performance, leaving Jennie and Geraldine in London.
The opera was first produced on 18 April and was well received by the
Hamburg public and press:

---

[56] *Cambridge Review*, 12 Mar. 1884, p. 241.

[57] *Cambridge Review*, 4 Mar. 1885, p. xcii.

[58] *Cambridge Review*, 13 Feb. 1884, p. 184.

[59] Stanford to Tennyson, 25 Feb. 1884, LCL, item 4266

[60] Stanford to Tennyson, 9 June 1884 (approx.), LCL, item 6992.

[61] Perhaps, after the damning criticism he was to receive from the British press for his
contribution to *Savonarola*, A'Beckett decided to give up writing libretti. Any musical
ideas Stanford had for an opera on *Beckett* may have been used in his incidental music
to Tennyson's play, staged at the Lyceum Theatre in 1893 (see Ch. 5).

[62] Parry to Jenkinson, 6 Mar. 1884, CUL Add. MS 6343, item 315.

> In point of musical content [it was] skilful and, at the same time, solid constructive art [and] surpasses all novelties of the kind which we have witnessed in Hamburg for a long time back ... Altogether the work betrays so much talent and such honest endeavour that we need not hesitate to prophesy a good future for its author.[63]

Stanford was pleased with the Hamburg production and stayed for the two subsequent performances on 22 and 24 April before returning to London.[64]

Stanford was barely back in England when he saw *The Canterbury Pilgrims* given for the first time at Drury Lane by Carl Rosa's company on 28 April. The press notices were generally favourable and Hans Richter, who was to conduct the British première of *Savonarola*, wrote that he thought the opera 'a quite splendid work'.[65] Parry, however, was less impressed: 'The Pilgrims' Song is the most attractive thing in it for me. The fugal entry of [the] Pilgrims [is] taking too. I didn't think anything else particularly noticeable.'[66] Grove too was at the performance and expressed equally reserved opinions to Parry:

> Charlie's music contains everything but sentiment. Love not at all – that I heard not a grain of. However did he make love to his wife? That spoiled the opera to me very much ... And I do think that there might be more *tune*. Melody is not a thing to be avoided surely, only its abuse ... *Savonarola* ought to be more to his hand I think.[67]

More serious for Stanford was the reaction of John Boosey, who left the performance disappointed shortly after the end of the overture.[68]

John Boosey's impression of *The Canterbury Pilgrims* boded ill for Stanford. It was clear that this financial commitment was a mistake and Boosey set about disengaging himself. When Stanford appeared in the firm's offices to arrange payment of the £500 which would be due to him when Richter performed *Savonarola* at Covent Garden, William Boosey refused payment on the grounds that the opera was being produced in German. This was a foolish excuse since John Boosey had made performance in London the condition for payment, not performance in English. Stanford made it clear that he expected to be paid when the opera was performed. Boosey was not, however, easily put off: he decided to thwart Stanford by preventing the performance.

---

[63] *Hamburger Nachrichten*, quoted in translation in *Era*, 26 Apr. 1884, p. 7.

[64] Stanford, *Pages*, 244.

[65] Hans Richter's diary, 3 May 1884, quoted in Christopher Fifield, *True Artist and True Friend: A Biography of Hans Richter* (Oxford, 1993), 206.

[66] Parry's diary, 28 Apr. 1884, ShP.

[67] Grove to Parry, 30 Apr. 1884, ShP.

[68] William Boosey, *Fifty Years of Music* (London, 1931), 32.

In May the firm registered its interest in the libretto at Stationers' Hall (Stanford having made his own entry some time previously), anticipating that this would oblige Stanford to pay them for its use in performance. By charging £500 for this 'service', for example, Boosey could cancel out his second payment, but he reckoned without Stanford's legal background and Stanford made it clear that the performance would proceed regardless of Boosey's objections. On 10 June Boosey applied to the Chancery Division for an injunction preventing the performance of the opera, pending the result of an action to vary Stanford's entry at Stationers' Hall so that it agreed with the firm's own entry. The application was refused on the ground that, if the performance went ahead and Boosey later won the action to vary Stanford's entry, Boosey could then sue for damages.[69]

This was not Stanford's only problem regarding *Savonarola*. Illness and lack of preparation were hampering the German Opera season at Covent Garden. The première was fixed for 18 June, but a week earlier the soprano playing the dual role of Clarice/Francesca pulled out and the performance was postponed until 27 June. A second soprano was brought in but, unable to master the part, soon withdrew. Stanford wrote to Richter twice on 24 June, after attending rehearsals at Covent Garden:

> The reading (of the 3rd and 4th Acts) was, as you said, very bad. However, in spite of that, it will be better tomorrow and Thursday. Perhaps, in your opinion and mine, the performance will not be tremendous; but the choir is excellent, and the players are enthusiastic, so we will at least survive. I feel it to be highly important that the Deutsche Oper meets its promise this time anyway as it was such a firm one, even if it does not go especially well. So do what you can, I can only give you my gratitude. Everyone will understand that the opera was given under very difficult circumstances.[70]

> I have just received your letter. I've already written to you once today and so our letters have crossed in the post. My opinion is this: do the rehearsals tomorrow and Thursday. *If they go badly* then do the opera on 2nd July, on Wednesday, but no later, otherwise no-one will think it will ever come out. As far as I'm concerned, you know I would never do anything in my own interest in the face of your well-meant opinions. But I do feel it very important, for the sake of the German Opera this season, to do the opera, if possible, on a specific day; all the more so as it has been postponed already. We can discuss it tomorrow after the rehearsal.[71]

---

[69] *Era*, 14 June 1884, p. 11. Mr Justice Pearson also felt that Stanford would not have been able to bring an action for damages if the injunction were granted because it would be impossible to calculate the profit margin of a performance which had not taken place.

[70] Stanford to Richter, 24 June 1884, RCM MS 4826, item 41.

[71] Stanford to Richter, 6.30 p.m. 24 June 1884, RCM MS 4826, item 43.

Stanford's reference to 'my own interest' is disingenuous, to say the least: not only would his reputation be harmed if the performance were cancelled, but he would lose the £500 due from Boosey regardless of the result of the legal action (one wonders whether Richter knew of this arrangement). His actions also show a certain naivety since press and public most certainly *did* expect a good performance and would not excuse a poor one on the grounds of 'circumstances'. Despite Stanford's hopes, the production was subsequently postponed again.

Finally, with a third soprano who had learnt the part in a week, the opera was given at Covent Garden on 9 July. Reaction was initially neutral but rapidly turned hostile. It was given in German and, because of Boosey's lawsuit, the libretto was available to the audience only in German, in Gothic script, and most had no idea what was going on. Francis Hueffer's comments in *The Times* show the direction of critical opinion. On 10 July he wrote: 'Leaving a more detailed account of the work to a later occasion we may briefly state that it was favourably received and the performance was, on the whole, satisfactory.'[72] With the benefit of a night's sleep, Hueffer's opinion matured: 'The performance, although far from perfect, was much better than could have been given a week ago ... Certain characteristics of the music may, however, be pointed out without hesitation. One of these is the almost total absence of any dramatic qualities properly so-called.'[73] Parry was less happy still and wrote:

> It seems very badly constructed for the stage, poorly conceived and the music, though clean and well-managed, is not striking or dramatic. The claque, which was tremendously strong, overdid their business, and by being too eager to bring CVS before the curtain as early as the Prologue, caused a sensation which prevented them from being able to make any effort over the later acts. At the end there was very little applause except from his personal supporters [and] ... the thing was a decided failure in every way.[74]

The best review was lukewarm and most were damning. Stanford himself was unhappy and he 'scarcely recognised the opera I had seen at Hamburg a few weeks before'.[75] Rosa was dismayed too, since he could see the failure of *Savonarola* crushing *The Canterbury Pilgrims*; he gave few performances of the opera on his provincial tour, including it only in Birmingham, Manchester, Glasgow, Dublin and Liverpool.

The failure of the two operas, particularly *Savonarola*, is understandable. Stanford made several misjudgements and showed that he did

---

[72] *The Times*, 10 July 1884, p. 6.
[73] *The Times*, 11 July 1884, p. 4.
[74] Parry's diary, 9 July 1884, ShP.
[75] Stanford, *Pages*, 254.

not have a keen enough dramatic perception to plan an opera successfully. This remained true throughout his life since, while his last four
performed operas (that is, from *Shamus O'Brien* onwards) were all quite
successful and have since unjustly lain neglected, Stanford was – though
he himself was unaware of the fact – always crucially reliant on the
dramatic awareness of his librettist and the strength of the original
literary source. If the scenario was well constructed for him, Stanford
could match this with appropriate and often very beautiful music, and
produce a credible opera. Thus an inexperienced librettist such as Barclay
Squire could produce a fairly good libretto by taking Moore's scenario
wholesale and writing in a straightforward literary style. But, in contrast
to Verdi or Puccini, Stanford could not see the weaknesses of a libretto,
and the two by Gilbert A'Beckett were simply awful. A'Beckett's lack
of dramatic perception was exacerbated by his literary style, which
favoured mock antiquarian language and did not recognise the virtue of
brevity (see below).

Dramatically, *Savonarola* is indebted to French grand opera.[76] The
Prologue, set in Ferrara in 1475, tells how the young Savonarola is
forced to leave his lover Clarice because of her father's disapproval. He
decides to become a monk. The action in the subsequent three acts takes
place in 1498, when he has become *de facto* ruler of Florence. A group
of citizens, led by Rucello, and including Clarice's daughter, Francesca
(who closely resembles her mother and is played by the same singer),
plot to overthrow him. Francesca's hatred for Savonarola dissolves,
however, and she changes sides. One of Savonarola's followers,
Sebastiano, falls in love with Francesca, but she is devoted to Savonarola
and spurns him. Sebastiano is killed defending his leader. Although
Rucello's plot is foiled, Savonarola's days are numbered. He is captured
and burnt at the stake. Francesca watches his death and dies in a state
of heavenly ecstasy. Thus the opera mixes the intimate – Francesca's
love for Savonarola – with the wider context of Savonarola's overthrow
and matrydom in typical French style. The work requires a huge
chorus and opulent scenery and costumes, and contains rivalries,
passions and spectacle, for example, an enactment of the 'bonfire of the
vanities' in Act I.[77] The story has dramatic potential, but is weakened
by the lack of relief from tragedy and discord. There are also structural
weaknesses. Sebastiano exists only because Savonarola, as a monk,
cannot reciprocate Francesca's love and Savonarola, although portrayed

---

[76] There are several similarities with Wagner's *Rienzi*, but Stanford is unlikely to have
known this opera when writing *Savonarola*.

[77] The ceremony initiated by Savonarola in which the rich gave up their finery in order
to demonstrate their renunciation of decadence.

in a historically accurate manner, appears too austere on stage to engender an audience's sympathy or support. Nowhere is there an explanation of Francesca's decision to change sides, and there is an imbalance of male and female principals (four to one). The music tries to convey the extreme emotions demanded by the scenario; it often succeeds in the sections involving the chorus but is less successful in the solo passages. The most satisfactory solo section is in the Prologue, when the young Savonarola leaves Clarice. Francesca's chaste 'Liebestod', however, is a pale imitation of Isolde's and Savonarola's funeral march is too redolent of Siegfried's in the last act of *Götterdämmerung*. The opera appears to decline gradually, encouraging the perception that it really comprises one act and three epilogues.

There are also many musical weaknesses in the work. Stanford employed several character motifs (that of the Monks is based on the plainchant hymn 'Angelus ad virginem', a melody supplied by his friend the Cambridge University Librarian, Henry Bradshaw), but their usage is not consistent and in some cases identifying their relevance is difficult. Stanford tried to avoid the use of standard forms, but he was not yet sufficiently practised to manage without them and his *arioso* lacked direction. The harmonic language is often blatantly Wagnerian: rising sequences appear frequently (Ex. 3.10), while distant modulation and the use of augmented triads give an illusion of chromatic decadence; this, however, is belied on closer examination in that the modulations are Schumannesque but rapid, while all dissonances are 'correctly' resolved. The total effect is turgid and so inferior to its Wagnerian antecedents as to be embarrassing.

The scenario of *The Canterbury Pilgrims* is an original one with a background inspired by Chaucer. Thus Stanford and A'Beckett capitalised on the Victorian obsession with things medieval, which had manifested itself in so many different ways, from the Gothic architectural style inspired by Pugin to the chivalric writing of Tennyson, and values of the 'Young England' Movement.[78] In terms of the blocking of

---

[78] The preoccupation with medievalism in the Victorian period resulted from the convergence of many different strands and values. In architecture, the Gothic style had first reappeared in the mid-eighteenth century with the construction of Strawberry Hill by Horace Walpole. It took, however, the pioneering theoretical work of Augustus Welsby Pugin to transform this architectural style from an eccentric byway to common currency. Pugin's theories, which linked Gothic architectural style directly to medieval Christianity, were expounded in *Contrasts* (1836), and *An Apology for the Revival of Christian Architecture in England* (1843). 'Gothic' soon became the most widely used architectural style, from suburban villas to great public and semi-public buildings, for example, Keble College, Oxford, Bradford and Manchester Town Halls, and St Pancras Station and Barry's Houses of Parliament, in London. The link with medievalism was soon established in other

Example 3.10   *Savonarola* (1884), Prologue, bars 627–35 (text: Gilbert A'Beckett)

Example 3.10 *(cont.)*

the scenario, and specific incidents, however, one can see direct parallels with *Die Meistersinger* and *Le nozze di Figaro*. The influence of Wagner notwithstanding, A'Beckett stated in the published libretto that he wished to write an English story for an English composer.[79] Hubert,

---

areas too: St Pancras appears more as a cathedral than a railway station in the well-known painting by John O'Connor, while in politics the 'Young England' movement, a small group of young Tory MPs, advocated a rejuvenation of the feudal system which would reduce the influence of radicals and *nouveau riche* manufacturers, thus restoring the 'proper' relationship between gentry and peasantry. This group had also been influenced by various sources: Walter Scott's medieval romances such as *Ivanhoe* (1819), Kenelm Digby's *The Broad Stone of Honour or Rules for the Gentlemen of England* (1822), and the Catholic convert priest Frederick William Faber (now best remembered as the author of many hymn texts, such as 'Sweet Saviour bless us ere we go', and 'O come and mourn with me awhile'). From the early years of Victoria's reign the cross-currents between various groups of scholars, politicians and artists become ever more complicated, and one can see elements of medievalism in nearly all areas of endeavour, for example, the Oxford Movement, Disraeli's novel *Coningsby* (1844), Tennyson's poems *The Lady of Shalott*, *Le Morte d'Arthur*, and *The Holy Grail*, many paintings by pre-Raphaelites, and aspects of the philosophies of Ruskin, Pater and William Morris, to name just a few examples. Throughout Victoria's reign this flowering was encouraged by the uneasy tension between the development of an industrial and manufacturing society on the one hand, aided by various scientific developments, and a desire for spiritual and social renewal on the other, the latter providing fertile ground for medievalists and medievalism. Indeed, the artistic genre in which the medieval passion was weakest was music itself, although here too there was a steady growth in interest, especially in plainchant. For a useful study of this issue, with principal reference to literature, see Raymond Chapman, *The Sense of the Past in Victorian Literature* (London and Sydney, 1986).

[79] The fact that Stanford was Irish does not seem to have struck A'Beckett; in fact, in Victorian society 'English' was synonymous with 'British' and was the more commonly used word.

an apprentice, is determined to win the hand of Cicely, daughter of
Geoffrey, landlord of the Tabard Inn, Southwark. Geoffrey disapproves,
however, and sends Cicely on a pilgrimage to Canterbury. Cicely has
also caught the eye of Sir Christopher Synge, who, with his steward
Hal, plans to abduct her. The plan is foiled by Dame Margery, Sir
Christopher's wife, with help from Hubert and Cicely, and Sir
Christopher is humiliated. While fleeing, however, Cicely and Hubert
are caught by Sir Christopher's men, and Hubert is tried for theft of
Cicely, with Geoffrey as plaintiff and Sir Christopher sitting in judgement as local magistrate. Hubert is sentenced to six years' imprisonment,
but denounces the philandering Sir Christopher. The verdict is withdrawn, and Geoffrey reluctantly bestows his approval on the lovers.

The Canterbury Pilgrims contains many of the same weaknesses as
Savonarola but is altogether a stronger work. The libretto is again too
long and has, for modern taste, an irritating 'olde Englishe' air ('I wot
thou seest how thou canst trust my wit' being an especially excruciating
example), although this style was widely praised at the time, being
referred to as 'crisp and vigorous [with] felicitous use ... made of old
English words without any suggestion of affectation or pedantry'.[80] Act
III (the trial) is dramatically superfluous and the opera could be brought
to a satisfactory conclusion at the end of Act II – unfortunately A'Beckett
and Stanford were too wedded to the model of *Die Meistersinger* and
the creation of a parallel to the singing competition. Some of the characters and drama are incongruous with the style of the music: the pact
between Cicely, Hubert and Margery, for example, is put into action by
the two women reversing roles in front of a blindfolded Christopher and
is akin to traditional British pantomime, lacking only an audience
shouting 'she's behind you'. This buffoonery, again paralleling Act II of
Die Meistersinger, is diminished by over-earnest music, with Stanford
afraid to display his natural wit and standing too much on the dignity
supposedly required of grand opera.

The music is again indebted to Wagner, and there are particular overtones of *Die Meistersinger*, as in Sir Christopher's serenade (Ex. 3.11;
cf. Beckmesser) and the fugal entry of the Pilgrims in Act I (Ex. 3.12;
cf. the entry of the Mastersingers). The reminiscence motifs (which
include 'Sumer is icumen in' for Hubert; see Ex. 3.13) are not used as
leitmotifs but are employed consistently and consequently work much
better than in *Savonarola*, but the *arioso* sections again lack direction,
and Stanford failed to create a dramatic impetus in the music which
reflects what is happening on stage. There is much less chromatic inflection than in *Savonarola* and the melodic material is stronger. Grove's

---

[80] *Athenaeum*, 3 May 1884, p. 575.

Example 3.11 *The Canterbury Pilgrims* (1884), Act II, Sir Christopher's serenade (text: Gilbert A'Beckett)

assertion about the lack of melody is plainly wrong: the opera has a
superabundance of it, but in homing in on melody as a constituent of
music Grove was going in the right direction. The problem in *The
Canterbury Pilgrims*, as in so much of Stanford's music, is not the lack
of melody, but rather that he did not construct it carefully. His melodies
frequently wander, seemingly without harmonic direction or sense of
coherence. Quite why Stanford found this so difficult is not evident; his
knowledge of Irish folk music, Italian opera and Schubert meant he knew
of the importance of periodisation, motif and forward impetus. But it
may be that this knowledge, coupled with his admiration of Schumann
and Brahms and, less strongly felt, of Wagner, led him to believe that
the hallmark of a progressive and sophisticated composer was the avoidance of the obvious and the use of more complex formulae. What
Schumann, Brahms and Wagner appreciated, but Stanford does not
appear to have done, is how motifs could be used to give coherence and

Example 3.12   *The Canterbury Pilgrims* (1884), Act II, opening (text: Gilbert A'Beckett)

structure when four-bar phrases and harmonic clichés were eschewed; Stanford, however, failed to exploit this degree of motivic coherence and without this sense his music often loses tautness and the listener's attention wanders because s/he is not supplied with the indefinable balance of predictability and surprise which fulfills the wish to be both secure and confounded. Given that melody was of primary importance to Stanford and that he always made it central to any composition, this weakness often thoroughly undermined what he was trying to achieve.

Stanford hoped that Richter would secure a performance of *The*

Example 3.13 *The Canterbury Pilgrims* (1884), Act I, bars 25–32 (text: Gilbert A'Beckett)

Canterbury Pilgrims in Vienna that would restore his reputation, but this aspiration came to nothing. The trail of events surrounding the operas left him depressed; the episode had been his first major setback and it could have hardly been more spectacular. Parry wrote to Jenkinson:

> I am very sorry he takes it to heart so. He certainly looked very glum at me. But I really was so fearfully disappointed that I could not for the life of me say a word. I daresay [*Savonarola*] will be better in English. The public of course could not make out what it was about. Perhaps if Rosa does it it will have a different result.[81]

---

[81] Parry to Jenkinson, 25 July 1884, CUL Add. MS 6343, item 333.

A fresh burst of adverse press comment came at the end of the opera season when many journals and newspapers ran review-articles, and it was the last nail in *Savonarola*'s coffin. After noting the remarkable fact that an opera by a British composer was given its British première by a German company in German, Hueffer described the work as bearing 'the trace of impending failure on almost every page ... the libretto being very uninteresting, and the music ... showing absolute want of dramatic power'.[82]

Press interest then declined, but Stanford was still waiting for a judgement in the action brought against him by Boosey. According to a letter from Stanford to Novello, an attempt to settle the matter privately had failed:

> [Mr Littleton] expressed regret that I had not made some pecuniary compromise with Boosey as to the sum he agreed to pay me for *Savonarola*. I think it is right for you to know and for myself to tell you that my solicitor did make a very liberal suggestion, more liberal in fact than the one your father suggested, and it was peremptorily refused.[83]

The hearing took place on 6 August. The firm argued that, in paying A'Beckett for the libretto, it had purchased the copyright, including the right of representation and therefore, under section 11 of the Dramatic Copyright Act 1842, it had the power to vary Stanford's entry at Stationers' Hall, so that he retained only the right of representation of the music. The defence argued that the right to represent the music would be useless without the right to use the words. The matter hung on a contradiction between a letter from Boosey to Stanford of 9 June 1881 and one from A'Beckett to Boosey of 15 June 1882. The former stated that Boosey would buy from Stanford 'the English copyright of the opera for £1000 ... this not to include the right of representation'.[84] The letter from A'Beckett to Boosey stated 'Received of Boosey & Co. the sum of £200 for the whole of my copyright and the right of performance of my book of the opera *Savonarola*'.[85]

The judges found in Stanford's favour. Confirming that there was doubt in the question, they concurred with the argument that the opera would be of no use to Stanford unless he had the right to use the words as well as the music. They gave Boosey the exclusive right of publication and Stanford the exclusive right of representation, and awarded

---

[82] *The Times*, 28 July 1884, p. 3.
[83] Stanford to Littleton, 13 July 1884, CUL Add. MS 9370, item 25.
[84] Quoted in *The Times*, 7 Aug. 1884, p. 3.
[85] Quoted in *Era*, 14 June 1884, p. 11.

costs against Boosey. The firm did not publish *Savonarola* but did publish *The Canterbury Pilgrims*. The legal action had, not unexpectedly, soured relations between composer and publisher, and Stanford dealt principally with Novello for the next ten years. It appears that Stanford had conceded to himself that *Savonarola* was dead, though he did later include the finale of the Prologue in a concert in Cambridge (14 March 1890). He later revised *The Canterbury Pilgrims* and tried to secure a production at Karlsruhe.[86] This failed, but the revised Act II love duet was later performed at the Philharmonic Society on 21 April 1887. Stanford became more sanguine and conceded to Joseph Bennett that even the revised version was 'destined for the wastepaper basket'.[87] In 1914 Parry noted that Stanford had 'hinted about getting *The Canterbury Pilgrims* into shape for us to do next year'.[88] Fate was against him, however, and the outbreak of war led the RCM to cancel the annual opera in order to save money.

Spring and summer 1884 were a chastening experience for Stanford and he did not return to operatic composition for over two years and did not work with A'Beckett again. In the short term there is no doubt that his reputation was greatly tarnished. His response to the legal action, albeit fully justified given Boosey's failure to deal with him straightforwardly, and his determination to see his works performed were the first public display of the reputation for awkwardness for which he was later notorious. The potential for this had always been there, for he did not take kindly to being thwarted, but had hitherto not been very evident since at Cambridge most were carried along by his enthusiasm and were happy to defer to him on musical issues.

In considering the six years between Stanford's marriage and the failure of *Savonarola*, however, one can see a sure and steady rise in both status and confidence. His reputation at Cambridge was sealed and works such as the Service in B flat, Op. 10 brought his name to an audience far beyond the university town. His appointment to the Royal College of Music is especially significant: for Stanford himself this work took him to London regularly and made him known and gave him contacts in the capital hitherto unavailable – the provincial musician thus became unequivocally part of the cosmopolitan world of the metropolis. But also, of course, Stanford's appointment to the RCM is significant for all those who followed him, since it allowed both him and Parry the opportunity to try to impart their aesthetics and values

---

[86] Stanford to Richter, 28 Feb. 1886, RCM MS 4826, item 46.
[87] Stanford to Bennett, 1 Apr. 1887, PML MS MFC S785.B4716, item 2.
[88] Parry's diary, 10 June 1914, ShP.

to the majority of British composers born between 1870 and 1900. And stylistically Stanford showed a real move towards maturity, progressing from an essentially pastiche approach to composition to one of some distinction, such that his music really did begin to sound like his own.

CHAPTER FOUR

At Cambridge
Triumphant

The years 1884–93 were a period of consolidation and enhancement for Stanford. When he finally left Cambridge for London, he had composed his most famous symphony, the 'Irish', plus another one in F major, and completed two full-length oratorios (*The Three Holy Children* and *Eden*), as well as three shorter secular cantatas (*The Revenge, The Voyage of Maeldune* and *The Battle of the Baltic*). *The Revenge* and the 'Irish' Symphony are works of real importance in his output, and demonstrate most convincingly the growth of an individual voice. As an academic his work was recognised at Cambridge by his election to the Professorship of Music in 1887, whilst his abilities as a conductor were further acknowledged by his taking up the baton of the Bach Choir in 1885.

After the debacle of *Savonarola* Stanford licked his wounds and went to Germany on holiday, which included visiting Ernst Frank at Hanover. There was good news on a personal front, as Jennie became pregnant again in August, and the couple returned to Cambridge in September, with the première of his *Elegiac Ode*, Op. 21 following at the Norwich and Norfolk Festival on 15 October 1884. The timing was apposite: the work was well received and partially restored Stanford's reputation, but it is not easy – critics viewed it not as a potboiler but rather as a demonstration of Stanford's ability to write serious but good and engaging music.

The *Elegiac Ode* is a setting of part of Walt Whitman's 'When Lilacs Last in the Dooryard Bloom'd' (1865–6). Quite how Stanford had come across Whitman's poetry, which was not well known in Britain at this time, is unknown. More curious still is that Stanford should have found Whitman's work appealing. This text is dark and brooding and exhibits a strongly individual style. Stanford returned to Whitman for three of the *Songs of Faith*, Op. 97, suggesting that this choice was no accident, but one cannot help feeling that it should have been Parry, well known for his interest in more liberal, philosophical and eclectic writing, who looked to Whitman, rather than Stanford. The prevalent attitude to Whitman was illustrated well by the *Musical Times*: 'There are some who look upon Whitman as a poet of genius, while others regard him as little better than a lunatic. It is not our duty to discuss this question but we must say that it is long since we met with anything more eccentric than the words which Dr Stanford has selected in his ode.'[1] No doubt these commentators were disturbed by Whitman's characterisation of Death as a fine, benevolent and powerful female, whose approach was to be relished and saluted as she brought peace and calm after the hectic pace of life. Although the Victorians were used to dealing with death they were unfamiliar with this laudatory approach:

> Come lovely and soothing Death,
> Undulate round the world, serenely arriving, arriving,
> In the day, in the night, to all, to each,
> Sooner or later, delicate Death . . .
>
> The night, in silence, under many a star;
> The ocean shore, and the husky whispering wave,
>   whose voice I know
> And the soul turning to thee, O vast and well-veil'd Death,
> and the body gratefully nestling close to thee.

While reservations were expressed about Whitman's poetry, praise was directed at Stanford's music:

> Dr Stanford has written an extremely effective and pleasing work, and in many parts, especially in the opening chorus, the music possesses real charm . . . Taken all in all we consider the *Elegiac Ode* the best work the composer has yet given us.[2]

> The introduction was not especially striking but the first chorus at once drew the attention. The undulating rhythm admirably expressed the words . . . The choric setting of the words 'From me to thee glad serenades' was very effective, if somewhat unelegiac . . . The gem of the composition was the last part 'The night, in silence under many a star', especially when the undulating rhythm recurred in the passage 'Over the rising and sinking waves'.[3]

By Festival commission standards of the time the *Elegiac Ode* is refreshing, not least because of Stanford's choice of Whitman's verse. Although his setting is prosaic in places and is cast in the shadow of the oratorio tradition, it also includes much skilful writing and some inspired passages which raise it well above the standard of many contemporaneous works. It comprises four numbers: an opening chorus, baritone solo, soprano solo with female chorus accompaniment, and a final chorus (consisting of a slow section, an extended fugue and a closing section which recapitulates material from the opening chorus). The two solo sections are not as strong as the choruses although both contain an easy flow of melody. The *Cambridge Review* correctly referred to the

---

[1] *Musical Times*, 15 Oct. 1884, pp. 633–4.
[2] Ibid.
[3] *Cambridge Review*, 29 Apr. 1885, p. ci.

Example 4.1 *Elegiac Ode*, Op. 21 (No. 1), opening

soprano solo as being 'somewhat unelegiac' and the same is true of the rumbustious fugue in the fourth movement which, with its strong primary-chord harmonies, sits uncomfortably in its surroundings, although in itself it is a successful use of a well-worn formula, and reflects the sentiment of the words ('Over the treetops I float three a song / Over the rising and sinking waves / over the myriad field, prairies wide'). These sections show one of Stanford's abilities as a two-edged sword: in a localised context he was very sensitive to the meaning of words and phrases and often translated these into effective musical settings, but the obverse was that he often did not appreciate the overall mood of the poetry and some individual passages sit awkwardly in their larger works as a result. Once again one is struck by a problem prevalent in other early works: over-sectionalisation. Despite these weaknesses, however, Stanford captured some of the spirit of Whitman's poetry and there are several effective passages.

The outer sections (including the orchestral introduction) are a successful evocation of serenity characterised by a succession of lilting triplet chords (Ex. 4.1), but the most striking part of the work is the opening of the final chorus. Here Stanford created a masterly picture of the sea – the first of many in his output – by the use of gently undulating strings and some striking harmonic progressions and inflections (a development of those first used in *God is our hope and strength*, Op. 8) (Ex. 4.2). The stressed minor sixth (fig. *a*, recalling the previous movement), the progressions starting at the words 'the ocean shore', and the subsequent settings of 'O vast and well-veil'd Death', (especially the suspended fourth in the second invocation) show how sensitive Stanford could be to the nuance and localised power of certain words and phrases, but here, in addition, he stayed truly within the overall mood of the poetry, giving the passage congruence and effect. It is readily apparent why contemporary reviewers were impressed and the *Elegiac Ode* went some considerable way to redeem Stanford's reputation.

Stanford's duties at Trinity were made less onerous at this time by the appointment of a Deputy Organist, which was financed principally by a donation from the Vice-Master E. W. Blore. Stanford took a cut

Example 4.2 *Elegiac Ode*, Op. 21 (No. 4), bars 11–28 (text: Walt Whitman)

in salary in recognition of the reduction of his duties, but he must have been pleased with the new arrangement. As the College Council noted, the proposal

> at a comparatively small sacrifice gives Mr Stanford a large amount of freedom whilst it seems calculated to secure the due training of the boys and the performance of the Chapel service by a responsible deputy on the frequent occasions when Mr Stanford is liable to be called away on professional duties. At the same time the

Example 4.2   *(cont.)*

Council desire to express their deep obligation to Mr Cobb for having for a long period so efficiently discharged the duties of the organist in his absence at so great a sacrifice of his own time.[4]

The minute carries an implication that Stanford had been neglecting his duties, but the Council were keen not to lose a man whose presence was conferring prestige on the College. Trinity College records show that Stanford continued to be a conscientious organist in this latter part of his tenure: he wrote a long letter to the Master in 1885 regarding the decline of the abilities of the choirmen.[5] He remained trenchant in his views on the selection of music, however, leading to another battle with the Precentor, Louis Borrissow, which Stanford lost, the Choir Committee determining unanimously that the Precentor alone was

[4] Minutes of Council (Domestic) 1882–97, p. 82 (23 May 1884), TCC.

[5] See Stanford's letter dated 23 Nov. 1885 in the Choir Committee Minute Book (MS REC.44.a.1) TCC; he recommended that five men be retired in the medium term. It took until 1892 (Stanford's resignation) for four of the men to go and Bilton, whose retirement Stanford most earnestly requested, survived him.

responsible for the selection of music and that Stanford had to make any objections to the Committee.[6]

At home, Jennie gave birth to their second child, christened Guy Desmond, on 10 May 1885. These domestic events did not, however, distract Stanford from his other work or from taking on new tasks – indeed Guy's arrival probably gave him more reason to commit himself to his profession. The latest addition to his work was his election as conductor of the London Bach Choir, facilitated by the retirement of Otto Goldschmidt. Stanford was encouraged to stand by his friend Arthur Coleridge, founder of the Choir and President at the time of Goldschmidt's resignation. Stanford was evidently well prepared for the election, which took place on 20 May, as he proposed a programme for his first concert at this meeting. Goldschmidt, however, was not in favour of Stanford's candidature and cut both Stanford and Coleridge afterwards.[7] For Stanford this appointment was a major achievement. The conductorship of the Bach Choir did not carry the cachet of that of the Philharmonic Society, but it was one of London's leading amateur choirs and gave Stanford a new capital-based ensemble to conduct. Over the years, up to his resignation in 1902, he was to conduct many works both old and new which the choir had not previously attempted, and the concerts remained an important feature of London musical life throughout nearly all of his tenure (see also Ch. 5).

Stanford completed *The Three Holy Children*, Op. 22 on 10 February 1885 and the work was premièred at Birmingham on 28 August, conducted by Hans Richter. Richter's appointment at Birmingham had caused ill-feeling among many in the British musical community – Sullivan had referred to the appointment as 'a bitter humiliation for all of us English'[8] – but Stanford, mindful and appreciative of all Richter had done to promote and support him over the previous few years, especially in regard to *Savonarola*, supported him from the beginning and was happy for him to conduct the oratorio. Critical reception of the work was qualified. The *Musical Times* commented: 'In his new oratorio our only regret is that the second part, which affords so excellent an opportunity for displaying invention and dramatic feeling, should be decidedly inferior to the first, in which we really have some charming and melodious writing for solo voices, chorus and orchestra.'[9] *The Three Holy Children* did not achieve a lasting place in the choral repertoire. To an extent this is due to the insatiable thirst for novelty that was a

---

[6] Choir Committee Minute Book (MS REC.44.a.1), 17 June 1885, TCC.

[7] See Stanford to Joachim, 6 Aug. 1885, BerSt (Tiergarten), MS SM 12/40, item 4695.

[8] Sullivan to Bennett, 8 May 1884, PML, MS MFC S949.B4714, item 5.

[9] *Musical Times*, 1 Oct. 1885, p. 592.

Example 4.3   *The Three Holy Children*, Op. 22, no. 1, 'Chorus of Jewish Women', bars 64–7

key ingredient of the British Festival movement of the late nineteenth century: no oratorio entered the standard repertoire between *Elijah* (1846) and *The Dream of Gerontius* (1900), although one or two other works survived beyond the normative couple of years. That *The Three Holy Children* did not establish itself, therefore, partially reflects the cultural conditions of the time, and there is also no doubt that, when compared with the offerings of many other composers, this oratorio stands fairly high.

Despite these considerations, the work is a long way from being Stanford's best. It is cast on traditional lines with the stereotypical mixture of arias, choruses and *recitativo accompagnato*, and both parts end with a virtuosic extended fugue. That Stanford followed the traditional model set out in *Elijah*, *The Creation* and *The Messiah* is unsurprising: it would have been a brave man who cast this format aside. Together with his friend and librettist Percy Hudson, Stanford had chosen a subject with good potential in the story of Azarias, Ananias and Misael and had framed it with adaptations of Psalm 137 ('By the waters of Babylon') to set the scene and a compressed version of the 'Benedicite' to act as a rousing conclusion. The text was substantial yet appropriate for a concert-length oratorio, but in comparison to the adventurous choice of text in the *Elegiac Ode*, it was drearily conventional and wedded to stereotypes, one of many factors which proved to be its undoing. Deprived of the unusual imagery which Whitman's work had provided, the oratorio is undermined by the slender and conventional nature of its musical material: too much of the music is uninspired or formulaic. The work starts well: the opening chorus of the Jewish

Example 4.4   *The Three Holy Children*, Op. 22, no. 13, bars 22–30

women conjures up the image of the waters of Babylon very successfully (Ex. 4.3),[10] and the idea of balancing this with a male chorus
representing the Assyrians was good, providing potential for contrast in
melody, harmony, timbre and orchestration. Unfortunately, the Assyrian
music, although appropriately martial in character, is insufficiently
stirring to be effective. The remainder of the oratorio continues worthily
but without the power and variety needed to sustain such a long
work. This is especially noticeable in the two fugues which, despite the
pyrotechnics of augmentation, *stretto*, dominant pedals and double
chorus, lack vitality and drive. The exceptions, apart from the Prelude
and opening chorus, are No. 13, in which an Angel appears to the
three children before they are cast into the fire, and No. 14, which relates
the building of the furnace. The former manages to conjure up something of the mystical atmosphere required by the angel's appearance
through its use of a six-part chorus (SSAATT) and Renaissance polyphony (Ex. 4.4); the latter, founded on a ground bass, acquires a sense
of drive and momentum as it builds up to a major-key cartharsis
when the fire consumes those around it. In this work more than many
others, one feels that Stanford was too conscious of precedent and that
he subordinated himself too overtly to established traditions and

---

[10] For modern ears the music has strong overtones of Smetana's *Vltava* but this work
had made little headway outside of Bohemia before 1885 so it is very unlikely that Stanford
knew Smetana's work when he was writing his oratorio.

formulae, especially in the work's overall conception, resulting in a piece which self-evidently could not stand comparison with its competitors.

Stanford's other work from 1885 is the incidental music for the Cambridge Greek Play Committee's production of Aeschylus's *Eumenides*, completed in May. The Greek plays were a recent innovation at Cambridge, instigated by J. W. Clark in 1882 by a performance of Sophocles's *Ajax*. Macfarren had composed that music and Parry wrote incidental music for Aristophanes's *The Birds* in the following year. The music to all of these plays (and subsequent ones, the most famous of which is Vaughan Williams's setting of *The Wasps*) is highly unusual in setting the original Greek and reflects an exclusive, Victorian Oxbridge, aesthetic. The performances took place from 1 to 5 December with Stanford conducting. Written for actors, the vocal lines are declamatory rather than melodic, and the work also includes melodrama. Aural interest lies in the orchestration, in the instrumental movements, and in the use of leading motifs, the treatment of which is similar to that of *The Canterbury Pilgrims*. The *Cambridge Review* referred to the music as being 'Dr Stanford's most successful effort hitherto',[11] and performances in London, under Richter, followed on 17 May 1886 and at Cambridge by CUMS on 15 June, but unsurprisingly, given its format, the work did not establish itself (the play, with Stanford's music, was, however, given again at Cambridge in 1906).

Stanford completed his Piano Quintet in D Minor, Op. 25 in February 1886, which Joachim and others played through informally at Harvey Road on 18 March, prior to Joachim's annual CUMS concert the following day.[12] The work was premièred at the CUMS Chamber Concert on 10 June, which also included a performance of the Toccata, Op. 2. The reception of the Quintet was mixed:

> It is difficult to speak confidently of the work at a first hearing, but the general impression given is that the last two movements are not equal to the first and second, which are undoubtedly fine, and more easily appreciated, especially the Scherzo. In the Adagio and Finale we seemed occasionally to trace the composer of the *Eumenides* music, but the slow movement is not wholly satisfactory, although the effect of the Irish melody is good ... Each movement was warmly applauded and at the conclusion the composer was twice called ... The Toccata was brilliantly played; but we were not particularly struck by it, and believe it to be an early work.[13]

These comments are deserved. Much of the Quintet is overly indebted to Teutonic composers; the soundworld of the first movement, with its

[11] *Cambridge Review*, 9 Dec. 1885, p. 131.
[12] Jenkinson's diary, 18 Mar. 1886, CUL, Add. MS 7409.
[13] *Cambridge Review*, 16 June 1886, p. 391.

frequently thick scoring in the tenor register, is strongly redolent of Brahms. The 'hop-jig' scherzo never quite builds up to the hell-for-leather momentum it needs. The slow movement too fails to cohere, with rather too much meandering and a startling quote from Mendelssohn's 'Wedding March' towards the close (possibly a reference to Francis Jenkinson and Stanford's sister-in-law Marian, who married after a long and halting courtship in July 1887). In retrospect one can see that the Piano Quintet, like the Piano Quartet, Op. 15, was something of a dry run for the 'Irish' Symphony, especially in its hop-jig scherzo, but, unlike the later work, the mode of expression is generally turgid, despite some grand moments.

In London, Stanford made his first appearance as conductor of the Bach Choir with Joachim as soloist on 25 March 1886 in a programme comprising Bach's cantata 'Gott ist mein König' (No. 71), the British première of Joachim's *Hungarian Concerto*, Beethoven's *Elegischer Gesang* and Part III of Schumann's *Faust*; *The Times* commented that 'the wisdom of the Bach Choir in choosing for its new conductor so experienced and able a musician as Mr C. Villiers Stanford was proved by an interesting programme and a fairly good performance at Thursday's concert given at St James's Hall before a numerous audience.'[14] Lest people thought that Stanford was concentrating too much on modern music with the Bach Choir, he put together a programme comprising works by J. C. Bach, Praetorius and Anerio for the concert on 14 December. Over at the RCM, students gave their first complete opera, Cherubini's *Les Deux journées*, at the Savoy Theatre on 24 June. The performance attracted much attention, with Grove ensuring that many musical luminaries, plus the Prince and Princess of Wales, were present. He subsequently wrote to his confidante Edith Oldham: 'The opera was a complete success and a most brilliant affair: not a hitch from beginning to end, acting and singing much better than at rehearsals. House full and most brilliant to look at. P. and Princess of Wales with a box full of children and peers dotted about all over the place.'[15]

While Stanford's visit to Birmingham in 1885 for *The Three Holy Children* was only a partial success, his appearance at the 1886 Leeds Festival, for the première of his setting of Tennyson's *Revenge*, was greeted with acclaim. Of all the works dating from the 1880s it was this which brought Stanford's name to the attention of a mass audience and finally secured his reputation. *The Revenge* was given on 14 October and Stanford wrote to Hallam Tennyson, urging his attendance: 'a line to tell you that *The Revenge* comes off at Leeds on Thursday evening

[14] *The Times*, 27 Mar. 1886, p. 4.
[15] Grove to Oldham, 25 June 1886, RCM, Grove–Oldham correspondence.

next. I wish you could come. The chorus is *magnificent*, also the band. You will never hear it anywhere else so splendidly done.'[16] Stanford's optimism was justified – both choir and orchestra did justice to his work and *The Revenge*, along with Sullivan's setting of *The Golden Legend*, were the hits of the Festival. Critical reaction to *The Revenge* was very positive:

> The effect of this fine and bold composition more than justified anticipatory remarks. We have not often met, in music, with a happier and, at the same time, more daring thought than that carried out by Mr Stanford when he employed melodies redolent of the sea and smacking unmistakably of the forecastle.[17]

> Thrice Dr Stanford was recalled to receive the approving cheers of the gathering . . . we think it may be safely predicted that this choral ballad will become a favourite study with provincial choral societies.[18]

Unusually for this type of secular cantata, the work was not written to commission. Stanford's name was one of fifteen which had been considered by the Leeds Festival Committee as potential composers from whom works might be commissioned, but they had settled instead on Rubinstein, Dvořák, Sullivan, Stainer and Mackenzie.[19] Stanford was then one of fourteen composers who offered works to Leeds unsolicited; *The Revenge* was the only piece accepted. For both Stanford and the Leeds Festival Committee this turned out to be a good decision and *The Revenge* subsequently became one of Stanford's best-selling compositions, remaining popular well into the 1930s and cementing his reputation with a huge number of amateur singers (120,000 copies were sold by 1914 and 195,000 copies by 1939).

Why was *The Revenge* so popular? There are many reasons for Stanford's success. First, the work is a 'practical' one – it was well within the technical grasp of many amateur choral societies, did not require soloists, and was, for a festival cantata, short, at about thirty minutes in length. The choral lines are grateful to sing and each line has its moments of glory. Secondly, the piece takes an accessible and popular subject, capitalising on the perceived English love of the sea and heroism during the Spanish Wars of the reign of Elizabeth I, interest in whose reign was resurgent in the 1880s. There is an unashamed patriotism about the work and HMS *Revenge* was in the so-called favourite position of the English, that of the underdog; even though the ship goes

---

[16] Stanford to Hallam Tennyson, 10 Oct. 1886, LCL, item 6993.

[17] *Musical Times*, 1 Nov. 1886, p. 655.

[18] *Yorkshire Post*, 15 Oct. 1886, p. 5.

[19] See Frederick Spark and Joseph Bennett, *History of the Leeds Musical Festivals* (2nd edn, Leeds, 1892), 272.

Example 4.5 *The Revenge*, Op. 24, bars 214–23 (text: Tennyson)

down, it only does so after routing most of the Spanish navy. Thirdly, the poem is a rapid narrative full of changing scenes and themes which Stanford captured well by eschewing the repetition of words and extensive development. Consequently the interest of the audience is maintained throughout as the story is told rapidly with plenty of contrast and, by British cantata standards of the time, directly, through, for example, transparent rhetorical devices (the rocking of the sea; see Ex. 4.5). This compares favourably to *The Three Holy Children*, which stood on its dignity, relied too much on bland formulae, and moved ponderously. Finally, Stanford had found a hole in the market: *The Revenge* proved popular because it had so few successful counterparts; the poem and music's lack of sentimentality probably helped to extend its shelf life as other works fell victim to the changing social attitudes of post-Great War Britain.

Stanford's music balances Tennyson's poem excellently. Here there is no problem about a localised sensitivity to text overbalancing the overall ethos of the piece, since rapid contrast is what the poem requires. The work contains many simple and telling melodies (Ex. 4.6), effective orchestration (Ex. 4.7) and, although some of the writing is formulaic,

Example 4.6 *The Revenge*, Op. 24, bars 58–68 (text: Tennyson)

the directness of expression and multitude of short passages avoids any feeling of stagnation or predictability. The preference for syllabic word-setting is also a plus (see Exs 4.5–4.7): the music gains a 'no nonsense' directness which emphasises the bluff heroism of the narrative and captures the same spirited mood as the earlier *Cavalier Songs*. Above all, the work is successful because Stanford set a text which spurred his own imagination and suited his abilities: he was at home with tales of bravado and heroism. Tennyson's poem allowed Stanford to play to all of his strengths and required no display of his weaknesses; as with the *Songs of the Sea* almost twenty years later, Stanford had found his metier.

With a highly satisfactory year behind him, 1887 was destined to be one of Stanford's busiest and most productive years. Although some of the music he wrote during this year is undistinguished, the 'Irish' Symphony in F minor, Op. 28 and parts of the incidental music to *Oedipus Tyrannus*, Op. 29 contain fine music, and the former established Stanford's reputation in Britain as an essayist in the symphonic

Example 4.7   *The Revenge*, Op. 24, bars 104–21 (text: Tennyson)

genre, balancing his success behind the rood screen and on the choral society benches. But it was not just as a composer that he worked hard: he also found time for much performance and a spate of correspondence on the Irish Question, which had once more bubbled to the top of the political agenda.

Example 4.7   *(cont.)*

Stanford's setting of Psalm 150, *O praise the Lord of Heaven*, Op. 27 was premièred at the Manchester Exhibition on 3 March 1887. The exuberant nature of the text did not leave him much scope for contrast and the music is not his best, but it is characterised by an accessible jollity and incorporates the hymn tune 'Tallis's Ordinal', which is used as a chorale and as the basis of the fugue which constitute the third section. For the 'Exhibition' genre – which required concise, confident and morally uplifting music – the work is appropriate, and Stanford was asked to compose similar pieces on later occasions (*East to West*, Op. 52 and *A Welcome Song*, Op. 107).

The year 1887 was also the year of Queen Victoria's Golden Jubilee and the opportunity for composing a commemorative piece (a possibility exploited by most composers with any commercial nous) also came Stanford's way. Charles and Jennie started the year by visiting the Tennysons on the Isle of Wight, and it was probably here that Tennyson suggested to Charles that he set the recently completed poem *Carmen saeculare*.[20] If this was when the proposal was made, Stanford worked quickly, for his setting was completed on 4 February and it was premièred in private to the Queen on 11 May. Despite the rash of works

---

[20] See Stanford, *Pages*, 233.

written in her honour, *Carmen saeculare* received special treatment due
to the Queen's long-standing admiration of Tennyson. Stanford wrote
to Hallam Tennyson: 'It was really very well done, in spite of Albani
not being able to sing and the whole thing being necessarily done on a
small scale ... The Queen expressed herself very much pleased, and I
hope she meant what she said. However, without disrespect, the verdict
of the musicians is the most valuable.'[21] The Queen was indeed pleased
and wrote to Tennyson (who had been too ill to attend the performance):
'I am anxious to tell you that your beautiful Ode was performed at
Buckingham Palace ... and conducted by Mr Stanford himself ... We
greatly admired the music, which was very descriptive and well adapted
to the words – and it was extremely well executed. I wish you could
have heard it.'[22]

Despite these plaudits, *Carmen saeculare*, both words and music, is
best forgotten. The poem is fawning and imperialist (hardly surprising
in the circumstances and conforming to the national mood of the time)
but is also badly written:

> She beloved for a kindliness rare in fable or history,
> Queen and Empress of India,
> Crown'd so long with a diadem never worn by a worthier.
>
> Nothing of the lawless, of the despot.
> Nothing of the vulgar or vainglorious.
> All is gracious, gentle, true and Queenly.
>
> Henry's fifty years are in shadow,
> Gray with distance Edward's fifty summers,
> Even her grandsire's fifty scarce remembered.

It is not surprising that Stanford could do nothing with this and the
music, in the form of a multi-section anthem, is dull and at times flails
desperately. The beginning and end are cast as 'Pomp and Circumstance'-
type marches, but while Elgar could perhaps have made a tolerable
success of such a work (witness the *Coronation Ode* of 1902), Stanford,
despite his avowed loyalty to the Crown, could not replicate the bombast
and pageantry of the words in the music. In a nineteenth-century version
of hype exceeding reality the work was a commercial failure, selling only
200 copies.

While *Carmen saeculare* may have fulfilled any patriotic duty Stanford
held, his most important (and financially successful) work produced in

---

[21] Stanford to Hallam Tennyson, 12 May 1887, LCL, item 4296.
[22] Queen Victoria to Tennyson, 14 May 1887, quoted in Hope Dyson and Charles
Tennyson (eds), *Dear and Honoured Lady – The Correspondence between Queen Victoria
and Alfred Tennyson* (London, 1969), 130–31.

Example 4.8   'Irish' Symphony, Op. 28, Scherzo, principal theme, bars 1–4

Example 4.9   'Irish' Symphony, Op. 28, Scherzo, 'B' section of Trio, bars 13–16

1887 was the 'Irish' Symphony. Richter had asked Stanford for the piece, which was completed on 30 April, and it was Richter who conducted the première at St James's Hall on 27 May. Critical reaction was very favourable, although *The Times* neglected to review it until 1 July, and the *Musical Times* failed to review the work at all. When *The Times* review did come, however, it was flattering:

> The rhythm and the type of melody prevailing throughout belong to the Green Island ... The result is an extremely pleasing and in many respects remarkable work, which was acclaimed with enthusiasm by the audience ... The gem of the symphony is undoubtedly the slow movement, the dreamy melancholy of which conveys an intense poetic impression.[23]

In subsequent months the symphony was performed throughout England, across Europe (including the inaugural concert of the Amsterdam Concertgebouw on 3 November 1888), and in the United States. It became a standard in the symphonic repertory until the First World War when it was eclipsed briefly by Elgar and then by the works of Stanford's pupils. More than any other work, the 'Irish' Symphony made Stanford's music known in international musical circles.

The work comprises the usual four movements, with the scherzo and slow movement reversed. The first movement is the least successful, its form being unduly perceptible and, although containing some melodious and well-orchestrated material, not evidently Irish in character. The

---

[23] *The Times*, 1 July 1887, p. 4.

Example 4.10   'Irish' Symphony, Op. 28, Scherzo, 'B' section of Trio, bars 23–6

remaining three movements, however, are different. The Scherzo is cast as a 9/8 hop-jig with a slower-paced trio. Here Stanford captured excellently the *perpetuum mobile* nature of Irish dance music as the jig rushes forward, almost tripping over itself through its energy (Ex. 4.8). The frenetic mood of the music recalls the diabolical nature of the 'Witches Sabbath' in Berlioz's *Symphonie fantastique* and the coda, in which the scurrying violin quavers build relentlessly to the closing cadence, is exhilarating. The trio has a more Brahmsian flavour to it (especially one falling phrase with walking pizzicato bass; see Ex. 4.9) but is still essentially Stanford, containing an easy flow of melody and some characteristic harmonisation, particularly, in one passage, the anticipation of a modulating seventh on the previous chord (Ex. 4.10).

The slow movement has been dogged by some argument, as one melodic cell appears to quote the main subject of the slow movement of Brahms's Fourth Symphony (Exs 4.11(*a*) and (*b*)). Stanford later refuted the accusation, claiming that the source was 'an old Irish lament in Petrie's MSS', but muddied the waters by getting his dates wrong, claiming that the two works were written simultaneously, whereas Brahms's symphony had been completed and premièred in 1885. In fact, the only melody in Petrie which contains a similar motif is 'The Lament of Owen Roe O'Neill' (Ex. 4.11(*c*)) and Stanford evidently modified this to produce his motif prominently displayed in the oboe;[24] furthermore, the crucial ingredient of Brahms's melody is that it starts on the mediant, whereas Stanford's does not, so the relationship is no

---

[24] See Stanford, *Pages*, 262. 'The Lament for Owen Roe O'Neill appears in Stanford's *Songs of Old Ireland* (1882) but not, curiously, in his edition of the Petrie Collection (1902–5). Further confusion was created by John Porte when he claimed that the source was the 'Lament of Deirdre for the Sons of Usnach' (see *Sir Charles Stanford* (London, 1921), 34); this melody does appear in Stanford's edition of Petrie (vol. 2, no. 1019) but is not the melody he used in the 'Irish' Symphony.

Example 4.11 (*a*) 'Irish' Symphony, Op. 28, third movement, bars 66–78; (*b*) Brahms, Fourth Symphony in E Minor, Op. 98, second movement, bars 1–3; (*c*) *Songs of Old Ireland* (1882), 'The Lament of Owen Roe O'Neill'

more than superficial. Ireland is evoked through the opening harp passage (a reference to the ancient Irish harping tradition, though the $B\flat^7$ and F^9 chords are almost impressionistic in effect) and the D major oboe theme, which represents Irish bagpipes. Apart from this the Irish character is somewhat lacking, and although one can see a portrait of an Irish lough on a rainy day, this would not be so readily apparent if

Example 4.12 'Irish' Symphony, Op. 28, fourth movement, bars 32–9

one did not know that the symphony carried the 'Irish' moniker. Nevertheless, the music is effective, aided by delicate orchestration and leisurely pacing which imbue it with a sense of freshness and space, with a 'thunderstorm' in the middle providing contrast.[25]

The final movement is the only one in which Stanford quoted directly from Irish folksong, using 'Remember the Glories of Brian the Brave' and 'Let Erin Remember the Days of Old' in a three-subject movement (the second theme is original; the two Irish songs were well known from *Moore's Irish Melodies*).[26] The opening of the movement (Ex. 4.12) shows how much his pupils owed to Stanford, since both Vaughan Williams and Holst in their military band music reproduce an English version of this Stanfordian style and, if one were to look for an exemplar of Constant Lambert's complaint about the use of folksong, here it is, since at the opening the first subject is given three times, first in

---

[25] Showing an affinity with Dvořák's Seventh Symphony, which Stanford may have known as it was premièred by the Philharmonic Society in April 1885.

[26] 'Remember the Glories' had previously been published under the name 'Molly Macalpin' in Edward Bunting, *A General Collection of the Ancient Irish Music* (London, 1796).

fragments, second complete but *piano*, and finally *tutti* and loud. Shaw, on hearing the Philharmonic Society perform the symphony in May 1893, criticised the movement for not containing proper development:

> The essence of the sonata form is the development of themes; and even in a rondo a theme that will not develop will not fit the form. Now the greatest folk-songs are final developments themselves: they cannot be carried any further. You cannot develop 'God Save the Queen', though you may, like Beethoven, write some interesting but retrograde variations on it. Neither can you develop 'Let Erin Remember'. You might, of course, develop it inversely, debasing it touch by touch until you had 'The Marseillaise' in all its vulgarity; and the doing of this might be instructive, though it would not be symphony writing. But no forward development is possible.
>
> Yet in the last movement of the 'Irish' Symphony, Stanford the Celt, wishing to rejoice in 'Molly MacAlpine' ('Remember the glories'), and 'The Red Fox' ('Let Erin Remember'), insisted that if Stanford the Professor wanted to develop themes, he should develop these two. The Professor succumbed to the shillelagh of his double, but, finding development impossible, got out of the difficulty by breaking Molly up into fragments, exhibiting these fantastically, and then putting them together again. The process is not in the least like the true sonata development.[27]

Arguably, however, Shaw missed the point, because the movement is not in true sonata form; the first two subjects set up this expectation but the passages using 'Let Erin Remember' (the third subject) replace the 'normal' development and coda. On the face of it, Shaw may have a valid complaint, since this implies that Stanford was trying unsuccessfully to compose in sonata form, but Shaw's thesis about the conflict between 'Stanford the Celt' (spontaneous and orgiastic) and 'Stanford the Professor' (stiff and formulaic) does not exist here: Stanford recognised, just as Shaw did, that folk tunes do not lend themselves to development, and did not attempt it; rather Shaw seems to be projecting here his own feeling that final movements ought to be in sonata or rondo form and does not entertain the possibility of other plans (see p. 385 for further discussion on Shaw's views on Stanford's Irishness). Stanford did not eschew thematic manipulation entirely – in the bridge passages between each subject both Irish melodies are broken up into fragments and juxtaposed, just as Shaw stated – but in essence he modified the formal stereotype to an episodic structure; it was a sound judgement and the second statement of 'Let Erin Remember', with full and triumphant orchestration, is a rousing conclusion to the symphony. Of principal satisfaction in this work is that one feels that Stanford has

---

[27] Shaw, *Music in London 1890–94*, ii, 319 and 322.

'arrived' in terms of maturity – here is a work which is both fresh in most of its utterances, showing a marked amount of individual style (no one but Stanford could have produced the scherzo or the slow movement), and a degree of technical accomplishment which prevent the freshness and idiosyncrasy from losing coherence. From this point on Stanford's style was both mature and stable.

Ten days before the première of the 'Irish' Symphony Stanford conducted the première of Parry's *Blest Pair of Sirens* with the Bach Choir (17 May), further evidence of his positive approach to Parry's music, and at the CUMS orchestral concert on 7 June Stanford's general advocacy of new British music was demonstrated by his securing another première, that of Frederic Cowen's Symphony No. 5 in F, with Cowen conducting. At the same concert Frederick Bridge conducted his setting of *Rock of Ages*, while Richard Gompertz was the soloist in Alexander Mackenzie's Violin Concerto, also conducted by its composer. Stanford concluded the concert with *The Revenge* and Goring Thomas's *Suite de Ballet*.

It was in the summer that the Irish Question reared its head in Stanford's world, when he initiated an acrimonious correspondence with the former President of the Cambridge Union, Edmund Garrett, over the issue of Home Rule. The seven letters were published in the *Cambridge Review* and caused quite a stir in Cambridge circles, even to those used to Stanford's flashes of temper.[28] The precise subject of his irritation was Garrett's conduct in trying to secure an invitation to a member of the Irish National Party to address the Cambridge Union, but as Garrett surmised in one of his replies, it was not so much this that annoyed Stanford, but the presence of a Nationalist speaker at all. The question of Irish government concerned Stanford throughout his life: inevitably, as a member of the Anglo-Irish ascendancy, he was very sensitive about the position of Ireland in the Union. Although Stanford believed that British governments had ruled Ireland badly,[29] he regarded the Irish National party as troublemakers who whipped up the emotions of the Catholic majority.

Stanford's reaction to Garrett's doings was exacerbated by political events over the preceding two years. The National party, led by Parnell, had supported, to varying extents, acts of civil disobedience, especially non-payment of rents by rural tenants, and was associated in many minds, Stanford's included, with the Phoenix Park murders of 1882.[30] The attitude of Gladstone's Liberal Party, which, until the mid-1880s,

---

[28] See *Cambridge Review*, 15 June 1887, pp. 385–7.
[29] See Stanford, *Pages*, 101–2.
[30] Ibid., 254–7.

he appears to have supported, also greatly upset Stanford.[31] Two events, one Irish, one not, disillusioned him. First had been the murder of General Gordon at Khartoum in January 1885. Francis Jenkinson records a whimsical way in which Stanford's response to this event manifested itself:

> I had an hour with [Geraldine] before dinner yesterday, and anything like her quickness and understanding I never saw . . . Her father had taught her to say 'Gladstone is a traitor' and she said it to me with great energy, but tho' she repeated it over and over again, I could not make out what she said until Mrs S. came and understood.[32]

The second event was Gladstone's conversion to Home Rule. Liberal Unionists, led from different ends of the party by Lord Hartington and Joseph Chamberlain, took their supporters away from Gladstone into the middle ground. Stanford went with them, principally because he believed that Home Rule in Ireland would pass power to the Catholic majority with few safeguards for his own constituency, the Anglo-Irish enclave in Dublin. Little of this turmoil is recorded by Stanford personally, but the spate of letters in 1887 shows how strongly he felt. The original motion at the Cambridge Union on 7 June, 'that in the opinion of this house it is desirable to concede Home Rule to Ireland', was bogged down in procedural wranglings and members later voted on whether to invite a Nationalist speaker to address them, a vote which was won convincingly. Stanford was, however, convinced that Garrett (who was pro-Home Rule), had acted inappropriately as President by canvassing in favour of the motion to invite the Nationalist speaker. Although Stanford's letters were written in the usual brusque – but also verbose – manner he employed when annoyed, here his tone was especially fierce. Stanford's first letter to Garrett stated:

> I could have wished in the interests of the Society that its president were not a party to this underhand proceeding [of selective canvassing], which, however much it may be in accordance with the novel traditions of your party, is scarcely what is expected of persons who have had the advantage of a University training . . . As it is, I can only hope that increasing years will lend you a graver sense of the responsibilities of any position which you may hold, and of the

---

[31] Stanford's political affiliations during his early years are unknown but he certainly signed a public affirmation of support for Professor James Stuart, who stood in the Liberal interest in the Cambridge University by-election in 1882; see the *Cambridge Review*, 22 Nov. 1882, p. 122.

[32] Francis Jenkinson to Eleanor Jenkinson, 27 Feb. 1885, CUL, Add. MS 7671, item III C 143. The murder of Gordon disillusioned many other Liberals and contributed significantly to Gladstone's loss of power at the 1886 General Election.

value of ensuring the respect of your adversaries by 'hitting above the belt' only.[33]

Garrett was no less adept in wielding an acerbic pen, and replied:

I stand astonished today at the grotesque pettiness of some of the charges which I find are current among a small and angry minority. I shall try to avoid them simply by not stooping to so low a plane of thought. To yours I have replied because I owed a reply to your position and to mine, not to the intrinsic nature of the charge – in itself ludicrously absurd.[34]

Stanford showed his true colours in his next letter: 'I . . . firmly believe that the whole arrangement was made in order to provide a political platform for one of the Irish party, and that the addition of an invitation to a Unionist was made in order to lend an air of apparent fairness to the plan'.[35]

The correspondence was drawn to a close by William Cunningham, the Trinity College chaplain, who gently rapped both men on the knuckles, and E. B. Birks, who relayed something approaching a grudging acknowledgement from Stanford that his charges were not fully justified.[36] The whole series of letters demonstrate just how strongly Stanford felt about the question of Home Rule, an issue to which he later returned (see pp. 285–6). It was unfortunate that he could not bring himself to apologise directly to Garrett as the distinct impression was created in Cambridge that Stanford was lacking in gallantry and that his behaviour had not conformed to the standards expected of a gentleman.

After the hectic first six months of 1887 the Cambridge Long Vacation must have come as a welcome relief. On 6 July there was a family celebration when Francis Jenkinson, one of Charles's closest friends in Cambridge, married Jennie's sister Marian. Jenkinson had been courting Marian gently for several years previously, so it was with great pleasure that Charles, along with other friends, including Grove and Parry, saw the couple marry at last. Stanford was also making plans for performances of the 'Irish' Symphony in Germany and lobbied both Richter

---

[33] Stanford to F. E. Garrett, 4 June 1887, quoted in the *Cambridge Review*, 15 June 1887, p. 386.

[34] F. E. Garrett to Stanford, 7 June 1887, quoted ibid.

[35] Stanford to F. E. Garrett, 9 June 1887, quoted ibid.

[36] For both letters see the *Cambridge Review*, 20 June 1887, pp. 402–3; the *Review* added, 'The Editors do not wish to take any further part in this controversy. They consider that the intervention of the Long Vacation between now and the issue of the next number of the *Review* will afford ample opportunity for the smoothing down of the feelings of all parties concerned.'

and Joachim. The latter had given up conducting the Berlin Philharmonic but recommended that Stanford try his successor Hans von Bülow, to whom Stanford duly sent the score. Bülow subsequently replied with a promise to give performances of the 'Irish' Symphony in Hamburg and Berlin. Joachim had also heard a rumour that Stanford was to be knighted, but the truth came quickly by return: 'I have (Gott Sei Dank!) only been knighted by Betts, critic of the *Figaro*, who having the control as well of *Truth*, the *Graphic* and now even the *Daily News*, invented the gilded lie out of his own head, put it in all four papers, and spread it to ends of the earth! Thus is history manufactured in the 19th century.'[37]

During this summer break Charles and Jennie travelled to Italy via Switzerland and back to England via Cannes and Paris. The visit to Italy enabled him to see one of the first performances of Verdi's *Otello*. Although he had earlier had little time for Italian opera, Verdi's gradual evolution of style through the 1860s and 1870s had led Stanford to take a greater interest in him. *Otello* greatly impressed him and he wrote to Parry:

> It is *quite splendid*. So spontaneous and fresh and big all through. Quite new too and unlike anything else I know. Not Wagner at all, except that it goes ahead without stopping. The book is superbly done. It opens with a storm at Cyprus and the curtain goes up at the 3rd bar! A startling effect and he has managed to write a new storm altogether. It was beautifully done.[38]

While away Stanford worked on the first act of a new opera, *The Miner of Falun*. It is not known why Stanford chose E. T. A. Hoffmann's short story *Die Bergwerke zu Falun* but it probably appeared to him that the story was fresh to the operatic stage.[39] It is unlikely that the opera was written to commission; Stanford showed Act I to Carl Rosa but it is not clear whether he expressed an interest in the work or not (see p. 137). Stanford asked Barclay Squire to write the libretto, and another of Stanford's Cambridge friends, Harry Wilson, also became involved in the project.[40] The reason for Wilson's involvement is unclear,

[37] Stanford to Joachim, 25 July 1887, BerSt (Tiergarten), MS SM 12/40, item 4609.

[38] Stanford to Parry, 4 Oct. 1887, ShP.

[39] Wagner's libretto for Dessauer was unknown at this point and whilst it is possible that Stanford knew Holstein's *Der Haidenschacht*, premièred in 1868 and popular in Germany in the early 1870s, the fact that the opera dropped out of the repertory quickly would have caused Stanford to be unworried by the duplication of the story.

[40] Henry F. Wilson (1859–1937) gained a first in Classics (1882) and was elected a Fellow of Trinity (1884). A member of the Cambridge Apostles and a friend of Prince Albert Victor (Edward VII's first son, d. 1892), he later became a civil servant, working mainly in the Colonial Office. He retired in 1907 and was knighted in 1922.

although it is possible that Squire's professional commitments as a librarian prevented him from taking on the project without help. The libretto of Act I at least was finished by June 1887 and, by 30 September, Stanford was able to write to Wilson that he had 'sketched' half of the first act.[41]

On 31 October, George Macfarren, the Professor of Music, died. Affectionate tributes for his contribution to British music followed but at Cambridge minds soon turned to the election of his successor. Since his election in 1875 circumstances had changed greatly: it had been the last for which any man could put his name forward and all members of the Senate were eligible to vote.[42] Due to the inevitable abuses of this system (at Macfarren's election another candidate offered to pay the train and cab fares of London residents if they committed themselves to going to Cambridge to register their vote[43]) the Senate approved the founding of Boards of Electors for each post. At the 1887 Music election the Board was asked if it wished to make any changes to the Professor's conditions of employment.[44] Regrettably, the Board did not avail itself of this opportunity, its minutes implying that it felt that the University would neither afford nor accept an increase in salary and, as a result, it did not feel that the duties could be more onerous than those specified for Macfarren, that is, that the Professor should examine MusBac and MusDoc candidates, and give at least four lectures in the University each year, with no requirement to be resident. In retrospect they would certainly have wished to have been more assertive – Stanford was stuck with the basic salary of £200 per annum until his death (and even in Macfarren's time all other University professorships attracted salaries of between £400 and £800) and the lack of a requirement of residence did music in Cambridge no good as, especially after 1900, Stanford steadily loosened his ties with the university, a situation which led to rumbling dissatisfaction in various quarters until his death (see pp. 326–7 and 334).

The election took place on 7 December and there were four candidates: George Garrett (organist of St John's), E. M. Lott of Toronto, Ebenezer Prout and Stanford. The Board was, coincidentally, packed with Stanford supporters (hardly surprising given that Stanford was friendly with nearly all of the leading musical men of Cambridge), and

---

[41] Stanford to Wilson, 30 Sept. 1887, TCC, Add. MS 1 103.

[42] Membership of the Senate was conferred on all men holding an MA; voting was in person.

[43] See MS O.XIV.53, fol.75^r, and MS CUR.39.10, CUL.

[44] See MS Min.V.11 (Minute Book, Board of Musical Studies), CUL, and the *Cambridge Review*, 16 Nov. 1887, p. 82.

included Austen Leigh (Fellow of King's College and CUMS President), Gerard Cobb and Sedley Taylor (both Trinity). These, together with George Grove, almost certainly backed Stanford with enthusiasm. In the event the other three electors (Frederick Gore Ouseley, William Pole[45] and the Vice Chancellor, Charles Taylor) backed Stanford as well and he was elected unanimously. On the day after the election Stanford 'appeared at the Vice Chancellor's room, made the declaration of office and was admitted on his knees into the Professorship'.[46] It would have been extremely surprising if Stanford had not been elected Professor: Cambridge showed a marked preference for electing its own men to such posts and the prospect of a resident Professor (the first since Walmisley, who had died in 1856, Sterndale Bennett and Macfarren having both lived in London) must have also been enticing. Garrett was also a Cambridge resident but his achievements were pale beside those of Stanford, who came with a national reputation and the certain achievement of having transformed music in the university. Stanford's family and friends celebrated and he took up a post which he was to occupy for the next thirty-six years.

In the midst of this process, on 22 November, the Cambridge Greek Play Committee's production of Sophocles's *Oedipus Tyrannus* opened for a run of seven performances, concluding on 26 November. After the praise Stanford received for his music for the *Eumenides* it was hardly surprising that he was asked to compose music (completed on 11 June) for this production, especially as the committee included Stanford himself and friends such as Austen Leigh, Oscar Browning, J. W. Clark, Francis Jenkinson and A. W. Verrall. As had been the case two years previously with the *Eumenides*, both the production and music were enthusiastically received, the *Cambridge Review* commenting: 'From beginning to end we felt that every incident of the play was pictured and brought home to us by the addition of the music ... We are convinced that no small share of the success of the *Oedipus* [*Tyrannus*] as a whole belongs to Mr Stanford and to those performing under his baton.'[47] The two sets of incidental music are the same in structure and intention; once again Stanford made use of leading motifs (but here more intensively), simple choral writing and some short sections of 'melodrama', but the music is conceived on a larger scale than the *Eumenides*

---

[45] Like Grove, William Pole (1814–1900) was trained as an engineer and was Professor of Civil Engineering in the University of London (1859–76). He was also a talented organist, gaining both B.Mus. and D.Mus. degrees from Oxford, and was an Examiner for the music degrees at London (1879–90).

[46] MS O.XIV.53, fol. 75^r, CUL.

[47] *Cambridge Review*, 23 Nov. 1887, pp. 99–100.

Example 4.13   *Oedipus Tyrannus*, Op. 29, prelude, bars 11–20

and is more demanding technically for the performers; again the aesthetic of the work is that of Victorian Oxbridge, so its lack of long-term success is hardly surprising (the play, with Stanford's music, was given again at Cambridge in 1912). *Oedipus Tyrannus* also includes two fine orchestral movements – the Prelude and the Entr'acte between Acts I and II; the latter was incorporated in the second movement of the Fourth Symphony (see pp. 143–4). The Prelude is elegiac, simple in form, and conveys a nostalgic sense of gravitas, and it contains an almost Elgarian turn of phrase (Ex. 4.13). This is one of Stanford's finest slow movements and enjoyed subsequent success as an independent concert work.

The following year opened far less auspiciously. On 5 January 1888 Marian Jenkinson, Jennie's sister, died after a short illness, aged 29. Francis and Marian had been married for just six months and her unexpected death must have been a severe blow to both Francis and Jennie. Parry, who was also close to Francis, could not bring himself directly to express his condolences and wrote to Stanford instead:

> This is most fearfully distressing news! I am afraid you must all feel it grievously. Both you and your wife. But of poor Jenkinson it is terrible to think. It's just a nipping in the bud of a life which was only just beginning. Poor soul, how I wish one could do anything to comfort him. Perhaps you or your good little Mrs. might send me a line sometime to say how he is. I scarcely like to write to him. The blow seems so even more than usually heavy.[48]

Marian's illness and death had prevented Stanford from travelling to Germany, as he had intended, for the performances of the 'Irish' Symphony. He did, however, travel to Hamburg a few days later for the performance conducted by Bülow:

> Walter Ford and I found out the concert-room, went on the sly after breakfast, and ensconced ourselves in the dark under the gallery. Hans was hard at work on the symphony. Whether it was second sight or brain-wave I know not, but we had not been there for a few minutes before he turned around, peered into the dark recesses

---

[48] Parry to Stanford, 7 Jan. 1888, CUL, Add. MS 6343, item 868.

at the back of the room, and called out my name. He had not heard a syllable about my coming.[49]

Bülow used the Hamburg performance as a dry run before conducting it in Berlin and persuaded Stanford to go there with him and hear the performance given by the Berlin Philharmonic. He was received enthusiastically, being called onto the platform six times, and was required to conduct the symphony himself the following evening before catching his train home. Jennie stayed at Cambridge in mourning whilst Geraldine and Guy were sent to Dublin to see their grandmother.

With all this activity, it is not difficult to see why Stanford's composition rate slowed at this time: between June 1887 and July 1888 he wrote only *A Child's Garland of Songs*, Op. 30, a short and easy work dedicated to Guy and Geraldine, and the remainder of the first act of *The Miner of Falun*. This was completed on 26 March; the remainder of the opera either does not survive or was not written. Stanford intended to write more but his enthusiasm was sporadic. In May 1889 he wrote to Joseph Bennett, music critic of *The Daily Telegraph*:

> I see from *The Athenaeum* that you are going to collaborate with Cowen on an opera which is Scandinavian in subject; please oblige me so as to give me without telling me name or story, the origin of it or character.
> The fact is I have been for some time at work upon an opera on a Scandinavian plot of which the book is finished and the music half done; and it would be a pity if we did the same story for both our sakes. You will keep my secret and I will keep yours. I showed the 1st Act to Rosa when I finished it and he alone knew the plot.[50]

Obviously little progress had been made.[51] It is not known why Stanford abandoned work on the opera, especially as the libretto was complete; it was not because of Cowen's opera (*Thorgrim*), and the most likely reasons are the death of Carl Rosa on 30 April 1889 or that Stanford simply lost interest. Rosa's death was a blow to all: he had been the only producer of opera by British composers for over thirty years (with the Sullivan-specific exception of Richard D'Oyly Carte) and Stanford probably felt that any possibility of production in England had disappeared.[52] His failure to interest any theatre in Germany or Austria in

---

[49] Stanford, *Pages*, 261.

[50] Stanford to Joseph Bennett, 18 May 1889, PML, MS MFC S.785.B344 item 6. The opera by Cowen and Bennett was *Thorgrim*, which was based on Scandinavian legend (premièred Covent Garden 22 Apr. 1890).

[51] Had Act II been completed it would surely have been bound with Act I in the autograph, RCM MS 4156.

[52] Although Augustus Harris carried on Rosa's work in a smaller way, Stanford, assuming he tried to interest Harris in *The Miner of Falun*, evidently failed.

The Canterbury Pilgrims (see pp. 104–7) probably disinclined him to try abroad; his one overseas advocate, Ernst Frank, had retired due to mental illness in April 1887 and died in August 1889.

Stanford, Wilson and Squire made several modifications to Hoffmann's story but not advantageously: Hoffmann's central character, Elis, is a complex introverted character who is engaged upon a mission of personal fulfilment but, in the opera, he is the archetypal hero who becomes a miner in order to find and wreak revenge on the father who abandoned him. It is apparent from this that the view of Stanford and his librettists was bound by operatic stereotyping and the power of Hoffmann's story is weakened by cliché. In the music Stanford retreated from the proto-Wagnerian style of *Savonarola* and returned to the number opera of *The Veiled Prophet*, giving the music a lighter touch. He also eschewed the use of reminiscence motifs.[53] It is likely he was influenced by seeing *Otello* at Parma; although the libretto was written before this the arrival of Elis's ship at Gefle (modern spelling Gävle) is strikingly similar to that of Otello in Cyprus, especially as both are opening scenes. Despite moving away from the sub-Wagnerism of *Savonarola*, however, the opera remains limited in its accomplishment. Most significantly, Stanford's adherence to operatic character stereotypes is a clear illustration of the limited and conventional field of vision to which he adhered too frequently in his musical output.

In spring 1888 Stanford became interested in Parry's *Judith*, commissioned for the 1888 Birmingham Festival, and the episode is a good demonstration of his overwhelming enthusiasm, tactlessness and lack of sensitivity to others, the three in combination provoking awe, admiration and resentment in almost equal proportions. On first reading through the score Stanford was critical; Parry wrote: '[Stanford] didn't take to it and played much of it as if he didn't see the sense of it and made some very severe criticisms ... He read the things very quickly but played them abominably without the very least sense of the meaning. It was pernicious!'[54] Stanford's lack of tact was lamentable but it was typical that he made these comments and this shows his failure to consider the feelings of others, for Parry was very sensitive about others' perceptions of his work. Stanford could easily have couched his criticism in a more constructive form and not as if Parry were a dilatory pupil. Over the coming months, however, Stanford's opinions changed: Parry later noted that 'Stanford ... looked at some more *Judith* and professed to change his mind.'[55] Now Stanford was almost equally

[53] As only Act I of the opera is extant firm conclusions in this area are impossible.
[54] Parry's diary, 14 Feb. 1888, ShP.
[55] Parry's diary, 13 Mar. 1888, ShP.

embarrassing to Parry in his advocacy of the work: in June 1888 it became apparent that the Birmingham Festival Committee believed *Judith* was too long and wanted it cut. Parry noted: '[Stanford] kicked up such a row and went at Richter so vigorously that Beale [Festival Secretary] . . . began to cave in somewhat, and at the end of the evening Richter promised to write from Bayreuth to try and arrange matters, and Beale promised to do what he could to have the work done complete.'[56]

In July Stanford intervened again, writing to Richter:

> I see today in the programme for the B'ham Festival, with much regret and deep concern that Piercy is singing tenor in Parry's oratorio. This will undoubtedly murder the work. The man has a voice like a drain and no hint is there of any dramatic élan. It is a highly dramatic part and I know that he wrote it for Lloyd. I find it most unjust that the Committee has engaged Lloyd for Sullivan's *Legend* (a work which established his success a long while ago) and a second rate singer (I'd rather say sixth rate) for a new work. If I were Parry, I would probably withdraw my work. The Committee always treat the artists who are too shy like this.
>
> But you, my dear fellow, can save the day, and I beg you to do it. I know the work and what it demands. With Piercy there isn't a hope. He sang my *Three Holy Children* in Liverpool so dreadfully that I wanted to remove the entire tenor part; and Hallé told me he'd never give him an important part again. Please forgive me; I have said nothing to Parry and I only received the programme today. I cannot write to the Committee myself as I am quite ignored by them.[57]

Stanford's letter paid off: Lloyd was given the job. He showed further support for *Judith* by publishing a highly complimentary article on it in which he referred to Parry's career as having 'been one of hard work and few opportunities; nor have the difficulties in his path been lessened by the fact that not one of the powers that preside over the discovery and encouragement of rising composers has given him a helping hand'.[58] *Judith* was praised for its 'freshness, clearness and directness [which] will hit the public taste more and more every time it is brought to a hearing'.[59] Stanford subsequently performed *Judith* with the Bach Choir on 4 May 1889 and with CUMS on 11 June 1889; no doubt Parry was grateful for Stanford's support and advocacy but equally embarrassed by the manner in which it was given.

---

[56] Parry's diary, 9 June 1888, ShP.
[57] Stanford to Richter, 8 July 1888, RCM MS 4826, item 20.
[58] 'Hubert Parry's *Judith*', subsequently reproduced in Stanford, *Studies and Memories*, 139–55.
[59] Ibid.

Stanford gave his first series of lectures as Cambridge Professor in the May term 1888 (starting on 28 April) and chose the string quartet from Gibbons to Haydn as his subject. The texts do not survive; indeed it is probable that he only used notes, so it is impossible to gauge the academic content of this or any subsequent series, although the fact that most of the music covered in these lectures was written for viol consort does not inspire confidence (but reflects general nineteenth-century scholarship). One critique does survive, however: in a series of articles, 'Letters to Lecturers', in the *Cambridge Review*, Stanford is addressed as follows:

> We cannot accord to you that unqualified praise [as a Lecturer] which our devotion to yourself, and admiration of your music, would fain have us mete out to you. Your lectures are marvels of erudition. Facts, dates, and sound criticism are there in unimpeachable array, but in this very strength lies their only weakness. Their massive solidity overwhelms us. Our poor mental digestion is hardly equal to disposing, at one sitting, of the tremendous intellectual meal which any one of your lectures so lavishly provides ... Your elaboration of details causes us to carry away only a confused and hazy impression of the point which you really wish us to remember. Then your hour is up, with half your story untold, and straightway you cast agonised glances at the blandly smiling clock, as if it were to blame, poor thing.[60]

No doubt this mistiming arose from inexperience, but it seems unlikely that Stanford enjoyed lecturing (although in the early years of his Professorship he gave eight lectures per year rather than the prescribed four). There is no evidence that he ever lectured at the RCM or that he gave public lectures outside Cambridge; in later years he persuaded (with some difficulty) the Board of Musical Studies to allow him to give a tutorial class in Composition in place of his lectures (see p. 278).

During summer 1888 Stanford wrote the Fourth Symphony in F, Op. 31, the movements being dated 4 June, 23 June, 15 July and 31 July respectively. Immediately after this he started writing a work for Joachim, to whom he wrote on 20 July: 'I am evolving in my head a suite for violin and orchestra with Pavans and Gagliardos and such like things which may take shape this summer and perhaps you may like it if I have the courage to send it to you.'[61] 'Evolving' seems to be an understatement on Stanford's part since, despite having to travel unexpectedly to Dublin to see his mother who had become ill, it was barely more than a month later that he wrote again: 'I have nearly finished a suite for violin and orchestra which I should vastly like you to see. It is probably full of impossibilities! But on the other hand you might like

[60] *Cambridge Review*, 21 Nov. 1889, p. 83.
[61] Stanford to Joachim, 20 July 1888, BerSt (Tiergarten), MS SM 12/40, item 4611.

it enough to try it at my concert in January.'[62] The concert to which Stanford referred in this letter was a reference to a real coup which he had, with Joachim's (and possibly Bülow's) help, managed to secure – a concert of his own music in Berlin. Conscious of the opportunity the concert gave him, Stanford intended that it should be used to bring more new work to the Germans.

Domestic life at Harvey Road was enhanced at this time by the family's acquiring a pet cockatoo (as well as the dogs which the Stanfords appear always to have had) but, despite this novelty, Charles and Jennie travelled as usual to Europe during the long vacation, going once again to Germany and Italy. This time they visited Bayreuth, Stanford's first time there since 1876. Only *Die Meistersinger* and *Parsifal* were given at the 1888 Festival, so it seems likely that he went to both operas, although he only mentioned *Die Meistersinger* in a letter to Joachim, referring to it as 'superb'.[63] It is a pity that he did not say anything about *Parsifal*, since it had a profound influence on him, most greatly evidenced in *The Travelling Companion*; it was his second favourite opera by Wagner (see pp. 298–300). From Bayreuth Charles and Jennie travelled south to San Martino in the Dolomites before returning home.

On 6 November 1888 Cambridge conferred honorary doctorates on Stanford and Mackenzie, recently appointed Principal of the Royal Academy of Music. These were the first honorary degrees given to musicians since Parry's in 1883, although Stanford's was essentially an award to make his professorship look more tenable (and belated in view of Oxford's award in 1883). Nevertheless many musicians attended the ceremony to give recognition to the contribution made by both men to British music. CUMS, however, was in a parlous state. In October it was announced that the Chamber concerts, which had been a regular feature of Cambridge life since the mid-1870s, were losing money and would cease unless attendance improved. Quite why the concerts were going through a rough patch is not apparent: the programming had remained remarkably consistent (although this may itself have been the problem) since the mid-1870s. There had been grumbles periodically about ticket prices but Cambridge may have become complacent about having so much music on its doorstep, and the poor performance of the Chamber Concerts had been preceded by some loss-making orchestral concerts (see p. 85). The CUMS committee stated that the 1888/89 season would run as planned but the following season would be held in abeyance until the success or otherwise of the present year's concerts could be gauged.

---

[62] Stanford to Joachim, 28 Aug. 1888, BerSt (Tiergarten), MS SM 12/40, item 4612.
[63] Ibid.

More positively, CUMS decided to celebrate the fiftieth anniversary of Joachim's first public appearance in Britain. It must have given Stanford great pleasure to have a hand in this *quid pro quo*, but the anniversary was one which many in Cambridge wanted to mark. Stanford wrote to Joachim:

> The real date [of the anniversary] is March 17 but that is a Sunday (which won't do!) On the other hand you are here on March 14 and 15. The 15th is the concert, and on the 14th we want to have the Dinner. I have been asked to find out informally if you would accept. Please do. It would be a most interesting meeting; the society is now 45 years old and we mean to get as many old members together as we can lay hands on.[64]

Joachim's positive reply soon arrived and planning for the event started in earnest.

On Boxing Day 1888 Charles and Jennie left Cambridge for Berlin; curiously, the cockatoo went to Berlin while Geraldine and Guy were left at home. The concert took place on 14 January 1889, allowing plenty of time for socialising and rehearsal. The programme included the premières of the Fourth Symphony, Op. 31 and the Violin Suite, Op. 32, plus the Prelude to *Oedipus Tyrannus*. The concert went well and Stanford was well received by both audience and press. The *Berliner Reichsbote* noted that 'last night's performance puts [Stanford] in the front rank of composers of our own day' whilst the *Kreuz Zeitung* stated: 'The compositions of Dr Villiers Stanford have taken us altogether by surprise. We did not expect such mature work from a man who has not yet left his youth behind him [the youth was now 36] and there is real ground for astonishment in his powerful handling of larger forms and masses ... His work is masterly.'[65] The Berlin concert was significant in that no British man had previously given a concert of his own music there, but it was achieved with the help of Joachim and did not make a lasting impression. It should not, therefore, be regarded as the landmark it first appears to be. For Stanford at the time, however, the feeling of elation was great and he wrote to Joachim:

> I must write to you one more line to thank you from Herzen for all your goodness and kindness to me and Jen in Berlin. It was and will always be the highest spot in both our lives and for me one of the greatest honours that I ever received that you played my work for me and that you helped me so much in making it presentable. You know me well enough to know that I am truly grateful to you for it all, more so than my poor pen will properly express. Take the will for the deed please![66]

[64] Stanford to Joachim, 26 Nov. 1888, BerSt (Tiergarten), MS SM 12/40, item 4615.
[65] Both quoted in translation in the *Musical Times*, 1 Mar. 1889, p. 153.
[66] Stanford to Joachim, 20 Jan. 1889, BerSt (Tiergarten), MS SM 12/40, item 4616.

The British première of the Fourth Symphony at Crystal Palace on 23 February brought a similar eulogy: '[the symphony] fully justified the praise bestowed upon it by the Berlin Press ... In conclusion we have no hesitation in pronouncing this Symphony to contain the best and maturest work which Professor Stanford has yet done.'[67] But the favourable impressions of the symphony soon faded and the work never established itself. Any feeling that the Fourth Symphony was stronger than the 'Irish' was soon forgotten and the latter work remained Stanford's sole symphonic success. Stanford, notably, did not mention the Berlin concert in his autobiography, suggesting that he recognised its long-term failure. Reaction to the Violin Suite was lukewarm; following its London première by the Philharmonic Society on 28 March at St James's Hall, the *Musical Times* referred to it as 'lacking in spontaneity'.[68] Stanford was somewhat unlucky with this piece although it is too calculating to be truly successful. It is a tribute to Joachim and his musical loves, most transparently Bach, but also Beethoven and Brahms. The opening of the Overture, for unaccompanied solo violin, with its dotted French rhythms, reflects Joachim's love for Bach's solo violin music. The Tambourin, its rhythmic pedal D articulated throughout, mainly on the timpani, requires some assured harmonic footwork from Stanford as the reiterated D necessitates the avoidance of dominant harmonies; perhaps because of this, however, the music never gathers a real momentum of its own. There are other masterly strokes – at the opening of the Ballade the spacing of the melody in oboe and cello three octaves apart creates a particularly poignant soundworld – but over all the work never lifts off in the way one would hope.

The Fourth Symphony, however, deserves more recognition than it has obtained. The two weaknesses of the symphony are its overall form and its strong overtones of Brahms, Dvořák and Beethoven but, despite this, it contains much fresh and moving music. Stanford prefaced the score with a motto 'Thro' Youth to Strife, thro' death to life'.[69] This was later suppressed, as the implied programme, each movement representing one of the four themes, is not readily manifest in the music. The first two movements do appear to portray their themes (the *effects* of strife being shown in the intermezzo rather than strife itself) but the third movement conjures up a confused image of death while the finale suggests new-born life rather than eternity. The greatest problems with the symphony arise from formal considerations. The second movement (an extended version of the entr'acte from *Oedipus Tyrannus*) is too wistful and melancholy to balance the elegiac slow movement which follows it and the symphony

[67] *Musical Times*, 1 Mar. 1889, pp. 151–2.
[68] *Musical Times*, 1 May 1889, p. 278.
[69] These words are a highly condensed version of lines from Goethe's *Faust*.

sags seriously in the middle as a result. The slow movement comprises
an orchestral recitative as introduction, a double binary-form movement,
and coda; the recitative is an overlong experiment and there is too much
literal repetition in the movement proper whilst the coda unconvincingly
exposes the main theme of the finale. The finale, although spritely, is
based on slender material and Stanford employs an uncharacteristically
large amount of counterpoint which, though technically impressive,
sounds forced. The second weakness is the stylistic similarity to other
composers: most of the intermezzo sounds, even by Stanford's standards,
overwhelmingly redolent of Brahms (specifically the intermezzo of the
Third Symphony), whilst the first and last movements contain substantial echoes of Beethoven and, to a lesser extent, Dvořák, as well as
Brahms – the second subject of the first movement is almost literal quotation of the first of Brahms's *Liebeslieder*, Op. 52 (Ex. 4.14). There are
also anticipations in the work: the theme of the elegiac slow movement
(Ex. 4.15), like the Prelude to *Oedipus Tyrannus* which it resembles,
foreshadows Elgar, especially in the leaps and appoggiaturas, whilst the
rhythmic recasting of the main theme of the finale foresees a similar
procedure in the finale of Glazunov's Sixth Symphony (1896).[70]

Despite these handicaps there is much good material in the Fourth
Symphony. The opening of the first movement has a real *joie de vivre*
and captures the mood of 'youth' very well and the intermezzo, despite
its Brahmsian voice, is excellently written. The entr'acte from *Oedipus
Tyrannus* was imported complete, with an extra section for strings just
before the coda, and the movement has a beautifully wistful quality, as
well as showing that Stanford could write evocatively for string
orchestra, a rarity in his output. The elegiac sections of the slow movement also contain a degree of nobility and resignation rare in Stanford's
music and each is built to a great climax. The major-key sections which
follow these are somewhat trite by comparison; it seems that Stanford
was trying to evoke the entry of the soul into Heaven but the impression is facile and nothing compared to the close of the later *Stabat Mater*
(see pp. 251–3). Conversely, the triumphant brass chorales in these
sections make an impressive impact and have a real sense of pathos. The
last movement, despite its functional pyrotechnics, captures a spirit of
drive and jollity which is exhilarating. Although Stanford's own voice
is muted in the Fourth Symphony it is still a piece with many touches
of brilliance and inspiration, deserving of a better fate.

The dinner to celebrate the golden anniversary of Joachim's first

---

[70] The brass cries at the end of the slow movement also anticipate those at the close
of the scherzo of Rachmaninov's Second Symphony, but it is highly unlikely that Stanford's
symphony was known by the Russian.

Example 4.14 Fourth Symphony in F, Op. 31: (*a*) Intermezzo, bars 1–9; (*b*) first movement, second subject; (*c*) Brahms, *Liebeslieder*, Op. 52 No. 1, opening theme

Example 4.15 Fourth Symphony in F, Op. 31, third movement, first theme

British appearance took place on 14 March 1889 at Caius College. The speeches were reproduced *verbatim* in the *Cambridge Review* (covering nearly five pages) and recalled both Joachim's career and CUMS's history with much celebration.[71] Stanford received many plaudits himself, including a backhander from Sedley Taylor, who remarked that 'those who have sat with him on committees of any kind know very well that he ... possesses qualities which, had his profession carried him into the paths of war rather than of peace, would have made him a brilliant strategist in the field'. Stanford's speech exemplified this as he looked forward to CUMS's fiftieth birthday in 1893 and signalled his intention

---

[71] See the *Cambridge Review*, 25 Apr. 1889, pp. 287–91.

to make it a special occasion. The seeds, therefore, of the conferment of honorary doctorates on Boito, Saint-Saëns, Tchaikovsky and Bruch were sown at Joachim's dinner. Despite this declaration of confidence, however, CUMS was in financial difficulties due to the long run of losses made on concerts. This was nothing new: the society had been losing money since the late 1870s (even the first Cambridge performance of Beethoven's Ninth Symphony was a financial disaster; see p. 85), but now action was taken. A new appeal for guarantors took place and was successful; one substantial guarantor, however, wanted more orchestral concerts, and it was decided that from 1889/90 there would be four of these each term and that they should be run by an organisation separate from CUMS. Attendance did not improve, however, even though Stanford secured the services of men such as Sullivan, and the committee battled against the conservatism of the Cambridge population as CUMS had done before it. For Stanford it was yet another proof that there was insufficient support for contemporary music in the town and no doubt gave him occasion to question his future there.

In October 1889 it appears that Stanford fell out with his long-standing friend, Gerard Cobb. The matter was trivial, as was often the case, but the effects were permanent. Stanford wanted a fund of £100 to mount a series of concerts which would illustrate the works upon which he lectured. The Board of Musical Studies divided evenly on the issue but Cobb, as Chairman, gave his casting vote against.[72] A fund of £50 was allowed, but Stanford was livid about being crossed so directly and cut Cobb thereafter. This was both petulant and stupid on Stanford's part: Cobb had supported him for almost twenty years, but this counted for little with Stanford at this point and, in this case, no one induced him to apologise or restore relations.

In the same month the cantata *The Voyage of Maeldune*, Op. 34 was premièred at the Leeds Festival (11 October). Following the success of *The Revenge*, a commission from Leeds was unsurprising, although Stanford was not amongst the committee's first choices (who were Brahms, Corder, Cowen, Goring Thomas and Parry). Stanford turned once again to Tennyson: he started planning the work just after returning from Berlin and wrote hastily to Hallam Tennyson asking for permission to set the poem and to incorporate a passage from *The Sea Fairies*;[73] the cantata was completed on 1 May 1889. Although well

[72] See Minutes of the Board of Musical Studies, 19 Oct. 1889, CUL, MS Min.V.11, fol. 88. Cobb, Junior Bursar of Trinity, no doubt thought £100 would be viewed as excessive and that it would not pass the Senate; his instinct was right as the Senate tried, unsuccessfully, to reduce even the £50 proposal.

[73] Stanford to Tennyson, 31 Jan. 1889, LCL, item 4270.

received it never made the same impression as *The Revenge*.[74] There are several reasons. The piece is longer and more ambitious than *The Revenge*, which was advantaged by its brevity and lack of soloists. More important, however, are the structure of the piece and the quality of the music. Stanford may have chosen this poem because it was founded on an Irish legend, but there is no trace of the Celtic inflections found in the 'Irish' Symphony. The cantata comprises a number of tableaux, each of which corresponds to the islands visited by Maeldune and his followers as they try to find the man who killed Maeldune's father; consequently there is none of the unfolding drama of *The Revenge*, but rather a series of loosely connected movements. This plan could have worked had Stanford correctly mixed the vigorous and the serene, but, for popular appeal, he misjudged the balance of the music: there is too much slow, contemplative writing and too little of the active writing which vitalised *The Revenge* while the choral writing is declamatory rather than melodic and less rewarding to sing. Finally, much of the music is too formulaic, and brings to mind Frank Howes's comment '[Stanford] knew only too well how that sort of stuff was written'.[75] This is especially true of the 'Isle of Witches', an anticipation of the Goblins' Dance in *The Travelling Companion* (to which Howes was referring).

Of the other works dating from 1889 the Service in F, Op. 36 and the Three Motets, Op. 38 are the most important. The former is of interest because the organ is optional and the choir split into *decani* and *cantores*, harking back to Baroque antiphony. It may be this unusual requirement which led the Service to be less popular than Stanford's other settings: the optional organ part is a support to the choir and lacks the distinctive role of the two earlier services, reducing colour and harmonic possibilities. Harmonic progressions and modulations are far more restrained than previously; as most of the writing is for full choir (preserving the full harmonisation Stanford favoured) the contrast between *decani* and *cantores* is the primary interest of the work. As in the earlier Services, there is a common 'Gloria Patri' and, as in the Service in B flat, unity across the work is created by the recurrent use of a

---

[74] See for example, the *Musical Times* (1 Nov. 1889, p. 661): 'Professor Stanford's treatment of [the] series of scenes are admirably dealt with by the composer, who has brought to bear upon them all his orchestral skill and ingenuity ... The narrative which carries on the main thread of the story is forcible and picturesque; only in the earlier part being too persistently harsh and rugged. This the Leeds audience appeared to regard rather coldly, but the island pictures ... and the conclusion ... won every heart and established the success of the work.'

[75] Frank Howes, *The English Musical Renaissance* (London, 1966), 151.

Example 4.16   Service in F, Op. 36, common doxology

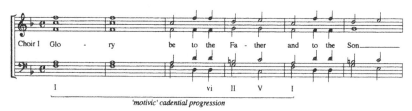

'motivic' cadential progression

motif, here a circular harmonic one based on the progression I–vi–II–V–I (Ex. 4.16). The restrictions Stanford placed upon himself by sidelining the organ inevitably reduce the impact of the music, and the style is not as rich or dynamic as the slightly later antiphony in *Coelos ascendit*, but the setting is impressive nonetheless.

Some confusion surrounds the provenance of the Three Motets, Op. 38 (*Justorum animae*, *Beati quorum via* and *Coelos ascendit hodie*). Originally published as Op. 51, they were later reassigned to Op. 38, but the mystery is unlikely to be solved as the autographs do not survive. The motets are dedicated to Alan Gray and the Choir of Trinity College, which has led to the assumption that they were written just after Stanford left the Trinity organ loft, Gray being his successor. It seems certain, however, that they were not composed as a set (the keys of the three motets, G, A flat and A, and the miscellaneous selection of liturgical uses – All Saints, a general text, and Ascension – do not suggest this),[76] and *Justorum animae* appears on the Trinity service list for 24 February 1888 (Feast of St Matthias) while the other two motets do not appear during Stanford's tenure (although it is possible that the entry *Beati omnes* on 1 February 1890 was, in fact, a misprint of *Beati quorum* since no motet of the former name survives). Although the works are short and generally straightforward, they occupy a special place in Stanford's output since they are still frequently performed by amateur choirs, and are rare examples of pieces by Stanford that have never left the repertory. Frank Howes described them as 'masterly examples of spacious writing with unerring recognition of the capabilities and the limitations of unaccompanied voices, and because functionally they do not require an intensity of personal expression they stand out as sheer splendid compositions'.[77] The motets are, indeed, some of Stanford's best work, each exemplifying different skills. In *Justorum animae*

---

[76] Stanford had also put together an *ad hoc* selection of songs for publication purposes before, that is, Six Songs, Op. 14.

[77] Howes, *English Musical Renaissance*, 156.

Example 4.17   *Justorum animae*, Op. 38 No. 1: (*a*) bars 1–14; (*b*) bars 41–6

Stanford realised perfectly all the different moods suggested by the text and shows great sensitivity both to the minutiae of meaning and declamation, especially in the varied restatement of the opening (Ex. 4.17). Remarkable too is his absolute command of harmony. Truly unexpected harmonic shifts are few, usually provoked by just one note (asterisked in Ex. 4.17(a)); the implications of these shifts are followed through so meticulously that throughout the music appears effortless yet simultaneously interesting and satisfying. *Beati quorum* is an evocation of tranquillity and devotion in which Stanford showed to the full his ability to write for voices, and built to a superb climax before an equally perfect valedictory coda; again the subtly varied recapitulation of the opening is an excellent instance of exemplary and effective workmanship. Equally impressive is Stanford's ability to found the motet on one simple concept (accompanimental stepwise movement in flowing crotchets) and to maintain this throughout the work with hardly any exceptions, all of which enhance the musical sense of the piece. *Coelos ascendit* recalls the *decani–cantores* opposition of the Service in F (and anticipates the later double-choir works, for example, Three Motets, Op. 135, *On Time*, Op. 142 and the *Magnificat*, Op. 164) and, although it is the least profound of the set, the antiphonal effects are splendid, with a brilliant final cadence starting on a unison E and broadening out rapidly to a plagal cadence in A with the final chord spread over two and a half octaves.

The other pieces composed in 1889 may be passed over briefly: in the Piano Trio in E♭, Op. 35 and Second Cello Sonata in D minor, Op. 39, Stanford falls victim to his periodic prolixity, although the latter piece was well received when premièred by Stanford and Piatti, its dedicatee, at St James's Hall on 18 November 1889.[78] Of the Two Anthems, Op. 37, 'And I saw another angel' is successful but 'And I shall confess' is handicapped by an unwieldy text.[79] As well as producing these smaller pieces, Stanford remained in demand as a composer of large-scale works. While Leeds had taken another cantata from him for its 1889 Festival, Birmingham commissioned a second oratorio for its 1891 meeting. This could be taken as a remarkable statement of faith on the Festival's behalf since its previous commission, *The Three Holy Children*, had not established itself. It also shows that Stanford's combative manner, on full display during the preparations for the performance of Parry's *Judith*, had not alienated the Birmingham Committee. The commission came in 1889 and Stanford asked Robert Bridges to write the libretto in May of that year. Stanford had an idea for his oratorio (*Eden*, Op. 40), based on Milton's *Paradise Lost*, a manuscript draft of which was in Trinity College Library. Bridges, despite an interest in Milton, needed some wheedling encouragement from Stanford and tried to pull out in November, but Stanford talked him round.[80] The two men did not know each other well and were not obvious collaborators: Bridges worried about the portrayal of Hell and how it could be repugnant spiritually but not unattractive musically; Stanford simply wrote to Bridges that 'the libretto will come all right I expect if I don't persecute you'.[81] At Bridges's suggestion, according to Stanford, Heaven might best be portrayed musically by the use of the old church modes, so, while Bridges wrote

[78] See *Musical Times*, 1 Dec. 1889, p. 726.
[79] The text is proper to St Andrew; Stanford may have needed to fill a gap in the liturgical calendar.
[80] See Bridges to Stanford, postmarked 19 Nov. 1889, RCM MS 4253, item 29.
[81] Stanford to Bridges, 12 July 1889, Oxford University, Bodleian Library, MS Dep Bridges 116, fol. 67.

the libretto, Stanford went back to the schoolroom and persuaded W. S. Rockstro, an acknowledged authority on the subject, to teach him modal counterpoint.[82] The course of tuition made a great impact on Stanford and he persuaded Grove to employ Rockstro to teach modal counterpoint at the RCM and, after Rockstro's death in 1895, Stanford incorporated the technique into his own course of composition (see pp. 356–8). Rockstro's lessons were fully employed by Stanford in *Eden* (see pp. 157–60).

Back in Cambridge, Stanford continued to encourage the performance of little-known music and conducted five performances of Gluck's *Orfeo* (13–17 May 1890). A letter from Grove to Edith Oldham shows that 'early music' was still a minority interest and that Stanford was being innovative in producing the work: '[*Orfeo*] ought to be very interesting though I fear (from the rehearsals) that the music will be heavy to modern ears. However I am prepared to like it.'[83] Stanford won plaudits, however, for his spirit of adventure: 'It was a happy if somewhat bold idea of Professor Stanford to produce *Orfeo* in Cambridge ... Prof Stanford has reason to be proud of his undertaking and Cambridge has a right to be grateful to him for giving her an opportunity (almost unattainable nowadays) of seeing this great opera.'[84] The success encouraged Stanford to produce the same opera at the RCM in 1892 and 1893, and clearly earlier criticisms of his explorations beyond the canon had made no difference to him.

In November 1890 Stanford embarked on another acrimonious quarrel, this time over the relationship between CUMS and 'Dr Mann's Festival Choir'. Stanford's relationship with Augustus 'Daddy' Mann, organist of King's, had never been an easy one, and each rubbed the other the wrong way. The situation had recently been exacerbated by Mann's decision to run a large-scale choir in Cambridge for the purpose of giving sacred oratorios. CUMS, which, under Stanford's direction, tended towards progressive and adventurous programming, had suffered from Mann's more populist approach. The quarrel was reported in full in the *Cambridge Review* (covering seven pages), which reproduced all the correspondence and an aural statement Stanford made to the CUMS.[85] As in Stanford's argument with Edmund Garrett on the

---

[82] See Stanford, *Pages*, 273–5. William Rockstro (originally Rackstraw) (1823–95) studied with Sterndale Bennett and then at Leipzig, where he met Mendelssohn. On returning to England he made his living as an organist and accompanist, wrote musical primers, and contributed to Grove's dictionary, as well as maintaining his research interest in sixteenth-century polyphony.

[83] Grove to Oldham, 3 May 1890, RCM, Grove–Oldham correspondence.

[84] *Cambridge Review*, 15 May 1890, p. 320.

[85] See the *Cambridge Review*, 20 Nov. 1890, pp. 105–9, and 27 Nov. 1890, pp. 124–5.

Cambridge Union (see pp. 130–2), matters of fact were in dispute between the two sides, but the root of the problem was that CUMS had been losing money in preceding years whilst Mann's Choir had been raising money for Addenbrooke's Hospital. CUMS attributed this success to the timing of the Mann's Choir's concert (held in King's College Chapel in May) and its own dismal showing to its concerts being held in a cold King's Chapel in February. Being advised that it was highly unlikely that the permission of the Council of King's for both societies to give concerts in King's Chapel in May 1891 would be granted, and Mann's Choir having rebuffed the CUMS proposal that they should take the Chapel in alternate years, the CUMS Committee approached the Provost of King's, Austen Leigh, directly:

> We beg to accompany this request [for the use of the Chapel in May 1891] with a short statement of the reasons which have led [CUMS] to ask for leave at that time of the year and of the negociations [sic] which we opened with Dr Mann's Festival Choir. Hitherto the Society has confined itself to an occasional request for the use of the Chapel in the Lent Term: a time which did not clash with the more recent applications of the Festival Choir for a day in the May Term. The experience of the Society however is, that, owing to the cold weather and consequent discomfort, it is impossible to expect a sufficiently large attendance in the winter even to meet expenses. We therefore entered into communication with the Committee of the Festival Choir, seeking their coöperation in asking the use of the Chapel in the May terms of alternate years. Our communication is enclosed with this letter, together with the refusal received by us from Dr Mann's committee. Our committee would beg to point out with regard to the reason alleged for that refusal, namely the assistance to Addenbrooke's hospital, that we would most willingly fall in with any suggestion of the Council for the application of the profits for the benefit of that institution.
>
> With regard to the claims of the University Musical Society, we would venture to point out, firstly, that we are far the older institution of the two, having been founded in 1843; secondly, that we were the first Society who gave any complete oratorio in the chapel; and thirdly, that we are essentially a University Society and are therefore exceptionally entitled to consideration in the matter of the application.[86]

For whatever reason, Stanford next felt that it was a good idea to take action on behalf of the Society; in his personal statement he said:

> I now leave for a moment the action of the committee, and I come to my own personal action, taken without consultation with you and without consideration with the committee, and for which I accept entire responsibility. I feel, and I always have felt, that in a

---

[86] Stanford to Austen Leigh, 27 Oct. 1890, quoted ibid., 107.

town of this size the co-existence of two choral societies of any magnitude is not a desirable thing. (Loud applause). I feel that it is not quite certain that they will flourish even if they both live ... The only way in which we can hope to get the best results in a town like this is by unity of action. You will say immediately after that statement 'Why did you not, when this Festival Choir was started, say something or do something, to ensure unity?' I will explain why I did not. As long as there is a Chair of Music in this University, no matter how unworthily it is occupied, it seems to me that if the Professor is resident and takes an active part in Music in Cambridge, that it is at any rate due to the Chair, if not to its occupant, I will not say to consult, but at any rate to inform him, if any such move is about to take place as the founding of a large choral society. (Applause). No such communication was made to me. The first knowledge that I had of the foundation of the Society, as a Society, was when I got this book of words of *Elijah* in Cambridge last May term. I there saw that it had been formed into an Association in the autumn of 1889, two years after I was made Professor of Music. I have also to point out another difficulty which was in my way if I wished to enter into communication with that Society. I was necessarily stopped by the fact that when I looked at the list of honorary members I saw that it contained practically every professional and amateur name of any musical importance in the town, with the exception of my own. I therefore was quite precluded from communicating, as I should have liked to have done, direct with any member of Dr Mann's Festival Choir. In matters of this kind, it seems to me that all personal considerations, if they exist, should be put on one side. (Applause). I therefore took the next best step, in my opinion – you may not endorse it – I had communications with three old friends of mine, and laid before them a set scheme which I was prepared to abide by – an offer of fusion with Dr Mann's Festival Choir. I would ask your notice to these terms of fusion. The conductorship was to be divided, I being prepared to hand over the entire salary of the conductorship to Dr Mann, and to take my part gratuitously for the love of the Society – (applause) – not as a compliment, but as my duty as Professor. I felt that this might, at all events, promote the much-needed unity. My friend, Mr Sedley Taylor ... kindly undertook the position of ambassador ... Mr Taylor kindly communicated with Mr Nixon, of King's, and proceeded to have an interview with him. The result of that interview at first promised possibly to be a favourable one, but subsequent communications from Mr Nixon made it clear that it was refused, and refused – I say it very deliberately – without any reason being given.[87]

Subsequent to this action, both Societies placed their applications for the use of the King's Chapel before the Council, which decided to grant Mann's application, and also rejected a motion to allow each society to give a concert in the chapel in alternate years. A subsequent exchange

---

[87] Stanford's statement to CUMS, 13 Nov. 1890, quoted ibid., 105.

of letters between Stanford and Nixon gives ample illustration as to why the committee of Mann's Choir would have resisted any growth in Stanford's influence:

> Dear Nixon, As a necessary consequence of the action of the Festival Choir to-day, you will of course expect that I shall make public the fact that I offered to use my influence to fuse the CUMS and the Festival Choir, and, if that was agreed to, to divide the conductorship with and resign the salary in favour of Dr Mann. This offer has, like our previous more official request, been refused without reasons of any sort being given.
>
> Feeling as I do that I only did what was right in sacrificing anything of personal feeling for the sake of unity here in matters musical, I have now no option but to let it be known what I did and how my offer was received. The responsibility of the split and the consequent danger to music here is now on other shoulders than mine.
>
> While Stainer has just succeeded in joining two similar societies in Oxford, you and Dr Mann have succeeded in spite of the fairest and frankest of offers in making a split here, which I can only still hope will not be permanent.
>
> In one matter I must from personal knowledge correct you. You said to Sedley Taylor that you believed that Dr Mann made no effort to get University men. I happen to know for a fact that for the past three years he has used his position at Caius to secure every respectably-voiced undergraduate there he can. When this is systematically done, as it has been, the contention that the two societies walk in different ways falls to the ground.[88]

> Dear Stanford, I am sorry to receive your letter of the 8th instant. I believe that you are entirely mistaken in thinking that anyone in Dr Mann's Choir Committee wishes to make 'a split' in our little musical world here. Many of them, I know, including myself are not only interested in, and supporters of the CUMS but grateful to you for all that you have succeeded in doing for Music in Cambridge. I must therefore repudiate with much surprise your statement that 'I and Dr Mann have succeeded in spite of the fairest and frankest of offers in making a split.'
>
> You are mistaken in every way about it. I communicated to Dr Mann the suggestions of Sedley Taylor, discussed them fully with both, and put the advantages to be got, fully and strongly, which Dr Mann seemed quite sensible of. I even went a little farther than perhaps Sedley Taylor's informal suggestions seemed to justify . . .
>
> You are mistaken entirely in saying that any offer, *such as you mention*, was made at all, or 'refused without reasons'. *No such offer was made.* Of your three points (i) fusion *was* mentioned (ii) division of the Conductorship was mentioned but indefinitely only – It was not *clear* that you meant a division of the *whole* of the

---

[88] Stanford to Nixon, 8 Nov. 1890, quoted in the *Cambridge Review*, 20 Nov. 1890, p. 108.

Conductor's work of the fused societies, i.e. oratorios and CUMS concerts, &c., as you now imply in your letter. Indeed a friend of yours who had talked to you about it has assured me that you had no such intention, as far as he could judge. (iii) *Not a word* was said about resigning your salary in favour of Dr Mann. Lastly I am surprised at your statement that the offer was refused without reasons of any sort; which, I suppose, is meant to imply an abrupt refusal. The fact is that I wrote to Sedley Taylor that the proposal had been considered by Dr Mann and several of the Committee, and was thought impracticable for many reasons which I would explain when we met.

No informal negotiations in this world can ever be carried on satisfactorily if one side is to confine itself to oral and somewhat vague proposals, and the other side expected to give formal reasons at once in writing for not acceding to them; explicit reasons *were* given in declining the explicit proposals made to the Committee as regards alternate performance of oratorios by the two societies . . .

As to Caius it is perfectly natural that two or three members of a choir trained by Dr Mann should wish to join his larger society. I doubt if you would find more than three or four cases in Caius.[89]

Quite why Stanford felt compelled to publish his statement and the associated correspondence is unclear. What is apparent, however, is the clear division of musical loyalties in Cambridge. Not only did Stanford and Mann not get on, but each had their own groups of supporters. Additionally, the contrasting aesthetic approaches of the two choirs – CUMS's academic and rarified, Mann's populist – divided the followers on musical as well as personal grounds (it is notable that there is no trace of Stanford ever having performed the two choral-society standards, *Messiah* and *Elijah*, at Cambridge). On top of this, several prominent Cambridge musicians were tied up in the dispute: Austen Leigh, Provost of King's, was also President of CUMS and thus wearing two particularly divergent hats, whilst Tilley, the CUMS Treasurer, was also on the Council of King's. Louis Borrisow, meanwhile, was not only the recently retired President of Mann's Choir but also, of course, Precentor of Trinity. Consequently, the dispute put many people in an awkward position and caused merriment and gossip in Cambridge circles. Stanford does not come out of the dispute with much credit. The publication of the letters seems to be self-interested and his tone became more combative as the correspondence progressed. Clearly he had a strong band of supporters and had CUMS under his thumb, but a large body of people did not like his approach or his personality, and there was a fear that a merger of the two choirs would be, in reality, a CUMS takeover; despite Nixon's assertions, one cannot help feeling that, for

---

[89] Nixon to Stanford, 10 Nov. 1890, quoted ibid.

several members of Mann's Choir, Stanford's dominance of CUMS was one of the main reasons for not entertaining the prospect of a merger. Many people felt that Stanford had over-professionalised music at Cambridge and had forgotten to cater for amateurs; this, they thought, had caused CUMS's financial problems. The bad relationship between Stanford and Mann made it unlikely that a joint conductorship would have succeeded. What the dispute made clear to Stanford was that Cambridge was restricting his ambition too much. He had already felt this to be the case at Trinity, but this had been solved by substantially increasing the role of his deputy, while his teaching at the Royal College and his conductorship of the Bach Choir had given him two platforms in London. Now it was evident that while CUMS would back him, Cambridge overall was not sufficiently big, liberal or enamoured to support the type of music he wished to produce. It seems likely, therefore, that it was about this time that Stanford, with a degree of regret, began seriously to consider leaving Cambridge when the opportunity arose.

Regardless of any disillusionment he may have felt, Stanford continued to advance music in Cambridge by inducing the Senate to give Antonin Dvořák an honorary doctorate, which he received on 16 June 1891. On the preceding day CUMS had given a concert of his music, including the *Stabat Mater* and the Eighth Symphony, which Dvořák conducted. If Stanford had felt chastised by his debacle with Augustus Mann the previous year, this event must have lifted his spirits. The CUMS chorus and orchestra was greatly credited for its achievement, and Stanford had succeeded in bringing to Cambridge one of Europe's most successful composers; the *Cambridge Review* was rapturous:

> The performance of Monday was in every way worthy of the great occasion; the soloists [Emma Albani, Hilda Wilson, Edward Lloyd and George Henschel] were, of course, beyond criticism, and we are all most grateful to them for the great pleasure they gave us ... To conclude in the words of an eminent London critic, Professor Stanford 'deserves very hearty congratulations on having brought the musical resources of Cambridge up to the high level at which such performances as that of Monday last become possible'.[90]

The Dvořáks stayed with Charles and Jennie and it is obvious that Stanford found them bizarrely provincial. Ironically, in his critique of Dvořák as a composer, Stanford accused him of weaknesses of which he himself was guilty: 'He did not show much interest, however much he felt, in anything outside his own metier. This may account to some

---

[90] *Cambridge Review*, 18 June 1891, p. 395.

extent for the lack of self-criticism, and the necessity for the pruning knife which is obvious even in his very best work.'[91] The strength of Dvořák's individual voice, of course, has overborne any truth there may be in Stanford's appraisal.

On 20 July 1891 *The Battle of the Baltic*, Op. 41 was premièred at St James's Hall under Richter, and was followed by a second performance at the Hereford Festival on 8 September. Based on a poem by Thomas Campbell about a naval battle during the Napoleonic Wars, the cantata tried to capture the same nautical mood as *The Revenge*. To an extent Stanford succeeded, but Campbell was not as good a poet as Tennyson and although reception was good – the *Musical Times* referred to 'breeziness and vigour that never degenerate into boisterousness or vulgarity'[92] – the piece was too similar to but not as good as *The Revenge*. Furthermore, the historical events portrayed were viewed, in the 1890s, as a shameful episode in British history, and Stanford's taste in choosing the poem was questioned.[93]

The Battle of the Baltic was, however, overshadowed by the première of *Eden*, given at Birmingham on 7 October. 'Brilliant balderdash' was Shaw's judgement,[94] and his opinion was echoed, albeit more politely, by many others. The work left many puzzled; the *Musical Times* stated 'it is a work to be dealt with in a calm and judicial spirit and to be heard again and again before final judgement is passed upon it'.[95] Amongst his close friends reaction was more positive; Parry, the dedicatee, wrote 'the reminiscences are too strong but the . . . balance of it all [is] admirable. It is much more evenly good than anything else of his'.[96] Francis Jenkinson, however, was more perceptive:

> The fact is it is too long, both in point of time and effect I think! . . . I was quite surprised to find it so beautiful. The opening so soothing and restful . . . the serpent wriggling in on Adam and Eve is very funny and Carl-like – otherwise I seldom felt him pure. There is a good deal of refined Wagner and his trips with old music are charming. Not much of his mannerism in any part of it I thought.[97]

[91] Stanford, *Pages*, 271.

[92] *Musical Times*, 1 Aug. 1891, p. 473.

[93] Ibid. The Battle of the Baltic (1807) was an unprovoked attack on Denmark by Britain which was recognised as unjustified almost as soon as it took place.

[94] Shaw, *Music in London*, i, 272.

[95] *Musical Times*, 1 Oct. 1891, p. 599. (Scores of festival works were normally circulated in advance; a full review of the work was published in the *Musical Times* on 1 Nov., p. 661.)

[96] Parry's Diary, Oct. 1891, ShP.

[97] Francis Jenkinson to Eleanor Jenkinson, 19 Nov. 1891, CUL, Add. MS 6343, item 1862.

No wonder critics were left in awe and puzzlement, since *Eden* is, indeed, the strangest piece Stanford ever wrote. It comprises three 'Acts', the first set in Heaven, the second in Hell – in which Satan looks upon the newly created Earth and decides to avenge himself upon God by corrupting Adam and Eve – and the third on Earth, which portrays the Fall and Banishment of Adam and Eve and the vision of the future given to Adam by St Michael. The libretto does not quote from the Bible or from Milton at all and Bridges created muses and angels at will. The portrayal of Hell and of Satan in Act II was the first such in a British oratorio and was no doubt viewed by some as an infringement of good taste; 'Vox Dei' in Act III was an innovatory way of solving the problem of representing of God.[98] Stanford also made use of representative themes (one based on the Sarum plainchant 'Sanctorum meritis') and attempted some tentative thematic transformation, both aspects sustaining the British trend of appropriating Wagnerian devices into oratorio and cantata (Ex. 4.18). He also made use of the augmented fourth in Act II, recalling 'mi contra fa Diabolus est in musica' (Ex. 4.19). The echoes of Handelian oratorio which appear periodically (recitative, *fugato* and some arias) sit uncomfortably, however, as do the echoes of 'Waldweben' from *Siegfried* at the beginning of Act III.

Most of Act I is modal (the product of Rockstro's lessons), including substantial sections of pastiche polyphony (which, nevertheless, are thoroughly nineteenth-century in conception) and vexed Shaw greatly, who declared that he would not accept that the choir were angels 'merely because they persistently sing B flat instead of B natural in the key of C major'.[99] Shaw could not, however, deny *Eden*'s uniqueness: no other British composer was writing in this style at this time and few contemporary composers had shown such an interest (although *Parsifal* must have influenced Stanford, and Bruckner had tentatively explored similar territory in his Mass in E Minor of 1866, almost certainly unknown to Stanford). Most significantly, the modal writing in *Eden* predates the interest shown in sixteenth-century music by Vaughan Williams in the 'Tallis' Fantasia by twenty years and the Mass in G Minor by thirty. For this innovation Stanford has received less than his due – while *Eden* turned out to be unimportant because of its lack of success, the lessons with Rockstro taken for its preparation convinced him of the importance of schooling his composition students in modal counterpoint. Not only did modes become part of their education but their experiments

---

[98] For a further discussion on this subject see Barbara Mohn, '"Personifying the Saviour?": English Oratorio and the Representation of the Words of Christ', in Bennett Zon (ed.), *Nineteenth-Century British Music Studies*, 1 (Aldershot, 1999), 227–41.

[99] Shaw, *Music in London*, i, 273.

Example 4.18   *Eden*, Op. 40 (text: Robert Bridges): (*a*) 'Heaven' motif (Act I, opening); (*b*) 'All Angels' motif (Act I, no. 1); (*c*) Chorus of all Devils (Act II, no. 7, bars 48–54); (*d*) 'Satan' motif (Act II, no. 9, bars 1–6); (*e*) 'Satan' motif (Act II, no. 14, bars 91–8)

Example 4.19   *Eden*, Op. 40, Act II, no. 7, bars 1–9

with modal writing must have suggested to them that this was a feasible manner of expression, if only it could be manipulated into an acceptable frame – which *Eden* was not. The concurrent interest in English folksong and growing research into the music of British composers working before 1600 reinforced the potency of the modes; such a varied advocacy impressed and influenced nearly all British composers working over the next fifty years – even if, in some cases, the result was an avowed determination to avoid modes like the plague. (See also pp. 355–7.)

One might describe *Eden* as a noble failure as much as 'brilliant balderdash', since Stanford showed real vision in this work. One must credit him with taking *Paradise Lost* as his basis and with incorporating an older style of composition (high Renaissance polyphony) alongside one of the most modern (leitmotif) and writing a piece with no parallel. Why did the work fail? It is, as Jenkinson wrote, far too long, and too much of the music, though academically ingenious, lacks interest. Its nearest relative is *The Dream of Gerontius* and with it some useful comparisons may be drawn. Elgar's work failed at its first performance, while Stanford's did not, but it is the vivid nature of Elgar's music which redeemed *Gerontius* and his visions of heaven and purgatory outstrip Stanford's by miles. While Stanford's hell was daring in 1891, Elgar's hell was terrifying in 1900; similarly Stanford's Heaven was appealing but Elgar's was radiant. Shaw summed up the position neatly:

> Take any of the British oratorios and cantatas which have been produced recently for the Festivals, and your single comment of any of them will be . . . 'Oh! Anybody with a bachelor's degree could have written that.' But you cannot say this of Stanford's *Eden*. It is as insufferable a composition as any Festival committee could desire; but it is ingenious and peculiar; and . . . in it you see the Irish professor trifling in a world of ideas.[100]

Eden is indeed 'ingenious and peculiar', but Stanford treated the ideas thrown up by his subject superficially and academically rather than with passion or conviction: the result is that, while the piece has far greater

---

[100] Ibid., ii, 319.

originality of concept and execution than *The Three Holy Children*, it is anodyne and unconvincing.

In mid-December 1891 news came that Stanford's aunt Susannah had died of influenza. She had lived with her sister Kate and Charles's mother, Mary, at 26 Fitzwilliam Square, Dublin, for many years, Mary having moved there after John Stanford's death. Charles and Jennie travelled to Dublin to attend the funeral. Unsurprisingly Kate and Mary, both aged over 74, also contracted the disease. Their decline is shown in letters from both Jennie and Charles to Francis Jenkinson:

Dec 26th [1891]   26 Fitzwilliam Square, Dublin

Dear Francis,

You will want to know what is happening. I feel as if I hardly knew. Our beloved Mother has influenza and although it is not bad at present, she is fearfully weak and we have the greatest difficulty in making her take anything: with her it is simply a question of strength at present. We are not very anxious about her as there are no complications and she is sleeping a great deal and is very quiet. Kate lives on, for two days she was to all purpose dead, her spirit was most certainly away. Then came a curious change and when she saw Carl she said 'I've come to life again'. Since then she has appeared to be getting better, although it seemed quite mad to hope. It has been quite impossible not to do so. This afternoon there seems to be another change, and I do not believe she is so well. The strain is very dreadful. I do trust it will end soon. I am longing with my whole heart to hear of the safe arrival of the babes, it is so wretched to be away from them ...

Your loving

Jen[101]

Dec 28, 91.   Royal Marine Hotel, Kingstown.

Dear Mr Jinks,

The dear Aunt died on Sunday quite peacefully. She knew me and spoke to me up to Saturday night. In fact I was the only one she did recognise at the end. That's a comfort. My mother has influenza coupled with a great shock and break down of strength. But she was better yesterday. Still it is anxious work until she begins really to mend. To add to my troubles Jen got a chill on Xmas Eve, and has been in bed at Kingstown for 2 days and again today. She was rheumatic and feverish (Temp 102°). Not influenza. Today she is 99.4 and is on the mend eating a chicken. Still you may imagine what a time it is for poor me running up and down between two invalids. I am quite happy about J. today. She is determined to take care of herself happily and not run risks.

---

[101] Jennie Stanford to Jenkinson, 26 Dec. 1891, CUL, Add. MS 6343, item 1921.

'Thanks ever so much for yr letter' from her. The funeral is tomorrow. I may be kept here yet for ages. I can't tell. I hope Trinity won't sling me out.

Yrs. aff,

C.V.S.[102]

Jan 1, 92.   Royal Marine Hotel, Kingstown.

Dear Jinks,

. . . I have been with my dear Mother and saw the end at 6 o'clock this morning. Quite peaceful and gentle. Now all my links to the old country and blessed family are practically gone. You will be sorry for us. Three such losses in a short fortnight. Jen bears up wonderfully and is better today. I must ask you to try and arrange a matter of great importance for me. The MusBac exercises are beginning to come in and the fees: due Jan 20. Can I possibly be given a substitute to examine them? I cannot really see how I can do them. I shall be overwhelmed with work (two executorships) . . .

I shall ask Hubert to conduct the [CUMS] concert on Feb 10.

Will you also like a good man put a notice in the *Reporter* for me cancelling my lectures this term (they happen to be optional). I should not be able to command my voice yet a while. E. S. Thompson wd do this if you cannot sign it on my behalf . . .

Ever yrs aff.

C. V. S.[103]

This was a distressing time for both Charles and Jennie and even though all the dead were elderly the shock of them dying in a short period was great. Charles was subsequently saddled with executing Susannah's will as well as the other two. There was sympathy for him in Cambridge, and Trinity gave him leave until the end of February. Charles and Jennie decided to spend time with his godfather, Bishop Graves, at Limerick and they then, together with Geraldine and Guy, spent most of February at St Leonard's, Sussex. To cap it all Geraldine caught influenza, and Charles wrote to Jenkinson that, 'coming on top of all the other things it makes us, of course, doubly anxious. But to my mind she is better tonight and her skin is beginning to perspire, a good sign. Guy's cold is better I think, but he may be going in for the plague too.'[104]

Things gradually returned to normal: Stanford returned to Cambridge to find the subscription concerts in financial straits once again (a problem

[102] Stanford to Jenkinson, 28 Dec. 1891, CUL, Add. MS 6343, item 1922.

[103] Stanford to Jenkinson, 1 Jan. 1892, CUL, Add. MS 6343, item 1931.

[104] Stanford to Jenkinson, 26 Jan. 1892, CUL, Add. MS 6343, item 1956.

solved by the summer) and another link with his past cut since George Phillips, President of Queens' College and Stanford's first contact with the university, had died whilst he was away. But there was one new circumstance which was to affect Charles's life greatly: he had been a beneficiary in the wills of his two aunts and in his mother's estate and was richer by about £13,000.

Whether by accident or design, rumours about Stanford's status began to circulate shortly afterwards, most notably that he was likely to be a candidate for the post of Music Master at Eton.[105] Stanford felt obliged to write:

> As many wholly imaginary rumours relating to me are being printed in the newspapers and are involving me in much unnecessary correspondence, will you kindly allow me space to say that:-
>   1. I am still alive.
>   2. I am thankful to say that I have not been, and am not ill.
>   3. I have not gone to Ireland for two months' rest and change.
>   4. I am not an applicant for a post at Eton College, which is not vacant, and for which, if it were, I should not be a candidate.
>   5. I have no intention whatever of resigning the Professorship in Music in Cambridge University.
>
> I remain your obedient servant,
>
> C. V. Stanford[106]

But his denials were selective: it is significant that he referred only to his Professorship and to neither CUMS nor Trinity. Over the Easter vacation he and Jennie went to Florence but unfortunately he contracted malarious neuralgia whilst there and was confined to Harvey Road upon his return home. Despite this illness much pondering took place and shortly afterwards he told Trinity that he would resign as organist at Christmas 1892 because he had decided to move to London. In accordance with the letter above he did not resign his Professorship and did not, at this time, resign as conductor of CUMS; evidently he felt that Trinity took up the greatest time and gave the least musical reward and the most musical frustration. Moreover, the interest from his inheritance could replace the lost income, while neither CUMS nor his Professorship required that he be resident in Cambridge.

As if to confirm Stanford's continuing relationship with CUMS, another great concert took place on 16 June 1892 following the installation of the university's new chancellor, the Duke of Devonshire. The concert was conducted by Stanford, Richter and Parry, and included

---

[105] See the *Pall Mall Gazette*, 9 Feb. 1892, p. 3
[106] *Pall Mall Gazette*, 15 Feb. 1892, p. 2.

the latter's *The Lotos Eaters*, but the piece which drew attention was Stanford's *Installation Ode*. It showed him at his wittiest, as it included 'Do ye ken John Peel' (a reference to the University's Vice-Chancellor), 'Gaudeamus igitur', the 'Cambridge Chimes', and combined 'Auld Lang Syne', 'Rule Britannia' and 'Let Erin Remember' in counterpoint.

The death of Alfred Tennyson on 6 October 1892 brought a renewed sense of bereavement. Tennyson had supported Stanford since first being associated with him in the mid-1870s when Stanford wrote the incidental music to *Queen Mary*. Stanford sent his condolences to Hallam:

> I know only too well alas! the terrible days you have gone through. I went through them twice less than twelve months ago. The same illness and the same end. No one can be with you more in it all than can I: and it is to me as real a grief as if I were of his own people. Like me you will find the memory so sweet that in time you will live on it and find it the greatest of all comforts. I can never forget his never varying kindness to me, and I can only promise you the double of the devotion as long as I live. These terrible moments bring hearts together more than anything; and you will never have to look farther than me for an affection as deep as of your own people. I can only write lame words, but you will know they are genuine. As for the dear lady I can only send her my love. She knows how we both will be feeling with her and sorrowing for her. It seems as if the world had turned over a leaf into a new chapter. I cannot help feeling that his grand influence will make it a better one than the last. That will be his greatest monument. God bless him and you all.[107]

There was, doubtless, a hope in Stanford that Tennyson's death would be the last of a close friend or relative for some time.

Stanford ended his occupation of the Trinity organ loft on Christmas Day 1892. No doubt he, and those around him, regarded this with mixed feelings. For Stanford, Trinity was too conservative and too unpliable for his liking; for Trinity, Stanford was a temperamental and irascible genius. The nub of the problem was the view of the Council of Trinity that the organist was merely a college servant[108] who was required to bend to their wishes despite his undeniably superior knowledge in his field (a problem which, of course, has afflicted many organists both before and after him) and this was a subject which Stanford addressed in public later. He had not tried to revolutionise the role of organist during his tenure but had consistently argued for a higher standard of music, both in terms of performance and repertory. He had,

[107] Stanford to Hallam Tennyson, 6 Oct. 1892, LCL, item 4271.
[108] A view partly reflected by salary: at his resignation Stanford received £270 per annum while Trinity's Chief Clerk received £200.

inevitably, been frustrated by a predilection for mid-Victorian sentimentality and a residual low-church mode of thought. The frustrations
he felt in the post are clearly revealed in a paper read to the Church
Congress in 1899:

> The rapidly increasing elimination of the works of our old masters
> from the [church music] lists means the destruction of all history
> and tradition, and the undermining of taste. While other countries
> are not only preserving their great works, but by research adding
> those which have dropped out or been forgotten to their stores, we
> are locking up and forgetting volumes of treasures and retaining for
> use only a few of the most obvious and best known ...
>
> The real root of the mischief is ... the trammelled position of the
> man who is responsible for the performance of the music, and who
> is, perhaps, in many cathedral bodies the only representative of thor-
> oughly trained knowledge of the subject – the organist. In most
> cases the responsibility for the choice of music is not centred in him,
> the expert, but either altogether in the hands of one of the clergy,
> or divided between a precentor and the organist ... This custom is
> a survival of ancient times, when the conditions were wholly
> different. Formerly the monk was a more learned and cultivated
> musician than his servant, the organist or choir-trainer. He there-
> fore rightly dictated the choice of music, of which he was a master.
> The positions are now reversed. The organist is the learned and
> cultivated musician, and the clerical official has not (save in a very
> few instances) qualified either by study or research for a task
> demanding exceptional musical skill and routine. But he retains a
> power for which he has in the lapse of time lost the necessary equip-
> ment, and the result is a far-spread amateurishness of taste, which
> if it is permitted to rule, will inevitably destroy the best traditions
> of English Church music ...
>
> I am not speaking of those matters merely from hearsay, but also
> from personal experience. I was for many years an organist. I ven-
> ture, therefore, to recount, as shortly as possible, my own experi-
> ences. When I entered upon my duties, I found that the choice of all
> music was made by the precentor. To this choice I was expected to
> sign my name with his. But when I found that I had practically no
> voice either in insertion or elimination, I declined to append my name
> to a list of music with the selection of which I had nothing to do.
> For many years, although the university to which I had the honour
> to belong had thought me worthy in knowledge and experience of
> being elected to their Professorship of Music, in my own college
> Chapel I was absolutely powerless to control or direct the choice of
> works which were to influence the tastes of hundreds of students.[109]

Probably Stanford should have resigned earlier than he did: no one in
Trinity could have expected him to acquire a national reputation as a

---

[109] See 'Music in Cathedral and Church Choirs', reproduced in *Studies and Memories*,
61–9, and *Pages*, 307–11.

composer whilst still its organist, and the College was, unsurprisingly, unable to deal with the demands he made of it. It seems likely that it was for financial reasons that Stanford stayed as long as he did, for he left as soon as he had the financial wherewithal to do so, and at a time when other projects in Cambridge were still to come to fruition (see pp. 170–3), suggesting a degree of opportunism in his relocation. Relieved at the time of his resignation, the College knew, in retrospect, that it had gained greatly from his service. Stanford was less charitable towards his erstwhile employers, and the College's failure to make him a Fellow nettled him until his death.[110]

What of Stanford's legacy as an organist *per se*? His work in this area was essentially transitory, rather than the realisation of a professional ambition (it is notable, incidentally, that he composed no solo organ music in his entire career at Trinity except for the early Prelude on 'Jesu Dulcis Memoriae' (1873)). As he did not, it seems, publicly play the organ again, it is worth considering his achievement in this area at this point.[111] There is no doubt that he brought a new degree of commitment and enthusiasm to chapel music in Cambridge in the 1870s from which the whole university benefited. His most significant attribute in the organ loft was the way in which he approached registration: he viewed the instrument as an orchestra, a perspective encouraged by his early teacher Sir Robert Stewart; Stanford recalled that Stewart himself preferred to play his own arrangements of orchestral pieces as voluntaries rather than music originally written for the instrument,[112] and Stanford replicated this preference in his own recitals at Trinity, where his programmes included, for example, arrangements of the slow movement of Beethoven's Second Symphony (24 May 1872) and the finale of the Fifth Symphony (30 May 1874), the last two movements of Schumann's Second Symphony (24 May 1873), the slow movement of Brahms's Third Symphony (21 May 1884), and Wagner's 'Huldigungsmarsch' (9 May 1877). No wonder Stanford's playing caused some consternation amongst senior academics: W. H. Thompson, the Master of Trinity when Stanford became organist, was heard to

[110] Although certainly a cause of resentment, it is difficult to see how he could have become a Fellow as at this time Fellows were only elected following examinations, a process upon which Stanford never seemed prepared to embark; his holding a Class III Bachelor of Arts would hardly have helped matters. Colleges were also empowered to confer Honorary Fellowships, but appear to have given these to members of the University employed (solely) at other institutions.

[111] Possibly he was bored with the instrument by this time and had neither the need nor the inclination to take another church post, necessary to facilitate frequent access to an instrument.

[112] Stanford, *Pages*, 49.

comment, 'Mr Stanford's playing always charms, and occasionally . . . astonishes: and I may add that the less it astonishes, the more it charms.'[113] Stanford also took some interest in organ building, having given advice on the restoration of the Trinity College organ towards the end of his tenure, and designing the new organ at the Church of Our Lady and the English Martyrs in Hills Road, Cambridge.[114]

As Stanford's move to London also put a stop to his appearances in Cambridge as a pianist, and, just as with the organ, he appears generally to have eschewed public appearances at the piano keyboard from this point, it is worth considering his work in this area also. In his long-standing role as CUMS's most regular chamber ensemble pianist and accompanist, Stanford undoubtedly played a very important role, bringing much new music to CUMS and its audience, especially before his appointment to the RCM in 1883, and it is in this respect that Stanford's contribution was most significant. His credentials as a performer *per se* were also high, and these concerts were undoubtedly of a far higher standard than Cambridge had enjoyed before he arrived, and he gained frequent plaudits for his sensitive playing (see pp. 39 and 66). He was not a virtuoso and appears only once to have taken the solo role in a concerto[115] and very rarely as a solo pianist, almost always appearing instead as an accompanist or chamber musician. This preferred role may have influenced his view on piano technique, on which he had robust views, feeling that warmth of tone had been sacrificed by some in the quest for virtuosity; in 1914 he wrote: 'It is the age of the hit instead of the pressure. If it is old-fashioned to prefer the pressure, I am happy to be still in the ranks of the out-of-date. I shall always prefer beauty of tone to strength of muscle. And beauty of tone was precisely what I found to be the predominant quality in both Liszt and Rubinstein.'[116]

This view is consistent with Stanford's other aesthetic views (see pp. 357–64 and 411–14), which always emphasised what he perceived to be substance over superficial attractiveness or empty showmanship. After relocation to London, he only occasionally appeared as a pianist in a professional context; Greene related an amusing incident when Stanford was accompanying him in *An Irish Idyll* at the Aeolian Hall in 1915: 'Harold Samuel . . . was turning over for him, and in the rapid

---

[113] Ibid., 122.

[114] See Gerard Cobb, *A Brief History of the Organ in the Chapel of Trinity College, Cambridge* (Cambridge, 1913), and N. Thistlethwaite, *The Organs of Cambridge* (Oxford, 1983), 56.

[115] The performance of his own Concerto in B flat with CUMS on 3 June 1874 (see p. 39).

[116] Stanford, *Pages*, 59.

ascending passage at the end of "Cuttin' Rushes" I distinctly heard behind me, *sotto voce*, in lightning thrust and parry, the words "Fake!" and "Liar!", neither being in the original text.'[117]

The years 1884–92 transformed Stanford from an up-and-coming young composer to one of national and almost international stature. He was then regarded, at the age of 40, as a member of the front rank of British composers, who had laboured hard to transform the reputation of Britain as a barren musical land, and he followed the nineteenth-century European tradition of being a performer, composer, conductor and pedagogue. The twin successes of *The Revenge* and the 'Irish' Symphony had established his name in the minds of nearly all the musically minded British, a success which was reflected in the continued demand for his services. The overall failures of such works as *The Three Holy Children* and *Eden* did not damage him in the long term; unlike his two earlier operas, both oratorios were cordially received even though they failed to capture the public imagination. Most importantly, it was in the late 1880s that Stanford's style settled into its mature mode of expression: although the influence of other composers is readily apparent in some pieces, it was increasingly the case that his music sounded like his own, since there was now a distinctive mix of melodic primacy, careful orchestration, passing interest in quasi-modal harmony, and a balance of lively spirits, contemplation and bluff heroism. He was still inclined to be insufficiently self-critical and the greatest strengths of works such as *The Revenge* and the Fourth Symphony are painfully absent in *Eden* and *Carmen saeculare*. This was, unfortunately, a defect that he never conquered. But, for all his faults, Stanford now stood amongst the greatest composers of late Victorian Britain, and his success as a composer was increasingly recognised both by reputation and by honours. A move to London was the next logical step in his career and there, it appeared, success could only continue.

---

[117] Greene, *Stanford*, 213.

CHAPTER FIVE

A Man about
London Town

Charles, Jennie, Geraldine and Guy moved to 50 Holland Street, Kensington (see Pl. 2), in early 1893 and it was to remain home to Charles and Jennie until the middle of the Great War. Stanford was now in the heart of London, within walking distance of the RCM, and it was there he concentrated his efforts as conductor and teacher. While many in Cambridge breathed a sigh of relief at his departure, his arrival in London was viewed by many with trepidation. Grove viewed the situation warily and had written to Edith Oldham before the Stanfords moved to town:

> I came in from a very tiresome Board Meeting at 11 last night where somehow the spirit of the d___l himself had been working in Stanford all the time – as it sometimes does, making him so nasty and quarrelsome and contradictious as no one but he can be! He is a most remarkably clever and able fellow, full of resource and power – no doubt of that – but one has to purchase it often at a very dear price.[1]

> I did not know how you felt towards Stanford before. I am afraid this feeling is pretty general, someone said to me the other day that he was the most disliked man in England. He can be very disagreeable; but I have never yet seen that side of him towards myself – As to his music I cannot honestly say that I ever cared for any of it, but on the other hand he is a very valuable member of College. His energy and vigour and resource are quite extraordinary. He is now rehearsing the first act of *Fidelio* for the examination and he is an *excellent* stage manager and, above all, he is always so affectionate to me and I am so fond of his wife, whom I knew when she was 8 or 9 (and did much towards making the match) that I hope I shall never experience his rough side.[2]

> What an energetic creature CVS is. He must have been most hard working last holidays – 30 songs, Gray's *Bard*, several Tennyson pieces &c. Parratt tells me the songs are some of them beautiful. Did you know that they were coming to live in Kensington? Charlie has a strong eye to money and I fear that when he's on the spot he will be constantly urging me to let him do work at College which will not always be advisable and will lead to his treading on the toes of the other Professors. It's astonishing how clear he and I have

---

[1] Grove to Oldham, 2 (?) July 1891, RCM, Grove–Oldham correspondence.
[2] Grove to Oldham, 21 Feb. 1892, RCM, Grove–Oldham correspondence.

kept of anything like a row. I think he really loves me which is more than I can say of him; though I like him much – there's a good deal of difference isn't there?[3]

At first Stanford maintained his links with Cambridge. The opportunism of his move is shown by there being two important schemes in progress at Cambridge, the first being CUMS's golden jubilee celebrations, the second the reform of Music degrees. For the first few months of 1893 it seemed as if little had changed: revisions to music degrees proposed by Stanford were debated in the Senate (see p. 172), while he appeared with Joachim at the latter's annual concert on 2 March and conducted CUMS Choir in Trinity College Chapel on 8 March. But the break with Cambridge became more apparent when it was announced in May that Stanford was resigning the conductorship of CUMS after its golden jubilee.

The seeds of this celebration had been sown by Stanford at Joachim's anniversary dinner in 1889 and had developed into a scheme to award honorary doctorates to Europe's leading composers. Brahms had been approached, but had refused again, as had Verdi, regretfully, on account of his age, and Gounod was unable to enter the country for legal reasons.[4] Acceptances were secured, however, from Saint-Saëns, Tchaikovsky, Boito, Grieg and Bruch.[5] A last-minute hitch occurred as Grieg was ill and was unable to attend, but otherwise all preparations went smoothly. At the concert on 13 June, Bruch conducted the Banquet scene from his opera *Odysseus*, and Boito his Prelude to *Mefistofele*. Saint-Saëns played the piano in the British première of his Fantasie for Piano 'Africa', Stanford conducting, with the first British performance of Tchaikovsky's *Francesca da Rimini* following it. In Grieg's absence Stanford then conducted the *Peer Gynt Suite No. 1* and the concert concluded with his own *East to West*, Op. 52. A dinner at King's College followed with speeches from Stanford, Saint-Saëns, Mackenzie and others and then a *conversazione* at the Fitzwilliam Museum. Here Stanford was presented with his farewell present from CUMS – eight silver candlesticks for him and a silver tea service for Jennie.[6] The four graduands were presented at the Senate House on the following day for the conferring of their degrees which they received with five others, including

---

[3] Grove to Oldham, 6 Nov. 1892, RCM, Grove–Oldham correspondence.

[4] A Cambridge degree could not be conferred *in absentia* (see pp. 57–8) and, in any case, the presence of the recipient was one of the primary reasons for the celebration.

[5] For extended and whimsical, but frustratingly unacademic, coverage of the CUMS Jubilee see Gerald Norris, *Stanford, the Cambridge Jubilee and Tchaikovsky* (Newton Abbot, 1980).

[6] The candlesticks are now the property of Trinity College, having been bequeathed to it by Guy Stanford.

Lord Roberts of Kandahar and the Maharajah of Bhaonagar, Sir Takhtsinhji Bhaosinhji. The whole event was deemed a triumph and there was a general feeling that Cambridge had shown how things could and should be done. For Stanford it was a great moment at which to bring his formal association with CUMS to a close; and it seems that all in Cambridge were prepared to recognise how much he had done for music in the town.

Stanford's contribution to the concert, *East to West*, a setting of words by Algernon Swinburne, was a short cantata grandiosely dedicated to the 'President and People of the United States' and had been completed in January 1893 and premièred by the Royal Choral Society at the Albert Hall on 10 May, although it was written for the World's Fair celebrations at Chicago.[7] It gained the qualified approval of Bernard Shaw:

> The two qualities needed for a good ode are tunefulness and bounce; and there is an allowance of both in *East to West*, though it is certainly stinted by the professorism which is Stanford's bane ... But the native audacity of the composer asserts itself more freely than in any of his recent compositions; and the entire welcomeness of the change was proved by a tremendous ovation at the conclusion of the performance [by the Royal Choral Society], very different in spirit from that which greeted the mixolydian angels at Birmingham.[8]

Stanford's other ongoing Cambridge project was the reform of musical degrees, which he had long felt to be a bar to the advancement of the music profession. His first moves to improve the syllabus had taken place in 1889 when he and George Garrett had succeeded in increasing the importance assigned to a knowledge of musical history at MusBac level, but his main campaign to reform the syllabus started in December 1891. Some proposed changes were technical but three were particularly important. They were:

1. that undergraduate candidates for the MusBac should be required to be resident in Cambridge for three years preceding graduation;
2. that MusBac graduates should proceed automatically to the MA;
3. that the 'Exercise' for the MusDoc should be scrapped and that candidates merely be required to submit scores of pieces upon which a claim for the degree could be based.

---

[7] Despite extensive enquiries, the late Frederick Hudson failed to trace a performance in Chicago.

[8] Shaw, *Music in London*, ii, 326–7.

The first of these was the most important. MusBac degrees had been unique in that they were conferred by both Oxford and Cambridge without a student having to have studied at the university: all that was required was for the candidate to sit and pass the exams.[9] Stanford felt that this devalued the MusBac as a musician was informed and improved by a general education which included knowledge of classics, literature and mathematics, and by the experience of living in a college in a university town.[10] And, indeed, this was required of students in all other disciplines. The inferiority of the MusBac was further demonstrated by the fact that a holder did not progress automatically to the MA, which conferred the right to vote in the Senate; Stanford's proposal of residence, however, changed the status of the MusBac and made the award of an MA a logical progression. For the MusDoc the removal of the 'Exercise' (an extended composition, usually an oratorio, which had, until 1878, to be performed to the examiners by an orchestra and choir paid for and conducted by the candidate) would, Stanford hoped, encourage more leading musicians to apply for it.

Debate in the Board of Musical Studies over Stanford's proposals took place throughout 1892; Garrett had serious reservations, principally on the grounds that it was unfair to impose residence on MusBac candidates when the university failed to provide adequate tuition. His lack of success led to his resignation from the Board and his opposing the recommendations when they were debated by Senate. Cobb may also have had reservations; he had chaired the Board since 1878 but resigned both the chair and his seat in February 1893. The reasons for his decision are unknown, although Stanford had barely spoken to him for the previous four years. The Senate debated the issues during early 1893 and Stanford's reforms were passed, with the qualification that both new and old regulations were to run concurrently for seven years (five years for MusDoc) to allow the University time to build up its teaching of music.

There is no doubt that Stanford did both Cambridge and musical education a great favour by pushing through these reforms. Music had always been a peculiar case in the universities up until this point: a degree in music had existed since the Renaissance (as music was part of

---

[9] This was also the pattern followed by other British universities in the nineteenth and early twentieth centuries; Stanford's opponents' principal argument against the change was that compulsory residence would prevent many potential MusBac candidates from taking the degree due to an inability to pay the fees required for residence; within Cambridge it was further argued that to become the sole British university requiring residence would drive potential candidates (and their examination fees) to other universities.

[10] Whether Stanford appreciated the irony of arguing for compulsory residence for undergraduates just at the time when he had ceased to be a resident is unknown. His proposals, however, were originally tabled before he elected to move to London, and his later absence became a source of frustration in Cambridge (see Chs 6 and 7).

the quadrivium) but it had always been inferior, with no residence being required and no examinations until the mid-nineteenth century. Other newer disciplines, for example English, History and Modern Languages, had stolen a march on Music and had become fully-fledged BA subjects at that time. Stanford's reforms put the MusBac on a par with the BA and laid the foundations for music's becoming a respected academic subject: from this point Cambridge built up its music teaching and this encouraged the fledgling fields of musicology and analysis. The requirement for residence was particularly important, since this changed the whole tone of the MusBac, and the lead given by Cambridge was followed by all British universities in the twentieth century (Oxford rejected a move to compulsory residence in 1898 but capitulated later; see p. 198). Although the anomaly of non-residential music degrees was bound to be removed sooner or later, it is to Stanford that Britain owes a debt for his move in this sphere.

As Grove noted, Stanford was productive throughout 1892 and 1893. He completed his setting of Thomas Gray's *The Bard* on 22 September 1892 (although this was not premièred until three years later; see p. 183) and his first part-songs also date from this time (Four Part Songs, Op. 47, and two sets of *Six Elizabethan Pastorales*, Opp. 49 and 53), as does the Mass in G, Op. 46 and a second collection of folksong arrangements, *Irish Songs and Ballads*. Stanford's First String Quartet in G, Op. 44 also received its première at Newcastle (22 January 1892).

In some respects, the Mass is an oddity. As Shaw noted, the idea of a mass written by an Irish Protestant was intriguing,[11] but it is a demonstration that Stanford was not anti-Catholic, as is often supposed, and he appears to have considered writing a mass before.[12] The Mass was

---

[11] Shaw, *Music in London*, iii, 151.

[12] There are, in fact, only one or two later comments about Elgar to substantiate the thesis that Stanford was anti-Catholic (see for example, Dent's Diary, 11 June 1909, KCC: 'We spoke of Elgar. S[tanford] said he had been merely bored by the new symphony and that Elgar was run by the Catholics and by Richter for his own ends)' and the oft-quoted 'it stinks of incense' (referring to *Gerontius*), a comment which does not sit well with his conducting it on several occasions (see Michael Kennedy, *Portrait of Elgar*, 2nd edn (Oxford, 1982), 151–3); it seems unlikely that he would have written the Mass and three more post-war Masses had this really been the case. In fact, Stanford's attitude to Catholicism was essentially a tolerant one; he occupied the Trinity College organ loft at a time of high Anglicanism and never embraced the low Church anti-popery of some of his relatives (see pp. 9 and 32–3).

There is, also, evidence to suggest that Stanford was tolerant of non-Christian religions. An anecdote from Edgar Bainton illustrates this: 'At a meeting of the Council of the RCM in the early days the late Archbishop of Canterbury proposed that a chapel should be added to the College buildings. Stanford immediately rose and said that if the proposal was carried, the Council would have to erect one altar for the Roman Catholics, another for the High Churchmen, a third for the Low Churchmen, a shrine for the Buddhists and

composed at the request of Thomas Wingham, organist of Brompton Oratory and an Examiner for the Cambridge MusBac (to whom it is dedicated, in memoriam, Wingham having died on 24 March 1893) and was first performed at the Oratory on 26 May 1893.[13] Few European composers wrote masses after about 1830 and British masses were a rarity after 1600, so Stanford turned to the Viennese composers of the late eighteenth century for guidance on the form of each movement. Despite this anachronism, the Mass is underrated and contains fine and appropriate music; even though the Kyrie follows the classical convention of lightness rather than supplication, it is extremely effective. The closing fugue of the Gloria is simplistic (and similar to that of Stanford's setting of Psalm 150 and clearly modelled, in part, on the same passage in Beethoven's Mass in C) but the preceding 'Qui tollis' is very moving and carefully written, Stanford effectively exploiting the yearning effect of the minor sixth (Ex. 5.1). The final three movements are especially good. Stanford dealt well with the text of the Credo, with its long statement of doctrine; evidently based on the Credos of Haydn, it maintains momentum and interest throughout by a mixture of rhetoric and overt theatricality. The opening of the Sanctus is eerily effective in its sense of awe, and the major-key catharsis at 'Pleni sunt coeli' is simple in conception but immensely powerful in execution (Ex. 5.2). The Agnus Dei is more contemplative than its classical predecessors but Stanford captured the meaning of the words excellently and there is some captivating vocal writing, notably the solo soprano entry on the word 'miserere' (Ex. 5.3). Possibly it was the success of this excursion into ordinary Catholic texts that led Stanford to set other ones later in life (for example, the *Requiem*, Op. 63); in any case, this piece is a perfect example of his mature style – conservative certainly, but with ample

a bath for the Baptists, and that within half an hour of the opening there would be bleeding noses all round. This incident, related to me by Sir Charles himself, is typical of the man. His broadmindedness in religious matters, his keen sense of humour, and perhaps a latent fear that the zeal of the students might outrun their discretion, were three dominant qualities in his character.' See 'Sir Charles Stanford and his Pupils', *Music & Letters*, 5 (1924), 200. (See also Ch. 8 n. 14.)

A letter to Parry from his father Thomas Gambier Parry suggests that Stanford had considered setting the Mass ordinary before: 'Stanford offered to finish specially a Mass Service [for the Gloucester Festival of 1883] – which, to be written specially for our Cathdral, was seriously objected to – an old mass, as a *study* of music of established high class for sacred purposes was placed in a totally different category. We cannot regard such matters merely and nakedly from the musical side alone. We very much regret Stanford not caring to produce anything else ... '. Thomas Gambier Parry to Hubert Parry, 20 Feb. 1883, quoted in Dibble, *C. Hubert H. Parry*, 207–8. If Stanford had started to compose such a work there is no evidence of its completion or survival.

[13] Feast of St Philip Neri, founder of the original and Patron of all Oratories.

Example 5.1   Mass in G, Op. 46, Gloria, bars 94–103

Example 5.2   Mass in G, Op. 46, Sanctus, bars 9–16

personal inflection and skill to mark him out among his contemporaries, and, above all, eminently satisfying to listen to.

The next major project was valedictory. Sixteen years after writing the incidental music to Tennyson's *Queen Mary*, Stanford returned to the genre when he was invited to compose music for Tennyson's *Beckett*. The play had been written several years earlier (see p. 74) and when Henry Irving finally persuaded Tennyson to allow him to produce it,

Example 5.3   Mass in G, Op. 46, Agnus Dei, bars 44–9

Tennyson insisted that Stanford should write the music; Stanford recalled Irving's business methods in his autobiography.[14] The music was composed in August 1892 and the play opened at the Lyceum Theatre on 6 February 1893 although, of course, Tennyson did not live to see it. The play was well received (possibly out of respect for Tennyson's memory) and the incidental music was also reviewed quite favourably; Stanford subsequently extracted the Funeral March as an independent concert piece.

Stanford's fourth completed opera, *Lorenza*, Op. 55, is a curiosity. Almost nothing is known about the circumstances of its composition and it has never been performed. Completed on 6 January 1894, it was the first work Stanford wrote after moving to London, and comprises two acts and a prologue. The libretto, very unusually for a British opera, is in Italian, written by Antonio Ghislanzoni and Ferdinando Fontana.[15] It may have been in February 1893 that Stanford met Ghislanzoni, when he went to Milan to review the première of Verdi's *Falstaff* for the *Fortnightly Review* and the *Daily Graphic*. Certainly Stanford met both Boito (again) and Verdi on this occasion and enjoyed the company of

---

[14] Stanford, *Pages from an Unwritten Diary*, 230–31.

[15] Michael Balfe had earlier composed to Italian libretti but he was exceptional among British composers in attaining a reputation in Italy. Ghislanzoni (1824–93) is chiefly remembered for his work on *La forza del destino* (1869) and *Aïda* (1876), plus Gomes' *Fosca* (1873) and Ponchielli's *I lituani* (1874). Fontana's most noted libretti are those for Puccini's *Le villi* (1884) and *Edgar* (1889).

both. For *Falstaff* itself Stanford had great praise. All aspects of the work and its production drew commendation, above all the way in which Verdi made the orchestra a quintessential part of the musical foundation of the opera without letting its importance detract from the dramatic action on stage. Stanford admired the pace of the drama too but regretted that this did not allow Verdi to introduce 'some one broad melody, which, without being necessarily too obtrusive, would give a rest point to the ear, and would clamp and cement together the whole'.[16]

It is not clear why Stanford chose an Italian libretto for *Lorenza* but Rosa's death in 1889 – removing the only impresario who had produced new British works – may have influenced him; although Covent Garden, under the aegis of Augustus Harris, was moving forward (producing works in the original French and German), it was still generally unready to take on British work.[17] This fact was brought home forcefully to Stanford when Harris agreed to produce *The Veiled Prophet* at Covent Garden, but only in an Italian translation. The single performance, on 26 July 1893, made little impression, even though Stanford had revised the opera (mainly by reducing its length) and written a new Prelude. Almost certainly, then, it was pragmatism that directed Stanford's choice.

Ghislanzoni's scenario is stereotypical, containing elements of the emerging *verismo* tradition; Fontana's involvement is unclear, but it may be that he completed the libretto after Ghislanzoni's death on 16 July 1893. Set in seventeenth-century Venice, the opera follows Lorenza in her quest to win back her lover, Soranzo, who has jilted her after he discovered that she had behaved improperly with a brother of his friend Lando. She hopes to achieve this by manipulating Lando and his new lover Gabriella, a former prostitute. Her plans go awry, however, and she is erroneously killed by the gondolier Isepo, who was pursuing Gabriella.

Ghislanzoni's libretto relies on simple design and clean divisions, and Stanford took on board these implications. Periodisation and melodic structure are simpler than in *The Canterbury Pilgrims* and *Savonarola*, though thematic interest is still found mainly in the orchestra. Stanford's lack of familiarity with Italian is demonstrated by the abundant revisions made to the vocal lines.[18] The extreme emotions portrayed in

---

[16] Stanford, 'Verdi's *Falstaff* (I)' in *Studies and Memories*, 170–83.

[17] Harris produced Isidore de Lara's *The Light of Asia* (11 June 1892) and *Amy Robsart* (20 July 1893), but this was the result of the intervention of his patron, the Princesse de Monaco (see p. 207).

[18] See the autograph, NUL, MS 12. Stanford had fairly good German and passable French but no Italian; his understanding of this libretto was probably based on his knowledge of French and Latin.

Lorenza – passion, neurosis, fear, anger, hysteria and the desire for revenge – are not ones which sit well with Stanford's contained and chaste aesthetic. Just as *Savonarola* failed because of his inability to translate the extreme emotions of the libretto into effective music, so does *Lorenza*. Indeed, in *Lorenza* the situation is worse, since the whole scenario is premised on *verismo* extremism. The opera is further weakened by the minimal role assigned to the chorus, which had hitherto provoked most of Stanford's best operatic music. There is no evidence that Stanford ever attempted to secure the opera's production and, if he showed the work to Augustus Harris, the result was obviously negative.[19]

Stanford's next major project was his Fifth Symphony in D, Op. 56, subtitled 'L'allegro e il penseroso', and contains some of his most sophisticated symphonic writing, inspired, like *Eden*, by Milton. Each movement of the symphony is prefaced by selected quotations from the two poems, lines from *L'Allegro* for the first and second movements, and from *Il Penseroso* for the third and fourth movements. Thus the symphony is not a programmatic representation of the whole poem but is a musical illustration of the lines quoted (similar to the manner of Vivaldi's *Four Seasons*).[20] The first and last movements are the most complex in structure and there are also thematic cross-references between movements: Stanford took a leaf here from his operas and oratorios. (The relationship to Milton's *L'Allegro* and *Il Penseroso* is charted in the appendix to this chapter, together with the musical themes.)

The symphony was premièred by the Philharmonic Society on 20 March 1895 and was well received, the *Musical Times* noting 'that a large part of it appealed to one's sense of satisfaction, by the charm and propriety of the themes and their skilful as well as picturesque treatment'.[21] Like all of Stanford's symphonies from the Fourth onwards, however, the Fifth enjoyed only brief favour with British audiences and soon disappeared from the repertory; it was not published until it was the subject of a Carnegie Trust award in 1923. Of all of Stanford's later symphonies this one shows some truly inspired writing, however, and the neglect is undeserved, though a tendency towards austerity of

---

[19] There is no evidence to suggest that Stanford tried to produce the work in Italy either. Although Cowen's *Signa* was produced at Milan (12 Nov. 1893), Italy was unreceptive to British opera and *Signa* was the first such work to be produced in Italy since Balfe's *Pittore e duca* (Trieste, 21 Nov. 1854; Trieste was part of Austria-Hungary at the time, but avowedly Italian in spirit). Henry Wood's assertion that he saw *Shamus O'Brien* produced in Milan (see Greene, *Stanford*, 195) has proved impossible to confirm.

[20] Although Stanford almost certainly did not know Vivaldi's work and, unlike Vivaldi, does not quote the texts above the musical score.

[21] *Musical Times*, 1 Apr. 1895, p. 233.

style, especially when compared with a work such as Tchaikovsky's
Pathétique, then immensely popular in British concert halls, is a probable explanation for the work's long-term failure. One wonders,
however, if the symphony might not have had more influence than hitherto supposed, for the vision of heaven at the close of the finale seems
strongly to anticipate the close of Vaughan Williams's Fifth Symphony
fifty years later.

Stanford did not allow the complexity of the structure required by the
poetry to banish good writing. While the Fifth Symphony does not have
the immediate appeal of the 'Irish' Symphony, it still contains a great deal
of effective and individual music for which Stanford did not receive due
credit. The middle two movements are relatively simply structured and
reflect the chosen lines of the poem well, though the Scherzo is derivative
in style and strongly Germanic in voice. The slow movement contains a
gravitas already seen in Stanford's work (for example, in the Fourth
Symphony and in *Oedipus Tyrannus*) but has advanced one stage further
in its sense of poise and stature. In the outer movements Stanford encountered a problem in reconciling the recapitulatory nature of musical forms
with the narrative thrust of the poems. In both cases the poem is compromised (though less so in the finale), but the resulting musical effect is
a good one: Stanford adapted themes, reorchestrated them in order to
attach a different meaning to them and struck just the right balance of
variation and subtlety needed to achieve this – a parallel with the way in
which he applied such structures in the Services of fifteen years earlier.
Both movements are modified versions of sonata form with the first movement remaining truer to the stereotype. The finale is also in sonata form,
but Stanford placed the development, which draws most heavily on the
bridge theme, after the recapitulation of the first subject, thus allowing
one to read the movement not only as a modified sonata form but as a
four-subject binary form in which the restatement of the second subject
is treated developmentally. In both cases Stanford adapted the form to fit
the poetry and the results are coherent. Possibly, without the Irish inflection, this symphony is a little less distinctive in musical style than the
'Irish', but Stanford's individuality still comes through in the elegance and
expansiveness of his melodies, the pertinent orchestrations, which take
their cues from references in the poems, and suave conception.

In October 1894 an era ended when Grove resigned the Directorship
of the RCM. He had long been pondering on who his successor should
be but found the choice unappealing. He communicated his thoughts on
several occasions to Edith Oldham,[22] showing a preference for either

---

[22] See Grove to Oldham, 17 Jan. 1892, 19 May 1894, 21 Oct. 1894 and 11 Nov. 1894,
RCM, Grove–Oldham correspondence.

Parratt or Parry, but with reservations in both cases. A newcomer, Grove felt, was an impossibility; 'Fancy', he wrote to Joachim, 'any outsider trying to make [Franklin] Taylor or Stanford go any other way than what they themselves wish.'[23] It is clear from Grove's writings that Stanford was never seriously considered: his letters quoted above make it clear that however much College colleagues admired his energy, they found it at best exhausting and at worst intolerable; his reputation had taken another dive earlier in the year after he had railed against a bad newspaper review of the Bach Choir and browbeaten, amongst other people, Grove, Parry and Parratt to sign a repudiation penned by Fuller Maitland.[24]

Earlier in 1894 it had appeared that Trinity College, Dublin might have been interested in Stanford as a successor to Sir Robert Stewart, who died on 24 March. Grove wrote to Oldham that he doubted whether Stanford would go and *'entre-nous* I don't think that the choice would be a wise one'.[25] Grove was surely right to assume that Stanford would have refused the post: his connection to Ireland was now only sentimental and he was unlikely to leave the capital for a provincial city so soon. Although Grove had considerable and justifiable doubts about Stanford's position, his name went forward as a candidate to succeed to him, along with those of Parry, Parratt, Bridge and Taylor, but only because the College Charter required five names to be submitted; the Council had virtually chosen Parry before the meeting which appointed him. It seems certain that Stanford did not want the job and viewed it as far too oner- ous a task: this is certainly implied in a letter from Stanford to Grove, which salutes Grove's contribution to the college:

> I must just write you one line of the most heartfelt gratitude for all the love and kindness you've shown me all these years at the College and for making the last 10 years the happiest I have ever spent. Any good I have done has all been from your loyal help and splendid initiative and the effect of that will last longer than you or I. I've always felt somehow as if your influence was like Arnold's at Rugby and certainly he was not loved or honoured more than you. You dear, bless you.
>
> We'll try to keep up to your standard if it is only for your sake and for what you have done. And forgive me for having often been a hotheaded and worrying chap always turning up at yr. busiest moments and making your life a burden to you generally.
>
> And to preach to Hubert to be methodical and not to wear himself out and to keep some of his time always for his own work . . .
>
> Goodbye, dear G, till Monday. For we must all, as Parratt says,

[23] Grove to Joachim, 31 July 1894, BerSt (Tiergarten), MS SM/12, item 2116.
[24] See Dibble, *Hubert Parry*, 313–14.
[25] Grove to Oldham, 1 Apr. 1894, RCM, Grove–Oldham correspondence.

keep a special armchair in our rooms for you to drop into at any hour of the day or night.[26]

The warmth with which Stanford wrote demonstrates his feelings and includes recognition that he did indeed hector and besiege his master. He also wrote to Parry declaring his support: 'Dear old man it is the greatest pleasure I could have to be under your thumb.'[27] To Joachim, Stanford wrote more circumspectly, but more out of concern for Parry than for any other reason: 'Hubert seems happy and gets on admirably. I only hope that it won't stop his private work. It's no place for a composer. You want a letter writing machine for such a place.'[28]

Whatever he may have written at this point, the relationship between Parry and Stanford, generally supportive hitherto but a long way from being problem-free, changed irrevocably. The basic reason was simple: Parry moved from being a colleague to a manager, a role which he was obliged to fulfil and which Stanford was only happy to accept when they agreed with each other. Over the years that followed, their relationship became steadily more fractious, a progression which was aided unwittingly by both men, Parry because his disagreements with Stanford prompted a dislike and distrust which he did not reconcile with the need for the Director to rise above politics, and Stanford because he seemed to believe that his friendship with Parry entitled him to expect capitulation to his every demand. Stanford's explosions and Parry's subsequent resentment led each man further into his own bunker, which both men left increasingly infrequently.

Upheavals at the RCM appear to have slowed Stanford's rate of composition. In 1893/94 he produced, as well as the works discussed above, the *Irish Fantasies*, Op. 54, the Fantasia and Toccata for Organ, Op. 57, the *Suite of Ancient Dances*, Op. 58 and the First Piano Concerto, Op. 59. From January 1895 to September 1896, however, he produced only the opera *Shamus O'Brien*, Op. 61, the short cantata *Phaudrig Croohore*, Op. 62 and the *Requiem*, Op. 63. Several notable performances took place in 1895, however, including the premières of the First Piano Concerto (Richter Concert, 27 May) and *The Bard* (Cardiff Festival, 19 September; see p. 183) and Stanford conducted the Bach Choir in performances of both Bach Passions and the B Minor Mass on 2, 4 and 6 April (all three concerts attracting critical comments from Parry, who referred to Stanford's tempi in the St Matthew Passion as 'quite incredibly bad').[29] He also directed RCM students in

---

[26] Stanford to Grove, 21 Nov. 1894, RCM, Grove–Oldham correspondence.

[27] Quoted in Charles L. Graves, *Hubert Parry*, 2 vols (London, 1926), i, 355.

[28] Stanford to Joachim, 9 Jan. 1895, BerSt (Tiergarten), MS SM12/40, item 4622.

[29] Parry's Diary, 2 Apr. 1895, ShP.

a production of *Dido and Aeneas* on 20 November to commemorate the tercentenary of Purcell's death and, although interest in Purcell's music had been growing steadily over the previous decades, Stanford's production helped spur interest in the composer's music to a significant extent (in an appropriately contemporary spirit, however, he included additional orchestral parts by Charles Wood).

The solo role in the First Piano Concerto was taken by Leonard Borwick, who subsequently premièred and promoted several of Stanford's other works. Stanford later reflected that the programming of the concert was unfortunate, as the concerto was placed between the Prelude from *Tristan und Isolde* and Tchaikovsky's Sixth Symphony: 'the effect was like handing round a *vol-au-vent* immediately after two large helpings of turkey and corn beef'.[30] Critical reaction to the concerto was qualified and one can detect the accusation of academicism in the comments of the *Musical Times*:

> the slow movement at once secured a host of friends by reason of its depth and sincerity of expression and the breadth and dignity of its melodic outlines and harmonic progressions. The themes of the first and third movements struck one at first hearing as scarcely worthy of the bold handling and undeniably clever treatment to which they are subjected.[31]

Stanford himself viewed the concerto as having a 'light and butterfly nature'[32] and it rejects the heroics seen in the concertos of Brahms, Liszt and Grieg, in the same manner that the earlier Serenade in G rejected the profundity of the nineteenth-century symphony. The outer movements are almost frivolous in their sparkle and show Stanford in expansive and playful mood; his piano writing is decorative icing on a dancing cake. The length of the first movement is at odds with the strength of its material but does not deserve the criticism above since it remains engaging throughout, but the last movement, whilst the shortest, loses its way and the jerky modulations from B♭ to G and back again which characterise the opening are distracting. The slow movement, a contemplative romance, offsets the vivacity of the outer movements perfectly, creating an excellent sense of symmetry across the work. Never hysterical or over-demonstrative, the material is treated with a restrained respect which adds to the gentle poignancy rather than emasculating it. After performances in Berlin (see p. 183) and at the Philharmonic Society in 1897, the concerto was undeservedly neglected and the good showing of the Second Piano Concerto (see pp. 287–8) overshadowed it.

---

[30] Stanford to Francisco Berger, 1 Jan. 1897, BL, MS Loan 48.13/32, fols. 244–5.
[31] *Musical Times*, 1 July 1895, p. 455.
[32] Stanford to Francisco Berger, 8 Dec. 1896, BL, Loan 48/13/32. fol. 243.

While the First Piano Concerto was later overtaken by its successor, Stanford's setting of Thomas Gray's *The Bard* failed to push past its antecedents. Although an appropriate subject for a Welsh festival (the poem tells of the alleged slaughter of the bards by Edward I in 1283), the style of poetry does not lend itself well to musical setting as the narrative is too deeply embedded in the text; this was a big disadvantage compared to the transparent structures of *The Revenge* and *The Voyage of Maeldune*. Gray's writing, by contrast to Tennyson's, is dense, and incorporates both flashbacks and predictions, as well as the bard's cries for vengeance, and becomes difficult to follow when music is added to it. Although he tried his best, Stanford could not get past the problems thrown up by the poem, and the work which, as usual, is well crafted, failed to excite.

On 30 December Stanford was once more in Berlin to conduct a concert of British music, although he himself was disproportionately represented. Both the new symphony and piano concerto were performed, but also included was music by Mackenzie ('Britannia' Overture), Sullivan ('MacBeth' Overture), Parry, Purcell, Maurice Greene and John Field. Stanford was hopeful that the Kaiser might attend the performance: 'The Embassy are extremely kind about it all and there is some probability of Caesar himself being able to come, at any rate von Seckendorff is going to see what can be done. So Gosselin writes to Greene. It would be a good thing for the sake of English music. (Unless he has us all guillotined after).'[33] The concert went well and both Charles and Jennie (along with Greene and Borwick, who took solo roles in the concert) spent an enjoyable two weeks in Berlin.

It is not clear whether the Kaiser attended the concert but Stanford met Brahms once again, in more convivial circumstances than in 1874; in his next letter to Joachim, however, Stanford wrote: 'It was most interesting to meet Brahms, though – shall I dare say it – I have no affinity for him! A big brain I know, and a small heart I think. Somehow I felt he had none of the divine sympathy which we meet with in our best beloved J[oseph] J[oachim].'[34] What impact this meeting with Brahms made on Stanford can only be guessed at; it must have been disconcerting, however, for Stanford to find that the composer whom he had idolised most consistently through his adult life was a man with whom he could feel little personal compatibility. The Kaiser's infamous 'Kruger telegram' sent on 3 January 1896, marred his visit more: 'We had a glorious time in Berlin and that last supper was a delightful end. We had a capital journey and a smooth sea. England is in a fever but

[33] Stanford to Joachim, 5 Dec. 1895, BerSt (Tiergarten), MS SM12/40, item 4625.
[34] Stanford to Joachim, 14 January 1896, BerSt (Tiergarten), MS SM12/40, item 4626.

is cooling. It was a pity, that telegram. No-one in Berlin knows what harm it did.'[35]

On returning to London, Stanford had to throw his energies into preparations for the première of *Shamus O'Brien*, which took place on 2 March 1896 at London's Opéra Comique Theatre. Followed by a run of eighty-two performances, this was Stanford's most successful opera and subsequently enjoyed more revivals than any of his other stage works. It was a long time in gestation. Based on a poem in mock-Irish dialect by Joseph Sheridan Le Fanu (whom Stanford had met in 1859; see p. 25), it was, according to Greene, Stanford's own idea that the poem could be turned into a libretto and he originally approached William Gorman Wills with the idea.[36] Wills, however, died in December 1891, and Stanford then turned to the Irish-American playwright George Jessop.[37] The date of Stanford's approach is unknown, and he did not start writing the music until late 1894, Act I being completed on 24 December and Act II on 14 January 1895; the subsequent delay between completion and performance may be explained by the time needed to form a company for the opera's production. For such a venture native singers were preferable and an Irish opera company did not then exist. Stanford secured the services of Augustus Harris as producer and Henry Wood as conductor.

When *Shamus* opened it was received enthusiastically. Critical reaction to the opera was almost unanimously favourable, though the surprise of some critics is exemplified by the back-handed compliments in the *Theatre*: 'Dr Stanford has condescended to be absolutely tuneful. His ballads are marked by simplicity and grace, his dances by rhythmic spirit and "go" and all alike are imbued with Irish character to a degree that makes it difficult to realise that they are only imitations and not the real thing itself.'[38] After the respectable run in London there was an extensive provincial tour starting in autumn 1896, a run in New York in early 1897 and a resumed tour through Britain for the remainder of 1897.

---

[35] Ibid. The telegram was sent by the Kaiser to Kruger and congratulated him for repulsing the Jameson Raid, thus maintaining the independence of the Transvaal. The raid resulted in the resignation of Cecil Rhodes as Premier of Cape Colony and the telegram led the Boers to believe that Germany would support them in an armed conflict with Britain.

[36] See Greene, *Stanford*, 198. William Gorman Wills (1828–91) was a rather eccentric and bohemian Irish playwright who had written plays for production by Henry Irving. He is better remembered today as a painter of portraits.

[37] George Jessop (d. 1915) was educated at Trinity College, Dublin, and emigrated to America in 1873. He made a career as a journalist and playwright in San Francisco but returned home on inheriting an estate in Ireland.

[38] *Theatre*, 1 Apr. 1896, p. 224.

Opera-goers were confronted by a much lighter work than Stanford had produced hitherto and the work harks back to the mid-nineteenth-century operas of Balfe and Wallace, but also sought to capitalise on the success of the Savoy operas and such similar works as Cellier's *Dorothy*. The action takes place in 1798, shortly after the abortive Irish Rebellion. The hero, Shamus, is in hiding following his involvement in the rebellion; British soldiers attempt his arrest but Shamus, in disguise, leads them into the countryside and loses them. During a village cele-bration later in the day the banshee is heard crying in the distance, signalling impending doom, and Shamus is captured by the British troops, who have been led to him by Mike Murphy, the frustrated former suitor of Shamus's wife Norah. The villagers go to the trial and see Shamus condemned to death and he is subsequently led to the gallows. The local priest, Father O'Flynn, blesses Shamus for the last time and suddenly undoes the ropes which tie Shamus, who escapes. Mike tries to stop him and the soldiers shoot but hit Mike. Shamus escapes and Mike dies: the banshee was crying for him.

Shamus includes some of Stanford's finest music and is the most inter-esting example of his 'Irish' style. Only two authentic melodies are used in the opera, both of which are used as character motifs: Stanford could not resist including 'The Top of the Cork Road' as a motif for the priest (the song had become well known as 'Father O'Flynn' after he had published an arrangement of the tune with words by Alfred Graves in *Songs of Old Ireland* (1882)); the other melody is an English marching song, 'The Glory of the West', and is associated with the English soldiers. Stanford also used pastiche Irish melodies, this approach taking two forms. First is the use of traditional Irish genres and melodic inflections. Two numbers exemplify this technique, the caoine (lament) 'A grave yawns cold', and the instrumental Jig. The caoine, like that of the later Clarinet Sonata, employs the rapid ascending and descending scalic orna-mentation found in Irish folk music as an essential characteristic, although Stanford did not take on the quarter-tone slides which are also common (Ex. 5.4). The Jig takes both the traditional form of the dance (the 'tune' and the 'turn', which follow each other in potential perpe-tuity) and the characteristic melodic inflections, that is, the use of tonic and dominant arpeggios, simple scales (cf. this melody and 'Father O'Flynn', Ex. 5.5), the flattened seventh, and the thrice-iterated tonic at the ends of phrases (which also appears in Kitty's 'Where is the man?'). Stanford also employed the drone (noted in the score to be played on Irish bagpipes). The second technique Stanford used was the aping of whole traditional melodies: two numbers ('I've sharpened the sword for the sake of ould Erin' and 'Pass the Jug around') borrow strongly from two songs in *Moore's Irish Melodies* ('Cruachan na feine' and 'Bob and

Example 5.4 *Shamus O'Brien*, Op. 61, Act I, no. 8, bars 100–104 (text: George Jessop)

Joan') and acquire Irish characteristics by this impersonation (Ex. 5.6).

The opera also succeeds because the scenario captured Stanford's imagination and the score demonstrates that the simplest ideas can prove to be the most effective; many who saw the opera recalled the long side drum ostinato based on 'The Glory of the West' which accompanies the long walk to the gallows in Act II.[39] Other numbers too are attractive and dramatically appropriate, especially Kitty's 'Where is the man that is coming to marry me?', Mike's 'Ochone when I used to be young' and the extended passage in the Finale of Act I which follows Shamus's arrest, all of which capture the light, sentimental nature of the play.

The strength of the music comes through despite the weakness of the libretto. Jessop's verse is often forced and contains some excrutiating accentuation, syntax and rhymes:

> Girls do not cringe to him,
> Yield not an inch to him,
> Sure you heard death in the banshee's shrill keen.
> Only rear Paddy here
> Up like his daddy here,
> To worship his country and die for the Green. (Act I Finale)

---

[39] See Greene's quotation of Henry Wood's reminiscences, *Stanford*, 197.

Example 5.5 *Shamus O'Brien*, Op. 61: (*a*) 'Father O'Flynn' motto; (*b*) Act I,
no. 8 (Jig), bars 182–98

Example 5.6 (*a*) *Shamus O'Brien*, Op. 61, Act I, no. 6, bars 7–15; (*b*) 'Cruachan
ne feine' (*Moore's Irish Melodies*); (*c*) *Shamus O'Brien*, Act I, no.
8, bars 6–13; (*d*) 'Bob and Joan' (*Moore's Irish Melodies*)

The sentimentality is overplayed too, in a cloying Victorian fashion,
although there are also moments when the action is enthralling and
when Stanford took hold of the dramatic implications of the scenario
and developed them with real power and mastery. Characterisation
was praised at the time as shedding the 'stage-Irish' clichés of Dion
Boucicault's *The Colleen Bawn* but now appears stereotyped, as does
the dull-witted but honourable Englishness of Captain Trevor.

Today the opera is also transparently the work of two Anglo-Irishmen
writing from an angle now unacceptable, while the twee language and

sentimentality sully the work beyond redemption. For the music this is unfortunate, but the opera was bedevilled by politics almost as soon as it was premièred and Stanford became resigned to this problem (see pp. 386–9, where this issue is discussed *in extenso*). In 1896, however, *Shamus O'Brien* brought Stanford the operatic success for which he had searched for fifteen years. By producing a work which aimed at the middle-brow theatre-goer who watched Gilbert and Sullivan, and Cellier, and who still demanded performances of *The Bohemian Girl* and *The Lily of Killarney*, Stanford ensured both popular acclaim and financial reward.

Having seen the great success of *Shamus O'Brien*, it must have appeared to Stanford that his choral setting of another Le Fanu poem, *Phaudrig Croohore*, would have been destined for a similar success. The work was conceived as an Irish equivalent of *The Revenge*: a short, vigorous cantata, designed for choral societies of average ability. It was premièred at the Norwich Festival on 8 October 1896. Parry heard a rehearsal of the work in London three days earlier and wrote that it 'struck me as superficial and scarcely up to his usual level of scoring'.[40] Stanford's hopes were dashed. The work made little impact and Parry was quite right to assert that Stanford appeared to have lost his touch. *Phaudrig Croohore* tells of a hero who elopes with his sweetheart on her wedding day after which they live happily until he is killed in the 1798 rebellion; the similarities with *Shamus O'Brien* are obvious and Le Fanu wrote the poem in the same mock-Irish style. The music too is simply constructed with a recurring battle-song theme, similar in nature to Shamus's 'I've sharpened the sword', as its anchor. Stanford's work falls short on two essential points. First, the music, despite its references to Irish folk music, has little of the melodic strength or melodrama of *Shamus O'Brien*; indeed, one cannot help agreeing with Parry that the music is, by Stanford's standards of workmanship, almost slipshod. Secondly, it is hard to see how any English choir could ever capture the Irish brogue and sentimentality that such a work would have needed to provide a convincing performance; it is strange that Stanford, with so many years of choral experience behind him, did not realise this, specifically as the company put together for *Shamus O'Brien* had been especially populated mainly by Irish actors in order to avoid this problem.

Two months after the première the work got caught up in a farcical display of English puritanism following a satirical paragraph written by Herbert Thompson in the *Yorkshire Post*:

> It must be a cause of satisfaction to the people of Manchester to know that in the chorus of the Hallé concerts there are those who

---

[40] Parry's Diary, 5 Oct. 1896, ShP.

at all risks will uphold the cause of pure morality ... Phaudrig
Crohoore may have been a 'broth of a boy' but his conduct was in
many respects such as is 'most intolerable and not to be borne' at
least in Manchester circles. A nice hero, indeed, of whom the poet
tells us – and this without apology – that 'there wasn't a girl from
thirty-five under, Divil a matter how cross, But he could round her'!
It is a mere subterfuge to defend this improper Phaudrig on the
ground that, as stated in the following lines, 'But of all the sweet
girls that smiled on him, but one was the girl of his heart, and he
loved her alone'. For it only illustrates the demoralised state of the
society to which he belonged that its feminine members smiled upon
a bachelor so promiscuously – possibly too without the necessary
formality of an introduction ... Sad to say the grave immorality of
the poem escaped notice at Norwich, where the piece was first
produced, and at Bradford, where it was given a few weeks ago.[41]

Choral societies in Manchester and Southport took Thompson at his
word and declared that the poem was indecent. Stanford wrote to
Thompson:

> Now Boosey [who was publishing the work] wants to change the
> words! Which will mean acknowledging that Le Fanu wrote an inde-
> cent line, a thing which he never did in his life. The poem is recited
> even by parsons at penny church readings. William Le Fanu
> used to recite it in every drawing room in Dublin from the Lord
> Lieutenant's down, and to children.
>   They object to 'divil a matter', an expression used by every man,
> woman, and child in Ireland from the priest of the parish down.
> 'Divil' has no meaning. 'Devil' in The Revenge has a great deal of
> meaning and they sing it every day without a word of objection ...
> only bad minds could see anything indecent in it. 'Good morning,
> have you used Pear's soap?' I suppose wd be indecent to some
> because it suggests a bath and no clothes on.[42]

The spat blew over and Boosey published Phaudrig with Le Fanu's original words, but the work never caught on and certainly never achieved
the success for which Stanford had hoped.

Shamus's success did not distract Stanford from work or leisure: he
spent the summer of 1896 in Malvern and it was here that he first cultivated Edward Elgar's friendship. That the two men had a difficult
relationship has long been known, and both were at fault. In some
respects they were too much alike to be friends: both were hypersensitive
to criticism, but had a tendency to dole it out in a blunt and uncom-
promising fashion. In the early days, however, they got on well and
formed something of a mutual admiration society; Stanford, as far as

[41] Yorkshire Post, 16 Dec. 1896, p. 6.
[42] Stanford to Thompson, 30 Dec. 1896, LUL, MS 361, item 262.

available evidence allows one to judge, continued to admire and respect Elgar for the next five or six years,[43] but Elgar's opinion of Stanford declined more rapidly, though he concealed this from all but close friends for some time.

Stanford's composition rate increased: after the *Requiem* was completed in September he composed the String Quartet in D Minor, Op. 64 (finished on 29 September), settings of three songs from *Twelfth Night* (Op. 65), and a Latin setting of the *Te Deum* (Op. 66; completed on 30 January 1897). The songs from *Twelfth Night* are particularly striking, Stanford capturing the nuances and sentiments of the text excellently. 'O Mistress mine' is a dark reading of the poem while 'Come away Death' is striking in its *cortège* rhythms and bold harmonies, especially the persistent ♭VII–♭ii⁷ progression, which is declaimed throughout. 'The rain it raineth every day' is also fine, with eighteenth-century overtones in its melismas on the words 'wind' and 'rain'. The RCM Orchestra gave its first out-of-London concert at the Cambridge Guildhall on 4 November 1896, and produced *Falstaff* under Stanford's direction on 11 December, while he visited Dublin to conduct *Shamus O'Brien* on 28 November – a rare triumph on his home patch with the Anglo-Irish enclave attending *en masse* since 'God save the Queen' was triumphantly sung by the audience at the end, 'a thing', Stanford wrote to Sedley Taylor, 'which had not been heard in the theatre for years'.[44] Stanford also hoped to go to Berlin once more but the political situation in South Africa was causing difficulties in Anglo-German relations; Stanford wrote to Joachim, 'I suppose Deutschland hates the Britisher too much just now'[45] (to which Joachim replied 'we do *not* hate the British, though we disapprove of Rhodes, Jameson and that lot').[46] Stanford did, however, travel to Holland and Germany in the following spring and conducted *The Revenge* in Berlin on 21 April 1897.

Stanford next tried to capitalise once more on the success of *Shamus O'Brien* (as he had attempted with *Phaudrig Croohore*), this time by writing another light opera. The result was *Christopher Patch* (also known as *The Barber of Bath*), Op. 69, and represents another move towards the operetta style of Sullivan and Cellier; as Stanford wrote to his librettist, Benjamin Stephenson, 'the whole thing wants the lightest of touches'.[47] The work was composed during spring and summer 1897,

---

[43] See Stanford's correspondence with Elgar, WRO, 5427: 7390–7410.

[44] See Stanford to Sedley Taylor, 30 Nov. 1896, CUL, Add. MS 6260, item 236.

[45] Stanford to Joachim, 6 Oct. 1896, BerSt (Tiergarten), MS SM12/40, item 4627.

[46] Joachim to Stanford, 9 Oct. 1896, quoted in Joseph Joachim, *Letters to and from Joseph Joachim*, trans. Norah Bickley (London, 1914), 456.

[47] Stanford to Stephenson, 7 Sep. 1896, Moldenhauer Archive, Northwestern University, Evanston, Ill., MS MA 193.

Act I being completed on 16 June and Act II on 4 September. Stanford hoped for an early production, but these aspirations were unfulfilled and the opera has never been performed. Edward Dent and Cyril Rootham examined the opera after Stanford's death but concluded that 'it was too obviously an attempt at the popular light opera style of Sullivan and Edward German and its old-fashioned humour would have made us all feel uncomfortable'.[48]

Set in eighteenth-century Bath (and carrying, therefore, overtones of such literary works as *The Rivals, Humphry Clinker, Persuasion* and *Northanger Abbey*) the scenario of the work remains unclear since the spoken dialogue has not survived. It is clear, however, that the plot is modelled on the Savoy operas and centres on four lovers who, after various shenanigans and intrigues, are paired off with their 'correct' partners. Much of this activity is facilitated by the doings of a fifth character, the barber Christopher Patch. The scenario was very much a product of Stephenson's mind, and followed the style of his earlier work, for example Cellier's *Dorothy* (1886) and *Doris* (1889).[49] Quite why the opera was not immediately produced is unclear, but neither the libretto nor the music matches the standard reached by the Savoy operas. Patch's patter songs – implying that the inane chatter of barbers was just as well-established a cliché as it is today – are acceptable, but hardly rival those of Gilbert:

> Please take a posture more reclining
> While this towel I am twining
> To save your satin lining
> From an accidental smirch.
> So I suppose you heard young Waring
> Has been soundly caned for staring
> At some ladies out a-charing
> Why, he winked at one in church! (Act I, No. 5)

Stanford too fell short of what was required; there are some charming songs in *Christopher Patch* but often the quality of melodic writing, so essential in this genre, fails to match up to that of Sullivan. This is partly because Stanford failed to capture the apparent simplicity of Sullivan's style and shifted towards the developmental structure of his own art songs; in *Shamus O'Brien* this was acceptable because of its novelty and

[48] Undated note by Dent attached to Stanford's letter to Stephenson (see n. 47), presumably written some time after Jennie Stanford had sent the manuscript to Cambridge after her husband's death.

[49] Benjamin Stephenson (1840–1906), sometimes known by the *nom de plume* 'Bolton Rowe', also supplied the libretto for Sullivan's *The Zoo* (1875) and, with Frederick Corder, for Goring Thomas's *The Golden Web* (1893), as well as many other stage comedies.

subject, but in *Christopher Patch*, which is pure comedy, this approach failed. The Gamblers' chorus, 'Give him three times three', contains some lively writing, however, as does the coy minuet in which soprano Betty Marsham confronts her army of suitors (Ex. 5.7); Stanford also antici-pated the use of the street-sellers' cries in Lionel Bart's *Oliver* (1960) by over sixty years (Ex. 5.8). The work is a missed opportunity since an operetta set in eighteenth-century Bath has the potential to be very funny, but in the end Stephenson did not have the ability, nor Stanford the flex-ibility, to beat the masters of the genre.

The *Requiem*, Op. 63, was premièred at the Birmingham Festival on 6 October 1897 and attracted both critical acclaim and some curiosity about its style. The *Musical Times* addressed the issue straightforwardly:

> The composer did not shrink from the task of preparing a Requiem which should reflect the spirit and feeling of Roman Catholic ceremonial. He was justified in this boldness for we have no more versatile musician than Dr Stanford. I will not say that he is a 'quick change artist' but that he can change, and do so thoroughly. From the evidence of the new work he might have been all his life engaged in writing church music for the sensitive and passionate Latin peoples ... Sincere the Requiem surely is, or it would not convince.[50]

Parry's reaction was more qualified and curious: 'Felt puzzled myself what he is driving at. Such an absence of detail in the inner working. Almost Italian in method. Some of it rather cheap [and] very dull.'[51] Hearing the piece again at the Royal Academy on 16 December Parry was more positive: 'The work tells despite its Italian style. Effective and well planned. Orchestration quite admirable in effect.'[52]

The work proved a big contrast with *Eden*, Stanford's previous Birm-ingham commission, and it is unsurprising that the *Requiem* provoked curiosity. As illustrated, Stanford's choice of text raised eyebrows in a country where residual anti-Catholicism was still common; there was probably an element of pragmatism as well: it was becoming increas-ingly difficult to find suitable yet unused biblical stories to set as oratorios and he had seen no oratorio of his own or of any other British composer establish itself in his lifetime. Both the Festivals and the general public had shown a greater willingness over the previous fifteen years to accept compositions based on Catholic Latin texts (for example, Gounod's *Mors et vita* (Birmingham, 1885) and Dvořák's *Requiem* (Birmingham, 1891)) and such texts were freely available and required neither librettist

---

[50] *Musical Times*, 1 Nov. 1897, p. 746.
[51] Parry's Diary, 6 Oct. 1897, ShP.
[52] Parry's Diary, 16 Dec. 1897, ShP.

Example 5.7   *Christopher Patch*, Op. 69, Act II, no. 15, bars 165–95 (text: Benjamin Stephenson)

continued overleaf

nor payment for their use. Finally, Stanford may have viewed this as a way in which he could discard the 'Festival oratorio' style, with which he had enjoyed no previous success. Having made this decision for the *Requiem*, Stanford returned to the Catholic liturgy for two subsequent Festival works, the *Te Deum* (1897) and *Stabat Mater* (1906).

Example 5.7   *(cont.)*

Example 5.8   *Christopher Patch*, Op. 69, Act I, no. 3, bars 73–80
(text: Benjamin Stephenson)

Stanford looked to other models for guidance, most notably those of Verdi and Dvořák, and he too conceived the *Requiem* for concert, not liturgical, use. Parry's perception of Italianate writing refers to a general simplicity of construction at both macro and micro levels. This aids a directness of expression, which Stanford achieved by a strong preference for homophonic choral textures, recurrent use of antecedent and consequent phrasing, some brilliant orchestration with particularly Verdian use of brass instruments, clear definition of sections, and antiphonal contrast between choir and soloists. Complex thematic relationships are avoided; there are few recurring themes in the work and none are used as leitmotifs. The most notable characteristic of the *Requiem* is its optimism, possibly attributable to Stanford's decision to commemorate the artist Lord Frederic Leighton (died 25 January 1896), with whom he had been acquainted.

Stanford's inspiration sagged at times: the Offertory is too monochrome for its length, while the galumphing 'Quam olim Abrahae' fugue which follows is ungainly both in its subject matter and its execution – the most obvious concession to Festival convention thus backfires. Conversely there is much exemplary writing; the early restraint of the Introit makes the *fortissimo* entries on 'Et lux perpetua' all the more impressive (Ex. 5.9), and the polyphonic Kyrie which follows here sounds appropriate, in contrast to the affectation of the 'Madrigale Spirituale' in *Eden*, so loathed by Bernard Shaw. The Sequence text is difficult for any composer to hold together because of its length, and Stanford started with an unorthodox approach: the 'Dies Irae' is treated by most composers in an explosive manner, but Stanford set it as an approaching storm starting with quiet thunder in the distance and building up to the simultaneous thunder and lightning clap at 'Tuba mirum'. The middle sections meander but once one reaches the 'Lacrimosa' one sees that this was deliberate, for here Stanford brought the Sequence to its biggest and most sustained climax before the 'Pie Jesu' coda; thus it becomes obvious that he viewed the Sequence as one unit and postponed catharsis and closure until the very end.

In the latter part of 1897 Stanford made a politically astute move by accepting the conductorship of the Leeds Philharmonic Society and made his first appearance there on 27 October, conducting Mendelssohn's *Erste Walpurgisnacht* and Parts I and II of *The Creation*. Stanford considered the Leeds chorus to be the finest in the country but, more importantly, the post placed him in geographical proximity to the conductorship of the Leeds Festival, then held by Sullivan, whose health was on the wane. Cowen had already got his foot in the door at Bradford but Stanford usurped him by getting into Leeds itself. The move paid off: Stanford was duly appointed Sullivan's successor in 1900 (see p. 205).

Example 5.9   *Requiem*, Op. 63: (*a*) Introit, bars 1–17; (*b*) Introit, transition to 'Et lux'

Stanford also found himself drawn into three debates on education at Cambridge. The first of these was the ongoing campaign to admit women to degrees. Women had been able to sit the same exams as men for some years, and their ability to do so had been supported by the foundation of Newnham and Girton Colleges, but, although their results were published, they were not placed in the formal class lists and not permitted to graduate. A campaign to admit women to degrees had rumbled on throughout the 1880s and 1890s and reached one of its periodic *crescendi* in 1896–7. Stanford wrote twice to *The Times* on the subject; his second letter is a thorough demonstration of his opposition to the proposed reform:

> The case against giving women degrees or titles to degrees in the older resident universities seems simple enough and can be put very shortly. The more outspoken supporters of the scheme admit that the title of a degree is only an instalment [leading to the conferment of the MA degree and voting rights in Oxford and Cambridge's sovereign bodies] and can only be accepted as such, therefore the question can be dealt with as that of a degree only. If the lesser is accepted the greater will follow as a matter of course.
>
> The reasons which impel many who wish well to the higher education of women to oppose the principle are in plain language the following:-
>
> 1. That the University towns are already overcrowded with students.
>
> 2. That the endowments of the universities can scarcely keep pace with the requirements of those who are new members of them.
>
> 3. That it is a more dignified course for women, who have now learnt at the ladies' colleges how a university is worked, to start one on their own account, where the lectures can be given on all subjects without regard to the difficulties involved by mixed classes, and where the standards of proficiency will be (as is proved by the success of women in the class lists) no lower than that of the Universities for men.
>
> 4. That it is well known that, if women were to accept the principle of a University of their own, ample funds would be subscribed for its endowment.
>
> 5. That competition between the sexes is a most injurious principle, the results of which [i.e. physiological and mental] cannot be measured perhaps for decades.
>
> 6. That the endowments of the older universities were intended for the education of men in theology, law, medicine and arts. Women cannot be ordained, cannot be called to the bar, or practise as solicitors, and can only to a very limited extent practise in medicine; if however they become members of the university they must logically share in all its endowments, even in faculties where no career is

open to them, and moreover must also share in its more disagreeable functions of discipline and home government.

7. That if the principle of mixed education is to be adopted, it must
logically be made applicable to the schools also.

> I have every respect for those who unhesitatingly approve of a
> mixed education; but to apply it at first at the University is to begin
> at the top rung of the ladder, instead of at the bottom. In Cambridge
> at all events, the machinery for working a mixed university requires
> a larger space than the place can supply. Therefore, as a strong
> supporter of the higher education of women, I oppose their admis-
> sion to a degree or to the title of a degree.[53]

The other two debates were of direct relevance to Stanford in his capacity
as Professor of Music; one was blatantly public, one almost completely
private, but both involved Stanford's RCM colleague Sir Frederick
Bridge. The public debate was on the subject of compulsory residence
for music degrees; Cambridge had approved Stanford's proposals, but
in 1898 Oxford's Hebdomadal Council, supported by Bridge, had
rejected a similar proposal there. During this process, Bridge had made
statements about the quality of musical education at Cambridge which
Stanford felt bound to refute:

> [A] serious statement has been made by Sir Frederick Bridge in a
> recent letter sent to every member of the Hebdomadal Council of
> Oxford University, which has been published in a musical periodi-
> cal. He has stated that 'the work demanded from candidates
> [at Cambridge] is not by any means equal to that exacted from myself
> when I passed at Oxford 30 years ago nor in one subject – viz. coun-
> terpoint – is it equal to that recently set at the Universities of Oxford,
> Durham, and Victoria; when I have acted as Examiner' . . .
> I deny absolutely that the standard of Cambridge musical exam-
> inations is one whit inferior to that of any other University, as
> can be proved by the fact that candidates who have failed in these
> 'easier' papers have shortly after passed on the 'severer' papers of
> other universities; and, moreover, I am in a position to affirm that
> the standard has been considerably raised of late by the excellence
> of the candidates themselves (not by any additional requirements
> from the examiners) who have entered under the new conditions of
> residence and general education, and who have in music, as in other
> branches of learning, have naturally profited by the results of
> residence and that education.[54]

Bridge's reply claimed that Cambridge's experiment had failed and has,
to anyone who has followed any debate about the quality of education,
a familiar ring:

---

[53] Stanford to *The Times*, 18 Mar. 1897, p. 8. See also Stanford to *The Times*, 5 Feb.
1896, p. 11.
[54] Stanford to *The Times*, 28 Nov. 1898, p. 10.

Under the old scheme in 1894 no fewer than eight gentlemen passed their final and took the MusBac degree, [whereas] in the present year, under the new arrangement only two have presented themselves and passed. If the Cambridge Professor is satisfied with this result of the change, and considers it augurs hopefully for the future of the faculty at his University by all means let him think so; he will find few serious musicians to agree with him, and happily, the Oxford authorities have shown that they do not.

With reference to my statements as to work demanded of candidates at Cambridge, as compared with that exacted from me at Oxford 30 yeas ago, I desire to say:- Besides the paperwork, I had to compose a long cantata, containing among other things five part fugues &c, the whole accompanied by string orchestra – as a matter of fact, mine was scored for full orchestra. This I had to perform, and had also to show my practical ability by conducting it in public. At Cambridge this exercise is swept away, and instead the candidate composes some ridiculously easy tests – a minuet and trio for strings being the only example of his powers of scoring.[55]

Three more letters followed in the same vein – as usual Stanford had the last word, and the match might be declared a draw.[56] The bad-tempered tone of the exchange may reflect the fact that in the other falling-out with Bridge, earlier in the year, Stanford had accused him of betraying the confidentiality of the Cambridge Board of Examiners – in a manner which just happened to show Stanford in a bad light.[57]

---

[55] Bridge to *The Times*, 30 Nov. 1898, p. 11.

[56] See *The Times*, 2 Dec. 1898, p. 8 (Stanford); 4 Dec., p. 10 (Bridge) and 6 Dec., p. 8 (Stanford).

[57] In the *Musical Times* (1 May 1898, p. 307) the following anecdote had appeared: 'Here is an examination story for the authenticity of which we can absolutely vouch. Its 'behind the scenes' nature will doubtless make it of special interest to those who seek to get on, or get honours, by degrees. Wild horses will not drag [from us] the name of the University where the incident occurred. The examiners were the Professor of Music, a distinguished foreign musician, and an eminent Cathedral organist, who related to us the story in the following abridged form: The Professor in composing an oratorio, had undergone a course of special reading with _____ (Ah! the name must be withheld) on the Old Church Modes. With a natural desire to test the candidates in his newly acquired knowledge, he had set some Old Church Mode questions in the paper. When the *viva voce* examination came on, the distinguished foreigner said (somewhat confidentially) to the eminent cathedralist, 'I don't know anything about Old Church Modes.' 'No more do I', was the frank reply of his colleague. It may therefore be assumed that when the examiners came up for their *viva voce*, the *modus operandi* of two out of the three learned examiners was to *look* very wise as the Professor put his Old Church Mode interrogatories to the luckless candidates.' It was obvious to Stanford, as it was doubtless to many others, that the University was Cambridge and that Stanford was the Professor. The other two examiners were Joachim and Bridge – evidently Bridge was the source of the anecdote. In two letters to F. G. Edwards (editor of the *Musical Times*) Stanford railed against this breach of confidentiality; while technically true, it is clear that he really took exception because he was the butt of the joke; see Stanford to Edwards, 3 and 11 May 1898, BL, MS Egerton 3090, fols 179–83.

Though the detailed facts of the matter are trivial, the incident appears to have led to an animosity between Stanford and Bridge which lasted for the remainder of their lives.

The frustrations Stanford had experienced in the operatic field (*Shamus O'Brien* being the sole exception) may have spurred him into launching his campaign for the foundation of a National Opera House in spring 1898. The campaign took the form of a memorial sent to the London County Council supported many prominent musicians and citizens. Mackenzie chaired the committee which drew up the memorial and Parry did much administrative work; Stanford, as was his wont, concentrated on chivvying and lobbying. The memorial deprecated the lack of state support for music, and specifically opera, in Britain, and contrasted this with the policy of other countries, providing detailed figures in support. It asked the LCC for an annual grant to subsidise the running costs of a National Opera House when it was established. Signed by Sullivan, Stainer, Parratt, Grove, Cowen, MacCunn, Bridge, German, Fuller Maitland, plus eleven peers, the MPs Joseph Chamberlain, Herbert Asquith and Charles Stuart Wortley, and also Arthur Conan Doyle, George Watts, Henry Irving and Squire Bancroft, the memorial was presented to the LCC on 21 June. The Council subsequently found in favour of the scheme but would not fund the institution from its own budget. Stanford tried to revive the scheme by writing a long letter to *The Times* in March 1899 and stimulated some media interest but he was unsuccessful in gaining anything substantive.[58]

Composition continued relatively slowly; following the *Te Deum*, the Variations on 'Down among the Dead Men', Op. 71 were completed in March 1898. Stanford also set lines from Tennyson's *The Princess* (Op. 68), Heine's *Die Wallfahrt nach Kevlaar* (Op. 72) and completed the second Piano Trio in G minor (Op. 73) on 23 January 1899 and the First Violin Concerto (Op. 74) on 12 November. In addition to this work and his regular teaching and conducting, Stanford also became a director of the Philharmonic Society, but when Mackenzie gave up the conductorship a year later Stanford resigned on the grounds that it would be invidious to be both a director and a candidate for the vacant post.

---

[58] See Stanford to *The Times*, 11 Mar. 1899, p. 10. This letter was followed by others from Mackenzie (27 Mar. 1899, p. 8), Lord Dysart and Sir Martin Conway (both 28 Mar. 1899, p. 10) and a leading article (28 Mar. 1899, p. 9). Stanford was subsequently drawn into a debate about the scheme with A. P. Herbert (see *The Times*, 1 Apr. 1899, p. 10 (Herbert), 4 Apr. 1899, p. 6 (Stanford), 11 Apr. 1899, p. 10 (Herbert) and 19 Apr. 1899, p. 4 (Stanford)).

Cowen was appointed, to Stanford's chagrin, and Stanford's resignation led to a third spat with Frederick Bridge.[59]

The *Te Deum* was premièred at the Leeds Festival on 6 October 1898. Dedicated to Queen Victoria, as a recognition of her diamond jubilee, the work is cast in the same 'Italianate' style as the *Requiem* and was well received by the *Musical Times*: 'The work must be pronounced among the best balanced and best sustained of all Dr Stanford's compositions. Though the *Te Deum*, as a text for music, does not afford the same opportunity for emotional treatment [as the *Requiem*] it is perhaps more evenly sustained and better balanced.'[60] Once again Stanford concentrated on simple thematic material, episodic and transparent construction, and some brash orchestration to capture the mood of the text. Although, as the *Musical Times* remarked, the predominantly laudatory nature of the text restricted Stanford's variety of expression, the work still captures an appropriate sense of celebration and praise.

In April 1900 Stanford asked Cambridge to confer three more honorary doctorates, this time on Elgar, Cowen and the American composer Horatio Parker. His letter of recommendation indicates that he was more politically astute than many have given him credit for: 'Do try and get them all if you can but *in especial* try and get Elgar in with Cowen. The musical profession is a curious mixture and I think I am gauging it right in saying that they ought both to be in the list to keep the balance [presumably between 'old' and 'new'] right.'[61] All three recommendations were accepted; Elgar and Cowen received their degrees on 22 November 1900, but Parker had to wait until 10 June 1902, on which occasion, coincidentally, Richard Henn-Collins, Fellow of Downing College, Master of the Rolls, and a cousin of Stanford's, also received an honorary doctorate. Stanford was unable to attend the congregation at which Elgar and Cowen received their degrees due to a meeting in Leeds about the Festival (see p. 205); it has been suggested that he wished to avoid Cowen, with whom he did not get on (and who was his rival to succeed Sullivan),[62] but Stanford had already advised Elgar that other commitments would prevent him from being present.[63]

On 4 May 1900 the 'Dead Men' Variations were premièred by the Philharmonic Society, with Leonard Borwick taking the solo role. This, and the Clarinet Concerto, are Stanford's most successful works for soloist and orchestra, and the earlier work benefits from the concision

[59] See Stanford to Francisco Berger, 19 July 1899, BL, MS Loan 48.13/32, fols. 256–9.
[60] *Musical Times*, 1 Nov. 1898, pp. 731–2.
[61] Stanford to Austen Leigh, 26 Apr. 1900, CUL, MS CUR 39.10.1.
[62] See Jerrold Northrop Moore, *Edward Elgar: A Creative Life* (Oxford, 1984), 337.
[63] See Stanford to Elgar, 24 Oct. 1900, WRO, 5247: 7398.

Table 5.1　Variations on 'Down among the Dead Men', Op. 71

Variation	Key	'Movement'	Comments
Introduction	c	Introduction leading to:	Fragments of theme displayed
Theme	c	*Allegro*	
I	c		Variations I and II are given out in the normal fashion; Variation III, with its shifts between tonic and relative major and legato writing, suggests the second subject of a symphonic exposition
II	c		
III	c and E♭		
IV	c	*Scherzo*	Both characterised by staccato scalic quaver movement
V	C		
VI	C	*Trio*	Contrast by broad, sweeping melody
VII (Intermezzo)	c to V of E♭	Bridge from *Trio* to:	Staccato of Scherzo and legato of Trio combined; second half a dominant pedal preparation for Var. VIII
VIII	E♭	*Andante tranquillo*	Legato melody with filigree decoration
IX	E♭ to V of c	*Andante* and bridging *Allegro*	*Andante* more decorative than preceding; bridge a dominant pedal introduction to Var. X
X	c	*Allegro* restatement	Closest to restatement of Theme but altered from 4/4 to 6/8
XI	A♭	Introduction leading to:	Quasi 'Marcia Funèbre' followed by modulating transition to Var. XII
XII (Finale)	c to C	*Finale*	Compressed sonata form with coda

demanded by the variation concept. Although the work is divided into an introduction, theme and twelve variations, it is more successfully read as an abridged and continuous symphony (see Table 5.1). Stanford's skill lay in running variations into each other so that they form not only a satisfactory whole, but groups or 'movements' within the piece (similar to the procedure used by both Dvořák and Parry in their Symphonic Variations). The simple dispersal of keys also helps in this as all the bridging variations lead on and prevent the piece from becoming over-sectionalised; the concern to create a cohesive whole is also demonstrated in Variation X, which, although in 6/8 and significantly altered in other ways also, is intended to be the clearest recall of the Theme, and here the melody is presented in its clearest form since – and with similar orchestration to – the beginning. This, in turn, neatly sets up the penul-timate variation and the Finale, which is itself in a compressed sonata form. This cross-breeding of forms, despite its apparent complication, is successful – the whole piece, which lasts about twenty-five minutes, is wrought into a coherent and satisfying episode which, despite the variety of *tempi* and textures, never lacks direction. The piece shows that, when Stanford applied himself to the consideration of form, he could both adapt existing stereotypes and bring cohesiveness over long stretches, producing successful extended compositions; one can see further instances in later pieces (for example, parts of *Much Ado* and the Seventh Symphony) and can only wish that he had had the time and inclination to apply this skill more frequently. Not only is Stanford's command of form at its best here, but his writing genuinely seems to look forward: here, partly because of the piano and orchestra combi-nation, one can see fleeting glances of the Rachmaninov/Adinsell 'film' style. It appears to be a nice coincidence that the opening of the theme presented in Variation VI is almost a quotation of the first theme of the Finale of the Fifth Symphony and even more curious that such an inven-tive piece in this format should be composed in the same year as Elgar wrote the 'Enigma' Variations; while Elgar undoubtedly got the fame he deserved for his work, it is a pity that Stanford did not do as well with a piece that deserved more attention than it has received.

On 15 May 1900 Stanford completed a short cantata, *The Last Post*, Op. 75, a setting of words by W. E. Henley. The work was first given at a state concert at Buckingham Palace on 25 June, but received its first public performance at the Hereford Festival on 11 September. It is an elegy for those killed in the Boer War, then at its height. The crisis in South Africa had been a running sore for Stanford for over four years, ever since the 'Kruger telegram' (see p. 183), but by May 1900 the dispute had just turned in Britain's favour (Ladysmith was relieved on 28 February, Mafeking on 17 May, and Lord Roberts reached

Johannesburg two weeks later; Stanford also commemorated the role of Irish troops in South Africa by publishing a new version of 'The Wearing of the Green' (see p. 389)). Henley's words are valedictory but unashamedly imperialist and the music is in sympathy with this mood – realising, perhaps, that the Boer War had some distance to run – and anticipates Great War works such as Elgar's *For the Fallen* in spirit if not in style. The music is not profound but the slow sections have a sense of nobility which is appropriate; the off-stage bugler playing the 'Last Post' at the beginning and end of piece imbues it with an air of poignancy. Inevitably, given the highly individual political circumstances which gave rise to it, the work did not stay in the repertory; in the Great War, when it might have come back into frequent use, it was overtaken by other works.

In the midst of these events, Stanford's attention was drawn much closer to home by the death of George Grove on 28 May 1900. Grove had been one of his great mentors, and Stanford, along with many others from the RCM and elsewhere, attended his funeral at Sydenham three days later. No doubt the event was a deeply moving one for Stanford: although Grove had had equivocal feelings about him for a long time, Stanford had worshipped Grove almost without qualification, and was one of the few people with whom he had never quarrelled.

During summer 1900 Stanford turned once again to composing opera, this time setting Shakespeare's *Much Ado about Nothing*. Edward Dent indicates that Stanford's choice was highly pragmatic:

> Lloyd told us of Stanford's forthcoming opera for Covent Garden: Beatrice and Benedick. 'I asked him – I said – "Where do you get all your ideas from?" and he said "Well, to tell ye the truth I got that one as I was sitting on the water closet." '[64]

In fact indirect inspiration probably came from a number of sources: Stanford had been impressed by Verdi's two Shakespeare operas, *Otello* and *Falstaff*, and he also had soft spots for Nicolai's *Die lustigen Weiber von Windsor* and Goetz's *Der Widerspänstigen Zähmung*, both of which he produced at the RCM in the late 1880s. Shakespeare's plays themselves were enjoying increased popularity, *Much Ado* being produced in London five times between 1891 and 1901.[65] Stanford asked Julian Sturgis to write the libretto.[66] He started composing the work while he and Jennie were on holiday in Malvern, the four acts being dated

---

[64] Dent's Diary, 21 Nov. 1900, KCC.
[65] See J. P. Wearing, *The London Stage 1890–99*, 2 vols (Metuchen, NJ, 1976).
[66] Julian Russell Sturgis (b. Boston, Mass., 1848, d. London 1904) came to England at the age of seven months; he was educated at Eton and Balliol, taking a BA in Classics, 1872. He practised as a barrister but, well provided for, spent most of his life writing

7 August, 21 August, 9 September and 27 September 1900 respectively. Stanford told David Bispham, who played Benedick in the Covent Garden première, 'it ran right out of the end of my pen'.[67]

In December 1900 Stanford was appointed to succeed Sullivan as conductor of the Leeds Festival. His candidature appears to have received broad support from the Festival Committee although others had expressed an interest in the post. Sullivan's vulnerability had been well known since the 1898 festival, when illness had rendered his attendance uncertain and it was made clear to him in 1899 that the Committee was not prepared to reappoint him on this account; his resignation was announced in December 1899.[68] Sullivan was furious but the committee was proved correct in its judgement as he died on 22 November 1900 – ironically, perhaps, Stanford was in Leeds on the same day discussing the festival, and his rival Cowen was in Cambridge receiving his honorary doctorate. There had already been some jockeying for position. Elgar had written to Percy Buck to urge his contacts on the Committee to support either Cowen or Elgar himself for the post; it is a reflection of the strange relationship between Elgar and Stanford at this point that Elgar wrote that the Committee ought 'to appoint anyone rather than Stanford – it will about kill the Festival artistically if he gets in'.[69] Stanford's conductorship of the Leeds Philharmonic Society placed him foremost in the mind of the Festival Committee and this must have aided his candidature. But any overt suggestion that Stanford had only taken the Philharmonic post merely to get a foot in the door annoyed him extremely: in February 1900 he had nearly launched a libel action again Henry Labouchere, publisher of *Truth*, after it printed a paragraph which implied that he had curried favour with Leeds by using some of its singers to bolster the Bach Choir.[70] In the end Stanford let the matter go but legal advice he received from both Richard Henn-Collins and from Sir George Lewis, 'Labby's' lawyer and an acquaintance of Stanford, suggested that the article was indeed a bad

---

novels. He also wrote the libretti of Sullivan's *Ivanhoe* (1891) and Goring Thomas's *Nadeshda* (1885).

[67] David Bispham, *A Quaker Singer's Recollections* (New York, 1920), 294.

[68] See Arthur Jacobs, *Arthur Sullivan* (2nd edn, Oxford, 1986), 389–90.

[69] Elgar to Buck, 17 Nov. 1899, quoted in Jeremy Northrop Moore, *Edward Elgar – Letters of a Life Time* (Oxford, 1990), 81–2.

[70] See *Truth*, 1 Feb. 1900, p. 277: 'The Bach Choir will give only one concert this year, namely a performance of Bach's great Mass in B Minor. For this, as I understand, a strong contingent from Leeds will come to London. The employment of the Leeds singers has, of course, nothing – no, absolutely nothing – to do with the vacant conductorship of the Leeds Festival.' In fact, the implied compliment to Leeds reads more as if it might be a measure of desperation, taken to shore up a declining Bach Choir (see pp. 236–7).

libel.[71] In retrospect Stanford's denials seem suspicious and it is tempting to believe that his acceptance of the Philharmonic conductorship was premeditated. But his assertions were adamant and he would have been on thin ice had he taken Labouchere to court;[72] perhaps, therefore, his motives were more altruistic than one might suppose – notably, he remained conductor of the Leeds Philharmonic for several years after he had been appointed Festival conductor, suggesting a genuine enjoyment of the task.

Whatever the circumstances of his appointment, Stanford looked forward to the 1901 Festival with pleasure, and wrote to Herbert Thompson:

> I am coming down tomorrow morning to see T[homas] Marshall and Spark [Chairman and Secretary of the Festival Committee respectively]. I hope we shall all be on velvet, and keep so. We shall if they consult with me as a rule. I don't mean if they agree with me as a rule, which is a very different thing, and which I don't expect. But consultation means confidence . . .
>
> It would be great fun to do the Verdi *Requiem* (with the Sanctus up to time!) And as you love Italians like me, how splendid would be the Final to Act II of Tell. I heard it done in the concert room (at the Gewandhaus) and it made a terrific effect. But perhaps they will have none of these things which we love![73]

Stanford's relationship with the Committee turned out to be a variable one but for once this was not all his own fault, for his complaints (see p. 240) were the same as those of Sullivan before him.

On 7 March 1901 Stanford's First Violin Concerto was premièred at Bournemouth. While the form of the 'Dead Men' Variations had encouraged brevity, Stanford's return to the standard three-movement concerto format provoked prolixity. The work appears to suffer from something of an identity crisis: the opening of the first movement presages a light, sparkling piece, but the movement as a whole is long-winded and vacillates between the opening levity and the need to make a serious

---

[71] For an account of Stanford's encounter with Labouchere see Stanford, *Pages*, 289–98. A denial also followed after a similar suggestion was made by B. W. Findon (*Sir Arthur Sullivan* (London, 1904), 164–6); see Stanford to *The Times*, 26 Sept. 1904, p. 4. Findon subsequently withdrew the book and rewrote the offending page (see Findon to *The Times*, 27 Sept. 1904, p. 6).

[72] Stanford failed to press the matter, he wrote, because Labouchere did insert an apology of sorts (see Stanford, *Pages*, 298); but even if he had not been as magnanimous as he himself implies, probably a libel action would have been more trouble than it was worth since the defence could have argued that an apology had been printed and that the prosecution was vindictive.

[73] Stanford to Thompson, 17 Dec. 1900, LUL, MS 361, item 268.

statement. The second movement has a length more appropriate to the strength of its material, but in the last movement again there is too much padding. The work was not taken up by violinists and, although Fritz Kreisler performed it at the Leeds Festival in 1904 and Rivarde gave it with the Philharmonic Society in 1905, the concerto never established itself.

In London, meanwhile, Stanford secured the première of *Much Ado* at Covent Garden. He had, however, a sanguine opinion of the management and wrote to Elgar, 'I am told that *Much Ado* will come out in the second week of the season, that is the week beginning May 20th [1901]. But I don't quite expect it; it depends on rehearsals.'[74] The first performance was set for 24 May and he was surprised about the time being spent on his work, writing to Elgar once more, 'It's going very well, and they are actually rehearsing it hard.'[75] The inevitable hitches followed, however, and the opening night was postponed twice to 30 May with a second performance on 3 June. The opera was well received and got good reviews but there were no more performances. Rumours circulated that Stanford was not happy with the way in which he had been treated.[76] Stanford's explanation for the opera's withdrawal and for his annoyance were reported by Edward Dent:

> A certain illustrious – or moderately illustrious – lady was interested in the performance of *Messaline*, a French opera by Isidore de Lara ... and according to Stanford's story she refused to pay the deficit on De Lara's opera unless Stanford's was set aside as a failure. Stanford had definitely been promised three performances, but he was only given two.[77]

Stanford's fortunes turned, however, and it was later announced that the Moody Manners Opera Company would take the work on a provincial tour in autumn 1901 and that it had been booked for future production at Leipzig.

Despite only receiving two performances at Covent Garden the opera was generally well received by the press; unsurprisingly, Fuller Maitland waxed lyrical in *The Times*: 'It is beyond question that [Stanford's] newest work reaches a higher degree of beauty, of sustained dramatic

---

[74] Stanford to Elgar, 11 Apr. 1901, WRO, 5247: 7403.

[75] Stanford to Elgar, 12 May 1901, WRO, 5427: 7405.

[76] *Era* (3 Aug. 1901, p. 11) reported that 'Dr Villiers Stanford may feel that two performances of *Much Ado About Nothing* hardly did justice to himself or his work'; it is not clear whether this was merely a relay of Stanford's feelings or that the *Era* felt he was justified in feeling badly done to.

[77] Edward Dent, *Selected Essays* (Cambridge, 1979), 233. The 'moderately illustrious lady' was the Princesse de Monaco (see Isidore de Lara, *Many Tales of Many Cities* (London, 1928)).

interest, and of real distinction of style than any of his former operas.
The action is carried on with very great skill in a flowing and really
vocal style and with such rich and individual orchestration as is most
rare.'[78] There were also positive comments in the *Era* and the *Sketch*;[79]
other reviews were complimentary but qualified, the *Athenaeum* and the
Musical Times both being more guarded:

> Dr Stanford's music seems to us to lack soul, and then again the
> influence of other composers argues against marked originality, but
> the manner in which he expresses himself is so direct, the varied
> moods are so appropriate, the contrasts so striking, that his work,
> though not masterly, is full of excellent effective music, and is one
> of which the composer has good reason to be proud.[80]

> [Stanford's] catholic tastes, his wide musical knowledge and his
> power of assimilating various styles have prevented him from slav-
> ishly imitating one master.[81]

Only John Runciman of the *Saturday Review* condemned the opera, but
he did so with gusto:

> There are pretty moments, as for example the earlier part of the
> second act; but the attempts in the grand manner hopelessly fail to
> come off. The effect of bells and organ and plainchant is exceed-
> ingly cheap at this time of day and it is carried out in a shockingly
> perfunctory manner – it almost suggests that Dr Stanford, being a
> busy man, had asked one of his pupils to do the job. But, whether
> fine or poor, the music struck me as always second hand. It is the
> least original thing Dr Stanford has written.[82]

Is this press comment fair? Overall, Stanford deserved to do better
than this; although not as successful as *Shamus O'Brien*, *Much Ado* has
stood the test of time better and is his first mature opera and the first
with an adequate book. Sturgis left Shakespeare's basic scenario almost
unaltered, although several subsidiary characters are eliminated or amal-
gamated and several scenes are cut, including the whole of Act I (although
some dialogue is transplanted into Act II, that is, Stanford's Act I).
Episodes reported in Shakespeare are added into the direct action of the
scenario, notably Hero's infidelity; the result is well balanced dramatically. More notable is Sturgis's extensive use of Shakespeare's dialogue,
which is important, as much of *Much Ado* was written in prose rather
than blank verse (Benedick and Beatrice generally speak in prose). The

[78] *The Times*, 31 May 1901, p. 4.
[79] See *Era*, 1 June 1901, p. 9, and *Sketch*, 5 June 1901, pp. 277–8.
[80] *Athenaeum*, 8 June 1901, p. 733.
[81] *Musical Times*, 1 July 1901, p. 388.
[82] *Saturday Review*, 8 June 1901, p. 735.

result is unusual since the prose libretto was a rarity in 1900. The most striking instance is Stanford's Act III (based on Shakespeare's Act IV, Scene 1) in which Benedick and Beatrice finally profess their love for each other and Beatrice tells Benedick that he must kill Claudio to avenge Hero. Sturgis's amendments to the original are minimal, although it is a telling comment on Victorian preferences that Sturgis used 'thou' where Shakespeare wrote 'you'. Sturgis's own words (for example, in Claudio and Hero's Act II Love Duet) have a spirit of Victorian romanticism but sit reasonably comfortably with those of Shakespeare. Stanford coped well with the irregular metrical structures implied by the use of prose; periodisation is highly irregular but structural integrity is preserved throughout by the use of short motifs (for example, Act III, in which most motifs are given out in the orchestral prelude).

Stanford had also made good progress with characterisation. The verbal sparring of Beatrice and Benedick suited his wit and these are the most successful characters, but Claudio, Hero, Pedro and John are also more than stereotypes. The treatment of Dogberry and the constables is less successful: they form a running thread of comedy in the play but are reduced to a single appearance in Act IV in the opera and do not, consequently, have chance to establish themselves; additionally, Stanford does not underline the difference between 'high' and 'low' characters, an essential part of Shakespeare's play.

In terms of musical construction *Much Ado* was by far the most sophisticated of Stanford's operas to date. Cast in number format, the opera achieves a greater sense of musical unity through the use of large-scale musical constructions and the repetition and development of a number of themes and motifs. Hero and Claudio's Act II love duet exemplifies this; the orchestral introduction is influenced by the 'Waldweben' section of *Siegfried* (like *Eden*), while Claudio's Serenade is an example of Stanford at his best, with delicate orchestration, including liberal use of mandolin and harp, and an almost impressionistic use of secondary sevenths creating a degree of tonal ambiguity and impressionistic haziness reminiscent of some French song. The movement in the second stanza from A major to an unprepared $G\natural$ in the bass, with the attendant blur between E minor^7 and G^6 is a perfect Stanfordian shift of tonality (Ex. 5.10). The remainder of the scene, the love duet proper, is based on varied strophic form, with Stanford using subtly modified phrase lengths and harmonic progressions to provide a balance of coherence and variation (Ex. 5.11). The 'Waldweben' and mandolin motifs supply an overarching sense of unity across the whole scene. While the means of construction are relatively simple, it is the wide span of the music and the conception of it as a unified whole which are worthy of attention. Stanford had attempted this in opera before but this was the

Example 5.10 *Much Ado about Nothing*, Op. 76a, Act II, bars 68–76, Claudio's Serenade (text: Julian Sturgis)

Example 5.11 *Much Ado about Nothing*, Op. 76a, Act II, Love Duet, skeleton harmonic structure of refrains 1–3

Example 5.12 *Much Ado about Nothing*, Op. 76a, Act I, bars 230–32

Example 5.13 *Much Ado about Nothing*, Op. 76a, Act III, bars 12–14

first time he met with success. This is also the only successful love duet in any of Stanford's operas (neither *The Critic* nor *The Travelling Companion* contains love duets); it is not coincidental that this is also the only one of Stanford's love duets in which the characters are not living in fear of external menace, but are at peace with themselves and their surroundings.

Much Ado does not just depend on localised standard forms for structural coherence: the opera is the first in which Stanford approached a truly Wagnerian system of leitmotifs. The technique is not as thorough as that found in Wagner's mature works but there are examples of variation, transformation and combination of motifs which he had not attempted hitherto. The motifs of Pedro and Hero are combined in Act I to show Claudio's love for Hero and his admiration for Don Pedro (Hero's father) (Ex. 5.12). In Act III Hero's motif is transformed from the wistful sighing quality it first exhibits to a tempestuous minor subject, while in the prelude to the act it is combined with Don John's curse motif – thus indicating the source of the 'ado' and its victim (Hero in a minor key) (Ex. 5.13). Two further examples link Acts III and IV: the motif which represents the effects of Don John's curse at the opening of Act III reappears in Act IV when Pedro and Claudio realise that they have been the victims of John's treachery (Ex. 5.14), and the passage in

Example 5.14   *Much Ado about Nothing*, Op. 76a: (*a*) Act III, bars 62–8; (*b*)
              Act IV, bars 471–4 (text: Julian Sturgis after Shakespeare)

Act III in which the Friar suggests that Leonato's family should pretend
that Hero is dead (also based on the 'effects of the curse') reappears in
Act IV when Claudio begs the Friar's forgiveness for slandering his lover,
thus bringing both the plot and the music full circle. Stanford's attention to detail extends beyond this since he connected Beatrice's lament
(the preceding section in Act IV) to Claudio's repentance (Ex. 5.15), and
thus all the consequences of John's actions are worked out through the
development of these two motifs.

   None of the musical techniques noted above was new: Stanford built
on developments of others, principally Verdi and Wagner, but *Much
Ado* does show that he was possessed of an undoubted technical mastery
and a degree of inspiration which, when directed by a good libretto,
could lead him to compose a fine, coherent, dramatic and moving opera.

Example 5.15   *Much Ado about Nothing*, Op. 76a: (*a*) Act III, bars 320–23;
(*b*) Act IV, bars 545–53 (text: Julian Sturgis after Shakespeare)

Although the spirit of *Die Meistersinger* hovers above it (for example, in the 'music for a summer's evening' nature of the music, the innocence of Claudio and Hero paralleling that of Walther and Eva, and the fumbling comedy of Beckmesser and Dogberry), the opera is none the worse for it.

The 1901 Leeds Festival occupied the four days commencing 9 October. The arrangements had been falling into place steadily over the previous few months and the programme, designed to be a retrospective of the nineteenth century, had been approved in outline in May (though, as Stanford wrote to Elgar about the 'Enigma Variations' in June, 'You must not talk about this to anyone, as the Committee may play all sorts of variations on my theme yet').[83] The whole package represented a balanced and varied programme (see Table 5.2).

---

[83] Stanford to Elgar, 30 June 1901, WRO, 5427: 7406.

Table 5.2 Principal works performed at the Leeds Festival, 1901

9 October		
(morning)	Sullivan	Overture 'In Memoriam'
	Handel	*Messiah*
(evening)	Coleridge Taylor	*The Blind Girl*
	Brahms	Piano Concerto No. 2
10 October		
(morning)	Verdi	*Requiem*
	Stanford	*The Last Post*
(evening)	Beethoven	Overture 'Leonora No. 2'
	Rossini	Finale of Act II of *William Tell*
11 October		
(morning)	Mendelssohn	Psalm 98
	Schumann	Symphony No. 4
	Wagner	Finale of Act I of *Parsifal*
(evening)	Cherubini	Overture 'Les Deux journées'
	Brahms	*Rinaldo*
	Elgar	'Enigma' Variations
	Glazunov	*Memorial Cantata*
12 October		
(morning)	Beethoven	*Missa Solemnis*

Many other composers were also represented: Palestrina, Schubert, Bach, Tchaikovsky, Parry, German, Charles Wood, Rossini, Auber, Sterndale Bennett, Saint-Saëns, Gounod, Mackenzie, Cowen, Bruch, Mozart, Weber, Haydn, Goring Thomas, Pearsall and Dvořák. Nearly all of this mammoth programme was conducted by Stanford himself and it is indeed a view of the previous hundred years with very few then popular names missing. One can see also that Stanford had exercised considerable influence in the choice of the programme: the works by Rossini and Elgar were definitely a result of his lobbying and one can be fairly certain that much of the other English music, and the works by Brahms, Glazunov and Bruch (all composers for whom he had a high regard) were also included as a result of his advice. There were adverse comments from some quarters that Sullivan was under-represented and that there was a dearth of novelties compared with a typical Leeds or Birmingham Festival.[84] Stanford's reading of the *Messiah* was also a novelty to some

---

[84] See *The Times*, 10 Oct. 1901, p. 8.

since he revived what he understood to be the Dublin traditions of the first performance, generally characterised by much faster *tempi*. Overall, however, Stanford had chosen well to give an overview of the previous century and was praised for his first attempt; Joachim was presented with a silver salver to commemorate his first appearance at Leeds in 1858. Many felt that all this activity gave Leeds a new breath of life after Sullivan's long stewardship and the Festival Committee had no reason to complain about a profit of over £1,600.

It seems strange, given the status that Stanford enjoyed at this time, that he should feel neglected by the public and by musicians. But in November 1901 he wrote a long letter to Richter asking for help:

> I am going boldly to ask you if you can see your way some day to do my *Requiem* at Manchester, or failing that, the *Te Deum*. When the *Requiem* came out at Birmingham, Forsyth told me that he wanted it done at Manchester: but that Cowen (because at that time he had not got an *honoris causa* degree at Cambridge!) refused to do it. In London there is but one Choral Society now, the Albert Hall: no chance for anything which is not published by Messrs. Novello, or is not *The Messiah* or *Elijah* or composed by Sir F[rederick] Bridge. These two works are, I know, my best: whether that best is good enough is not for me to say, but I think they are at any rate no worse than other choral works which are being given elsewhere: and they have never been given a chance. You can, if you like, give them, or one of them, that chance: but I know the difficulties and you may find them impossibilities. If so, say no more: I shall not expect anything. You know probably how things are going musically here. Tschaikowsky *Pathetic*, and Wagner, and 3 symphonies or 4 of Beethoven. Of the Englishmen of my generation next to nothing. The younger generation is excellent *Gott Sei Dank*, but it should not in justice cut out entirely the men who prepared the way for them, and who got rid of the Mendelssohn and *Wasser* for them out of this country. Moreover, any Englishman who has the courage to think that Sullivan was not a second Beethoven or Bach is attacked by all the crew who pretend that he was: therefore if some one does not back up the people who have the courage of their opinion (and I have, as you know) we shall go to the wall.
>
> Your answer is obvious: that if the music is good in itself it will eventually take its right place. Quite true: and of that I am convinced as you are. But I am human, and should like a little of it before I am in the next world. I don't say that my miserable compositions are not given at all; but I do say that the best of them are not. And that is why I ask you to give these two things or one of them, a chance.[85]

Was Stanford justified in this appeal? His letter raised a number of points

---

[85] Stanford to Richter, 12 Nov. 1901, RCM, MS 4826, item 31.

about the British musical scene at the turn of the century. There is an evident bitterness directed at both Cowen and Bridge; he had strained relationships with both of them and Bridge, by virtue of being Organist of Westminster Abbey, and Cowen, newly appointed conductor of the Philharmonic Society, both exercised real influence in London. Stanford was about to resign the conductorship of the Bach Choir (see pp. 236–7) and in any case, the programmes of both that organisation and of the RCM Orchestra show that he was fairly reticent about scheduling his own works. His comments on Sullivan may well be a reaction to the criticisms made of the Leeds Festival programme. More significant, however, was the British audience's strange mixture of conservatism and thirst for novelty. The work of Henry Wood had widened the taste of the British audience for music from eastern Europe, and this popularity and the rise of the 'younger generation' (Stanford must have been thinking particularly of Elgar and, to a lesser extent, Coleridge Taylor), was pushing him, Parry and Mackenzie out of the concert halls. Here was the heart of the problem: some works had been taken to the audience's heart but those of Stanford and his contemporaries generally had not: typically works were performed once or twice and then dropped. Stanford was justified in feeling some of this neglect since some of the works which had fallen by the wayside were worthy of regular performance. But in the 'market economy' which he both accepted and applauded the composer had to hit precisely the moving target of popular opinion. Stanford had, of course, done this on occasion (*The Revenge*, the 'Irish' Symphony) and would do so again (*Songs of the Sea, Irish Rhapsody No. 1*) but not often, and not often enough for his own liking. The music-consuming public, meanwhile, did not feel bound to prefer a product simply because it was home-grown.

During autumn 1901 the Moody Manners Company took *Much Ado* on a successful provincial tour but Stanford was still unhappy about the loss of his London performance, and bullied Parry into sanctioning the production of *Much Ado* by the RCM on 29 November. Parry put a brave public face on this decision but it is more likely that he capitulated to pacify Stanford's ongoing campaign to have his teaching fees raised.[86] His diary refers to *Much Ado* as being 'brilliantly clever in parts and bright, but . . . totally inadequate in all the emotional crises'.[87] While Stanford may have been grateful to Parry for this action, Parry should

---

[86] In his report to the RCM Executive Parry said that the opera was chosen 'in view of the the great services which have been rendered to the College by Professor Stanford, as well as for its artistic qualities' (see RCM Executive Committee Minutes, 23 Jan. 1902, RCM).

[87] Parry's Diary, 30 May, 1901, ShP.

have known better than to try to pacify Stanford in this way. Stanford had acquired an increase in his hourly rate of pay in 1897 but he was now campaigning for a salary, similar to that which he received from Cambridge and which Parry received from the College. The first salvo was launched by Stanford in a letter to Parry on 27 October 1901:

> My position at the college, from the point of view of emolument, is and has been for some time on the downward grade. The actual composition teaching is very small and by the nature of things (for composers are scarce) has to be so. During this term it sank lower than ever, to three hours a week; and at the rate of work which I have had to do this term the whole year's teaching at the College, including everything, represents to me only some £350 (in rough terms) as against £450 to £470 some three or four years ago. It is, I imagine, about 50% lower than the income of most of the professors who care to take much teaching. I cannot think that the work which I do for the Orchestra, some seventy-two rehearsals and six concerts, is adequately met by the £170 which I get for it; and I am perfectly certain that if I were incapacitated tomorrow, no one of the position and experience necessary for that work could be induced to take it for less than three times that amount. The fee for concerts is the same as that which is paid to a principal wind player at a [professional] concert, and less by one half than that paid to a leader of the violins. If Richter were engaged to conduct a College Concert his fee would be fifty guineas. I get three.
>
> I feel, moreover, that the wear and tear involved in Orchestral and Operatic Rehearsals is very much greater than that of ordinary teaching, and ought to be dealt with in a different way . . .
>
> Therefore I think that the post of Orchestra and Opera Conductor deserves to be taken out of the payment-by-hour principle, and be paid for by a proper and reasonable salary, which would, to some extent, equalise the position which the Conducting Professor holds with that of his colleagues who, from the nature of their work, are able to earn a more 'living wage'.
>
> I have worked since the opening of the College at this department, and have devoted myself entirely to tuition there, refusing all outside pupils (which are of course a much more renumerative asset) in order to keep myself for its duties. When I gave up my Cambridge work, the then Registrar . . . told me that I could count on getting not less than £150 a term for my College work. For a time this was so, but it has now fallen 25%. Men of my age in full possession of their working powers do not expect their incomes from the profession to decrease largely as they get older and more experienced.[88]

Parry laid the letter before the RCM Executive on 5 December. Stanford's case was somewhat undermined by the production of statistics

---

[88] Stanford to Parry, 27 Oct. 1901, RCM Executive Committee Minutes, 5 Dec. 1901, RCM.

showing that his income from the college for each year since 1896–7 had been £380, £480, £469, £419 and £427 respectively (the increase in 1897–8 reflecting the increase he had then negotiated), although his assertion that his income had recently fallen and that he was not making the £450 he had been led to expect in 1893 was true. The Executive decided that they could not accede to the request for a salary but approved instead increased fees: an orchestral rehearsal would increase from £2.2.0 to £2.10.0. The biggest increases, however, were to apply to the rarest occasions so the package amounted only to about £60 extra each year.

On the following morning Parry wrote to Stanford communicating the Executive's decision. Stanford was livid:

> A long and extremely disagreeable interview with Stanford who is furious at the proposals for increasing his fees without granting his request for a fixed independent stipend. He maintained that his work was quite of a different nature and value to all the other professors, and should be treated on a different footing, which I could not admit, as we should have no hold on him.[89]

A typical sulk followed. On the following day Parry wrote 'saw Stanford at orchestral practice and he was thunderous',[90] and three days later, 'final orchestral concert ... went very well, though Stanford was even more black and gloomy than ever. Mrs. Stanford tried to cut Maude and me.'[91] Perhaps what infuriated Stanford more than anything else was the fact that Parry made clear his support of the Executive's policy. Further exchanges of correspondence followed and Parry reported to the Executive on 23 January 1902 that Stanford had resolved that as

> the policy of the Committee was also the policy of the Director he was not going to press what he considered to be the justice of his claims in the teeth of the opposition of the Director. He preferred to leave the responsibility for the decision with the Director and Committee feeling that to push the matter further would be futile and would be to urge his case beyond the point which personal friendship or loyalty to the head of the College would allow.[92]

This may have been what Stanford had *written* to Parry, but Parry, in the face of Stanford's behaviour of the preceding months, could only have concluded that Stanford had given up in the face of overwhelming odds and that loyalty to either him or the College had nothing to do

---

[89] Parry's Diary, 9 Dec. 1901, ShP.
[90] Parry's Diary, 10 Dec. 1901, ShP.
[91] Parry's Diary, 13 Dec. 1901, ShP.
[92] RCM Executive Committee minutes, 23 Jan. 1902, RCM.

with it. Arthur Coleridge, a committee member and long-standing friend of Stanford's, felt similarly annoyed; Parry noted, 'Arthur Coleridge spoke to me with some bitterness about Stanford's quarrelsomeness. He mentioned instances and said he had done what he could "but Charlie will have his quarrel"'.[93] Parry proposed a compromise at the meeting which all parties – with varying degrees of grace – accepted. The proposed increases were cancelled but Stanford was to receive instead an annual retainer of £100 in addition to the established fees.

Clearly Stanford's behaviour was characteristic and stupid but were there any grounds for his complaint? It seems certain that there were: Parry's objection to Stanford receiving a salary was that the College would 'have no hold on him' and reflected an unease which bordered on distrust. Parry was unusual amongst the RCM's academic staff in that he received a salary for his work (set at £800 per annum in 1895), so in that sense Stanford was not treated atypically, but it could not have been beyond the College to draw up a contract for Stanford laying down specific duties and hours had it so wished. That the College did not do this seems primarily due to Parry, whose attitude was affected far more by his personal relationship with Stanford than professional propriety ought to have allowed. And Stanford certainly had a point when he argued that freelancers of a similar stature received better pay than he did and that he received better pay in respect of other work he took on, for example, £315 for conducting each Leeds Festival and £200 per annum at Cambridge for minimal duties, the latter being poor in comparison with the salaries attached to other Cambridge Professorships. Unfortunately for both men the awkwardness continued throughout the winter until they finally made up, with generosity on both sides, at the end of March 1902. Parry's diary entries are illuminating:

> [18 February] Prepared to take Stanford's place [at Orchestra] this afternoon as he had intimated he would not be well enough to come. Asked Arbós if he would like to take the rehearsal of Bruch's Concerto with his pupil Winifred Smith. At last moment to my astonishment Stanford walked in ... I couldn't turn out Arbós then and he seemed so pleased to take a turn conducting. Stanford furious, went off to leave the College. I fetched him back with difficulty and he took the last part of the practice. However his temper was violent and when Frank [Pownall?] innocently asked him after how many tickets he would like for the function on Monday he snapped 'I don't want any.'[94]

> [27 March] Up to Coll before 10 for Executive. A huge list which I tried to force through against time. Unfortunately I came into

---

[93] Parry's Diary, 24 Jan. 1902, ShP.
[94] Parry's Diary, 18 Feb. 1902, ShP.

conflict with Stanford who disputed a suggestion of mine in a most offensive manner and caused me, worn out . . . to break into furious wrath. He also turned green with rage. Tableau! Very unfortunate and upset me frightfully.[95]

[29 March] Made up my mind to face the situation with Stanford and went to see him soon after 10. We set too and shouted our mutual opinion of each other without blinking. Mrs. came in and after over an hour of it came to terms. He behaved very well and so did she.[96]

In April Stanford travelled to Leipzig to see *Much Ado*. He was pleased with the performance and his reception, and wrote to Herbert Thompson: 'The performance was quite admirable. You will also be glad to hear that it was quite an extraordinary reception, for C. V. S. had to come out sixteen times, and the singers about sixteen more. This, for Leipzig, is, I am told, quite unusual.'[97] Stanford also came up against anti-British feeling, however, due to the Boer War, which reinforced his dim view of the German nation: 'The Leipzig papers (which have been all through the war the most virulent Anglophobists), and I refer to two only of our four daily papers, and to the *Signale*, which is connected, I understand, with one of their pro-Boer papers, have been trying all they know to explain away the success.'[98] Despite this, however, Stanford was elated by his reception and was well entitled to be pleased that his opera had been successfully performed in the city in which he had studied almost thirty years earlier.

Returning to England, Stanford embroiled himself in yet another argument, this time over the music for the coronation of King Edward VII, the arrangements for which were controlled primarily by Parratt and Bridge, arising from their roles at Windsor and Westminster. Parry, only a spectator this time, left an extensive account in his diary containing a mixture of revulsion, fascination and enjoyment:

Extraordinary development on May 22 about the Coronation music. Some time ago Stanford made up his quarrel with Bridge, obviously because he foresaw if he didn't he might get left out of the Coronation Service and he was naturally rather sold when he found he had been left out all the same. Parratt, who was much worried about it told me after luncheon on May 22 that he had been told by Francis Knollys [the King's Private Secretary] that one of the ladies attached to one of the Princesses had received a packet from Stanford containing two letters, one private for herself and the other

[95] Parry's Diary, 27 Mar. 1902, ShP.
[96] Parry's Diary, 29 Mar. 1902, ShP.
[97] Stanford to Thompson, 27 Apr. 1902, LUL MS 361, item 275.
[98] Stanford to F. G. Edwards (Editor, *Musical Times*), 9 May 1902, BL, Egerton MS 3090, fols. 190–92.

a tremendous long rigamarole though addressed to her obviously
meant for the King, and to the King it was submitted. Knollys asked
Parratt if it was not a great mistake that Stanford had been missed
out and he quite rightly said it was. He also asked if it would
lengthen the service if Stanford's Te Deum [in B♭, from Op. 10] was
put in instead of Smart's and he said it would not. Parratt had just
told me this when Stanford came in and Parratt told him frankly
of the communication which had been due to him and Stanford
instantly began volubly to explain that he did not wish any music
of his to be performed but only that the King should know that he
had not refused to write anything for the coronation, but that he
considered what Bridge (under remonstrances) had offered him as
the only thing available, namely a fanfare, was altogether too lean
and inadequate. He went on saying to Parratt 'do you see my point'.
Parratt only saw it too well and if Stanford was sincere in what he
said I never saw a more complete instance of a man imposing upon
himself. It was perfectly transparent that his eagerness to get into
the Coronation Service was so great that he would stop at nothing
to get in, and his expression . . . put in for my benefit, clearly showed
that he knew we saw through the whole business. It made me
feel sick.[99]

The following day Parry saw Parratt again and discovered that the
proposed revisions to the service had been accepted but that 'the King
was not favourably impressed' by Stanford's conduct.[100] *Truth* commented (sarcastically?) that 'for nights at a time the worthy Westminster
organist [Bridge] was unable to obtain his proper modicum of sleep and
tossed about the pillows, racking his brain to discover how he could
possibly introduce into the Coronation service some music by his friend
Dr Stanford'.[101] While Parry's account reflects the nature of his own
recently strained relationship with Stanford it is certainly the case that
Stanford did not acquit himself well on this occasion. For Stanford,
however, the coronation turned into a happy affair. In musical terms he
was as well represented as anyone else but, more importantly, he received
a knighthood in the King's Coronation Honours List, published on 26
June.[102] In the same list Conan Doyle also received a knighthood and
Parry was raised to a baronetcy. Unsurprisingly, Stanford was elated by
his honour and was received with cheers by the RCM orchestra, though
Parry noted that he was 'trying to excuse his condescension in accepting it'.[103] In fact Stanford was the last of the Royal College knights:
Parry, Parratt, Grove and Bridge had all received theirs in previous years

[99] Parry's Diary, appendix to 1902, ShP.
[100] Parry's Diary, 23 May 1902, ShP.
[101] *Truth*, 5 June 1902, p. 1453.
[102] The Coronation was scheduled for 26 June but the King developed appendicitis and
was operated on a couple of days earlier; the Coronation was postponed until 9 August.
[103] Parry's Diary, 27 June 1902, ShP.

(as had Mackenzie). On the other hand, their honours had all been received primarily due to the posts they held rather than for their compositions *per se*. Stanford was the first man to be honoured for his music since Sullivan in 1883.

In the ten years following his move to London Stanford stood at the height of his powers. Well established as a composer, he produced several works of significance and some truly great pieces; recognition of this achievement came ultimately in his knighthood. He developed a surer touch in much of his music: this can be seen in the two performed operas and in the craftmanship of works such as the Mass in G, the *Requiem* and the Fifth Symphony. At the same time, however, several of his smaller works are weak and suggest that he was undiscriminating in his choice of texts and sometimes unconcerned with the quality of the work he was producing: there are several pieces which are misjudged in conception and which amply justify the charge of academicism. Around the turn of the century it becomes apparent that Stanford's position was beginning to slip: the letter to Richter quoted above exaggerated his plight, but he was having to wait longer for first performances and several of his works were queued up. The rise of Elgar most certainly damaged Stanford – the *Requiem* was the last commission he received from Birmingham, which was then dominated by Elgar – although Stanford remained equally dominant at Leeds. He was also steadily being eclipsed by his pupils, again a development he mentioned to Richter – as the first generation built individual careers, most notably Samuel Coleridge Taylor. As he approached his fiftieth birthday, therefore, Stanford might have had reason to feel uneasy about the future, but he could look back on the previous decade with great satisfaction.

Appendix: The Relationship of the Fifth Symphony to Milton's *L'Allegro* and *Il Penseroso*

Music	Milton's text	Example
1st Movement – Sonata Form		
Introduction I	Hence loathèd Melancholy	*a*
	Of Cerberus and blackest midnight born ...	
	In dark Cimmerian desert ever dwell	
Introduction II	But come thou Goddess fair and free,	*b*
(transition to first	In Heaven yclept Euphrosyne,	
movement proper)	And by men, heart-easing Mirth	

Exposition

1st subject	Haste thee nymph and bring with thee	
	Jest and youthful jollity	*c*
Bridge subject	[new subject, treated in a quasi-fugato manner]	*d*
End of bridge	And Laughter holding both his sides	*e*
2nd subject	Come and trip it as you go,	*f*
	On the light fantastic toe ...	
	Mirth admit me of thy crew	

| *Development* | [built on earlier material, including music from the introduction] | |
| End of development | [not quoted in Stanford's score but evoking 'the dull night', allowing a lead in to the recapitulation] | *g* |

Recapitulation

1st subject	[not quoted in Stanford's score but evoking 'To hear the lark begin his flight / And singing startle the dull night' as above]	*h*
Bridge subject	as in exposition	
2nd subject	as in exposition	
Coda	as in exposition, drawing particularly from the bridge subject	

2nd movement – Scherzo and Trio Form

Scherzo 'A' section	Oft listening how the hounds and horn	*i*
	Cheerly rouse the slumbering morn,	
	From the side of some hoar hill,	
	Through the high wood echoing shrill.	
Scherzo 'B' section	While the ploughman, near at hand,	*j*
	Whistles o'er the furrow'd land,	
	And the milkmaid singeth blithe,	
	And the mower whets his scythe	
	... the hawthorn in the dale.	
Trio	Sometimes with secure delight,	*k*
	The upland hamlets will invite,	
	When the merry bells ring round,	
	And the jocund rebecks sound ...	
	With stories told of many a feat,	
	How Faery Mab the junkets eat;	
	[Remainder of movement recapitulates the Scherzo section with an allusion to the Trio towards the end in Beethovenian fashion]	

Music	Milton's text		Example
3rd movement – Episodic Form			
1st theme	But hail thou Goddess, sage and holy		*l*
	Hail divinest Melancholy,		
	Whose saintly visage is too bright		
	To hit the sense of human sight		
2nd theme	Come, pensive nun, devout and pure,		*m*
	Sober, steadfast and demure . . .		
	And looks commercing with the skies		
3rd theme	But first, and chiefest, with thee bring,		*n*
	Him that yon soars on golden wing . . .		
	In her sweetest saddest plight		
4th theme	Sweet bird that shunn'st the noise of folly,		*o*
	Most musical, most melancholy! . . .		
	Riding near her highest noon		
4th movement – Modified Sonata form			
Introduction	Oft on a plat of rising ground	d	*p*
	I hear the far-off curfew sound		
	[use of chord ii^7 as the curfew]		
Exposition			
1st theme	Sometime let gorgeous Tragedy,	d	*q*
	In sceptre'd pall come sweeping by		
2nd theme	[declamatory brass chorale]		
3rd theme	And as I wake sweet music breathe	F	*r*
	Above, about, or underneath		
4th theme	But let my due feet never fail	F	*s*
	To walk the studious cloister's pale,		
Development fused with Recapitulation			
1st theme	And love the high-embowéd roof	d	
	With antique pillars massy proof		
	[simple restatement but with heavier		
	orchestration; aural impression of		
	recapitulation]		
2nd theme	And storied windows richly dight	~~	
	Casting a dim religious light		
	[traditional development by fragmentation		
	of theme]		

Recapitulation
  proper

3rd theme		D
4th theme	There let the pealing organ blow	D
	To the full voiced quire below	
	[reorchestrated by replacing horns with organ]	
1st theme	[full restatement with heavier orchestration	
	including organ]	d
Coda	Dissolve me into ecstasies	D *t* and
	And bring all Heaven before mine eyes	see *n*
	[references to the curfew chord (in the	
	major) and to the 3rd theme of the slow	
	movement]	

Example 5.16   Themes in the Fifth Symphony, Op. 56

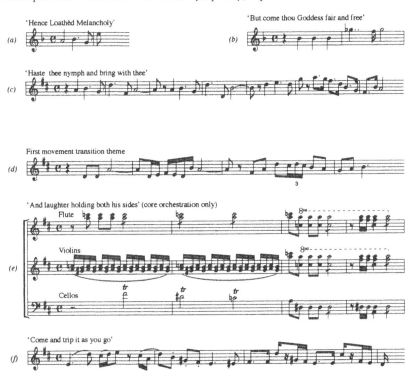

Example 5.16   *(cont.)*

'The Dull Night'

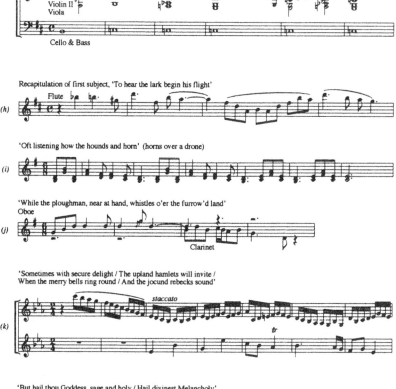

Recapitulation of first subject, 'To hear the lark begin his flight'

'Oft listening how the hounds and horn' (horns over a drone)

'While the ploughman, near at hand, whistles o'er the furrow'd land'

'Sometimes with secure delight / The upland hamlets will invite / When the merry bells ring round / And the jocund rebecks sound'

'But hail thou Goddess, sage and holy / Hail divinest Melancholy'

'Come, pensive nun, devout and pure' (oboe)

Example 5.16   *(cont.)*

'But first, and chiefest, with thee bring / Him that yon soars on golden wing'

(n)

I _____   ♭viib   ♭VIc   ♭III⁷ ♭VI (4–3)

'Sweet bird that shunn'st the noise of folly'   Flute

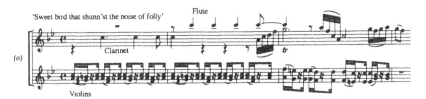

(o)

Clarinet

Violins

Curfew Chord (Brass)   'Sometime let gorgeous Tragedy / In sceptre'd pall come sweeping by'

(p)   (q)

'And as I wake sweet music breathe'

(r)

'But let my due feet never fail / To walk the studious cloister pale' (core orchestration)

Horns

(s)

Cellos and Basses (pizzicato)

'Dissolve me into ecstasies / And bring all Heaven before mine eyes'

'Him that yon soars' (inverted)

(t)

          6   7   6   6   8
                  4   5   5
      3⁴   3   'Him that yon soars' (original)

[Trombone]

CHAPTER SIX

A Long Edwardian
Summer

The years 1902–16, from Stanford's knighthood to his move to Lower
Berkeley Street, cover both his pre-eminence and decline. Stanford moved
seamlessly to the role of elder statesman in British music: one who was
to be honoured for his achievements and regularly invited to do more,
but who was also steadily being eclipsed by the following generation.

In 1902 the RCM was almost twenty years old and had established
itself as the principal centre for study of both performance and composition in Britain, surpassing the RAM. In composition this rise was due
to the work of both Parry and Stanford, but it was not until the post-
Victorian period that the product of their teaching became part of the
mainstream of British music. The rogue element in this RCM hegemony
was Elgar. The 'Enigma' Variations transformed his status to one of
national pre-eminence. The poor première of *The Dream of Gerontius*
at Birmingham in 1900 set him back only briefly and did not prevent
Gerontius from becoming the first oratorio since *Elijah* to establish itself
in the repertory. These two successes ensured that Elgar's star catapulted
past those of Parry and Stanford, and Elgar became, for many, the quintessential Edwardian composer. Possibly the death of Sullivan helped in
this: as Stanford commented to Richter, Sullivan had been deified by
many music-lovers,[1] and now this role – that of 'classical' musician with
the gift of the compositional 'common touch' – was vacant. With no
establishment figure appearing as an obvious successor, Elgar bounded
past and became, almost instantly, the classical composer who was able,
in music, to speak to and for much of Edwardian England.

The success of Elgar had one direct consequence for Stanford. He
received no commissions from the Birmingham Festival after the
Requiem for 1897 and his falling out with Richter in 1908 cemented
this exclusion. Festival commissions generally became thinner after 1902;
even at Leeds only the *Stabat Mater*, Op. 96, premièred in 1907, was
directly commissioned. The trend in Stanford's output, therefore, moved
away from the large-scale works which had dominated between 1884
and 1901 and towards solo and small ensemble music. Stanford was not

---

[1] See Stanford to Richter, 12 Nov. 1901, RCM, MS 4826, item 31, quoted on p. 215.

often at his best in this area so some works from this period have limited appeal. Conversely, however, some of his best works also date from these years, including *Songs of the Sea*, *Songs of the Fleet*, the Service in G, the *Stabat Mater*, and his last two symphonies and operas.

The *Irish Rhapsody No. 1*, Op. 78 was Stanford's first première after the announcement of his knighthood. It had been written at the request of Hans Richter, a practical response, perhaps, to Stanford's plea for more performances (see pp. 215–16), and was dedicated to him, although it was Stanford himself who conducted the première at Norwich on 23 October 1902. Despite the implications of the title, the rhapsody is carefully constructed, and rooted in Beethovenian scherzo form. Stanford incorporated two Irish melodies, both from the Petrie Collection, which he was then editing for publication, 'Leatherbags Donnell' (used as the 'scherzo' theme) and a second popularly known as the 'Londonderry Air' (used in the 'trio').[2] He treated the material with the romanticised Classicism typical of his other work; there is an extended restatement of the 'trio' theme but here 'Leatherbags Donnell' is used as a accompanying motif to the 'Londonderry Air', providing a sense of thematic integration (Ex. 6.1). The 9/8 D major coda is also based on the air but takes in elements of 'Leatherbags Donnell' as well. This careful, but straightforward, construction serves as an excellent basis for Stanford to bring out the emotive qualities of the melodies, and for the music to incorporate a sense of forward momentum. The proportions of the piece are well judged and the material used is ideally contrasted. For modern ears the setting of the 'Londonderry Air' sounds a little pale, since the melody has become irredeemably associated with an overly sentimental picture-postcard image of Ireland, but Stanford

---

[2] Subsequently the veracity of the Irish roots of the 'Londonderry Air' have been called into question; Greene stated that Stanford found the melody in the Petrie manuscripts (see *Stanford*, 180–81) and it had been included in the selection of melodies published in 1855 (George Petrie, *The Petrie Collection of the Ancient Music of Ireland* (Dublin, 1855), a publication sponsored by the Society for the Preservation and Publication of the Melodies of Ireland, founded in 1851; Thomas Rice Henn, Stanford's uncle, was a member of the society's council). Petrie stated that he received the melody ('name unknown') from a Miss J. Ross of Limavady, Co. Londonderry, 'a lady who has made a large collection of the popular unpublished melodies of that county, which she has very kindly placed at my disposal, and which has added very considerably to the stock of tunes which I had previously acquired from that still very Irish county' (Petrie, 57). Stanford and Graves also included it in *Songs of Old Ireland* (1882) under the title 'Emer's Farewell to Cucullain'. Stanford did not include the melody in his own edition of the Petrie Collection when it was published a few years later; more important here than the true history of the air is that Stanford himself believed it to be Irish. For further discussion see Brian Audley, 'The Provenance of the Londonderry Air', *Journal of the Royal Musical Association*, 125 (2000), 205–47.

Example 6.1   *Irish Rhapsody No. 1*, Op. 78, bars 492–5 (core orchestration
only)

derived from 'Leatherbags Donnell'

captured its beauty and sentiment almost perfectly, although a sudden
Straussian burst with screaming echoing horns sits at one point incongruously amidst the remainder of the material. This is one of Stanford's
most successful orchestral pieces and deserved its popularity; Fuller
Maitland's review of the first performance stated that the piece was
'scored with all possible richness of effect and is a typical and most
successful example of the master's work'.[3]

The *Irish Rhapsody No. 1* is the greatest of four Irish works which
Stanford produced at the turn of the century, the other three being
vocal works: *Songs of Erin*, Op. 76 (another collection of arrangements
for voice and piano with words by Alfred Graves), *Six Irish Folksongs*,
Op. 78 (excellent choral reworkings of tunes from *Moore's Irish
Melodies*), and a set of solo songs to words by Moira O'Neill,[4] *An Irish
Idyll*, Op. 77.[5] O'Neill's poetry is, one hundred years on, an embar-
rassment, being cast in mock Irish dialect, and ranging from sentimental
to bathetic in mood. Stanford was touched by the mood of the poetry,
however, as was Plunket Greene, who performed the cycle, and it caught
the spirit of the time, at least for Anglo-Irish emigrants nostalgic for the
Ireland of their imagination.[6] The emigrant experience is dealt with in

[3] *The Times*, 24 Oct. 1902, p. 8.

[4] Moira O'Neill (1865–1955), *nom de plume* of Agnes Skrine, published her collection
Songs from the Glens of Antrim in 1901. Extremely populat at the time, O'Neill's poetry
fell into disfavour in the reappraisal of Anglo-Irish literature after independence, though
it retained some advocates in the new Ireland.

[5] It is not apparent why Stanford confused his opus numbers at this time – *Much Ado*
was published as Op. 76a, and he used Op. 78 both for the *Six Irish Folksongs* and the
Irish Rhapsody No. 1. Confusion arose later when one version of the *Four Irish Dances*,
Op. 89 was published as Op. 79; Stanford had used this number for a rejected *Irish
Rhapsody No. 2* (see pp. 237–8), but did not reassign the number after abandoning the work.

[6] Although in the *Cambridge Review* (1 Dec. 1915, p. 129) it is claimed that Stanford
and Greene had only just given the première of the work, at the Aeolian Hall on 27
November.

Example 6.2 'The Fairy Lough' (from *An Irish Idyll*, Op. 77 No. 2, bars 24–41 (text: Moira O'Neill)

the first and last songs ('Corrymeela' and 'Back to Ireland') but Stanford did not rise to the occasion in either, while 'Johneen' is excruciating in its sentimentality. 'The Fairy Lough' is easily the best of the six, and Greene cited it on several occasions as one of Stanford's most perfect Irish songs.[7] It is a good piece of wistful writing and fairly captures the

[7] See Greene, *Stanford*, 206–13.

other-worldliness of the lough through the juxtaposition of unrelated chords – the frequent moves from tonic to flat mediant creating a sort of Anglo-Irish impressionism (Ex. 6.2). The song is immaculately crafted and engaging throughout, and although Stanford's accompaniment is sometimes a little obvious, its delicacy and variegation are ample justification of Greene's claim.

The Clarinet Concerto, Op. 80, completed on 17 July 1902, was the first work composed after the announcement of Stanford's knighthood and was premièred at Bournemouth on 29 January 1903 by Charles Draper. The name of Richard Mühlfeld, the original dedicatee, was scratched out of the score; once again, it seems, Stanford growled intemperately, causing offence which he either could not or would not undo. Stanford had met Mühlfeld at Cologne in April 1902 when on his way to the Leipzig performances of *Much Ado*. According to Stanford, Mühlfeld asked him to write something for clarinet and Stanford responded with the concerto, which he sent to Mühlfeld to peruse.[8] Knowing that the Meiningen Orchestra, of which Mühlfeld was a member, was coming to England in November 1902, Stanford hoped that Mühlfeld might find the opportunity to play the concerto during the tour. Unfortunately, Stanford took umbrage over a laudatory article which appeared in *The Times*.[9] He sent a vitriolic letter purporting to defend English orchestral players who, he argued, had been derided by reports that the Meiningen Orchestra had brought music to life in a way in which others had failed to do:

> I have waited for someone of the public rather than of the profession to come forward ... to record his gratitude for the splendid work of English orchestra players, to protest against this wholesale slur cast upon them, and to remind your readers of the results of the labours ... of Hallé, of Richter, of Wood and ... of Manns, whose conducting of a permanent daily band in the palmy days of the Crystal Palace Concerts resulted in an ensemble in no way inferior to that of any other orchestra, and in a quality of tone, wind and strings, vastly superior to any of that our recent visitors could claim.[10]

---

[8] See Stanford to Joachim, 15 May 1906, BerSt (Tiergarten), MS SM 12/40 item 4651.

[9] See *The Times*, 18 Nov. 1902, p. 5. The article began "'I have never heard an orchestra before" was the remark which many habitual concert-goers were prompted to make last night .... Even those who knew [Brahms's First Symphony] must have been unprepared for the surprises that awaited them, many of which were the result of a slightly different balance between wind and strings from that to which we are accustomed. The delicate gradations of pace and the play of light and shade lent to every movement a new beauty and meaning.'

[10] Stanford to *The Times*, 2 Dec. 1902, p. 4.

Stanford's outburst was ludicrous although it did represent the position of a few others. *The Times* replied that it had in fact only printed 'the remark which many habitual concert-goers were prompted to make last night'.[11] If Mühlfeld saw this letter he could only have found it extremely offensive; he did not play the concerto and returned the score without comment. Stanford responded by removing his dedication. Four years later he remained oblivious of the offence he had caused and wrote to Joachim:

> If [Mühlfeld] says that it is I who have offended him ... he is wholly wrong. He has shown excessively bad manners to the composer of a country which has always received him with the warmest hospitality and appreciation and he probably labours under the delusion that he may snub any Englishman with impunity. But I expect from German artists the same courtesy which I have always shown to them. The fault was his and he must know it: and he can't get away from that fact by throwing dust in the eyes of others.[12]

Stanford added that he had no objection to Joachim's showing the letter to Mühlfeld; one hopes that Joachim had more sense than to do so.

It is a pity that these circumstances arose, for the Concerto is an engaging work and shows Stanford in declamatory, urbane and playful moods. His sense of humour is shown in its construction, which, as Tovey argued, is simultaneously a single-movement sonata form and a standard three-movement concerto with each movement linked;[13] this compression results in a concerto of only twenty minutes' duration. It is the three-movement structure which is most apparent to the listener, but closer examination shows the sonata principle. The first movement is set up as a straightforward sonata form: a first subject in the tonic, A minor, and second subject in the relative major. An obvious development commences but this peters out in mid-flow and the slow movement follows. After this fully worked-out section comes the brisk finale, in which the two subjects – variations on those of the first movement – are presented in recapitulation format, that is, in tonic minor and major (Ex. 6.3). The genius of the work is that both levels function independently: if one fails to perceive the sonata principle the work still presents its material coherently, while, for those who notice, the arousal and subversion of expectations show an entertaining sense of erudition and wit. These academic games would backfire, however, without the high spirits of the material itself, but the subjects are well wrought, the

---

[11] Ibid.

[12] Stanford to Joachim, 15 May 1906, BerSt (Tiergarten), MS SM 12/40 item 4651. See also Stanford to Joachim, 16 May 1906, BerSt (Tiergarten), MS SM 12/40 item 4652.

[13] See Donald F. Tovey, *Essays in Musical Analysis*, 5 vols (London, 1936), iii, 197–200.

Example 6.3　Clarinet Concerto, Op. 80: (a) First movement, first subject, bars 1–4; (b) First movement, second subject, bars 81–8; (c) Second movement, principal subject, bars 3–7; (d) Second movement, subsidiary subject, bars 36–43; (e) Final movement, first subject, bars 47–55; (f) Final movement, second subject, 'anticipation' at bars 129–35; (g) Final movement, second subject, 'authentic' at bars 151–6

1   2 Herbert Street, Dublin

2   50 Holland Street, Kensington, London

3 Photograph of Stanford in the 1880s

4   Portrait of Jennie Stanford by Hubert von Herkommer

5   'Spy' drawing of Stanford (*Vanity Fair*, 14 April 1904)

6   'Physical Energy' by George Frederick Watts

7 'Love and Life' by George Frederick Watts

8 'Love and Death' by George Frederick Watts

9 'Good Luck to your Fishing' by George Frederick Watts

10 Stanford with Parry, Mackenzie, German, Elgar and Godfrey at Bournemouth, 1910

11 Stanford with Elgar, Brewer, Bantock, Hadow and others at Gloucester, 1922

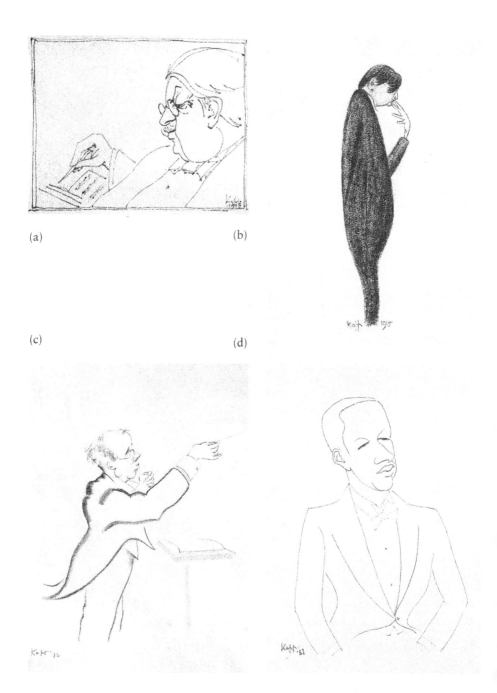

(a)

(b)

(c)

(d)

12 Drawings of (a) Stanford, (b) Vaughan Williams, (c) Holst and (d) Goossens by Eric Kapp

writing for the clarinet is grateful and varied, and the orchestration typically meticulous (Stanford dispensed with clarinets and trombones and
ensured that the clarinet was appropriately supported in all registers and
at all dynamic levels). In view of these strengths the concerto's lack of
contemporary success is a surprise – the review of the London première
in *The Times* is unusually acerbic for that newspaper:

> In [Stanford's Clarinet Concerto] ingenuity and knowledge may
> almost be said to bristle yet, in spite of this and of [Charles Draper's]
> great skill, the concerto failed to make a deep impression. It is, of
> course, superbly scored – in fact, an object lesson in scoring for a
> solo instrument – but the part for the latter is of far more interest
> to the player than to the hearer. The concerto has the merit of being
> short – it is, as a fact, in one movement only – or rather, without
> a break in its three movements. But, even though the composer
> himself conducted, it was felt that the concerto was deficient in
> contrast of effect and in real musical interest.[14]

Although it was occasionally played by Draper's pupil Frederick Thurs-
ton in subsequent years, it was not published until 1977 – but more
recent interest (it has been recorded twice since 1985; see App. 2) has
partially redressed the balance.

Two works, the Service in G, Op. 81 and *The Triumph of Love*, Op.
82, date from the latter part of 1902. The former is written in much
the same style as Stanford's earlier accompanied services, but here the
organ reaches an even greater orchestral expansiveness. Stanford's usual
unifying devices appear, for example, the opening theme of the *Te Deum*
is used for the each of the doxologies, but it is the Magnificat and Nunc
Dimittis which stand out. In the former Stanford looked upon the text
from the Marian point of view, setting it for treble solo with a delicate
organ accompaniment of running quavers. Although the organ part is
indebted to such works as Schubert's 'Gretchen am Spinnrade' and Saint-
Saëns's *Le Rouet d'Omphale*, this application of the music of the
spinning wheel to the text of the Magnificat, with its implicit picture of
Mary singing to God whilst at her work, is a typically Stanfordian flash
of inspiration (Ex. 6.4). A domestic image, atypical of Magnificat
settings, breathes new life into the text, making this one of Stanford's
most ingenious Anglican works. The effect is only weakened by the
restated doxology: its grandiose nature sits uncomfortably with the
domesticity and it is ironic that here Stanford fell a victim to the cyclic
unity he pioneered in the Service in B flat. The Nunc Dimittis is the
perfect foil to the Magnificat. The earlier treble solo is balanced by a

[14] *The Times*, 3 June 1904, p. 6.

Example 6.4   Service in G, Op. 81, Magnificat, bars 1–13

baritone and joyfulness and activity by solemnity and calm while the slower tempo and static organ part create an excellent contrast. Here Stanford solved the problem of the doxology appropriately since it is modified to maintain the serene mood of the former section.

While the Service in G contains much of Stanford at his best, *The Triumph of Love* is a failure. Stanford was probably inspired to set these five sonnets written by Edmund Holmes, then HM Chief Inspector of Schools, because Holmes was a cousin by marriage and the two men were close friends. Holmes produced a steady stream of prose and poetry but these sonnets were wholly unsuited to Stanford's contained emotional language: he could do nothing with lines such as 'O wounded heart / Bleed on, exultant in love's agony / Bleed on, defiant of Time's healing art' and the poems contain no narrative passages evocative of natural scenery which Stanford handled well. The fourth song, 'I think that we were children', requires some of the naive simplicity which Stanford could manipulate, but the remainder of this cycle is poor.

In late 1902 Stanford decided to resign the conductorship of the Bach Choir. It appears that the choir had been on the slide for some time: Stanford had conducted a three-concert Bach Festival in 1895 which was widely feted, but in 1900 only one concert was given. Ironically, Stanford's importation of singers from Leeds to stiffen the choir on this occasion led to the spat with Henry Labouchere which almost led to Stanford launching a libel action (see pp. 205–6). It appears that in 1902 the society gave no concerts at all – the *Musical News* reported that 'it is rumoured that there is considerable difficulty in reorganising the Bach Choir. The Society has given no performance for some time past.'[15] This report suggests that the problems were long-standing and in January 1903 Stanford's resignation was announced. It would appear that at this point dissolution was likely, but it was reported that 'lovers of choral music will be glad to learn that this society is not to be disbanded',[16] and Walford Davies was appointed the new conductor. To what extent Stanford contributed to this malaise is unknown: given what it is known of his temperament and conduct in other situations it is difficult to conclude that he was wholly innocent in the matter, but there is no known evidence to substantiate this hypothesis. It is equally possible that the ebb and flow of musical activity may have taken its toll on the choir at this time; the episode remains obscure.

Also in early 1903 Stanford returned to the idea of the Irish Rhapsody. He had already tried to capitalise on this in March 1902, writing to Richter that he was already working on a second rhapsody,[17] six months before the première of the first, but he abandoned it after seventy-two bars. The *Irish Rhapsody No. 1* had quickly become Stanford's most successful orchestral work since the 'Irish' Symphony, and the Dutch conductor Willem Mengelberg commissioned a similar work from Stanford which became the *Irish Rhapsody No. 2*, Op. 84, completed on 23 February 1903 and premièred by Mengelberg at the Concertge-bouw, Amsterdam, on 25 May 1903, with a second performance three days later. The British première was given by the same orchestra and conductor on 8 June at St James's Hall when they were in Britain to mount a Richard Strauss Festival – an irony, given Stanford's antipathy for Strauss's music and Strauss's declaration a year earlier that 'Meister Elgar' was the only British composer worth listening to. Fuller Maitland gave the work a good review, calling it 'one of the composer's most happily inspired works', and showed his like distaste for Strauss by declaring that the concert including Stanford's work gave the audience an opportunity to listen to 'some music that was in one key at a time

---

[15] *Musical News*, 29 Nov. 1902, p. 467.
[16] *Musical News*, 14 Feb. 1903, p. 151.
[17] Stanford to Richter, 26 Mar. 1902, RCM, MS 4826, item 34.

and that conformed to the usual canons of beauty'.[18] Dan Godfrey
conducted the work at Bournemouth on 26 October but it did not
replicate the success of the *Irish Rhapsody No. 1*. The piece draws from
Gaelic legend and bears the subtitle 'The Lament for the Son of Ossian'.
Stanford may have been inspired by the fabricated 'Ossianic poetry'
of James MacPherson (1736–96) which, although largely discredited by
scholars by the mid-nineteenth century, had remained popular as literature.[19] Stanford took the death of Oscar, son of Ossian, Ossian's
demand for vengeance, and Oscar's burial as a programme for the music,
and used three traditional Irish melodies as material, 'The Lament for
Owen Roe O'Neill', 'Awake Fianna' and 'Lay his Sword by his Side'.[20]
As the programme suggests, the mood of the piece is sombre, and this
probably contributed to the work's lack of long-term popularity: anyone
expecting the careful mix of romanticism and bravado presented in the
Irish Rhapsody No. 1 would have been disappointed. Even without
the earlier piece acting as a yardstick, the latter is weak. Stanford did
not show a clear sense of direction and this error is compounded by the
weak treatment of the melodies, and unusually pale orchestration.

Also dating from 1903 are all the other works Opp. 83 to 90 inclusive. These include Stanford's only two string quintets (Op. 85 in F and
Op. 86 in C minor, completed on 21 April and 3 June respectively)
and the *Four Irish Dances*, Op. 89. The first of the String Quintets was
performed by the Kruse Quartet with E. Tomlinson at St James's Hall
on 11 January 1904 (for whom Stanford wrote the Fourth String Quartet
in 1906), while the second was given by the Joachim Quartet at Berlin
on 30 March and at St James's Hall on 5 May. The C minor Quintet
was intended to be a present to Joachim to celebrate the sixtieth anniversary of his first visit to England; Stanford's subsequent wheedling to
ensure that Joachim performed the work probably took the gloss off the
tribute.[21] In the music Stanford fell, as usual, into his chamber music
'trap': the material is too slight to sustain the length, and the scoring is
too thick and lacking in variation. Fuller Maitland's review of the C
Minor Quintet, although positive, was restrained by his standards; the

---

[18] *The Times*, 9 June 1903, p. 12.

[19] Ossian was an Arthur-like figure in Irish history, alleged to have lived in the third
century AD, although no substantive evidence proves his existence.

[20] 'The Lament for Owen Roe O'Neill' is taken from the Petrie Collection and had been
published by Stanford and Graves in *Songs of Old Ireland* (1882) (see also pp. 126–8);
'Awake Fianna' is found in Petrie's 1855 volume (see above, n. 2) under the title 'The
Monks of the Screw' and as 'Awake Fianna' in *Moore's Irish Melodies* and *Songs of Old
Ireland*; 'Lay his Sword by his Side' is taken from *Moore's Irish Melodies*.

[21] See Stanford to Joachim, 24 Mar. 1904 and 7 Apr. 1904, BerSt (Tiergarten), MS SM
12/40, items 4646 and 4647.

best he could say of the first movement was that 'the themes ... seem a little wanting in contrast [but] the working-out section is interesting throughout'.[22] The *Four Irish Dances* became well known thanks to the several different versions in which they exist: for solo piano, violin and piano, orchestra, and later arranged for solo piano by Percy Grainger. It is not certain which version came first but Stanford's version for solo piano is most likely; the first recorded public performance was of the orchestral version at Bournemouth on 12 January 1905, but they achieved greatest renown in Grainger's virtuoso arrangement.

During 1903 and 1904 there was some improvement in Stanford's relationship with Elgar before its collapse in 1905. Despite Stanford's overtures Elgar had remained wary, although the conferment of the honorary doctorate at Cambridge and Stanford's genuine enthusiasm for the 'Enigma' Variations and the 'Pomp and Circumstance' marches had helped to reassure Elgar about Stanford's motives.[23] A brief contretemps over the role of the Society of Authors had annoyed both men in November 1902,[24] but in April 1903 Stanford wrote to Elgar putting forward a new proposition:

> May I put you down for the Athenaeum? I know you are not very much in town, but it is a place which is very welcome to persons of your tastes; the best private library in London and some very choric souls, and a club where you are left alone if you wish to be and can rest and snooze if you wish.
> Also it is important to have music of the best represented there ... and the supply is small ... Parry is on the Committee and I should like you to be put down before he goes off.[25]

This letter probably caused Elgar mixed emotions; the proposal could be taken as a genuine gesture by Stanford, and Elgar was always gratified by the conferment of some distinction upon him. Conversely, Elgar could have seen himself as a pawn in Stanford's game to advance the political status of music; Stanford's comment that 'the supply is small', which could be read derisively, was probably a slip of the pen.

As with the Cambridge doctorate, worries about cost preoccupied Elgar, and Stanford wrote again a few days later:

> I am sorry but Rule 2 [allowing for the election of members on the grounds of an outstanding contribution to British life] does not let anyone off the entrance fee. It is 30 guineas, however, (not 40 or

---

[22] *The Times*, 7 May 1904, p. 9.

[23] See Stanford's correspondence with Elgar during 1901, WRO, 5427: 7403–10.

[24] See Stanford to Elgar, 8 Nov. 1902, WRO, 5427: 7416 and 3 Nov. 1902, WRO, 5427: 7417.

[25] Stanford to Elgar, 20 Apr. 1903, WRO, 5427: 7414.

50) and honestly I do think you will find it worth the squeeze . . .
But of course I can't move until I hear from you to say yes or no.
I hope, however, that it will be yes. Write a couple of songs and
get the entrance fee on account for royalties.[26]

Elgar took the invitation as a genuine gesture of goodwill, and by
the time of the Hereford Festival of 1903 the two men had become
sufficiently friendly to play golf together at Malvern. Parry duly proposed
Elgar's membership but the wheels of the Athenaeum moved slowly and
Elgar's nomination was not considered for another year. At the ballot
on 12 March 1904 Elgar was defeated by the architect Aston Webb,
but a month later he was duly elected.

Stanford continued to support Elgar's music. He had already performed the 'Enigma' Variations with the RCM Orchestra and at Leeds
in 1901. The Leeds Festival Committee had commissioned a work from
Elgar – hopefully a symphony – for 1904 and, although Stanford had
not been consulted, he recognised Leeds's coup. Elgar had difficulties
with the work, however, and in November 1903 he notified Leeds that
he was withdrawing from the festival.[27] When Stanford discovered this
he wrote to Elgar:

> I was very sorry to hear from them that you had withdrawn your
> symphony. I asked [the Committee] if it was irrevocable and they
> said that it was, and that they had already accepted another novelty
> in its place. As this was the first occasion since 1901 that I have
> seen or heard from the Festival Committee, I had no opportunity
> of knowing their policy or actions, and I could say nothing beyond
> expressing my great regret, in fact it was evidently a sore subject
> with them (which I regret also) so there was nothing to be done.
> As (in all Festivals) the Conductor is more or less 'au fait' of what
> is being done, I think it is only right that you should know that at
> Leeds it is not so . . . the election of the Conductor is not until next
> Saturday and while I was delighted to hear from you that you were
> doing a symphony for them, I was extremely disappointed to hear
> that it was withdrawn.[28]

Stanford's uncharacteristically temperate tone shows a desire to find out
what had happened, while not chiding Elgar. Elgar apparently gave no
answer but rumours that he had withdrawn from Leeds because he
preferred to write a new work for Richter made him unpopular with
the committee and he was only included in the Leeds programme as a
result of lobbying by Stanford and Parry. Stanford's growing frustration
with Elgar shows in a letter written to W. S. Hannam, a Leeds Committee

---

[26] Stanford to Elgar, 24 Apr. 1903, WRO, 5427: 7415.
[27] See Moore, *Edward Elgar*, 420 and 444–5.
[28] Stanford to Elgar, 23 Nov. 1903, WRO, 5427: 7419.

member: 'Fair play, old chap, and a man's artistic work ought to rank independently of his personality. If it had not been that Hans von Bülow had taken this view of Wagner, the Bayreuth theatre would not be standing now.'[29] In the event Elgar conducted his new overture, 'In the South', at Leeds, but he left before Stanford conducted either his Violin Concerto or the première of Songs of the Sea, and had avoided Stanford when the Te Deum was given at the Gloucester Festival a few weeks earlier.

In December 1904 Stanford's friendship with Elgar collapsed completely. Stanford wrote an offensive letter, the tone of which Elgar put down to Stanford's resentment of Elgar's appointment to the newly created Chair of Music at the University of Birmingham.[30] The letter does not survive and it is still unclear why or what Stanford wrote to Elgar, although there has been periodic speculation. According to Alice Elgar, her husband sent Stanford a temperate reply.[31] In other cases the situation might have been retrievable: Stanford offended many people and most (wearily) accepted the amends that usually followed. But Elgar could not be treated in this way; he had always been suspicious of Stanford and often felt patronised by him. If Stanford ever did feel inclined to apologise, Elgar's later decision to bite back put an end to this. At his first lecture at Birmingham, on 15 March 1905, Elgar named Parry as the sole English composer of any stature and went on to say: 'Twenty, twenty-five years ago, some of the Rhapsodies of Liszt became very popular. I think every Englishman since has called some work a Rhapsody. Could anything be more inconceivably inept? To rhapsodise is one thing Englishmen cannot do.'[32] Stanford may have been neither English nor the only composer of rhapsodies but no one had any doubt that it was Stanford's Irish Rhapsodies to which Elgar referred. Faced with the sort of vicious comment to which he more often subjected others, Stanford reacted badly, taking grave and permanent offence. He wrote a letter of general comment to The Times, arguing that Elgar's statement that English music was held in no respect abroad was 'an unjust disparagement of the influence which has long been exerted by the music of his own country'.[33] Justifying his avoidance of Elgar subsequently, Stanford argued that the offence was not the attack itself but

[29] Quoted in Greene, Stanford, 155.

[30] See Moore, Edward Elgar, 449–50. The letter was received by Elgar on 27 Dec. 1904.

[31] Ibid.

[32] See Edward Elgar, 'The Inaugural Lecture', in A Future for English Music, ed. Percy Young (London, 1968), 22–65.

[33] Stanford to The Times, 3 Nov. 1905, p. 11.

that it had been made in public. A year later, when a rapprochement
was attempted, Stanford turned down an invitation to a party at which
Elgar was to be present and wrote:

> I quite saw, and believe me, thoroughly appreciated the kindly
> motive which underlay your invitation, and if this had been a private
> or personal matter no one would have responded quicker to it than
> I. But it is unfortunately a public one. The gross disloyalty and
> ingratitude to those professional colleagues whose identity was all
> the more clearly pointed out by the exceptions which were publicly
> named, can't be obliterated in private. I am not in the least affected
> in this respect by the obvious fact that the remarks were mainly
> directed at myself. They were made in general terms which affected
> us all . . .
>
> Perhaps [Elgar] has forgotten that Cambridge University was
> somewhat ahead of Richard Strauss in its tribute to his musical
> gifts.[34]

Neither man comes out of the affair with much credit. Both could have
behaved better if they had so chosen and kept their respective feelings
to themselves. Equally, however, it seems inevitable that two men with
such mercurial temperaments would have come to blows sooner or later;
as it was, the break between Stanford and Elgar was permanent and led
to a breach within the British musical profession that festered beyond
Stanford's death (see p. 405).

Perhaps due to the preparations for Leeds and the end of Guy's schooldays at Eton,[35] 1904 was a remarkably fallow year for composition:
Stanford produced only the *Songs of the Sea*, Op. 91 and, probably, the
Three Rhapsodies from Dante, Op. 92. The latter work was written for
Percy Grainger – Stanford had been much impressed by the Australian
since he had arrived in Britain and had cultivated his friendship; Grainger
reciprocated and they appeared together as conductor and soloist on
several occasions over the next few years. Grainger gave the première
of 'Beatrice' and 'Capaneo' at Bechstein Hall on 13 February 1905 and
of the full set on 25 March. Stanford took his inspiration from *The
Divine Comedy* and the three rhapsodies depict Francesca, Beatrice and

---

[34] Stanford to Littleton, 25 June 1906, CUL, Add. MS 9370. Elgar's comments may
have struck Stanford even more forcibly since Elgar gave his lecture wearing his Cambridge
MusDoc gowns.

[35] It is clear from the diaries of Herbert Thompson (LUL, MS 80) that Guy then went
to study in Leeds (from Oct. 1904). He may have studied at the newly founded University
of Leeds, but does not appear in the list of graduates. Stanford later wrote to Francis
Jenkinson that Guy had settled upon architecture as his chosen profession, but there is
no evidence that he ever practised as an architect (see Stanford to Jenkinson, 27 Apr.
1906, CUL, Add. MS 6343, item 6084).

Capaneo respectively. The two movements performed on 13 February were well received by *The Times*:

> In the expressive nature of the first theme and the dreamy chords that come later on we find a most picturesque reflection of the first appearance of Beatrice to Dante in the second canto of the *Commedia*. The other is a vigorous and defiant movement suggested by the figure of Capaneo in the 14th canto ... its manly character makes it extremely effective.[36]

In view of Grainger's ability as a pianist it is unsurprising that the three pieces are technically demanding; 'Francesca' nods to Liszt in style as well as virtuosity, but Stanford returned to home territory in 'Capaneo', where the declamatory style of Brahms's Rhapsody in E flat (Op. 119 No. 4) and the early Sonata in C (Op. 1) are in evidence.

With the exception of the problems surrounding Elgar, the Leeds Festival of 1904 (5–8 October) was generally judged a success. There were several novelties: Mackenzie's *The Witch's Daughter*, Walford Davies's *Everyman*, Holbrooke's *Queen Mab* and Charles Wood's *Ballad of Dundee*, plus Parry conducting his *Voces Clamantium*, while Stanford conducted Glazunov's Sixth Symphony, extracts from *Parsifal*, *Meistersinger* and *Lohengrin*, Beethoven's *Missa Solemnis* and the obligatory performance of *Elijah*. The *Musical Times* commented:

> In the purely instrumental works, when under Sir Charles Stanford's direction, the band produced a superb volume of tone; when required they roared as lions, at other times in the softest *pianissimi*, they cooed like doves, but in nearly all the modern choral works the orchestra frequently overpowered the choir, still more the soloists ... Can eighty-two strings ever be necessary to accompany a single voice?[37]

In the midst of the Festival, on 6 October, Stanford, Elgar, Parry, Mackenzie, Walford Davies and Charles Wood all gathered for the inaugural ceremony of the new University of Leeds at which they all received honorary doctorates.

As well as a performance of his Violin Concerto with Fritz Kreisler, Stanford was represented at the Festival by his new *Songs of the Sea*. The work was one of the hits of the Festival, and it is easy to see why: the five settings of poems by Henry Newbolt[38] were not only perfect

---

[36] *The Times*, 14 Feb. 1905, p. 10.

[37] *Musical Times*, 1 Nov. 1904, p. 730.

[38] Henry Newbolt (1862–1938), educated at Clifton College and Corpus Christi, Oxford, is remembered principally for his nautical ballads (the first set of which, *Admirals All and Other Verses*, was published in 1897), and the public school paean 'Vitaï Lampada' ('There's a breathless hush in the close tonight ... '). He also worked as a civil servant and published *A Naval History of the War, 1914–18*, in 1920.

representations of how Edwardian Britain wished to see to itself, but are also a romantic and vibrant illustration of the sea, Stanford's best attempt since *The Revenge*. Newbolt had not written the poems as a cycle and Stanford appears to have selected them for their varied moods. The work's importance, like that of *The Revenge*, derives from its popularity which, in turn, grew out of Stanford realising precisely what was wanted and supplying it. The emotional direction of the cycle is exactly right in conception: noble determination and eternal vigilance in 'Drake's Drum', followed by wistful parting in 'Outward Bound', bravado in 'Devon, O Devon', thankful return in 'Homeward Bound', and daring triumph in 'The "Old Superb"'. Stanford managed to run the gamut of emotions within fifteen minutes and each song capitalises on a different aspect of the contemporaneous perception of Britain as a brave, patriotic and sea-faring nation.

The formal construction of the songs is simple – all are in strophic form, though the slow ones with various added subtleties – and this transparency is part of their appeal, but, equally, Stanford introduced some dramatic effects which illustrate once again how he could capture exactly the spirit of the text and produce its musical foil. Thus in 'Drake's Drum' the tonic major catharsis for the last stanza evokes Drake as a sleeping giant ready to be wakened when England is in peril, the steadily moving chords in 'Homeward Bound' illustrate the slightly unpredictable undulations of a calm sea, while in the final song the words 'the Old Superb is old and foul and slow' are set to crotchets within a melody otherwise constructed of quavers, and 'round the world' is shown by a repeated circular melody (Ex. 6.5). The standard of craftmanship is outstanding throughout: the perfect match between the speech rhythm and inflection and the melodic line of 'Drake's Drum' is just one example of this (Ex. 6.6). This technical excellence, allied with an exact balance between tried and trusted formulae and vigour and conviction, are the essential ingredients in the work's success and led Herbert Thompson to write: 'In this type of work the composer is supreme. He understands the importance of lightness of touch and is never guilty of over-elaborating his score, yet never misses a point that can be enforced by musical means ... and, in spite of his success in other lines I cannot help thinking that he is at his very best in miniature work.'[39] This warm welcome was typical or the work's reception and ensured another place for Stanford in the heart of the choral-society repertory.

In 1905 Stanford managed to regain some impetus in his composition, and he completed the *Five Characteristic Pieces for Violin*, Op. 93

---

[39] *Yorkshire Post*, 8 Oct. 1904, p. 10.

Example 6.5 'The "Old Superb"' (from *Songs of the Sea*), Op. 91 No. 5, bars
114–21 (text: Henry Newbolt)

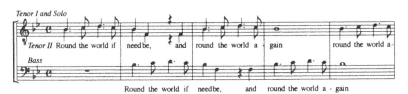

Example 6.6 'Drake's Drum' (from *Songs of the Sea*), Op. 91 No. 1, bars 3–9
(text: Henry Newbolt)

(1 February), the Sixth Symphony, Op. 94 (19 June), and the Serenade,
Op. 95 (often referred to as the Nonet; 16 July). He travelled to
Düsseldorf to hear the *Requiem*, conducted by Julius Buths, on 24
February, and also remained in demand as a conductor: as well as his
work at the RCM he conducted his Violin Concerto (this time with
Rivarde) at the Philharmonic on 26 May, plus Parry's *Symphonic
Variations* and Grieg's Piano Concerto with Percy Grainger at Queen's
Hall on 11 November. More surprisingly, in view of the collapse of his
relationship with Elgar, he conducted successful performances of *The
Dream of Gerontius* on 22 March (substituting for Elgar, who was ill),
and *King Olaf* on 8 November, both at Leeds.

On 11 January 1906 Stanford conducted the newly formed London
Symphony Orchestra in Paris with a chorus from the Leeds

Philharmonic;[40] a week later the Sixth Symphony was given under his baton by the same orchestra at Queen's Hall and a week after that the Serenade was given at a Broadwood Concert in the Aeolian Hall. The Sixth Symphony was written 'in honour of the life-work of a great artist', George F. Watts, who had died in 1904. The instrumental form (unlike the text-based *Requiem* commemorating Frederic Leighton) allowed Stanford to draw inspiration, loosely, from some of Watts's work. Apart from 'Good luck to your fishing' which inspired the Trio of the Scherzo, Stanford was not specific about which works inspired which sections but mentioned the equestrian statue 'Physical Energy' in Kensington Gardens, and two paintings, 'Love and Life' and 'Love and Death' (see Pls 6–9). Although the four movements of the symphony follow the normal order, two themes – one representing love, the other death (Ex. 6.7) – reappear in different movements and provide a degree of thematic integration and cross-referencing. Stanford was not attempting a programmatic narrative, but apparently an illustration of the initial displacement of life by death and its eventual reconciliation with love; this idea weaves its way through the symphony, most prominently in the second and fourth movements. Throughout, the most prominent characteristic of the music is its freshness and overt romanticism; the fast movements are all characterised by bold, sweeping gestures, the result of which is an invigorating symphony which is ultimately optimistic. Here Stanford came closest to Elgar's mode of expression in the mixture of elegy and confidence; the similarity between the openings of Stanford's symphony and Elgar's later Second Symphony is striking. One can also see touches of Glazunov and an unintentional reference to Berlioz (the brass chorale rendition of the 'Dies Irae' in the *Symphonie fantastique*) at the end of the scherzo. Like the Clarinet Concerto of three years earlier, the symphony's lack of success is puzzling; the explanation may have been the runaway success in Britain of Elgar's First Symphony less than two years later, but for Stanford – who produced some of his best music, both skilful and engaging, in this work – its failure to last must have been a cause of frustration.

In the Serenade Stanford maintained this vitality and it is his most successful piece of ensemble chamber music. The comparatively large number of instruments (the work is scored for flute, clarinet, bassoon, horn, two violins, viola, cello and double bass, that is, the same as Schubert's Octet with the addition of the flute) gave him a larger degree of flexibility than in his string quartets and quintets, and he made full use of the greater variety of timbres. The work is pervaded throughout

---

[40] For an account of this concert and the chaotic journey which preceded it see Greene, *Stanford*, 135–6.

Example 6.7   Sixth Symphony, Op. 94: (a) 'Love' theme (second movement, opening, solo cor anglais); (b) 'Death' theme (second movement, solo trumpet)

(a)

(b)

by a classical urbanity but this never becomes stuffy, as wit and *joie de vivre* are also present in abundance, the former most evident in the stop-start eleven-bar theme of the finale, the latter in the hell-for-leather succession of Variations in the scherzo, which is constantly pushed forward by a two-bar see-saw ostinato.

Composition continued steadily throughout 1906. Stanford completed the *Stabat Mater*, Op. 96 on 15 March and the Fourth String Quartet, Op. 99 on 30 October. The *Songs of Faith*, Op. 97, and the Magnificat and Nunc Dimittis on Gregorian Tones, Op. 98 also date from this year. The *Songs of Faith* contains the most successful music of the smaller works. Stanford turned once again to Tennyson and also returned to Whitman. The Tennyson settings are a little stolid, but for the Whitman poems (from *Leaves of Grass*) he produced heartfelt music. Compared with when Stanford composed the *Elegiac Ode* in 1884, Whitman's work was by this time regarded as mainstream and was attracting the attention of other composers.[41] The rhythmic intensity of the outer two songs ('To the Soul' and 'Joy, Shipmate, Joy') shows a heavy Brahmsian influence, although both are wrought in Stanford's own style. 'To the soul' shows his one of his own rhythmic fingerprints, that of accompanimental silence on the first beat of each bar, here creating a resigned plodding which evokes the slow, incessant journey into the unknown (Ex. 6.8). The static middle section would be banal in its simplistic illustration of the words ('I know it not, O soul / Nor dost thou / All is a blank before us / All waits undream'd of in that region / that inaccessible land') if it were not for Stanford's carefully calculated harmony, first circular and then based on a bass line descending by step from B♭

---

[41] Vaughan Williams set the same poem as Stanford's 'To the Soul' as *Towards the Unknown Region* in 1907, and again in 1925; there are also settings by Charles Wood and Holst. Vaughan Williams also set 'Joy, Shipmate, Joy'.

Example 6.8   'To the Soul' (from *Songs of Faith*), Op. 97 No. 4, bars 1–9 (text: Walt Whitman)

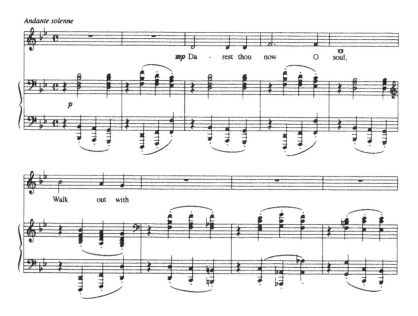

to E♮ (Ex. 6.9). Stanford's ability to manipulate simple concepts with facility and skill is evident in all three songs, in 'Tears' by a constant reworking of the sighing figure in the bass line and in the final song by a circulating *moto perpetuo* figure which spins into the distance with its protagonist, who repeats the words 'Joy, shipmate, joy' as if an incantation. Again Stanford demonstrated an awareness of catharsis, as the foreboding and sorrow of the previous two songs are countered by the confidence of the last.

Relations with Parry were becoming more strained once again: in May 1906 Parry was amazed by Stanford's conduct in respect of the series of Sunday Concerts at Queen's Hall. Stanford's complaint was, as usual, with regard to his fees as he had detected that Charles Wood was receiving more. Parry referred to Stanford's behaviour as 'a positively disgusting exhibition of humbug and ... of sordid selfishness with fine abstract principles',[42] and then happily noted that the concerts conducted by Wood had made a profit of £200 whilst those conducted by Stanford and Mackenzie had lost £800. Stanford's indignation may have been

---

[42] Parry's Diary, 7 May 1906, ShP.

Example 6.9   'To the Soul' (from *Songs of Faith*), Op. 97 No. 4, bars 31–46
             (text: Walt Whitman)

brought up short by the premature death at the age of 30 of his former student William Hurlstone on 30 May,[43] but it must have been a relief to Parry at least when Stanford went to Inverness-shire on holiday in late July. Spirits were better the following term, mainly, in Parry's view, due to the fact that the annual RCM opera, performed on 23 November, was *Shamus O'Brien*.[44]

The following year, 1907, saw the completion of the *Ode to Wellington*, Op. 100 (10 February), *Six Short Preludes and Postludes*, Op. 101, the Fantasia and Fugue, Op. 103, both for organ, and the incidental music to Laurence Binyon's play *Attila the Hun* (Op. 102, 29 June). The play opened on 4 September but only managed thirty-two

---

[43] According to Fritz Hart, 'Sir Charles Stanford always said [Hurlstone] was his best pupil. Hurlstone's relations with Stanford are further emphasised by a characteristic incident. He had submitted to the Professor a piano sonata, and Sir Charles was so pleased with the work that he called [Ernst] Pauer ... [to] hear it and pass his opinion on its merits. Pauer liked the sonata but thought it was too much in one key – a view which Stanford did not share. Hurlstone was dismissed to the common room whilst the two professors discussed his efforts in private. Now the threshold of the common room is never crossed by a professor, but on this occasion, Stanford managed to put his head round the door whispering defiantly "Stick to your key, my boy, stick to your key"' (Fritz Hart, quoted in Katherine Hurlstone (ed.), *William Hurlstone: Musician* (London, 1947), 15–16). Stanford, along with Parry, Bridge and Coleridge Taylor, attended Hurlstone's funeral at Mitcham Cemetery on 1 June 1906.

[44] See Parry's Diary, 9 Oct. 1906, ShP.

performances before it closed; the quality of the music suggests that Stanford did not empathise with the subject and Parry commented that the music 'did not seem of much account'.[45] Earlier in the year Stanford had been on the stage once again, this time for a production of *Shamus O'Brien* in Breslau (now Wroclaw, Poland). This production caused Stanford particular pleasure for the Breslau Opera House had expressed an interest in performing the work in 1898 but there had been many postponements, not least because of the Boer War, when it was felt that giving an English work in Germany would be inopportune. The production finally opened on 12 April 1907; Stanford took the opportunity to make revisions to the opera and was obliged (probably against his better judgement) to set the spoken dialogue as *secco* recitative – he was entertained, however, by having to teach the chorus how to dance a jig and reel.[46]

An era closed on 15 August when Joseph Joachim died in Berlin, aged 76; he had been an essential part of European and especially British musical life since the 1850s and had been a close friend of Stanford's for over forty years. The relationship, which had been remarkably free of strife, had benefited Stanford enormously, starting with Joachim's securing Stanford's tuition by Kiel in 1876. Stanford had engaged Joachim to play on countless occasions in Cambridge, London and Leeds, and helped to maintain his links with England. In commemoration Stanford wrote his Fifth String Quartet (Op. 104 in B flat) over the weeks following Joachim's death and the work was performed in Leeds and London on 3 and 4 March 1908 respectively. In a letter to Herbert Thompson, Stanford gave an indication of the general character of the work:

> The motto ... is the first phrase of his Romance for Violin. He often played it an as encore. He played it the last time I ever heard him. The figure marked J.J. .... is the passage he always tried his fingers with before he went up on the platform; and it used to be a kind of signal ... that he had arrived from Germany when it was heard from below, which all the public knew and smiled and got ready to yell when he came up. It gets higher up as the movement goes on ....
> The work is not meant to be sad (except the Elegy in the third movement). He was not the sort of man whose memory could be associated with sadness, at least not to me.[47]

Although commemorating Joachim in an appropriate genre, Stanford's work fails to tell and is marred by the thick scoring which pervades his quartets.

---

[45] Parry's Diary, 27 Sept. 1907, ShP.

[46] See Greene, *Stanford*, 198.

[47] Stanford to Thompson, 28 Feb. 1908, LUL, MS 361, item 276.

Less than two months later Stanford was embroiled in the 1907 Leeds Festival. A wide-ranging programme included the premières of Somervell's *Ode on the Intimations of Immortality*, Boughton's *Choral Variations on Two English Folksongs*, Bantock's *Sea Wanderers*, Glazunov's Eighth Symphony and Vaughan Williams's *Towards the Unknown Region*. Other works included Bach's Mass in B Minor (the solos of which Stanford directed from a piano, with a small orchestra accompanying), and Beethoven's Ninth Symphony. Elgar conducted *The Kingdom*, but a big attraction, the presence of Grieg to conduct his Piano Concerto, fell through as he died on 4 September.[48] Stanford took his place on the rostrum with Percy Grainger once more at the keyboard.

Stanford's contribution, the *Stabat Mater*, was performed on 10 October. As in the *Te Deum* and the *Requiem*, he wrote in an 'Italianate' style, exemplified in the work's straightforward episodic construction, and the dramatic Verdian orchestration (although he also made good use of a most un-Verdian instrument, the organ). The work comprises five movements of which the first is an orchestral prelude and the third an intermezzo; this justifies the designation 'symphonic cantata'. The text is divided into three sections and is dealt with succinctly, the second movement setting stanzas 1 to 8, the fourth stanzas 9 to 14 and the finale stanzas 15 to 20; the division follows the subjects of the text – the Virgin kneeling at the cross of her crucified son, a prayer to the Virgin by the narrator, its continuation, in which the supplicant asks for the Virgin's protection as he faces the Day of Judgement and aspires to entry into Heaven. Both instrumental movements use material employed in other movements; the prelude is exactly that and, in abridged sonata form, presents the 'lacrimosa' motif and harmonic progression used in the second movement, and the 'paradise' theme of the finale (Ex. 6.10), contrasting their anguished and peaceful natures as first and second subjects. A bridge passage links the Prelude and first chorus, and in the latter Stanford showed once again his appreciation of the emotive potential of individual words and phrases. The inter-mezzo functions as an entr'acte, preparing the audience for the 'second act' but, unfortunately, interest nods in the fourth movement and there is a lack of direction. As in the Sequence of the *Requiem*, however, this serves to throw as much dramatic weight as possible into the finale. Stanford appears to make a theatrical interpretation of this section of text; as the Day of Judgement approaches, the mood is of fervent antic-ipation, building relentlessly. At 'Quando corpus morietur' the soul looks in terror over the precipice into Hell (Ex. 6.11), before being reprieved

---

[48] Stanford's invitations to Grieg appear to be ill-fated: Grieg had been unable to come to Cambridge in 1893 to accept his honorary doctorate due to illness.

Example 6.10   *Stabat Mater*, Op. 96, 'Paradise' theme

Example 6.11   *Stabat Mater*, Op. 96, no. 5, bars 198–206

and drawn up steadily to Heaven, the gates of which are reached at the most triumphant declaration of 'paradisi gloria' (Ex. 6.12). In Heaven the soul experiences infinite paradise.

The result is immensely effective. The work has a sense of balance between strife, sorrow, tranquillity and triumph which is admirable and the dramatic impetus of the finale is terrifying. Stanford echoed Verdi's 'Dies Irae' in his view of death, and the term 'Italianate' refers to the especial primacy of melody, preference for homophonic writing and simple periodisation. Sensibly, Stanford eschewed the obvious temptation to ape the Renaissance polyphonic style or to slip in pastiche plainchant, with just two brief exceptions: first the melisma on 'plagas' in the finale and secondly the Mixolydian (but not contrapuntal) portrayal of heaven at the close. In the latter case one cannot resist the thought that Stanford was deliberately cocking a snook at George Bernard Shaw's withering comments about 'mixolydian angels' in *Eden*. Parry disliked the piece, calling it a 'singular work, very Italian in style [with] more colour than texture',[49] and later derided it as 'very much on the cheap [and] R-C [in] style'.[50] Critical reaction in general, however, was positive: Fuller Maitland declared that Stanford had 'touched a far higher point of his art' than previously,[51] while Herbert Thompson wrote:

---

[49] Parry's Diary, 2 Oct. 1907, ShP.
[50] Parry's Diary, 30 Jan. 1908, ShP.
[51] *The Times*, 11 Oct. 1907, p. 10.

Example 6.12   *Stabat Mater*, Op. 96, no. 5, bars 221–5

If one may venture upon comparisons with Stanford's previous works, this one has the emotional feeling of the best parts of his *Requiem*, together with a construction which reminds us of the *Te Deum*, while in dramatic intensity and conciseness of expression it surpasses both ... The interest never slackens but the ideas, while fully developed, are concisely stated. The final pages might perhaps be considered rather protracted, but it is easy to understand the continuous repetitions when one remembers they not only form the conclusion of an elaborate work of art, but may be meant to symbolise the endless peace of a future state of existence.[52]

Unfortunately, the work did not achieve the popularity it deserved; the reasons are unclear although in 1908 John Hedley, secretary of the Albert Hall, told the Leeds Festival Committee that there was a lack of interest in Latin works generally and declared that only *Elijah* and the *Messiah* could be guaranteed to make a profit for concert promoters.[53]

For his next work Stanford turned to a satirical vein, completing the *Ode to Discord* on 19 January 1908. Over the remainder of the year the works Opp. 105–14 inclusive followed; the last of these, *Ave atque vale*, was completed on New Year's Eve. Stanford also conducted the premières of *A Welcome Song*, Op. 107 at the Anglo-French Exhibition

---

[52] *Yorkshire Post*, 11 Oct. 1907, p. 7.
[53] See Leeds Festival General Committee Minutes, 3 Nov. 1908, WYAS.

at Shepherd's Bush on 15 May and the *Ode to Wellington*, Op. 100 at the Bristol Festival on 14 October. The former is a light work but was good for his public profile (the Exhibition was the biggest event of its kind in Britain since the Great Exhibition of 1851); the latter, based on lines by Tennyson, is badly proportioned and lugubrious, which, while reflecting the poetry, results in a dreary piece with insufficient contrast. Parry noted that '[many] of the words [are] now unfit to be set'.[54] The most unusual of Stanford's works from 1908 is *Bible Songs*, Op. 113. Designed for sacred use, the work comprises six settings of biblical texts (four psalms, and excerpts from Isaiah and Ecclesiasticus), plus choral arrangements of six well-known hymns which Stanford later interspersed between them. The songs resemble cantata arias in aesthetic terms, and the orchestral organ writing and the succeeding hymns reinforce this impression, recalling Bach and the Lutheran tradition. Despite the interest shown by Harry Plunket Greene in the work, the songs, perhaps because of their unusual format, did not make much progress.

1908 was less successful from a personal perspective since in April Stanford's relationship with Richter broke down. The event which triggered the collapse was a minor one, and then blown out of proportion. Stanford had written a letter of introduction to Richter for James Friskin, but the meeting had not gone as planned.[55] Friskin duly related the events to Stanford who, furious at Richter's behaviour, shot off a sharply worded letter. Richter had a different recollection of the meeting and sent Stanford an icy response putting his side of the situation. The original letter of introduction does not survive, but the subsequent correspondence is worth reproducing as it shows both a typically Stanfordian outburst and one type of response:

> Dear Richter,
>
> I wrote to you some time since a letter introducing to you a young English musician of very great gift. I expected some kind of reply, but have had none. In my letter I told you of his remarkable talent for composition, and asked you to let him to play something of his own for you; and I laid stress on the fact that he was very shy and modest, and would need encouraging treatment at your hands if you wanted to see the best of him. As far as I could gather from his own very guarded account of the interview, you did not go further about his own music than to ask him whether he wished to play as a composer or as a pianist, a question which, as my letter made clear to you, would certainly result in your not hearing any work of his own, and that your reception of him was exactly the

---

[54] Parry's Diary, 10 May 1907, ShP.

[55] Friskin was regarded by Stanford as a promising composer; he later became known principally as a pianist and married another Stanford pupil, Rebecca Clarke.

reverse of what I asked, and as I could see, made him uncomfortable and nervous.

Even if you think this is the proper attitude to take to a young artist, it was not exactly courteous to his master and friend who sent him, and made me much regret that I had taken any steps in the matter. He told me that you were annoyed at his coming late for the appointment. He arrived at the Queen's Hall at 12.25, and the hour fixed by Mr Forsyth in a letter to me was 12.30. You began therefore by blaming him for an unpunctuality which did not exist, and to start with undeserved reproach was not exactly calculated to encourage him to steady his nerve.

I am sorry about this, but I cannot say that I am surprised. Your position in this country, gained primarily by your own gifts, was assured by the unflinching support of men like myself, whose goodwill has now become unnecessary to you, and which you therefore have dispensed with.

But there would be no great harm done (from a personal as distinct from an artistic standpoint) if you kept up even so much show of respect for them, as to acknowledge important letters when they write them, or to fall in with such small requests as personal kindliness to a boy, in whom several of those on whose opinion in musical matters you apparently used to get some value, are exceptionally interested.[56]

Dear Sir Charles,

Your letter was an unexpected, nay an unpleasant surprise to me: and I regret you should have considered it necessary to write it. I imagine that it would have been worth your while to make some enquiries, to have satisfied yourself that the state of things was not such as you describe, before writing in this fashion, for I can only assure you that the young man has misrepresented things entirely. I had to finish at 12 o'clock upon the day in question because the members of the orchestra had other business which demanded their attention and simply remarked to your protege that I was sorry that the half hour between this and the time of his appointment should have been wasted, thereby meaning that had I known of this, I could have arranged to let him come earlier and thus hear more of him; it could certainly not have been a question of impatience or discourtesy as I had myself fixed the hour of meeting.

I further asked him whether he wished to be heard as a soloist or as a composer and this because I should be more able to help him in the former capacity than in the latter. He elected to play for me and after he had done so, I told him that it was unfortunately too late to make him a definite promise of engagement because many of the next season's arrangements had already been settled, adding however, that I would bear him in mind in the event of any date becoming free; upon my return to Manchester, I likewise asked Mr Forsyth to take a note of his name.

[56] Stanford to Richter, undated (but written in mid/late April 1908, judging from the two following letters quoted), RCM, MS 4826, item 38.

Unfortunately I deserve to be called a negligent correspondent, but my busy life and numerous journeys are to a great extent answerable for this; in any case intentional under-estimation has nothing to do with the present case.

Your remark 'I am sorry ... and which you therefore have dispensed with' contains the undeserved accusation of ingratitude. As far as my memory of our correspondence of earlier days serves me, I always proved myself worthy of your goodwill. That you however permit yourself to write 'but I cannot say I am surprised' throws a curious light upon our relations, for you insinuate that you have always regarded me as an ungrateful egotist, one who was open to accept favours but never to return them.

Now I know that it is not necessary for me to tell you that I have never used my friends in this way: on the contrary, I have always tried to help them to the best of my ability and as far as it lay in my power. Your letter has robbed me of an illusion, but it has enriched my experience – which is a bad exchange! And in order to avoid future misunderstandings of this sort, I may add that in spite of the unpleasant effect of your letter, I shall always be at your service musically if I can do so without prejudice to my artistic feelings.[57]

My dear Richter,

I should like you clearly to understand that Mr Friskin made no complaint to me whatever about your reception of him, and that the impression I received was the result of questions which I put to him. He evidently tried hard to make the best of it, but I could not help seeing that he was not happy about it. A letter from you would have helped to explain matters, and the absence of it naturally confirmed the impression. I never used the expression which you put in quotation marks 'intentional under-estimation', as you will see if you refer to my letter, nor did I say anything to suggest it.

Neither have I 'insinuated' anything whatever. What I said I said frankly and straight. I do not deal in insinuations.

Your final sentence I confess that I do not understand. I said no word implying a lack of musical consideration 'in earlier days' on your part, or asking for it with or without prejudice to your artistic feelings in present of future days.

What I regretted was your entire lack of personal consideration for me in this particular instance, and your ignoring of my letter.

In a word I expected the same courtesy from you with which I, who am also a busy man, should certainly treat you or any of my colleagues under such circumstances.

We can now allow this matter to rest.[58]

Richter's annoyance is amply illustrated by his starting the letter 'Dear Sir Charles' but what really made Stanford's behaviour so bad was his

[57] Richter to Stanford, 23 Apr. 1908, RCM, MS 4826, item 37.
[58] Stanford to Richter, 25 Apr. 1908, RCM, MS 4826, item 39.

insistence on replying to Richter, reinforcing many of his earlier accusations, several of which were quite outrageous. It is unsurprising that people found Stanford offensive when he would not let a matter rest: the final sentence rubbed salt into the wound, implying that the matter could only be closed when Stanford had had the last word and was not required to apologise. Richter's annoyance was so great that he refused to deal with Stanford after this and one more friendship – this one of almost thirty years' standing and of great benefit to both men – came irrevocably to an end.

Richter was not the only person to feel the lash of Stanford's tongue in 1908; Stanford also got into a heated correspondence with H. V. Higgins, Chairman of the Covent Garden Opera Syndicate, over the Ricordi Opera Competition, first in his paper 'The Case for National Opera' and then in the columns of The Times.[59] The dispute revolved around whether the competition's winner, The Angelus by Edward Naylor, was to be performed at Covent Garden in Italian or English. Although Higgins was probably correct in detail, Stanford certainly had a valid general point, that is, that it was a sad state of affairs when operas in English had to be translated into a foreign language for performance in London. No doubt memories of his own experiences with Savonarola and The Veiled Prophet informed his view. The article which offended Higgins, 'The Case for National Opera', was another of Stanford's attempts – well argued and practical – to encourage the foundation of a state-supported opera house and company; as usual the pleas fell on deaf ears.[60] Despite having carefully costed his scheme, drawing information from other Continental opera houses, Stanford found no state enthusiasm for such a project and, like the proposal to the LCC ten years earlier (see p. 200), his plans proceeded no further.

The two biggest works premièred in 1909 were the choral overture Ave atque vale, Op. 114 (Bach Choir, Queen's Hall, 2 March), and the Ode to Discord (Queen's Hall, conducted Landon Ronald, 9 June). The former was inspired by the centenaries of the death of Haydn and birth of Tennyson and the words are drawn from chapters 43 and 44 of the Book of Ecclesiasticus. The most notable feature is the opening harmonic progression, which reappears throughout the piece, a distorted cycle of

---

[59] Stanford, 'The Case for National Opera', in Studies and Memories, 3–23; in The Times see 19 Dec. 1908, p. 13 (Higgins), 21 Dec., p. 11 (Stanford), 25 Dec., p. 11 (Higgins), 26 Dec., p. 9 (Stanford), 29 Dec., p. 9 (Higgins), and 30 Dec., p. 9 (Stanford).

[60] An attempt, at a roughly similar time, to secure a state-funded concert hall, also failed. Despite an interview with the Prime Minister, Henry Campbell-Bannerman, the scheme was dismissed by the Treasury because encouraging those without ample means to go to concerts smacked of socialism (see Stanford, Pages from an Unwritten Diary, 315); quite how the quintessentially conservative Stanford viewed this can only be imagined.

fifths which shows Stanford's preference for flatward movement (E♭–A♭–D♭–G–C, that is, in C major, ♭III–♭VI–♭II–V–I) (Ex. 6.13). The tritonal relationship between the third and fourth chords is always preserved and becomes a motto; the preference for flatward movement is complemented by the choice of flat keys: only the opening choral entry, in G major, is a sharpwards move from the tonic C while the remainder of the piece is orientated to C, A♭, E♭ and F minor.

The *Ode to Discord* was a skit on trends in modern composition and showed, satirically, Stanford's view of contemporary developments. The poem, by Charles Graves, opens with a reference to Milton's *L'Allegro* ('Hence, loathèd Melody'), which had inspired the Fifth Symphony. The words give an indication of the music in their sights:

> Let drum (bass, side and kettle)
> Add to the general welter, and conspire
> To set our senses furiously on fire.
> Noise, yet more noise, I say. Ye trumpets blare
> In unrelated keys and the affrighted air
> Nor let the shrieking piccolo refrain
> To pierce the midmost marrows of the brain.
> Bleat, cornets, bleat, and let the loud trombone
> Outbay the bloodhound's awe-inspiring tone.

Fuller Maitland's review in *The Times* summed up both the strengths and weaknesses of the work perceptively:

Example 6.13   *Ave atque vale*, Op. 114: (*a*) bars 1–5; (*b*) bars 203–11 (text: Ecclesiasticus)

It is notoriously difficult, almost an impossible thing, to make a successful musical parody or skit of any length or elaboration; and the announcement of an *Ode to Discord* by Sir Charles Stanford created no small stir among those who knew his firm attitude of opposition to the 'advanced' school of music and the tendencies of the present day . . .

A good deal of the 'Chimerical Bombination in four Bursts' . . . proceeds from the kind of high spirits that most of us associate with schooldays; but in the music . . . there are many hits that are sure to reach the mark. The typical melody that is banished in the opening soprano solo is Schubert's 'An Die Musik' and the choral invocation to cacophony has a succession of bare fifths for the female voices which are quite worthy of the most-admired modern writers. The only fault, indeed, that can be found with the music is that it has no touch of the exaggeration which parody requires . . . At the beginning of the solo in the second 'burst' Debussy's favourite six-tone scale . . . is introduced with deafening effect, and the baritone solo supplies musical relief of a very beautiful kind in a song which laments the departure of the 'ancient fane which stood foursquare for thrice an hundred years'. Some Miltonic allusions find appropriate musical counterpart in quotations from Parry's *Blest Pair of Sirens*. And after the extinction of Beethoven has been celebrated in the funeral march from the 'Eroica', Wagner's attainment of 'the limbo of back numbers' is illustrated by the 'Walhall' theme followed by that which is associated with the central idea of *Götterdämmerung*. The 'Preislied' from *Die Meistersinger* is interwoven with a quotation from Parry before we reach the fifth burst in which the Chromatic Brigands have a midnight orgy in a fugue built on a perversion of 'We won't go home till morning', a fugue which is hardly a parody since it is technically much better and so much more effective than the weak fugal efforts of the new school.

The simultaneous playing of the notes G and A flat together with the appalling effect of a similar kind at the end are, like the direction *Nobilmente*, in another place, special satires on individual composers; but as a whole the work . . . is deficient in the pure unqualified ugliness and dullness of most of the new music.

The joke was a huge success and the very large audience called the composer, Mr Graves, and the soloists again and again.[61]

Stanford also parodied the huge orchestra beloved of Strauss and the rhythmic freedom that was becoming popular in a bass clarinet 'quasi cadenza' (Ex. 6.14(*a*)), while the whole-tone scale attributed to Debussy destroys the opening of Beethoven's Ninth Symphony. Two other passages, however, curiously imply that Stanford was criticising composers long dead: the 'Orgy of the Chromatic Brigands' is modelled on the fugal section of the 'Witches' Sabbath' of Berlioz's *Symphonie*

---

[61] *The Times*, 10 July 1909, p. 12.

Example 6.14   *Ode to Discord* (1908): (*a*) Bass Clarinet 'quasi cadenza'; (*b*) 'a feverish pulsation of the approved pattern on the wind'

fantastique and a rhythmically irregular figure used elsewhere closely resembles one of the motifs associated with Alberich in *Der Ring* (Ex. 6.14(*b*)) (Stanford and Graves describe this as 'a feverish pulsation of the approved pattern on the wind' in the 'analytical notes' published in the vocal score under the pseudo/acronym 'CaLGaCVS'). Fun though the work is, its weakness is as Fuller Maitland surmised and the message fails to tell. Stanford was defeated by the problem faced by any conservative wishing to satirise radicalism: it can only be achieved by outdoing the radical, and the product is anathema to the conservative, since it is even more offensive than that which is satirised. Just five years later it would have seemed pale indeed to any musician familiar with Stravinsky and Schoenberg.

Compared with the previous year, Stanford wrote little new music in 1909, completing only the Service in C, Op. 115 and the *Te Deum and Canzona for Organ*, Op. 116. His output picked up again in 1910, and he completed all works with opus numbers from 117 to 123 inclusive plus the Festal Communion Service in B flat, Op. 128 (the Gloria of which was first heard at the coronation of George V on 22 November 1911). Four works are significant from these two years: the Service in C, *Songs of the Fleet*, Op. 117, *Cushendall*, Op. 118, and Eight Part-songs, Op. 119; one other work, the Sixth String Quartet, Op. 122, does not appear to have been performed publicly until 1980 – a demonstration of Stanford's now variable fortunes.

The Service in C earned a lasting place in the Anglican repertory due to its ease of performance and its simple sense of nobility; the Credo, Sanctus and Gloria are particularly well written. The work was evidently intended for smaller or less proficient choirs, since it contains much more unison writing than previously; the organ part too is much simpler and Stanford was careful to ensure that all lateral modulations are carefully prepared in the organ before the choir sings. Nevertheless, the opening

Example 6.15   Service in C, Op. 115, Sanctus, bars 1–9

of the Sanctus (Ex. 6.15) exemplifies how Stanford's contained aesthetic could still produce highly evocative and well-wrought music and how his simplest ideas were often the most effective in execution.

Cushendall, which comprises six songs to words by John Stevenson, was Stanford's first collection of Irish songs since *An Irish Idyll* and, like the earlier work, does not really succeed. Three of the songs, 'Did You Ever?', 'The Crow' and 'Daddy Longlegs', are bland affairs; the quotation of Brünhilde's Fire motif in the latter at 'You try to moderate your legs in lamp or candle flame' sits incongruously in its surroundings, and while Stevenson's comparison of a crow with a lawyer would have tickled Stanford, his setting did not add to the poetry. The other three, 'Ireland', 'Cushendall' and 'How does the wind blow?', are better but still lack intensity; 'Cushendall', with its long procession of secondary sevenths, has a gentle sense of sorrow, but the climax, despite the poignancy of the words for Stanford, fails to hit the mark (Ex. 6.16).

Most of the Eight Partsongs, Op. 119 are inconsequential, but the setting of 'The Bluebird' is an exception. Deserving of its renown, Stanford's skill here led to a piece little short of perfection. The slow-moving choral parts, replete again with secondary sevenths, create a perfect picture of a still, hot day, while the solo soprano soars above playing the role of the bluebird (Ex. 6.17). The length of the piece is excellently judged and there are clear affinities with Vaughan Williams's later *Lark Ascending* (1914); this type of natural scene came easily to Stanford and inspired him here to genius – the detailing and concept of this miniature are faultless. The remainder of the set unfortunately failed to meet this standard. Stanford's only attempt at illustrating modern technology appeared here ('The Train') but is a fragmentary affair; one wonders if he appreciated the irony of Mary Coleridge's words in 'The Inkbottle' ('Well of blackness, all defiling / Full of flattery and reviling

Example 6.16   'Cushendall' (from *Cushendall*), Op. 118 No. 3, bars 45–53
(text: John Stevenson)

/ Ah what mischief hast thou wrought / Out of what was airy thought / What beginning and what ends / Making and dividing friends').

In summer 1910 Stanford was involved in a brief spat with the leading suffragist Millicent Garrett Fawcett (widow of Henry Fawcett, late Professor of Political Economy at Cambridge) on the subject of votes for women, then a rising issue. He opposed the change (which, incidentally, put him on the opposite side of the argument to the Liberal Parry), arguing that a General Election should be held on the issue; despite his assertion to the contrary it is tempting to believe that Stanford favoured an election because he believed that the (then exclusively male) electorate would reject candidates who favoured votes for women:

> Will Mrs. Henry Fawcett answer the following question with a simple 'yes' or 'no'? Is she or is she not, in favour of a bill involving not only an enormous increase of the electorate, but also a fundamental alteration of its constituents being passed into law before the country has been given an opportunity of expressing its views upon it?[62]

Mrs Fawcett replied:

> In answer to the inquiry of my old friend Sir Charles Stanford I would respectfully point out that he has worded it in a manner which begs the questions, and therefore it is impossible for me or anyone sharing my views to answer it by "a simple yes or no."

---

[62] Stanford to *The Times*, 16 July 1910, p. 12.

Example 6.17   'The Bluebird', from Eight Partsongs, Op. 119 No. 3, bars 1–13
(text: Mary Coleridge)

But I may perhaps be allowed to say that, while I do not take the 'mandate' view of the duties of members of Parliament, but believe that the House of Commons is bound to deal with political questions as they arise, according to what seems best, it is a matter of common knowledge that the question of woman's suffrage has been before the country for some 40 years, and that during the last four or five of these it has been more discussed both in public and in private than perhaps any other public question outside the range of party politics . . .

Sir Charles Stanford asks me if I am in favour of "an enormous increase of the electorate." I reply that we are advocating a moderate increase of the electorate. There are more than seven and a half millions of men at present upon the register. The Bill now before Parliament would add to these about one million of women. The addition would be important, but by no means numerically enormous . . . [63]

Stanford pressed his point, however:

I cordially appreciate the kindly tone and the admirable temper of Mrs. Fawcett's letter, which is in every way an object lesson in controversial method. But with all respect I must point out that Mrs. Fawcett alters my question. I did not ask if she was in favour of an enormous increase in the electorate, but if she was in favour of passing into law such an increase . . . without an appeal to the country . . . .

---

[63] Millicent Garrett Fawcett to *The Times*, 19 July 1910, p. 14.

She, one of the shining lights in the small firmament of political honesty, would be the last to wish England to be governed by an electorate framed in opposition to its wishes ... Why then should she object to making dead sure of its endorsement? I am not arguing the question of women's franchise; I am asking whether she would approve in any such momentous question the taking of the most fractional risk of passing a bill against what, for all she or I can possibly tell and still less positively know, may be the feeling of the country.

It is quite true that the question has been before the country for many years. So have plenty of other questions, which remain academic inasmuch as they have not been made a dominant issue at a General Election. To put it direct to the country is a very different matter from passing resolutions in societies and associations: and I am asking Mrs. Fawcett if she would approve a course with regard to this Reform Bill, which she would, I feel confident, she would have disapproved with regard to the Reform Bill of 1831, or of that of 1866, and which so ardent a reformer as Mr Gladstone did not dream of adopting in the case of the Irish Church Bill of 1868.[64]

Conservative though these views are, one should bear in mind that they were by no means uncommon among men and women of Stanford's class and generation, and they should not come as a surprise. What is clear once again, however, is Stanford's temperamental conservativism in the true sense of the word: he never embraced change for change's sake, and often opposed change because it implied consequences elsewhere – this is seen not only in his attitude to social issues but also to the evolution of music (see pp. 358–64).

As well as maintaining his steady output of music and keeping up with current affairs, Stanford also conducted his fourth Leeds Festival. The Festival Committee had been planning the event for the previous two years and for this Festival Stanford was consulted extensively about the programme. He attended at least three committee meetings; an extract from the minutes of 22 June 1909 (when he was not present) show the extent of his input:

[Extract from a letter from Stanford]

"I can't see how you can get in the Tchaikovsky 4th Symphony. It is a bit hackneyed and does not wear too well and you have four symphonies as it is – quite enough and all far better stuff than the Tchaikovsky. My other suggestion I hope you will for many reasons agree to viz. Parry's *Pied Piper*. It is excessively lively and jolly and just fits the joviality of Saturday evening. Parry saves us lots of sovereigns by getting us of the loan of the College Concert Room but

[64] Stanford to *The Times*, 21 July 1910, p. 9. See also Fawcett to *The Times*, 23 July 1910, p. 12.

independently of this it is right and proper to represent him. It is very doubtful if he would conduct. Has Rachmaninov been asked yet? Neither he nor the orchestral engagements ought to be postponed for long."

[Committee discussion]

The following objections were raised to the Programme as revised:

1. For Thursday evening Act III of *Die Walkyrie* was the original suggestion of the Committee, and not Act I, and the Committee prefer Act III to Act I.
2. Strong objection was taken to the Programme for Friday morning. Mr Hannam and Mr Atkinson expressed their opinion that the overture *Manfred* and the *Faust* Part III should be omitted from the Programme.
3. The Committee did not approve of the exclusion from the programme of a Symphony by Tchaikovsky and suggested that his 4th or 5th Symphony should be included in the works to be given.
4. The inclusion of *The Pied Piper* in Saturday evening's programme was not unanimously approved and suggested that if a work of Hubert Parry's was to be included something else should be selected.

A discussion took place as to the new works to be included in the programme and the Secretary was instructed to write to Mr Vaughan Williams and say that the Committee would be glad to see the score of the new work which he offered for performance and upon receipt of the score the Secretary was instructed to forward it to Sir Charles Stanford and ask his opinion and advice upon the work.

The question of the inclusion of a work by Mr Basil Harwood was directed to stand over until after the meeting with Sir Charles Stanford on the 30th inst.[65]

At subsequent meetings the committee accepted Stanford's suggestion of including Palestrina's *Missa O admirabile commercium* and his approval of Vaughan Williams's *Sea Symphony* (electing to pay Vaughan Williams 30 guineas), and did replace Act III of *Die Walkyrie* with Act I. Stanford made more suggestions at subsequent meetings, some of which were adopted, some not: the inclusion of Rachmaninov's Second Symphony (its British première) and Debussy's *Blessed Damozel* ('fascinating stuff' according to Stanford[66]) were based on his recommendations.

Stanford was pleased with the final programme. On holiday in Northumberland, he wrote to Herbert Thompson criticising Robin Legge for declaring the programme dull:

I am concerned to hear from you that the serials [that is, subscriptions] are below the level. But it really is not surprising when people

[65] Leeds Festival Programme Committee Minutes, 22 June 1909, WYAS.
[66] Stanford to Hannam, 21 Oct. 1909, quoted in Greene, *Stanford*, 143.

like Legge, who ought to know better, slang the programme in the
D[aily] T[elegraph] and, when there are 12 English to 12 German
works in the programme, curse the Commee for asking Rachmaninoff. All these things tell. Considering that one can't get everything
exactly as one wants with a body of men of widely different tastes,
I think the programme is wonderfully interesting and representative. I expect Legge's programme would be this:-

Wednesday mng	Elektra – Strauss.
Wed evg	New Symphony – Cyril Scott
	Choral Symphony – Mahler.
Thursday mng	New Oratorio "The Loan Guarantee Assocn
	Bankruptcy" – Granville Bantock
Thursday evg	Sinfonia Domestica – Strauss
	New Choral Work "The Fens" – Hathaway.
Friday mng	Acts 1, 2, 3 'Pelléas and Mélisande'– Debussy.
Friday evg	Acts 4, 5 'Pelléas and M.' – Debussy
Sat mng	Oratorio "The Black Country" – Rutland
	Boughton
	Part I. Smoke
	II. The Pit Mouth
	III. The explosion.
Sat evg.	Cantata – Julius Harrison "The diversion of
	Messaline"
	Double Concerto for Penny Whistle and
	Tuba. – A. Bax

'God Help the Audience'

Receipts for the festival £1. 13. 4[67]

Stanford's version of Legge's preferred programme shows his own biases;
the inclusion of works by Strauss (*Don Juan*) and Debussy in both the
real programme and Stanford's 'Legge alternative' show that he was
prepared to go a certain distance with both composers but that his toler-
ance was strictly limited. His consignment of Bax, Bantock, Boughton,
Harrison, Hathaway, Mahler and Scott to the 'Legge alternative' shows
a contempt for music he perceived to be overly redolent of Wagnerian
indulgence and exoticism.

The real Festival was very successful. The presence of Rachmaninov,
who played his Second Piano Concerto and conducted his Second
Symphony, was a great coup and, of the indigenous works premièred,
Vaughan Williams's *Sea Symphony* was his first large-scale work to
achieve prominence. Stanford's conducting and organisation were
praised also and, unusually, Parry wrote positively about his conducting of the *St Matthew Passion*.[68] A difficult encounter with Elgar was

---

[67] Stanford to Thompson, 7 Aug. 1910, LUL, MS 361, item 277.

[68] Parry wrote 'At 11 Matthäus Passion very finely dealt with. Stanford treated it authen-
tically. Chorales *forte*. "O Mensch bewein' dein Sünde gross" *forte*. Final chorus *forte*

avoided since the Committee had declined to pay him the £100 he demanded for conducting his First Symphony; in light of the famous incident at Bournemouth in August when Stanford had refused to shake Elgar's hand (see Pl. 10), Elgar's absence from Leeds was fortunate indeed. Despite this Stanford conducted Elgar's *Variations* and *Sea Pictures*. Stanford escaped neither the obligatory performance of *Elijah*, nor Tchaikovsky's Fourth Symphony, but Parry's *The Pied Piper* and Act I of *Die Walkyrie* both made the final programme, and Stanford also conducted the *German Requiem*, Handel's *Ode on St Caecelia's Day* and the Third Symphonies of Beethoven and Schumann.

Stanford's own works – the *Wellington Ode* and the new *Songs of the Fleet*, Op. 117 – were heard respectfully but did not raise great enthusiasm. The latter had originally been intended to be sung by the Leeds Chorus at the International Congress of Naval Architects, which was to have taken place at Queen's Hall in July 1910, but the Congress was cancelled due to the death of King Edward VII. As a result the Songs, already learnt by the chorus, were slipped into the Festival programme instead, and performed on 13 October. Like *Songs of the Sea*, *Songs of the Fleet* comprises five settings of poems by Henry Newbolt but on a bigger scale and requiring a mixed chorus. Comparison with the earlier work was inevitable and was not positive: Herbert Thompson wrote, 'The new series of sea-songs must inevitably undergo the test of comparison with its predecessor, and, while not suffering the fatality which attends most sequals, can hardly be regarded as any advance upon them.'[69] In the new set Stanford wrote three slow and two quick songs which, for many, made the pace pedestrian. This does not, however, endow the work with an inferior nature but a different

(but slow). The effect however was good. Elwes best I have ever heard as Evangelist' (Diary, 15 Oct. 1910, ShP). The performance of his own work, *The Pied Piper*, was awful in rehearsal; Parry later wrote 'The Leeds rehearsal of *The Pied Piper* of Oct 10 was one of the most dreadful things I have ever experienced. In the first 6 bars I saw they did not know anything about it. Then they sang wrong notes and bungled leads. And finally at the words 'shut fast' the whole choir went completely off the rails. I felt an extraordinary sensation as if the bottom was falling out of everything. And turning at that moment saw Rachmaninoff and remembered that he was waiting his turn, and feeling the whole affair an utter farce went on without correcting the colossal blunder. Stanford afterwards tried to make them sing it right, but they were so utterly out of touch with the whole thing that it was hardly worthwhile. Stanford had gone on first at 7.30 and took near three quarters of an hour and he had told me he wanted Rachmaninoff to go on at 8.30! I saw Friskin afterwards and he told me that they had had such difficulty with Vaughan Williams's work that they had not ever been able to go through *The Pied Piper* once since the chorus came back from their holidays, and they had forgotten it' (Diary, Appendix to 1910, ShP). Fortunately, the problems were sorted out by the performance: '*Pied Piper* went very well indeed. But the public did not care for it' (Diary, 15 Oct. 1910, ShP).

[69] *Yorkshire Post*, 14 Oct. 1910, p. 7.

one. Once again the five songs are well written and deftly orchestrated. 'The Middle Watch' paints an eerie picture of the sea at night by the use of simple undulating triplets, long-held pedals, and slowly descending bass lines – old hat from Stanford by now but no less effective than the *Elegiac Ode* of 1884. 'The Song of the Sou'Wester' captures the mood of Newbolt's poetry excellently; as the character of the wind sweeps all before it so the music is restless and violent with perpetual running triplet quavers, sudden crashes, and blustering *crescendi*. 'The Little Admiral' does not quite gel, and the earlier part of 'Farewell' is overly static, but the last seventeen bars, in which a steady succession of chords builds superbly to the final cadence, more than make up for this. Although lacking the bluff jollity of the earlier set, *Songs of the Fleet* has been underrated, for it shows Stanford almost at his best both technically and creatively.

1911 saw Stanford compose his last symphony, as well as the Four Songs, Op. 125 the Second Piano Concerto, Op. 126, Eight Partsongs, Op. 127 and the Clarinet Sonata, Op. 129. The two vocal works do not require attention (the former being a lacklustre set of royalty ballads, dedicated to Clara Butt and her husband Kennerley Rumford, and the latter an uninspired collection of settings of Mary Coleridge), but the three instrumental works are more significant.

The Seventh Symphony in D minor, Op. 124 was completed on 6 February 1911 and premièred at the Philharmonic Society on 22 February 1912. Its most notable feature is its brevity – it takes about twenty-five minutes to perform – and Stanford is said to have been delighted that he managed to compress the whole symphonic argument into the time typically taken by Haydn or Mozart:[70] as the First Piano Concerto is the antithesis to the heroic and virtuosic Romantic concerto, so this symphony refutes the expansiveness of the period – neoclassicism almost before it was invented. Fuller Maitland was delighted with the result:

> While it is evident that Sir Charles Stanford has in this symphony set a conscious limit upon his means, the whole work cannot be passed by as an academic essay in an old style. He has said what he wanted to say and produced a beautiful result, and while there is nothing new in its technique, there is nothing stale or secondhand in its feeling.[71]

---

[70] See Thomas Dunhill in Greene, *Stanford*, 225: 'I think he was more particularly pleased that in the seventh, and last, he had succeeded in writing a full blown Symphony which took less than twenty-five minutes to perform! It was a clever concession to modern requirements, but he did not concede a particle of classical convictions. He dearly loved the sport of riding over difficulties without sacrificing his principles.'

[71] *The Times*, 23 Feb. 1912, p. 10.

This is misleading since it implies an adherence to classical forms, whereas the symphony includes some formal innovations. The work comprises the usual four movements, with the inner two reversed as Stanford preferred, and the fourth runs straight on from the third. The first movement looks to Mendelssohn and Schubert (especially to the 'Unfinished' Symphony at the opening) in its clarity of texture. The movement is Brahmsian in structure, although Stanford greatly compressed the development and transition passages. Interest is maintained by presenting exposition material differently in the recapitulation by extensive reorchestration, and continuing thematic and tonal manipulation. This use of Brahms's 'developing variation' technique is taken further in the next movement, a structural ingenuity. The movement opens with a B flat stately minuet, imbued with classical figures but with nods to both Beethoven and Brahms, and is followed by a 'trio' in the tonic minor, still light in texture. The restatement of the minuet follows as expected but transformed into 6/8 and hinting at a light Tchaikovskian waltz. The trio is also restated but this time in 2/4, with an attendant 'fairy' character found in some Tchaikovsky and Glazunov scherzi, before the movement concludes with brief references back to both the 6/8 and 3/4 versions of the minuet. This Cook's Tour could be distracting but the disparate styles are kept together through careful reworking which preserves a judicious balance between varying ambiences and thematic continuity.

Despite these ingenuities, the Variations and Finale were Stanford's formal *tour de force*. The third movement comprises a theme followed by six variations, each of which develops material in the Brahmsian manner, especially five constituent elements of the theme (Ex. 6.18). Stanford took this process much further, however: Variations V and VI act not only as an integral part of the preceding but as a transition into the Finale (by virtue of a change of tempo and time signature, previously consistent). The Finale itself has a dual personality: it is a sonata-form movement, but also a massive seventh variation of the third movement. A variant on *x1* is the first subject, while a development of Variation III forms the second. The development is more a reminiscence: Variation IV and the first subject of the first movement reappear, followed by *x1* again, this time treated in a manner redolent of the finale of Brahms's Second Symphony. The recapitulation is compressed but straightforward; brief references to Variations IV and VI of the preceding movement herald the coda.

Stanford had shown occasional interest in structural innovation previously (for example, the Cello Sonata, Op. 9, the Violin Sonata, Op. 11, the 'Dead Men' Variations and the Clarinet Concerto) and the reasons for this recurrence are unknown. Lewis Foreman views the Classical and

Example 6.18   Seventh Symphony, Op. 124: (a) Theme; (b) Variation I, opening; (c) Variation II, opening; (c) Variation III, opening; (d)
Variation IV, opening; (f) Variation IV, climax; (g) Variation V;
(h) Variation VI; (i) Finale, first subject; (j) Finale, second subject (cf. also (d))

early Romantic overtones of the texture and the 'light' substance of
the music as a reaction to the self-indulgence and blatancy, as Stanford
saw it, of Elgar's symphonies.[72] This is probably true since Stanford had

---

[72] Lewis Foreman, sleevenotes for Stanford's Seventh Symphony, recorded by the Ulster
Orchestra, conducted by Vernon Handley, Chandos Records, CHAN 8861.

disliked Elgar's First Symphony[73] and always delighted in debunking the grandeur of others (for example, in the *Ode to Discord*), but this does not explain the structural complexity of the Seventh Symphony. Although the internal relationships facilitated his brevity, they are more intricate than this sole object requires, and it is probable that he was influenced by the intricate relationships within Rachmaninov's Second Symphony, the British première of which had taken place at Leeds four months earlier; the extensive thematic cross-references between the movements, especially in the Finale, show a strong resemblance to the practices of the Russian. Notably, however, Stanford used these intricacies to a different end, for while Rachmaninov's work is the apotheosis of the expansive, thematically integrated Romantic symphony, Stanford's is virtuous in its economy and brevity. Stanford looked not only to Rachmaninov, however, but also to his own work, for the Variations and Finale are similar to the 'Dead Men' Variations in their overall conception; the recall of specific passages is the new ingredient in the Seventh Symphony. Although the spirits of other composers hover over the work, Stanford produced music which was very much his own and which showed his skills to great advantage; throughout the Symphony is pleasing and the lightness of touch, its strongest characteristic, is uplifting. Despite the eschewal of emotional intensity the work is never trite and the occasional climax, especially Variation IV of the third movement, is made more powerful by its brevity – Stanford succeeded in maintaining the emotional balance of the work amidst the formal manipulations. Although the construction of the work is meticulous and calculated, and a perfect example of academicism, this is surely a work Shaw would have found difficult to criticise for lack of spirit.

In his other big work of 1911, the Second Piano Concerto, Op. 126, Stanford also nodded in the direction of Rachmaninov, again reflecting the Russian's presence at Leeds. The concerto is less successful than the Seventh Symphony since he did not manage to make the movements cohere so well but there is much beautiful writing, even if parts of the first movement echo the second piano concertos of both Rachmaninov and Brahms. The influence of the former is particularly evident in the exposition, the first subject paralleling exactly that of Rachmaninov in key and in rapid piano arpeggios set against an imposing theme in the tenor range of the orchestra, while the second subject echoes both Rachmaninov's piano figuration and lyricism (Ex. 6.19). Brahms's stylistic influence is evident in other sections of piano writing and in some of the orchestration. The remaining two movements are less derivative

---

[73] Parry wrote, 'Stanford seemed immensely pleased because he disliked Elgar's symphony. Said Friskin and Benson also disliked it' (Parry's Diary, 8 Dec. 1908, ShP).

Example 6.19   Second Piano Concerto, Op. 126, first movement, second subject

but materially weaker; the theme of the slow movement, for example –
again influenced by Rachmaninovian lyricism – is too slender to support
the movement's length. In the finale, Stanford, in Herbert Howells's
words, 'turns his face to the west [and] fills his mind with the thematic
cut-and-thrust of melody and rhythm innately Irish'.[74] This is true insofar
as the principal theme is modelled on the Irish war songs which also
influenced 'I've sharpened the sword' in *Shamus O'Brien*, but the second
subject is weak, and the movement does not capture the same momentum
as many of Stanford's other finales. The concerto was tried out at the
RCM on 29 September 1911 but, despite the interest showed by Moritz
Rosenthal and Willem Mengelberg, Stanford had to wait until 1915 for
the première and until 1916 before he heard it himself (see pp. 287–8).

The final work of 1911, the Clarinet Sonata, Op. 129, was completed
on 28 December. It has remained Stanford's most popular chamber
work, and is his only sonata for a wind or brass instrument. It is an
easy and graceful piece, placid if not always purposeful in mood; its
relative popularity arises not least from its being a rarity as a pre-First
World War British clarinet sonata. The slow movement is the best
known, and is cast as an Irish 'Caoine', similar in manner to 'A grave
yawns cold' in *Shamus O'Brien*, and makes effective use of the timbre,
agility and different registers of the instrument. Once again Stanford had

---

[74] Howells, 'Address to the Royal Musical Association', 30.

to wait a long time for the première, given by Charles Draper and Thomas Dunhill at Steinway Hall on 14 March 1916.

Throughout 1911 discussions had taken place over arrangements for the 1913 Leeds Festival, the financial situation of which was causing concern. During Stanford's conductorship the results had declined steadily and in 1910 the Festival had finally slipped into deficit, losing £162. Now the contrary motivations of Stanford and the Committee came into sharp relief. Stanford, though financially aware, had always believed that the primary function of the festival was artistic; the committee was more conscious of the Festival's original *raison d'être*, raising money for local charities. The failure of the 1910 Festival to raise any money led the committee to look hard at its arrangements; its principal conclusion was that the Festival needed more than one conductor:

> The Management Committee believe that it is impossible for one man to be in sympathy with each individual school of music represented at a Festival and that it would add very considerably to the interest taken in the Festival if each school were represented by a conductor who had made the music of that school his special study and whose fame chiefly rested upon his ability to conduct such music and his method of interpretation.[75]

The Committee decided to ask Stanford to be joint conductor with two or three others. Its letter, followed by Stanford's reply, sets out their respective positions:

> Dear Sir Charles,
>
> It is now necessary that a beginning should be made to the arrangements for the Leeds Musical Festival of 1913 and the Management Committee have just held their first meeting. The financial results of the last Festival naturally occupied our attention and it was unanimously felt that the methods hitherto adopted required careful reconsideration and that some entirely new departure would probably have to be made ... We considered ... the conductorship and ... it was resolved that it would be desirable to abandon the practice of having a sole conductor and instead to retain the services of more than one conductor, each of whom should be responsible for certain concerts or certain works. The plan involves no doubt a serious departure from the past, but the Committee think that it will have the effect of stimulating interest in future Festivals and thus conduce to their success. The details have yet to be considered and nothing has been decided as to the names of the gentlemen who will be invited to take part, except that the Committee, who are very sensible of the value of your services in the past and most anxious to preserve your long connection with the Leeds Festivals,

[75] Leeds Festival Management Committee report arising from its meeting on 7 Dec. 1911, filed in the Minute Book of the General Committee, p. 54, WYAS.

have desired me to express the hope that you will accept the appointment of one of these conductorships.[76]

My dear Mr Ford,

You and your Committee will, I am sure, understand that I could not give a clear answer to your letter without expressing my views about the policy which has given rise to it.

As a general principle I cannot think that a division of musical control at a great Festival could be to its advantage, and I am convinced that it would be a very gross injury to the cause of British music, dealt by one of its most representative institutions, and as I hold this view so strongly, I should be false to my trust if I endorsed such a policy by taking a share in the conducting.

To pass to lesser matters, the Committee will, as business men of experience, see that a man who has had the sole control of the musical forces for four festivals could not accept a lesser or limited position. An Admiral who has commanded a fleet in action can never again become a captain of a battleship.

I offer no opinion as to whether the policy adopted by the Committee is likely to result in financial success at Leeds, or to stem the tide of financial failure from which all Festivals, Musical Societies, and practically every serious musical enterprise, public or private, in the country has been suffering for some years.

I am happy to think that of all the Festivals of recent times in various parts of the country, even the oldest and soundest, Leeds has shown by far the most successful balance sheet. If it has been no exception to the prevailing depression, it can at any rate point to the smallest item on the debit side. Whether the committee's solution to the problem is the right one time alone can show. I hope very sincerely that in due course the pendulum may swing back both for Leeds and for all the other musical ventures of artistic value in the country.[77]

Subsequently, on 25 January 1912, a deputation went to London to discuss the matter with Stanford further, but neither side moved. The arguments which Stanford advanced for the decline were principally that all Festivals were in difficulty and that Leeds had alienated part of the potential audience by limiting, from 1901, the chorus to Leeds residents only.[78] His arguments had some merit. Expenses during his tenure had fallen from £9,903 in 1901 to £7,912 in 1910, showing prudence. Income, however, had fallen more sharply, from £11,555 in 1901 to

---

[76] J. Rawlinson Ford to Stanford, 14 [?] Dec. 1911, filed in the Leeds Festival General Committee Minutes of 20 Dec. 1911, p. 128, WYAS.

[77] Stanford to J. Rawlinson Ford, 18 Dec. 1911, filed in the Leeds Festival General Committee Minutes of 20 Dec. 1911, p. 128, WYAS.

[78] Whereas, for several previous festivals, many West Riding towns had sent a contingent.

£7,749 in 1910 (it is unknown how much this decline was attributable to the change in the constitution of the chorus). The Committee was not minded to accept these arguments, however, and Stanford's assertion that all Festivals were in difficulties was hardly comforting to a committee with a £162 deficit; it decided to thank Stanford for his previous work and to move on.

Stanford's attitude was unsurprising. Even Parry was understanding and wrote to W. S. Hannam:

> I'm afraid it's rather dangerous my being let in behind the scenes, especially at the moment when Stanford has been making himself so absolutely impossible here that I can only hold formal business communications with him . . . It is very much to be regretted that his tenure of the stick must come to an end. You say you have given him the option to take part of the Festival. If it was decided to split up the days between different conductors you couldn't do less, in view of his services and association with Leeds – but it was to be expected that he would not accept. He could hardly step down from boss to an inferior position in the same show![79]

The Committee approached Elgar, who accepted on the mistaken assumption that he was being offered broadly the same terms and conditions as existed previously.[80] On discovering that the Committee was offering something different, Elgar withdrew. Nikisch was subsequently engaged for four concerts, along with Hugh Allen and Elgar, who had reconsidered, for two concerts each. Ironically, the 1913 Festival lost more money than that of 1910 (£628 compared to £162); whilst the decline in income was stopped, expenditure increased, especially on 'principal artists'.[81] The Committee was satisfied but Stanford doubtless felt vindicated.

Despite the unfortunate way in which the relationship between Stanford and Leeds ended, it is clear that Stanford did the Festival a great deal of good. As in Cambridge, he used his extensive contacts to entice famous musicians to Leeds, increasing its stature. He also worked hard with the choir to maintain its reputation; press comment indicates that he was successful in this endeavour. Most importantly, however,

---

[79] Parry to Hannam, 6 Feb. 1912, McMaster University, Hamilton, Ont., Canada.

[80] Elgar asked the Committee to announce his appointment in the following terms: 'The Committee of the Leeds Festival have engaged Sir Edward Elgar O.M. as Conductor and Musical Director of the Leeds Festival; Sir Edward will be consulted as to the engagement of some celebrated conductors for special performances &c.' (letter from Elgar to the Festival Committee filed in the Leeds Festival Management Committee Minutes of 27 Feb. 1912, p. 164, WYAS).

[81] Unfortunately, no distinction is made between conductors and other principals in the accounts.

he broadened Leeds's musical horizon beyond that contemplated by Sullivan, and pushed the Festival Committee tentatively to explore some of the modern trends in music, both British and foreign. Stanford's perspective remained contained but his promotion of such composers as Rachmaninov and Vaughan Williams was of great importance, especially for the latter. Even though Stanford was not prepared to consider the most radical music, he brought Leeds into the twentieth century, urging the committee to be more innovative and to stop pandering to ever-present demands to give old favourites and certainties. In this one can see a continuation of the approach he had espoused in Cambridge since the 1870s; Leeds benefited from the same energy and determination thirty years later.

1912 produced little new music: Stanford completed only the *Six Characteristic Pieces for Piano*, Op. 132 on 17 January, the incidental music for Louis Parker's play *Drake* (Op. 130) on 7 August and three partsongs for female voices entitled *Fairy Day*, Op. 131 on 6 November (dedicated to Victor Harris and the St Cecelia Choir of New York but apparently unperformed by them). The piano pieces were dedicated to Moritz Rosenthal and the work was Stanford's first for piano solo since the *Three Rhapsodies from Dante* of 1904. They contain some deft and attractive writing; the first piece, 'In modo Dorico', was later rearranged for use as the Prelude to *The Travelling Companion*. *Drake* was Stanford's most successful attempt at theatrical music; Parker's play opened on 3 September 1912 at His Majesty's Theatre and ran for 221 performances.[82] Wisely, if unoriginally, Stanford employed 'Drake's Drum' as the main theme in the music, along with 'Devon, O Devon' in the Entr'acte to Act III, a traditional melody 'Since First I saw Your Face', and a tune from *Ravenscroft's Psalter* ('Bristol' in *The English Hymnal*). While the Overture treats 'Drake's Drum' in much the same way as the song, Stanford also set it as a calm and mournful theme at the opening of Act I by use of cor anglais and static wide-spread strings (Ex. 6.20) and the suite contains a good mixture of vigour, serenity and pageantry.

An unexpected blow came on 1 September 1912 when one of Stanford's most successful former pupils, Samuel Coleridge Taylor, died. Stanford was greatly saddened as he had always regarded Coleridge Taylor as one of his best students; soon after, in late November an appeal was made for the composer's family, who were living in straitened circumstances. Coleridge Taylor's relative poverty, and his death at the age of 37, had caused consternation in the musical world, not least

---

[82] It closed on 12 Mar. 1913.

Example 6.20   *Drake*, Op. 130, *Adagio* from Scene I, bars 1–6

because of the profits made by Novello from *Hiawatha's Wedding Feast*, which had been sold to them for 15 guineas. S. Squire Sprigge, who initiated in the appeal, argued in *The Times*: 'It is fair to the composer's memory as a hard working and careful man that the public should know that he did provide with his brains a work which under the royalty method of dealing with literary and artistic property, would have supported his family after his death, while making him more comfortable during his life.'[83] Over subsequent days Novello responded to the implicit charge of unfair dealing, and Stanford waded in. Although the subsequent exchange of letters concentrated specifically on Coleridge Taylor and the assignment of the copyrights and the *Ballade in D Minor*, Op. 4, Stanford was really focusing on how Novello treated young composers wishing to make a mark:

> *Hiawatha* was published in two sections. The first, *Hiawatha's Wedding*, the composer (gladly, of course) sold outright. For how much? Will Messrs. Novello deny that he asked for a royalty of Parts II and III in consequence of the great success of Part I, and was refused it? What were the terms which he gladly accepted, and what were the profits which Messrs. Novello no less gladly have made? Do they number *Hiawatha* among his less successful works?[84]

The arguments presented by Stanford are somewhat one-sided but the quotations from correspondence between Coleridge Taylor and Novello in respect of the *Ballade* make it clear that the publishers were quite

---

[83] S. Squire Sprigge to *The Times*, 26 Nov. 1912, p. 21.
[84] Stanford to *The Times*, 2 Dec. 1912, p. 9. The other letters published were on 28 Nov., p. 9 (Novello), 30 Nov., p. 8 (Sprigge), 4 Dec., p. 8 (Novello), 6 Dec., p. 10 (Stanford), and 7 Dec., p. 8 (Novello).

prepared to try to intimidate him into accepting inferior conditions. Stanford's essential point, that Novello had knowingly exploited Coleridge Taylor's youth and pliability, was well made, and the publishers did not come out in a good light; one suspects that, on this occasion, many other musicians felt that Stanford's acerbity was more than justified.

At Cambridge, Stanford became involved in a debate about the provision of music teaching for undergraduates. Since the introduction of compulsory residence in the 1890s a few changes had taken place – not least the conversion, in 1899, of Stanford's general lectures into a series of composition classes.[85] In 1913 the extent of this composition teaching became an issue – no doubt prompted in part by Stanford's general absence from Cambridge. The Board of Musical Studies voted in favour of increasing provision, with Stanford and Charles Wood vehemently opposed. The exchange of letters between Stanford and Sedley Taylor shows how the sides shaped up, while also showing Stanford's failure to appreciate irony, and his dislike of Cyril Rootham:

> [Stanford to Taylor] The extent of the composition teaching in the University is not measured by the length of the lecture list in print. The Harmony and Counterpoint lectures cover also a good deal of preliminary composition. But apart from that fact there is no earthly use in giving lectures of the usual type in composition alone. It can only be taught by individual criticism and advice. You can't preach it from a high desk. My lectures are an individual lesson, man by man. I may claim to have some judgement upon this, and upon the ground covered at present as I have had 30 years' experience in the best ways of training in the craft, and most of the young composers of the day have come from my teaching room ... All this and much more I would have talked over with you if you had given me the opportunity for doing so: and I must say I think if it were only on the grounds of old friendship it would have been more fitting to talk the matter over with me, if not as Professor at any rate as a friend before it appeared in the agenda of a dry board meeting.

> [Taylor to Stanford] Let me say at once that your gentle approach has gone straight to my heart and made me feel that in this matter I ought to have begun by communicating with you as Professor, and

---

[85] See Sedley Taylor to Stanford, 5 Feb. 1899, CUL, Add. MS 6255, item 134. Evidence from Edward Dent suggests that by the late 1890s Stanford's 'history' lectures were poorly attended and then by greater numbers of non-students than by undergraduates: 'Stanford's first lecture in the afternoon though there were not many men [that is, undergraduates] there. A very good lecture indeed' (Dent's Diary, 6 Nov. 1897, KCC); at the first of the new style classes, Dent noted, 'At 2.15 I went to Stanford and was delighted to find I was his only audience. Two ladies came but he choked them off' (Dent's Diary, 29 Apr. 1899, KCC).

still more, as old friend. I earnestly ask your forgiveness for not having done so.

[Stanford to Taylor] Say no more: to get such a generous letter from you was a real joy to me: but not to anyone who knows you long and well anything of a surprise. Prosit!

[Stanford to Taylor] I wish *à propos* the proceedings of yesterday [a meeting of the Board of Musical Studies] to make one or two things clear.

1. I should like it to appear in the minutes that the Professor and the lecturer in Harmony and Counterpoint voted in the minority on the motion to extend the composition teaching.
2. I wish you to know that I was not going to explain at the bidding of a junior member of the board [Cyril Rootham], the conditions and reasons which were clearly understood when the salary of the Professor was fixed at £200. The question was discussed fully by Cobb and others at the time of Macfarren's appointment and I was cognisant of them. The salary was so fixed because it was imperative in the interest of the University exams to have one of the Heads of the Profession in England as professor and it was considered impossible to ensure that, or proper for the University to offer less than that sum as a retaining fee. The exams were the main feature of the question, and the four lectures were added presumably because Bennett did not lecture at all. This arrangement stood exactly as it was in 1887 when I was appointed and Austen Leigh ... clearly stated to me that the conditions were the same as those which Macfarren accepted. Such methods therefore as dividing two hundred pounds by four to shew that the Professor's lectures cost £50 apiece (which leaves out the examination work altogether) are wholly beside the mark. The salary is, after deducting the lecturing and exams, a retaining fee as originally intended.
3. If there is a lectureship in form and analysis the appointment should go first to the person who both in seniority and experience and grasp of the subject stands first: Alan Gray. It would be almost an insult to pass over him.
4. I considered the question of giving some extra lectures in Composition in the October and Lent terms and inquired carefully into the question some little time ago ... But the result of my doing so would in all likelihood be the draining of the pockets of others to a very considerable extent [who offered and charged for preliminary tuition in composition], without any preponderating advantage; and I am not prepared to risk doing such an injustice to anybody, especially in a profession which is the worst paid existing ... [Gratuitous music tuition] gets no thanks from the University, though its members are very free in censuring their colleagues if they do not give it. You may take it however that if the Musical Board encourage gratuitous teaching as their main plank instead of adhering to the principle that the University is bound to support it if it wants it, even their request for an adequate salary for the lecturer will go into the wastepaper basket.

My chief impression yesterday was the urbanity and courtesy with which Dr Rootham upheld the best tradition of his college. There used to be days when such men as Blore and Austen Leigh put discussions on a high, dignified, and gentlemanly plane.[86]

While Stanford failed really to appreciate that it was his own absence from Cambridge *versus* the requirement for compulsory residence which had led to this situation, one can have sympathy with his argument that, if the University wanted more tuition to be provided, it should be prepared to pay for it, rather than trying to provoke current appointees to provide lessons out of a sense of guilt. Within two months the dispute had moved on and been partially resolved by Sedley Taylor's decision to fund a lectureship in form and analysis himself[87] – conveniently supporting the teaching of composition without explicitly increasing it. It was perhaps inevitable that Stanford got involved in another spat, by arguing for advertisement of the post nationally, while members of the university preferred an internal appointment in order to secure a Cambridge resident.[88] Asked later informally which of Stewart MacPherson and Cyril Rootham would be the better appointee, Stanford replied 'MacPherson';[89] the Board appointed Rootham, no doubt to Stanford's fury. While the argument was, in itself, a matter of detail, the tone of the dispute (the correspondence gives several indications of Stanford's lack of availability to go to Cambridge to discuss matters, and one blank refusal) and its nature shows that his relationship with the university and his supporters and friends had become distant at best and very strained at worst.

1913 was a much more fertile year for composition, Stanford completing all works Opp. 133 to 141 inclusive. Four works are Irish-inspired (see pp. 281–5); the others are chamber and choral music. The Second Piano Quartet, Op. 133 (completed 10 January and premièred 14 March 1914 at Bechstein Hall) includes an idiosyncratic slow movement in 8/8, split into 5 + 3, but the most important of the non-Irish works is the Three Motets, Op. 135, the elaborate choral settings later inspiring Parry's *Songs of Farewell*.[90] The standard of all three pieces is high but the first, 'Ye holy Angels Bright', is the best. Based on the

[86] Respectively, Stanford to Taylor, 2 Feb. 1913, CUL, Add. MS 6260, item 169; Taylor to Stanford, 3 Feb. 1913, CUL, Add. MS 6255, item 147; Stanford to Taylor, 3 Feb. 1913, CUL, Add. MS 6260, item 170; Stanford to Taylor, 18 Feb. 1913, CUL, Add. MS 6260, item 171.

[87] See Stanford to Taylor 16 Apr. 1913, CUL, Add. MS 6260, item 174.

[88] See Stanford to Taylor, 21 July 1913, CUL, Add. MS 6260, item 177.

[89] See Stanford to Taylor, [undated], CUL, Add. MS 6260, item 182, and Stanford to Taylor, 21 Oct. 1913, CUL, Add. MS 6260, item 183.

[90] See Dibble, *Hubert Parry*, 478.

associated hymn tune 'Darwall's 148th', it looks backwards for inspiration and exploits Baroque contrapuntal techniques in the first stanza, *cantus firmus* in the second and double choir antiphony in the fourth (echoing the Service in F, Op. 36 and anticipating the *Magnificat*, Op. 164).

The rash of Irish-inspired works composed in the latter part of 1913 (*A Fire of Turf*, Op. 139, *A Sheaf of Songs from Leinster*, Op. 140 and the third and fourth Irish Rhapsodies (Opp. 137 and 141 respectively)) reflected Stanford's concerns about Home Rule for Ireland. Home Rule had last been attempted by Gladstone in 1893; the Conservative administrations of Salisbury and Balfour opposed it and Campbell-Bannerman's Liberal government, elected in 1906, had been apathetic. This changed after the General Election of 1910; the Liberals had become actively pro-Home Rule once again and needed the support of the Nationalists and/or Labour to get their programme through parliament. Accordingly a Home Rule bill was introduced in April 1912 and had a good chance of becoming law, since the newly passed Parliament Act prevented the Lords from scuppering the bill as they had previously. For Stanford this prospect was horrifying. He had always opposed Home Rule and now the situation was exacerbated by Ulster Protestants who, under Sir Edward Carson, actively campaigned for the exclusion of at least four north-eastern counties from Home Rule. The issue rumbled on until the outbreak of war in both parliament and Ireland, causing Stanford considerable anger and anxiety.

The two groups of Irish songs are settings of poetry by Winifred Letts and are pieces of political escapism. Miss Letts,[91] according to Stanford, was 'a quick little mouse of a lady living in Monkstown ... Such poets are rare birds: and the ones which smell of the real genuine turf are rarer still.'[92] While the poems are apolitical, they are rather more down to earth than other poetry Stanford had used for his Irish songs. Letts's poetry is relatively plain and unsentimental, and not so encumbered with the dialect which taints Moira O'Neill's writing. Unfortunately, Stanford rose to the occasion only sporadically. All the songs have something to offer, with 'A Fire of Turf' and 'The Chapel on the Hill' standing out as particularly responsive to the nuances of the texts. 'The Fair' is modelled on Stanford and Graves's arrangement of 'Trottin' to the Fair' in *Songs of Erin* and does not quite match its progenitor in execution. In *A Sheaf of Songs from Leinster*, 'Grandeur' and 'A Soft Day' are the most effective. The former, which reflects on the life of a woman at her

---

[91] Winifred Letts (1882–1972) published *Songs from Leinster* in 1913. Born in Co. Wexford, she was educated in London before returning to Ireland, where she worked for a time at both the Abbey and Gate Theatres.

[92] Stanford to Sir John Mahaffy, 5 May 1917, Trinity College, Dublin, MS 2075/270.

Example 6.21   'Grandeur' (from *A Sheaf of Songs from Leinster*), Op. 140, bars 1–8 (text: Winifred Letts)

wake, is simple and straightforward, and Stanford responded in kind, conjuring up the air of passive reflection which the poem demands (Ex. 6.21). Stanford later referred to the poem as being 'one of the most touching things I know',[93] and his setting, deeply felt yet curiously detached, is perfectly judged. A typically Stanfordian moment appears in the last stanza when, after having dwelt in C minor and E flat for the rest of the song, there is a fleeting and unique inflection of G flat at the words 'angels' – an excellent instance of chromatic colouring (Ex 6.22). 'A Soft Day' also shows Stanford's immaculate crafting, appearing to be deceptively simple on the surface but with every note and harmonic turn considered. Again the music balances the mood of the poetry very well. In the rest of the set, however, Stanford failed to capture the poet's spirit adequately: 'Little Peter Morrissey' deals in a

---

[93] Ibid.

Example 6.22   'Grandeur' (from *A Sheaf of Songs from Leinster*), Op. 140, bars
42–50 (text: Winifred Letts)

quite realistic vein with a neglected boy, but it is difficult to see what
Stanford's *parlando* recitative, technically accurate though it is, adds to
the words. The final song, 'Irish Skies', in which the London-based
emigrant dreams of Ireland, should have touched a nerve, but the music
remains curiously detached despite its evidently careful setting.

Of the two orchestral works, it is not clear why the *Irish Rhapsody
No. 3* should have lain so neglected – there is no evidence of any public
performance before its recording in 1987. One of two Rhapsodies for
solo instrument and orchestra (this one for cello, No. 6 for violin), it is,
despite the political background of its composition, an optimistic and
extrovert piece. Although it is well scored and quite gracefully written
for the solo cello, the proportions of the piece are badly skewed in favour

of the first section while the following jig, 'The Black Rogue', vigorous
and archetypally Irish, is scantily treated and followed by a brief Aeolian
melody which is discarded as soon as it is presented.

The *Irish Rhapsody No. 4* is a much stronger work. Completed on
10 November 1913, when strikes were disrupting Ireland and the Home
Rule bill was still crawling through parliament, Stanford's sympathy
with the Unionist cause is readily visible on the score: it is prefaced by
a quote from Thomas Moore's 'The Minstrel Boy' ('"Land of Song!"
said the Warrior-bard / "Tho' all the world betrays thee / One sword
at least thy rights shall guard / One faithful harp shall praise thee!"')
and followed by the words 'Dark and true and tender is the North' from
Tennyson's *The Princess*. The work also bears a subtitle, 'The Fisherman
of Lough Neagh and what he saw'. Stanford's musical plan is similar
to the previous rhapsodies; traditional Irish melodies are used as the
basis of the music, in this case 'I will raise my sail black, mistfully into
the morning' and 'The Death of General Wolfe'.[94] The subtitle and form
of the music imply a programme; a long extended opening section seems
to evoke early morning on Lough Neagh as the mist rises from the water,
and is followed by a brass chorale and a long 6/8 march illustrating an
approaching army, a bloody clash (including gunshot), and a hollow
triumph. When the work was premièred on 19 February 1914, *The
Times* had no doubt about the political message of the work:

> What did the Fisherman see? Some people will say that he saw a
> political pamphlet on the Ulster question. Certainly were we to try
> to put into words the programme which the combination of folk-
> tunes, mostly from the North, and the quotations from Moore and
> Tennyson written in the score suggest, the result would read very
> like a political pamphlet, perhaps 'another' solution. But Sir Charles
> Stanford has just avoided putting it into words; he has put it into
> music which is better, and we prefer to leave it there.[95]

Although the programme of the work is undeclared, there is no doubt
that Stanford was fervently involved with the Irish Question at this time
since rarely did his music sound so passionate and emotionally charged;
the opening is almost impressionistic until the entrance of the cor anglais,
whose melody brings one firmly back into Stanford's soundworld, here
calm and sad (Ex. 6.23). The later approach of the army is momentous
in its steady build but whereas, on many other occasions, one feels that

---

[94] Both to be found in Stanford's edition of the Petrie Collection (nos 365 and 377);
'The Death of General Wolfe' is stated as having been collected by the Revd J. Mease of
Rathmullen, Co. Donegal, and 'I will raise my sail' as having been supplied by Mary
O'Malley and James Gill of Arranmore on 8 Sept. 1857.

[95] *The Times*, 20 Feb. 1914, p. 8.

Example 6.23   *Irish Rhapsody No. 4, Op. 141, bars 1–13*

Stanford stepped back from a savage statement because it might be coarse, here he showed no such reservations: the last statement of the march theme is fully and aggressively orchestrated, while the anguished wailing which follows the gunfire (three bars of *fortissimo* timpani and side drum solo) is one of the best examples of Stanford casting aside the 'stiff upper lip' and caoining with abandon. It is this overt emotionalism which distinguishes the music: here is absolute commitment to the score and the rhapsody carries an unmistakable dynamism which makes it one of his finest works.

The Irish Question continued to preoccupy politicians in the first half of 1914. Stanford himself became involved in the Spring and sent a series of six letters to *The Times* outlining his opposition to Home Rule and the proposed exclusion of parts of Ulster from it; in the course of this correspondence he locked horns with both Henry Newbolt and Erskine Childers.[96] Stanford's attitude was simple: Home Rule as proposed was not wanted and would split Ireland into two, making Unionists outside Ulster highly vulnerable:

> [Home Rule] was a bone of contention thrown into a rapidly recuperating country by a government which could not stand alone without the support of the so-called Nationalist Party . . .
>
> The fact is that Ireland does not want Home Rule . . . The farmers who have purchased their land dread it . . . The priests are sitting

---

[96] Erskine Childers (1870–1922) was born of Anglo-Irish parents and educated at Haileybury and Trinity College, Cambridge. He worked as a Clerk in the House of Commons from 1895 to 1910 but then devoted himself to the cause of Home Rule. After the War he returned to Ireland permanently to campaign for independence. He joined the Republican Army in pursuance of this and was executed in 1922, a victim of the Irish Civil War.

on the stile ... The dreamers and the schemers are the only Irish
supporters of the bill. If it were dropped tomorrow there would be
a sigh a relief from the Giant's Causeway to Valentia.

People clamour for an alternative policy. It has been there ever
since Wyndham's Act. The alternative is consistent and accelerated
land purchase. If this were carried through Home Rule would be as
dead as mutton in a decade ...

In India we have Mahomedans and Brahmins who would be at
each others' throats if the rule were not in trusty hands outside and
above them. In Ireland we have the same situation in the equally
strong antipathies of Christian sects. We could not exclude
Mahomedans from Indian Home Rule, any more than we can
exclude Protestants from Irish Home Rule. To exclude a section of
them in the North would be a gross, and cowardly desertion of
those who are in the south, who are in smaller numbers and in greater danger.

The true feeling of Ireland was voiced this week by an Irish
Railway Porter from Limerick, a nationalist and a Roman Catholic
who said to me:- 'What are they doing with us all? Why can't they
leave us alone?'[97]

Childers declared Stanford's view to be 'delightfully old-fashioned'[98] and
unsubstantiated: just where was this great pro-Union majority, he asked.
Stanford could only come back with anecdotal evidence, but stuck to
his guns and to his caste (and missing the falsehood of his comparison
between India and Ireland in that 'the rule' in Ireland was not entrusted
to a group 'outside and above' everyone else).

Ireland remained on tenterhooks while the international situation too
declined. Stanford composed little during 1914 and was no doubt occupied by these issues and the completion of his autobiography, *Pages
from an Unwritten Diary*. A short setting of words by Milton, *On Time*,
Op. 142, was completed in May and followed by the *Thanksgiving Te
Deum*, Op. 143. The latter piece is quite effective in its solemnity, and
includes a quotation from the 'Last Post', but it is not clear for what
Stanford was giving thanks.[99] The declaration of war in August came

---

[97] Stanford to *The Times*, 9 Apr. 1914, p. 10. Wyndham's Act 1903 made provision
for Irish tenant farmers to buy their land and its provisions, alongside acts introduced
over the previous thirty years, had gradually established a class of Irish farmers unbe-
holden to absentee landlords. Stanford's comments about India are ironic since, ultimately,
partition on religious lines was exactly what did happen. The full series of correspondence
is: 23 Mar. 1914, p. 5 (Stanford), 26 Mar., p. 10 (Stanford), 1 Apr., p. 9 (Newbolt), 6
Apr., p. 6 (Stanford), 7 Apr., p. 10 (Newbolt), 9 Apr., p. 10 (Stanford), 11 Apr., p. 10
(Childers), and 13 Apr., p. 10 (Stanford).

[98] See previous note.

[99] The manuscript of the work does not survive and it is not possible to date the piece
more exactly than 1914, which is the date of copyright: the work could commemorate
those killed in the civil unrest in Ireland in 1913 and 1914. Also conceivable, but less
likely, it may refer to those killed early in the war, although this suggests more unfounded
optimism than is credible.

as just one more blow: Stanford wrote to Richter for the first time in six years:

> I must send you a note on this terrible day. I have not forgotten the old times, and everything that you have done for music in England. Thank God that in music we do not have political or military questions.
>   I do not know whether this letter will get as far as Bayreuth. I have sent it via Boito in Milan. I can well imagine what you will experience like all of us will. I won't forget my student days in Leipzig, or the happy times in Vienna, or Hans.[100]

His benevolent attitude did not last for long; as the war progressed his attitude to Richter and to Germany became more entrenched and hostile.

For the first year or so of the war Stanford was able to view it, like the Boer War, as something distant. Greene recalled that Stanford put immense faith in gossip received from 'respectable' sources and quoted a postcard received in September 1914: 'A letter from the Provost Marshall on ___'s staff came to ___ yesterday saying that we are to "be of good cheer" and that he has such good news he must not say what it is. This from a Boss at Headquarters.'[101] Parry viewed Stanford's claims to be privy to important information with sardonic pleasure: 'Stanford very amusing at luncheon and indeed in afternoon. Very important telling people in secret all the latest rumours of the clubs, with the air of their being the latest from headquarters which he had been privileged to hear.'[102] At this stage Stanford was able, like many others, to retreat from reality because of the 'business as usual' spirit and the conviction that it would 'all be over by Christmas'. That the British Army took several months to sort itself out postponed the impact of the war becoming apparent until well into 1915.

The effects of the war were brought home to Stanford in the events leading to the première of his Second Piano Concerto, which took place on 3 June 1915. Completed in 1911, its performance had been planned by Stanford since May 1913: he had written to Horatio Parker that he would like, with Leonard Borwick, to première the work in the USA during Borwick's next visit in October 1914 (thus replicating the team which had premièred the First Piano Concerto in 1895).[103] By March 1914, however, this plan had fallen through.[104] In November Parker

---

[100] Stanford to Richter, 15 Aug. 1914, RCM, MS 4826, item 40. Translated from German.

[101] Greene, *Stanford*, 268.

[102] Parry's Diary, 24 Sept. 1914, ShP.

[103] Stanford to Parker, 8 May 1913, Yale University Music Library.

[104] See Stanford to Parker, 21 Jan. 1914 and 5 Mar. 1914, Yale University Music Library.

invited Stanford to visit in June 1915 to take part in the Norfolk Music Festival. This prestigious event was held at the estate of Carl Stoeckel, in Connecticut,[105] and it had become the practice to invite a well-known composer: Coleridge Taylor and Sibelius had visited previously. Stanford was delighted with the idea:

> Your charming and very tempting letter arrived this morning. It is too tempting too resist (in spite of the ghastly sea!) [although] many things may happen between now and then. But, all things being well, as in my unfailing optimism I believe it will be, I will with pleasure accept the very kind invitation of Mr and Mrs. Stoeckel, to whom my best thanks for their proffered hospitality. I shall, however, ask to bring my wife with me: to keep up my spirits on the sailing and to give her a view too of the new country . . . I would like very particularly for my new Pianoforte Concerto to be done, and I wd also reserve the first performance of it for Norfolk if they wd consider it . . . I have all the material ready. Rosenthal as you know, wanted to do it in N. Y. this winter, but his visit fell through.[106]

The arrangements for the visit were made and Stanford was happy to assume that the war would not prevent his journey. His optimism was misplaced. His and Jennie's passage was booked on the *Lusitania* on 15 May, returning on 26 June, but on 7 May the Germans torpedoed the ship off Ireland. Stanford wrote to Parker:

> Double D____ those Huns. It has upset the whole thing: for they are unanimous here that I must not risk it: especially in returning, for anything might happen in five weeks and I might be marooned on your side. Also the wife would not let me go alone, she wd be miserable if I did . . . Alas! Alas! But it will all come right in the end. But I do so hate upsetting all [Stoeckel's] plans, and (if possible) I love Wilhelm even less than before. Brutus: and to go and hit your good people like that! I am so grieved for them and for you all.[107]

The performance of the Piano Concerto went ahead as planned, with Harold Bauer taking the solo role and Arthur Mees conducting. It was Stanford's first direct brush with the consequences of war and frustrated the only visit he had hoped to make across the Atlantic. The British première of the concerto was planned for October 1915 but was cancelled and finally took place on 7 December 1916 at Bournemouth.

---

[105] The festival survives now as the Yale Chamber Music Festival; Carl Stoeckel's father had been Professor of Music at Yale.
[106] Stanford to Parker, 12 Nov. 1914, Yale University Music Library.
[107] Stanford to Parker, 9 May 1915, Yale University Music Library.

If one seeks an example of how the war started to affect Stanford, his article 'Music and the War', written in 1915, is it.[108] He tried to retain a sense of impartiality in his argument and his discussion of the effects of war echoes a common position taken by many intellectuals, that is, that occasional wars were necessary cathartic purifications:

> The unmistakable influence which national convulsions and international wars have had at all times in awakening the highest forces of musical art is one of the most interesting problems of the historian and the psychologist ... At no time has a great country failed to produce great composers when its resources have been put to the supreme test of war, provided ... that the ideals of the nation are high, that its principles of action are just, and that it possesses a sound incentive to call forth a genuinely patriotic effort.

When he turned his attention to Germany, however, Stanford's argument turned polemical, accusing the Germans of 'admit[ting] no rivalry, however friendly' in respect of music and of using 'her all-powerful Press Bureau to stamp out any sign of appreciation of good foreign work'. Stanford's personal agenda becomes obvious in his next comment: 'Treated with respect, courtesy, and admiration when they come to this country as our guests, the Germans persistently made it clear that in none of these qualities will they show the least approach to reciprocity.' Here he was clearly thinking of the problems he had experienced with *Much Ado* in Leipzig, the long postponed production of *Shamus* in Breslau, and his brush with Mühlfeld over the Clarinet Concerto (see pp. 232–3). Strong as this is, Stanford left his most vicious comments for German music and composers. This issue had caused real problems for British musicians; German music formed such a large part of the repertory and British musicians had clearly paraded their affinity with and admiration for German music and musicians throughout Stanford's life. Some, like Parry, detached Prussian militarism from German artistic achievement,[109] but Stanford argued that there was an explicit link:

> The modern developments of German music since the death of Wagner and of Brahms throw a light, if a lurid one, upon the trend of the German character ... The essence of German militarism has been reliance upon numbers, rapidity of concentration, perfection

---

[108] Charles Stanford, 'Music and the War', *Quarterly Review*, 1 Apr. 1915, pp. 393–408.

[109] In his address to the RCM students and staff at the beginning of the Autumn Term 1914, Parry said 'I have been a quarter of a century and more a pro-Teuton. I owed too much to their music and their philosophers and authors of former times to believe it possible that the nation at large could be imbued with the teaching of a few advocates of mere brutal violence and material aggression'; see Parry, *College Addresses*, ed. Henry Colles (London, 1920), 222.

of machinery, repression of individual initiative, and in action the attack in close formation of which this repression is the necessary corollary. In their recent music, all these elements can be traced. Richard Strauss is the counterpart of Bernhardi and the General Staff. He relies increasingly upon the numbers of his executants, upon the technical facility of his players, upon the additions and improvements to musical instruments, upon the subordination of invention to effect, upon the massing of sounds and the super-abundance of colour to conceal inherent poverty ... He sets Bernhardi to music in *Ein Heldenleben* not indeed taking him or even a Napoleon for his hero, but with sublime egotism glorifying himself. To succeed in this he uses old themes of his own, obviously because, as the context shows, he was unable to hit upon any so good.

The attack is so hysterical that it is almost entertaining; the extravagance is typical of its time, but to anyone who could view the situation with detachment, the article could have done Stanford no good at all.

For unknown reasons Stanford appears to have written no music in the first half of 1915, but in July or August he started to set Sheridan's *The Critic*, his first opera for fifteen years. He worked quickly; Act I was completed at Loch Rannoch on 14 August and Act II on 8 September at Malvern. His reasons for the choice of text were straightforward: 'it is all so delightfully characteristic and funny; and at the moment most topical'.[110] Sheridan's play depicts, in Acts II and III, a play by Puff, the subject of which is the approach of the Spanish Armada.[111] Sheridan had been inspired by rumours of an invasion fleet of French and Spanish ships, following Spain's declaration of war on Britain in June 1779; the parallels with the situation in 1915 are obvious. Stanford may also have

---

[110] Stanford to Greene, summer 1915, reproduced in facsimile in Greene, *Stanford*, opp. p. 192.

[111] The 'theatre play' was particularly popular in the 1770s but could claim an ancestry dating at least as far back as Buckingham's *The Rehearsal* (1671), and its most celebrated antecedent is probably the Mechanicals' enactment of the tragedy of Pyramus and Thisby in Shakespeare's *A Midsummer Night's Dream* (published in 1600 but possibly dating from the early to mid-1590s). There were broadly two types of 'theatre play' and Sheridan used elements of both. The first is the 'trailer', a short play given at the beginning of the evening, deliberately contemporary in context, which drew upon recent gossip and parodied dramatic practices; these were used as a means of advertising other plays to be given at the same theatre during the season and also for actors and actresses who were playing there – these people often appeared as themselves. The second type was a longer burlesque, which often used the 'play within a play' technique, and satirised genres rather than specific works. M. S. Auburn argues that four plays in particular influenced Sheridan: *Occasional Prelude* (1772) and *New Brooms* (1776), both by Colman, and *The Meeting of the Company* (1774) and *A Peep Behind the Curtain* (1767), both by Garrick – the latter had been revived by Sheridan at Drury Lane in 1778 (see Auburn, *Sheridan's Comedies: Their Contexts and Achievements* (Lincoln, Nebr. and London, 1977), 149–75).

been spurred by the sinking of the *Lusitania* and been encouraged by the revival of *Drake*.[112]

The Critic was taken up by the Beecham Opera Company, and Eugene Goossens was engaged to conduct both it and Ethel Smyth's new opera *The Boatswain's Mate*, as Beecham preferred to go on holiday in Italy. Goossens recalls,

> Later Stanford himself attended orchestral rehearsals, but interfered remarkably little with them, though he seemed surprised at finding his twenty-two year old former pupil in control of his affairs . . . I went ahead and conducted my first opera without mishap . . . dear old Stanford literally shook with excitement at the end of the evening when, hand in hand with his erstwhile pupil, he took many curtain calls.[113]

The opera was premièred at the Shaftesbury Theatre on 14 January 1916 with Debussy's *L'Enfant prodigue* as a curtain-raiser, interest having been stimulated by two trailing articles in *The Times*.[114] According to Percy Heming, who played Sir Walter Raleigh, disaster nearly struck:

> During the first performance there was an elaborate change of scenery, and all the cast and chorus had to crowd to the side of the stage. The dresses of the ballet were of muslin and were wired out and around. One of these wires happened to touch an electric cable which was cracked and exposed. There was a big flash and in a second the flimsy material was on fire. By a stroke of luck I happened to be near the girl and whipped off my cloak and pulled it tight around her and got it out just in time. History repeated itself – Sir Walter Raleigh's cloak had come in handy once again.[115]

Although cordially received and given thirteen performances in London and five in Manchester, the opera failed to enter the repertory.

The Critic was adapted for Stanford by Lewis Cairns James, the producer of the RCM operas, and is skilful in its execution. Sheridan's Act I (dispensed with by James) is a curtain-raiser leading to the performance of the play-within-a-play in Acts II and III ('The Spanish Armada'). Dangle, Puff and Sneer (theatre manager, playwright and critic respectively) watch the play from the side of the stage and comment on its dialogue, dramaturgy and *mise en scène*. In the opera, 'The Spanish Armada' was transformed into an opera-within-a-play, with libretto by Puff and music by Dangle, who remain, with Sneer, at the side of the

[112] The revival opened on 19 Aug. 1914 at His Majesty's Theatre and ran for 101 performances.

[113] Eugene Goossens, *Overtures and Beginners* (London, 1951), 116–17.

[114] See *The Times*, 8 Jan. 1916, p. 9, and 13 Jan. 1916, p. 11.

[115] Quoted in Greene, *Stanford*, 194.

stage. The conductor is required to take the part of Thomas Linley, but remains in the pit.[116] Most notably in James's adaptation, Sheridan's words were barely altered and the opera almost entirely comprises the original play set to music.

Sheridan wrote *The Critic* in the same farcical style as *The School for Scandal* and *The Rivals*. Puff's tragedy 'The Spanish Armada' is appallingly bad and the scenario is nonsensical: the characters have contradictory motivations (if any at all) for their actions, crucial 'facts' are omitted, an irrelevant subplot is introduced, and exits are omitted so characters are left stranded on stage. Puff, an expert in 'puffing up' his own achievements, believes he has written a masterpiece; to Sneer his folly is all too obvious. Some of Sheridan's references were contemporary 'in-jokes' (Dangle, for example, is a representation of Sheridan himself, who was then owner of the Drury Lane Theatre) but others are timeless: there are parodical references to *Othello*, *Hamlet* and Milton's *Lycidas*. Stanford took the dramatic devices as Sheridan intended and added musical ones, quoting from Bach, Beethoven and Wagner, parodying other composers, and adding 'mistakes' to the score.

This 'straight' adaptation is essential. Sheridan's play is not a masterpiece but it is a superlative example of its kind; to alter any aspect would have ruined it. The preservation of the original did, however, throw up problems for Stanford: there are few opportunities for choruses or diegetic songs, and clear delivery of the text is essential. Stanford recognised this and adapted his style accordingly: the remnants of 'number opera' remain, but the text is minutely reflected and formal structures are loose. His ability to respond locally to texts has been discussed previously, but in drawing that sensitivity into a coherent macro-structure he sometimes failed. In *The Critic*, however, Stanford effected a sense of direction and cogency, achieved through regular phrasing in the orchestra with vocal parts crossing at will – a common approach, but one used successfully here, especially in Leicester's 'Prayer to Mars' and Tilburina's Act I monologue. In Tilburina's Act II 'Mad Scene' Stanford abandoned regular periodisation in the orchestra as well, and to good effect. Tilburina's mood oscillates wildly and her utterances are disjointed and nonsensical; Stanford reflected all of this by word-painting, frequent use of tremolo, and rapid contrast between broad legato phrases and short staccato ones. The reappearance of the opening theme at the end creates a sense of closure (Ex. 6.24).

The greatest challenge was to sustain, amplify and complement the wit of Sheridan's play. Stanford did this well: while Sheridan parodied

---

[116] Sheridan married Thomas Linley's daughter Elizabeth.

Example 6.24   *The Critic*, Op. 144, Act II, *Scherzino Passo* (Tilburina's Mad
Scene): (*a*) opening; (*b*) reprise (text: Lewis Cairns James after
Sheridan)

Shakespeare in Tilburina's 'mad scene', Stanford parodied French grand
opera in Leicester's 'Prayer to Mars'. Similarly, while Sheridan mocked
theatrical convention by stranding characters on stage, Stanford did the
same by the use of incorrectly copied parts (Ex. 6.25). His use of quotations from other composers varied in motivation just as Sheridan's did
– he used his own 'Drake's Drum' for the appearance of Drake at the
end of Act II, quoted 'Ein feste Burg' when Raleigh refers to England's
Protestantism, and 'Blest Pair of Sirens' at the Beefeater's line 'O curs'd
parry'. A more cunning example is the quotation from Beethoven's Ninth
Symphony to match Sheridan's from Shakespeare (Ex. 6.26).

The perception of the listener is crucial: J. S. Shedlock, reviewing the
première in the *Athenaeum*, declared: 'Sir Charles had undoubtedly a
splendid field for his particular talents, and, above all, his sense of
humour. But the subject had in its own excellence the danger that it
might tempt him to exaggeration in treatment and especially in parody

Example 6.25   *The Critic*, Op. 144, Act I, bars 251–62 (text: Lewis Cairns
James after Sheridan)

DANGLE: Major, major, trombones!
PUFF: Here, now you see, Sir Christopher did not in fact ask any one question for his own information.
SNEER: No indeed; his has been a most disinterested curiosity!
PUFF: New then for the Commander-in-Chief, the Earl of Leicester, who, you know, was no favourite but of the Queen's.
We left off in amazement lost!
(The Band correct their parts.)
CONDUCTOR: Go to letter K.
(Sir Christopher returns and repeats business.)

and quotation. Sir Charles, however, observed the "mean" to an
admirable degree.'[117] Gervase Hughes, on the other hand, questioned
whether Stanford should have set Sheridan at all:

> Some of the jokes (like Sheridan's) were simple to the point of
> crudity; others, less well-matched with the burlesques of the orig-
> inal, were sufficiently abstruse to strain the mental capacity of a
> Doctor of Music ... It meant nothing to the audience at the
> Shaftesbury Theatre, and many musicians will be relieved to learn
> that Scott Goddard (who was erudite enough to catch all the allu-
> sions but too modest to admit it) felt as though he were a street
> urchin looking through a window at the goings-on among the gentry
> in a big house.[118]

These comments are a manifestation of a long-running musical debate:
Shedlock's opinion that Stanford avoided the temptation to obvious
vulgarity is countered by Hughes's assertion that the wit was too obscure

---

[117] *Athenaeum*, 22 Jan. 1916, p. 49.
[118] Gervase Hughes, *Composers of Operetta* (Oxford, 1962), 207.

Example 6.26   *The Critic*, Op. 144, Act II, Beefeater's Entrance, bars 249–54
(text: Lewis Cairns James after Sheridan)

Per - di   tion catch my soul,   but I   do   love thee.

for most people to see, let alone appreciate. Both men reflect the change
in attitudes to popular culture that had taken place between the eighteenth and twentieth centuries: Sheridan's play contains the same
combination of 'high' and 'low' references as Stanford's score, but
Sheridan would have expected an audience mixed in its education and
expectations. That Stanford could not may leave him open to the charge
of misjudgement and John Runciman, who had previously condemned
Much Ado about Nothing, took up this point with characteristic directness:

> This fantasia of Sheridan's, this phantasmagoria of sheer fun,
> boyishness, perversity, malice and the rest – what on earth has it
> all to do with opera? What can it prove but a hindrance to the
> opera? . . . Most of the music is neither good nor bad; it serves. One
> or two rather good melodies make their appearance and melt away,
> leaving us longing for some more of that sort of thing . . . Quotations
> from his own works seem to me . . . quite senseless; for the music
> possesses no marked individuality by which it can be recognised,
> and many of his pieces are altogether unknown.[119]

Should Stanford have set *The Critic*? In the case of his other operas
a judgement can come quite easily from an examination of the score,
but here the lack of opportunity to see the work on stage is a real
hindrance. That Stanford set Sheridan so exactly was a necessity, but
whether he brought anything extra to the play is more debatable.
Partly the problem is dealing with two works which were so fixed in
their own time; any piece which contains so many up-to-the-minute
references as Sheridan's play loses its edge quickly, and Stanford's opera,
being so much an allusion to the Great War, falls into a similar trap.[120]
Despite this, however, it would be interesting to see *The Critic* on stage,
and to see what Stanford had achieved; it is certainly one of his most
intriguing works.

Stanford completed his final opera, *The Travelling Companion*, Op.
146, on 7 July 1916. The end product both reflects and rejects the bleak

---

[119] *Saturday Review*, 29 Jan. 1916, pp. 106–7.
[120] Notably *The School for Scandal* and *The Rivals* are now much more performed
than *The Critic*.

situation in which he found himself at this time. The rejection is evident in the tranquillity of the work, which is written on a timeless subject and which is underpinned by belief in redemption and the goodness of humanity. The work reflects the spirit of the age in that it is tinged with sadness, a feeling of remote other-worldliness and of unreality. It is a piece of escapism, written at a time when war was revealed as grim and harsh, and not the purifying struggle Stanford had previously believed (see pp. 289–90).

It could well have been different, for *The Travelling Companion* was first contemplated by Stanford as the subject of an opera in 1911. Harry Greene claims the credit for the idea:

> I was reading through Hans Anderson [*sic*] for the hundredth time when I came upon [*The Travelling Companion*]. I actually heard it say, 'Make me into an opera,' and I took it at its word on the spot. I jumped into a taxi and rushed off to [Stanford] with the book and that evening we worked out the whole thing together practically as it appears in print to-day.[121]

Greene claimed that these events took place in 1917,[122] but his dating is manifestly inaccurate. Sir Henry Newbolt, the librettist, writing in 1915, referred to the project as having been commenced 'about four years ago',[123] but, according to him, Stanford and Greene constantly changed their minds about the scenario. Eventually, Newbolt wryly recalled, they ended up with the framework he had originally proposed.

Little progress, it appears, was made between 1911 and 1915; possibly, after completing *The Critic*, Stanford pressed Newbolt for completion, as he found himself in an operatic frame of mind. By January 1916 Newbolt was able to write:

> This morning I spent an hour with Stanford – in seventh heaven over the still more brilliant performance of *The Critic* ... *The Travelling Companion* handed over to him and he is to begin soaking it in at once: no doubt he read it within the hour after I left. He was in a delightful mood for it and kept looking into it and liking what he saw. He wants it at once to sandwich between *The Critic* and another eighteenth century opera which he wrote long ago and couldn't get performed.[124]

---

[121] Greene, 'Stanford as I Knew Him', 80.
[122] See Greene, *Stanford*, 194.
[123] Henry Newbolt to Lady Alice Hylton, 7 Dec. 1915, quoted in Margaret Newbolt (ed.), *The Later Life and Letters of Sir Henry Newbolt* (London, 1942), 219.
[124] Henry Newbolt to Lady Alice Hylton, 19 Jan. 1916, quoted ibid., 221. Newbolt's latter comment implies that Stanford was hoping that Beecham would also take up *The Travelling Companion* and then *Christopher Patch* (the 'eighteenth century opera') for production.

Work commenced early in 1916; Act I was completed on 21 April, Act II on 15 May, Act III on 25 June and Act IV on 7 July. This timing is important; by now the war was extracting a real toll on life at home and this affected Stanford deeply. Although, in many respects, life carried on as normal – food was plentiful, for example – casualty lists were mounting and tempers fraying. Conscription of all men aged between 18 and 41 was introduced in May 1916, which was a further signal that the war still had a long course to go. On 5 June Kitchener was killed whilst travelling to Russia; although generally held now to have been a hindrance to the war effort, his death dealt a blow to British morale. Less than a month later the most wasteful and unproductive battle of the war started on the Somme and at home the 'blackout' was intro- duced in mid-1916 in an attempt to hamper air raids. The Easter Rising in Dublin (25–9 April) distracted attention from the Western Front for a few days, but for Stanford these events brought more distress than relief: his home town had just self-destructed.

The impact of the war was felt keenly at the RCM too, since student numbers had collapsed. The College began to maintain a 'Roll of Honour' as its students, past and present, became casualties. For Stanford, still paid by the hour, the decline in student numbers had financial as well as psy- chological consequences. His relationship with Parry declined further and, ironically, their latest disagreement focused on opera. Stanford wanted an organised opera class introduced into the college syllabus and pro- posed this at a meeting of the Board of Professors on 15 October 1915 (see pp. 306–7). On 9 December the College Executive, doubtless with advice from Parry, rejected the scheme. Given the war, this is hardly unreasonable but it did not appear so to Stanford. Meanwhile Parry accused Stanford of defrauding the College by claiming for lessons he had not given.[125] Later, on 20 June 1916, an all-out public row was only just avoided at a meeting of the Associated Board. Walter Parratt wrote to his former pupil Craig Lang, 'college is rather tense. The friction between those two great men is severe and things are difficult for all of us.'[126]

Stanford's greatest worry, however, was over Guy, who was in France. Guy had signed up as a Second Lieutenant with the Devonshire Regi- ment, the First Battalion of which was posted to the Somme in July 1915.[127] The Somme did not become a major part of the front line until

---

[125] See Parry's Diary, 8 Jan. 1916, ShP, quoted and discussed pp. 305–8.

[126] Quoted in Donald Tovey and Geoffrey Parratt, *Walter Parratt: Master of the Music* (Oxford, 1941), 122.

[127] War records are fragmentary and none of Stanford's surviving war correspondence mentions Guy. His war record is based mainly on C. T. Atkinson, *The Devonshire Regiment 1914–1918* (London and Exeter, 1926).

the offensive of July 1916; Guy's battalion went to the front line on 22 July but sometime within the next seven days he succumbed to appendicitis, was invalided out, and did not fight again. Although Guy's excursion onto the Somme was brief and the main offensive did not take place until after *The Travelling Companion* was finished, this must have been an unnerving time for both Charles and Jennie. Newspapers gave limited information and communication with the Front was haphazard, so they must have had very little knowledge of what was happening. Guy, of course, was lucky; over 400,000 men were killed in the Somme offensive and within days Arthur Bliss was injured, Ivor Gurney gassed and George Butterworth killed.

Andersen's story *The Travelling Companion* was first published in Denmark in 1835 and based on a Danish folktale, *The Dead Man's Help*. John, the hero of Andersen's tale, has just lost his father. He leaves his home and in a church protects the body of a dead man from robbers; the dead man is subsequently 'resurrected' and becomes John's friend. He helps John solve the three riddles set by the Princess with whom John has fallen in love; by solving the riddles John emancipates the Princess from her allegiance to a Wizard and brings the skeletons of her former suitors back to life. John and the Princess are married but the Travelling Companion, his debt to John paid, returns to the grave.[128] Newbolt's scenario took all the essentials of Andersen's story and the differences between the two versions are minor.

Edward Dent once alleged that it was Stanford, and not Wagner, who had composed *Parsifal* and, while self-evidently untrue, Dent was perceptive, as there is a lot of *Parsifal* in *The Travelling Companion*.[129]

---

[128] *The Travelling Companion* shares ingredients with other tales, and there is an obvious parallel between this opera and Puccini's *Turandot* in the role of the frigid Princess and the solving of the riddles. Molière's *La Princesse d'Élide* is also based on the Turandot story and the German folktale *Das Rätsel*, collected by the Brothers Grimm, is Turandot in reverse, that is, the suitors pose the riddle but the Princess always knows the answer. The idea of solving three riddles to win a Princess's hand also appears in the English folktales *The Princess of Canterbury* and *Silly Jack and the Lord's Daughter*. Another British folktale, *Four Eggs and a Penny*, tells of a dead man returning to repay a debt to the living and is based on the same idea as *The Dead Man's Help*; see Katherine Briggs, *A Dictionary of British Folktales*, 4 vols (London, 1970).

[129] See Hugh Carey, *Duet for Two Voices* (Cambridge, 1979), 96. Eugene Goossens recalls conducting *Parsifal* at Covent Garden in the early 1920s: 'Stanford sat behind me during the whole evening and afterwards came back to tell me how much he'd enjoyed the performance. So affected was he by the music that he burst into tears – something I'd never seen him do before! . . . "Damned beautiful, me bhoy, but ye took the Grail march a mite too fast. Maybe though {ap}tis myself's been playing it too slow these last years. The Old Man's spirit surely hovered over ye this night." And he wiped his glasses, took up his hat and left. That was the last time I saw him' (see Goossens, *Overtures*, 149).

Example 6.27   *The Travelling Companion*, Op. 146, developments of the
Companion's motif

Wagner's last opera was, in Stanford's view, surpassed only by *Die Meistersinger*. Stanford's use of motifs betrays the influence of Wagner's mature style most clearly and *The Travelling Companion* contains his most successful and comprehensive use of Wagnerian leitmotif technique. Motifs are related to each other, combined, developed from each other and anticipated before they appear in their 'true' form. The motif

which represents the Travelling Companion is given first at the beginning of the Prelude and appears in modified versions throughout the
opera (Ex. 6.27). Three more motifs grow out of this opening and they
are then developed, modified and combined with the parent motif; the
combination at Act I, bars 374–6, shows a notable closeness (presumably coincidental) to the 'Good Friday' music of *Parsifal*. Other motifs
represent John, the skeletons of the Princess's former suitors, the
Princess, the King, the Wizard, and the Riddle. Throughout the opera
the motifs are used with great care, suggesting that Stanford may have
made sketches of the opera, although none are known to survive. He
also used the Wagnerian tendency to assign keys. This approach is
systematic since there are several modulations which are superfluous
apart from their function of delivering him into the 'correct' key. Again
one can see the influence of *Parsifal*: although the assignment of G minor
to the storm music and the skeletons and of F and B flat to the People
has no parallel, the use of A flat, C and E flat for John and the
Companion, and of B minor, D and F sharp minor for the Wizard and
goblins clearly parallels Wagner's keys for Parsifal and the Knights on
the one hand, and for Klingsor and the Flower Girls on the other.

As in *Much Ado*, Stanford thought in long time spans when composing
The Travelling Companion and each number is carefully planned, while
transition sections 'blur' the edges, giving a sense of continuity. This was
his best attempt to take on board the changes Wagner had wrought,
even though he preferred to think much more in terms of closed numbers
than truly continuous music. The Act I song 'All in a Morning Glory',
for example, was conceived as a ternary-form movement, lasting over
two hundred bars, but a blurred edge is achieved by the initial emphasis
that part of John's motif is a retrograde of part of the song theme which
follows (Ex. 6.28). A second method of long-scale planning is exemplified in Act III; here two identical sections of text, appearing several
minutes apart, are set with altered harmony and the change transforms
the atmosphere. In both cases John is trying to go to sleep; in the first
instance the Travelling Companion reassures him and the harmony is
diatonic (A flat to C major via F minor); in the second the Princess
comes on to the balcony above, spurring his interest, and the harmony
moves non-diatonically (A flat to F minor and then D major[7]) (Ex. 6.29).
The Companion's comment 'If the stillness last' takes on a different function: the first time it is conversational, almost irrelevant; the second time
it becomes conditional and menacing. A third method is the postponement of cadence points with a view to heightening dramatic tension; the
final cadence in Act IV is delayed for over eighty bars (8 minutes in
performance) as the Travelling Companion rejects John's request that
he stay with him, and is one of the most beautiful, moving and skilful
pieces of writing in Stanford's operatic output.

Example 6.28   *The Travelling Companion*, Op. 146, Act I, bars 402–18

While *The Travelling Companion* is not problem-free, it is Stanford's strongest opera. Newbolt's lack of experience as a librettist and dramatist is a plus since the plot and verse dispense with some hidebound conventions. Some characterisation, however, is weak: the Wizard is a pantomime cliché and neither the Princess nor the King is satisfactory, it never being apparent why the Princess wants to avoid marriage or why she falls in with the Wizard, or why the King lets her do so.[130]

The central focus of the opera, however, is the relationship between John and the Companion, and this is well handled and extremely moving. The real subjects are male bonding, trust and support, and parallel life on the Front. The Companion's lines at the end of Act I could easily be directed at a departing soldier:

> No gold! No guide! No swinging steel,
> Only a dream and a song to win the world!
> Go forth! O gallant heart!
> O heart of youth that will not count the cost!
> A flash of morning sunlight,
> A call of the wand'ring wind,
> And alone thou art gone to dare the death!

---

[130] Turandot's frigidity is accounted for by the rape of one of her ancestors; in Andersen's story the Princess is the victim of a spell which is broken by John in an episode omitted by Newbolt, thus removing the reason for her behaviour.

Example 6.29 *The Travelling Companion*, Op. 146, Act III: (*a*) bars 31–7; (*b*) 126–30 (text: Henry Newbolt)

It is doubtless this aspect of the opera which encouraged the good reviews it received when it was finally premièred professionally at Bristol on 29 October 1926.[131] *The Times* remarked that Stanford and Newbolt were aiming at 'the stuff which Englishmen like to feel has made England what it is',[132] and was surely referring to the understated and 'light' nature of the music, and the emphasis on comradeship and loyalty.

---

[131] The opera was first performed by an amateur company at the David Lewis Theatre, Liverpool, on 30 Apr. 1925, and received critical reviews due to the performers not being able to meet the demands of the score. There is evidence that Stanford did at least hear the opera played through at the RCM in 1920 (see Stanford to the Carnegie Trust, 21 Jan. 1920, Scottish Record Office, File GD 281/41/36, item 9).

[132] *The Times*, 26 Oct. 1926, p. 14.

There was also an element of puzzlement: the restraint and simplicity of Stanford's style (that is, in tonality and lieder-like textures) by this time was seen not only as old-fashioned but distinctly strange. Critics often referred to the music as being derivative (a claim that cannot be refuted) and found Act III, in which the Wizard appears, to be incongruous with the rest of the opera. For once, the distance of time proved to be an advantage; when Sadler's Wells took up the opera in 1935 *The Times* wrote:

> The impression left by last night's performance was one of such singular beauty and of so much deftness in the musical design that it would be a wonder that it could have been so long neglected. Stanford's music rises to each opportunity. The sombre prelude which introduces the scene in the church where the young man defends the corpse from thieves, the freshness of the girls' chorus, 'All in a morning glory', which lures the young man to take his chance with the Princess, the scherzo of rattling bones of dead lovers, the nocturne in which the Travelling Companion brings sleep to his friend are passages of such a diverse beauty as cannot escape the attention of every musical listener.[133]

The years 1902–16 were ones of mixed fortune. Stanford had some successes and remained in demand as a composer and conductor. It is notable, however, that the time between the completion of a composition and its first performance was sometimes very long, and that fewer of his pieces resonated with audiences: his reputation depended more on the works composed in the 1880s and 1890s than those of the Edwardian age. There is an extent to which this was inevitable: Stanford reached his mature style of composition in his thirties, after which there was little change. Inevitably, therefore, a composer who was conservative in his outlook was easily outdated and outshone by others who appeared more exciting and original. It is also the case that Stanford's reputation for being rude and acerbic did not help him: his breaks with Elgar and Richter are the most dramatic demonstrations of this, but his constantly strained relations with Parry, although concealed from the public eye, were just as, if not more, damaging. Greene argued that Stanford's real decline started in the latter stages of the war;[134] in mental terms that is a credible view, but his status as a composer and performer had turned some years previously. How Stanford viewed this is unclear, but his attitudes to the RCM and the Leeds Festival suggest that he remained convinced of his own status and worth, at least until the outbreak of the war. From this time, with the Irish Question exacerbating

---

[133] *The Times*, 4 Apr. 1935, p. 12.
[134] See Greene, *Stanford*, 269, and pp. 309–10.

the situation, he became much less certain of everything and started to recognise that he was getting old. In *The Travelling Companion* there is an air of finality about the story which appears not only as a farewell from the character beyond the grave, but from Stanford himself.

CHAPTER SEVEN

Last Years

July 1916 signalled a low point for Stanford from which he never fully recovered. The impact of war had grown steadily and was most forcefully felt during Guy's posting to the Somme. The Easter Uprising in Dublin had also caused much distress as Stanford saw parts of his home city implode due, in his view, to the mischievous activities of Nationalists and Home Rulers. In summer 1916, however, these difficulties were reinforced by a purely domestic problem: Stanford decided that he had to leave 50 Holland Street. It seems inconceivable that this relocation was undertaken for positive reasons: Charles and Jennie had spent twenty-three years there and it was a large, well-located and characteristic house to which they had become attached. By comparison, the house to which they moved, 9 Lower Berkeley Street (now Fitzhardinge Street) was, although in a desirable neighbourhood north of Oxford Street, smaller and further away from the RCM.[1] The move almost certainly arose out of financial necessity: just as Stanford had forecast to Parry in 1915, prices rose while his income declined.[2] Stanford probably held Parry partly responsible for this decline in income and it was a factor which led to their most explosive row at the end of 1916. Parry had caught Stanford fiddling his teaching claims in order to counteract the effects of the war:

> I led [Stanford] onto the subject of his false entries on the 'professors' slips' to his charging for lessons he had not given because he was talking in other professors' rooms when he ought to have been giving them, and to his having a string quartet to play his own

---

[1] Stanford tried to interest Oscar Sonneck in his 1773 Kirchmann harpsichord on the grounds that he had no room for it in his new house; in all probability he needed the money too. See Stanford to Sonneck, 7 Nov. 1916, Library of Congress, Washington DC, shelfmark ML 94.S Case. The house in Lower Berkeley Street has since been demolished.

[2] Prices rose sharply during the course of the war: by July 1916 prices stood about 50% higher than in August 1914 and would more than double by November 1918 (these figures are derived from the government's 'All Items Cost of Living Index' which commenced in July 1914; although it is a crude calculation by today's standards, it was the first systematic attempt in the United Kingdom to chart price fluctuation over time). Stanford's income fell in both real and absolute terms over the same period; his annual salary from Cambridge remained fixed at £200, whilst his income from royalties fell. At the RCM he continued to be paid by the hour and so, as the number of students fell due to army recruitment, so did his income.

> compositions which he charged for as an hour's wind ensemble, and
> a few more things of the kind . . . He concluded by saying 'I always
> believe in being straight. I am straight' – which I did not endorse,
> thinking the exact opposite. It was a tiring hour.[3]

This accusation was serious and not new: five years earlier Stanford had
been accused of charging for lessons he had not given.[4]

This disagreement was exacerbated by Parry's opposition to Stanford's
proposal for a fully-fledged Opera Class at the RCM. The RCM
Executive had cancelled the annual opera in 1915 due to the war, a
decision which, whilst Stanford may have understood the circumstances,
ended a run of thirty-two productions given since 1885, every one of
which he had conducted. Possibly as a result of the cancellation, Stanford
put forward his proposals in October 1915. These included classes not
only in the musical aspects of opera but also in acting, elocution, diction,
gesture, deportment, dancing and fencing, plus a mixture of staged and
concert performances.[5] The scheme was seconded by Parratt, passed by
the Board of Professors and referred to the Executive for approval.
Parry's personal attitude to the scheme is unclear,[6] but he was quite
certain about Stanford's motives:

> At 4 Stanford came in by appointment. He began by emphasising
> his financial difficulties, said he would be forced to give up 50
> Holland Street, and that his college fees were seriously collapsing.
> He laboured this for a quarter of an hour, as if to impress the oblig-
> ation of the College to assist him financially, and then proceeded to
> discuss the opera question. He produced a scheme for a permanent
> opera class, by which he was to get vast increase of work.[7]

It would be difficult to conclude that Parry was wrong in his cynicism
but the scheme itself was a good one and, had relations between the
two men not been so strained, he would, no doubt, have sympathised
with Stanford's straitened finances. Unsurprisingly, however, the Executive concluded that circumstances were not conducive and rejected the
scheme, while retaining the option of reconsideration after the war

---

[3] Parry's Diary, 8 Jan. 1916, ShP.

[4] Parry wrote 'Also a very unpleasant [interview] with Stanford about Hayles's indis-
cretion in the office, when Stanford says that H said "don't charge for lessons you haven't
given."'! Tried to accommodate matters. Hayles saying he had not said it' (Diary, 28 Nov.
1911, ShP).

[5] See Minutes of the Board of Professors, 15 Oct. 1915, RCM.

[6] Parry felt bound to oppose the scheme because of the College's financial position. His
well-known comments about opera being 'the shallowest fraud man ever achieved in art'
(Notebook, [?1918], ShP) did not mean that he was blind to the importance of teaching
opera in the institution of which he was Director.

[7] Parry's Diary, 18 Oct. 1915, ShP.

ended. Stanford was not to be put off and a subcommittee was set up by the Board of Professors to consider the matter further. On 7 June 1916 the subcommittee's report was examined, despite Parry's protests that too many board members were away. The scheme was much more detailed than the original and also dealt with its financial implications.[8] Once again the Board commended the scheme to the Executive and once again the Executive resolved to postpone further consideration until after the end of the war.[9]

The Executive's decision, in the face of declining student numbers and fee income, is hardly surprising, but doubtless Stanford viewed it as just one more incidence of Parry's lack of support. At the end 1916 tempers on both sides boiled over. Stanford wrote a long letter to Parry (which does not survive) defending himself against the earlier charges of impropriety. Parry considered it at some length, hesitated, and then replied, taking the opportunity not only to deal with the issue at hand, but to give vent to all the frustration and resentment which had built up over twenty years:

> The facts to which I called your attention have not been disproved and cannot be. The slips you signed, with the time charged for entered in your handwriting are at the College now, and so are my notes, showing that the amount of time you entered and signed for was not in accordance with the facts. These are the documents to which I called your attention, and I put no gloss on them, but merely presented them as incontestable facts and such they are. No member of the Council could form any opinion of them because no 'charges' were made against you either to Council or Executive. When I presented my scheme for the revision of the system of making returns on the slips to preclude such amounts in future I did not mention your name ... [but] it was my duty as Director of the College to call attention to things which were not business-like ...
>
> I read the first page of your letter and think that is sufficient ... But I will take the opportunity to say a few words about the relations which your attitude towards me in the last 20 years has brought about. I always gladly and heartily acknowledge the wonderful generosity and kindness with which you treated me in early days. I owed you more than it was possible to put into words. There is hardly anyone I can think of who helped me so much. It is a delightful memory to look back to. They were great days and joyful days. But alas you are quite a different person now. As your old friend Arthur Coleridge said to me 'you must have your quarrel'. And in spite of everything I could do to humour you and shut my eyes to your growing ill will you forced a quarrel upon me. I did

---

[8] See Minutes of the Board of Professors, 7 June 1916, RCM. The subcommittee comprised Stanford, Plunket Greene, Cairns James, Albert Visetti, Sydney Waddington and Charles Wood.
[9] Executive Committee Minutes, 12 Oct. 1916, RCM.

not take part in it, but you had your quarrel, and ever since I have been enduring with all the patience I could muster your constant use of every thing available as a handle to represent things in an injurious light . . .

So by degrees it has come about that the delightful relations of the Cambridge days have been destroyed. To what an extent can be gauged by two incidents. Near the end of Christmas term 1915 I went into the office to speak to Perry and found you and Cairns James there. I went straight up to you and held out my hand. You turned your back and walked out, before the Clerks and boys. On May 25 of this year we were invited with several representative musicians to Courtnege's room at the Shaftesbury to discuss ways of helping poor MacCunn. I came in late, and shook hands with them all and came up to you and held out my hand, and you, before all of them, refused it. To talk of friendship after such behaviour is ridiculous. To me it is final.

As long as I am Director of the College and you a Professor of it I shall continue to treat you with all the consideration due to a member of the Staff: if either of us cease to be in either of those positions I shall feel no longer bound to keep to myself the reasons why our early friendship came to an end.

Only as a forlorn hope I would ask if you thought it possible to reconsider your ways of behaving to your fellow men – your habits of making accusations against them and quarrelling and treating them offensively – then perhaps you might then become something more like what you were thirty years ago![10]

Faced with someone biting back as savagely as he himself had bitten, Stanford was shocked. Some days later Parry wrote:

After tea Lady Stanford made her appearance with a letter from C. V. S. It was very plucky of her and she behaved very well. I told her it was impossible to discuss a man with his wife. But she stuck to it. She brought a very slippery and tortuous letter from C.V.S., evading the issues as usual. We got hot now and then, but in the end she induced me to write a letter for her to take. I couldn't climb down much, but she thought it would do and went off after an hour's discussion and promptly came back with C.V.S. who advanced with his hand out. His face with something more of his old expression, and I made the best of it.[11]

Not, therefore, a full reconciliation, but something of a patch-up. Stanford may have felt the matter resolved but, if so, he was being naive; Parry was unable to forgive Stanford instantaneously for disputes spreading back over twenty years and their relationship remained strained until Parry's death.

Why did Parry find Stanford so difficult to deal with? Their relationship illustrates very well the difficulties encountered by anyone dealing

---

[10] Parry to Stanford (draft), [Dec.] 1916, ShP.
[11] Parry's Diary, 3 Jan. 1917, ShP.

with Stanford who, in Cyril Rootham's words, 'did not always . . . realise that other people could be as sensitive as he was himself'.[12] While some people, such as Greene, found Stanford's directness a forgivable part of his personality, most found it hypocritical, chiefly on the grounds that he could take grave offence if addressed in the same manner as he would expect others to accept in good part when he himself passed the comments. In his dealings with Parry, however, their working relationship coloured every encounter and conversation. Parry referred to the change to their friendship over the previous twenty years and this coincided with Parry's appointment as Director of the RCM. Hitherto Stanford had been able to regard Parry as a colleague and equal with whom ideas could be debated and frank criticisms could be exchanged. Parry sometimes felt Stanford's criticisms were harsh and insensitive but his respect for and gratitude to Stanford usually prevailed. After succeeding Grove, however, Parry's perspective, of necessity, changed. His duty then was to think primarily from a College perspective and be accountable to the Executive. Stanford failed to recognise this change and still expected an ally in every battle and supporter of every proposal. Above all he still perceived Parry to be an equal, not a superior, and Parry's failure sometimes to support him led to suspicion and resentment. This situation was compounded by the fact that, in most other parts of his life, Stanford was himself the primary centre of power (most notably in CUMS and in the early years of the Cambridge professorship). On previous occasions when he had dealt with a superior it was usually someone for whom he had a long-held respect, leading to a more temperate expression of opinions. It was this difference in status which allowed him to maintain good relations with Grove but led to disaster with Parry. Neither man was without fault in his conduct: Stanford remained totally insensitive to Parry's changed status and to his sensibilities, while Parry did not always rise above his resentment of Stanford, which compromised the impartiality of some decisions he made as Director of the RCM.

In Greene's view, the stresses of war and age now started to take their toll. Air raids commenced in 1917 and affected Stanford greatly; he often stayed at Windsor with Parratt, only coming to London during the day. Parry viewed this as cowardice,[13] but Greene believed that the retreat to Windsor was on doctor's orders,[14] and that this was the beginning of Stanford's decline:

---

[12] 'Sir Charles Stanford and his Pupils', *RCM Magazine*, 20 (1923–4), 55–61.

[13] See Parry's Diary, 19 Feb. 1918, ShP: 'Stanford didn't come [to a meeting of the Associated Board], being afraid of air raids, but committed his interests to other members of the board who were not afraid to come.'

[14] See Greene, *Stanford*, 269.

> Looking back on it now, it becomes plain that from this time he headed slowly downward. It was imperceptible at first. He carried on with his work and taught and conducted as well as before, but as time went on the boundaries of his interest seemed gradually to shrink, giving one the feeling that he was concerned only with the things in front of him and that those on either side passed him by unnoticed.[15]

The end of the war did not bring relief:

> As time went on outside things began to fade out of the picture. Politics, fishing and cards did not play their old part. There was no more piquet or poker-patience and even bridge seemed to have lost its interest. All honour to those good men of the Savile who played with him and followed his pace and never said a word. Recreations meant nothing to him anymore; the only thing that absorbed him was the routine of his daily work. His creative brain continued to function in a semi-miraculous manner.[16]

One event in 1917 did lift Stanford's spirits, however: the marriage of Guy to Gwendolyn Dalrymple on 6 January, at St Mary's, North Eling, near Gwendolyn's family home at Cadnam, Hampshire. Guy's occupation is still given as '2nd Lieutenant, Devonshire Regiment' on the marriage certificate, suggesting that recall was a possibility. In other respects, 1917 seems to have been a year of little distinction. Once again he annoyed Parry, this time in respect of his treatment of May and Beatrice Harrison:

> Stanford has taken it upon him[self] to be entirely offensive to the Harrisons ... when [Beatrice] Harrison came back to the College recently and became Rivarde's pupil, Rivarde wanted her to play with the orchestra, but knew Stanford would refuse to allow her. So he deliberately devised a trap and told us of it. His account of its complete success was that he broached the subject to Stanford, and S. altogether refused to allow 'Baby' to play; and that then Rivarde airily mentioned that he thought she would play Stanford's Violin Concerto very well and he had already begun to work at it with her. The effect was instantaneous – Stanford changed his tone altogether immediately and welcomed the idea of 'Baby's' playing with the orchestra; and so great was the momentum of the change that he welcomed May and Baba to renewed friendship and himself invited them to come and play Brahms's double concerto.[17]

---

[15] Ibid.

[16] Ibid., 273.

[17] Parry's Diary, [25 May] 1917, ShP. Parry comments that Stanford had previously fallen out with the Harrisons, but the reason for this is unknown. May (1891–1959) and Beatrice (1892–1965) Harrison were both child prodigies (May, a violinist, won an RCM Gold Medal aged 10; Beatrice, a cellist, made her first appearance as a soloist with orchestra aged 14) and went on to have successful professional careers, often appearing with each other.

Beatrice Harrison performed Stanford's Violin Concerto with the RCM Orchestra on 12 July 1918 and Parry caustically noted that it was 'very good and artistic. What's called absolute music. Reflections of other people's sayings with no particular point. Admirably played by Baby Harrison.'[18]

Stanford composed consistently and turned out an impressive volume of work after the move to Lower Berkeley Street, aided, ironically, first by the decline of student numbers at the RCM during the war, and then, from about 1921, by his gradual running down of professional commitments, both of which freed up more time. Dating the works written between 1917 and 1924 is often difficult as many manuscripts are missing – some pieces such as the Masses, Opp. 169 and 176, are missing altogether, other opus numbers (for example, 185, 186, 188) have no known works assigned to them. To complicate matters several other works (such as *Songs from the Elfin Pedlar*) have no opus number and printed editions are not dated (the best, but scarcely satisfactory, estimate of the date of composition is, therefore, the year of copyright). Finally, the manuscripts of many published works are lost (for example, *Songs of a Roving Celt*, Op. 157, and the Third Piano Concerto, Op. 171).[19]

From 1917 Stanford focused on the composition of solo and chamber music. No doubt there was an element of pragmatism in this: such music generated the best financial returns and he needed cash. Sometimes he was forced to give up royalties (which he preferred) in favour of a single payment with all rights signed away (for example, *Night Thoughts*, Op. 148 and Six Pieces for Violin and Piano, Op. 155, sold to the publisher Joseph Williams for £90 and £80 respectively).[20] Conversely, music which he wrote for larger forces was either rejected by publishers (such as the *Concert Piece for Organ*, Op. 181)[21] or, perhaps, not submitted to publishers at all.

The works of the earlier part of this period (up to 1921) show little change in style and do not require detailed comment in this regard. Stanford continued to compose much as before although, inevitably, several works referred in some way to the war. The first work which he completed after moving to Lower Berkeley Street was the *Irish Rhapsody No. 5*, Op. 147 (11 Feb. 1917). The form of the piece is similar to that of his first rhapsody and uses the tunes known as 'The

---

[18] Parry's Diary, 12 July 1918, ShP.

[19] A version for two pianos of this concerto does survive (NUL MS 70); the late Geoffrey Bush constructed an orchestral version in 1996.

[20] See Contract Nos 8723 and 8726, Stainer & Bell Archive, Finchley, London.

[21] See A. P. Watt to Stanford, 17 Oct. 1922, attached to the autograph manuscript of the *Concert Piece for Organ*, NUL, MS 73.

Return from Fingal', 'Oh for the Swords', 'Sweet Isle', 'The Green Woods of Truigha' and 'Michael Foy'.[22] The work is dedicated to the Irish Guards and their commander-in-chief, Lord Roberts, and once again there is an implicit Unionist statement in the music, since the importance of Irish regiments in the British army is highlighted.[23] At its première on 18 March *The Times* declared that 'Sir Charles Stanford has laid a wreath on the tomb of Lord Roberts in the form of the beautiful music of his *Irish Rhapsody No. 5* ... The rhapsody is a simple and chivalrous tribute to a great soldier and the regiment that called him its first colonel.'[24] Although lacking the passion of the Fourth Rhapsody, the fifth is an impressive setting, particularly in the opening section, in which the first two tunes are set with a martial dash and grim assertiveness, setting up effective picture of verve and determination complemented by the frequent use of bare fifths. In the slow middle section Stanford treated his material delicately but the final section flags slightly – the rhythmic impetus which gave the opening such character is lacking and the recalls of 'The Return from Fingal' fall slightly flat. The Rhapsody crossed the Atlantic and was given at the Norfolk Festival in Connecticut on 7 June.

Stanford's view of his home was, however, a pessimistic one; in May 1917 he wrote, 'I suppose some day I'll summon the courage to go and see my native soil. But the awful papers frighten me. I shall see ghosts all day and every day.'[25] With no close family left in Ireland there was no incentive to return, and Ireland continued to sit on a political knife edge as Sinn Fein worked for independence on the one hand, and Unionists argued for Ireland to play a full part in the war on the other; Stanford preferred to deal with the Ireland of his memories and not to contemplate what might happen in the future. Unsurprisingly, therefore, the two Irish works which came from Stanford's pen in 1918 (the *Six Irish Sketches*, Op. 154 and the *Irish Concertino*, Op. 161) echo the style and spirit he had established in the 1880s. Despite this, the *Irish Concertino*, a two-movement work for violin, cello and orchestra, is engaging. The themes (lyrical for the first-movement

---

[22] 'The Return from Fingal' was published by Stanford and Graves in *Songs of Old Ireland* (1882) and Stanford's piano accompaniment bears a remarkable resemblance to the style of his accompaniment in the *Irish Rhapsody No. 5*. It had previously been published by Petrie (see Ch. 6 n. 2) with a note that legend stated that the tune was played by Munster troops on their return from the Battle of Clontarf, 1014. 'Oh for the Swords' was published in *Moore's Irish Melodies*.

[23] Lord Roberts died in France in November 1914 and was primarily remembered for his service in India and in South Africa during the Boer War.

[24] *The Times*, 19 Mar. 1917, p. 5.

[25] Stanford to Sir John Mahaffy, 5 May 1917, Trinity College, Dublin, MS 2075/270.

Example 7.1   'The Pibroch' (from *Songs of a Roving Celt*), Op. 157 No. 1, bars
               1–5 (text: Murdoch Maclean)

variations, a vigorous jig for the second movement) are spirited and well
set off against each other, even though he tried to draw more out of the
jig than its strength justified. An arrangement of the *Irish Concertino*
for piano, violin and cello was performed on 4 December 1918 at
Wigmore Hall and Stanford conducted the orchestral première at
Bournemouth on 22 April 1920 with Rhoda Backhouse and Ivor James
as the soloists, but, despite a polite reception, the work did not stick;
the *Musical Times* noted that it was 'conceived in his customary scholarly vein' – hardly a ringing endorsement.[26]

Stanford also toyed with the Celtic fringe in his *Songs of a Roving
Celt*, Op. 157. This collection of five settings of poems by Murdoch
Maclean are, however, Scottish in mood. 'The Pibroch', the first song,
is the best of the set and has a welcome edge – the strong modal language
and reel-inspired accompaniment give the song a sense of drive (Ex. 7.1).

During the remainder of 1917 Stanford completed two works for piano
(*Night Thoughts*, Op. 148 and *Scènes de Ballets*, Op. 150) but his most
significant achievement in 1917 and 1918 was the set of five Organ
Sonatas (Opp. 149, 151, 152, 153 and 159). It may have been Stanford's
frequent stays with Parratt at Windsor (where he may have had access
to the organ of St George's Chapel) which spurred a renewed interest in
writing for the instrument (which, previously, had been sporadic, including only Opp. 57, 88, 101, 103, 105, 116 and 121, most of which are

---

[26] *Musical Times*, 1 June 1920, p. 417.

short pieces designed to be played before or after church services); certainly this group of works was his most significant contribution to the organ repertory. The sonatas are all cast in the normal three movements, although the first and second movements of the First Sonata run continuously, and all three movements of the Fifth Sonata are linked. The First Sonata, in F major, is the shortest and least satisfactory; dedicated to Stanford's successor at Trinity, Alan Gray, it is a functional piece but lacks a sense of purpose. The Second Sonata, dedicated to 'Charles Marie Widor and the great Country to which he belongs', is more successful.[27] It is one of several commentaries by Stanford on the war: the work is subtitled 'Eroica' and recalls the Battle of Verdun. The first movement is founded on the plainchant 'O filii et filiae' but it is the second and third movements which are linked with Verdun, first in a solemn and dignified march, and then in a confident allegro, to which Stanford appended the title 'Heroic Epilogue' when he orchestrated these two movements shortly afterwards, most notably adding a side drum ostinato which represents the phrase 'on ne passera pas'. The work is not intended to be a narrative of the events at Verdun (a 'battle' which lasted for most of 1916 and cost 400,000 French lives) but rather, as the dedication suggests, to commemorate and celebrate the French achievement: the principal theme of the finale is 'La Marseillaise'. The orchestrated (and slightly modified) movements were given the title 'Verdun' and were conducted by Landon Ronald at the Royal Albert Hall on 20 January 1918; *The Times* paid Stanford a backhander in its comment 'we seem to have heard it all before but we are very glad to hear it again'.[28] The remaining three sonatas draw substantially for their material on hymn tunes. The Third Sonata, dedicated to Parratt and subtitled 'Britannica', uses 'St Mary' and 'Hanover' in the first and third movements respectively and, despite the over-long middle movement, is the most successful of the five, executed with some panache and requiring great agility from the performer. The themes were treated by Stanford conventionally but with his usual dexterity, being broken down into constituent elements and manipulated by various means (for example, rhythmically and by transposition) to build up larger paragraphs. The Fourth Sonata, 'Celtica', uses the Irish tune 'St Patrick's Breastplate' for the basis of its

---

[27] Shortly after the composition of the 'Eroica' Sonata, Stanford consulted Widor about his membership of the Music Section of the Berlin Academy of Arts; Stanford was the sole British member and decided to act in concert with Widor and Saint-Saëns (see Stanford to *The Times*, 14 Nov. 1917, p. 9). Widor told Stanford that he and Saint-Saëns had decided to postpone consideration of the question until after the war; Stanford announced that he had decided to follow suit but, like Widor and Saint-Saëns, resigned in January 1919.

[28] *The Times*, 22 Jan. 1918, p. 2.

finale, while the Fifth, 'Quasi una Fantasia', employs Stanford's own tune
for 'For all the Saints', but neither work tapped an inspired vein, though
they both include imposing writing.

On 7 October 1918 Parry died. Although he had long suffered from
indifferent health, had just passed 70 and had taken the effects of war
hard, he had seemed relatively healthy during the summer. Despite his
doctor's best attempts, the blood poisoning which he contracted in early
September proved unresponsive to treatment. For Stanford, Parry's death
caused much soul-searching. He was undoubtedly conscious that he had
only partly patched up his relationship with him since their altercation
at the beginning of the previous year and Parry had continued to find
his behaviour difficult to deal with. Stanford had decided in September
to salve his conscience and to make amends by dedicating a new choral
piece to Parry, but time intervened. As a result the *Magnificat*, Op. 164,
although completed a few days before Parry's death, bears a posthumous inscription to his friend: 'Huic operi quod mors vetuit ne Carolo
Huberto Hastings Parry vivo traderem nomen illius moerens praescribo'
('To this work, which his death prevented me from handing Charles
Hubert Hastings Parry in life, I prefix his name in grief'). This was
Stanford's only Latin setting of the Magnificat and is an optimistic piece.
Cast in the double-choir format he had already exploited in the Three
Motets, Op. 135, it again draws heavily on Baroque antiphonal tradi-
tion, perhaps as a recognition of Parry's interest in music of the period,
and *decani–cantores* dialogue is the predominating feature (Ex. 7.2).
Like its models the work is episodic, each verse introducing a new theme
(apart from the recall of the opening at the doxology), and exploits other
Baroque devices such as hemiola, contrast between upper and lower
tessituras, and voice-leading. Despite this antiquarian framework, the
piece is very much Stanford's own – it is expressed throughout in his
own tonality (no Mixolydian angels here!) and is a vocal *tour de force*,
a declamatory and exuberant interpretation of the text, operatic in its
drama and completely removed from his poised Anglican settings.
Whether it would have been enough fully to reconcile Parry is unknown;
hopefully the work would have been offered and received at face value.

Parry's funeral took place on 17 October at St Paul's Cathedral and
a memorial concert, conducted by Stanford at the RCM on 8 November, included Parry's *Elegy for Brahms* and the 'English' Symphony.
Stanford's feelings about this concert are unrecorded but there was
doubtless a sense of grief tinged with guilt. Three days later the armistice
came into effect. It must have seemed paradoxical to Stanford that two
very different eras should have ended so close together, and he did not
find himself looking to a 'brave new world' but rather to a strange
mixture of new and old. There were some obvious changes to civilian

Example 7.2   *Magnificat*, Op. 164, 'Fecit potentiam', bars 115–24

life – with the end of air raids, for example, Stanford returned to living in London full time – but in many respects there was a desire in Britain to get back to life as usual, as if the war had been an aberration, an unpleasant interruption of the normal pattern. In reality it was not nearly so simple; merely adapting to demobilisation had major consequences. Nowhere was this more apparent for Stanford than at the RCM. Hugh Allen was appointed Parry's successor and, although Stanford supported him, the changes which Allen instigated transformed the college in a way which Stanford could scarcely have expected. Preparation was made for a vast increase in student numbers as men returned home, and Allen made twenty-six new appointments within the first two years of his tenure, including Vaughan Williams, Holst and Howells. Male and female students, long since treated almost as separate species who only mixed when necessary, were allowed to use the same staircases, a reform which Stanford, who retained a thoroughly Victorian attitude to the status of the sexes, probably abhorred. Student common rooms were introduced, and second and third orchestras founded. The young Adrian Boult became involved with orchestral conducting from July 1919 and took an increasing role over the next two years. Stanford crossed swords with Allen over the policies he disliked, although he could hardly find fault with Allen's ambitious plan to build a fully-fledged theatre at the College and to dedicate it to Parry's memory.

Stanford could also begin to see that the fortunes of his own music were changing. In the post-war world it became harder than ever to secure performances of his works and many, mainly larger, works, such as the Second Violin Concerto, Op. 162, Third Piano Concerto, Op. 171 and *Missa Via Victrix*, Op. 173, were disregarded. The same fate also befell some smaller works, for example the Eighth String Quartet, Op. 167 and the Two Sonatas for Violin, Op. 165. Stanford was a long way from being disregarded, however, and many works did come to the public platform, even though none of them established themselves in the long term.

In addition to the earlier works produced as a result of the war (the *Irish Rhapsody No. 5* and the 'Eroica' Sonata), Stanford composed four others, starting with the Third Piano Trio, Op. 158 (completed 22 April 1918), which was dedicated to members of the Royal Flying Corps who were killed in action, and concluding with *At the Abbey Gate*, Op. 177 (completed in November 1920), Stanford's last work for choir and orchestra. The Piano Trio, despite its noble aspirations, is curiously emasculated in its emotional voice and the second and third works of the set (*A Song of Agincourt*, Op. 168 and the *Missa Via Victrix*, Op. 173) also leave something to be desired, though they are both stronger. *A Song of Agincourt*, which takes as its basis the song believed to have been sung at Henry V's victory (and later famously used by William Walton in his incidental music to Laurence Olivier's 1944 film), was written to mark members of the RCM killed and wounded. Despite the commemoration, the work was Stanford's victory song. It was premièred at the RCM on 25 March 1919 but Stanford was unsatisfied and revised it extensively before giving it again at the RCM on 4 July; Dan Godfrey, who continued to give Stanford generous support after the war, conducted the work at Bournemouth on 16 October.

The *Missa Via Victrix* (completed 14 December 1919) was, from Stanford's point of view, his definitive commentary on the war, written both to commemorate the dead and to celebrate victory. If noble intentions could be satisfied by length then Stanford would have done well, but the piece has many weaknesses which outweigh its strengths. Although published by Boosey & Hawkes, no performances of the work have been traced. The Kyrie, dominated by a sarabande rhythm, successfully evokes both the battlefield and the funeral march, and recalls the *Stabat Mater* in its sense of anguish, and here Stanford captured a real sense of supplication in the face of great loss. In the Gloria he aimed at an imposing splendour but consequently lost the intimacy of the Mass in G; the 'Qui Tollis', a fully-fledged Funeral March, is better, but he fell back onto formulae in the 'Quoniam' and 'Cum Sancto' fugue, which are too derivative and lack impact. After a weak Credo, the Sanctus shows some improvement, but the quotation of the 'Paradisi gloria' theme from the *Stabat Mater* in the Benedictus is more distracting than helpful, feeling almost like a commercial for the earlier work. The Agnus Dei has the merit of brevity, but the march which intervenes before the final invocation (as in the earlier *Requiem*) is, like the reference to 'Paradisi gloria', a superfluous distraction. Overall, the piece is a disappointment and Stanford must have been frustrated that so much work led not even to one performance. Having had no experience of war, he could not imagine the horror of life in the trenches; it was not until Vaughan Williams, who had spent time in France, produced his *Pastoral Symphony* (premièred in 1922) that anyone came close to composing a work which dealt with the war satisfactorily.

Stanford was more successful, however, with his final war work, *At the Abbey Gate*. It is a setting of a short poem by C. J. Darling, very much in the spirit of its time:

> Stay – Who goes there?
> 　A friend –
> What friend – Whence come you?
> 　From a dark cave beneath a ruined street.
> Oh friend, where fare you,
> Why wouldst thou pass further?
> 　To lay my heart down at our mother's feet.
>
> Whom call you Mother?
> 　England – Nelson's; thine;
> 　Her whom we proudly serve, in life, in death –
> Her do I guard, friend –
> Canst thou also serve her?
> Aye, when they fail her who do yet draw breath.
>
> Who art thou friend. then?
> 　I was – and am – No One –
> 　No name is ours – An unknown host are we.
> Pass on, brave spirit.
> Oh 'tis Christ that passes
> In thee, poor soldier, who didst die for me.

With the advantage of greater distance from the war, Stanford left the bombast of his earlier works behind and captured an elegiac vein. The music is redolent of the end of *The Travelling Companion* in manner

Example 7.3 *At the Abbey Gate*, Op. 177, bars 143–9 (text: Judge Darling)

and bears some passing resemblances to it also. Through-composed, the work comprises an orchestral prologue and epilogue and a central choral episode, all *'in modo di marcia funebre'*; the character of the music is one of simple dignity and directness. As in some earlier choral works (such as *The Voyage of Maeldune*) attention is focused on the orchestra with functional choral writing above it (Ex. 7.3). Premièred on 5 March 1921 (see p. 325), it is one of Stanford's finest choral pieces and has been undeservedly neglected; at the time, however, it was clearly felt to be inferior – Alfred Kalisch wrote:

> The words are simple and dignified and simple dignity is also the keynote of the music. The composer might, however, have been less studiously simple without sacrificing the dignity necessary in dealing with so great a subject. The most impressive part of the whole is the Funeral March with which the composition opens. At a first hearing, however, it seemed too lengthy in proportion to what follows. Mr Plunket Greene sang the music allotted to the solo with extraordinary dramatic intensity, a quality in which the singing of the choir was unfortunately deficient. As the composer conducted, however, it may be presumed that his intentions were carried out.[29]

There is a thorough spirit of patriotism in both words and music, but the work is completely lacking in jingoism and emphasises above all the importance of loyalty – another echo of *The Travelling Companion*. The banishment of vacuous sentiment and triumphalism adds to the work's stature; although the music was old-fashioned by the standards of the time, explaining the lack of success, Stanford came nearest here to an appropriate summation of the war.

Despite the increase in student numbers at the RCM, following demobilisation and Allen's extensive restructuring, Stanford showed no sign

---

[29] *Musical Times*, 1 Apr. 1921, pp. 270–71.

of slowing his rate of composition in the immediate post-war years. As
well as the works discussed above he produced a setting of Tennyson's
Merlin and the Gleam (Op. 172, completed August 1919), the Seventh
and Eighth String Quartets (Opp. 166 and 167, completed 27 February
and 25 June 1919 respectively), the two lost Masses (Opp. 169 and
176), the Third Piano Concerto, Op. 171 and two sets of songs (*Songs
from the Glens of Antrim*, Op. 174, settings of poetry by Moira O'Neill,
and a miscellaneous selection in Op. 175).

Merlin and the Gleam and *Songs from the Glens of Antrim* show
Stanford far behind the times. In the former piece his style is exactly the
same as that of his earliest settings of Tennyson written in the 1880s;
even the choice of Tennyson strikes one as being regressive and of all
of Stanford's post-war works it is this one which demonstrates his
Victorian outlook most clearly. *Songs from the Glens of Antrim* shows
the same tendency only here with an Irish tinge. As in *An Irish Idyll*,
O'Neill's use of dialect is twee and the songs vary in quality; 'Denny's
Daughter' has a gentle melody which is appealing and Stanford captured
the Irish lyrical style well (Ex. 7.4), but 'The Sailor Man', 'Lookin' Back'
and 'I mind the Day' are formulaic. 'At Sea' is formulaic too but the
sea never failed to stir Stanford's compositional facility and the song's
minimalist construction, comprising simple arpeggios over a B♭ pedal,
evokes the sea effectively. It is the final number, however, which demonstrates how completely Stanford was out of touch with his home. 'The
Boy from Ballytearin' leaves his home to seek his fortune, returning only
to find that his love has died, so he leaves again, this time for ever.
Transposed to England, this theme might have been permissible but set
in Ireland, where emigration due to poverty had been a running sore
since the 1840s, both the poem and Stanford's setting of it suggest a
disengagement from Irish reality which is quite amazing.

Some of Stanford's best post-war work, on the other hand, is found
in his two sets of Preludes for the Piano, Opp. 163 and 179. Taking his
starting point from Bach, he covered each key in both sets, thus
producing a '48'. Stanford had, of course, been exposed to Bach's music
in his youth – Robert Stewart and Michael Quarry both had a high
regard for Bach – and it had formed an important part of his studies
with both Reinecke and Kiel, both of whom were advocates of Bach's
music. Subsequently Stanford himself encouraged performances of
Bach's music, most obviously in his conductorship of the Bach Choir,
but also in Cambridge and Leeds.[30] The most obvious manifestation of

[30] For further discussion of these pieces of music, the influence which Bach had on
Stanford, and of the British context into which Stanford's '48' falls, see Allis, 'Another
"48"'.

Example 7.4 'Denny's Daughter' (from *Songs from the Glens of Antrim*), Op. 174 No. 1, bars 4–13 (text: Moira O'Neill)

Bach's influence is seen primarily in the tonal plan of the two sets; beyond this it is rather more sporadic, making some specific appearances (for example, no. 9 in E subtitled 'Humoresque', a latter-day two-part invention in spirit (Ex. 7.5(a)), and no. 18 in G sharp minor, subtitled 'Toccata') and some general ones (the use of Baroque dance forms, such as no. 41 in A flat, a gavotte, and no. 43 in A, a sarabande). The nineteenth-century prelude tradition is reflected too, as some pieces concentrate on a specific aspect of piano technique, for example, nos 3 and 8. Romantic composers also make their influence felt more directly, most notably Chopin (no. 2 in C minor (Ex. 7.5(b)) and no. 22 in B flat minor (Ex. 7.5(c)), the latter a funeral march dedicated to Maurice Gray, the son of Alan Gray, killed in service in August 1918), Liszt (no. 8 in E flat minor; Ex. 7.5(d)), Schumann (no. 7 in E flat and no. 17 in A flat (Ex. 7.5(e)), the latter recalling the 'Davidsbündlermarsch' of *Carnaval*) and Schubert (no. 15 in G (Ex. 7.5(f)), a perky piece redolent of the *Moment musical* in F minor). Stanford evoked many

Example 7.5   Preludes for Piano, Op. 163: (*a*) No. 9 ('Humoresque'), bars 1–6;
(*b*) No. 2, bars 1–5; (*c*) No. 22, bars 1–6; (*d*) No. 8, bars 1–9; (*e*)
No. 17, bars 1–10; (*f*) No. 15, bars 1–10

Example 7.5   *(cont.)*

different moods in both sets of Preludes, many of which are highly
effective pieces. Although he appeared to have designed each set for
continuous performance – such is the disposition of moods prelude by
prelude – all can exist as independent pieces or could be selected as sets,
and all are designed as character pieces, though not of a cyclic nature.
Thus one visits the imposing (no. 1 in C), tender (no. 2 in C minor),
lyrical (no. 19 in A), goblinesque (no. 20 in A minor) and elegiac (no.
24 in B minor) in a manner which is well balanced and satisfying. The
second set explores similar territory to that of the first, although it
remains varied and original; here too Stanford found occasion to use
specific ideas, for example, a musette (no. 42 in G sharp minor), recitative (no. 40 in G minor), ostinato (no. 38 in F sharp minor) and a whole
movement based on a tonic pedal (no. 35 in F). The final prelude is
subtitled 'Addio' and here Stanford brought both sets of preludes to an
impassioned and poignant conclusion.

Although Stanford continued to compose consistently he was slowly
weakening physically. He happened to be staying in Malvern when Alice
Elgar died and went to her funeral on 10 April 1920. W. H. Reed related
the event to Harry Greene:

> When I emerged from the gallery at the end of the church ... [I
> found] Sir Charles Stanford standing inside the door. As the coffin
> was being borne from the church to the grave he impulsively caught
> hold of my arm and said, 'Tell Elgar I *had* to come. I daren't go to
> the graveside as the doctor has absolutely forbidden me to stand in
> the open air without a hat, but tell him how sorry I am and that I
> just felt I *must* come.' At this he broke down and went away. He
> was far from well and I firmly believe that he had toiled all the way
> from Great Malvern contrary to the doctor's orders.[31]

Whatever Stanford's motives for attending, Elgar was furious and wrote
to Frank Schuster a few days later:

> Of Stanford's presence at the funeral I was unaware until after the
> ceremony. I only regard it as a cruel piece of impertinence. For years
> (?16) he has not spoken to me and has never let me know why,
> although we have several friends in common.
>
> His presence last Saturday was a very clever trick to make it
> appear that after all, he is really a 'decent fellow' etc. and that I am
> the culprit – that the fault (if any) of our difference (which only
> exists by his manufacture) is wholly mine and not his. As to his
> wanting to show respect, and the like, I do not believe a word of
> it and never shall do. It was a mere political 'trick'.[32]

It was over two years before the two men encountered each other again.
They both went to Gloucester in September 1922 for the Three Choirs

---

[31] Quoted in Greene, *Stanford*, 158.
[32] Elgar to Frank Schuster, 18 Apr. 1920, WRO, 705: 445: 6976.

Festival, at which Parry was to be commemorated. Stanford's *Fantasia on a tune of Parry*, Op. 187 was premièred and in the cathedral a memorial tablet was unveiled. Herbert Brewer made Elgar and Stanford shake hands, but it could mean little to either man after so many years of hostility and could not, as Greene thought, be called a reconciliation (see Pl. 11).[33]

As he aged more visibly Stanford began to run down his professional engagements. In February 1921 Greene hints that he suffered a mild stroke and that this led to a reduction in his confidence.[34] On 5 March the Royal Choral Society gave the première of *At the Abbey Gate*, but Greene recalled that Stanford was nervous:

> He came to me the day before and asked me pitifully if I would mind if he got someone else to conduct it. I knew by experience the danger of giving way to your nerves and I over-persuaded him. I promised him that I would see him through. I arrived in the afternoon with two strong doses of sal volatile in my pocket. One of these I made him take on the spot and the other just as he was going on to the platform; and I told him to remember that I should be standing close beside him and that if he felt shaky he was to put his hand out and lean upon me. The moment he took up the stick he forgot it all and carried it through triumphantly; but he never conducted again.[35]

In fact, Stanford conducted one more concert with the RCM Orchestra, on 3 June 1921, but after that, though it does not appear to have been announced formally, he handed the baton fully on to Adrian Boult, having held it in his own hand for thirty-eight years.

One final opportunity to travel to Ireland presented itself to Stanford in early 1921 when Trinity College, Dublin voted to confer on him an honorary doctorate; the ceremony was to take place on 30 June 1921.[36] The situation in Ireland, however, was still very tense; Sinn Fein had swept the board in the 1918 General Election (winning all Irish seats outside Ulster except the four allocated to Dublin University) and had set up the Dail as an alternative parliament, moving Ireland inexorably towards the Free State and to partition. Sporadic unrest broke out, despite continued negotiations with the British government about the future.[37] Nevertheless, and although he must have had many reservations about returning to Dublin after such a long time, Stanford was, according to Greene, only stopped from going there on doctor's

---

[33] Greene, *Stanford*, 58.

[34] Greene, 'Stanford as I Knew Him', 82–8.

[35] Ibid. Greene's later account (see Greene, *Stanford*, 273–4) is slightly different in detail.

[36] See the *Musical Times*, 1 May 1921, p. 364.

[37] The period between 21 Jan. 1919 and 11 July 1921 is now commonly referred to as the Anglo-Irish War and saw extensive guerilla warfare by the Irish Republican Army and reprisals by government agencies.

orders.[38] As the degree could not be conferred *in absentia* he failed to receive this honour from his home town.

Relations with Cambridge, Stanford's first English home, had long been distant. He had loosened his links when he moved to London in 1893 and over the succeeding years his involvement with Cambridge had steadily reduced, such that his involvement had come down to the bare minimum. As long ago as 1902 the *Musical News* had remarked that 'with an absent Professor [music students] cannot properly study music while in residence there ... and so unfortunately the Faculty appears to be absent'.[39] By 1920 discontent in Cambridge over the absentee professor was less muted than hitherto. Peter Warlock reported in the *Sackbut* that '130 junior members of the University of Cambridge have signed and presented to the Vice Chancellor a petition that Cambridge should have a resident Professor of Music "who shall by force of his enthusiasm and daily example give the lead and sympathy which is now provided by others"'.[40] In fact Stanford had long been aware of the disadvantages of a non-resident Professor but clear about the reasons for the situation. Tackled by Edward Dent on the subject in 1902 Stanford had written:

> I am afraid that your ideal notion of the Professor of Music resident in Cambridge is knocked on the head by the base fact that it is worth £200 a year less income tax, and certainly the present Professor could not afford to keep up a Cambridge establishment on that footing! And Cambridge made it sufficiently clear to my experience that unless the Professor was also an organ grinder he had nothing to supplement it. Perhaps they'll give the next £1000 and then there may be some chance of your hope being realised.[41]

The statement may in one respect be disingenuous: although Stanford was quite right in his assertion about the poor salary, one doubts whether he would have moved back to Cambridge even if the University had offered to increase his salary to £1,000 per annum. The students' petition was sidelined when presented but was a portent of things to come: in 1924 the Senate did start to look at the status of the Professor of Music, but Stanford died before they had agreed on any changes (see p. 334). Stanford was not, however, wholly disengaged from music in Cambridge and continued to give his annual course of composition classes and to examine degrees. In June 1921 there was a brief exchange

[38] Greene, *Stanford*, 274–5.
[39] *Musical News*, 7 June 1902, p. 541.
[40] *Sackbut*, 1 May 1920, quoted in *The Occasional Writings of Philip Heseltine*, ed. Barry Smith, 3 vols (London, 1997), i, 84.
[41] Stanford to Dent, 18 Nov. 1902, Fitzwilliam Musuem, Cambridge.

of letters with Francis Jenkinson regarding the conduct of Cyril Rootham as a Cambridge examiner:

> I am very sorry to worry you. But this affair of the MusBac Exam is getting *very serious*. One of the candidates, Armitage of Christ's, came to me today and told me about the *circs* and exactly what C.B.R. said, even criticising papers which we others had not seen! The whole matter of the MusBac will fall into disrepute if it goes on; or as Allen said 'it is in R's interest to put him right as to how examiners have to behave' ... I feared this w[oul]d be the result of [Rootham's] appointment (from old experience). You can't make silk purses out of some people's ears.[42]

The outcome of this incident is unknown and part of his annoyance was probably prompted by his personal dislike of Rootham, but, as Stanford was responsible for the conduct of examinations in Cambridge, he was right to be worried and the incident demonstrates that he still took the responsibilities of his job, minimal as they were, seriously.

In the music produced by Stanford in his last three years he moved further towards an austerity of expression. A certain emotional detachment in some works has already been noted; in these last works there was also a tendency for his music to become minimal in means. Stanford had long preached the virtues of economy to his students (see pp. 355–7) and reacted badly to what he viewed as extravagance, for example the use of 'extra' orchestral instruments and the proliferation of subject material; in the pre-war period this reaction is exemplified in such works as the Seventh Symphony, although his practising of this doctrine was inconsistent. In many of his songs, also, especially the Irish settings, he had shown a recurrent interest in paring down the accompaniment to its essentials, using simple figuration and sparse chords, leading to a transparency of texture. In the post-war years this was a dictum he put increasingly into effect and executed in a more extreme manner than hitherto; many post-war works, especially those of the 1920s, carry an almost puritan ethos, so minimal are the means of execution. This trend is most apparent in smaller pieces, such as the *Songs from the Elfin Pedlar* (1923) and the two unpublished Piano Sonatinas (1922). In these not only is the piano writing pared down to the minimum but the gestures are small and restrained (Ex. 7.6); as in the late compositions of Saint-Saëns, there is a spirit almost of neoclassicism in the music, resulting from a reaction to the luxuriant romanticism of Elgar, the extremity of Strauss and the German Expressionists, and the primitivism of Stravinsky. Stanford's neoclassicism was not expressed in the

---

[42] Stanford to Jenkinson, 17 June 1921, CUL, Add. MS 6343, item 9006.

enfant-terrible style of Prokofiev, however, but like Saint-Saëns, in a manner of emotional and practical understatement.

Stanford completed his last orchestral work, the *Irish Rhapsody No. 6*, Op. 191, on 17 September 1922. Two weeks after finishing the Rhapsody he celebrated his seventieth birthday but in November came further evidence of his declining health. Greene recalled:

> He dined at the Savile – his family being at the theatre – and played bridge until a fairly late hour. When he started to go home he found a thick fog outside, so thick that the traffic had stopped. There was no possibility of getting a taxi, and he started to walk home to Lower Berkeley Street [a distance of about one mile]. This was one of the emergencies with which he was constitutionally unfitted to grapple; he was lost in the fog from the moment he walked down the steps of 107 Piccadilly. An hour later he was brought back to the Club by a friendly stranger who found him wandering about, completely bewildered, in Down Street. What had happened in the interval nobody knows; he did not know himself. In all probability he had never been more than a hundred yards or so from the Club. Major Butson ... put him to bed in his own room ... and telephoned home to say that he was safe and sound and that he would bring him back himself the next morning ... He was manifestly ill when he got there, and was put to bed at once under the doctor's orders. He probably had had a slight stroke on this occasion; from this moment it was evident that he was heading downhill.[43]

Despite this physical frailty Stanford was still able to compose, although more slowly. In his last eighteen months he produced five small works: the Three Anthems, Op. 192, Three Preludes and Fugues, Op. 193, Three Idylls, Op. 194 (these latter two works are both for organ), *Songs from the Elfin Pedlar*, and settings of Edward Lear's *Nonsense Rhymes*. There were also some brighter moments; Greene related that Stanford was invited to a celebratory concert at Guildford in February 1923 which included performances of the *Irish Rhapsody No. 4*, the Sixth Symphony and *Songs of the Sea*.[44] In April 1923 the Carnegie Trust announced that it was to publish the Fifth Symphony in full score, only the third of his symphonies to be printed in this format (although a postcard to the Carnegie Trust implies that Stanford had handed over the symphony for publication several years previously).[45] Finally, Greene also recalls the final family party, at Lower Berkeley Street, in July 1923: 'It was a tropical night, 92 in the shade. Sybil Eaton ... and Leonard Borwick

---

[43] Greene, *Stanford*, 276.

[44] Ibid., 277–8.

[45] See Stanford to the Carnegie Trust, 25 Apr. 1923, Scottish Records Office, Edinburgh, File GD 281/41/36.

Example 7.6   Sonatina in G for Piano (1921), first movement, bars 1–15

played, and I sang. The room was crammed with people, and the old
Guildhall spirit seemed to be abroad. He seemed rejuvenated for the
occasion.'[46]

The last Irish Rhapsody was given its first performance in the version
for violin and piano by Sybil Eaton, for whom it was written, and
Sir Edward Bairstow at a concert of the York Musical Society on 10
October 1923. The orchestral première took place a month later at a
special concert of Stanford's music given by the Leeds Philharmonic on
13 November. Stanford travelled to Leeds for the occasion, and was
feted at a dinner on the previous evening. The concert included the *Stabat
Mater*, *Phaudrig Croohore*, *Songs of the Sea*, and a number of songs,
as well as the new Rhapsody. The shortest of the six at ten minutes, the
final Rhapsody shows immense promise in its opening, a truly rhapsodic
exposure of 'The Lament for Owen Roe O'Neill'; Stanford had used this
tune in the Second Rhapsody but whereas in the earlier work it had
been treated in a declamatory manner, giving the impression of mass
mourning, in this last rhapsody the solo violin turns the melody into an
intensely personal statement. The solo line is complemented by a sense
of space and orchestral palette that were as keen as ever. Stanford lost
his way in the middle of this slow section, however, and the sudden
modulation to D major, which sets up the transition to the following
reel, is a jolt and unsatisfactory. In the reel and march which form the
quick music Stanford fortunately pulled himself back together and they
are executed with some panache and concision; the opening lament and
the final dash set a good seal on Stanford's last orchestral work.

The settings of Edward Lear's *Nonsense Rhymes* demonstrate that he
retained his facility and wit until the end. The work was not published

---

[46] Greene, *Stanford*, 276.

until 1960 and, as Stanford intended, does not contain any direct reference to him. The composer's name is only thinly disguised, however
('Karel Drofnatzki'), and further clues to his identity are given in the
references to the River Yeffil and the province of Retsneil. Stanford chose
fourteen of Lear's limericks, and most of his settings quote or satirise
the works of other composers: the violin concertos of Mendelssohn and
Beethoven in 'The Compleat Virtuoso', Grieg in 'The Handy Norsewoman', and Mendelssohn again in 'Limmerich ohne Worte'. Handel,
Henry Bishop, Brahms, Bach, Johann Strauss and Tchaikovsky are also
pressed into service, though Stanford's most daring mockery is directed
at Wagner (Ex. 7.7). Frivolous it may be, but this late work of Stanford's
is also one of his most endearing.

Stanford wrote once more on the subject of opera to *The Times* in
February 1924. It turned out to be his last letter to the newspaper and
it seems appropriate that it should deal with the musical genre closest
to his heart and that it should again advocate, if slightly incoherently,
state support for a national opera company:

> The British National Opera Company is doing its very best for
> its art and its country. Like all foreign companies, it produces all
> operas of all countries all in our own English language. That is
> the first great step. To produce new operas by English composers
> means more money and consequently more risk. They must give the
> familiar works in order to be able to take that risk. They must take
> time to ensure that the risk is not too great to be borne without
> damage to the structure as a whole. The word 'National' is now
> justified by the language in which they sing. It would be further
> justified when the music itself bears its due proportion in nation
> ality also. It cannot be so justified unless it gains the support and
> encouragement which all other countries financially support, thereby
> showing their belief that music is an essential part of education and
> not a mere luxury.[47]

Stanford continued to make plans and to socialise: Hermann Klein
recalled seeing him at a dinner of the Society of English Singers in early
March and that although 'he could no longer make a speech ... his
mind was as alert and his conversation as lively as ever'.[48]

According to Greene, Stanford suffered a second stroke on 17 March,
and was confined to bed.[49] Two days later Frederick Bridge died, aged
79. Stanford and Bridge had never got on well and crossed swords on
several occasions, most notably over the status of Oxbridge music

[47] Stanford to *The Times*, 21 Feb. 1924, p. 13.
[48] Hermann Klein, *Musicians and Mummers* (London, 1925), 302.
[49] Greene, *Stanford*, 278.

Example 7.7   *Nonsense Rhymes* (1923), no. 14 ('A Visit from Elizabeth'), bars 1–15 (text: Edward Lear)

degrees in 1898 and over the music for Edward VII's coronation (see Ch. 5).[50] Stanford also took pleasure in undermining Bridge's composure: Greene related how Bridge had been the victim of one of Stanford's witticisms:

> Bridge had been voluminously explaining all through luncheon, and afterwards in the smoking-room, a system of his own invention for teaching the Abbey choir-boys the elements of music. It was a series of physical 'stunts' symbolising the intervals . . . Three fingers of the right hand extended represented a major third, three of the left hand a minor third; the two fists together signified the common chord,

---

[50] Their lack of regard for each other may be seen in their autobiographies: Bridge (*A Westminster Pilgrim* (London, 1918)) mentioned Stanford only four times and Stanford, in *Pages from an Unwritten Diary*, did not mention Bridge at all.

and so on. When at last Bridge stopped for a moment to take breath, Stanford said very seriously: 'There's one ye've forgotten, Bridge.'

'What's that?' said Bridge, indignantly.

Stanford put his thumb to his nose and slowly extended the fingers of both hands in a long snook. 'Consecutive fifths, my boy,' he said.[51]

Despite their distant relationship, Bridge's death was another hint of mortality and the passage of time: he, like Stanford, had been on the staff of the RCM since its foundation.

Stanford's own illness prevented his attendance at Bridge's funeral on 21 March, and he was still confined to bed when Walter Parratt died, aged 83, on 27 March. Stanford had known Parratt since the early 1870s when he had come to Cambridge to give organ recitals at Trinity. They had been close friends for many years and Parratt had been Stanford's greatest ally at the RCM apart, perhaps, from Greene, even though Stanford had, in Parry's view, bullied Parratt and manipulated him for his own ends.[52] Stanford had much reason to be grateful to Parratt, however, not least for his hospitality in the latter years of the war when Stanford had spent so much time at Windsor. Like Bridge, Parratt had been on the staff of the RCM since its foundation.

Whether Stanford was able to take in the news of Parratt's death is debatable since by this time he too was mortally sick. On 28 March *The Times* described him as lying 'very seriously ill'[53] and stated that his condition 'shows no sign of improvement'. On the following day *The Times* reported that his condition was 'unchanged'[54] and he died on that same day, 29 March. His death was not reported in *The Times* until 31 March, by which time his funeral had been fixed to take place at 11 a.m. on 2 April at St Mary's, Bryanston Square, Stanford's parish church since he had moved to Lower Berkeley Street.[55] In recognition

---

[51] Greene, 'Stanford as I Knew Him', 85.

[52] For example, 'Found Parratt had sent in notice of proposals he was going to move on Wednesday at Board of Professors which had evidently been dictated by Stanford' (Diary, 18 Oct. 1915, ShP). Also, 'At 5.30 the Professors' Board meeting about which there were such disagreeable anticipations. All the agenda bristled with danger. Stanford did a great deal of talking and of lighting matches ... [and then] letting out his pipe. Parratt made a very lame show with his motions, which had been prompted by Stanford. In the end I had to draw up all the resolutions to the Executive ... myself and the threat of rebellion fizzled out, and came away without so much as a grumble' (Diary, 20 Oct. 1915, ShP). Two days later Parry wrote 'Parratt actually standing up to Stanford at luncheon. Stanford looking churlish!' (Diary, 22 Oct. 1915, ShP).

[53] *The Times*, 28 Mar. 1924, p. 17

[54] *The Times*, 29 Mar. 1924, p. 12.

[55] See *The Times*, 31 Mar. 1924, p. 12; an editorial (p. 13) and obituary (p. 14) also appeared in this issue.

of his status, however, the plans were changed; on 1 April *The Times* announced that these arrangements had been cancelled and that the funeral would take place at Westminster Abbey two days later.[56]

On 2 April Stanford's body was cremated at Golders Green and his ashes taken to Westminster for the funeral. The abbey was full – as well as his close family, friends and colleagues the mourners included Lady Parry, Mackenzie, Sir Squire Bancroft, Cecil Sharp, Samuel Coleridge Taylor's widow Jessie and A. Tilney Bassett, presumably a descendant of the Dublin schoolmaster who had terrorised Stanford sixty years earlier. The service was led by Bishop Ryle, Dean of Westminster, with music provided by the abbey choir, conducted by Sydney Nicholson, a former pupil, and the RCM Orchestra, directed by Boult, played the Prelude of the *Stabat Mater*, the slow movement of the Fifth Symphony and the Funeral March from *Beckett*. His ashes were buried in the musicians' aisle, near the organ.[57]

At Bournemouth Dan Godfrey conducted the latest Irish Rhapsody on the day of the funeral and tributes followed in newspapers and magazines. The *RCM Magazine* devoted most of its Spring Term issue to reviewing the careers of the three men – Bridge, Parratt and Stanford – who had done so much to secure its reputation over such a long period. Stanford's work was covered in articles and tributes by Mackenzie, Greene, Marion Scott, and by a group of reminiscences by former pupils. In Cambridge comments were more muted. A short obituary appeared in the *Cambridge Review*[58] and the Funeral March from *Beckett* was included in a CUMS concert on 13 June, but, in view of the distant relationship which had developed between Stanford and the University over the previous twenty years, it is unsurprising that his death caused less distress – by this time nearly all of his friends from the Cambridge days were themselves dead.

At both institutions moves were made to appoint successors. Adrian Boult formally took on the role of Conductor of the RCM Orchestra, while Stanford's composition teaching was taken on by Ireland, Vaughan Williams, Holst, Howells and Frank Bridge, all former pupils. Despite the RCM's tendency to prefer appointing former students, and a relative lack of choice of graduates from other institutions, the success of Stanford's work at the RCM can be amply seen in the appointment

---

[56] See *The Times*, 1 Apr. 1924, p. 17.

[57] A full account of the funeral was given by *The Times* (4 Apr. 1924, p. 15); a copy of the Order of Service is held at the British Library (pressmark: D–3406. c.26). His ashes are in good company, with Gibbons, Blow, Sterndale Bennett and Balfe close by; he was later joined by Elgar, Howells and Vaughan Williams.

[58] *Cambridge Review*, 11 June 1924, p. 414.

of his successors. Although they were less rigid and more progressive than Stanford, elements of his aesthetic – economy of means, clarity of expression, and secure technique – continued to be central parts of the RCM's approach to composition teaching (see Ch. 8).

At Cambridge the decline in Stanford's health, his general detachment, and complaints from students about a non-residential professorship had led the Senate to initiate a review of the status of the Professor of Music in spring 1924. At his death Stanford was still only required to give four lectures each year (long since transformed into one-to-one composition classes but not, contrary to popular rumour, given in the Station Hotel) and to take charge of examining the MusBac and MusDoc degrees, for all of which he received £240 *per annum*, almost identical to the conditions imposed when he was appointed in 1887. On 25 February the Senate was presented with a Report of Council which recommended changes to the professorship – the appointment was to be quinquennial with optional renewal, the salary was to be raised to £500 per annum, and the Professor was to give eight lectures per term and be available for consultations for a further two hours per week in the Lent and Michaelmas Terms; there was, however, still to be no requirement to be resident.[59] In the debate on 4 March reservations were expressed about this last condition but it was approved.[60] Notice of the election was given on 13 May and Charles Wood – another former pupil and the most senior musician linked to Cambridge after Stanford – was elected to succeed him under the new rules on 10 June but, although Wood was only 58 when he was appointed, he died two years later, and was succeeded by Edward Dent.

Although Stanford's direct influence at Cambridge had long since declined, the impact of his work was still felt; Dent wrote to Greene in 1934:

> I believe I can honestly say that I think of Stanford every day at Cambridge; I am always trying to pass on to my composition pupils what he taught me, and I know that the immense respect in which Music (as a University Department) is now held by the Council of

---

[59] See the *Cambridge University Reporter*, 26 Feb. 1924, p. 650.

[60] See the *Cambridge University Reporter*, 11 Mar. 1924, p. 706: Dr Burkitt was reported as remarking that 'they had all been suffering in the last few years from all the evils that come from a non-resident professor. It was not the fault of the professor, it was the fault of the system which had been found unsatisfactory, as was admitted in the preamble to these recommendations ... He would be sorry that the absence of any kind of protest or regret should give the Senate the impression that those concerned with the study of music in this University were at all satisfied with the further provision that had been made for the endowment of the teaching of music ... A non-resident Professor was always unsatisfactory. It was to be hoped in the future that it might be avoided.'

the Senate and similar authorities (even when they are individually unmusical) is all due to Stanford's struggles in the face of opposition long ago.[61]

Given the long-strained relationship between Stanford and Cambridge this tribute may seem surprising, and Dent may have amplified his sentiments for Greene's benefit, but Stanford's contribution to musical life in Cambridge in the 1870s and 1880s and his reform of music degrees in the 1890s had a profound effect on the role and status of music in Cambridge and helped direct the faculty towards the status it enjoys today.

Of Stanford's family little remains to be said; indeed details are scarce. Jennie was granted a pension by George V in recognition of her husband's work and left Lower Berkeley Street soon after his death for a smaller house in Westminster; she died at a nursing home in Wimborne Minster in 1941. Guy became an antique dealer with a shop on South Audley Street in Mayfair; he was widowed in 1949 and died, childless, in Brighton, in 1953. Geraldine, always a figure in the shadows, died a spinster in 1956. Their interests in Stanford's copyright were bequeathed to the Royal School of Church Music and the British Empire Cancer Campaign respectively; on a more intimate note Guy gave his father's signet ring to Herbert Howells in 1952, and bequeathed the CUMS presentation candlesticks to Trinity College. And at this point the history of Stanford's life and his family line ends.

*   *   *

'They don't keep that [College] Guestroom at all in the proper state,' he said. 'When I got out of bed this morning and walked about with bare feet I found the carpet full of gravel – little pebbles ye know! It was horrid – so I went across to Sedley [Taylor].' 'In bare feet?' 'No, and I said to him, "Who took the guest room for me?" and he said, "I did." "What did ye pay for it?" I said. "Well, if ye wish to know, I paid five shillings for the two nights." So I fished out five bob and plonked them down and said, "There's yer money: and now I'm my own host!" and I told him "They've left the traces of everybody who's been in that room."' A characteristic bit of Stanford I think.[62]

Characteristic, indeed. This blunt speaking, illustrated here by Edward Dent, is the personality trait most commonly associated with Stanford. Cause of amusement, cause of frustration, cause of fascination and cause

---

[61] Quoted in Greene, *Stanford*, 82.
[62] Dent's Diary, 24 May 1899, KCC.

of offence, Stanford's distinctly un-Victorian frankness seems to have been remarked upon by everyone. Abundant instances of this acidic language, wit and frankness have been given elsewhere; there is certainly no doubt that Stanford had the 'gift of the gab' and that he used it to both lively and deadly effect. What for pupils was both kindness and brutality, and for Parry and many others was lack of consideration, was defended by Greene, who argued that Stanford merely told the truth; his fault was to fail to realise that this could hurt:

> He followed his instincts and spoke the truth that was in him. He said to his pupil: 'This is damned ugly, my boy' (no thought of the victim), because it was true and it was the shortest way to say it; but he said to the girl whom he had wrongly accused of talking [in an orchestral rehearsal]: 'I believe you, my dear, I'm sorry' (no thought of himself), because it was just and the only way to say it.[63]

The perception, articulated by Greene, of a mercurial temper, potentially vicious tongue, reactionary conservatism, wit, extraordinary frankness manifesting itself in both kindness and brutality, loyalty, boyish enthusiasm, modesty and lack of self-consideration is countered, especially by Parry, who laid charges of arrogance, boorishness, social climbing, dishonesty and lack of consideration for others at Stanford's feet. As Dent's anecdote shows, however, Stanford was well aware of his directness and almost revelled in it; clearly some of the differences between him and Parry are explained by this and are a reflection of the different temperaments of the two men.

Beyond this, however, Stanford remains, in so many personal matters, a figure of mystery. Many aspects of his life remain shrouded – for example, the happiness of his marriage, and his relationships with and aspirations for his children. For nearly all of this information one still depends on Greene; Stanford himself was scrupulously silent about his private life, except for that of his childhood, in *Pages from an Unwritten Diary* and his surviving correspondence brings little illumination. Greene mentioned various friends; those friendships made with other professional musicians have tended to be the best documented, but others, such as those with the amateur musicians Robert Finnie McEwen and Gerard Cobb, remain tantalisingly obscure due to lack of documentary evidence. Of Stanford's wider circle of friends, and of the nature of his relationships with them, similarly little is known. Also obscure are Stanford's recreational activities; nearly all our knowledge of this too comes from Greene: Stanford was a keen player of whist (and later bridge) and a keen, if erratic, angler (from around 1900 most summer

---

[63] Greene, 'Stanford as I Knew Him'.

holidays were spent in the Scottish highlands). In the mid-1880s there is also evidence that he was a regular tennis player, including at least one match with Parry – an intriguing prospect,[64] and he is also known to have played golf with Elgar at Malvern.[65] He was a member of the Athenaeum and Savile Clubs in London – both haunts of those whose primary interest was the arts – and was in this respect a typical male member of the upper middle classes, and in the Savile in particular he clearly spent much leisure time.

These are but fleeting glances into the domestic side of Stanford's life, however, and overall it seems destined to remain obscure. Does this matter? All information adds something to an assessment of a person's character and actions, so the lack of reliable information on so many domestic points is frustrating. On the other hand, enough survives to build up an impression which is of great value and upon which an assessment of his contribution to music can be based. And of one thing there can be no doubt: for all his strengths and weaknesses it seems that he was a man to whom no one who met him could be indifferent. As such, one can accord him the accolade of being a stimulator of thought and debate, a characteristic which should never be dismissed, for from debate and experiment comes the impetus to change and progress.

---

[64] See Francis Jenkinson's diaries for 1886 and 1887 (CUL, Add. MSS 7409 and 7410) and Francis Jenkinson to Eleanor Jenkinson, 10 Feb. 1885, CUL, Add. MS 7671, item III C 141.

[65] See Moore, *Edward Elgar*, 414.

PART TWO

Appraisal and Conclusions

CHAPTER EIGHT

Stanford
the Pedagogue

Stanford's obituarist noted that 'a man who is a composer does not want to be remembered by anything else'.[1] Stanford has always, however, been noted as a pedagogue – in the widest sense of the word – as well as a composer, and, in the view of many, his work as a teacher of composition is of greater significance than his own music. Certainly the list of his pupils (discussed below; see Table 8.2) is very impressive and few teachers can have claimed to have had a bearing on so many of their country's future composers as Stanford. Within the British Isles it is certain that a claim that he taught more successful composers of later generations than any other person is irrefutable. The extent of his influence on his pupils has been subject to rather more debate and it is the aim of this chapter to examine all of Stanford's pedagogical work and to set it within the context of British and European music of the late nineteenth and early twentieth centuries, coming to conclusions on the extent and value of his contribution and influence.

Conductor and Writer

Although, from a pedagogical perspective, Stanford's work as a teacher of composition is of greatest significance, he also made important contributions as a conductor and writer. In an era where 'star' conductors were relatively few and the time of the 'virtuoso' only coincided with the tail-end of his career, Stanford, like many of his contemporaries, was expected to undertake, and was happy to do so, extensive work as a conductor. He directed choirs and orchestras from the early 1870s until his tacit retirement from the RCM Orchestra in 1921. As one would expect, his technique was old-fashioned when compared with the full-time professional conductors who emerged in the 1900s; Marion Scott wrote:

> His beat when conducting was clear. Though he never employed much variety of gesture, or left-hand delineation, and though his

---

[1] *The Times*, 31 Mar. 1924, p. 17.

style was that of the old school, he always conveyed clearly what
he wanted, and that without any strain to himself or fuss for the
players ... Ordinarily when conducting Stanford's face was in-
expressive. But there came times when, in some passage of a noble
work, the beauty of the music seemed to rouse him to a passion
of high love and reverence; then the hidden fires glowed in his
look.[2]

According to Scott he was also very attentive to detail (see pp. 346–7)
and always well prepared; he appeared to her to be happiest when
conducting Brahms:

> In especial his understanding of Brahms was a remarkable combi-
> nation of intellect and intuition. I have spoken with many who
> played under him; one and all agree in placing his Brahms' [sic]
> interpretations as his finest performances. Mr Claude Hobday
> [leader of the double bass section of the LSO], intimately connected
> with the College orchestra for years, writes: 'I always felt he was
> happiest when interpreting Brahms; he had such a fine sense of the
> Brahms' [sic] rhythms and a perfect understanding of the tempi.'[3]

These positive sentiments were not echoed by everyone: Parry, in particular, often found Stanford's interpretations, especially of Bach,
unbearable (see p. 181) and Shaw too disparaged Stanford's conducting
on several occasions (though he criticised nearly all conductors at some
point).[4] Technically, as well as chronologically, Stanford was halfway
between the earlier generation of Sullivan and Costa, whose technique
was essentially undemonstrative, and the later generation of such men
as Nikisch, Boult and Harty, the first generation of men known as
virtuosi of their profession. Looking at his contemporaries, Stanford
himself wrote that, ultimately, he preferred what he viewed as
Richter's predictable solidity to Bülow's brilliant but somewhat erratic

---

[2] Marion Scott, 'Sir Charles Stanford and the RCM Orchestra', *RCM Magazine*, 20
(1923–4), 48–52 at 51.

[3] Ibid.

[4] For example: 'There must be still alive in [Stanford] something of the young Irishman
of genius who wrote those spirited Cavalier tunes ... before he was forced back into the
dismal routine of manufacturing impossible trash like *The Revenge* for provincial festival
purposes, and into conducting, which is so little his affair that when I lately described his
Bach choir work in my unliterary way from the point of view of a person whose business
it is to use his ears, the only champion who ventured to say a word in his defence did
not dare to sign it. [Cowen] also, is no more fitted to be a conductor than the majority
of brilliant and popular writers are to be editors. My interest in getting both gentlemen
back to their proper work, which I take to be intelligent and vivacious dramatic composition, is that it would then become a pleasure to criticise them, instead of, as it generally
is at present, a disagreeable duty' (Shaw, *Music in London*, i, 239).

abilities[5] – a clear parallel with his anti-virtuosic sentiments regarding pianists (see p. 167). Clearly, however, he did not believe in the almost *laissez-faire* method of conducting adopted by Sullivan and Costa, the former being witheringly portrayed by Eduard Hanslick in 1886:

> Sullivan presides on the podium from the comfortable recesses of a commodious armchair, his left arm lazily extended on the arm-rest, his right giving the beat in a mechanical way, his eyes fastened to the score. [The Philharmonic Society] played Mozart's Symphony in G Minor. Sullivan never looked up from the notes; it was as though he were reading at sight. The heavenly piece plodded along, for better or worse, listlessly, insensibly. At the end the audience applauded long and loudly, but it apparently never occurred to Sullivan to turn around and face the audience. He sat stolid and immovable in his armchair.[6]

Hanslick went on to cite the solid Richter as the best conductor working in Britain at the time, followed by August Manns and Charles Hallé, noting that 'it is significant that both are Germans'. Given his own friendship with and admiration for Richter, it is probable that Stanford modelled his own technique on Richter's to an extent. Eugene Goossens remembered :

> Richter's stick technique was simplicity itself. He used a short, thick piece of cane with a padded grip and indulged in few superfluous gestures. The elaborate arabesques of contemporary conducting were totally unknown – and superfluous – to him. The beat was a square one, vehement, simple, and best suited to classic and romantic styles. Especially in long sustained rhythmic patterns did he preserve a marvellous continuity of style ... His manner was the antithesis of the Nikisch school, and little the worse for that.[7]

Stanford's style appers to have been close to this, so it is unsurprising that, just as Costa and Sullivan's approach had been by-passed by the 1880s, so, later, was Stanford and Richter's. Harty, whose career took off just before the First World War, and who was appointed to the Hallé in 1919, is a good exemplar of this new style:

> Few conductors could, without asking, so exactly indicate by the beat the kind of staccato, or the pulse of the vibrato, or the length of the note required ... His left hand directions were an inspiration. I have heard conductors admit how terrified they have been

---

[5] See Stanford, 'On Some Conductors and their Methods', in *Interludes, Records and Recollections*, 29–38.

[6] Eduard Hanslick, *Hanslick's Musical Criticisms*, trans. and ed. Henry Pleasants (New York, 1988), 263.

[7] Goossens, *Overtures and Beginners*, 54.

to beat the opening bar of Strauss's *Don Juan*, wondering if the orchestra would get off the ground after the impact of the first beat. Often the philosophy has been, 'Give the beat and hope for the best.' But when Harty conducted the work, there was no doubt what was expected. His timing was so exact that the cascade of seven semiquavers that follow the downbeat sounded like a tornado.[8]

It is rather difficult now to be sure of how effective Stanford's conducting was – the comment by Scott that he 'absolutely banned the use of a penny instead of a mute [by his string players]'[9] does not inspire huge confidence in the overall standards of the time, and nor does Stanford's lauding of Richter for finally persuading English orchestras that dynamic markings were of some significance[10] – clearly, however, Stanford was able to hold his own with most of his British contemporaries, with no greater number of strengths or weaknesses than such men as Cowen, Elgar or Mackenzie.

More important than technique, however, was the repertory Stanford conducted. His work at Cambridge and Leeds and with the Bach Choir has been discussed in previous chapters, but it was at the RCM that he made the most important long-term impact because it was here that so many future professional British orchestral players were trained. Under his thumb for thirty-eight years, the RCM Orchestra programmes inevitably reflect his own preferences, but still included a wide variety of music. Between 1905 and 1921 (for which a complete run of programmes survives)[11] he conducted a huge variety of music from Bach onwards; predictably, Brahms and Beethoven are the best represented, while Tchaikovsky, Berlioz, Bach, Mozart, Schumann, Glazunov, Wagner, Saint-Saëns, Franck, Bruch and Dvořák are all given reasonable prominence. The favouring of Glazunov arose from Stanford's personal admiration for him; conversely, the poor representations of such composers as Elgar and Richard Strauss are surely also the result of his personal antipathies. Other gaps are a reflection of contemporary mores: Haydn, Schubert, Borodin and Mussorgsky all appear only occasionally, but in line with much programming of the time.

While Stanford might be congratulated for giving his students a solid grounding in what was then canonic repertory, the lack of contemporary music reflects poorly on him. Works by former RCM students appear with reasonable frequency and gave British composers

---

[8] Leonard Hirsch, 'Memories of Sir Hamilton', in David Greer (ed.), *Hamilton Harty: His Life and Music* (Belfast, 1979), 68.

[9] Scott, 'Sir Charles Stanford and the RCM Orchestra', 50.

[10] Stanford, 'On Some Conductors and their Methods', 33.

[11] See the *RCM Magazine* for this period for complete details.

Table 8.1   RCM opera productions conducted by Stanford,
1885–1914

Date		Composer	Work	Theatre
1885	July 22	Mozart	*Le nozze di Figaro* (Acts I and II)	Empire
1886	June 24	Cherubini	*Les Deux journées*	Savoy
1887	June 27	Weber	*Der Freischütz*	Savoy
1888	July 11	Nicolai	*Die lustigen Weiber von Windsor*	Savoy
1889	July 10	Goetz	*Der Widerspänstigen Zähmung*	Prince of Wales
1890	July 16	Mozart	*Così fan tutte*	Savoy
1891	Dec. 9, 16	Cornelius	*The Barber of Bagdad*	Savoy
1892	Dec. 10	Gluck	*Orfeo*	Lyceum
1893	Mar. 11	Gluck	*Orfeo*	Lyceum
1894	Dec. 13	Délibes	*Le roi l'a dit*	Prince of Wales
1895	Feb. 26	Délibes	*Le roi l'a dit* (command performance)	Windsor Castle
1895	Nov. 20	Purcell	*Dido and Aenaes*	Lyceum
1896	Dec. 11	Verdi	*Falstaff*	Lyceum
1898	Jan. 27	Mozart	*Don Giovanni*	Lyceum
1898	Dec. 9	Wagner	*Der fliegende Holländer*	Lyceum
1899	Dec. 12	Mozart	*Die Zauberflöte*	Lyceum
1900	Nov. 30	Weber	*Euryanthe*	Daly's
1901	Nov. 29	Stanford	*Much Ado about Nothing*	Lyceum
1902	Nov. 25	Beethoven	*Fidelio*	His Majesty's
1903	Dec. 4	Humperdinck	*Hänsel und Gretel*	Lyric
1904	Dec. 2	Gluck	*Alcestis*	His Majesty's
1905	Dec. 7	Mozart	*Le nozze di Figaro*	His Majesty's
1906	Nov. 23	Stanford	*Shamus O'Brien*	La Scala
1908	Jan. 23	Verdi	*Falstaff*	His Majesty's
1908	Dec. 3	Goetz	*Francesca*	His Majesty's
1910	Feb. 18	Gluck	*Iphigénie en Tauride*	His Majesty's
1910	Nov. 18	Schumann	*Genoveva*	His Majesty's
1911	Nov. 21	Cherubini	*Les Deux journées*	His Majesty's
1912	Dec. 9	Mackenzie	*Colomba*	His Majesty's
1913	Nov. 28	Verdi	*Falstaff*	His Majesty's
1914	Dec. 7	Humperdinck	*Hänsel und Gretel*	Royal College

Source: Henry Colles and John Cruft, *Royal College of Music: A Centenary Record* (London, 1982), 99–100.

a creditable representation but the works of other indigenous writers are conspicuous by their absence; the appearances of Mackenzie are in due proportion to his national standing but works by RAM students hardly ever appear. Whilst Stanford may have felt that the RAM itself was the appropriate place for these pieces to be performed, he did the RCM Orchestra a disservice by not exposing it directly to the school of composition fostered at Tenterden Street. Surprisingly, but perhaps commendably, works by both Stanford and Parry appear only rarely; whether Parry felt neglected or not is not clear, but Stanford's reluctance to promote his own music shows a (rare?) eschewal of self-promotion. His greatest fault was his avoidance of contemporary foreign composers, whose works were woefully neglected: the works of Ravel and Debussy are almost entirely disregarded, and Mahler and Stravinsky do not appear at all. Given that a substantial proportion of Britain's post-war orchestral players were trained at the RCM in the Edwardian period, this tendency to conservative programming must have handicapped the performance of contemporary music in Britain in the 1920s and 1930s.

The RCM Opera productions do Stanford more credit, for here he brought many then obscure operas into the public arena. Composers such as Strauss and Puccini remain unrepresented, but the limitations of the singers with whom Stanford was dealing would have rendered many operas impractical: Wagner and Verdi were given only three performances between them but this did not arise from personal disaffection (see Table 8.1).

The especial importance of a number of these productions is the willingness to explore beyond the operatic canon; the best examples are *Genoveva*, *Les Deux journées*, the two operas by Goetz, the three by Gluck, the revival of *Colomba* and the first modern performance of *Dido and Aeneas*. The list remains heavily biased towards Germany but Stanford appears in a better light here than as an orchestral conductor, not least because the repertoire of the commercial opera companies was so conservative at this time: between the commercial and college worlds, RCM students would have seen a reasonably broad cross-section of work. Whatever his failings, Stanford kept the operatic flag flying at the RCM despite the lukewarm attitudes of Grove and Parry, and for this he should be given credit, both for his dedication and for the educational benefits derived by his students. Marion Scott recalled both his relentless rehearsals and their results:

> Stanford was unsparing, enthusiastic, almost ruthless in the thoroughness of his preparations and rehearsals. Though we in the band often felt rueful as he issued his final orders: 'Now, ye're not to look at the stage, ye're to look at *me*'; of course he was perfectly right!

> One reward of his thoroughness was that when at a performance
> (*The Magic Flute*, I think it was), all lights failed in the Lyceum
> Orchestra, the band played on as if nothing had happened, and
> played by heart for a page till the lights came on again.[12]

Stanford's achievement as a conductor was to help broaden the repertory performed in Britain. His pioneering performances of Brahms and
Schumann at Cambridge are the most celebrated instances, but other
events too, such as the performances of Handel's *Hercules* at Cambridge
and of *Dido and Aeneas* at the RCM, are further examples, as is his
advocacy of a variety of new works at Leeds. From the 1890s Stanford's
notable achievements tended to be in the sphere of new British music
of a non-radical type, while conductors such as Henry Wood and
Thomas Beecham explored the works of adventurous Continental
composers. Despite this conservative tendency, however, Stanford played
a significant and positive part in broadening the established British
orchestral repertory.

In another pedagogical field, Stanford also made some important
contributions to musical debate as a writer. The most significant of these
are his pronouncements on composition, which are considered below,
but other subjects attracted his attention at various times; these articles
were mainly published in the two collections *Studies and Memories*
(London, 1908) and *Interludes, Records and Recollections* (London,
1922).[13] He never, however, aspired to be a musicologist and did not
write substantial tracts on musical history as Parry or Fuller Maitland
did, or on theory, as exemplified by Ebenezer Prout. Nor did Stanford
contribute to Grove's dictionary, either in its first edition, directed by
Grove himself, or the second edition edited by Fuller Maitland.

In fact, Stanford's two biggest historical monographs are both somewhat disengenuous; an examination of *A History of Music* (London,
1916) shows that two-thirds of the chapters were actually written by
his former student Cecil Forsyth, with Stanford supplying only five (those
covering the period from Monteverdi to Wagner), while in his mono-
graph on Brahms (London, 1912), Stanford openly admits that most of
the material is a rehash of the biographies by Florence May and Max
Kalbeck. Indeed this book is strangely skewed as it concentrates principally on Brahms's life up to 1872 and deals with the entire musical
output of his last twenty-five years in a mere two paragraphs. As an

---

[12] Scott, 'Sir Charles Stanford and the RCM Orchestra', 49–50.

[13] In both collections the articles may be grouped into three categories: commentary on
individual pieces of music, memoirs of musicians and commentary on issues of the day
(some of which originated as speeches). See Bibliography for a list of the contents of each
book.

independent piece of historical research or commentary, therefore, the book has little value, although his reflections on speculation about the possibility of Brahms's being Jewish are of interest to the extent that they show that Stanford was not anti-Semitic.[14] Stanford's other biographical study, that on Sterndale Bennett, also concentrates on Bennett's life with both factual and anecdotal commentary, rather than discussing his music to any extent.[15]

The articles dealing with 'issues of the day' are of the greatest interest; the most important of these are mentioned in other chapters, for example 'Music and the War', and below. In these articles Stanford brought some erudition and wide knowledge to his arguments, but not systematic research as is now understood – and which would not have been expected at the time. Rather, he wrote on subjects which interested him, or of which he had had some direct experience. One frequently finds analogies with other disciplines (discussed below in relation to composition) and aspects of the quintessential Stanford appear from time to time: in the article 'Music in Elementary Schools' (1889) he wrote:

> My proposition is this: that the first effect of education upon the uneducated masses is the development of socialistic and even revolutionary ideas amongst them. We are now carrying out a species of repetition of the story of man's fall: but with a difference. When Adam ate of the fruit of the tree of knowledge, he was under no compulsion, unless indeed you can apply such a term to the

---

[14] 'One of the most polemic questions ever imported in to the realms of art was first crystalised by Wagner in 1850, when, at first under a pseudonym, he promulgated his "Judaism in Music". It was as dangerous a weapon to play within art, as in politics and finance. Aimed at a race to which no honest man can deny pre-eminent and very special gifts in the very art with which this pamphlet dealt, it produced, perhaps even more by its title than by its contents, a heated controversy which should never have been allowed to arise. Wagner had expanded into a general theory a personal dislike of Mendelssohn and an artistic detestation of Meyerbeer, and so committed himself to the dangerous maxim "E duobus disce omnes." He allowed this prejudice to lead him to hint at a Semitic strain in Brahms, founded on a wrong conception of his name. The name, of course, has no more connection with Abraham than Mozart with Moses. It is purely Teutonic, and has many forms in Germany, such as Bram, Brahm, Brahms or Brahmst, and is the same as Broom or Reed in English nomenclature ... [Brahms] was too broad minded a judge of his art not to appreciate the value of Jewish influence in its history, and of Jewish masters in its performance. He knew, as all unprejudiced critics know, that if a national work of art is good in itself, it cannot become less so if investigation detects some foreign strain in the family of its creator; and he experienced in his own career, the immeasurable help and encouragement which that brilliant race, which evolved the grandest piece of literature in existence, could by its rapidity of appreciation and its almost unrivalled power of expression bring to his aid.' Charles Stanford, *Brahms* (London, 1912), 11–12.

[15] Charles Stanford, 'William Sterndale Bennett', in *Interludes, Records and Recollections*, 161–209.

persuasive powers of a wife ... The gentle persuasion of woman has given place to the official compulsion of the School Board [following Forster's Education Act of 1870]. Those of you who have watched with interest the home policy of Germany will not fail to have noted that Prince Bismarck was alive at once to the necessity and to the danger of popular and compulsory education. He accompanied his measures of improvement by measures of precaution ... he passed laws for the repression of socialism almost simultaneously with his laws for general compulsory education.[16]

Most of his writings have been superseded either by events or by the statements of others; the comments which still resonate now can be both the most cheering and depressing, whether it be on the status of church musicians (see pp. 164–6) or on the perception of schoolboys that music is a 'effeminate' subject.[17] The most significant aspect of Stanford's published writings is, however, that they are the comment of a significant musician on the state of the world around him and it is in their status as contemporary comment that they are most illuminating – both for what they tell us about the world around him and, more importantly, for what can be deduced from them about his views of his surroundings.

'Damned ugly me bhoy' – Stanford the Teacher

That Stanford's reputation as a teacher of composition has predominated over his renown as a composer was, perhaps, inevitable, as he taught so many people who became significant composers in their own right, their plurality overshadowing his singularity. At the RCM, Stanford was the primary composition teacher after Parry became Director and remained so for nearly twenty-five years: avoiding Stanford was, therefore, not easy. The list of pupils who passed through his hands at Cambridge and the RCM remains impressive (see Table 8.2). Many of his pupils left accounts of his teaching and he himself left extensive writing on the approaches and values he tried to inculcate in his students, principally in his book *Musical Composition*, but also in *Pages from an Unwritten Diary* and in the paper 'On Some Recent Tendencies in Composition'.[18] The students' reminiscences published in the *RCM*

---

[16] Charles Stanford, 'Music in Elementary Schools', in *Studies and Memories*, 43–60.

[17] See 'Some Notes upon Musical Education', in *Interludes, Records and Recollections*, 1–17.

[18] 'On Some Recent Tendencies in Composition' was given as a paper to the Royal Musical Association in 1920 and reproduced in *Interludes, Records and Recollections*, 89–101.

Magazine[19] shortly after his death should be treated with some caution; whilst they are not hagiography as such, they form a tribute in which direct criticism would have been almost unacceptable. Nevertheless, the accounts show the good and bad sides of his personality. Notably, many former pupils, especially Vaughan Williams, Dunhill and Howells, remained remarkably loyal to their teacher, at least in public, in later years, suggesting that these early 'tribute articles' are a reasonably realistic reflection of how Stanford's pupils viewed him.

Stanford's approach to teaching can be conveniently divided into three areas: the manner in which he taught, the course of exercises and tasks he set, and the aesthetics which he tried to inculcate. His personal approach to pupils varied, although it is unclear whether this was calculated or haphazard. To Vaughan Williams, Stanford was blunt and to the point, and criticisms were made straightforwardly or even brutally, contrasting with Parry's methods:

> Stanford was often cruel in his judgements and the more sensitive among his pupils wilted under his methods and found comfort under a more soft-hearted teacher. I remember I once showed Stanford the slow movement of a string quartet. I had worked feverishly at it, and, like every other young composer, thought not only that it was the finest piece that had ever been written, and that my teacher would fall on his knees and embrace me, but that it was also my swan song. Now what would Parry have done in a case like this? He would have pored over it for a long time in hopes of finding something characteristic and, even if he disliked the piece as a whole, would try to find some point to praise. Stanford dismissed it with a curt 'All rot, me boy!' This was cruel but salutary. So far as I can remember, he was quite right. Luckily the piece was lost years ago.[20]

This directness is corroborated by Cyril Rootham and John Ireland.[21] To Herbert Howells, however, Stanford's criticisms were made obliquely:

> I was under [Stanford] for five years and at the end of that time he told me that I was probably the only pupil who hadn't experienced the rough edge of his tongue. He took to me personally – he used to refer to me as his 'son in music' – and this I think softened the blows when they did fall. If Stanford didn't like you he could be merciless. However, his criticisms were generally indirect.[22]

---

[19] 'Sir Charles Stanford and his Pupils', *RCM Magazine*, 20 (1923–4), 55–61. Another article under the same name, but with substantially different contents, appeared in *Music and Letters*, 5 (1924), 193–207.

[20] Ralph Vaughan Williams, 'Vaughan Williams's Talk on Parry and Stanford, 1957,' in Ursula Vaughan Williams and Imogen Holst (eds), *Heirs and Rebels: Letters of Ralph Vaughan Williams and Gustav Holst* (London, 1959), 94–102 at 100.

[21] See p. 309 (Rootham) and p. 354 (Ireland).

[22] Quoted in Christopher Palmer, *Herbert Howells: A Study* (London, 1978), 12–13.

Table 8.2 Selective list of Stanford's composition students
(RCM and Cambridge)

Name	Years taught	Name	Years taught
Arthur Somervell	1880–83	Harold Samuel	*1897–1900*
Emil Kreuz	1883–8	Haydn Wood	*1897–1900*
Hamish MacCunn	1883–6	Edgar Bainton	*1898–1901*
Sydney Waddington	1883–8	Herbert Fryer	*1898–1901*
Charles Wood	1883–7	Frank Bridge	1899–1903
Henry Walford Davies	1890–94	Edward Dent	1899–1900
Richard Walthew	1890–94[a]	George Dyson	1900–4
Alexander Cecil Forsyth	*1891–4*	Herbert Hughes	1901–4
		Ernest Farrar	1905–8
Samuel Coleridge Taylor	1892–7	James Friskin	1905–8
		Harold Darke	*1906–9*
Katherine Ramsay	*1892–5*	Rebecca Clarke	1907–10
Thomas Dunhill	1893–8	Ivor Gurney	*1908–11*
Fritz Hart	1893–6[b]	Eugene Goossens	1910–12
William Hurlstone	1894–8	Arthur Benjamin	1911–14
Martin Shaw	*1894–7*	Herbert Howells	1912–*15*
Gustav Holst	1895–8	Arthur Bliss	1913–14
Ralph Vaughan Williams	1895–7	Ernest Moeran	1913–14
		George Thalben-Ball	*1914–18*
Rutland Boughton	*1896–9*	Maurice Jacobson	*1916–22*[c]
Nicholas Gatty	*1896–1901*	Margaret Nosek	*1916–18*
Sydney Nicholson	*1896–9*	Leslie Heward	1917–20
Marion Scott	1896–1904	Thomas Wood	1918–20
John Ireland	1897–1901	Gordon Jacob	*1918–21*
Cyril Rootham	1897–1900	Hugh Ross	*1918–21*

Source: This table is derived principally from the list given in Greene, *Stanford*, 93. Dates in italics are unconfirmed; where no information could be traced a hypothetical three-year period from the age of 18 has been inserted.

[a] Appears in Greene's list, but actually taught by Parry and perhaps not by Stanford at all.
[b] Not taught by Stanford but influenced considerably by him at the RCM.
[c] Studies interrupted by the War.

Stanford's admiration of Howells's talents is well known and exempli-fied by his insistence that his Piano Quartet be submitted to the Carnegie Trust in 1917. Howells was not unique, however, as both Edgar Bainton and Rebecca Clarke were also treated carefully:

> [Bainton:] Kindliness and geniality were his most characteristic qualities, and his oft-repeated comment (often the sole remark at a

lesson), 'this is d_____d ugly my boy' was given in such dulcet
tones and with such a gentle motion of the eyelid that it came to
be regarded almost as a tribute of affection, and the few occasions
when it did not occur left a feeling of blankness, as of something
essential having been lost.

[Clarke:] I shall always remember with gratitude and affection the
lessons he gave me, feeling myself fortunate to have been his pupil.
From the very beginning he was entirely charming to me. I remember
so well how I waited outside the glass door of his room before my
first lesson, too nervous to go in; and how an older student, chancing
to pass by, advised me to speak up for myself and not give him the
impression of being frightened. Sir Charles's amused quizzical glance
of course took in the situation in an instant, and we were friends
from that moment. I can see now the hovering of his familiar gold
pencil, and hear the picturesque exaggerations of his praise or
blame.[23]

Margaret Nosek's recollections imply that Stanford's attitude to Clarke
was coloured by her gender; he had strong views about the role and
education of women (see pp. 64 and 197–8) and believed that the sexes
should be treated differently. With Nosek, however, Stanford made an
exception, showing in passing another example of his directness:

[I] was told that Sir Charles Stanford had done me the honour of
accepting me as a pupil. This was indeed an honour, for amongst
other things, Sir Charles always refused to take female pupils. He
explained all this to me the first time I went to him, and I gathered
that his chief objection to women pupils was that he did not feel
enough at ease in their presence to take his coat off or shout at
them. But with me, he said, it was entirely different. It was not my
fault that I was a girl, indeed, I should have been a boy. 'You were
born wrong' he said, and went on to tell me that my way of thinking
and speaking was much too direct for a girl and that it would prove
a great handicap to me in later life, a prognostication which has
proved to be only too true. Whereupon, having asked my permission to do so with old world courtesy, he took off his coat, and
from that moment treated me as though I were a boy.[24]

Inevitably, however, there were students with whom Stanford failed to
sympathise. Cyril Rootham, whom Stanford personally disliked, was one
case, but the most prominent example is that of Arthur Bliss, who wrote:

I prefer to forget the hours I spent with Stanford; they were not
many and from the first moment when he scrawled on my manuscript, 'He who cannot write anything beautiful falls back on the
bizarre,' I felt the lack of sympathy between us. He was a good

[23] 'Sir Charles Stanford and his Pupils' (*RCM Magazine*), 55 and 58 respectively.
[24] Margaret Nosek, 'From a Destroyed Autobiography II', *RCM Magazine*, 80 (1984),
29–36 at 33.

teacher when he was in the mood ... but his own disappointments as a composer perhaps affected his outlook and he had a devital-ising effect on me.[25]

This reference to mood was corroborated by Edward Dent:

> [29 April 1899] I greatly enjoyed my lesson though [Stanford] was severe and said that the trail of the Cathedral organist was all over my work, in the style of writing not being string writing: he admitted that it was not once my harmony.

> [6 May 1899] Stanford's new variations at the Philh[armonic] on 'Down Among the Dead Men'. So I wrote in some haste a theme for variations in the English folksong style: feeling rather ashamed of it, as being trivial and almost vulgar. When I took it to Stanford at 2.15 he said it was the best of the lot and considered it an excel-lent tune. I still feel rather ashamed of it.

> [13 May 1899] [Stanford] seemed fairly pleased with my variations and was most amusing. Unfortunately he could not come to tea. After[wards] tea, to which I made Howard come, as there was buttered toast for Stanford and no Stanford to eat it.

> [20 May 1899] I took my variations to Stanford at 1/4 to 1. He was very full of municipal opera – the L.C.C. being more favourable than he expected – so that he looked very well and was cheerful. He was most encouraging and asked me to bring him the variations later when they were all finished. I only hope the municipal opera wave will last over next week!

> [28 July 1900] I went up to London by the 12 train to see Stanford at the RCM at 2. He was tired and out of sorts and seemed to take no interest in my work at all.[26]

That these notes were made contemporaneously and not intended for publication mean that they are a particularly valuable record of Stanford's approach – and show that his mood could vary and his crit-icisms be unexpected. Thomas Wood, who studied with Stanford after the war, wrote that he had by then lost some of his redeeming features:

> If I could have gone to him ten years earlier I should have less uncomfortable memories ... he was not the Stanford of the legends. The old truculence was there, but not the warmth or the tenderness or the wit. These had died in the War. He had changed. So had we all. I found him bitter ... He made me angry, he made me unhappy, he made me rebel, but he taught me my job; and I still do not know whether he whole-heartedly wished to do so or whether he could not help himself. He was Irish; and the Irish have ever been the puzzlers.[27]

---

[25] Arthur Bliss, *As I Remember* (London, 1970), 28–9.
[26] Edward Dent's Diaries, KCC.
[27] Thomas Wood, *True Thomas* (London, 1936), 195 and 199.

Viewed with hindsight, Stanford's methods seem harsh: John Ireland recalled the way in which Stanford taught him orchestration:

> Week by week he would let a score progress with practically no comments. When it was finished he would say 'Now me bhoy, go home and copy out the parts and we'll try it over.' In due course, one's piece was tried over by the orchestra. I stood beside Stanford whilst he conducted it. When the more or less appalling sounds had subsided, the Master would close the score, and handing it back with a grin, would say 'Well, you see, it won't do, you'll have to find some other way.'[28]

Arnold Bax went through a similar baptism of fire at Stanford's hands, as a conductor, when he was invited to have some of his music played at an RCM Patrons' concert. It is a reminiscence which also illustrates an outsider's perception of the RCM, and the experience may have affected Bax's attitude to Stanford later.

> Now, hitherto I had never been near the RCM and I had no idea of its manners and customs, though I always had a vague notion that it was a more aristocratic and pompous place than our old Academy ...
>
> The heat was intense during my journey to Kensington Gore, and I arrived at the intimidating portals of the RCM already perspiring not a little. Shyly entering the concert hall, I started back, appalled at finding the place crammed with students and visitors.
>
> It appeared that I had come in the nick of time, for Sir Charles Stanford approached me at once, and said brusquely, 'So here ye are, you're Bax, aren't you? Well now, ye can go up there and work your wicked will on the orchestra.'
>
> At these dreadful words my knees knocked together and I stammered out in a very small voice, 'But I have never conducted in my life.' 'Never mind that,' retorted the ruthless Stanford. 'You've got to begin some time, my bhoy. Go on with ye.' There was nothing for it but to obey.
>
> Over-harrowing it would be to resuscitate in any detail the pity and terror of that scene ... The orchestra players, I must admit were stoically long-suffering, and only once did a politely ironic voice query, 'Excuse me, but are you beating in twos or threes?' After some forty-five minutes of mental and physical misery Stanford applied the closure, and I stumbled off the platform, not far from collapse. 'Ye look warm, young man,' observed 'CVS' and taking me aside chatted very amiably for some time, incidentally giving me no doubt excellent advice on the subject of conductor's technique. But I remember nothing of that discourse, nor would it have served me in after life, for ... in that hour I made my firm resolve, 'Never again!'[29]

---

[28] Quoted in John Longmire, *John Ireland; Portrait of a Friend* (London, 1969), 10–11.
[29] Arnold Bax, *Farewell my Youth* (London, 1943), 26–7.

A century later this approach would be frowned upon, but in Stanford's time learning by trial and error, with the prospect of public humiliation after an inferior effort, was viewed as character-building. Though brutal, play-throughs by the RCM Orchestra gave Stanford's pupils the invaluable experience of hearing what they had written, even if the exercise was consigned immediately to the wastepaper basket.

There are discrepancies between the accounts left by Stanford's students about the syllabus he followed but, taking them altogether, it is clear there was a general plan which varied according to each student's needs. Margaret Nosek left one of the fullest accounts:

> As a teacher, Stanford was severe and old fashioned in his methods. For him there were no short cuts to perfection: the pupil began at the beginning and worked out the whole evolution of music from Palestrina till today in his own person. After experimenting with modal writing and the pure tone scale he was set to write an imitation of a Mass of Palestrina, the *Missa Brevis*, and only after having learned to do this satisfactorily was he allowed to approach Haydn and Mozart and then Beethoven. Stanford's method of teaching the secrets of Mozart's and Beethoven's Symphonies and their orchestration was to make the pupil initiate himself in them by writing them for orchestra as he thought Mozart and Beethoven would have written them, with only a four hands piano version of the symphony to guide him. After finishing several pages, the pupil had to take the original full score and copy it above his own version in red ink. This was a most painful and laborious business, yet I doubt if it is possible to gain an intimate knowledge of Mozart and Beethoven by any other means. Having had to do all this for a long time, and having survived, I am very grateful for the lessons I learned from it, although I am just as grateful that I do not have to do it again.
>
>   Side by side with the drudgery, the pupil was allowed a certain amount of free play and urged to produce original compositions. Though he could write what he liked, the beginner was encouraged to write variations for the piano on an original or borrowed theme. The writing of variations teaches you to express the same thought in as many ways as your ingenuity suggests; to put the most varied complexions on the same old home truth, for although there may be a right and a wrong way of doing everything, infinite are the ways in which a thing may be expressed. It teaches you, therefore, facility of expression, a greater asset, no doubt, in this everyday world, than the power to utter original thoughts, which is inborn and cannot be learned. There was only one form of composition to which Stanford objected to his pupils attempting – the writing of songs. Writing a song is the most difficult thing in the world to do well, and the easiest to do badly, for which reason, no doubt, all young people yearn to write them, the words giving a much needed stimulus to their halting and untried imaginations. Sir Charles used to say that song writing called for the highest pitch of perfection on the part of the composer, and was therefore the

last thing that the pupil should attempt. One day, however, I discovered the real reason for this ban, which was that he could not
endure the poems which most of his pupils chose to set to music.
In a burst of confidence he told me that the taste of most of his
pupils in poetry was lamentable, and that it was incomprehensible
to him that a man with a keen ear for music should have a poor
one for poetry.[30]

Modal counterpoint and piano variations figured in most students'
studies; for John Ireland, Stanford believed that a study of the modes
was the best way to broaden his musical palette beyond nineteenth-
century Germanic harmony:

> At my first lesson, after looking over the manuscripts I had brought,
> he turned to me and said, 'All Brahms and water me bhoy and more
> water than Brahms.' After a pause; 'Study some Dvořák for a bit
> and bring me something that isn't like Brahms.' I followed his
> instructions and wrote him, as time went on, two sets of piano vari-
> ations, and a sextet in four movements for clarinet, horn and string
> quartet. Stanford had this tried over; it sounded well and when I
> occasionally look at the score I feel rather a nostalgic affection for
> the old piece. But the master was not satisfied; he said 'The last
> movement isn't organic me bhoy.'
> After one or two further tentative experiments on me he said one
> day 'I shall have to try another way with you me bhoy but you'll
> find it a hard one.' He then started me on an exhaustive study of
> the modes and modal counterpoint based on Palestrina. He kept me
> at this for a whole year, not allowing me to write a bar of music,
> even secretly, except in the strict style. Stern discipline indeed but I
> have since had every reason to bless him for it. I believe I was the
> first pupil to whom he applied this modal treatment, at any rate in
> such a drastic way.[31]

It is significant – and perhaps ironic – that Stanford did not want Ireland
to write in a neo-Brahmsian manner; he was aware that the modern
composer needed to have a broader palette than that of the recent
Germanic canon, and believed that an introduction to the modes was
one acceptable way of achieving this. It is significant too that Ireland
used the same approach with Britten in the 1930s and that Britten
admitted its value.[32] For Vaughan Williams, who was already conversant with modes when he arrived at Stanford's door, Renaissance
counterpoint was eschewed and instead Stanford encouraged him to

[30] Nosek, 'From a Destroyed Autobiography', 34–5.
[31] Interview with John Ireland, quoted in 'Every Inch an Irishman', RTE Broadcast 4
Oct. 1974 (RTE Archive Accession No. S 85/74).
[32] See Humphrey Carpenter, *Benjamin Britten: A Biography* (London, 1992), 37–8.

broaden his musical perspective by going to Italy; Vaughan Williams elected to go to Berlin instead.[33]

While knowledge of the modes broadened the harmonic horizon, the composition of piano variations taught, as Nosek noted, the twin virtues of economy of material, and facility of development and manipulation. For Eugene Goossens this laid the foundations for bigger projects:

> [Stanford] started me off on a theme and variations for piano, as he claimed that the supreme test of creative ingenuity lay in extracting the last ounce of variety from a good tune. With Beethoven, Mozart, and Brahms as models, I set out on what seemed a thankless task, but eventually succeeded in squeezing thirty-two variations from an utterly barren tune. Stanford liked them, and this gave me a feeling of great superiority. Some of the more 'modern' ones he erased on the ground of 'cacophony' – a subject which made him foam at the mouth. ('Damned ugly, me bhoy! Take it out!') From variations I graduated to sonatas, and string quartets, and by the time I left the College in 1912 I had turned out a creditable number of student efforts in many of the smaller forms, all of which bore the blue-pencilled excisions and comments of a strict and often intolerant mentor.[34]

Another maxim which appears to have been a constant in Stanford's teaching was that of the virtue of rests; even Arthur Bliss acknowledged that this was a wise truism.[35] Stanford often preferred to teach this technique by metaphor; Herbert Howells recalled that this indirect approach passed him by:

> In my very first lesson we stood at the windows of his room, from which in those days we could see across to the Imperial Institute as it then was, and he discoursed on architecture, particularly on windows. He then sent me away to write the first movement of a string quartet, which I did and was duly pleased with. I took it to him. He read it through in complete silence as was his wont, and then said to me, 'I see that our first lesson was entirely in vain'. No windows – not a single rest anywhere.[36]

Stanford's writings give further insights into his methods and aesthetics. At the opening of *Musical Composition* he wrote: 'To tell a

---

[33] Vaughan Williams recalled that 'Stanford wanted me to go to Italy and hear opera at the Scala. He thought I was too Teuton already. He did not want me to take definite lessons with anyone. But I disregarded his advice and went to Berlin. My reason for this choice, I believe, was the extraordinary one that Berlin was the only town at that time where they performed the *Ring* without cuts!'; *National Music and Other Essays* (2nd edn, Oxford, 1996), 187.

[34] Goossens, *Overtures and Beginners*, 80–81.

[35] Bliss, *As I Remember*, 28–9.

[36] Palmer, *Herbert Howells*, 12.

student how to write music is an impossible absurdity. The only province of a teacher is to criticise it when written, or to make suggestions as to its form or length, or as to the instruments or voices for which it should be designed.'[37] The accounts of his pupils give ample proof to this assertion. Stanford was firmly of the opinion that he could not teach inspiration or originality and saw his role as one of nurturing talents, by instilling a technical knowledge which would allow the fluent expression of inspiration, and of encouraging certain aesthetic values which he held to be inviolate. The importance of technical facility was emphasised in *Musical Composition* by another metaphor:

> The house cannot stand if it is built upon insecure foundations, and its security depends upon a knowledge of technique which involves the hardest and at times the driest drudgery. It is often disheartening, often apparently superfluous, but the enthusiasm which is not strong enough to face the irksome training and lasting enough to see it through to a finish had better be allowed to die out.[38]

In part this assertion could be read as a sideswipe at Bernard Shaw and other commentators who had criticised Stanford and other Victorian composers for 'academicism'; if this is the case, Stanford went on to justify his belief:

> A composer who has full knowledge of his technique, and can play about with a canon or fugue, has got to a point where he can utilise his knowledge to make experiments. A man who knows he is writing consecutive fifths can write them if he is convinced of their appropriateness, and can convince the hearer of their beauty, without being pulled up by the old formula of infringement of rule; for in composition *per se*, there is no rule save that of beauty, and no standard save that of taste.[39]

This advocacy of beauty exposes the other of Stanford's fundamental aesthetic beliefs. A subjective concept, this standpoint created far more difficulties for pupils, especially in Stanford's later years when his concept of beauty appeared increasingly old-fashioned. George Dyson, however, felt that students could respond to such dogmatic beliefs positively:

> [Stanford] was impatient, blunt, and frankly hostile to much of what we are pleased to call modernity. To him music was, as it were, a body of truth, and what was not true was false. To deny truth was heresy. To be lukewarm was to betray one's poverty of soul ... And though few of his ablest pupils could embrace his particular

[37] Stanford, *Musical Composition*, 1.
[38] Ibid., 2.
[39] Ibid., 3.

dogmas, the best of them caught from him the stimulus of a faith of some kind, without which there can be little strength or merit in work.[40]

Stanford repeated his view in the last chapter of *Musical Composition*, ominously entitled 'Danger Signals':

> It is not necessary, in order to depict an ugly character or a horrible situation, to illustrate it with ugly music. To do so is the worst side of bad art. Ugly music is bad music. No great painter would paint even a Caliban badly. He draws the line at characterisation. When Beethoven wrote music for one of the greatest villains in opera, Pizarro, he did not pen an ugly or even a crude bar, and yet it is a masterpiece of delineation ... No composer of inherent nobility will so sacrifice the most noble of the arts. For music stands alone among the arts in one respect, it is incapable without association with words or action of being in itself indecent or obscene.[41]

By 1911, however, this belief in beauty was being questioned by many composers. While British music remained almost at one with Stanford on this point, the German Expressionists had started to explore emotion through deliberately harsh sound and discordant tonality, and this was one reason why Stanford hated such works as *Elektra* and *Salome* and, a little later, the music of Arnold Schoenberg. *Musical Composition* was also published only a year before the première of *The Rite of Spring*; whether he ever heard or examined Stravinsky's work is unknown but his reaction is easy to predict.

Inevitably, the more adventurous of his pupils heard these new works and wanted to emulate their radicalism and difference. For Stanford, not only was their work 'damned ugly', it was technically faulty: chromatic language, for example, had to be carefully controlled lest it destabilise the modal and tonal systems established in previous centuries, and any attempt to usurp these essential building blocks undermined the 'foundations' of the 'house' upon which invention and originality had to sit. With some shrewdness and originality Stanford turned to Wagner to demonstrate his point:

> There remains the question as to the diatonic or chromatic treatments of melodies. We possess in western music no interval less than a semitone (except in the form of *portamento*). Chromatics are, as their name implies, colour and not drawing. If we use in excess the only means we have of heightening effect, we have nothing further to fall back upon for intensifying contrast ... *Tristan* itself, which teems with chromatics, becomes immediately diatonic at its

[40] George Dyson, 'Charles Villiers Stanford', *RCM Magazine*, 20 (1923–4), 43–6 at 45.
[41] Stanford, *Musical Composition*, 186–7.

moments of climax, such as the coming of the ship in the third act (where the scale and chord of C pounds away with the insistence of Beethoven himself), and wherever the healthy, muscular, kindly figure of Kurwenal comes to the front. Practically all the bigger and most important motives of the Nibelungen are also diatonic, such as the Walhalla theme and the sword theme.[42]

Whether intellectually justified or not, Stanford's pupils steadily disregarded his beliefs as he became more disenchanted with the course of modern music: 'I'm afraid I'm getting old, dear boy, I can't accustomise my nostrils to these modern stinks', he reportedly said to Howells when discussing the latter's *Fantasy String Quartet*.[43]

By the early 1920s Stanford appeared as a dinosaur in the composition field. In a short article entitled 'Sanity (?) in Composition' written in 1917, he appointed himself, and other members of his profession, as a kind of nurse, whose responsibility it was to wean the public away from indigestible music:

> There is often, in these days of quick travelling, rapid action, and high pressure, a hankering after something to tickle jaded palates, and to astonish rather than to elevate taste. Anything which gives a shock is liable to appeal to this hysterical tendency. The music which ministers to this abnormal craving is doing infinite mischief to those who sit and listen to it, and the degradation of good clean art is certain to ensue. Accustom a child to restrict its diet to sweets and curries, and he will suffer for the absence of good solid food in after life. So it is with those musical children, the public. They are just now in the mood to accept any imposture, if it is only exciting enough and sufficiently striking to arrest their attention. They would even revel in a lecture which set out to prove that black is white, or that the earth is flat. They set the quack above the physician. The cranks (like the poor) are always with us, but they are happily, in a minority. The majority, unfortunately, in northern climes do not hiss, and the minority, in consequence, claim that they accept what in their hearts they loathe, and only tolerate for the sake of a little extra excitement. The apostles of ugliness meantime prosper, and will continue to do so just as long as and no longer than the public will allow it.[44]

Clearly at this point Stanford felt that the extraordinary circumstances of war were leading people astray. Four years later, however, in 'On Some Recent Tendencies in Composition', his last substantive statement on the subject, he argued through his points in a more intellectual

---

[42] Ibid., 44–5.

[43] Quoted in Paul Spicer, *Herbert Howells* (Bridgend, 1998), 60.

[44] Charles Stanford, 'Sanity (?) in Composition', *Musical Herald*, 1 Mar. 1917, pp. 78–9.

manner; although there was essentially nothing new in what he said, the first paragraph almost beggars belief when compared with some of his behaviour:

> Let me begin by saying that I am, and always have been, essentially a Progressist, and welcome every innovation, however unfamiliar, provided it makes for the enhancement of beauty, as I consider it. I am not in the modern, perverted, sense of the word, now usually used as a term of opprobrium, 'academic', but I hope that I am 'academic' in the true sense, which cannot be too much insisted upon, of one who knows his business . . .

> [Consecutive] Fifths were prohibited because they were ugly, and they are as ugly now as they ever have been, and as they ever will be, world without end, because their ugliness most probably depends upon natural laws and not upon individual taste . . .

> For music which relies upon colour rather than upon drawing, it may have its fascinations; but as all pictures which have done so have failed to hold the field, so chromatic music will. They attract but only temporarily. They excite but often unwholesomely. They are useful as servants but dangerous as masters. Even post-impressionists and cubists have found it necessary to enclose their pictures in a square or a round frame to accentuate form; and not even they, perhaps unfortunately, have taken to exhibiting their palettes as their pictures. If chromatics prevail, good-bye to simplicity . . .

> We live in the days of Monteverde [sic], not those of Palestrina. Experiment is worshipped. It is not without its uses, nor was the music of Monteverde. But Palestrina lives; Monteverde is no more.[45]

Leaving aside Stanford's hopelessly inaccurate prophecy of the fortunes of Monteverdi, it is evident that his declarations were becoming more reactionary. His opening paragraph is especially interesting since it initially appears that he was a Liberal in Tory clothing, but the four words 'as I consider it' add more than enough qualification.

Stanford's paper was as manna from heaven for Peter Warlock's satirical pen, and he took full advantage:

> There was something quite pathetically fatuous about Sir Charles Stanford's recent address to the Musical Association. When it was announced that the venerable Professor was to read a paper on 'Some Recent Tendencies in Composition' we knew we were in for some fun, but we did not anticipate a more perfect caricature of a pedant proper than could be devised by the most malicious of his critics. One wondered how elastic the term 'recent' would be, whether 'modern music' meant Tchaikovsky – or perhaps Tovey . . . [but] Alas, in this latter respect we were doomed to disappointment.

---

[45] Stanford, 'On Some Recent Tendencies in Composition', *Proceedings of the Royal Musical Association*, 47 (1920–21), 39–54 at 45.

No contemporary names were mentioned. 'Modern Music' was just an aggregate . . .

Two of its chief characteristics were an inordinate love of consecutive fifths (with the suggestion that modern composers wrote them merely because they had been told not to do so – the dirty dogs!) and an excessive use of the whole tone scale! It is scarcely credible, in the face of twentieth century musical practice, that consecutive fifths can still be seriously discussed, where actual composition is concerned.

Of course while we were on the subject of scales, we were not allowed to escape without a dose of the usual twaddle about the so-called 'pure' or natural scale, together with equally stale blather about the supposed lack of rhythm and melody (neither term being defined of course) in modern music. Finally, dear Brethren, let us strive to attain beauty, nature and simplicity etc. etc. *in saecula saeculorum, ad nauseam perpetuam.* Amen.

Sir Frederick Bridge (Chairman) then came out with the shameless admission that in the old days he could settle down comfortably in his armchair by the fireside with a good cigar ('no harm in that') and read the score of a musical composition whereas now – on the other hand – when he turned to the scores of young fellows of the present time he found he couldn't do it anymore! Rounds of applause and roars of delighted laughter, the utter inferiority of contemporary music being thus incontestably proved.

No, it was not a dream but an exceedingly disagreeable reality which makes one realise more clearly than ever that music has no more poisonous enemy than the musical profession.

Is Sir Charles Stanford really acquainted at first hand with the work of Delius, Schoenberg, Van Dieren, Bartók, Stravinsky, Ravel, Scriabin, and the rest, or does he merely condemn, in terms of vague generality, things about which he knows nothing in particular? There was not one word in it to indicate that he had ever conscientiously applied himself to the study of a contemporary composition with a view to discovering its author's spiritual aims rather than his supposed technical shortcomings – which simply amount to his non-conformity with text-book regime.

It is high time for our pedagogues to try to realise a few simple little facts about the art they profess to teach: that music is an expression of the soul in terms of a more fluid and intractable medium than any of the other arts employ . . . that 'the artist creates not what others will consider beautiful but that which for himself is necessary' (Schoenberg) and that everything which is truly expressive of a significant state of the human soul must, of necessity, be beautiful to all who have eyes to see and ears to hear.[46]

Arthur Bliss took a similar view, though it was articulated in a much more moderate fashion. Bliss took Stanford's three central points and argued simply that he was wrong:

---

[46] *Sackbut*, 1 (1921), 418–20 (printed under the *nom de plume* Barbara C. Laurent).

Some acoustical authority declared [consecutive fifths] were ugly; the avoidance of them became a rule, and it is still cherished, although the ear has so developed (thanks to the composers) that it delights in consecutive seconds, sevenths, ninths, twenty-firsts, in fact in anything that it can conceive will further adorn any particular passage. Every master broke this rule at the bidding of his own ear and so will every master continue to break it ...

Even before [Stanford's] words were written, the greatly lamented Debussy was dead, and with him the whole-tone scale, its employment as the basis of tonality being a personal cliché. Others indeed experiment with it, but no one before or since has used it as a principle as he did, and with his death the whole-tone scale died out ... How well I remember the savage delight with which our master would rend us as imitators of Debussy, if we innocently placed three major triads in succession. No matter what the mood, no matter what the context, those little thirds did the trick; we were thereafter followers of Debussy ...

He mentions in addition to consecutive fifths and the whole-tone scale the tendency to overcrowding modulation. But what does he mean by that? Modulation presumes a basis of key system, and generally throughout Europe we find the principle of polytonality or atonality superseding the old key system. We can point to the Schoenberg school in Vienna, the Busoni school in Berlin, the Stravinsky and Milhaud school in Paris, not to speak of Goossens and Berners in London. What on earth has modulation to do with it?[47]

Stanford's convictions and aesthetics had simply been bypassed by time; his insistence that beauty could be defined absolutely prevented any progress or movement in his views (see pp. 370–1 and 411). In later years this pejorative view of Stanford's aesthetics has been restated by Peter Pirie:

His methods do not appear to have been subtle; his outlook was anything but liberal and constructive ... But the 'revolution' Stanford's pupils were advocating had already taken place in Europe decades before they ever went to Stanford; and the result of his teaching, in the majority of cases, was to reinforce a conservatism that was already present in all his pupils, the only one of whom showed any radical bent in later years was Frank Bridge.[48]

Pirie's argument also contains the seeds of its own undoing. Conservative Stanford's aesthetic certainly was but this was as much a reflection of the general compositional mores of pre-War Britain as an influence upon them; it is highly unlikely that pupils pushed along a revolutionary

---

[47] Arthur Bliss, 'Some Aspects of the Present Musical Situation', *Proceedings of the Royal Musical Association*, 49 (1922–3), 59–77 at 66–7.

[48] Peter Pirie, *The English Musical Renaissance* (London, 1979), 37.

path by a radical Stanford would have made much progress in Britain's
mainly reactionary and wholly commercial musical environment.

For all his weaknesses, Stanford was regarded by most of his pupils
as a good teacher. His success, contrary to Pirie's beliefs, was founded
in an uncharacteristic degree of flexibility for, whilst he was in many
ways prescriptive and brutal, his list of pupils contains an enviable
number of good and even great composers, most of whom were of the
opinion that they had moved towards their goals aided by Stanford's
guidance and not in spite of it. Crucial to understanding the strengths
and weaknesses of Stanford's legacy as a teacher is the appreciation of
his surroundings. Despite holding firm positions on so many aesthetic
issues, there was also a strong element of pragmatism in his motivation.
In his own career he had wanted, from his adolescence, to make his
living from music and, from his mid-thirties, without being an 'organ
grinder', a position achieved in 1893. This, in turn, meant composing
music which sold and was performed, and the very high proportion of
his music written between 1878 and 1914 which was published demonstrates his success in this endeavour and, as Stanford was never rich,
shows just how much music had to be produced in order to secure a
reasonable living. The purely commercial nature of the Victorian musical
world – unique in western Europe at the time – allowed its inherent
conservative values to flourish; the richest pickings were to be found in
music written for the choral societies and for the Anglican Church, both
of which were biased towards British composers because of the issue of
language (although the larger choral societies did venture into other
tongues towards the end of the century) and, in the case of the church,
the unique liturgy. But radical approaches to music did not flourish in
either area – partly from conservatism, partly from practicality – and
change was gradual. Stanford himself did well in both as they suited his
cautious gifts for composition, although he was frequently frustrated by
the extent to which the church and the choral societies played safe.

In turn, Stanford applied this pragmatism to his teaching and schooled
his students most closely in skills which could be best applied to the
genres flourishing in Britain. It was not just in his pupils' interests that
Stanford took this approach. He also wished, with many of his contemporaries, to raise the status of the music profession and to provide
better and more secure employment for native musicians. Stradling and
Hughes examine this aspect of the Victorian approach to music;[49] their
tendency to view the work of those employed by the RCM as a pre-
designed scheme is distracting, but their fundamental point is sound:
Grove, Parry, Stanford and many others viewed the mission of the RCM

---

[49] Stradling and Hughes, *The British Musical Renaissance*.

as the enhancement of the profession through the creation of a skilled workforce and a native school of composition, which would then become mutually self-perpetuating. This, in turn, meant imbuing music and its practitioners with the attributes of other professions and, in a superficially conservative society, this meant outward respectability, integrity and conformity. Stanford's work at the RCM contributed to this process (just as, in his own music, he aimed for the same goal, writing for the greater part in what Shaw had termed in frustration 'the manner and tone of good society'). A useful comparison may be made with the development of music in Russia: there, the construction of a profession was greatly enhanced, and protected, from commercial and moral pressures by the existence of the social rank of 'free artist'; this controlled the amount of competition and the restrictive social code allowed Russian musicians, ironically, a greater freedom than their British counterparts.

The criticisms made by Pirie and others do gain some currency when viewing the musical world of the *fin de siècle* and afterwards. The mission to transform the status of music ran into difficulties because the values of the musical world started to evolve much more rapidly. British audiences had been showing an interest in more adventurous music since the pioneering performances of Wagner by Hans Richter in the 1880s; Henry Wood took this further in the 1890s with the promotion of the Russians, especially Tchaikovsky. Stanford was not averse to this; his catholic interests led him to recognise the value of many of the 'new' composers, and he expected that this evolution of taste would benefit native composers as well. But by 1900 it was already too late for Stanford, and the composers who gained the greatest reputations were those whose music exhibited the more direct emotional expression which audiences wanted – in the first instance Coleridge Taylor with his setting of *Hiawatha's Wedding Feast* (1898) and then, spectacularly, Elgar with the 'Enigma' Variations (1899). The situation was exacerbated by British musical life catching up with that of the Continent so that, instead of being as much as twenty or thirty years behind Europe as it had been in the 1870s, in the 1900s new work would arrive in Britain within five years of its first Continental performance. For British composers this new radicalism was especially disconcerting. While the spirit of the *fin de siècle* and its decadent implications prospered in Europe until 1914, in Britain the trial of Oscar Wilde traumatised the artistic establishment into a puritanical disavowal of all that Wilde and his associates had stood for. In music, however, the art in which morality could only be explicit through the introduction of extra-musical elements, British tastes were not distorted by the Wilde débacle. The acceptance of outright expressionism and primitivism may have been resisted by audiences, composers and critics, but the louche, expressive and emotionally charged music of Strauss, Rachmaninov and Debussy, amongst others, was enthusiastically embraced by consumers, while the RCM-dominated world of composition viewed it with considerably more suspicion. While many of Stanford's pupils approached this new music with enthusiasm, albeit cautiously in some cases, for Stanford these changes were incomprehensible.

Despite this shortcoming, all of Stanford's pupils seem to have regarded him well. On one matter all were agreed: his technical prowess and ability to solve problems was unsurpassed. His competence in this area spurred on many to master the mechanical aspects of their discipline in order that they could acquire Stanford's great fluency. Sydney Waddington viewed Stanford almost as a god: 'I never thought of questioning [his] gifts. He could do things. Therefore what he said was right. And, indeed, now that experience has placed his personal glamour into correct focus, it still seems to me that it nearly always was.'[50] Cyril Rootham, one of Stanford's more ambivalent students, agreed: 'He had ... a cunning trick of altering or adding a phrase or a note here and there in a newly-written piece of work, which nearly always compelled one's admiration.'[51]

The unambiguous comments on students' work, however tactfully or tactlessly expressed, were often a boon too. If Stanford liked what he saw enthusiasm could carry him away, as Thomas Dunhill noted:

> Stanford's critical severity ... was balanced by a boyish enthusiasm for everything we did well, and that was indeed wonderfully stimulating. He would rush with our manuscripts into the teaching-room of any Professor who happened to be engaged on the same floor and insist upon the poor unoffending Professor hearing the work through from beginning to end – and many a conscientious Professor has had to work 'over-time' in consequence![52]

This behaviour endeared him to his pupils by increasing their self-esteem; as Dunhill hints, however, it could be equally vexing for Stanford's colleagues.

Stanford praised his pupils warmly when he felt it appropriate, and this confidence in their ability is reflected in performances of their works at RCM concerts. Student compositions appear mainly in the more informal concerts of chamber music, unsurprisingly since Stanford's course of composition was geared to smaller forms. He was also careful not to lionise his pupils too early; this may seem mean-spirited but he believed that, no matter how much confidence one had in one's early

---

[50] Sydney Waddington, 'Stanford in the Early Days', *RCM Magazine*, 79 (1983), 19–22.
[51] 'Sir Charles Stanford and his Pupils' (*RCM Magazine*), 60.
[52] Ibid., 56.

works, they came to be regretted later – just as he had withdrawn most of his own music composed before 1880. Occasionally, however, he did put student works into the RCM orchestral concerts; the most famous instance was the première of Coleridge Taylor's *Hiawatha's Wedding Feast* on 11 November 1898, which rapidly led the composer to national renown. He also gave Hurlstone's Piano Concerto (6 March 1896) but, as a rule, preferred to give orchestral works of former students who had, in his view, matured, and when exposure would be valuable.

Ironically, his conservative view of musical aesthetics was also a positive asset for many pupils since it caused them to investigate music which Stanford disliked with extra determination; Eugene Goossens wrote:

> Stanford laid most of the blame for the wildness of the young radicals on the pernicious influence of Strauss and Debussy, though secretly he grudgingly admired the more conservative efforts of both composers. He was irritated when I told him of being present at the *Elektra* performance earlier in the year, and that I considered it thrilling and masterful. He said frankly that were I to hear much more of that 'pornographic rubbish' he'd give me up as a lost soul. So when I saw that the première of Strauss's *Salome* was announced for the end of the year at Covent Garden, I was all the more determined to go.[53]

Although this approach caused problems and resentment, it also led students to question their own motives and provoked in many self-criticism and analysis that led to greater belief in the final product. Edgar Bainton's observation is of great significance:

> It is a curious paradox that in spite of Sir Charles Stanford's dominating personality (at times aggressively dominating), hardly one of his many pupils' works shows any influence of Stanford. Could any music be more dissimilar than that of Hurlstone and Holst, of Goossens, Rutland Boughton, and John Ireland? And this fact in itself is surely the finest tribute to his teaching, that he kept his own personality in the background, and helped them, whether they were conscious of it or not, to express themselves, to say clearly what they wanted to say.[54]

This wide variety of styles is perhaps the greatest testimony to his ability; no doubt the students whose names did not reach national prominence included some Stanford clones, but those who did come to the fore were not subjugated by their teacher but enabled to speak more freely. There are some Stanford pupils whose voice was somewhat closer to his, for example Coleridge Taylor, Hurlstone and Ireland, and a

---

[53] Goossens, *Overtures and Beginners*, 82. The British première of *Elektra* took place at Covent Garden on 19 Feb. 1910.

[54] 'Sir Charles Stanford and his Pupils' (*RCM Magazine*), 55.

different teacher might have encouraged different modes of expression from these students, although in respect of the first two this is an especially difficult question since their premature deaths prevented their styles developing to full maturity. Conversely, there are other pupils whose style is remarkably divergent from Stanford, such as Vaughan Williams, Holst, Bridge and Howells, whose only strong concordance with Stanford is their belief in economy of material.

This sense of economy and an almost classical purity or cleanliness which characterises Stanford's pupils, however, is especially significant. If one compares their styles with those of the students taught by Frederick Corder at the Royal Academy, this asperity is thrown into sharper relief; Bantock, Holbrooke and Bax all tend to exhibit a greater sensuality and colour in their music than Stanford's pupils. This, perhaps, demonstrates Corder's interest in Wagner, but Corder often failed to instil in his pupils an ability to manipulate form or an interest in the virtue of brevity. Stanford, though only considering classical forms, emphasised the importance of structure, and this is reflected in the work of his pupils.

The most damaging criticism levelled at Stanford as a teacher has been that his conservative aesthetics led him to overemphasise the German classical tradition and this restricted the growth of both a distinctive British musical style and the individuality of his pupils. There is some truth in this argument but the charges are overdone. In Stanford's youth the German classical tradition was viewed as the dominant and longest-established musical voice in Western Europe; Italian and French composers had almost exclusively confined themselves to the composition of opera in the earlier nineteenth century and there remained a clear distinction in British society between the opera house and the concert hall throughout the Victorian period; opera, by dint of its elitism and precarious financial position, was very much a minority interest. Not only had Britain been wedded to Germany in musical terms since the time of Handel, but it had been linked politically too; the accession of George I in 1714 created strong links between Britain and Germany, while France remained an enemy until 1815 and was still regarded as a potential aggressor in the 1850s. The Victorian religious revival led to a re-emphasising of moral purity, while French mores were often associated, whether for better or worse and regardless of factual accuracy, with decadence and a degree of moral laxity. Emerging racial theories in the late nineteenth century also led to an emphasis on the 'affinities' of the English and German peoples and their difference from the 'Latin' peoples of France and Italy. Possibly the anti-Wilde reaction after 1895 indirectly reinforced some of this suspicion. Unsurprisingly, therefore, British musical opinion looked to Germany in the late nineteenth century for both leadership and approval of its emerging school of composition:

> Whatever we may think of the present state of art in the Fatherland, all must agree that it is extremely desirable to obtain German approval for the productions of our composers. This is a very different case from that of French music in Germany. The productions of Gallic composers are often welcomed there for the relief and change they bring, as products of an entirely different school and a contrasted national temperament ... English music in Germany comes as the rival of German music on its own ground, and is naturally subjected to more than usual scrutiny when it has succeeded in engaging serious attention at all.[55]

In these circumstances it is unsurprising that Stanford and his contemporaries were drawn to the German tradition as composers (Mackenzie, Cowen, Parry, Sullivan and Stanford had all studied in Germany) and, in some cases, teachers, and that Stanford emphasised this inheritance to his students. This approach had the twin virtues of idealism and realism. Stanford's ideal was to create a compositional culture in Britain which would rival that of other European countries; in order to achieve this, he had to ensure that his students' works would be published and performed. The strongest markets were in the concert hall, especially for choral works, and in the church, and in both of these genres, for different reasons, the classical tradition was well established as the preferred model. Although Stanford may have encouraged the composition of opera – his own works are ample proof of his interest in the genre – and several of his pupils tried their hands at it, the highly exclusive and reactionary nature of opera audiences in Britain until after the Second World War made success in this area almost impossible. Hence schooling students extensively in the Italian tradition, which had been viewed in Britain as being exclusively operatic for two hundred years, would have brought them little tangible benefit. In fact Stanford did encourage the study of Italian music, especially for those students whom he felt had become over-Germanicised, as his advice to both Vaughan Williams and Dyson ('go to Italy, my boy, and sit in the sun') shows;[56] he believed that acquaintance with later Verdi in particular would encourage a sense of brilliance in his pupils' work, to counteract the potential stodginess of the Germanic tradition – importantly, however, Stanford was advocating bringing 'colour' to a potentially dry idiom, not the abandonment of Teutonic classical forms and disciplines.

While Stanford's interest in the Italian tradition is to be applauded (although one feels that he might have encouraged it more), a notable

---

[55] *Musical Times*, 1 Mar. 1888, p. 154.
[56] See n. 20 and 'Sir Charles Stanford and his Pupils' (*Music & Letters*), 197.

failure was his lack of engagement with French music. Earlier in his life, his avoidance of the French tradition might have been more justified; the mid-century French music scene focused principally on opera, and was dominated by Meyerbeer, for whom Stanford had only limited time, and then by Gounod, whose music Stanford despised. From the 1890s, however, his failure to encourage his students to look more extensively at French music was a significant failing on his part, since this would have introduced them to many composers at the cutting edge whose mode of expression differed notably from that of their German contemporaries.

Stanford's interest in the modes, dating from the course of lessons he took with W. S. Rockstro while composing *Eden* in 1890, did, however, partially ameliorate the influence of German music. The interest in modal writing shown by many British composers has generally been attributed to the folksong revival, but Stanford's teaching demonstrated to his pupils that modes could not only be applied to a 'pastoral' style, but could be used to extend the harmonic and melodic palette in all areas. He thus reinforced the idea that modal writing could be viewed as an alternative both to the loosening of tonality pursued by Strauss and Schoenberg, and the interest in the exotic shown by Debussy and Ravel. For composers looking to forge a distinctive British style, at a time when the concept of national characteristics was taken as a *sine qua non*, a thorough-going use of modes provided a means of expression yet to be exploited consistently in mainland Europe.

Stanford's greatest weakness as a teacher was his narrow and immutable definition of beauty. For him beauty was an absolute truth (see pp. 358–64), the tonality in which it was to be expressed being derived, in his view, from the 'pure scale'; there were, consequently, strict limits within which tonality and melody could be manipulated. His restricted view of what was beautiful was the greatest limitation on his pupils for which he was directly responsible, and his determination not to redefine his beliefs reinforced the conservative parameters in which British music existed at the turn of the century. It is important to recognise, however, that Stanford was by no means alone in this belief; the British musical scene was driven by its own unique history and commercial structure (see pp. 364–6) and this was reflected as much at the Royal Academy as at the RCM. Arnold Bax recalled the machinations of *his* teacher:

> Corder certainly admitted to a weakness for *Till Eulenspiegel* but, apart from his almost over-generous championship of the works of his own pupils, I never heard him express approval of any other music of modernistic tendencies.
>
> He could see nothing in Debussy. One of his pupils, entering the classroom for his lesson, found his old master seated at the piano frowning in puzzled absorption at the score of *L'Après-Midi d'un*

Table 8.3   Selective list of appointments held by former
Stanford pupils

Name	Dates	Appointment
Edgar Bainton	1901–33	Newcastle Conservatory (except 1914–18)
	1933–47	Director, New South Wales State Conservatorium
Arthur Benjamin	1926–?	Royal College of Music
Arthur Bliss	1939–41	University of California, Berkeley
	1942–4	Director of Music, British Broadcasting Corporation
	1953–75	Master of the King's Musick
Rutland Boughton	1905–11	Midland Institute School of Music (Birmingham)
Samuel Coleridge Taylor	1903–12	Trinity College of Music
	1910–12	Guildhall School of Music
Harold Darke	1919–69	Royal College of Music
	1945–9	Fellow, King's College, Cambridge
Edward Dent	1902–18	King's College, Cambridge
	1926–41	Professor of Music, Cambridge University
Thomas Dunhill	1899–1946	Royal College of Music
George Dyson	1911–14	Marlborough School
	1914–18	Rugby School
	1918–52	Royal College of Music; Director from 1938
	1924–37	Winchester College
James Friskin	1914–?	Juilliard School, New York
Eugene Goossens	1923–46	Conductor, Rochester Philharmonic Orchestra
	1947–56	Director, New South Wales State Conservatorium
Fritz Hart[a]	1915–36	Director, Melbourne Conservatory
	1936–42	University of Hawaii
Leslie Heward	1924–7	Musical Director, South African Broadcasting Commission
	1930–43	Conductor, City of Birmingham Orchestra
Gustav Holst	1905–34	St Paul's School for Girls
	1907–24	Morley College
	1919–23	Royal College of Music
	1919–23	Professor of Music, University College, Reading
Herbert Howells	1920–79	Royal College of Music
	1936–62	St Paul's School for Girls
	1950–64	Professor of Music, London University
William Hurlstone	1905–6	Royal College of Music
John Ireland	1923–39	Royal College of Music
Gordon Jacob	1926–66	Royal College of Music
Hamish MacCunn	1888–94	Royal Academy of Music
	1912–16	Guildhall School of Music
Sydney Nicholson	1928–56?	Founder and Director of (later Royal) School of Church Music
Ralph Vaughan Williams	1919–39	Royal College of Music
Sydney Waddington	1895–?	Royal College of Music
Henry Walford Davies	1895–1919	Royal College of Music
	1919–26	Professor of Music, University College, Aberystwyth
	1924–41	Gresham Professor of Music
	1934–41	Master of the King's Musick
Charles Wood	1888–1926	Royal College of Music
	1897–1924	Lecturer in Music, Cambridge University
	1924–6	Professor of Music, Cambridge University
Thomas Wood	1924–8	University of Oxford

[a] Not taught by Stanford but his influence was clearly acknowledged by Hart
(see Table 8.2).

Faune. Becoming aware of the lad's presence, Corder rose with that familiar volcanic sigh of his, and exclaimed, almost tearfully: 'I've tried, *honestly* I have, but I *cannot* understand it!'[57]

Stanford's inability to cope with modern music was, therefore, by no means unique. Similarly, his insistence on good technique, blamed by some for the emasculation of both his own style and that of his pupils, is an unfair accusation: Stanford's approach finds a parallel with that of Schoenberg, who was just as adamant that his students should have no weakness in their practical armoury. If anything, Schoenberg's approach to teaching composition was more conservative than Stanford's as he focused on just five composers: Bach, Mozart, Beethoven, Schubert and Brahms. But Schoenberg's method produced different results, first because he himself was writing radical work, leading him to be more sympathetic to the adventures of his pupils and, secondly, because the general ambience of Austrian and German musical education (and especially Vienna before 1914 and Berlin from 1920 to 1933) allowed difference and experimentation to flourish. In Britain, by contrast, the prevailing outlook was conservative and it would have taken far more even than one of the country's leading composers to alter that.

Though Stanford was undoubtedly a good teacher, one should not overestimate him. His pupils did not make their way in the world solely because they had been his pupils – quite apart from their own abilities, most of them benefited from being members of the RCM, which brought the twin advantages of an intensively musical atmosphere in which to study and, later, the possibility of exploiting its dominant position in the British musical world through contacts and associations, and the link with the institution itself. The RCM's preference (by no means unique amongst varied British institutions of the time) for appointing former students to its teaching posts helped to secure this hegemony and sense of continuity for many years. Even allowing for this, however, Stanford's achievement is still highly significant. Table 8.3 shows appointments held by a selective list of his students; those held in teaching institutions were particularly important since there was, in most cases, at least a partial imparting of some Stanfordian values and a sense of inheritance. Such a 'family tree' of teaching relationships does not necessarily mean that values pass forward 'generation' to 'generation' (although Ireland's tuition of Britten (see p. 356) shows that it is eminently possible), but it is notable that not only did Stanford teach most of the leading composers of the two generations which followed him, but they in turn dominated British, and to a lesser extent Empire,

---

[57] Bax, *Farewell my Youth*, 21.

composition teaching well into the 1960s. This hegemony was only diluted in the post-1945 period after the teaching of composition was taken up in British universities on a wider scale and the RCM's dominance was ended – an irony since Stanford's reforms in Cambridge sowed the seeds of this university expansion. The 'purity' of the RCM tradition was aided by an almost complete lack of cross-fertilisation between the RCM and RAM. Although one could not attribute the extent of Stanford's influence to a design of his own making, without him the direction taken by British composers in the first half of the twentieth century might have been very different.

CHAPTER NINE

Stanford
the Composer

Stanford's reputation as a composer has been gradually overshadowed by his reputation as a teacher. For Guy Stanford this caused some resentment: 'My reaction to all accounts of his life are chiefly that far too much emphasis has been given to his teaching and far too little on his composition.'[1] This change in status was, however, inevitable as Stanford's music fell out of fashion and the reputation of his pupils grew. With the exception of the Anglican church, in which Stanford's music remained a central part of the repertory, this primary perception of Stanford as a pedagogue remained strong until the 1980s, when the gradual revival of interest in the 'British Musical Renaissance' included a growth in interest in his music.

The legacy, inevitably, is a mixed one. With his education steeped in the German tradition, it is unsurprising that Stanford's style is closely related to that school and to the music of his German contemporaries.

The most notable characteristic of Stanford's music is the persistent use of melody as its basis. The bass line is always an important yet secondary line and anything in between was regarded as 'filling'. As he devoted much time to song-writing and opera, this emphasis on melody is unsurprising; in a letter to Greene describing the composition of song, one of Stanford's maxims was 'get a good voice part and a good bass part: the middle is texture and trimmings, though very important ones',[2] and this simplistic description exemplified his approach to most composition. For Stanford music was primarily melodic and all other aspects were subordinate to it; in contrapuntal writing the melodic strength of each line was viewed as crucial, just as it had been in the late sixteenth century when the contrapuntal ethos reached its apotheosis.[3] He believed that a good melody sprang from linear (and not vertical) thinking; his work takes on a vertical dimension because he made his contrapuntal lines obey a strict hierarchy. In fact Stanford did not have much time

---

[1] Guy Stanford to Susan Stanford, 7 Nov. 1952, quoted in Frederick Hudson, 'Stanford', in *New Grove Dictionary of Music and Musicians*, ed. Stanley Sadie, 20 vols (London, 1980), xviii, 72.

[2] Greene, *Stanford*, 242.

[3] See Stanford, *Musical Composition*, 9–11.

for (and was perhaps not very good at) strict imitative counterpoint; like Schubert he showed relatively little interest in true contrapuntal conversations in his music, and most of the exceptions occur on occasions when convention demanded the use of contrapuntal forms, for example, some of the works for organ or choir. Stanford's melodies are characterised by straightforward rhythms, and stepwise and other simple intervallic leaps. The preference for simple intervals may reflect the influence of Irish folk music and perhaps also classical composers. The avoidance of more distant intervals emphasises the classical qualities of his music and forms a notable contrast with the frequently angular melodies of Elgar. Stanford's melodies generally also avoid the motivic intensity associated with Schumann and Brahms, not, therefore, replicating the sometimes obsessive aspects of their melody construction.

This emphasis on melody sometimes accentuates a weakness in Stanford's armour, that is, that his themes were not always strong. Partly this is the result of eschewal of melodic and rhythmic motifs referred to above and also to a frequent avoidance of regular periodisation. Lack of orientation is the product. Why did he fail to appreciate this weakness? Three possible explanations can be cited. First, he argued that 'originality has far more to do with the treatment of melodies than the invention of them'[4] and this suggests that he placed more emphasis on manipulation of melody than on the strength of the source (also implied by his belief in the value of writing variations). Secondly, he was insufficiently rigorous in reviewing his own music; although financial considerations played a part in his need to produce music rapidly, Stanford often relied too much on technical facility to make up for lack of inspiration. Whilst criticising his pupils for covering up poverty of invention with orchestral and chromatic colouring, Stanford sometimes fell into a similar trap, using his immaculate technique to produce not inconsistent brilliance, but dependable blandness. Thirdly, he succumbed to the 'academicism' of which Bernard Shaw accused him: Stanford wanted to make his mark as a composer of high calibre 'art music' and this was equated with sophistication which, in turn, was equated with intellectual rigour. This move is most clearly seen in the contrast between the music composed in his early days at Cambridge (the naive style seen in the Queens' Service of 1872) and the music written after he returned from his sojourns in Berlin and Leipzig (for example, the Service in B flat, Op. 10) in which his whole style was informed by a greater technical accomplishment and knowledge than hitherto (see pp. 70–3). British mores of the time applauded this lack of simplicity – witness, for example, the dim view taken by the musical establishment of Sullivan's

---

[4] Ibid., 188.

operettas. Like Sullivan, however, Stanford remained at his best when, in the words of the *Theatre*, he 'condescended to be absolutely tuneful'.[5] And he certainly could be 'absolutely tuneful'; good and strong melodies characterise much of his music – the slow movement of the Sixth Symphony, *La Belle Dame sans Merci*, and parts of *The Revenge* are good examples of true inspiration producing impressive music. His frequent use of melodic quotations may be viewed as a form of gentle cheating but provided a secure foundation for many pieces (such as the First, Fourth and Fifth Irish Rhapsodies and the 'Dead Men' Variations). His ability to produce pastiche helped much more music (for example, the fast numbers in *Songs of the Sea*, several parts of *Shamus O'Brien*, and the scherzo of the 'Irish' Symphony). In all of these works, and in many others, Stanford's versatility as a melodist pays out in spades.

While Stanford's melodic style may avoid the intensity associated with Brahms and Schumann, his harmonic style is very much founded on that of the two Germans. He always viewed chromaticism as ornamentation, so the influence of radical Wagner appears relatively sparingly.[6] His music deals firmly with tonal centres and always retains a definite sense of key; chromatic language was used as colour, but such colouring never obscured the tonal centre. This stress on key is also seen in his insistence on explicitly harmonising all his music: unaccompanied lines or duets rarely occur and all harmonic implications are spelt out in full – this can lead to a feeling of density, especially in his chamber music, and a desire that he had taken his own maxim on the use of rests further. Despite occasional infatuations, Stanford's harmonic style remained remarkably consistent after it reached its maturity in the late 1870s. This progression from 'amateur' composer to 'professional', discussed in Chapters 2 and 3, was Stanford's main period of development but there was still his interest in the modes to come, its apotheosis reached in his studies with Rockstro in 1890. Although he was already interested in modal harmony in the late 1870s (exemplified in *La Belle Dame sans Merci* and 'There's a Bower of Roses' from *The Veiled Prophet*), the interest displayed and the extent to which modal harmony was employed increased during the 1880s. Two stimuli are apparent: his interest in Irish folksongs (see pp. 390–5) and his friendship with the Cambridge University Librarian Henry Bradshaw, who supplied the melody 'Angelus ad Virginem' used in *Savonarola*, provoking an interest in plainchant.

---

[5] *Theatre*, 1 Apr. 1896, p. 224, reviewing *Shamus O'Brien*.

[6] The exceptions are *The Canterbury Pilgrims* and *Savonarola*, but even here it remains clear that he viewed Wagner as a tonal composer who returned to diatonic security at dramatic climaxes.

That Stanford's harmonic language did not change much after the 1870s is partly attributable to his belief in the physical properties of the pure scale. It is not known when he acquired this knowledge (although the inclusion in the Cambridge music syllabus of a course on acoustics suggests that he must, at the very least, have been acquainted with this subject when he became Professor in 1887), but his belief in the 'absolute truth' of mathematical properties must have led him to conclude that his harmonic language could only develop further by undermining the scientific basis of music as sound. He did not entertain the possibility that quarter- or micro-tones might be employed[7] and used the same mathematical theory to argue against the whole-tone scale:

> The student of some interesting modern developments will also speedily discover that the adoption of the so-called whole-tone scale as a basis of music is, except upon keyed instruments tuned to the compromise of equal temperament, unnatural and impossible. No player upon a stringed instrument can play the scale of whole tones and arrive at an octave which is in tune with the starting note, unless he deliberately changed one of the notes on the road, and alters it while playing it.[8]

For Stanford, therefore, going against the laws of physics was an unnatural aberration or, as George Dyson might have put it, a heretical denial of a fundamental truth.[9]

Stanford's approach to rhythm is equally conventional by the standards of the time; he remained wedded throughout his career to the regular rhythms which had prevailed over the previous three centuries and did not even consider questioning their basis. This conservative approach is demonstrated in *Musical Composition*, in which the chapter on rhythm is the shortest of all, and in which he discussed rhythm primarily in relation to phrase length. The fundamental assumption throughout is that 'rhythm is the heartbeat or pulse which drives [music]',[10] and this implication of regularity is one he followed throughout his life – his most subversive uses of rhythm are the brief 5/4 passages in Act I of *Savonarola* and the 5 + 3 pulse used in the slow movement of the Second Piano Quartet. With such few exceptions, rhythm is treated in a thoroughly conventional contemporary manner which, while always clean and well managed, is neither unusual nor innovative.

An aspect of Stanford's writing that has not received much attention, but of which he was a master, is that of orchestration. His knowledge

---

[7] Stanford, *Musical Composition*, 44.
[8] Ibid., 17.
[9] Dyson, 'Stanford', 45.
[10] Stanford, *Musical Composition*, 23.

and use of orchestral instruments was irreproachable; although he modelled his style on the German Classical tradition he always avoided the thicknesses associated with Wagner, Brahms and Schumann, and in this respect his style is more closely related to the earlier models of Mendelssohn and Schubert and, ironically, the textual clarity of his music also bears affinities with the music of Strauss. As in other matters, his precepts were articulated didactically in *Musical Composition*; notably he used Mozart as the model upon which students should build their skills, and he took a sideswipe at the British disciples of Wagner by turning to Wagner himself for his proof:

> The full swell is a fascinating sound, and so is the richness of a densely-populated modern orchestra. But if one or other is to get full value for its effect, it must be used as a contrast only, and a rare contrast too. No one knew this better than Wagner did . . . He used his horns with great chromatic freedom, but never for padding, and never with disregard of their timbre. He subdivided his violins, but never allowed the wind-instruments to take advantage of their scattered numbers and wipe them out. He used his extra instruments, such as the cor anglais, bass clarinet, double bassoon, tuba, *et hoc genus omne*, not to fill up a general clatter and to add extra notes, but as exponents of passages which were written for and required their particular type of colour . . .

> This mastery he owed, as he would himself have been the first to admit, to his complete knowledge of Mozart, Beethoven and Weber. The so-called modern type of full-swell instrumentation owes nothing to any of them. It is only the natural result of revelling too much in Wagner's climaxes of polyphonic sound, which he used economically, and with which the less experienced of his successors gamble.[11]

His views on the use of 'colour' being well known, it is unsurprising that Stanford never used the orchestra in the multifaceted manner associated with either the Russian or neo-Wagnerian schools, but he still managed to exact an enormous variety of sound from the orchestra and his use of different instruments is invariably appropriate to the situation. Despite his reservations about 'colour for colour's sake', Stanford showed a marked interest in the cor anglais and bass clarinet (not regarded as standard in the pre-First World War British orchestra), and also made extensive use of the harp. Another notable characteristic was his frequent use of the trumpet as a melodic instrument, and in this treatment he viewed it more as a member of the woodwind than the brass. In accordance with his precepts, however, Stanford always used these extra instruments to vary the timbre of the orchestra and never as

---

[11] Ibid., 109–10.

padding. In view of this expertise, the heaviness of his chamber music for strings is a mystery, although this may be an unforeseen result of the explicit harmonisation referred to above. As in other aspects of his music, his orchestral style does sometimes display the influence of specific composers, as in the Intermezzo of the Fourth Symphony (Brahms), parts of the finale of the *Stabat Mater* (Verdi) and the finale of the Sixth Symphony (Elgar). Although he never luxuriated in the sensuousness of orchestral colour, he was more self-indulgent in this area than he would have admitted, and exemplary scoring invariably strengthens what would otherwise be weaker music.

Stanford's approach to form was also grounded in the Classical tradition; in *Musical Composition* he argued that forms evolved and that conscious innovation was bound to be sterile:

> A new form in music may require study and frequent hearing to understand it, but if it is logical and founded on a thorough knowledge and control of means, time will endorse it. Such modifications grow (like folk-songs in Hungary) and are not made. To have any value at all they must in their nature be children of their fathers. The laws of evolution apply as rigidly to musical art as they do to nature itself.[12]

Stanford was not averse to experimenting with form (for example, in the Cello and Violin Sonatas, Opp. 9 and 11 and the Seventh Symphony) but such adventures were atypical, based on precedent, and took place within strictly defined parameters. Generally, he preferred to work with established forms and to manipulate them according to need. The adaptations are not radical: he never, for example, experimented with cyclic forms, but he did fall in with general trends, such as the use of character motifs in opera (which eventually grow into fully-fledged leitmotifs in *Much Ado* and *The Travelling Companion*), and recalling earlier movements in symphonies (as in the Sixth and Seventh Symphonies). He also showed occasional genius in the adaptation of form, the best example of which is the Fifth Symphony, in which the narrative of Milton's *L'Allegro* and *Il Penseroso* is superimposed onto the conventional forms of the classical symphony.

Despite this historically informed approach to composition, which could easily lead to slavish imitation, Stanford's music is marked by a number of personal fingerprints. He was especially fond of melodic appoggiaturas resolving (more commonly downwards) by step; their liberal use imbues his music with a classical elegance that hints at the earlier styles of Mendelssohn and Schubert. It also suggests that he

---

[12] Ibid., 76.

Example 9.1   Fourth Symphony, Op. 31, first movement, bars 1–11

Example 9.2   Seventh Symphony, Op. 124, first movement, bars 1–10

thought, unconsciously, of melody in all genres as vocal melody – his awareness of speech rhythms, intonation and stresses was brought to bear across all of his music and with an almost Schubertian intensity. He was particularly fond of using appoggiaturas at the ends of phrases, echoing dactylic and trochaic accentuation common in English, Latin (in which he was, of course, well versed) and the Irish folksong he studied throughout his life. Appoggiaturas were the main source of chromaticism in Stanford's music, their careful resolution no doubt

Example 9.3 *Justorum animae*, Op. 38 No. 1, bars 8–21

satisfying his belief in chromatics as shading rather than colour *per se*. Not only melodic colour but also extensive harmonic colour can be found in his recurrent move from stressed/conflicting note/chord to unstressed/resolved note/chord (Ex 9.1 and 9.2); in his vocal music these stresses are invariably matched with stressed syllables.

As noted in previous chapters, Stanford showed a strong preference for flatwards over sharpwards modulation. This often reflects his interest in modal language and is most evident aurally in the apparent appearance of unexpected flattened sevenths, although these also appear because much of his music is skewed heavily towards plagal movement. As one would expect from such a technically exact composer, these notes are usually properly prepared, being approached from below and resolved downwards (Ex. 9.3). Stanford also engineered this flatward movement by the use of mediant–dominant pivots, (for example, C to E flat or E minor to C minor, both pivoting on G). Although this preference for flatwards modulation implies the possibility of drabness, he mitigated this by making the device his own particular version of local colour.

Stanford also had two rhythmic trademarks: he was fond of a one-sided dialogue between melody and bass in a rhythmic format, and of loud cadential progressions which burst out of his music as if shouting 'so there!' (Ex. 9.4). In terms of form his favourite device was the modified restatement of material: on many occasions recapitulations are subtly altered – for example by amending harmony, scoring or melody – changing the emotional landscape of the music and bringing a degree of fine distinction to his music which is often highly effective. He adopted

Example 9.4   (a) *Phaudrig Croohore*, Op. 62, bars 149–56 (text: Joseph Le
Fanu); (b) Variations on 'Down among the Dead Men', Op. 71,
variation 6, bars 21–35 (core orchestral parts)

Example 9.5   *Beati quorum via*, Op. 38 No. 3: (*a*) bars 1–17; (*b*) bars 49–62

this approach in all genres; on a small-scale *Beati quorum via* is an excellent example of how a modified recapitulation alters the tranquillity of the exposition to a more restless but ultimately triumphant restatement (Ex. 9.5). In a larger work, the continual modifications of the refrains of the Love Duet in *Much Ado* show how continual adaptation to the emotional nuances of the text avoids stagnation and creates propulsion towards the final climax (see pp. 209–11).

None of these fingerprints, or general stylistic points, marks Stanford out as a highly innovative composer. His gifts and attitudes were cautious – this can be seen in his pre-Leipzig compositions in which, rather than challenging rules or subordinating conventions through ignorance, he fought shy and wrote with a harmonic and formal naivety or timidity – but the disposition of those gifts and of the fingerprints do create a discernible musical personality. Stanford's harmonic language, for example, may be closely related to Brahms, but, as noted above, he rarely showed Brahms's obsession with generating whole musical paragraphs from small motivic cells – so while there is often a Brahmsian tinge to his writing, it never acquires the hothouse intensity of Brahms's music and can rarely be confused with him for long. Stanford's use of brighter scoring also quickly dispels Brahms's spectre. The melodic expansiveness which was Stanford's strongest characteristic brings Dvořák to mind, but Stanford never acquired the tangential method of thought that is an essential part of Dvořák's style, and nor did he employ the same rhythmic impetus. When one combines the different factors of style – melodic primacy with a preference for vocally influenced melodies, heavy reliance on speech-influenced appoggiaturas and the implied classicism which flows from it, Germanic harmony with modal overtones, normally leisurely rhythm, bright but not brilliant scoring, the use of conventional forms with a hint of 'developing variation' – in Stanford's proportions and then adds on factors of nationality and emotional involvement, one arrives at a mode of expression which can be highly individual and unmistakably Stanfordian.

Every Inch an (Anglo-)Irishman?

The most intriguing aspect of Stanford's personality and music is the extent to which they can be regarded as Irish. For the purposes of this discussion it is assumed that there are shared national characteristics and that nationality can be satisfactorily defined. Although, in recent years, it has become common to question these ideas, in Stanford's time the concept of nationality was taken for granted and it was normal to attribute common characteristics to national groups. National characteristics are not, however, a fixed concept: in 1887 *The Times* referred to the 'Irish' Symphony as having 'the rhythm and the type of melody [of] the Green Island'[13] while Frank Howes in 1966 dismissed it, remarking that 'the total effect is more like leaving and returning to Ireland from a holiday in Germany';[14] this is not merely a difference which arises because the comments were made by two different individuals but a reflection of the fact that perceptions of nationality change over time. Bernard Shaw, a fellow Anglo-Irishman, viewed Stanford's 'Irishness' differently again, arguing that he suffered from a split personality:

> The spectacle of a university professor 'going fantee' is indecorous, though to me personally it is delightful ... The 'Irish' Symphony, composed by an Irishman, is a record of fearful conflict between the aboriginal Celt and the Professor. The Scherzo is not a scherzo at all, but a shindy, expending its force in riotous dancing. However hopelessly an English orchestra may fail to catch the wild nuances of the Irish fiddler, it cannot altogether drown the 'hurroosh' with which Stanford the Celt drags Stanford the Professor into the orgy.[15]

Faced with these disparate opinions, and with Shaw's argument that Stanford was suffering from musical schizophrenia, it is no wonder that Stanford's Irishness has proved elusive.

The first issue to address is whether Stanford the *man* was Irish. This is a question fraught with difficulty since there has been more debate about the true nature of Irishness than, perhaps, that of any other western European nationality. The position of those born into the Ascendancy is often viewed as an equivocal one: Stanford was a member of a demographic group which had tried to maintain a social and religious aloofness from the greater part of Irish society since it arrived in the sixteenth and seventeenth centuries. Aloofness itself does not deprive one of nationality, but failure to integrate more fully into the indigenous population may do so. While, in the seventeenth century, the Anglo-Irish were viewed as invaders whose primary loyalty was to England (or, in the case of Ulster, Scotland), by the latter part of the eighteenth century the position had changed. Although still tending towards respective exclusivity, all three major Irish population groups (Catholics, Anglo-Irish and Ulster non-conformists) opposed English rule and, under the leadership of Henry Grattan, the powers of the Irish Parliament were enhanced in 1782. This was not independence, but

---

[13] *The Times*, 1 July 1887, p. 4.
[14] Howes, *The English Musical Renaissance*, 154.
[15] Shaw, *Music in London*, ii, 319 and 322.

many powers were devolved from London to Dublin. Crucially, however, the religious divide remained in Ireland: the Penal Code remained
in force and only members of the established church were entitled to
hold public office or to vote, excluding the great majority of the population. Catholic emancipation was advocated by some and some
relaxations made, but only to the extent that it did not compromise the
position of the Ascendancy. That the group which held the reins of
power was almost synonymous with the group descended from the
'invaders' set the Anglo-Irish apart and, in the view of many, their true
colours were seen after the 1798 Rebellion when, afraid of losing their
dominant position, the Anglo-Irish voted their Parliament out of existence and actively supported the 1800 Act of Union. Inevitably in the
nineteenth century, and especially after Catholic Emancipation in 1829,
the cause of Irish Nationalism was increasingly associated with the
Catholic majority. The path was a circuitous one – at times some Anglo-
Irish veered towards advocating decentralised government – but in
essence they remained Unionists (see also pp. 5–6).

Perceptions in the twentieth century have often been negative and the
Anglo-Irish have been viewed as lackeys, used by England to keep the
Catholic majority in subservience and to prevent Irish self-determin-
ation. Inevitably, however, the situation is far more complex than this
and to see if one can determine whether or not Stanford was Irish, one
must separate out the political and cultural dynamics of the nationalist
debate. No more potently are these complexities and intricacies articulated than in the history of the opera *Shamus O'Brien*; by examining
the background to the opera, Stanford and Jessop's development of the
scenario, Stanford's approach to the music and his attitude to its production, it is possible to go some way in deconstructing his national
affiliation.

The poem upon which Stanford based his work shows the early
Victorian ambiguities in the Anglo-Irish position. Joseph Le Fanu, its
author, was, like Stanford, an Anglo-Irish Protestant, raised in the
traditional manner, complete with education at Trinity College, Dublin.
Yet the poem appears to be overtly nationalist: Shamus is the hero
and the British soldiers are the villains. The poem was first popularised
in the 1840s by Samuel Lover, a travelling performer in Ireland and
America; both then, and after anonymous publication in 1850, many
assumed that Lover was the author. Lover was aware of this but did
not move to correct the error; he justified his inaction to William Le
Fanu, Joseph's brother, with the following reason: 'I would not wish to
wear a borrowed feather, I should be glad to give your brother's name
as author, should he not object to have it known but, as his writings
are often of so different a tone, I would not speak without permission

to do so.'[16] These other writings were Joseph's contributions to the high Tory, pro-Union *Dublin University Magazine*.[17] So what was Le Fanu doing? He had, at times, supported the Repeal Movement (which campaigned for the re-establishment of the Irish Parliament) and campaigns for land reform, but this support was really a manifestation of his dissatisfaction with the remoteness and harshness of rule from Westminster, and not an overtly nationalist statement. Le Fanu was unlikely to write such a poem seriously and Alfred Graves suggested it was a joke: 'We have heard it said (though without having inquired into the truth of the tradition) that *Shamus O'Brien* was the result of a match at pseudo-ballad writing made between Le Fanu and several of the most brilliant of his literary *confrères* at TCD.'[18] This theory has more recently been backed by William McCormack, who moved to explain the political dimension of the poem:

> Nationalism (at least in the form of a vigorous scepticism of English ideas) had some appeal for the protestant bourgeoisie ... *Shamus O'Brien* was in part a symbol of disenchantment with the alliance between an ascendancy (or sections of it) in Ireland and a government in England ... [Le Fanu's] ballad offers only ambiguous evidence of radical thinking. Its politics are overtly nationalistic, but its form is deliberate pastiche, and close to parody.[19]

Le Fanu's poem thus highlights the political ambiguity of the community into which Stanford was born, although the generational difference – Stanford was fifty years younger – must be taken into account. While the poem of *Shamus O'Brien* was written before the devastation caused by the Potato Famine, Stanford, when in his twenties, was confronted by an Ireland whose population had almost halved since his birth, which had experienced a surge of Fenian violence, and whose symbol of the Ascendancy, the Church of Ireland, had been disestablished. His support of the Liberal candidate in the Cambridge University by-election of 1882 suggests that he agreed with Gladstone's pre-Home Rule programme of social reform, but as soon as Gladstone declared for Home Rule, Stanford's approval turned to hostility and his political allegiance changed, although he continued to believe that reform was the best means of strengthening the Union, as his letters to *The Times* in 1914 show (see pp. 285–6).

---

[16] Quoted in Michael Begnal, *Joseph Sheridan Le Fanu* (Lewisburg, Pa., 1971), 16–17.

[17] Charles Stuart Stanford, the uncle of Charles Villiers Stanford, was one-time editor of this publication.

[18] Joseph Le Fanu, *The Purcell Papers*, ed. Alfred Graves, 3 vols (London, 1880), i, preface.

[19] William McCormack, *Sheridan Le Fanu and Victorian Ireland* (Oxford, 1980), 53.

Stanford and Jessop's adaptation of Le Fanu's poem needs to be seen in this broader context and it is significant that they moved to take as much of the nationalist sting out of the tale as possible, achieved by the introduction of the character Mike Murphy. By this action the British ceased to be the villains, and became mere incompetents who could not keep hold of a prisoner, whilst it was Mike, Shamus's betrayer and fellow Irishman, who was the real villain.[20] Crucially this allowed the nationalist message of the poem to be greatly diluted. Stanford and Jessop were also careful to ensure that Captain Trevor was shown as an upright, worthy, if bumptious man, who falls in love with Kitty, who reciprocates (and thus portrays love across the national and, presumably, sectarian, divide).

The opera could still be read as a pro-nationalist piece, however, since Shamus remained a strong hero who escapes from his captors and whose sedition goes unpunished. On seeing the opera shortly after its première Francis Jenkinson wrote, 'An erratic person named Weale, who failed to reach the actors before the curtain, gave Bunny a green pamphlet rolled and tied with cherry ribbon which she gave me. "Ireland and Africa". Quite cracked.'[21] Jenkinson's note is not conclusive evidence, but it does imply that the subject matter of the opera had, at the very least, provoked some debate. When *Shamus* toured Ireland in 1896 and 1897 reception was enthusiastic; although more perceptive nationalists could see that there was ambiguity in the meaning of the work, many who were less intellectually critical picked up on Shamus's heroism and Mike's betrayal in simple terms:

> On the opening night at Waterford, after O'Mara, who played the part of Mike the informer, had disclosed the identity of Shamus and led to his arrest, a shrill voice from an old lady at the back of the pit yelled out 'O ye dirthy blagyard' with such a fury of emotion that there was a yell of laughter from the whole house, audience, singers and orchestra alike, and the performance had to be temporarily suspended.
>
> On the night when O'Mara was presented with the freedom of the City of Limerick at the close of the last performance there the whole place was packed from floor to ceiling. They shouted for 'The Wearin' of the Green' and he sang it, unaccompanied, with overwhelming effect. There was not a dry eye in the house.[22]

In subsequent years Stanford was not inclined to take chances. Probably in 1912, when a Home Rule bill was once again presented to

---

[20] This change also created the love-interest which Stanford viewed as essential in an opera; Shamus's wife Norah was also introduced by Stanford and Jessop, thus setting up the rivalry between Shamus and Mike, who are both in love with her.

[21] Francis Jenkinson's Diary, 17 Mar. 1896, CUL, Add. MS 7419.

[22] Quoted in Greene, *Stanford*, 199.

Parliament, he banned performances of *Shamus*, and the ban remained until his death. This decision would not have been taken lightly, since *Shamus* was a good earner for him, but, interviewed by Herbert Antcliffe in 1917, Stanford made it quite clear why he had acted: 'At the present moment Sir Charles considers it is inopportune that *Shamus O'Brien* should be played, as it has sometimes led to a political misunderstanding.'[23] This highly unusual action – it is a rare thing for a composer to impose a ban on his own work for political reasons – illustrates how strongly Stanford felt on this matter and how important it was to him not to encourage or be seen to encourage anti-Union sentiment.

Yet, despite his pro-Union politics, Stanford remained adamant that he was an Irishman. Most people who have written about him later have included comments affirming that he was possessed of what they viewed as typical Irish character traits: a sharp sense of wit, a keen tongue and an easily lost, but quickly restored, temper. And Stanford was typical of the Anglo-Irish in his identification of Ireland as his true home. At the commencement of the new millennium, when nationalism in general has become almost solely identified with the desire to establish a commensurate sovereign state, this ambiguity is difficult to understand, but, for the Victorian Anglo-Irish, it did not cause a problem – their spiritual allegiance was to Ireland but their political affiliation was to the United Kingdom. This dual nationality is encapsulated in the setting of 'The Wearin' of the Green' published by Stanford and Charles Graves in 1900, celebrating both the recent relief of Ladysmith and the impending visit of Queen Victoria to Ireland (the first since 1849):

> And have you heard the joyful word that's flyin' round full blast?
> That Bullen and his boys are through to Ladysmith at last!
> And how, to march in first of all the soldiers of the Queen,
> He put the Dublin's playin' up 'The Wearin' of the Green'.
>
> On left and right, past General White, our Ulster hero grand,
> Went Bullen's twenty thousand deliverers, torn and tanned,
> Past women pale and patient, and defenders famine-lean
> Liftin' up the little childer for the glory of the Green.
>
> A heart of fire has Lancashire for fightin' inch by inch,
> But the Irish, though they started last, were first into the trench,
> They took the front, they bore the brunt o'er kopje and ravine,
> Till at Pieter's Hill, Majuba's ill they righted for the Queen.
>
> And so upon St Patrick's Days, Victoria she has said –
> Each Irish regiment shall wear the Green beside the Red;
> And she's coming to ould Ireland, who away so long has been,
> And dear knows but into Dublin she'll ride wearin' of the Green.

---

[23] Herbert Antcliffe, 'Sir Charles Stanford', *Music Student* (1916–17), 9, 211–15.

Although they are Graves's words, Stanford's approval is absolutely implicit in his arrangement of the melody and, as such, his imperial beliefs are evident: to him Ireland was as much a part of the Empire as England and, crucially, to be seen as an equal part. It is notable that, when W. B. Yeats wrote regarding Victoria's visit to Ireland and referred to her as 'the official head and symbol of an empire that is robbing the South African republics of their liberty, as it has robbed Ireland of hers',[24] Stanford wrote to Alfred Graves that he was resigning his membership of the Irish Literary Society, of which both he and Yeats were members, because 'they can't have this Yeats on the Committee if they wish to be considered non-combative and non-political'.[25]

One may debate the validity of Stanford's assertions but the crucial fact is that he *himself* believed that he was an Irishman first and foremost. This allowed him to identify himself as a 'cultural nationalist' but not a 'political nationalist' and for Stanford there was no contradiction in the concept of the 'Irish Imperialist'. Like many Anglo-Irish he was greatly interested in Irish culture and history and supported several organisations which promoted them, for example the Feis Ceoil Music Festivals, founded in the mid-1890s, and the Irish Literary Society mentioned above. On many occasions he cited the beauty of Irish folk music and sophistication of its culture in general with evident pride.[26]

The simplest example of Stanford's cultural interest is to be found in his arrangements and editions of Irish folksongs. Unlike Cecil Sharp and Vaughan Williams, Stanford never collected folksongs, but in contrast to England, large collections, such as those of Petrie and Bunting, already existed. Instead he arranged many airs from these works in collaboration

---

[24] Quoted in *The Times*, 5 Apr. 1900, p. 10, from a letter written by Yeats to several Dublin newspapers.

[25] Stanford to Graves, 19 Nov. 1900, NLI, MS 17797, item 40. Stanford's cousin Lord Justice Henn Collins, then Master of the Rolls, also resigned, after discussing the issue with Stanford. Here is an example of the concept that supporting the *status quo* is an apolitical act while questioning it introduces politics into an issue that had previously been somehow above the fray; Stanford and Charles Graves's work is no less political than that of Yeats; indeed, the adaptation of 'The Wearin' of the Green', which had the status of unofficial national anthem, might be taken to be more provocative than Yeats's letter.

[26] See, for example, Stanford, 'Music in Elementary Schools', in *Studies and Memories*, 43–60: 'In the British Isles you have the greatest and most varied storehouse of national music in existence. You have two distinct schools – Saxon and Celtic; and four distinct styles – English, Welsh, Scotch, and Irish. The English, strong, solid, and straightforward; the Welsh, full of dash and 'go'; the Scotch, a mixture of the humorous and the poetic, full of strongly marked rhythms, dry and caustic at times, full of a quality which I can best term 'lilt'; the Irish, which, to my mind, speaking as impartially as an Irishman can, is the most remarkable literature of folk-music in the world – there is no emotion with which it does not deal successfully, and none has more power of pathos or of fire.'

with Alfred Graves, who supplied the words, and the principal results were *Songs of Old Ireland* (1882), *Irish Songs and Ballads* (1893) and *Songs of Erin* (Op. 76, published 1901), plus *The Irish Melodies of Thomas Moore, restored and arranged* (Op. 60, published 1895). Altogether these four sets include 249 folksongs and Stanford published many more singly. By the standards of the time the arrangements are generally good; Stanford was particularly keen to preserve or restore what he took to be the original modality of the melodies and to ensure that his harmonisations followed these implications. This involved challenging many established assumptions, since John Stevenson, in the arrangements he made for *Moore's Irish Melodies* (published in sets between 1807 and 1834), was meticulous in diatonicising melodies and harmonies as much as possible. Subsequent rearrangements, such as that published by Michael Balfe in 1859, 'improved' Stevenson's harmony but let most of the diatonicisation stand, and Stanford, therefore, saw himself as restoring the original character of the melodies to a far greater extent than had previously been the case; and there is no doubt that his arrangements generally show far more skill and sensitivity than those of previous editors. An example of this can be seen in his version of 'The valley lay smiling before me', which is a clear improvement on both the versions by Balfe, and Moore and Stevenson's original (Ex. 9.6).[27] The words which Graves supplied for his and Stanford's collections are often twee by today's standards and hardly authentic, but as originally any words would have been in Gaelic, and as, at Stanford's birth, barely a quarter of the Irish population spoke any Gaelic, and only 5 per cent spoke it as a first language, Graves's labours can be defended: publication solely in Gaelic, whilst academically sound, would have been highly elitist and defeated the commercial motivations of both Graves and Stanford, who evidently hoped to create a new incarnation of *Moore's Irish Melodies*.[28] When editing Moore's collection Stanford left the words alone: after eighty years of good sales such poems as 'The Harp that once in Tara's Halls' and 'The Minstrel Boy' were viewed as an integral part of the whole and had acquired an authenticity of their own.

Stanford's other major contribution in this area was his edition of *The Petrie Collection of Irish Music*, containing 1,582 melodies, and published between 1902 and 1905.[29] In one sense the scale of the task is shown by the number of tunes incorporated, but, unfortunately,

---

[27] This melody had previously been issued under the name 'The Pretty Girl Milking the Cows' in Edward Bunting, *A General Collection of the Ancient Irish Music* (London, 1796).

[28] Stanford spoke no Gaelic; Graves appears to have had a rudimentary knowledge of it.

[29] Petrie published a volume of 140 melodies from his collection in 1855 (see Ch. 6, n. 2) but Stanford's edition was the first of the whole collection.

Example 9.6   'The valley lay smiling before me' (from *Moore's Irish Melodies*)
               with accompaniments by Stevenson (top), Balfe (middle), and
               Stanford (bottom)

Stanford did little work as a serious editor and only categorised the
melodies by basic character and failed to group together any but the
most obvious variants. He also failed to make any enquiries as to the
authenticity of the melodies, being content to assume that Petrie's scholarship was adequate. This is partly because he himself approached the
question of folksong from an amateur standpoint; in his article 'Some

Example 9.6   *(cont.)*

look'd   for the   lamp, which   she   told   me,   Should   shine,   when her   Pil-grim re - turned;   But, tho'

dark-ness   be - gan   to   en - fold   me,   No   lamp   from the   bat - tle - ments   burn'd!

Thoughts Concerning Folk-Song and Nationality' it becomes clear that he accepted a casual application of Darwinian evolution theory to the development of folksong, stating that

> [The origin of Celtic folksong] is lost in antiquity, and by some learned ethnographical pundits a connection has been traced between it and the music of India. Dr George Petrie ... found a

striking resemblance between Indian and Irish lullabies. The present
writer has often been surprised by the similarity between Hungarian
and Irish folk-song: a similarity which may be due to a joint Oriental
origin.[30]

This is not the place for a debate on the authenticity or otherwise of
various folksongs;[31] it is evident from this article, however, that Stanford
was prepared to rely on the work of others and more importantly
on his own instincts when judging folksongs, rather than careful
research.

This approach, together with some unfortunately slapdash methods,
resulted in a number of potential and actual weaknesses in the edition
of the Petrie Collection which were almost immediately criticised:[32]
Stanford was unable in practice, and probably unwilling in theory, to
check any of the transcriptions to see if they were accurate or to enquire
into the veracity of their sources and probity of the contributors. Petrie
himself had accepted many melodies from other collectors, accepting
their legitimacy if, in his judgement, the melodies appeared to be
authentic and if he believed the contributor was (socially?) reputable;
Stanford himself inexplicably excluded some melodies, such as the
'Londonderry Air'.[33] Stanford recognized the close relationship between
'Scotch' and Irish folksongs, as both belonged to the 'Celtic' tradition:[34]
many jigs and reels are found in both countries, with no certainty as to
which was the country of origin and, while there may be no means of
clarifying this ambiguity, Stanford could have done more to scrutinise
Petrie's methods in order to avoid errors. According to Greene, some

[30] Charles Stanford, 'Some Thoughts Concerning Folk-song and Nationality', *Musical
Quarterly*, 1 (1915), 232–45. In the same article he stated that 'Dvořák's explorations
into negro melodies, when he was in New York, give an example of this [interweaving of
national types]: for many of the tunes which he used in his compositions of that period
are really Irish tunes coloured with a negro brush.'

[31] For some examination of the general issue of the authenticity of English folksong
see, for example, David Harker, *Fakesong: The Manufacture of British Folksong 1700 to
the Present Day* (Milton Keynes, 1985).

[32] Some weaknesses are acknowledged by Greene, who appears to have played an unofficial role in examination and preparation: 'The collection, in its final form, has come in
for a good deal of criticism, and it must be acknowledged that some of it is deserved. In
spite of all our care there are a good many repetitions of the same tune, sometimes note
for note and sometimes in a different key, which escaped us. This should not have
happened, and I just as much as Stanford was responsible for letting them through' (Greene,
Stanford, 179).

[33] Petrie had, however, questioned Bunting's judgement in some instances, showing a
degree of academic scrutiny. Later debates on, for example, the authenticity of the
'Londonderry Air', found in Petrie's collection (see Ch. 6, n. 2), have led to questioning
of the scholarly reliability of both collections.

[34] Stanford, 'Some Thoughts'.

titles were mistranslated from Gaelic (although it is not clear in this instance with whom the fault lies).[35] Similarly, what has been perceived as an archetypally English folksong, 'Green Rushes' (or 'Green Bushes'), used by Vaughan Williams in the *English Folksong Suite* (in the *Allegretto scherzando* of the slow movement) and Butterworth in *The Banks of Green Willow* (coda section), is also to be found in Petrie and was reproduced uncritically by Stanford (vol. 1, nos 368–70), a weakness is also partially acknowledged by Greene.[36] The greatest problem that this presents is certain identification of a distinctive Irish style of folk music. Stanford's approach was to trust to his instincts in both 'correcting' Petrie's manuscripts and in accepting which melodies were authentic. Despite these undoubted failings, however – partly due to the accepted standard of scholarship prevalent at the time – Stanford's edition of Petrie did at least bring a multiplicity of (apparently) Irish melodies into wider circulation, and as, arguably, it was with the responsibility of producing an edition of this collection with which Stanford was charged, he could claim in his defence that he had done what was required of him.

Of greatest importance, however, in this discussion of Stanford's nationality, are his own Irish compositions. They span his entire career, from early works such as the 'Gigue' in the Suite for Piano, Op. 2 (which, despite its French nomenclature, displays melodic figurations typical of Irish jigs) to the *Irish Rhapsody No. 6*, Op. 191. Again, *Shamus O'Brien* serves as a representative and excellent exemplar. Here Stanford pulled what have been commonly viewed as many of the correct nationalist levers: he quoted a traditional Irish melody, 'The Top of the Cork Road', wrote elegant pastiche (see the examples given in pp. 185–7), and used Irish bagpipes to supply the drone in the Act I Jig. For contemporary critics he had done his job well and created a genuinely Irish soundworld:

> The characteristics of Irish music have been so assimilated by the composer that, although he has only used two actual traditional tunes, many of the themes in the work might easily pass for genuine treasures of national song.[37]

> We are bound to say that it exceeded even the anticipation of those who, knowing and admiring [Stanford's] 'Irish' Symphony and his arrangements of the songs of his native land, expected something

---

[35] See Greene, *Stanford*, 179–80; for example, 'I will raise my sail black mistfully in the morning' should read 'I shall set sail for Joyce's country in the morning.' (This melody is used at the opening of the *Irish Rhapsody No. 4*.)

[36] Ibid; Greene wrote 'Others [that is, other tunes] – only a few – are of non-Irish origin and appear under aliases.'

[37] *The Times*, 3 Mar. 1896, p. 12.

racy of the soil. Musically *Shamus O'Brien* is simply a little master-piece.[38]

A change in attitudes over subsequent years is hardly surprising; Fuller Maitland (*The Times*) had only the advantage of comparison with composers such as Smetana, Dvořák and Tchaikovsky, whose essential methods are similar to Stanford's, even if the end products are different in sound. One should also bear in mind Fuller Maitland's particular admiration for Stanford: on revising the entry on Stanford for *Grove III* in 1927, Fuller Maitland wrote:

> Stanford's Irish descent gives his music a strong individuality which is not only evident in his arrangements of Irish songs and in his works as a collector, but stands revealed in his Irish Symphony ... and in many other definitely Irish compositions. The easy flow of melody, and the feeling for the poetical and romantic things in legendary lore ... are peculiarly Irish traits.[39]

Fuller Maitland was not unique, however, in his perception that Stanford's music was truly Irish. When *Shamus* was produced in Dublin in 1924, shortly after Stanford's death and the first production since the self-imposed ban some twelve years earlier, the shift in views is highly significant: advances in the theatre initiated by such writers as Yeats and Synge led to criticism of the drama, perceptions of the nature of which had changed, but not of the music:

> The libretto belongs to the school of Dion Boucicault – that school which the Abbey Theatre has taught us now to call 'stage-Irish', the school whose work reminds one of the picture postcards sold to English tourists, showing the Irishman of caricature, with shillelagh, squat nose, green knickerbockers, and pig complete. It made a hero of the rebel, a fool of the British soldier, a heroine of the Irish colleen and a despised rascal of an informer ...

> Stanford's score, in its technique a model for many composers of its own time, and of the new generation, is remarkable for its flavour of Ireland, with rhythms and melodies all in the spirit of our native music.[40]

In Ireland dramatic tastes had changed as a direct result of developing cultural nationalism and through a conscious debunking of stereotypes, becoming more distinctive than in the nineteenth century, but musical tastes remained wedded to an earlier model based on the German tradition and Thomas Moore, there having been no real musical equivalent

---

[38] *Musical Times*, 1 Apr. 1896, p. 240.
[39] *Grove's Dictionary of Music and Musicians*, 3rd edn, ed. Henry Cope Colles, 5 vols (London, 1929), v, 119.
[40] *Irish Times*, 12 Aug. 1924, p. 4.

to the work of the Abbey Theatre playwrights. It was this same nine-teenth-century view which allowed Shaw to write in terms of 'Stanford the Celt' and 'Stanford the Professor' (see p. 385) and to accord him, at least in part, a real Irish pedigree as a composer. When Frank Howes wrote of Stanford's 'holiday in Germany' in the mid-1960s, he had the advantage of a knowledge of such diverse and highly distinctive composers as Bartók, de Falla, Poulenc and Szymanowski, all of whom moved further from the German classical tradition than Stanford ever practised or advocated. Thus Howes's view was informed by the same nature of cultural change which influenced the perception of drama displayed by the critic of the *Irish Times* in 1924, but now applied to music.

Attributing views of Stanford's nationalism to shifting taste and educa-tion only answers the question of his Irishness in part. So does answering the question in terms of Stanford's self-perception. In fact, the quest for labels stultifies the search for his character and the discussion of his music. Arnold Bax inadvertently summed up the problem by saying that 'Stanford was not Irish enough'.[41] He was talking then not of Stanford's music but of his nationality *per se*: Bax did not believe that Stanford, born into the Ascendancy, was truly Irish. Rather, he considered the Gaelic-speaking west coast to be the true Ireland, and was right in believing that Stanford was not part of it. Rather, Stanford was part of another Ireland: Protestant metropolitan Dublin, which was, in its own way, just as Irish as Co. Galway. But here is the rub – was it? Unless one completely disowns the concept of nationality, an argument is not advanced that London is less English than Gloucestershire or that Paris is less French than Burgundy, but the peculiar historical circumstances of Ireland with its religious, social, ethnic, linguistic and geographical sectorisation, which separated the Anglo-Irish in Dublin from those who were, literally, beyond the Pale, placed Stanford in a highly ambiguous position.[42] That he emigrated to England at the age of 18, never to return, and that he ardently supported political and religious positions held by a minority of the Irish population have emphasised this ambi-guity. For while London and Gloucestershire might be seen as two different but equally valid Englands, legitimising, therefore, both John Ireland and Herbert Howells as English composers, there has been a

---

[41] Bax, *Farewell my Youth*, 27.

[42] Looking further back than the seventeenth century, it is clear that Irish society was almost as much an ethnographic mix as English, but the position of the Anglo-Irish settlers who arrived in the Tudor and Stuart periods is somewhat clearer as they took, by and large, deliberate action to avoid intermarriage with those who could claim indigenous resi-dence for longer.

long-held perception that Stanford's Ireland, the Anglo-Irish Protestant world centred on Dublin, was an illegitimate Ireland when compared to that of the 'true' Ireland to which Bax alluded. This position is over-laden with significance because of the unique nature of Irish society and politics; strictly one can argue that both Irelands are valid since both existed and therefore that Stanford's experience is not compromised in the way in which Bax implied, but Bax's declaration, and the term 'Anglo-Irish' itself, echo a perception that the Anglo-Irish only ever played at being Irish, that they avoided assimilation and were never, therefore, the genuine article; this would in turn justify the British and Continental overtones apparent in Stanford's music since, had he been truly Irish, so would his music have been.

The assumption that Stanford's Ireland was a fallacy is compounded by the fact that he frequently tried to evoke in his music the Ireland of his dreams rather than the Ireland of his experience, and to this extent, Stanford's Ireland was indeed a fallacy. This is especially true of the songs, which partially explains why they are his least successful Irish works, for here Stanford usually evoked a peaceful, rural, peasant Ireland of which he knew little. In these works we see the Ireland that Stanford wished existed – and it jars against the Ireland evoked contemporane-ously in such works as J. M. Synge's *The Playboy of the Western World* (1907), which is an altogether grittier and harsher affair and which was soon perceived as the 'real' Ireland, a 'warts and all' view which has chimed with Irish mores to a far a greater extent than Stanford's idyll. In the instrumental works the lack of words emancipates both composer and listener from a pre-determined image and many become more convincingly Irish as a result, for example parts of the 'Irish' Symphony and some of the Rhapsodies. That the remainder are not convincing arises, however, from the issues of facility and emotional restraint which dogged Stanford's output (see pp. 407–16) rather than an inherent lack of Irishness. The complexity of the situation is equally illustrated by what one might term Stanford's 'English' works. These pieces, for example *Songs of the Sea*, *Songs of the Fleet*, and *The Revenge* on the nautical side, and the best of the church music, are as avowedly 'English' in spirit and sound as the Irish works are Irish. For Bax this would merely reinforce the idea that Stanford was faux-Irish; for Stanford this would be a demonstration of his Ireland being part of a larger whole; today we might see this as a demonstration that he was really a dual national – but, as for much of the twentieth century, Irishness has been defined as being an 'Other' to Britishness, or more specifically English-ness, this dual nationality has become an insurmountable obstacle.

The problem with Stanford is not that his Irish background was falla-cious but that it was atypical; one can draw a parallel with Samuel

Coleridge Taylor, whose life and education were stereotypically English apart from his being born of a West African father. In both cases there has been an extent to which the subjects became dual nationals or, alternatively, stateless, but, while Coleridge Taylor has been 'claimed' as a pioneering black composer, Stanford has been disowned as an Irish one; this reflects more on the attitudes of those looking on Stanford than on Stanford himself. For Stanford the issue is further highlighted because the mixed perceptions are aided by the lack of a comparator, since no other contemporary Irish composer succeeded to his extent; he was the sole example of a successful pre-War Irish composer to both his benefit – through being cited as *the* Irish composer of his time – and to his detriment: no equal against whose value his own could be assessed.

Nicholas Temperley has proposed a general framework for tracing the establishment of national music, in which he argues that there are three stages in its development.[43] Using Russia as his model, Temperley cites Bortnyansky as representing stage 1, in which composers demonstrate the credibility of the indigenous product by writing music in the same style and as good as that to be found in countries with established reputations. Glinka represents stage 2, in which the most basic of the nationalist elements are introduced, for example the use of folksong and dance music and the use of subjects of a national character, whilst still using 'classical' forms. Finally, Mussorgsky is the exemplar of stage 3, in which a radically different and individual style is forged. Applying this to the British Isles, one can cite Balfe, Wallace and Macfarren as embodying stage 1, Stanford, Mackenzie and MacCunn stage 2, and Vaughan Williams, Butterworth and Warlock stage 3.[44] Stanford used most of Temperley's devices (the principal exception being indigenous language, which was impractical) and yet there are still charges laid of a 'lack' of Irishness. Partly this arises out of the passage of time alluded to earlier but, compared with his 'nationalist' contemporaries, Stanford's music almost always remained too redolent of his German education and fell a victim to his own ability. In Shaw's terms, therefore, 'Stanford the Professor' won the battle – not, however, against 'Stanford the Celt', but against 'Stanford the Savage', for the problem is not that Stanford's music was insufficiently Irish, but that it was too often insufficiently passionate or intense in expression (see pp. 410–16). For 'Stanford the Celt', the problem was that he started and ended in a unique situation: an emigrant Irishman committed to a minority faith and political

---

[43] See Nicholas Temperley, *The Lost Chord: Essays on Victorian Music* (Bloomington and Indianapolis, Ind., 1989), 143–58.

[44] Parry and Elgar may also be given as representing stage 2 in Britain, but neither made extensive use of the devices which Temperley gives.

allegiance, as clear in his own belief in his position as that position now seems ambiguous.

Reception, Perception and Legacy

Stanford perceived a decline in interest in his music from the turn of the century and, after his death, his work steadily fell out of the repertory. This inevitable decline has not been a consistent one: the Anglican church bucked the trend and his services and anthems continue to form one of the bulwarks of that repertory; in this case the decline has only set in over the last thirty years and is attributable to the changing nature of Anglican worship. The Anglican Church is, however, atypical, and the general change in fortunes can be exemplified by tracing the years in which a selection of Stanford's works went out of print (see Table 9.1) and in the slowing sales of *The Revenge*, one of his most successful choral pieces (see Table 9.2). In this latter case it is notable that the decline started only in the 1930s and that sales, although smaller, remained roughly level between 1934 and 1954; in this instance Stanford was no doubt partly the victim of the general decline of the British choral societies.

In the face of this decline the inevitable predictions of a revival of interest in Stanford's music followed. In 1952, Vaughan Williams, speaking on the occasion of the centenary of Stanford's birth, took the opportunity not only to predict a revival, but to chastise the institutions around him:

> The bright young things of the younger generation do not seem to know much about Stanford, and not having had the advantage of his teaching are inclined to ignore what he did and what he taught. But I believe that he will return again. With the next generation the inevitable reaction will set in and Stanford will come into his own. His smaller works are still known and loved by our choral societies, and I cannot but believe that such splendid music as the *Stabat Mater*, *Requiem*, and *Songs of the Fleet* will not strike home as soon as opportunity is given to hear them. It is up to our concert societies, in this centenary year, to give us these works as well as the 'Irish' Symphony and Rhapsodies and the many fine songs. In any continental country the centenary of a composer of Stanford's calibre would have been celebrated in every opera house in the country. Covent Garden and Sadlers Wells cannot even give us an opportunity of hearing such splendid works with all the certainty of popularity as *Much Ado* and *Shamus O'Brien*. Instead of which they choose to shake the dead bones of *Norma* and *Samson et Delilah*.[45]

---

[45] Vaughan Williams, 'Charles Villiers Stanford', in *National Music and Other Essays*, 195–6.

Table 9.1   Selective list of Stanford's works with the year of
withdrawal from sale

Piano Quintet in D minor, Op. 25	1927
Blarney Ballads	1932
God is our hope and strength, Op. 8	1933
Three Intermezzi, Op. 13	1938
'Sweet Isle' (from Op. 1)	1942
Irish Songs and Ballads	1942
'Day is Dying' (from Op. 1)	1942
East to West, Op. 52	1943
The Battle of the Baltic, Op. 41	1945
Service in A, Op. 12	1945[a]
'Irish' Symphony, Op. 28 (sales of score and parts)	1946
Eden, Op. 40	1953
The Voyage of Maeldune, Op. 34	1955
Mass in G, Op. 46	1956
'Blue Wings' (from Op. 1)	1956
Communion Service in G, Op. 46a	1958
The Revenge, Op. 24	1974

Source: Novello Archive, British Library. The year in which Novello officially
withdrew a work from sale was the one in which the last payment of royalties
was made to Stanford's estate; the last print run may have been several years
earlier. On withdrawing the work from sale any remaining copies were destroyed.
Unfortunately, Novello's accounts only record these details for works on which
royalties were payable – no information is available for pieces whose copyright
was sold outright at the time of publication.

[a] Magnificat and Nunc Dimittis in A remains in print.

Herbert Howells added his voice to the cause,[46] but the centenary of
Stanford's birth was a low-key affair, although some special perfor-
mances were given. The great revival which Vaughan Williams and
Howells anticipated and hoped for did not then materialise.

In fact, Vaughan Williams's 'inevitable reaction' was far longer in
coming than he could have expected; he could not have foreseen the
spirit of radicalism that seized British music in the 1960s and which led
to a fall in the fortunes of his own works and those of many of his
contemporaries. He miscalculated by thirty years: the revival of interest
in Stanford's music did not get under way until the 1980s. In part this

---

[46] See Herbert Howells, 'Charles Villiers Stanford: An Address at his Centenary',
Proceedings of the Royal Musical Association, 80 (1952–3), 19–31.

Table 9.2   Sales of vocal scores of *The Revenge* in five-year periods

Five years to:	Copies sold
(1886–)1889	18,570
1894	13,318
1899	14,859
1904	18,794
1909	26,612
1914	19,832
1919	12,893
1924	21,456
1929	19,723
1934	11,427
1939	7,358
1944	4,420
1949	4,589
1954	5,363
1959	2,791
1964	1,834
1969	848
1974	823

Source: Novello Archive, British Library.

was due to the natural cycle to which Vaughan Williams alluded, but it was also spurred on by the general revival of academic interest in the 'British Musical Renaissance' (see Preface) and the advent of the compact disc, which led to an exponential increase in new recordings (see App. 2); several works long out of print have also been reissued.

Perhaps partly because of his abrasive personality and bluntly expressed views, critical opinion on Stanford has tended to fall into two sharply defined camps, pro and anti. Until the 1960s this tendency was also influenced by individual contact, as many commentators had known Stanford personally. On both sides of the argument the opinion of Stanford's music has centred on three issues: those of nationality (see pp. 384–400), facility, and his ability to express emotion. In these three issues, it has been felt, the 'problem' with Stanford's music has lain and, in the latter two the passage of time has made little difference to critical opinion. Facility has attracted attention because of a common perception that if a composer finds it all too 'easy' she or he is often neither sufficiently self-critical nor inclined to refine music through continuous redrafting. Emotional restraint has been a bugbear in the romantic and post-romantic ethos, which has generally required music to be frankly expressive rather than decorous or necessarily civilising. The two issues have become somewhat intertwined: music which was easily composed is often suspected of being superficial, both technically and emotionally. George Bernard Shaw articulated these issues pithily with regard to Stanford:

> [*Eden*] is as insufferable a composition as any Festival committee could desire; but it is ingenious and peculiar . . . [nevertheless] you find certain traces of a talent for composition, which is precisely what the ordinary professor, with all his grammatical and historical accomplishments, utterly lacks. But the conditions of making this talent serviceable are not supplied by the Festival commissions. Far from being a respectable oratorio-manufacturing talent, it is, when it gets loose, eccentric, violent, romantic, patriotic, and held in check only by a mortal fear of being found deficient in what are called 'the manners and tone of good society'. This fear, too, is Irish: it is, possibly, the racial consciousness of having missed that four hundred years of Roman civilisation which gave England a sort of university education when Ireland was in the hedge school.[47]

Disregarding his fixation with Stanford's Mixolydian angels, his national stereotyping and the reappraisal of Celtic civilisation which has since taken place, Shaw viewed Stanford's music as being ingenious, almost perfect, in its execution, but emotionally emasculated by its deliberate self-restraint.

On the pro-Stanford side, his compositional facility has always been a cause of admiration in itself, but recognised as a potential pitfall; the charge of emotional restraint has caused more problems which have proved difficult either to refute or explain. Thomas Dunhill, writing in 1927, gave a slightly diffident but essentially positive view: 'Musicians differ in their estimate of the value of his more extended creations, but they all agree that in the art of fashioning small things with polished grace and exquisite delicacy of touch no other modern British composer can be compared with Stanford.'[48] As a former pupil, one would expect Dunhill to side with Stanford. It is equally unsurprising that both Fuller Maitland and Harry Greene also advocated his cause, given their close friendships with him. Fuller Maitland's critique of Stanford and Parry, published in 1934, is more circumspect than one would expect, although one surmises that he was attempting to remain scrupulously balanced

---

[47] Shaw, *Music in London*, ii, 319–20.
[48] Dunhill, 'Charles Villiers Stanford: Some Aspects of his Work and Influence', 54.

between the two and consciously avoiding comparison.[49] Greene's biography, issued a year later, is, however, heavily biased in favour of its subject. His admiration of Stanford's music is almost unstinting and appears in its most distilled form in his response to Dunhill: 'If [Stanford] had not been a great composer, he would have been the greatest teacher this country has ever known. The whole of our modern school, which probably stands higher than that of any other country at the present moment, is absolutely founded on Stanford.'[50] Herbert Howells also held Stanford in high regard but attempted to assess his master's music impartially:

> There was about him and his music an uncanny, baffling ease. In an epoch of confused idioms, ill-defined styles, full-hearted theorizings and half-hearted loyalties – it had an anachronistic beauty. In his church works and his songs it was touched by genius. To everything he did it gave an untroubled fluency . . . But so often the same elegant, enviable ease seemed to be devoted to some other musical personality than his own. In the large-scale choral and orchestral works Stanford did not always come to terms with himself. The problem of the incompatibilities was never wholly resolved, for the sufficient reason that he himself never recognised them as such. And (it would seem) he was entirely unconcerned over what, to many of us, was his central dilemma.[51]

Howells's use of the word 'anachronistic' is a recognition of Stanford's old-fashioned aesthetics; Vaughan Williams too picked up on the more important point, that of facility:

> He has written some of the most beautiful music that has come from these islands . . . Of course in Stanford's enormous output there is bound to be a certain amount of dull music; but, after all, so there is in Beethoven and Bach. At times his very facility led him astray. He could, at will, use the technique of any composer and often use it better than the original, as in 'The Middle Watch', where he beats Delius at his own game. Sometimes he could not resist adding a clever touch which marred the purity of his inspiration, as in the sophisticated beautiful song 'Sailing at Dawn'.[52]

Frank Howes, in *The English Musical Renaissance* (1966), did not, unlike those cited above, know either Parry or Stanford personally, and this distance led to a greater frankness:

> No doubt Stanford wrote too much. His technical mastery was such that he could, like Haydn, sit down to a daily stint of composition

---

[49] John Fuller Maitland, *The Music of Parry and Stanford* (London, 1934).
[50] Dunhill, 'Stanford', 64.
[51] Howells, 'Stanford', 29.
[52] Vaughan Williams, 'Stanford', 195.

and never a bar of shoddy work in it. But his facility was not all good. It meant that he found the solutions to all problems too easily ... [This] also won him the reproach of being academic. The word ought not to carry a reproach, for it implies both erudition and skill, an approach to the things of the mind that regards them as intrinsically worthwhile for their own sake without ulterior purpose. Stanford caustically dismissed it as 'the latest catch-word for the works of all men who learn their business before they practise it'.[53]

Like previous commentators, however, Howes admired many of Stanford's works, referring to much of his Anglican church music as sounding 'exactly right without qualification' and to *Much Ado about Nothing* as 'delicious'.[54]

The anti-Stanford side comprised mainly those British composers and critics who were out of sympathy with Stanford's evolutionary view of music. For those who wished to progress more quickly than his conservatism allowed he became a *bête noire*, a reactionary whose Canute-like approach to the waves of musical progress could only be condemned.[55] Peter Warlock and Arthur Bliss subscribed to this view (see pp. 361–3), as did Cecil Gray, who believed that Stanford (and Parry) merely provided Britain with 'second-hand Brahms', while their pupils were just pale imitators of various Continental composers (perhaps, therefore, condemning Parry and Stanford as teachers as well as composers).[56] Already indelibly associated with conservatism, Stanford also fell victim to an irony after his death: Edward Dent's summary of Elgar in 1930 ('[Elgar] possessed little of the literary culture of Parry and Stanford ... for English ears Elgar's music is too emotional and not quite free from vulgarity')[57] had the unintended effect of reinforcing the perception: Dent represented the academic world of Cambridge and had been taught by Stanford, *ergo* Dent's opinion of Elgar was really that of Stanford voiced from beyond the grave (Stanford and Elgar's poor relationship being well known). In fact the perception of Stanford as malignant manipulator was, in this case, untrue: evidence shows both that Dent formed his opinion of Elgar without Stanford's help and that

---

[53] Howes, *The English Musical Renaissance*, 151–2.

[54] Ibid., 156 and 157 respectively.

[55] A slightly false analogy, of course, since Canute was trying to demonstrate that it was impossible to hold back the waves.

[56] Cecil Gray, *A Survey of Contemporary Music* (London, 1924), 251.

[57] Originally published in an article entitled 'Modern British Music' in Guido Adler's *Handbuch der Musikgeschichte* (Berlin, 1930), and noticed in Britain soon afterwards, leading to an open letter to the musical press in 1931 (see, for example, *Musical Times*, 1 Apr. 1931, p. 326 (plus discussion on pp. 326–8)) signed by most leading British musicians of the day, including several other former Stanford pupils.

he had not swallowed Stanford's beliefs whole.[58] Post-war perception was affected by the erosion of the RCM's virtual monopoly on composition teaching as university music departments expanded and took up a much more radical approach to composition than that practised at the RCM. For musicologists and composers trying to find explanations for British music's conservatism and adherence to tonality, Stanford and his contemporaries were easy targets. Such modern scepticism is to be found in the works of Peter Pirie and Michael Trend, in both of whose books Stanford is treated summarily.[59] For both men the 'Renaissance' started with Vaughan Williams, Holst, Delius and Elgar; Stanford and his contemporaries are viewed only as precursors. Pirie dismissed Stanford's music as being under a 'very heavy Brahmsian influence'; Trend was less inclined to judge but the stance of both men is clear: Stanford's contribution to music was limited.

With the exceptions of Pirie and Trend, assessments of Stanford published in the last twenty years have chimed more with the measured evaluations of Dunhill and Howells and with the original observations made by Shaw. Is there a truth somewhere between these two perspectives? Not absolutely, but there is an extent to which these opposing views can be reconciled by recognising that Stanford fell victim to his own early success as well as to his own failings and weaknesses, to changing tastes, to the commercial structure of the British musical world, and to his being a member of an establishment, the values of which changed in his lifetime, and the motivations and *raison d'être* of which were questioned by others.

Earlier chapters have shown how quickly, at a relatively young age, Stanford gained a national reputation, with the ensuing expectation that he would produce great things. Elgar personifies the new, brash, and emotionally explicit style which eclipsed him in the late 1890s, and the styles and successes of his pupils demonstrate the further change in taste of both audiences and the establishment. The unusual commercial circumstances facing musicians in Victorian Britain have also been alluded to and played a major part in shaping both Stanford and the British Musical Renaissance which has not been fully acknowledged.

---

[58] Dent's diaries (KCC) show that he did not like *Caractacus* ('a noisy thing', he wrote after hearing the first performance; 5 Oct. 1898) or the 'Enigma' Variations (14 Feb. 1902), for which Stanford professed great enthusiasm. Stanford's dislike of *Gerontius* exposed him to Dent (25 May 1904) but it is evident that Dent had made up his mind about Elgar without Stanford's help. Dent's notorious condemnation of Elgar has been reappraised by Brian Trowell; see 'Elgar's Use of Literature', in Raymond Monk (ed.), *Edward Elgar: Music and Literature* (Aldershot, 1993), 182–326, at 182–90.

[59] Pirie, *The English Musical Renaissance*, and Michael Trend, *The Music Makers* (London, 1985).

Since the strongest pressure was to succeed and the best way to achieve this was to conform and be predictable, the path to success led to the safe side of adventurous. Nigel Burton suggests that Stanford was unlucky to have the role of innovator thrust upon him when his compositional gifts were innately conservative,[60] but he was even more unlucky in being expected to create a distinctive and innovative style in a society so inclined to view cultural pioneering in the same manner as Hobbes's and Disraeli's 'leap in the dark' – as a foresaking of the tried, tested and established for a black unknown, with all the negative ramifications that implies. It is hardly surprising that Stanford, and his contemporaries, found their task almost impossible, as indeed did artists in other genres: in 1885 W. S. Gilbert admitted that 'English plays lacked strong dramatic interest because they had to be written to be morally suitable for a hypothetical fifteen-year-old girl, so easily and unnecessarily alarmed that English plays could contain nothing which might make her blush';[61] Gilbert, it would seem, would have liked to have been more adventurous in his subject matter, but capitulated to public pressure to produce more of the same.

Despite these surroundings, there is no doubt that Stanford was a composer of immense technical accomplishment and of occasional inspiration. Consequently, many pieces, with examples in most genres, are great achievements, and have the power both to move the listener emotionally and to engender admiration of their technical aspects – a highly successful combination of ends and means. The resultant issue which has preoccupied assessments of Stanford is why and how he did not hit the mark more often.

Facility is usually cited as the problem. That Stanford was possessed of a great musical adroitness was recognised by all of his contemporaries: many people have referred to his copious knowledge of music, efficient memory, and how easily he composed. Thomas Dunhill wrote:

> Until practically the end of his life the fresh morning hours of every day were set aside for musical composition. The writing of music thus became a regular habit with him. The result was the acquirement of a technical facility which was not possessed by any of his contemporaries. The ease with which he trampled over all difficulties and rode straight ahead with unhesitating purpose reminds one of Mozart. He scarcely ever made a sketch. Even complicated orchestral works were written straight into the score, in ink, without

---

[60] In Temperley (ed.), *Music in Britain*, 236.

[61] Jane Stedman, *W. S. Gilbert: A Classic Victorian and his Theatre* (Oxford, 1996), 223; Stedman summarises part of a speech Gilbert made at the Dramatic and Musical Sick Fund on 18 February 1885; the full text of his speech was published in *Era*, 21 Feb. 1885, p. 14.

previous preparation. He scarcely ever made an alteration, or needed
to make one.[62]

Faced with a work with such a complex motivic structure as *The
Travelling Companion*, it is difficult to believe that Stanford never made
sketches, but hardly any survive for any work, and the one or two that
do appear to be little more than aide-memoires,[63] suggesting that
Stanford rarely debated with himself which was the best structure to
adopt or method to use – a sign of insufficient self-criticism.

This facility created problems for Stanford of which he was seemingly
unaware. As Vaughan Williams wrote (see p. 404), it led him to be able
to imitate other composers with little difficulty and resulted in a
chameleon-like nature which, whilst admired by many at the time, often
proved, in retrospect, to be his undoing. Hence there are references to
Wagner (*Savonarola* and *The Canterbury Pilgrims*), to Verdi (*Requiem,
Te Deum* and *Stabat Mater*), Brahms (too many to mention), Elgar (the
finale of the Sixth Symphony) and Rachmaninov (the opening of the
Second Piano Concerto) to name but a few. Add to this the multifar-
ious quotations which were worked into his music, and it can become
difficult to find the real Stanford at all. The enduring impact of these
references is a frequent feeling that one could be listening to someone
else's work; in academic assessment which places greatest emphasis on
difference, originality and innovation, Stanford comes out particularly
badly.

This ability to transmogrify, almost at will, extended to nationality
also, for Stanford sounded as Irish in the Irish Rhapsodies as he managed
to sound bluffly English in *The Revenge* or *Songs of the Sea*, to say
nothing of catching the German, Italian and Russian spirits alluded to
above, or the pillorying of composers in the *Ode to Discord* and the
settings of Edward's Lear's *Nonsense Rhymes*. And it is this facility –
that which Shaw referred to as the 'Irish professor trifling in a world of
ideas'[64] – coupled, frankly, with a lesser degree of genius, which led to
some emasculation of his style, whilst composers equally imbued with
their own national traditions (Dvořák, Verdi) and, in some cases, lacking
Stanford's natural facility (Tchaikovsky, Elgar) became highly individual
and easily recognisable composers.

---

[62] Dunhill, 'Stanford', 45.

[63] See, for example, the sketch of the 1893 Prelude to *The Veiled Prophet*, RCM MS
4164. The statement that Stanford wrote straight into score is correct, as there are surviving
examples of pieces abandoned part-way through a fair copy (see the 'Benedictus' from the
Mass in G, Op. 46, BL MS Loan 69/14 and the first attempt at an overture to *The Veiled
Prophet*, RCM MS 4164).

[64] Shaw, *Music in London*, ii, 319.

Furthermore, Stanford's use of his facility was influenced by the nature of his own education. His music was most strongly indebted to Germany because it was this music which was cited, to the young Stanford, as the greatest modern achievement. British musical society expected its composers to emulate the German models – in oratorio by looking to the *Messiah* and *Elijah*; in cantata to such works as *Die Erste Walpurgis-nacht*; in song by looking to Schubert, Schumann and, later on, to Brahms. In Dublin, Stanford was reared on Bach, Beethoven, Mendels-sohn and Chopin at the keyboard and in the concert hall, and on Donizetti, Verdi, Meyerbeer, Gounod and Bellini in the opera house – and his general lack of respect at this stage for the Italian and French composers led him to face firmly towards Germany. In subsequent years his musical education remained geared to the Teutonic mode, and was especially reinforced by the three years he spent in Leipzig and Berlin. The affinity felt by British commentators with German culture (see pp. 368–9) and the desire to rid Britain of the image, if not the tag, of 'das Land ohne Musik', further emphasised the primacy of the German product and the advantages of a German education.

For German composers such an education caused few difficulties: they were expected to develop and further the tradition which they inherited. This motivated Wagner, Strauss and Schoenberg, leading the latter to proclaim that serialism was designed to 'ensure the supremacy of German music for the next hundred years'.[65] For those nations trying to develop their own distinct styles, however, such education could cause difficulties. The problems faced by Stanford are the same as those confronted by such composers as Grieg and Tchaikovsky (the latter being by far the best educated of his contemporaries, tutored by Rubinstein in the German school, but often criticised by 'the Five' for being overly reliant on Western forms and modes of expression).[66] But while in Russia Tchaikovsky and his contemporaries debated and questioned the value of the German tradition (though with variable results), Stanford and his British contemporaries became so firmly wedded to it that they often failed to keep it in its place. The British desire for German approval (see p. 368), at least up until 1914, led to an over-dependence on its values and traditions. In Stanford's case specifically his facility was largely to blame; because comprehension and the ability to emulate came easily

---

[65] Quoted in Hans Stuckenschmidt, *Schoenberg* (Zurich, 1974), 252; it is possible, however, that Schoenberg was being sardonic when he made this comment. Schoenberg's devotion to the Teutonic tradition of composition, is however, undoubted.

[66] This perception of Russian music comprising two composing schools, one of which was 'more Russian' than the other, has been challenged in more recent years. For exten-sive discussion and debate see, for example, Richard Taruskin, *Defining Russia Musically* (Princeton, 1997).

to him it was natural that the Teutonic musical mores held up to him since childhood should have become a central part of his compositional ethos, especially in a man conditioned to work for change from within rather than by discarding rules and values wholesale.

Ultimately, therefore, it was Stanford's facility which lay at the bottom of this problem of expression: his skill as a mimic outstripped his originality. It is tempting to speculate what would have happened to him had he not been endowed with such a broad musical education – perhaps, had he been musically isolated, or self-taught, his facility might have led him to compose well but without carrying all the baggage which his family and social background laid upon him and he might have produced works of far greater individuality. It is ironic that, having been hampered by his own broad education, he then advocated the same experience for his students and for all musicians, and that he became a pedagogue who impressed the importance of a secure technique upon his pupils. It is equally important to recognise, however, that he believed passionately in this breadth of education and did not view it as a problem or a possible cause of his 'weakness' – he was therefore not just a victim of his circumstances.

Then there is the question of emotional sterility. Bernard Shaw summed up the problem for Stanford in his comments on *The Revenge*:

> I do not say that Mr Stanford could not set Tennyson's ballad as well as he set Browning's *Cavalier Songs*, if only he did not feel that, as a professional man with a certain position to keep up, it would be bad form to make a public display of the savage emotions called up by the poem. But as it is, Mr Stanford is far too much the gentleman to compose anything but drawing-room or classroom music. There are moments here and there in *The Revenge* during which one feels that a conductor of the lower orders, capable of swearing at the choir, might have got a brief rise out of them; and I will even admit that the alternating chords for the trombones which depict the sullen rocking of the huge Spanish ship do for an instant bring the scene before you; but the rest, as the mad gentleman said to Mrs Nickleby, is gas and gaiters. It is a pity; for Mr Stanford is one of the few professors who ever had any talent to lose.[67]

Shaw was constantly frustrated by what he saw as Stanford's gentlemanly nature, which he sometimes castigated as academicism. But in essence he was recasting his point about Stanford suffering from national schizophrenia; just as Stanford could write real Irish music if he shrugged off the burden of his education, so he could compose heartfelt music if only he cast aside Victorian respectability.

[67] Shaw, *London Music as Heard in 1888–89*, 395–6.

There is a lot to be said for Shaw's case, for one can see many instances in Stanford's music when emotional expression is strong; works such as the *Irish Rhapsody No. 4* and parts of *The Travelling Companion* contain directly emotive language, whilst parts of the *Stabat Mater*, *Songs of the Sea* and *Songs of the Fleet* show that he was also capable of overt theatricality, both of which move his music beyond stereotypical Victorian reticence. Stanford could foresake the 'drawing room' but did not do so often enough, whilst his vast output makes it appear that such excursions were unusual; if he had managed to bring the same degree of intense expression manifested in some of his letters, his music might be pungent indeed. Herbert Howells argued (see p. 404) that Stanford's failure in this area arose from his own inability to see it as a problem. Howells's opinion seems naive, however, as it invites one to conclude that this commonly perceived weakness in Stanford's music was not a weakness of his at all, but rather a failing of the consumer. It does, however, provide an explanation for why Stanford himself did not appear to consider this a problem; Howells implied that Stanford would never have accepted Shaw's hypothesis of the Celt and the Professor.

One should not, however, give the impression that Stanford was merely a victim of circumstances. Not only was he a product of Victorian society, with all its restrictive mores, but he believed in its values and was a pillar of its establishment. His own conservatism was reinforced by being placed in the position of pedagogue, since he had continuously to invent rules and maxims to pass on to his students. Stanford's view of aesthetics did, therefore, become as George Dyson noted, a question of absolute truth, with the denial of truth being heresy.[68] Again on the opposing side are Peter Warlock and Peter Pirie. For the latter, Stanford's view of truth was medieval; 'that any body of doctrine could be only half true, or that facts are in constant flux, is incompatible with it',[69] whilst Warlock argued that 'the theory of a finite and absolute standard of beauty is the supreme obstacle to the progress of musical evolution. Every standard of beauty must necessarily lie in the taste of the individual.'[70] For Stephen Banfield this is the nub of Stanford's problem; Banfield argues that Stanford was, like Saint-Saëns,

> [trying] to maintain a moderate, mainstream approach to compositional technique in the late-Romantic period when there was no longer any mainstream to follow. Neither [man] was prepared to

---

[68] Dyson, 'Stanford', 45.

[69] Pirie, *The English Musical Renaissance*, 38.

[70] Peter Warlock (writing under his real name, Philip Heseltine), 'Some Reflections on Modern Musical Criticism', *Musical Times*, 1 Oct. 1913, pp. 652–4 at 653.

identify with a particular school, and both ended up with a curiously
emasculated style that contrasted painfully with a sometimes venom-
ous intellectual sharpness. In Stanford at least there is a pervasive
lack of focus that often overrides the positive qualities.[71]

This view, that European music in the late nineteenth century dealt
with a multiplicity of truths, all evolving and mutating, is now accepted,
but for Stanford the possibility of many truths was an anathema. Again
he faced, with his colleagues, the problem of Victorian society and its
attitude to musicians. In their aspiration to make music a respectable
profession Stanford saw that this could be achieved by endowing it with
the same value systems as those of other disciplines; his writings, like
those of many others, contain frequent allusions to other artistic genres,
especially painting and architecture, both of which were held in high
regard in Victorian society.[72] Science was also a model to which to aspire
and, as it then comprised a search for the discovery of absolute truths,
so musical composition had also to be based on a similar concept. For
Stanford, therefore, an octave had to be as inherently perfect and certain
as Newton's falling apple, for thus was respectability obtained.

While one may admire Stanford's attempts to create a respectable
profession, his belief in respectable music brought problems. For him it
was a means of avoiding corruption and immorality and, he argued, he
had history on his side:

> The regulators of [the composer's] work are a pure taste and a deep
> sense of nobility. Folk-songs are a treasure house of both. The simple
> soul of the people from which they spring is often richer in both
> these qualities than many accomplished and versatile composers give
> it credit for. There is no young writer, however gifted, who can

---

[71] Banfield, *Sensibility and English Song*, i, 32. Eugene Goossens had made a similar
comparison between Stanford and Saint-Saëns, together with Glazounov, although he
expressed it in more positive terms: 'Both Glazounov and Saint-Saëns were contemporaries whose musical make-up was practically identical. Both were prolific, academic,
resourceful, and often inspired. But now they are both undeservedly neglected by conductors, and underestimated by the concert-going public. Their creative fertility stemmed from
real genius, but I think that their chief claim to fame lies in their fine craftsmanship. Both
were cunning workmen. Saint-Saëns, economical of means and simple of expression;
Glazounov wallowing in the luxuriance of an exotic but always well-controlled range of
colour. Charles Villiers Stanford was their English counterpart, a fact which accounts for
his constant references to both composers in his composition classes, and his obvious
intense delight in performing their music, for Stanford combined both the orderliness of
Saint-Saëns and the romanticism of Glazounov. His music, little played nowadays, is a
disciplined product of both qualities' (see Goossens, *Overtures and Beginners*, 80).
[72] For extensive discussion of the use of comparison and analogy in nineteenth-century
music criticism see Bennett Zon, *Music and Metaphor in Nineteenth-Century British
Musicology* (Aldershot, 2000).

afford to ignore the lesson which they teach. They make for simplicity, for beauty, and for sincerity; and no composer who has grounded his early tastes upon them will lightly play with the fire of sensuality or vulgarity against which they are a standing protest. It is the old fight between idealism and materialism; and when music ceases to be ideal, it will abrogate its chief duty, the refinement and elevation of public taste.[73]

Leaving aside the doubtful assertion of the purity and nobility of folksong, and morally uplifting though Stanford's argument might be, his attitude is realised in his own music by an inability to deal with passion, and it is this lack which undermines many of his pieces. Anger, *joie de vivre*, nobility, chaste love, nostalgia, sorrow, conviction and sentiment are all emotions which Stanford could evoke and many pieces which require these are successful. Passionate love, however, was beyond his ken, or beyond his belief of music's purpose; in praising Humperdinck, he wrote that he had taken on 'the best in Wagner; the Wagner that knew and appreciated Palestrina, that laid his foundation upon folksong, the Wagner of the *Siegfried Idyll*, of the *Meistersinger*, and of *Parsifal*, not the Wagner of *unbridled excitement and sensuality*' [my italics].[74] This attitude would not have been a problem had it not been for three qualifiers. First, Stanford did not avoid the subject of sensual passion, especially in many songs and operas, many of which carry at least such undertones in their texts and scenarios, and his failure to engage with this level leaves much music appearing pathetic at best and sterile at worst. Secondly, this would not have been a problem had Stanford deliberately put himself forward as a composer of light music, which did not require this intensity of expression, and for which he had an undoubted genius. For Stanford, however, this was not an option: he wanted either to go head to head with or to be a successor to Sullivan, precisely because Sullivan was openly known to aspire to 'greater' things than the Savoy Operas. Furthermore, Stanford's desire to educate and ennoble the masses would not be satisfied by composing popular potboilers, even if they brought mass popularity and wealth. Thirdly, and most seriously, Stanford allowed his eschewal of sensual passion too often to spill over into lack of passion generally, for what one misses most often (but still inconsistently) in his music is intensity of expression. Again one must also conclude that he was unfortunate to live when such intensity became an ever more overt aspect of music; Stanford's purity sits uncomfortably with the works of Strauss, Tchaikovsky, Wagner and Brahms, all of whom either met the question

---

[73] Stanford, *Musical Composition*, 187.
[74] Stanford, 'Music and the War', 400.

of sensuality head-on and encouraged its portrayal and/or whose 'absolute' music always retains a sense of emotional conviction. An interesting comparison can be made between Stanford and Bruckner, whose naivety also led to a chaste mode of expression; Bruckner, however, managed to imbue his music with a sense of conviction while remaining pure and chaste. Similarly with the music of Sibelius, a passion exists within a soundworld which appears to exclude human presence. If one accepts Stanford's position – that of the desirability of not parading sensual emotions in music – as being acceptable, then one must conclude that his failures were not to realise that this value placed limits on what he could achieve and to allow the restraint to spread too far. He often showed poor judgement in choosing subjects with which to deal, his undoing on many occasions. This failure was his biggest handicap as a composer. In fairness to Stanford, however, it has to be acknowledged that changing tastes among listeners play a major part in determining fortunes: in the same time that Stanford's reputation has declined, so Bruckner's has risen – their music, of course, has stayed the same throughout.

The two most recent studies which deal with Stanford's music in any detail (Nicholas Temperley's edited volume *Music in Britain 1800–1914* and Stephen Banfield on English song) both acknowledge this sense of respectability.[75] The former work does not judge Stanford's overall legacy to music, but the writers[76] come to a generally consistent position on his gifts and support the concepts of great but conservative technical facility and emotional restraint. Nicholas Temperley reaches a particularly interesting conclusion as regards Stanford's church music, which underlines Shaw's frustrations with Stanford's self-control:

> The result [of listening to the Service in B flat], as most often with Stanford, is a thoroughly satisfying artistic experience, but one that is perhaps lacking in deeply felt religious impulse. Never does he, like [Samuel Sebastian] Wesley, cast aside all principles of musical structure to respond directly to the imperative demands of the text. And this, in religious music, makes him the lesser man of the two.[77]

In Temperley's argument one can see a parallel with Stanford's difficulty with sensuality: in both instances what is wanted is more passion, albeit of different types. Despite this shortcoming Temperley writes that 'it is

---

[75] See Temperley, *Music in Britain*, and Banfield, *Sensibility and English Song* respectively.

[76] Nigel Burton on oratorio, cantata and opera, Michael Hurd on part-song, Geoffrey Bush on solo song and chamber music, Percy Young on orchestral music and John Parry on piano music.

[77] Temperley, *Music in Britain*, 205.

especially due to Stanford that the service setting regained its full place beside the anthem as a worthy object of artistic invention',[78] thus praising Stanford's success in contributing to and furthering the Anglican Choral Revival. Again one stands on dichotomies: first, one could wish for a lesser sense of propriety in Stanford's music, yet it is this very quality which aided the acceptance and promotion of much of his music, especially in the Anglican Church; secondly there is the irony that Stanford is praised for fully imposing the coherence of formal thematic and recapitulatory structures on an Anglican ethos still founded on pre-Baroque episodic form, but that the vehicle by which he achieved this was a German classical model, diluting rather than concentrating the distinctiveness of British music.

The battle which Shaw identified, therefore, between emotion and respectability, or, less accurately, between 'Stanford the Celt' and 'Stanford the Professor', did indeed form the essential problem for 'Stanford the Composer'. If one accepts Herbert Howells's argument, this dichotomy was never faced by Stanford because he did not acknowledge it, but it is a problem to which most commentators have referred and Howells's answer is unsatisfactory. There has been a tendency to marry facility with shallowness in previous appraisals but the two issues are separate. Stanford's facility did most definitely prove his undoing on several occasions, first because of the tendency subconsciously to ape the styles of other composers whom he admired, but more often because he does not appear to have been sufficiently self-critical in reviewing his own work. That some of his prolixity is attributable to financial pressure is undoubted, as it is also true that some uninspired music resulted from the pressure of deadlines. On several occasions one feels that he fell victim to the poverty of invention for which he often berated his pupils but that he did not recognise the failing in his own work. His extreme sensitivity to criticism did not help in this since it inclined friends not to pass judgement on his music when moderating appraisals would have been beneficial. Gordon Jacob suggested that Stanford was overly conscious of 'the weight on his shoulders of the great Masters and what they would approve of and all that sort of thing, so much, that it rather inhibited him from expressing himself as freely as he might',[79] but, although Stanford was certainly conscious of tradition, his own writing makes it clear that he believed in a sense of restraint and this became the biggest problem – substitute the words 'the public and his fellow musicians' for the words 'the Great Masters' and Jacob's statement

---

[78] Ibid., 204.
[79] Gordon Jacob in conversation on RTE Radio Broadcast 'Every Inch an Irishman', 4 Oct. 1974.

becomes, in essence, the same as Shaw's. He chose deliberately to eschew the portrayal of some emotions, and to limit the intensity of expression of others; the extent of this considered language is especially emphasised by the music composed by his late Romantic contemporaries. Certainly Stanford's music is not devoid of emotion: he could 'do' fun, wit, pomp, solemnity and serenity with few problems. Anger and struggle came with greater difficulty although there are examples when a real ferocity does come to bear. The real gap in his emotional language is that of love and romance and, specifically, sex and sensuality. This had been picked up by Grove as early as 1884 when he had noted to Parry that *The Canterbury Pilgrims* contained 'everything but sentiment. Love not at all – that I heard not a grain of'.[80] In pieces in which love is not a motivating factor, such as *Songs of the Sea*, *The Revenge*, and much of the church music, this lack is not a particular weakness, but in many other pieces this inability or unwillingness to convey a sense of passion is a real handicap since its lack often renders the music pointless. Although this prudery chimed with the prevalent upper middle-class Victorian morality (one cannot resist that quintessential cliché of Englishness, 'the stiff upper lip'), it was clearly at odds with the ethos followed by many late nineteenth-century composers. Such a restrained emotional framework explains the sterility of such works as *Savonarola*, *Die Wallfahrt nach Kevlaar* and *The Triumph of Love*, whilst the chaste situations of *Much Ado about Nothing*, *The Travelling Companion* and the song 'Grandeur' are conversely successful. In line with this Victorian mode of expression is the sentimentality into which Stanford often falls, especially in his Irish songs, where bathos creeps in with the aid of nostalgic poetry. But, despite this self-imposed restriction on expression, Stanford left a substantial amount of beautiful, touching and well-wrought music, for which he has rarely gained due credit. For, while such works as the Mass in G, Fifth, Sixth and Seventh Symphonies, *Stabat Mater* and Nonet, to name but a few, may not show evidence of radical innovation or have changed the course of Western art music, they are still rewarding to hear and great in accomplishment.

What is Stanford's legacy? He was in some respects a brilliant composer, but in terms of his overal output, only occasionally was he brilliant enough. Many pieces are outstanding in every respect; many more, if one is not looking for subversive originality, are enticing and enjoyable; finally there is a swathe of lesser works which none of his technical ability could save from dullness. Despite this he achieved success in most genres; dealing with music composed after 1878, he maintained the most consistent high standard in his works for church

---

[80] Grove to Parry, 30 Apr. 1884, ShP.

and for orchestra, and the most consistent low standard in his chamber music. His achievement is most erratic in opera, with 'festival' choral music coming next – in both genres one sees the masterly (*The Travelling Companion*, *Songs of the Sea* and the *Stabat Mater*) and the dirge-like (*Savonarola* and the *Ode to Wellington*). In retrospect it is evident that Stanford's fixation with Shaw's 'manner and tone of good society' did the most harm; he had a gift for lighter music (seen, for example, in *Shamus O'Brien* and *Songs of the Sea*), but he failed to exploit it extensively, concentrating instead on grand statements which only matched worthiness with power or profundity occasionally. Like Parry, Stanford felt that this was not the area in which the true British tradition would be built – Britain had to achieve success in the 'serious' genres if it was to compete with its continental neighbours.[81] Here Stanford achieved much, both in terms of teaching and composing, and if he did not achieve as much as he deserved or we would like, it has to be acknowledged that this is due, in about equal proportions, to his own limitations and those of the society around him. Nevertheless, he made a substantial contribution to his profession and his art, being a leading light in and greatly raising the status of the former, and adding a substantial number of first-rate works to the latter. He gained a national reputation and international recognition in unpropitious circumstances due entirely to his own abilities and hard work. Pre-War British music would have been much worse off had he not existed, for, with other contemporaries, he showed that Britain was very much a Land *with* Music, and, for that, his successors owe him a debt of gratitude.

---

[81] This belief contains a measure of truth as well as snobbery – successful works in the 'serious' genres have tended to achieve a longer shelf-life than successful lighter works, where turnover and the thirst for novelty are always greater.

APPENDIX ONE

Select List of Works

The following list of works is not exhaustive but includes all works mentioned in the main body of the text plus many others. Stanford composed prolifically and frequently wrote and published short works and arrangements in order to raise money. Consequently, many of these smaller works, plus extracts he drew from larger works, are not listed; Stanford's extensive output of arrangements of folksongs, mainly Irish, are also omitted, with the principal exception of the major collections he published. In order to gain a sense of chronology the works are listed in order of opus number; works without opus numbers are integrated at appropriate points where the date of composition is known. Stanford obligingly dated most of his manuscripts and many published works have the completion date engraved below the final double bar; where none of this information has been given, and when the date of publication is posthumous, the relevant work has been listed at the end of this Appendix. The original publisher is given; in some cases works have been reissued by other companies in later years.

Appendix One: Select List of Works

Opus	Title	MS and date	Publication	Performance
—	March	—; ?1860	Musical Times, 1 Jan. 1898, pp. 785–93	1863? Dublin (Theatre Royal), Puss in Boots Pantomime
—	Once more my love (text: ?)	—; composed ?1863		16 Nov. 1863, Dublin (Philharmonic Society)
—	When green leaves come again (text: ?)	—; composed ?1864		Sept. 1864, Dublin (Exhibition Choir)
—	A Venetian Dirge ('We bear her home'; Barry Cornwall)	—; ?1864	Gunn & Son, Dublin	6 June 1864, Dublin (2 Herbert Street, private recital)
—	Heroes and chieftains brave (text: ?)	—; composed ?1867		15 Feb. 1867, Dublin (Choral Society)
—	Rondo for Cello and Orchestra in F	MA, MS MA 193, 17 Aug. 1869		
—	Concert Overture	—; completed 30 July 1870		
—	The IOUX Indians	—		Christmas 1870, Limerick (Bishop's Palace) (see Pages from an Unwritten Diary, 117–19)
—	Incidental music to The Spanish Student (Longfellow)	RCM 4143, 16 Sept. 1871		
—	Magnificat and Nunc Dimittis in F ('Queens' Service')	FWC, 20 Dec. 1872	Stainer & Bell	5 May 1877, Cambridge (Trinity College) (earliest traced record)
1	Eight Songs from The Spanish Gypsy (George Eliot) 1. Blue wings; 2. Day is dying; 3. Sweet springtime; 4. Spring comes hither; 5. Came a pretty	—; composed 1872/4	Novello (nos 1–3), Chappell (nos 4–8)	22 May 1872, Cambridge (CUMS) (No. 4 only); 18 May 1875, Cambridge (CUMS) (No. 8 only); 19 May 1876, Cambridge (CUMS) (No. 1 only)

maid; 6. The world is great; 7. Bright, o bright Fedalma; 8. The radiant dark

2	Suite for Piano Solo	—	Chappell	
3	Toccata for Piano Solo	—	Chappell	
—	Concerto for Piano and Orchestra in B♭	NUL 78, 11 Jan. 1873		3 June 1874, Cambridge (CUMS)
—	Magnificat and Nunc Dimittis in E♭	FWC, Mu MS 1006, 15 Nov. 1873		
—	Pater noster (8-voice setting of The Lord's Prayer)	NUL 79, 28 Aug. 1874		
4	Six Songs (Heine) 1. Sterne mit goldner Füschen 2. Mit deinen blauen Augen; 3. Dass du mich liebst; 4. Frühling; 5. Ernst ist der Frühling; 6. Der Schmetterling ist in die Rose verliebt	RCM 4339, 25 Sept. 1874 [No. 1]	Stanley Lucas, Weber & Co.	
5	The Resurrection (Klopstock)	RCM 4140, 21 Sept. 1874 (rescored 25 Oct. 1876)	Chappell	21 May 1875, Cambridge (CUMS)
—	Two Novelettes for Piano Solo	NUL 80, 30 Oct. 1874		
—	In memoria aeterna erit Justus	TCC, R.2.68a, 4 Nov. 1874		
—	Piano Trio in G	—; composed ?1874/75		4 Mar. 1875, Cambridge (CUMS);
—	The Golden Legend (Longfellow)	RCM 4145, 29 Jan. 1875 [part 1 only; remainder either not composed or lost]		8 Nov. 1878, Cambridge (CUMS)

Appendix One: Select List of Works

Opus	Title	MS and date	Publication	Performance
—	Concerto for Violin and Orchestra	NUL 81, 2 Sept. 1875		
6	Incidental music to Queen Mary	RCM 4139, 31 Jan. 1876	Stanley Lucas, Weber & Co.	18 Apr. 1876, London (Lyceum Theatre)
—	First Symphony in B♭	MA, MS MA 193.7, dated 'Cambridge, 1876'		8 Mar. 1879, London (Crystal Palace)
7	Six Songs (Heine) 1. Ich lieb' eine Blume; 2. Wie des Mondes; 3. An die blaue Himmelsdecke; 4. Der sterbende Almansor; 5. Ich halte ihr die Augen zu; 6. Schlummerlied	—	Stanley Lucas, Weber & Co.	24 May 1877, Cambridge (CUMS) (No. 6 only; earliest traced)
—	The Lord is my Shepherd	—; 1876	Novello	22 May 1877, Cambridge (CUMS);
8	God is our hope and strength (Ps. 46)	27 Nov. 1875	Novello	6 June 1881, London (St James's Hall, cond. Richter)
(9)	Six Waltzes for Piano Solo/ Fantasia Waltzes for Piano Duet	NUL 1, 27 Feb. 1876 (solo version); NUL 2, 28 Feb. 1876 (duet version)		21 Feb. 1879, Cambridge (CUMS) (duet version; Stanford and Fuller Maitland)
—	Prelude on the Ancient Melody 'Jesu dulcis memoriae' for Organ	TCC, R.2.68b, 19 Nov. 1876		
—	In memoria aeterna erit justus (second setting)	TCC, R.2.68c, 25 Nov. 1876		
—	Festival Overture	—		6 Sept. 1877, Gloucester; 17 Nov. 1877, Crystal Palace

No.	Title	Publisher	MS / Publication	First performance
—	Serenade for Piano Duet		—	7 Mar. 1877, Cambridge (CUMS) (Andante and Scherzo)
9	Cello Sonata in A Major	Bote & Bock	NLI MS 14091, 20 Apr. 1877	2 Oct. 1878, Vienna; 26 Mar. 1879, Cambridge (Stanford and Hausmann)
—	La Belle Dame sans Merci (Keats)	Stainer & Bell	—	30 Oct. 1877, Cambridge (CUMS) (earliest traced)
10	Service in B♭	Novello	—	Te Deum and Jubilate 25 May 1879; Kyrie, Gloria, Credo 10 Aug. 1879; Benedictus, Magnificat, Nunc Dimittis 24 Aug. 1879; all Cambridge (Trinity College)
—	The Veiled Prophet of Khorassan (Barclay Squire, after Thomas Moore)	Boosey	RCM 4164, 30 July 1878 (Act II), 8 Feb. 1879 (Act III) (revisions at BL Loan 84/38)	6 Feb. 1881, Hannover (Hoftheater, conducted Ernst Frank)
—	Three Ditties of the Olden Time 1. Out upon it (John Suckling) 2. Why so pale? (John Suckling) 3. To Carnations (Herrick)	Stanley Lucas, Weber & Co.	— (but published edition acquired by BL in July 1878)	
—	Concerto for Cello and Orchestra		NUL 82, 20 Oct. 1879 (version for cello and piano), NUL 83, 29 Aug. 1880 (full score)	13 Mar. 1884, Cambridge (CUMS) (slow movement only)
11	Violin Sonata in D Major	Ries & Erler, Berlin	—	24 May 1877, Cambridge (CUMS)
12	Service in A	Novello	—; Magnificat and Nunc Dimittis, 16 Feb. 1880; remainder delivered to Novello & Co., 27 Sept. 1894	

Appendix One: Select List of Works

Opus	Title	MS and date	Publication	Performance
—	Second Symphony in D Minor ('Elegiac')	NLI 14092, and Pendlebury Library, Cambridge (MS 42) (copy), 7 Aug. 1879, rev. Jan. 1882		7 Mar. 1882, Cambridge (CUMS)
13	Three Intermezzi for Clarinet and Piano	NUL 4a, 9 Dec. 1879	Novello	18 Feb. 1880, Cambridge (CUMS) (Stanford and Frank Galpin)
14	Six Songs 1. Requiescat (Matthew Arnold) 2. Ode to the Skylark (Shelley); 3. Sweeter than the Violet (Andrew Lang); 4. There be none of beauty's daughters (Byron); 5. Tragödie (Heine); 6. Le bien vient en dormant (Old French)	—; composed between 1873 and July 1881	Boosey	15 Nov. 1882, Cambridge (CUMS) (no. 1)
15	Piano Quartet in F	—; completed Apr. 1879	Bote & Bock	26 May 1880, Cambridge (CUMS)
16	Awake my heart (Klopstock)	—; completed Aug. 1881	Boosey	3 Nov. 1881, London, St Paul's, Church Choir Association; 2 Dec. 1882 Cambridge (CUMS)
17	Three Cavalier Songs (Browning) 1. Marching along; 2. King Charles 3. Boot, saddle, to horse and away	BL Loan 84/48 (later orchestral version)	Boosey	30 Nov. 1881, Cambridge (CUMS); 22 Mar. 1882, Cambridge (CUMS)
18	Serenade in G	NLI 14093, 11 Sept. 1881	Novello (arranged for piano duet)	30 Aug. 1882, Birmingham Festival

No.	Work	Manuscript	Publisher	First performance(s)
—	If Ye then be risen with Christ	—; ?1883		— ?, London
19	Six Songs 1. In Praise of Neptune (Campion); 2. Lullaby (Dekker); 3. To the rose (Herrick); 4. Come to me (Pollock); 5. Boat Song (Pollock); 6. The Rhine Wine (Pollock)	—	Boosey	25 Oct. 1882, Cambridge (CUMS) (no. 2)
—	Songs of Old Ireland (traditional Irish melodies arranged by Stanford with words by A. P. Graves)	—	Boosey	
20	Piano Sonata in D♭	RCM 4160 and 4161, 8 Mar. 1883		4 Feb. 1884, London (St James's Hall)
—	Savonarola (Gilbert A'Beckett)		Vocal score only, privately by G. P. Röder	18 Apr. 1884, Hamburg (Stadttheater)
—	The Canterbury Pilgrims (Gilbert A'Beckett)	RCM 4232, 2 Dec. 1883	Boosey (vocal score)	28 Apr. 1884, London (Drury Lane)
21	Elegiac Ode (Walt Whitman)	BL Loan 84/26	Boosey	15 Oct. 1884, Norwich Festival
—	Prospice (Browning)	—	Stanley Lucas, Weber & Co.	
22	The Three Holy Children	RCM 4162, 10 Feb. 1885	Stanley Lucas, Weber & Co.	28 Aug. 1885, Birmingham Festival (cond. Richter)
23	Incidental music to Aeschylus's Eumenides	FWC, Mus MS 693, May 1885	Stainer & Bell	1 Dec. 1885, Cambridge (Greek Play Committee); 17 May 1886, London (concert performance, cond. Richter)
24	The Revenge (Tennyson)	BL Add 41462	Novello	14 Oct. 1886, Leeds Festival
—	Blessed are the dead	—	Novello (*Musical Times*, 1 Aug. 1886, pp. 469–71)	15 Feb. 1886, Cambridge (funeral of Henry Bradshaw, Cambridge University Librarian)

Appendix One: Select List of Works

Opus	Title	MS and date	Publication	Performance
—	The Tomb	—; ?1886	Andrew, Guildford	
25	Piano Quintet in D Minor	NUL 6 (undated; completed ?Feb. 1886)	Novello	10 June 1886, Cambridge (CUMS)
26	Carmen saeculare (Tennyson)	NUL MS 7, 4 Feb. 1887	Novello	11 May 1887, Buckingham Palace
27	Praise ye the Lord (Ps. 150)	—	Forsyth Brothers	3 Mar. 1887, Manchester Exhibition
28	Third Symphony in F Minor ('Irish')	BL Add 60495, 30 Apr. 1887	Novello (full score, parts, and arranged for piano duet)	27 May 1887, London (St James's Hall, cond. Richter)
29	Oedipus Rex	Full score unknown; orchestral parts at FWC, Mu MS 693A	Novello	22 Nov. 1887, Cambridge, Theatre Royal (Greek Play Committee)
30	A Child's Garland of Songs (Robert Louis Stevenson) 1. Bed in Summer; 2. Pirate Story; 3. Foreign Lands; 4. Windy Nights; 5. Where go the Boats?; 6. My Shadow; 7. Marching Song; 8. Foreign Children; 9. My ship and Me	—	Curwen	
—	The Miner of Falun (Barclay Squire and H. F. Wilson, after E. T. A. Hoffmann)	RCM 4156, 26 Mar. 1888 (Act I only)		
—	Carmen familiare (Verrall)	—	MacMillan & Bowes (Cambridge)	7 June 1888, Cambridge, Trinity College ('Smoking Concert')
31	Fourth Symphony in F	NLI 14094, 31 July 1888	Novello (piano duet arrangement)	14 Jan. 1889, Berlin; 23 Feb. 1889, London (Crystal Palace)

No.	Work	Source	Publisher	First performance
32	Violin Suite	—	Novello (violin and piano arrangement)	14 Jan. 1889, Berlin
—	I heard a voice from Heaven	—; 1889	Novello	
33	Six Partsongs			
34	The Voyage of Maeldune (Tennyson)	RCM 4157, 1 May 1889	Novello	11 Oct. 1889, Leeds Festival
35	Piano Trio in E♭	NUL 8, 17 June 1889	Novello	16 Jan. 1890, London (Dannreuther Concert); 5 Mar. 1890, Cambridge (CUMS)
36	Service in F	—	Novello	
37	Two Anthems 1. And I saw another angel; 2. If thou shalt confess with thy mouth	—	Novello	
38	Three Motets 1. Justorum animae; 2. Beati quorum via; 3. Coelos ascendit hodie	—	Boosey	24 Jan. 1888, Cambridge (Trinity College) (Justorum animae); 1 Feb. 1890, Cambridge (Trinity College) (entry in College music lists for Beati omnes, but no work of this name survives)
—	Overture 'Queen of the Sea'	—; 1888, written to commemorate the Tercentenary of the Spanish Armada		
39	Cello Sonata in D Minor	NUL 9a, 19 Sept. 1889	Simrock	18 Nov. 1889, London (St James's Hall), Stanford and Piatti
—	Blarney Ballads (C. L. Graves) 1. The Grand Ould Man; 2. The March of the Man of Hawarden; 3. The Wearing of the Blue	—	Boosey	

Appendix One: Select List of Works

Opus	Title	MS and date	Publication	Performance
40	Eden (Robert Bridges)	RCM 4163, 1 Dec. 1890	Novello	7 Oct. 1891, Birmingham Festival
41	The Battle of the Baltic (Thomas Campbell)	RCM 4141, 11 Jan. 1891	Novello	20 July 1891, London (St James's Hall, cond. Richter); 8 Sept. 1891, Hereford Festival
—	Installation Ode	CUMS Orchestral Library, Pendlebury Music Library, Cambridge; autograph vocal score NUL 87		
42	Six Pieces for Piano Solo	NUL 10, 6 May 1894 (nos 4–6 only; nos 1–3 lost)		
43	Three Songs (Robert Bridges) 1. Since thou, o fondest and truest; 2. I praise the tender flower; 3. Say, o say!	—	Augener	
—	For ever mine (text: H. Boulton)	—; 1891	In Sir H. E. Boulton, Twelve New Songs, Leadenhall Press	
44	First String Quartet in G Major	NUL 11, 22 Aug. 1891	Eulenberg	22 Jan. 1892, Newcastle upon Tyne (Chamber Music Society)
45	Second String Quartet in A minor	NUL 12, 25 Sept. 1891	Eulenberg	13 Feb. 1894, London (Princes Hall)
46	Mass in G	BL Loan 69/14, 22 Oct. 1892	Novello	26 May 1893, London (Brompton Oratory)

46a	Service in G (arrangement in English of preceding)	—	Novello	
—	Tom Lemmin (text: Arthur Quiller Couch)	? 1893		
47	Four Partsongs 1. Soft, soft wind (Kingsley); 2. Sing heigh ho! (Kingsley); 3. Airly Beacon (Kingsley); 4. The Knight's Tomb (Coleridge)	—; composed July 1892	Novello	
48	Incidental music to *Beckett* (Tennyson)	NLI 14095, 20 Aug. 1892		6 Feb. 1893, London (Lyceum Theatre)
49	Six Elizabethan Pastorales (Set I) 1. To his flocks; 2. Corydon arise; 3. Diaphenia; 4. Sweet love for me; 5. Damon's passion; 6. Phoebe	—; composed Aug. 1892	Novello	
50	The Bard (Thomas Gray)	BL Loan 48/30, 22 Sept. 1892	Boosey	19 Sept. 1895, Cardiff Festival
51	no work attached to this opus number (Three Motets, Op. 38, originally published under this number)			
—	Crossing the Bar (Tennyson)	—	Stanley Lucas & Co.	
—	A Corsican Dirge (Corsican traditional, translated A. Strettell)	—	Stanley Lucas & Co.	
52	East to West (Swinburne)	RCM 4155; Jan. 1893	Novello	2 Mar. 1893, Cambridge (CUMS; Stanford and Marie Brema) 10 May 1893, London (Royal Albert Hall, Royal Choral Society); 13 June 1893, Cambridge (CUMS Golden Jubilee)

Appendix One: Select List of Works

Opus	Title	MS and date	Publication	Performance
53	Six Elizabethan Pastorales (Set II) 1. On a hill there grows a flower (Breton); 2. Like desert woods (?Dyer); 3. Praised be Diana; 4. Cupid and Rosalind (Lodge); 5. O shady vales (Lodge); 6. The Shepherd Doron's Jig (Greene)	—; composed Oct. 1893	Novello	
54	Six Irish Fantasies for Violin and Piano	NUL 15a, 31 Oct. 1893	Stanely Lucas & Co.	3 Feb. 1894, London (St James's Hall)
—	Irish Songs and Ballads (traditional airs, with new words by A. P. Graves)	—	Novello	
55	Lorenza (Ghislanzoni and Fontana)	NUL 12, 6 Jan. 1894		
56	Fifth Symphony in D 'L'allegro e il penseroso'	private possession	Stainer & Bell (Carnegie Trust Award)	20 Mar. 1895, London (Philharmonic Society)
57	Fantasia and Toccata in D minor for Organ	NUL 17, July 1894	Stainer & Bell	
58	Suite of Ancient Dances	—	Boosey	27 Feb. 1902, Bournemouth (arrangement for orchestra)
59	First Piano Concerto in G major	BL Loan 84/23, 18 Oct. 1894		27 May 1895, London (cond. Richter, piano Leonard Borwick); 5 May 1897, London (Philharmonic Society)

No.	Title	Source / Publication	Publisher	First performance
60	Moore's Irish Melodies Restored	—	Boosey	
—	Prince Madoc's Farewell (Hemans)	(published 1894)	Boosey	
61	Shamus O'Brien (Jessop, after Le Fanu)	BL Loan 84/42, 14 Jan. 1895	Boosey	2 Mar. 1896, London (Opéra Comique)
62	Phaudrig Crohoore (Le Fanu)	RAM 4, 2 July 1895 autograph vocal score NUL 18	Boosey	8 Oct. 1896, Norwich Festival
63	Requiem	RCM 4159 (undated; published vocal score cated Sept. 1896)	Boosey	6 Oct. 1897, Birmingham Festival
64	Third String Quartet in D minor	NUL 19, 29 Sept. 1896	Augener	
—	The Calico Dress (Jessop)	(published 1896)	Boosey	
65	Clown's Songs from Twelfth Night (Shakespeare)	—	Boosey	
66	Te Deum	BL Loan 48/31, 30 Jan. 1897, also RCM 4456	Boosey	6 Oct. 1898, Leeds Festival
67	Six Elizabethan Pastorales (Set III) 1. A Carol for Christmas (Bolton); 2. The Shepherd's Anthem (Drayton); 3. Shall we go dance? (Breton); 4. Love in Prayers (Breton); 5. Of Disdainful Daphne (Howell); 6. Love's Fire (Dyer)	—	Boosey	
—	The Battle of Pelusium (from *The Mad Lover*, Beaumont and Fletcher)	(published 1897)	Boosey	

Appendix One: Select List of Works

Opus	Title	MS and date	Publication	Performance
68	A Cycle of Nine Quartets from *The Princess* (Tennyson) 1. As thro' the land; 2. Sweet and low; 3. The splendour falls; 4. Tears, idle tears; 5. O swallow, swallow; 6. Thy voice is heard; 7. Home they brought her warrior dead; 8. Our enemies have fallen; 9. Ask me no more	—	Boosey	
68	Our enemies have fallen (Tennyson) (arrangement of no. 8 of preceding)	BL Loan 84/32, 15 Mar. 1899	Boosey & Hawkes	30 June 1899, London (Buckingham Palace); 28 Oct. 1899, London (Crystal Palace)
69	Christopher Patch *or* The Barber of Bath (Benjamin Stephenson)	RCM 4152, 4 Sept. 1897		
70	Violin Sonata (No. 2) in G major	—; copyist's MS: RCM 4088		
71	Concert Variations on 'Down among the Dead Men' for Piano and Orchestra	—	Novello	4 May 1899, London (Queen's Hall); 7 May 1900, Bournemouth
72	Die Wallfahrt nach Kevlaar (Heine)	NLI 4829, 22 Nov. 1898	Boosey	
73	Piano Trio (No. 2) in G minor	NUL 20, 23 Jan. 1899	Bosworth	
74	Violin Concerto in D major	NUL 21, 12 Nov. 1899	Breitkopf & Härtel	7 Mar. 1901, Bournemouth (Arbós); 7 Oct. 1904, Leeds Festival (Kreisler); 25 May 1905, London (Philharmonic Society; Rivarde)

75	The Last Post (W. E. Henley)	NUL 22, 15 May 1900	Boosey	25 June 1900, London (Buckingham Palace); 11 Sept. 1900, Hereford Festival
76	Songs of Erin (traditional Irish melodies arranged by Stanford with words by A. P. Graves)	—	Boosey	
76a	Much Ado about Nothing (Sturgis, after Shakespeare)	RCM 4165, 27 Sept. 1900	Boosey	30 May 1901, London (Covent Garden)
77	An Irish Idyll (O'Neill) 1. Corrymeela; 2. The Fairy Lough; 3. Cuttin' Rushes; 4. Johneen; 5. A Broken Song; 6. Back to Ireland	—	Boosey	? 27 Nov. 1915, London (Aeolian Hall), Stanford and Plunket Greene
—	Jack Tar (Tennyson)	— (published 1900)	Boosey	
—	The Wearing of the Green (Irish traditional with new words by C. L. Graves)	— (published 1900)	Boosey	
78	Six Irish Folksongs (Thomas Moore) 1. Oh breathe not his name; 2. What the bee is to the flower; 3. At the mid hour of night; 4. The Sword of Erin; 5. It is not the tear; 6. Oh the sight entrancing	—	Boosey	
78	First Irish Rhapsody in D minor	—	Boosey	23 Oct. 1902, Norwich Festival; 29 Jan. 1903, Bournemouth; 12 Mar. 1903, London (Philharmonic Society)
79	Second Irish Rhapsody (abandoned after 72 bars; see also Op. 84)	NUL 23, undated		

Appendix One: Select List of Works

Opus	Title	MS and date	Publication	Performance
80	Clarinet Concerto in A Minor	RAM 321; 16 July 1902	Cramer	29 Jan. 1903, Bournemouth (Charles Draper); 2 June 1904, London (Philharmonic Society)
81	Service in G	—	Houghton	
—	Flourish of Trumpets	—	Houghton	1 Jan. 1903, Delhi (Imperial Coronation Durbar)
82	Five Sonnets from *The Triumph of Love* (Edmund Holmes)	BL Loan 84/49 (later orchestral version)	Boosey	8 Jan. 1903, London (St James's Hall; Marie Brema and Stanford)
83	The Lord of Might (Reginald Heber)	—	Boosey	13 May 1903, London (St Paul's Cathedral; Festival of the Sons of the Clergy)
84	Second Irish Rhapsody in F minor	RCM 4831, 23 Feb. 1903		25 May 1903, Amsterdam (Concertgebouw); 8 June 1903, London (St James's Hall)
85	First String Quintet in F major	NLI 14096, 21 Apr. 1903	Houghton	11 Jan. 1904, London (St James's Hall)
86	Second String Quintet in C minor	NUL 24a, 3 June 1903		
87	A Welcome March	NUL 25c, 18 July 1903		Possibly on the occasion of Edward VII's State Visit to Ireland in 1903
88	Six Preludes for Organ	NUL 26, June 1903	Stainer & Bell	
89	Four Irish Dances	RCM 4136, Nov. 1903 (version for solo piano); RCM 4833 (version for full orchestra)	Stainer & Bell (version for piano and violin; autograph unknown)	12 Jan. 1905, Bournemouth (orchestral version)

No.	Title	Source	Publisher	Performance
90	Overture in the Style of a Tragedy	NUL 27, 7 Dec. 1903		
91	Songs of the Sea (Henry Newbolt) 1. Drake's Dream; 2. Outward Bound; 3. Devon, O Devon, in wind and rain'; 4. Homeward Bound; 5. The Old superb	RCM 4148, Mar. 1904	Boosey	7 Oct. 1904, Leeds Festival
92	Three Rhapsodies from Dante for Piano	—	Houghton	13 Feb. 1905, London (Bechstein Hall, Percy Grainger (nos 2 and 3); 25 Mar. 1905, London (Percy Grainger)
93	Five Characteristic Dances for Violin and Piano	NUL 28a, 1 Feb. 1905	Boosey	
94	Sixth Symphony in E♭ (dedicated to the memory of G. F. Watts)	NUL 29, 19 June 1905		18 Jan. 1906, London (Philharmonic Society); 24 Jan. 1907, Bournemouth
95	Serenade in F Major for wind and strings ('Nonet')	NUL 31, 16 July 1905		25 Jan. 1906, London (Aeolian Hall)
—	Dainty Davie (Burns)	— (published 1905)	Boosey	
96	Stabat Mater	BL Loan 48/33, 15 Mar. 1906	Boosey	10 Oct. 1907, Leeds Festival
97	Songs of Faith 1. Strong son of God (Tennyson); 2. God and the Universe (Tennyson); 3. Faith (Tennyson); 4. To the Soul (Whitman); 5. Tears (Whitman); 6. Joy, Shipmate, Joy (Whitman)	NUL 32, 19 Dec. 1906 (end of No. 6 missing)	Boosey	
98	Magnificat and Nunc Dimittis on 2nd and 3rd Gregorian Tones	—	Stainer & Bell	

Appendix One: Select List of Works

Opus	Title	MS and date	Publication	Performance
99	Fourth String Quartet in G minor	NLI 14097, 30 Oct. 1906		20 Feb. 1907, Cambridge (CUMS); 26 Oct. 1907, London (Bechstein Hall)
100	Ode to Wellington (Tennyson)	BL Loan 48/34, 10 Feb. 1907	Boosey	14 Oct. 1908, Bristol Festival
—	Choric Ode (J. H. Skrine)	RCM 4142, 2 June 1907		19 July 1909, Bath Historical Pageant
101	Six Short Preludes and Postludes for Organ (Set I)	NUL 36, Apr. 1907	Stainer & Bell	
102	Incidental Music to *Attila the Hun* (Laurence Binyon)	NUL 37, 29 June 1907		4 Sept. 1907, London (His Majesty's Theatre)
103	Fantasia and Fugue in D minor for Organ	NUL 38, 8 Aug. 1907	Stainer & Bell	
104	Fifth String Quartet in B♭	—; Sept. 1907	Stainer & Bell	3 Mar. 1908, Leeds; 4 Mar. 1908, London
—	Ode to Discord (C. L. Graves)	RCM 4146, 6 Jan. 1908	Boosey	9 June 1909, London (Queen's Hall)
105	Six Short Preludes and Postludes for Organ (Set II)	NUL 39, Feb. 1908	Stainer & Bell	
106	Four Partsongs for Male Voices 1. Autumn Leaves (Dickens); 2. Love's Folly; 3. To his Flocks (Constable); 4. Fair Phyllis ('J. G.')	—	Stainer & Bell	
107	A Welcome Song (Duke of Argyll)	BL Loan 84/35, 10 Mar. 1908	Boosey & Hawkes	14 May 1908, London (Anglo-French Exhibition, Shepherd's Bush)
108	Installation March	NUL 41, 17 June 1908	Stainer & Bell (arrangement for organ)	17 June 1908, Installation of Lord Rayleigh as Chancellor of University of Cambridge

No.	Title	MS ref	Publisher	Notes / Performance
109	Three Military Marches	NUL 44		
110	Four Partsongs / 1. Valentine's Day (Kingsley); 2. Dirge (Cory); 3. The Fairies (Cory); 4. Heraclitus (Cory)	—	Stainer & Bell; 'Heraclitus' also published by Stainer & Bell as a solo song	
111	Three Partsongs (M. Byron) / 1. A Lover's Ditty; 2. The Praise of Spring; 3. The Patient Lover	NUL 45, undated (Nos 1 and 3)	Curwen	
112	Four Songs (Tennyson) / 1. The City Child; 2. The Silence; 3. Spring; 4. The Vision	—	Stainer & Bell	
113	Bible Songs for Voice and Organ / 1. A Song of Freedom; 2. A Song of Trust; 3. A Song of Hope; 4. A Song of Peace; 5. A Song of Battle; 6. A Song of Wisdom / Plus six hymns designed for interspersal between the above (settings for choir and organ) / 1. Let us with a gladsome mind; 2. Purest and highest; 3. In Thee is gladness; 4. Pray Thee Jerusalem; 5. Praise the Lord; 6. O for a closer walk with God	—	Stainer & Bell	
114	Overture 'Ave atque vale' (Ecclus.)	NUL 47b, 31 Dec. 1908	Stainer & Bell	2 Mar. 1909, London (Queen's Hall; LSO and Bach Choir)
115	Service in C	—	Stainer & Bell	
116	Te Deum and Canzona for Organ	—	Schirmer	

Appendix One: Select List of Works

Opus	Title	MS and date	Publication	Performance
117	Songs of the Fleet (Henry Newbolt) 1. Sailing at Dawn; 2. The Song of the Sou' Wester; 3. The Middle Watch; 4. The Little Admiral; 5. Fare Well	RCM 4158, Jan. 1910	Boosey	13 Oct. 1910, Leeds Festival
118	Cushendall (John Stevenson) 1. Ireland; 2. Did you ever; 3. Cushendall; 4. The Crow; 5. Daddy Long-legs; 6. How does the wind blow?; 7. Night	—	Stainer & Bell	
119	Eight Partsongs (Mary Coleridge) 1. The Witch; 2. Farewell, my joy; 3. The blue bird; 4. The train; 5. The inkbottle; 6. The swallow; 7. Chillingham; 8. My heart is thine	—	Stainer & Bell	
120	Come ye thankful people, come	—	Stainer & Bell	
121	Fantasia and Idyll for Organ	—	Schirmer	
122	Sixth String Quartet in A minor	NUL 51a, 30 Oct. 1910		
123	Ye Choirs of New Jerusalem	—	Stainer & Bell	
—	Minuet for Flute, Clarinet, Horn, 2 Violins, Viola, Cello, and ad lib. Harp	NUL 96, 2 May 1911		20 July 1980, Bracknell
124	Seventh Symphony in D Minor	CUL Add 5349(c), 6 Feb. 1912	Stainer & Bell	22 Feb. 1912, London (Philharmonic Society); 14 Mar. 1912, Bournemouth
125	Four Songs 1. John Kelly (W. M. Letts);	—	Stainer & Bell	

No.	Title	Source	Publisher	First performance
	2. The Song of Asia (Shelley); 3. Phoebe (Thomas Lodge); 4. The Song of the Spirit of the Hour (Shelley)			
126	Second Piano Concerto in C Minor	Yale University Music Library Misc 105	Stainer & Bell	22 Nov. 1915, Norfolk CT; 7 Dec. 1916, Bournemouth; 29 Apr. 1919, London (Philharmonic Society)
127	Eight Partsongs (Mary Coleridge) 1. Plighted; 2. Veneta; 3. When Mary through the garden went; 4. The Haven; 5. The Guest; 6. Larghetto; 7. Wilderspin; 8. To a Tree	—	Stainer & Bell	
128	Festal Communion Service in B♭	NUL 53, 23 Oct. 1910 (Gloria); 27 Aug. 1911 (remainder)	Stainer & Bell	22 Nov. 1911 London (Westminster Abbey, Coronation of George V; 'Gloria' only)
129	Clarinet Sonata in F major	CUL 8341, 28 Dec. 1911	Stainer & Bell	14 Mar. 1916, London (Steinway Hall; Charles Draper and Thomas Dunhill)
130	Incidental Music to *Drake* (Louis Parker)	NUL 54, 7 Aug. 1912		3 Sept. 1912, London (His Majesty's Theatre)
131	Fairy Day (W. Allingham)	NUL 56, 6 Nov. 1912	Stainer & Bell	
132	Six Characteristic Pieces for Piano solo	NUL 57, 11 Jan. 1912	Stainer & Bell	
133	Second Piano Quartet	NUL 59, 10 Jan. 1913	Stainer & Bell	14 Mar. 1914, London (Bechstein Hall)
134	Blessed City, Heavenly Salem	—	Stainer & Bell	
135	Three Motets 1. Ye holy angels bright (R. Baxter); 2. Eternal Father (Bridges); 3. Glorious and powerful God	—	Stainer & Bell	
136	Five Caprices for Piano	—; composed May 1913	Stainer & Bell	

Appendix One: Select List of Works

Opus	Title	MS and date	Publication	Performance
137	Third Irish Rhapsody in D major (with solo cello)	RCM 4832, 18 June 1913		20 Oct. 1987, Belfast (Ulster Orchestra, cond. Handley)
138	Six Songs for Two Sopranos 1. A Welcome Song (Herrick); 2. To Music (Herrick); 3. Autumn (Shelley); 4. The Chase (Rowley); 5. Meg Merrilies (Keats); 6. Oh! sweet content (Dekker)	—	Curwen	
139	A Fire of Turf (W. M. Letts) 1. A Fire of Turf; 2. The Chapel on the Hill; 3. Cowslip Time; 4. Scared; 5. Blackberry Time; 6. The Fair; 7. The West Wind	—	Stainer & Bell	
140	A Sheaf of Songs from Leinster (W. M. Letts) 1. Grandeur; 2. Thief of the World; 3. A Soft Day; 4. Little Peter Morrissey; 5. The Bold Unbiddable Child; 6. The Irish Skies	—	Stainer & Bell	
141	Fourth Irish Rhapsody in A minor	NUL 63, Nov. 1913	Stainer & Bell	19 Feb. 1914, London (Queen's Hall; Philharmonic Society)
142	On Time (Milton)	—; composed May 1914	Stainer & Bell	
143	Thanksgiving Te Deum	—	Stainer & Bell	
—	The King's Highway (Newbolt)	— (published 1914)	Stainer & Bell	

144	The Critic (Lewis Cairns James, after Sheridan)	RCM 4153, 8 Sept. 1915	Boosey	14 Jan. 1916, London (Shaftesbury Theatre)
145	For lo, I raise up	—	Stainer & Bell	
146	The Travelling Companion (Henry Newbolt, after Andersen)	RCM 4151, 7 July 1916	Stainer & Bell	30 Apr. 1925, Liverpool (David Lewis Theatre)
147	Fifth Irish Rhapsody in G minor	Yale University Music Library Misc 66, 11 Feb. 1917; NUL 64, 11 Feb. 1917 (copy)		18 Mar. 1917 London (Royal Albert Hall); 7 June 1917, Norfolk CT; 22 May 1918, Bournemouth
148	Night Thoughts for Piano	—; composed May 1917	Joseph Williams	
149	First Organ Sonata in F major	BL Add. 54389, 29 May 1917	Augener	? 1 Dec. 1917, Cambridge (Trinity College)
150	Scènes de Ballet for Piano solo	BL Add. 54389, 11 June 1917	Augener	
151	Second Organ Sonata ('Eroica') in G minor	—	Stainer & Bell	? 9 Dec. 1918, Cambridge (Trinity College)
151	Verdun (second and third movements of preceding arranged for orchestra)	NUL 109		20 Jan. 1918, London (Royal Albert Hall); 22 May 1918, Bournemouth
—	The Grand Match (O'Neill)	— (published 1917)	Stainer & Bell	
152	Third Organ Sonata ('Britannica') in C minor	—	Stainer & Bell	
153	Fourth Organ Sonata ('Celtica') in D minor	—; Jan. 1918	Stainer & Bell	
154	Six Irish Sketches for Violin and Piano	NUL 66a, Jan. 1918 (but MS excludes second half of no. 1 and nos 2 and 4, which are missing)	Boosey	

Appendix One: Select List of Works

Opus	Title	MS and date	Publication	Performance
155	Six Easy Pieces for Violin and Piano	—	Joseph Williams	
156	Ten Partsongs	—		
157	Songs of a Roving Celt (Murdoch Maclean) 1. The Pibroch; 2. The Assynt of the Shadows; 3. The Sobbing of the Spey; 4. No More; 5. The Call	—	Enoch	
158	Third Piano Trio in A minor	BL Add. 54389, 22 Apr. 1918	Augener	
159	Fifth Organ Sonata ('Quasi una Fantasia') in A major	—; composed May 1918	Augener	
160	Ballata and Ballabile for Cello and Orchestra	NUL 67, 5 Jan. 1918		3 May 1919, London (Wigmore Hall) (arrangement for Cello and Piano)
161	Irish Concertino for Violin, Cello and Orchestra	NUL 68a, 22 Jan. 1918		4 Dec. 1918, London (Wigmore Hall) (arrangement for Violin, Cello and Orchestra); 22 Apr. 1920, Bournemouth (orchestral version)
162	Second Concerto for Violin and Orchestra	PML, Morgan Collection, 30 July 1918 (arrangement for Violin and Piano)		
163	Preludes in all the keys for Piano solo (Set I)	—(dated Sept. 1918 in printed edition)	Swan & Co.	
164	Magnificat	—	Boosey	

No.	Title	Manuscript/Date	Publisher	Premiere
—	The Fair Hills of Ireland (C. F. Smith)	— (published 1918)	Enoch & Sons	
—	Six Sketches for Piano (Elementary)	— (published 1919)	Williams	
—	Six Sketches for Piano (Primary)	— (published 1919)	Williams	
165	Two Sonatas for Violin and Piano	—		7 May 1919 (2nd Sonata)
166	Seventh String Quartet in C minor	NUL 69, undated		27 Feb. 1919, London (Royal College of Music)
167	Eighth String Quartet in E minor	RCM 4138, 25 June 1919		20 Mar. 1968, BBC Radio Three
168	A Song of Agincourt	NLI 14098; revisions completed 11 Apr. 1919, which involved removing the original ending and thus the original completion date		25 Mar. 1919, London (Royal College of Music); 4 July 1919, London (Royal College of Music) (revised version); 16 Oct. 1919, Bournemouth (revised version)
169	Mass	—	Ascherberg, Hopwood & Crewe	
170	Ballade in G Minor for Piano solo	—		
171	Third Piano Concerto in E♭	NUL 70, Jan. 1919 (version for two pianos; orchestral version unknown, later orchestrated by Geoffrey Bush)		
172	Merlin and the Gleam (Tennyson)	—; composed Sept. 1919	Stainer & Bell	
173	Missa Via victrix	BL Loan 84/36, 14 Dec. 1919	Boosey	

Appendix One: Select List of Works

Opus	Title	MS and date	Publication	Performance
174	Six Songs from 'The Glens of Antrim' (Moira O'Neill) 1. Denny's Daughter; 2. The Sailor Man; 3. Lookin' Back; 4. At Sea; 5. I mind the day; 6. The Boy from Ballytearim	—	Boosey	
175	Six Songs 1. A Song of the Bow (Heber); 2. Drop me a flower (Tennyson); 3. The Winds of Bethlehem (W. M. Letts); 4. The Monkey's Carol (W. M. Letts); 5. Lullaby (G. L. Gower); 6. The Unknown Sea (M. K. Clark)	—	Cramer	
176	Mass	—		
—	A Toy Story for Piano	NUL 100, undated (published 1920)	Stainer & Bell	
—	Six Song Tunes for Piano	— (published 1920)	Stainer & Bell	
177	At the Abbey Gate	BL Loan 84/37	Boosey	5 Mar. 1921, London (Albert Hall, Royal Choral Society)
178	Three Waltzes for Piano solo	—	Swan & Co.	
179	Preludes in all the keys for Piano solo (Set II)	— (dated Dec. 1920 in printed edition)	Swan & Co.	

No.	Title	Source / Date	Publisher	First performance
180	Variations for Violin and Orchestra	Dorset Rural Music School, Blandford Forum (version for violin and piano), 21 Jan. 1921; orchestral version unknown		19 June 1990, Belfast (Ulster Orchestra, cond. Handley, Gillian Weir)
181	Concert Piece for Organ, Brass and Drums	NUL 73, 15 Apr. 1921	Stainer & Bell	
182	Six Occasional Preludes for Organ	—		
183	Five Bagatelles in Valse Form for Violin and Piano	—	Cramer	
184	Three Nocturnes for Piano	NUL 74, May 1921		
185	unknown			
186	unknown			
—	Fantasy for Clarinet and String Quartet	NUL 100a, 27 Oct. 1921		
—	Fantasy for Clarinet and String Quartet	NUL 102a, 20 Jan. 1922		
—	Sonatina in G major for Piano	NUL 103, 19 May 1922		
—	Sonatina in D Minor for Piano	NUL 104, May 1922		
—	Fantasy for Horn and String Quartet	NUL 101a, 6 June 1922		
187	Fantasia upon a tune of C. H. H. Parry ('Intercessor') for Organ	NUL 75, undated	Stainer & Bell	5 Sept. 1922, Gloucester Festival
188	unknown			
189	Four Intermezzi for Organ	—	Stainer & Bell	
190	unknown			

Appendix One: Select List of Works

Opus	Title	MS and date	Publication	Performance
191	Sixth Irish Rhapsody in D minor (with solo violin)	BL Loan 84/24, 17 Sept. 1922	Boosey (arrangement for violin and piano)	30 Oct. 1923, York (arrangement for violin and piano); 3 Apr. 1924, Bournemouth (orchestral version; performed as an 'in memoriam')
192	Three Anthems 1. Lo! He comes (Wesley & Cennick); 2. While shepherds watched (Tate); 3. Jesus Christ is risen today	—	Novello	
193	Three Preludes and Fugues for Organ	—	Novello	
194	Three Idylls for Organ	—	Stainer & Bell	
—	How beauteous are their feet (Watts)	— (published 1923)	Novello	
—	Nonsense Rhymes (Lear)	PML, MS Cary 301	Stainer & Bell (published under the pseudonym Karel Drofnatzki)	
—	Queen and Huntress (Jonson)	— (published 1923)	Boosey	
—	When God of Old (Keble)	— (published 1923)	Stainer & Bell	

Works published posthumously where date of composition is unknown

—	The Earth is the Lord's	—	Stainer & Bell (1924)	
—	Three Fancies for Piano	—	Edward Arnold (1924)	
—	Songs from the Elfin Pedlar (H. D. Adam)	(?1923)	Stainer & Bell (1928)	
—	Be Merciful unto Me	—	Stainer & Bell (1928)	
—	How long wilt Thou forget me?	—	Stainer & Bell (1928)	

Discography

This discography lists nearly all compact disc recordings available in the United Kingdom in 2001 (the principal omissions are where the same work, performed by the same artists, has been released by the same company on more than one disc). The works are listed in order of opus number with works of uncertain date placed at the end. Unless marked to the contrary the complete work is available on each recording; in cases where only part of a work has been recorded (for example, one song from a collection) this is noted either at the beginning of the entry (in which case this annotation applies to all recordings of the work listed) or against each individual recording.

Appendix Two: Select Discography

Opus	Title	Recording
—	From the Red Rose (A. P. Graves)	Felicity Lott and Graham Johnson, Hyperion CDA66937
—	Magnificat and Nunc Dimittis in F ('Queens' Service')	1. Queens' College Choir, Cambridge, R. Woodward, A. Linn, Mirabilis MMSCD4 2. Christ Church Cathedral Choir, Dublin, A. Johnstone, M. Duley, Priory PRCD602
—	Magnificat and Nunc Dimittis in E♭	1. Winchester Cathedral Choir, David Hill, Christopher Monks, Hyperion CDA66964 2. Christ Church Cathedral Choir, Dublin, A. Johnstone, M. Duley, Priory PRCD602
—	Pater Noster	Winchester Cathedral Choir, David Hill, Hyperion CDA66964
1	Eight Songs from 'The Spanish Gypsy'	Stephen Varcoe, Clifford Benson, Hyperion CDA67123
4	Six Songs (nos 1, 3, 4 and 6)	Stephen Varcoe and Clifford Benson, Hyperion CDA67123
—	First Symphony in B♭	Ulster Orchestra, cond. Vernon Handley, Chandos CHAN9049
7	Six Songs (nos 1, 2, 5 and 6)	Stephen Varcoe and Clifford Benson, Hyperion CDA67123
—	The Veiled Prophet of Khorossan (Prelude; Act II Ballet Music; 'There's a Bower of Roses')	V. Kerr, National Symphony Orchestra of Ireland, cond. Colman Pearce, Marco Polo 8 223580/1
10	Service in B♭	1. Truro Cathedral Choir, S. Morley, A. Nethsingha (Magnificat and Nunc Dimitis), Priory CD553 2. Durham Cathedral Choir, J. Lancelot, K. Wright (complete), Priory, PRCD437 3. Winchester Cathedral Choir, David Hill, Stephen Farr (Morning and Evening Services complete), Hyperion CDA66964

4. Winchester Cathedral Choir, Waynflete Singers, T. Byram-Wingfield, Bournemouth Symphony Orchestra, cond. David Hill (Te Deum and Evening Service, orchestral version), Argo 430 836–2ZH

5. Durham School Chapel Choir, J. Newell, Gregory Williams (Te Deum), Abbey CDCA929

6. Trinity College Choir, Cambridge, Richard Marlow, Simon Standage (Te Deum), Conifer CDCF214

7. St Paul's Cathedral Choir, M. Blatchly, Barry Rose (Te Deum), Guild GMCD7102

8. I. Attrot, P. H. Stephen, N. Robson, Stephen Varcoe, Leeds Philharmonic Choir, BBC Philharmonic Orchestra, cond. Richard Hickox (Te Deum, orchestral version), Chandos CHAN9548

9. Hereford Cathedral Choir, Roy Massey, G. Bowen (Te Deum; Jubilate), Priory PRCD507

10. Ely Cathedral Choir, Paul Trepte (Te Deum; Jubilate), Chandos CHAN6603

11. Ely Cathedral Choir, Paul Trepte (Magnificat and Nunc Dimittis), Guild GMCD7117

12. Rochester Cathedral Choir, Percy Whitlock, C. H. Stewart (Magnificat), Amphibion PHICD147

13. Cambridge Singers, John Rutter, W. Marshall (Magnificat and Nunc Dimittis), Collegium COLCD118

14. Worcester Cathedral Choir, Donald Hunt, Paul Trepte (Magnificat and Nunc Dimittis), Hyperion CDA66030

1. S. Stanzeleit and G. Fenyö, Cala CACD88031

2. P. Barritt and Cathryn Edwards, Hyperion CDA67024

1. Janet Baker and G. Moore, EMI CDM5 65009–2

2. Ian Bostridge and J. Drake, EMI CDC5 56830–2

3. Stephen Varcoe and Clifford Benson, Hyperion CDA67123

11   Violin Sonata in D

—   La Belle Dame sans Merci

—   Second Symphony in D Minor ('Elegiac')   Ulster Orchestra, cond. Vernon Handley, Chandos CHAN8991

Appendix Two: Select Discography

Opus	Title	Recording
12	Service in A	1. St Mary Redcliff Choir, Bristol, C. Hunt, J. Marsh (Jubilate), Abbey CDDCA589
		2. Durham Cathedral Choir, J. Lancelot, K. Wright, Priory PRCD514
		3. Hereford Cathedral Choir, Roy Massey, G. Bowen (Te Deum), Priory PRCD507
		4. Ely Cathedral Choir, Paul Trepte (Te Deum; Jubilate), Guild GMCD7117
		5. Winchester Cathedral Choir, David Hill, Stephen Farr (Magnificat and Nunc Dimittis), Hyperion CDA66964
		6. Christ Church Cathedral Choir, Dublin, F. Grier, (Magnificat and Nunc Dimittis), ASV CDQS6019
		7. Lichfield Cathedral Choir, A. Lumsden, M. Shepherd (Magnificat and Nunc Dimittis), Priory PRCD505
		8. Trinity College Choir, Cambridge, Richard Marlow, P. Rushforth (Magnificat and Nunc Dimittis), Conifer CDCF214
13	Three Intermezzi for Clarinet and Piano	1. Emma Johnson and M. Martineau, ASV CDDCA787
		2. L. Merrick and Benjamin Frith, Serendipity SERCD4000
		3. G. de Peyer and G. Pryor, Radiant Mastery GDP1007
14	Six Songs (no. 5)	Stephen Varcoe, Clifford Benson, Hyperion CDA67124
—	Songs of Old Ireland	1. B. Greevy, H. Tinney (An Irish Lullaby), Marco Polo 8 225098
		2. Stephen Varcoe, Clifford Benson (My love's an arbutus; The Willow Tree), Hyperion CDA67123
		3. J. Griffet, Clifford Benson (My love's an arbutus; The Confession; Jenny; The Willow Tree), Campion CAMEO2001
15	Piano Quartet No. 1 in F	Pirasti Trio and Philip Dukes, ASV CD DCA 1056
—	If ye then be risen with Christ	New College Choir, Oxford, C. Plummer, E. Higginbottom, CRD CRD3497
—	The Lord is my Shepherd	1. Worcester Cathedral Choir, H. Bramma, C. Robinson, Chandos CHAN6519
		2. Trinity College Choir, Cambridge, Richard Marlow, P. Rushforth, Conifer CDCF214

Appendix Two: Select Discography

Opus	Title	Recording
38	Three Motets	1. Trinity College Choir, Cambridge, Richard Marlow (complete), Conifer CDCF155
		2. Queen's College Choir, Cambridge, R. Woodward (complete), Mirabilis MMSCD4
		3. New College Choir, Oxford, E. Higginbottom (complete), CRD CRD3497
		4. King's College Choir, Cambridge, Stephen Cleobury (complete), EMI CDC5 55535—2
		5. York Minster Chapter House Choir, J. Sturmheit (complete), Guild GMCD7140
		6. Winchester Cathedral Choir, David Hill (complete), Hyperion CDA66964
		7. His Majesties Clerkes, A. Heider (complete), Cedille CDR90000036
		8. St Paul's Cathedral Choir, London, John Scott (Justorum animae), Hyperion CDA66519
		9. Cambridge Singers, John Rutter (Justorum animae), Collegium COLCD113
		10. St Paul's Cathedral Choir, London (Coelos ascendit), Hyperion CDA66678
		11. Winchester Cathedral Choir, Martin Neary (Coelos ascendit), ASV CDQS6025
		12. Lincoln Cathedral Choir, C. Walsh (Coelos ascendit), Priory PRCD478
		13. Salisbury Cathedral Choir, R. Seal (Coelos ascendit), Meridian CDE84810
		14. Lincoln College Choir, Oxford, C. Walsh (Coelos ascendit; Beati quorum via), Regent REGCD110
		15. Southwark Cathedral Choir, John Scott (Coelos ascendit; Beati quorum via), Abbey CACA542
		16. Cambridge Singers, John Rutter (Beati quorum via), Collegium CSCD500
		17. St Paul's Cathedral Choir, London, Andrew Lucas (Beati quorum via), Hyperion CDA66374
		18. Marlborough Chapel Choir, Robin Nelson (Beati quorum via), Priory PRCD586

No.	Title	Recording
		19. King's College Choir, Cambridge, David Willcocks (Beati quorum via), HMV HMV5 72166–2
		20. New College Choir, Oxford, E. Higginbottom (Beati quorum via), Decca 488 870–2
		21. Worcester Cathedral Choir, Donald Hunt, Paul Trepte (complete), Hyperion CDA 66030
39	Cello Sonata in D Minor	Julian Lloyd Webber and John McCabe, ASV CDDCA807
—	For ever mine	Stephen Varcoe, Clifford Benson, Hyperion CDA67124
48	Incidental Music to *Beckett* (Funeral March)	London Philharmonic Orchestra, cond. Adrian Boult, Lyrita SRCD219
54	Six Irish Fantasies for Violin and Piano	1. Paul Barritt and Cathryn Edwards (no. 1), Hyperion CDA67024 2. F. Hunt and U. Hunt (nos 1 and 2) Continuum CCD1051
—	Irish Songs and Ballads	1. K. McKellar, R. Sharples (Trottin' to the Fair), Decca 466—415—2DM2 2. J. Griffet, Clifford Benson (Trottin' to the Fair; Colonel Carty; Londonderry Air; The Zephyrs Blest; A Lament; The Ploughman's Whistle), Campion CAMEO2001 3. C. Maltman, BBC Scottish Symphony Orchestra, cond. Martyn Brabbins (orchestral version of The Chieftain of Tyrconnel), Hyperion CDA67065
—	Prince Madoc's Farewell	C. Maltman, BBC Scottish Symphony Orchestra, cond. Martyn Brabbins, Hyperion CDA67065
56	Fifth Symphony in D ('L'Allegro e Il Penseroso')	Ulster Orchestra, cond. Vernon Handley, Chandos CHAN8581
57	Fantasia and Toccata for Organ in D minor	1. J. Rees-Williams, Abbey, CDCA902 2. K. John, Priory PRCD370
59	First Piano Concerto in G Major	Piers Lane, Scottish Symphony Orchestra, cond. Martyn Brabbins, Hyperion CDA66820
60	Moore's Irish Melodies Restored	Kenneth Tynan, D Collins Black Box BBM1022 (Silent, O Moyle; Song of the Battle Eve; Weep on, weep on)

Appendix Two: Select Discography

Opus	Title	Recording
61	Shamus O'Brien (Ochone when I used to be young)	Joseph O'Mara, PEAR GEMMCDS9050/2(1)
63	Requiem	Frances Lucey, Colette McGahon, Peter Kerr, Nigel Leeson-Williams, RTE Philharmonic Choir, National Symphony Orchestra of Ireland, Adrian Leaper, Marco Polo 8 223580/1
65	Clown's Songs from *Twelfth Night* (The rain it raineth every day; O Mistress Mine)	Anthony Rolfe Johnson, Graham Johnson, Hyperion CDA66480
—	The Calico Dress (Jessop)	S. Leonard and M. Martineau, Somm SommCD214
70	Second Violin Sonata in G Major	Paul Barritt and Cathryn Edwards, Hyperion CDA67024
71	Concert Variations on 'Down among the Dead Men'	Margaret Fingerhut (piano), Ulster Orchestra, cond. Vernon Handley, Chandos CHAN7099
73	Second Piano Trio in G Minor	Pirasti Trio, ASV CDDCA925
74	Violin Concerto in D	Anthony Marwood, BBC Scottish Symphony Orchestra, cond. Martyn Brabbins, Hyperion CDA67208
76	Songs of Erin	1. J. Griffet, Clifford Benson (The Blackbird and the Wren), Campion CAMEO2001 2. Stephen Varcoe, Clifford Benson ('Trottin' to the Fair), Hyperion CDA67123
77	An Irish Idyll	1. R. J. Leonard, M. Martineau (complete), SommCD214 2. B. Greevy, H. Tinney (no. 2), Marco Polo 8 220596 3. Kathleen Ferrier, F. Stone (no. 2), London 430 061—2LM 4. Roy Henderson, I. Newton (no. 2), Dutton Laboratories CDLX7038 5. Stephen Varcoe, Clifford Benson (no. 2), Hyperion CDA67124 6. C. Maltman, BBC Scottish Symphony Orchestra, cond. Martyn Brabbins (no. 2 orchestral version), Hyperion CDA67065

78 Irish Rhapsody No. 1
80 Clarinet Concerto in A Minor

7. J. Griffett, Clifford Benson (nos 2 and 6), Campion CAMEO2001
8. E. Suddaby, R. Paul (no. 3), Amphibion PHICD134
Ulster Orchestra, cond. Vernon Handley, Chandos CHAN8627
1. Janet Hilton, Ulster Orchestra, cond. Vernon Handley, Chandos CHAN8991
2. Emma Johnson, Royal Philharmonic Orchestra, cond. Charles Groves, ASV CDDCA787

81 Service in G

3. Thea King, Philharmonia, cond. A. Francis, Hyperion CDA66001
1. New College Choir, Oxford, E. Higginbottom, C. Glynn (Magnificat and Nunc Dimittis), Priory PRCD596
2. Durham Cathedral Choir, J. Lancelot, K. Wright (complete), Priory PRCD514
3. King's College Choir, Cambridge, Boris Ord (Magnificat and Nunc Dimittis), Belart 461 453–2
4. Winchester Cathedral Choir, David Hill, Stephen Farr (Magnificat and Nunc Dimittis), Hyperion CDA 66965
5. Cambridge Singers, John Rutter, W. Marshall (Magnificat only), Collegium COLCD118
6. St Paul's Cathedral Choir, London, Adrian Lucas, John Scott (Magnificat and Nunc Dimittis), Hyperion CDA66439
7. New College Choir, Oxford, E. Higginbottom (Magnificat and Nunc Dimittis), Proud Sound CD114
8. King's College Choir, Cambridge, J. Vivian, Stephen Cleobury (Magnificat and Nunc Dimittis), EMI CDC5 55535–2
9. Trinity College Choir, Cambridge, Richard Marlow, Simon Standage (Magnificat and Nunc Dimittis), Conifer CDCF214

84 Irish Rhapsody No. 2
— Tom Lemmin
88 Six Preludes for Organ

Ulster Orchestra, cond. Vernon Handley, Chandos CHAN9049
Stephen Varcoe, Clifford Benson, Hyperion CDA67124
1. Francis Jackson (nos 1 and 3), Amphibion PHICD126
2. J. Watts (nos 3 and 5), Priory PRCD414

89 Four Irish Dances

1. M.-A. Hamelin (piano) (nos 1 and 4, arr. Percy Grainger), Hyperion CDA66884

Appendix Two: Select Discography

Opus	Title	Recording
		2. Martin Jones (piano), Nimbus NI1767
		3. Percy Grainger (piano) (nos 1, 3 and 4, arr. Percy Grainger), Nimbus NI8809
91	Songs of the Sea	1. Benjamin Luxon, Bournemouth Symphony Chorus, Bournemouth Symphony Orchestra, Norman Del Mar, EMI CDM5 65113–2
		2. Peter Dawson, chorus and orchestra, PEAR GEMMCD9384
		3. Thomas Allen, London Philharmonic Chorus, London Philharmonic Orchestra, Roger Norrington, London 455 147–2LH
		4. Stephen Varcoe, Clifford Benson (voice and piano), Hyperion CDA67124
92	Three Rhapsodies from Dante	Peter Jacobs, Olympia OCD638
93	Five Characteristic Pieces for Violin and Piano	Paul Barritt and Cathryn Edwards, Hyperion CDA67024
94	Sixth Symphony in E♭	Ulster Orchestra, cond. Vernon Handley, Chandos CHAN8627
96	Stabat Mater	Ingrid Attrot, Pamela H. Stephen, Nigel Robson, Stephen Varcoe, Leeds Philharmonic Choir, BBC Philharmonic Orchestra, cond. Richard Hickox, Hyperion CDA66974
97	Songs of Faith	1. P. Leonard, M. Martineau (To the Soul), Somm SommCD214
		2. C. Maltman, BBC Scottish Symphony Orchestra, Martyn Brabbins (To the Soul; Tears), Hyperion CDA67055
		3. Stephen Varcoe, Clifford Benson (To the Soul; Joy, shipmate, joy), Hyperion CDA67124
101	Six Short Preludes and Postludes for Organ (Set I)	1. Francis Jackson (complete), Amphibion PHICD126
		2. J. Bate (nos 2 and 4), ASV CDQS6160
		3. C. Dearnley (no. 3), Morette CD10911
103	Fantasia and Fugue for Organ	Francis Jackson, Amphibion PHICD126

105 Six Short Preludes and Postludes for Organ (Set II)

1. Francis Jackson (complete), Amphibion PHICD126
2. Desmond Hunter (complete), Priory PRCD445
3. J. Bate (no. 2), ASV CDQS6160
4. C. Dearnely (nos 2 and 3), Motette CD10911
5. M. Williamson (no. 6), OxRecs OXCD–41
6. J. Bielby (no. 6), Priory PRCD298
7. Stephen Cleobury (no. 6), EMI CDC5 55535–2
Jesus College Choir, Cambridge, D. Phillips, T. Horton, Cantoris CRCD2367
J. Watts, Priory PRCD414

— For all the saints

— Idyll and Fantasia 'In Festum Omnium Sanctorum'

110 Four Partsongs (Heraclitus only)

1. Ionian Singers, T. Salter, USK 1220CD
2. J. Griffet, Clifford Benson (solo song version), Campion CAMEO2001
3. Canzonetta, J. W. Davies, SommCD204
4. Stephen Varcoe, Clifford Benson (solo song version), Hyperion CDA67123

113 Bible Songs for Voice and Organ (plus six hymns for choir and organ composed for interspersal between the songs)

1. Stephen Varcoe and I. Watson (songs only), Chandos CHAN9548
2. Winchester Cathedral Choir (songs and hymns), Hyperion CDA66965
3. Canterbury Cathedral Choir, M. Harris, D. Flood (nos 4 and 6 songs and hymns), York Ambisonic York AmbisonicCD120
4. John Mark Ainsley and Stephen Cleobury (nos 4 and 6 songs), EMI CDC5 55535–2
5. St Mary's Girls' Choir, Warwick, S. Lole, K. Bowyer, Regent REFCD112
NB: Several other recordings of single hymns have been issued and are not listed here

115 Service in C

1. Durham Cathedral Choir, J. Lancelot, K. Wright (complete), Priory PRCD437
2. Winchester Cathedral Choir, David Hill, Stephen Farr (Morning Service complete), Hyperion CDA66965; (Magnificat and Nunc Dimittis) Hyperion CDA66974
3. Cambridge Singers, John Rutter, W. Marshall (Te Deum), Collegium COLCD118
4. Chichester Cathedral Choir, A. Thurlow, J. Suter (Te Deum), Priory PRCD312

Appendix Two: Select Discography

Opus	Title	Recording
		5. Rochester Cathedral Choir, B. Ferguson, R. Sayer (Te Deum; Jubilate), Priory PRCD433
		6. Ely Cathedral Choir, Paul Trepte (Te Deum; Jubilate), Guild GMCD7117
		7. Trinity College Choir, Cambridge, Richard Marlow, P. Rushforth (Benedicite), Conifer CDCF214
		8. Greenwich Royal Naval College Chapel Choir, N. Johnson (Communion Service complete), Cathedral Classic CC002
		9. Truro Cathedral Choir, D. Briggs, H. Doughty (Magnificat and Nunc Dimittis), Priory, PRCD322
		10. Portsmouth Cathedral Choir, D. Thorne, A. Lucas (Magnificat and Nunc Dimittis), Priory PRCD527
		11. King's College Choir, J. Vivian, Stephen Cleobury (Magnificat and Nunc Dimittis), EMI CDC5 555353-2
		12. St Paul's Cathedral Choir, London, C. Dearnley, John Scott (Magnificat and Nunc Dimittis), Hyperion CDA66249
		13. Ely Cathedral Choir, A. Wills, S. le Provost (Magnificat and Nunc Dimittis), Meridian CDE84276
117	Songs of the Fleet	Benjamin Luxon, Bournemouth Symphony Chorus, Bournemouth Symphony Orchestra, cond. Normal Del Mar, EMI CDM5 65113-2
119	Eight Partsongs	1. Chester Music Society Junior Choir, M. Cook, C. White (The Bluebird), Regent REGCD117
		2. Cambridge Singers, John Rutter (The Bluebird), Collegium COLCD104
		3. Laudibus, M. Brewer (The Bluebird), Hyperion CDA67076
		4. Oxford Camerata, J. Summerly (The Bluebird), Naxos 8 553088
		5. Canzonetta, J. W. Davies (The Bluebird), Somm SommCD204

— O praise God in His holiness

6. Ionian Singers, T. Salter (The Bluebird, The Swallow), USK1220CD

123 Ye choirs of New Jerusalem

Christ's Hospital Choir, P. Allwood, Carlton Classics 30366 0085-2
1. Southwell Minster Choir, P. Wood, P. Hale, Abbey CDCA959
2. Trinity College Choir, Richard Marlow, Simon Standage, Conifer CDCF214
3. New College Choir, P. Plummer, E. Higginbottom, CRD CRD3497
4. Winchester Cathedral Choir, David Hill, Stephen Farr, Hyperion CDA66974
5. Worcester Cathedral Choir, Donald Hunt, Paul Trepte, Hyperion CDA66030

124 Seventh Symphony in D minor

Ulster Orchestra, cond. Vernon Handley, Chandos CHAN8861

125 Four Songs (Phoebe)

Stephen Varcoe, Clifford Benson, Hyperion CDA67124

126 Second Piano Concerto in C Minor

1. Malcolm Binns, London Symphony Orchestra, cond. Nicholas Braithwaite, Lyrita SRCD219
2. Margaret Fingerhut, Ulster Orchestra, cond. Vernon Handley, Chandos CHAN7099

127 Eight Partsongs (When Mary thro' the garden went)

1. Cambridge Singers. John Rutter, W. Marshall, Collegium COLCD118
2. Durham Cathedral Choir, R. Lloyd, York Ambisonic HAC832

128 Festal Communion Service in B♭ major

1. Christ Church Cathedral Choir, Dublin, A. Johnstone, M. Duley (complete), Priory PRCD602
2. Westminster Abbey, Choir, T. Farrell, George Guest (Gloria), Chandos CHAN6603
3. Westminster Abbey, Choir, M. Baker, English Chamber Orchestra, Martin Neary (Gloria), Cantoris CSAMCD3050
4. Trinity College Choir, Cambridge, Richard Marlow, S. Standage (Gloria), Conifer CDCF214
5. Winchester Cathedral Choir, David Hill, Stephen Farr (Gloria), Hyperion CDA66974

129 Sonata for Clarinet and Piano

1. Emma Johnson and M. Martineau, ASV CDDCA891
2. J. Denman and P. Fan, Britannia BML009
3. E. Johannesson and P. Jenkins, Chandos CHAN9079

Appendix Two: Select Discography

Opus	Title	Recording
		3. M. Khouri and John McCabe, Continuum CCD1074
		4. Thea King and Clifford Benson, Hyperion CDD22027
		5. V. Soames and J. Flinders, CLRI CC0025
132	Six Characteristic Pieces for Piano	Peter Jacobs, Priory PRCD449
135	Three Motets	1. New College Choir, Oxford, E. Higginbottom (Ye holy angels bright; Glorious and powerful God), CRD CRD3497
		2. Trinity College Choir, Cambridge, Richard Marlow (Eternal Father), Conifer CDCF503
		3. Winchester Cathedral Choir, David Hill (Eternal Father, Glorious and powerful God), Hyperion CDA66974
		4. Magdalen College Choir, Oxford (Glorious and powerful God), Abbey CACA913
		5. Worcester Cathedral Choir, Donald Hunt, Paul Trepte (Ye holy angels bright; Glorious and powerful God), Hyperion CDA66030
—	St Patrick's Breastplate	1. City of Birmingham Symphony Chorus, P. King, Simon Halsey, Conifer CDCF502
		2. Winchester Cathedral Choir, David Hill, Stephen Farr, Hyperion CDA66974
137	Irish Rhapsody No. 3	Rafael Wallfisch, Ulster Orchestra, cond. Vernon Handley, Chandos CHAN8861
139	A Fire of Turf	1. P. Leonard and M. Martineau, Somm SommCD214
		2. J. Griffett and Clifford Benson, Campion CAMEO2001
140	A Sheaf of Songs from Leinster	1. J. Griffet, Clifford Benson (Thief of the World; A Soft Day; The Bold Unbiddable Child; Campion CAMEO2001
		2. V. Baulard, S. Wright (A Soft Day), Max Sounds MSCB12
		3. Kathleen Ferrier, F. Stone (A Soft Day), London 430 061–2LM
		4. Roy Henderson, E. Gritton (A Soft Day), Dutton Laboratories CDLX7038

Appendix Two: Select Discography

Opus	Title	Recording
159	Sonata for Organ (No. 5) in A major ('Quasi una fantasia')	Desmond Hunter, Priory PRCD445
163	Preludes for Piano (Set I)	Peter Jacobs, Priory PRCD449
164	Magnificat in B♭	1. Trinity College Choir, Cambridge, Richard Marlow, Conifer CDCF214
		2. King's College Choir, Cambridge, Stephen Cleobury, EMI CDC5 55535–2
		3. Winchester Cathedral Choir, David Hill, Stephen Farr, Hyperion CDA66974
		4. Westminster Cathedral Choir, J. O'Donnell, Hyperion WCC100
174	Songs from the Glens of Antrim	Stephen Varcoe, Clifford Benson, Hyperion CDA67123
175	Six Songs (A Song of the Bow; Drop me a flower; The Winds of Bethlehem; The Monkey's Carol)	J. Griffet, Clifford Benson, Campion CAMEO2001
179	Preludes for Piano (Set II)	Peter Jacobs, Olympia OCD638
181	Concert Piece for Organ, Brass and Drums	Gillian Weir, Ulster Orchestra, cond. Vernon Handley, Chandos CHAN8861
—	Quick, we have but a second (from Moore's Irish Melodies)	Cambridge Singers, John Rutter, Collegium COLCD104
191	Irish Rhapsody No. 6	Lydia Mordokovitch, Ulster Orchestra, cond. Vernon Handley, Chandos CHAN7002
—	How beauteous are their feet (Watts)	1. New College Choir, Oxford, P. Plummer, E. Higginbottom, CRD CRD3497
		2. Winchester Cathedral Choir, David Hill, Stephen Farr, Hyperion CDA66974
		3. St Paul's Cathedral Choir, John Scott, Hyperion CDA67087
193	Three Preludes and Fugues for Organ	1. Francis Jackson (no. 1), Amphibion PHICD126
		2. Andrew Smith (nos 2 and 3), CRD CRD3497

Works where the date of composition is uncertain or unknown

	The Anglers' Song (Chalkhill)	Ionian Singers, cond T. Salter, USK USK1220CD
	At the Mid-Hour of Night (Moore)	J. McCormack and G. Moore, PEAR GEMMCDS9188
	The Beautiful City of Sligo (trad.)	A. Murray and G. Johnson, Hyperion CDA66627
	The Earth is the Lord's	Choir of St Mary Redcliffe, Bristol, C. Hunt, J. Marsh, Abbey CDCA589
	The Falling Star	A. Murray and G. Johnson, Hyperion CDA66627
	God and the Universe (Tennyson)	Ionian Singers, T. Salter, USK USK1220CD
	The Irish Reel (A. P. Graves)	J. Griffet, Clifford Benson, Campion CAMEO2001
	The Merry Month of May (Dekker)	J. Griffet, Clifford Benson, Campion CAMEO2001
	More of Cloyne	J. Griffet, Clifford Benson, Campion CAMEO2001
	The Poison on the Darts (Theocritus, trans. A. P. Graves)	J. Griffet, Clifford Benson, Campion CAMEO2001
	The Stolen Heart (trad.)	A. Murray, G. Johnson, Hyperion CDA66627
	Witches' Charms	J. Griffet, Clifford Benson, Campion CAMEO2001

Select Bibliography

The following bibliography contains details of the books referred to directly in the text and to other significant sources consulted. Stanford's own contributions to various periodicals were reproduced in the collections *Studies and Memories* and *Interludes, Records and Recollections* and only these books are fully recorded here. Numerous periodicals were consulted; specific references drawn from these and other periodicals are cited only in the main body of the text, but substantial biographical articles are also listed here.

Autograph Letters and Other Primary Sources

The following list gives the main collections of autograph letters consulted. Other substantial archives are also listed here. For details of the location of autographs of Stanford's music, see Appendix One. For full references to these collections, and to other smaller ones, see the relevant footnotes in the main body of the text.

1. Letters from Stanford

Joseph Bennett: Pierpont Morgan Library, New York, MS MFC S785.B4716.
Francisco Berger: British Library, London, MS Loan 48 13/32.
Bote & Bock (Publishers): Staatsbibliothek zu Berlin (Unter den Linden), MS Mus.ep.Stanford.
Oscar Browning: King's College, Cambridge (no MS nos).
Carnegie Trust: Scottish Records Office, Edinburgh, File Gd 281/41/36.
Edward Dent: Fitzwilliam Museum, Cambridge (no MS nos), and King's College, Cambridge (no MS nos).
F. G. Edwards: British Library, London, MS Egerton 3090.
Edward Elgar: Worcester Records Office, Accession 5247.
Alfred Graves: National Library of Ireland, Dublin, MSS 17797 and 21128.
George Grove: British Library, London, Add. MS 55239.
Francis Jenkinson: Cambridge University Library, Add. MSS 4251, 6343 and 8781.

Joseph Joachim: Staatsbibliothek zu Berlin (Tiergartenstraße), MS SM12/40.

Macmillan & Co. (Publishers): British Library, London, Add. MS 55239.

Robert Milward: Birmingham Central Library, Lee Crowder MS 1171.

Novello & Co. (Publishers): Cambridge University Library, Add. MS 9370.

Horatio Parker: Music Library, Yale University, New Haven, Conn., USA (no MS nos).

Hubert Parry: Shulbrede Priory, Lynchmere, West Sussex (no MS nos).

Philharmonic Society: British Library, London, MS Loan 48 13/32.

Hans Richter: Royal College of Music, London, MS 4826.

Society of Authors: British Library, Add. MS 56819.

Edward Speyer: British Library, London, Add. MS 42233.

Sedley Taylor: Cambridge University Library, Add. MSS 258 and 6260.

Hallam Tennyson: Lincoln City Library, Tennyson Archive.

Herbert Thompson: Brotherton Library, Leeds University, MS 361.

2. *Other Primary Sources*

Records of the Board of Studies (Music), Cambridge University: Cambridge University Library (includes information on election of Professors of Music, conferring of honorary degrees, and general management of the study of music within Cambridge University).

Letters from Gerard Cobb to Joseph Joachim: Staatsbibliothek (Tiergartenstraße), Berlin, MS SM/12.

Diaries of Edward Dent: King's College, Cambridge (no MS nos).

Letters from Harry Plunket Greene to Herbert Thompson: Brotherton Library, Leeds University, MS 361.

Letters from George Grove to Joseph Joachim: Staatsbibliothek (Tiergartenstraße), Berlin, MS SM/12.

Letters from George Grove to Edith Oldham: Royal College of Music, London (uncatalogued).

Letters from George Grove to Hubert Parry: Shulbrede Priory, Lynchmere, West Sussex (no MS nos).

Letters from Francis Jenkinson to Eleanor Jenkinson: Cambridge University Library, Add. MSS 6343, 7510, and 7671.

Archives of Leeds Musical Festival: West Yorkshire Archive Service, Leeds (no MS nos).

Letters from Hubert Parry to Francis Jenkinson: Cambridge University Library, Add. MS 6343.

Diaries of Hubert Parry: Shulbrede Priory, Lynchmere, West Sussex (no MS nos).

Diaries of Arthur Sullivan: Beinecke Library, Yale University, New Haven, Conn., USA.

Archives of Royal College of Music: Royal College of Music, London (includes records of Council, Executive Committee, and Board of Professors).

Archives of Trinity College, Cambridge: Trinity College, Cambridge (records of the Seniority relating to Stanford's appointment as College Organist, and of the Choir Committee).

Secondary Sources

Adams, B., 'Songs of the Spanish Gypsy', *George Eliot Fellowship Review*, 22 (1991), 46–50

Allis, Michael, 'Another "48": Stanford and "Historic Sensibility"', *Music Review*, 55 (1994), 119–37.

Antcliffe, Herbert, 'Sir Charles Stanford', *Music Student* (1916–17), 9, 211–15.

Atkinson, C. T., *The Devonshire Regiment 1914–1918* (London and Exeter, 1926).

Auburn, M. S., *Sheridan's Comedies: Their Contexts and Achievements* (Lincoln, Nebr. and London, 1977).

Audley, Brian, 'The Provenance of the Londonderry Air', *Journal of the Royal Musical Association*, 125 (2000), 205–47.

Banfield, Stephen, *Sensibility and English Song*, 2 vols (Cambridge, 1985).

Bax, Arnold, *Farewell my Youth* (London, 1943).

Beckett, James C., *The Anglo-Irish Tradition* (London, 1976).

Begnal, Michael, *Joseph Sheridan Le Fanu* (Lewisburg, Pa., 1971).

Bennett, Joseph, *Forty Years of Music* (London, 1908).

Bispham, David, *A Quaker Singer's Recollections* (New York, 1920).

Bliss, Arthur, *As I Remember* (London, 1970).

—— 'Some Aspects of the Present Musical Situation', *Proceedings of the Royal Musical Association*, 49 (1922–3), 59–77.

Boosey, William, *Fifty Years of Music* (London, 1931).

Breathnach, Brendan, *Folk Music and Dances of Ireland* (2nd edn, Dublin and Cork, 1967).

Bridge, Frederick, *A Westminster Pilgrim* (London, 1918).

Briggs, Katherine, *A Dictionary of British Folktales*, 4 vols (London, 1970).

Brooke, Christopher N. L. (ed.), *A History of the University of Cambridge*, 4 vols (Cambridge, 1992).

Burke, John, *A Genealogical and Heraldic History of the Extinct and Dormant Baronetcies of England* (2nd edn, London, 1844).

Burke, Oliver J., *Anecdotes of the Connaught Circuit* (Dublin, 1885).

Burke's Genealogical and Heraldic History of the Landed Gentry in Ireland, ed. L. G. Pine (London, 1958).

Burtchaell, George, and Thomas Sadler, *Alumni Dublinienses 1593–1846* (Dublin, 1924).

Carey, Hugh, *Duet for Two Voices* (Cambridge, 1979).

Chapman, Raymond, *The Sense of the Past in Victorian Literature* (London and Sydney, 1986).

'Charles Villiers Stanford', *Musical Times*, 1 Dec. 1898, pp. 785–93.

Cobb, Gerard, *A Brief History of the Organ in the Chapel of Trinity College, Cambridge* (Cambridge, 1913).

Coleridge, Arthur, *Reminiscences* (London, 1921).

Colles, Henry C., *Walford Davies* (Oxford, 1942).

—— and Gordon Cruft, *Royal College of Music: A Centenary Record* (London, 1982).

Colls, Robert, and Philip Dodds (eds), *Englishness, Politics and Culture 1880–1920* (London, 1986).

Cowen, Frederic, *My Art and my Friends* (London, 1913).

Daly, Mary E., *Dublin: The Deposed Capital* (Cork, 1984).

De Lara, Isidore, *Many Tales of Many Cities* (London, 1928).

Delong, Kenneth, and D. Salter, 'Stanford's Incidental Music to Henry Irving's Production of Tennyson's *Beckett*', *Theatre History Studies*, 3 (1983), 69–87.

Dent, Edward, *Selected Essays* (Cambridge, 1979).

Dibble, Jeremy, *C. Hubert H. Parry: His Life and Music* (Oxford, 1992).

—— 'Stanford's Service in B flat, Op. 10, and the Choir of Trinity College, Cambridge', *Irish Musical Studies*, 2 (Dublin, 1993), 129–48.

Dickinson, Page L., *The Dublin of Yesterday* (London, 1929).

Duggan, George C., *The Stage-Irishman* (London, 1937).

Dunhill, Thomas, 'Charles Villiers Stanford: Some Aspects of his Work and Influence', *Proceedings of the Royal Musical Association*, 42 (1927), 41–65.

Dyson, George, 'Charles Villiers Stanford', *RCM Magazine*, 20 (1923–4), 43–6.

Dyson, Hope, and Charles Tennyson (eds), *Dear and Honoured Lady – The Correspondence between Queen Victoria and Alfred Tennyson* (London, 1969).

Elgar, Edward, *A Future for English Music*, ed. Percy Young (London, 1968).

Eliot, George, *The George Eliot Letters*, ed. Gordon Haight, 9 vols (London and New Haven, 1954–78).

Fifield, Christopher, *True Artist and True Friend: A Biography of Hans Richter* (Oxford, 1993).

Findon, B. W., *Sir Arthur Sullivan* (London, 1904).

Forbes, Anne Marie, 'Celticism in British Opera 1878–1938', *Music Review*, 47 (1986–7), 176–83.

Foreman, Lewis, *From Parry to Britten: British Music in Letters 1900–45* (London, 1987).

Foster, Myles Birket, *History of the Philharmonic Society* (London, 1912).

Fuller Maitland, John, *A Doorkeeper of Music* (London, 1929).

—— *The Music of Parry and Stanford* (London, 1934).

Galloway, William J., *The Operatic Problem* (London, 1902).

Gerard, Frances A., *Picturesque Dublin, Old and New* (London, 1898).

Godfrey, Dan, *Memories and Music* (London, 1924).

Goossens, Eugene, *Overtures and Beginners* (London, 1951).

Graves, Alfred, *Irish Literary and Musical Studies* (London, 1913).

—— *To Return to All That* (London, 1929).

Graves, Charles L., *Hubert Parry*, 2 vols (London, 1926).

Gray, Cecil, *A Survey of Contemporary Music* (London, 1924).

Greene, Harry Plunket, *Charles Villiers Stanford* (London, 1935).

—— 'Stanford as I Knew Him', *Royal College of Music Magazine*, 20 (1923–4), 77–86.

Grove's Dictionary of Music and Musicians, ed. J. A. Fuller Maitland, 5 vols (2nd edn, London, 1904–10).

Grove's Dictionary of Music and Musicians, ed. H. C. Colles, 5 vols (3rd edn, London, 1927).

Hart, Fritz, *William Hurlstone as I Knew Him* (London, 1947).

Hauger, George, 'Stanford's Early Operas', *Opera*, 35 (1984), 724–9.

Henn, Thomas Rice, *Five Arches: Leaves from an Autobiography* (Gerards Cross, 1980).

Heseltine, Philip, *The Occasional Writings of Philip Heseltine*, ed. Barry Smith, 3 vols (London, 1997).

The History of the Theatre Royal, Dublin (Dublin, 1870).

Howells, Herbert, 'Charles Villiers Stanford: An Address at his Centenary', *Proceedings of the Royal Musical Association*, 80 (1952–3), 19–31.

Howes, Frank, *The English Musical Renaissance* (London, 1966).

Hudson, Frederick, 'C. V. Stanford: Nova Bibliographica', *Musical Times*, 104 (1963), 728–31.

—— 'C. V. Stanford: Nova Bibliographica II', *Musical Times*, 105 (1964), 734–8.

—— 'C. V. Stanford: Nova Bibliographica III', *Musical Times*, 108 (1967), 326.

Hudson, Frederick, 'A Revised and Extended Catalogue of C. V. Stanford', *Music Review*, 37 (1976), 106–29.

Hueffer, Francis, *Half a Century of Music in England* (London, 1889).

Hughes, Gervase, *Composers of Operetta* (Oxford, 1962).

Hurlstone, Katharine (ed.), *William Hurlstone: Musician* (London, 1947).

Hutchinson, John, *The Dynamics of Cultural Nationalism* (London, 1987).

Hynes, Samuel, *A War Imagined: The First World War and English Culture* (London, 1990).

Jacobs, Arthur, *Arthur Sullivan* (2nd edn, Oxford, 1986).

Joachim, Joseph, *Letters to and from Joseph Joachim*, trans. Nora Bickley (London, 1914).

Kennedy, Michael, *Portrait of Elgar* (2nd edn, Oxford, 1982).

Klein, Hermann, *Musicians and Mummers* (London, 1925).

Knight, Frieda, *Cambridge Music* (Cambridge, 1980).

Le Fanu, Joseph, *The Purcell Papers*, ed. Alfred Graves, 3 vols (London, 1880).

Longmire, John, *John Ireland: Portrait of a Friend* (London, 1969).

Lyle, W , 'Sir Charles Villiers Stanford – A Personal Impression', *Musical News*, 28 (Oct. 1922), 388–9.

Lynch, Patrick, *Some Members of the Munster Circuit* (Cork, 1946).

Lyons, Francis S. L., *Culture and Anarchy in Ireland 1890–1939* (Oxford, 1979).

M'Clintock, A. E., and C. Brady, *The Law Directory for Ireland 1846* (Dublin, 1846).

McCormack, William J., *Sheridan LeFanu and Victorian Ireland* (Oxford, 1980).

Mackenzie, Alexander, *A Musician's Narrative* (London, 1927).

—— 'Sir Charles Stanford – A Tribute', *RCM Magazine*, 20 (1923–4), 37–8.

Marwick, Arthur, *The Deluge: British Society and the First World War* (2nd edn, London, 1991).

Moore, Jerrold Northrop, *Edward Elgar: A Creative Life* (Oxford, 1984).

—— *Edward Elgar – Letters of a Lifetime* (Oxford, 1990).

Musgrave, Michael, *The Musical Life of the Crystal Palace* (Cambridge 1995).

Newbolt, Margaret (ed.), *The Later Life and Letters of Sir Henry Newbolt* (London, 1942).

Norris, Christopher, *Music and the Politics of Culture* (London, 1989).

Norris, Gerald, *Stanford, the Cambridge Jubilee and Tchaikovsky* (Newton Abbot, 1980).

Nosek, Margaret, 'From a Destroyed Autobiography II', *RCM Magazine*, 80 (1984), 29–36.

O'Brien, Joseph V., *Dear Dirty Dublin: A City in Distress 1899–1916* (Berkeley, Calif., 1982).

O'Flanagan, James R., *The Irish Bar* (London, 1879).

—— *The Munster Circuit* (London, 1880).

Palmer, Christopher, *Herbert Howells: A Study* (London, 1978).

Parry, Hubert, *College Addresses*, ed. Henry Cope Colles (London, 1920).

Petrie, George, *The Petrie Collection of the Ancient Music of Ireland* (Dublin, 1855).

Pirie, Peter, *The English Musical Renaissance* (London, 1979).

Porte, John F., *Charles Villiers Stanford* (London, 1921).

Power, T. P., and Kevin Whelan (eds), *Endurance and Emergence: Catholics in Ireland in the Eighteenth Century* (Dublin, 1990).

Rainbow, Bernarr, *The Choral Revival in the Anglican Church* (London, 1970).

Richards, Fiona, *The Music of John Ireland* (Aldershot, 2000).

Rodmell, Paul, 'A Tale of Two Operas: Stanford's *Savonarola* and *The Canterbury Pilgrims* from Gestation to Production', *Music & Letters*, 78 (1997), 77–91.

Rootham, Cyril, 'Music in the Universities', *Proceedings of the Royal Musical Association*, 48 (1922–2), 99–116.

Rosa, Carl, 'English Opera', *Murray's Magazine*, 1 (1887), 460–70.

The Royal Irish Academy of Music – A Centenary Souvenir (Dublin, 1956).

Scott, Marion, 'Sir Charles Stanford and the RCM Orchestra', *RCM Magazine*, 20 (1923–4), 48–52.

Self, Geoffrey, *The Hiawatha Man* (Aldershot, 1995).

Shaw, George Bernard, *London Music as Heard in 1888–89 by Corno di Bassetto* (New York, 1973).

—— *Music in London 1890–94*, 3 vols (New York, 1973).

Sheehy, Jeanne, *The Rediscovery of Ireland's Past: The Celtic Revival 1830–1930* (London, 1980).

'Sir Charles Stanford and his Pupils', *RCM Magazine*, 20 (1923–4), 55–61.

'Sir Charles Stanford and his Pupils', *Music and Letters*, 5 (1924), 193–207 (substantially different from the preceding).

Spark, Frederick, *Memories of my Life* (Leeds, 1913).

—— and Joseph Bennett, *History of the Leeds Musical Festivals* (2nd edn, Leeds, 1892).

Speyer, Edward, *My Life and Friends* (London, 1937).

Spicer, Paul, *Herbert Howells* (Bridgend, 1998).

Stanford, Charles Villiers, *Brahms* (London, 1912).

—— *A History of Music* (London, 1916).

Stanford, Charles Villiers, *Interludes, Records and Recollections* (London, 1922). [Contents: 'Some Notes upon Musical Education'; 'English Orchestras'; 'On Some Conductors and their Methods'; 'Beethoven's Ninth (Choral) Symphony and Some Common Misreadings of its Pace'; 'The Composition of Music'; 'A Sketch of the Symphony'; 'On Some Recent Tendencies in Composition'; 'Music and the War'; 'Three Centenaries: Jenny Lind, Pauline Viardot Garcia and George Grove'; 'Bayreuth in 1876'; 'Upon Some Amateurs'; 'William Sterndale Bennett'.]

—— 'Music and the War', *Quarterly Review*, 1 April 1915, pp. 393–408.

—— *Musical Composition* (London, 1911).

—— 'On Some Recent Tendencies in Composition', *Proceedings of the Royal Musical Association*, 47 (1920–21), 39–54.

—— *Pages from an Unwritten Diary* (London, 1914).

—— 'Some Thoughts Concerning Folk-song and Nationality', *Musical Quarterly*, 1 (1915), 232–45.

—— *Studies and Memories* (London, 1908) [Contents: 'The Case for National Opera'; 'The Development of Orchestras in England'; 'The Wagner Bubble'; 'Music in Elementary Schools'; 'Music in Cathedral and Church Choirs'; 'Some Aspects of Music Criticism in England'; 'The Ethics of Music Publishing in England'; 'Alfred, Lord Tennyson'; 'Ernst Frank'; 'A Few Memoirs of Johannes Brahms'; 'Joseph Robinson'; 'Joachim'; 'Hubert Parry's *Judith*'; 'Sullivan's *Golden Legend*'; 'Verdi's *Falstaff* I' (from the *Daily Graphic*); 'Verdi's *Falstaff* II' (from the *Fortnightly Review*); 'The Music of the Nineteenth Century'].

—— and Cecil Forsyth, *A History of Music* (London, 1916).

Stradling, Robert, and Merion Hughes, *The British Musical Renaissance: Construction and Deconstruction* (London, 1995; 2nd edn, Manchester, 2001).

Temperley, Nicholas, 'Schumann and Sterndale Bennett', *Nineteenth Century Music*, 12 (1988–9), 207–20.

—— (ed.), *The Lost Chord: Essays on Victorian Music* (Bloomington and Indianapolis, Ind., 1989).

—— *Music in Britain: The Romantic Age 1800–1914* (London, 1981).

Thistlethwaite, N., *The Organs of Cambridge* (Oxford, 1983).

Tovey, Donald, and Geoffrey Parratt, *Walter Parratt: Master of the Music* (Oxford, 1941).

Trend, Michael, *The Music Makers* (London, 1985).

Trowell, Brian, 'Elgar's Use of Literature', in Raymond Monk (ed.), *Edward Elgar: Music and Literature* (Aldershot, 1993), 182–326.

Vaughan Williams, Ralph, *National Music and Other Essays* (2nd edn, Oxford, 1996).

Vaughan Williams, Ursula, and Imogen Holst (eds), *Heirs and Rebels: Letters of Ralph Vaughan Williams and Gustav Holst* (London, 1959).

Venn, John A., *Alumni Cantabrigienses, Part II: 1752–1900*, 6 vols (Cambridge, 1940).

Waddington, Sydney, 'Stanford in the Early Days', *RCM Magazine*, 79 (1983), 19–22.

White, Terence de Vere, *The Anglo-Irish* (London, 1972).

—— 'The Stage Irishman', *Essays by Divers Hands*, 45 (1988), 59–72.

Winstanley, Denys A., *Later Victorian Cambridge* (Cambridge, 1947).

Wood, Thomas, *True Thomas* (London, 1936).

Young, Percy, *George Grove: A Biographhy* (London, 1980).

Zon, Bennett, *Music and Metaphor in Nineteenth-Century British Musicology* (Aldershot, 2000).

—— (ed.), *Nineteenth-Century British Music Studies*, 1 (Aldershot, 1999).

Index of Compositions
by Stanford

Only works referred to in the main body of the text are listed; if there is no entry here see Appendix I. For Stanford's writings see under Stanford – Writings in the main index.

General Index